Microsoft Defender for Endpoint

Endpoint security fundamentals deployment and
cross-platform defense with MDE

Shailender Singh

bpb

www.bpbonline.com

First Edition 2025

Copyright © BPB Publications, India

ISBN: 978-93-6589-402-8

LIMITS OF LIABILITY AND DISCLAIMER OF WARRANTY

To View Complete
BPB Publications Catalogue
Scan the QR Code:

www.bpbonline.com

Dedicated to

My Family!

About the Author

Shailender Singh is a seasoned technology leader with over 17 years of rich and diverse experience spanning cybersecurity, software development, and IT architecture. As a former Microsoft team member, he contributed extensively to the **Microsoft Defender for Endpoint (MDE)** and **Microsoft Defender for Application (MDA)** teams, where he spearheaded initiatives such as the development of a cross-platform lab that analysed millions of malware samples automatically. His career journey also includes pivotal roles at Symantec (now Broadcom), where he worked on cutting-edge security products like **Cloud Workload Protection (CWP)** and **Symantec Endpoint Protection (SEP)**.

Currently serving as an advisor - software architect in the core banking sector with Finxact (Fiserv), Shailender brings his deep expertise in hybrid cloud infrastructures, container security, DevOps, DevSecOps, and **site reliability engineering (SRE)** to drive innovation and efficiency. He is actively working on Agentic Mesh in the AI domain, creating fusion across security, system engineering, and AI/ML. With a background as a C developer on the Linux platform during his early career and now an active Python developer along with Polyglot programming languages, he combines hands-on technical proficiency with strategic vision. Additionally, his academic credentials include two master's degrees in IT and computer applications.

Shailender's professional footprint extends to prominent organizations such as McKinsey a business consulting firm and **Hewlett Packard (HP)**, where he contributed in various impactful roles. Passionate about leveraging his skills for problem-solving, he is currently focused on building solutions in the security domain and developing **Infrastructure from Code (IfC)** frameworks aimed at reducing engineering costs for budding startups. His expertise bridges the gap between engineering and innovation, making him a dynamic force in cybersecurity, software architecture, and AI advancement.

About the Reviewer

Taresh Mehra is a data protection & cyber security QA engineer with over 18 years of experience in Edison, New Jersey. He specializes in backup and storage solutions, ransomware mitigation, and data indexing, ensuring data integrity in modern IT environments. His expertise spans AI/ML applications in data security, REST API testing, and cloud technologies.

Taresh has also shaped industry standards through his leadership in the Cloud Security Alliance and extensive contributions as a cyber security publication reviewer. His work advancing the field through IEEE conference papers and technical evaluations at major hackathons earned him the prestigious 2024 SILVER GLOBEE® AWARD for Cyber Security Professional of the Year. As both, an IEEE Senior Member and RSA Fellow, he continues to influence the direction of enterprise security, helping define best practices and innovation benchmarks across the industry.

Acknowledgement

I want to express my deepest gratitude to my family specially my parents and wife for their unwavering support and encouragement throughout this book's writing as I spent my many weekends in articulating my thoughts into the chapters so that I can create value for my readers out from the haystack.

I am also grateful to BPB Publications for their guidance and expertise in bringing this book to fruition. It was a long journey of revising this book, with valuable participation and collaboration of reviewers, technical experts, and editors.

I would also like to acknowledge the valuable contributions of my past colleagues and co-worker during many years working in the tech industry, who have taught me so much and provided valuable feedback on my work.

Finally, I would like to thank all the readers who have taken an interest in my book and for their support in making it a reality. Your encouragement has been invaluable.

Preface

Security is a vast domain, having different products, services, technologies, tools, processes and involve people from 1st layer of defence in form of SOC analyse to extreame advance level research activities in indentification of malicious activities in the world. So this book is a attempt to help readers to understand all factors, roles, domains involed in the security management of a company. There are many different domains in IT infrastructure security in form of device including IoT and identity security, application security and this book is an attempt to help you to understand endpoint security management that is the major chunk in day to day management by security practioners and it mainly covers the device security part of it.

We have covered Microsoft technologies to help you to learn and start journey in security domain to manage the endpoints and specifically focused on **Microsoft Defender for Endpoint (MDE)** and briefly talked around other products those seamlessly runs around it in form of Micorosoft Intune Endpoint Manager and Cofiguration Manager and covered MDE security webportal in detail. Chapters around installation and configuration will help you to gain confidence while playing SOC and security administrator role as we have captured screenshots from major key areas and will help readers those who do not have access to security portal and will help in building their strong understanding on the produce before hand.

This book will help you to become good SOC expert or a security administrator in short span of time and will help you to quick start your journey in the security domain!

Personally, I like understanding things first from thousand feet view and then I go deep to understand something so same approch you will find in chapters and we have captured many architecture diagrams just crafted for our readers to build better understanding. You will find some material borrowed from Microsoft **Security Adoption Framework (SAF)**, **Microsoft CyberSecurity Reference Architecture (MCRA)**. We also covered hybrid cloud infrastructure management architectures, cross-platform product organization, SOC activities in graphical presentation.

As I directly worked inside the MDE and MDA teams so I brought up more clarity about how such products and services are built that will help you in gaining the insight about various features and the mindset behind it. This book not only help you to learn the MDE from end user point of view but will also help to develop such similar products in case you have special interest in development of security products and services in the market as most of the core technologies are stitched together from the open-source world.

Keeping the trends in shift left security approach we have also briefly touched on DevSecOps and its tools and given insight about exact coverage activities under it and such information will give you the confidence in implementation of such practices in your organization. Similarly, we have also briefly touched on Microsoft Defender for **Cloud** (**MDFC**), and container security techniques, **Microsoft Cloud Native Protection Platform** (**CNPP**). We also given insight about Kubernetes Platform security.

We given cheat sheet of many configuration that you can leverage to manage your MDE configuration and such configurations are brought up from real world consulting work done by my colleagues in the past. Atlast we covered the future solutions those are coming in the market in form Microsoft Security Copilot features that will help SOC analysts to perform their day to day activities with more confidence and will help in reducing MTTR of incident in hand.

Chapter 1: Introduction to Microsoft Defender Endpoint - Get an overview of endpoint security and explore the architectural landscape of Microsoft Defender Endpoint. Learn about its evolution, key features, capabilities, and the benefits it offers. Discover the journey towards a unified portal for enhanced security management.

Chapter 2: Understanding Endpoint Security Fundamentals - Dive into the threat landscape of endpoint security and address common challenges. Understand the significance of endpoint protection and learn best practices to mitigate risks. Explore the transition from traditional to proactive security measures and gain insights into the MITRE ATT&CK framework.

Chapter 3: Deploying Microsoft Defender Endpoint - Prepare for successful deployment by meeting system requirements and prerequisites. Follow a step-by-step guide for installation, configuration, and integration with existing security infrastructure. Explore various deployment options, including integration with Microsoft Intune, Microsoft Endpoint Manager, and Azure Security Center.

Chapter 4: Configuring Microsoft Defender Endpoint - Learn how to manage endpoint security policies and configurations, including those for macOS, Windows, and Linux. Customize real-time protection settings, antivirus, malware protection, and endpoint firewall configurations.

Chapter 5: General EDR with Respect to SOC - We will cover general EDR, different techniques that Threat actor uses and how security researchers help in resurfacing through tools like Defender. This chapter will give further heads up about Defender SOC capability and DLP label consideration.

Chapter 6: Monitoring and Alerting with Defender SOC - Explore **endpoint detection and response** (**EDR**) and real-time threat detection and analysis. Discover endpoint security analytics and reporting, leveraging threat intelligence, and considerations for regulatory compliance.

Chapter 7: Defender SOC Investigating Threats - EDR and real-time threat investigation. Learn about incident investigation on the endpoint, including the advanced threat hunting techniques.

Chapter 8: Responding to Threats with Defender SOC - Understand the Live Response feature. Learn more about escalation, reporting, recovery from incident. Regulatory compliance considerations, incident response and mitigation, case management in MDE, managing security incident response and recovery and responding to threats.

Chapter 9: Endpoint Vulnerability Management - Learn to identify and assess vulnerabilities and effectively manage patching and software updates. Implement vulnerability scanning and remediation using Microsoft Defender Endpoint. Understand risk based TVM lifecycle, TVM principles, remediation and tracking,web portal TVM menu and general CVE understanding.

Chapter 10: Cross-platform Endpoint Security - Gain an overview of the cross-platform journey with Microsoft Defender for Windows, Mac, and Linux. Understand unified endpoint protection strategies and explore dynamic malware behavior analysis using deep learning. Understand various terminologies in cross platform, Microsoft software release cycle rituals and gain insight into **mobile threat defense (MTD)** in cross platform security. There are special insights about Mac Hardware and expirences out while building the MDE lab that analyzed millions of samples.

Chapter 11: Endpoint Security for Cloud Environments - Understand DevSecOps, tools, understand container and kubernetes, understand security of containers and container platform,vulnerability management in the container, Microsoft Defender for Cloud, MCRA architecture for SOC, multi-cloud and hybrid protection in MD for cloud, onboarding non-Azure servers.

Chapter 12: Managing and Maintaining Microsoft Defender Endpoint - Learn security management using Microsoft Frameworks like **Microsoft Cybersecurity Reference Architecture (MCRA)**, threat modelling along with network attack vectors. Gain insight into MDE – training reference, types of network threat along with real-time threat detection and analysis with MDE.

Chapter 13: Future Ahead with AI and LLM - Understand **venture capitalist (VC)** involvement in security business. Explore Microsoft Security Copilot, threat research, and the use of AI in threat detection. Understand the MDE team's focus on WSL vs. container security and discover query languages used by security experts. Learn about the grading platform that leverages AI/ML for researchers.

Chapter 14: Practical Configuration Examples and Case Studies - Implement endpoint security configurations for small businesses and enterprises. Explore industry-specific endpoint security implementations, real-world deployment scenarios, and best practices. Engage in a practical lab evaluation on the MDE portal.

Code Bundle and Coloured Images

Please follow the link to download the
Code Bundle and the *Coloured Images* of the book:

https://rebrand.ly/a0vfhed

The code bundle for the book is also hosted on GitHub at **https://github.com/ bpbpublications/Microsoft-Defender-for-Endpoint**. In case there's an update to the code, it will be updated on the existing GitHub repository.

We have code bundles from our rich catalogue of books and videos available at **https:// github.com/bpbpublications**. Check them out!

Errata

We take immense pride in our work at BPB Publications and follow best practices to ensure the accuracy of our content to provide with an indulging reading experience to our subscribers. Our readers are our mirrors, and we use their inputs to reflect and improve upon human errors, if any, that may have occurred during the publishing processes involved. To let us maintain the quality and help us reach out to any readers who might be having difficulties due to any unforeseen errors, please write to us at :

errata@bpbonline.com

Your support, suggestions and feedbacks are highly appreciated by the BPB Publications' Family.

Did you know that BPB offers eBook versions of every book published, with PDF and ePub files available? You can upgrade to the eBook version at www.bpbonline. com and as a print book customer, you are entitled to a discount on the eBook copy. Get in touch with us at :

business@bpbonline.com for more details.

At **www.bpbonline.com**, you can also read a collection of free technical articles, sign up for a range of free newsletters, and receive exclusive discounts and offers on BPB books and eBooks.

Piracy

If you come across any illegal copies of our works in any form on the internet, we would be grateful if you would provide us with the location address or website name. Please contact us at **business@bpbonline.com** with a link to the material.

If you are interested in becoming an author

If there is a topic that you have expertise in, and you are interested in either writing or contributing to a book, please visit **www.bpbonline.com**. We have worked with thousands of developers and tech professionals, just like you, to help them share their insights with the global tech community. You can make a general application, apply for a specific hot topic that we are recruiting an author for, or submit your own idea.

Reviews

Please leave a review. Once you have read and used this book, why not leave a review on the site that you purchased it from? Potential readers can then see and use your unbiased opinion to make purchase decisions. We at BPB can understand what you think about our products, and our authors can see your feedback on their book. Thank you!

For more information about BPB, please visit **www.bpbonline.com**.

Join our book's Discord space

Join the book's Discord Workspace for Latest updates, Offers, Tech happenings around the world, New Release and Sessions with the Authors:

https://discord.bpbonline.com

Table of Contents

Introduction to Microsoft Defender Endpoint

Introduction

In this chapter, we will understand endpoint security and explore Defender Endpoint, a robust and comprehensive security product offered by Microsoft. We will begin by understanding the significance of endpoint security and how it plays a critical role in protecting organizations from modern cyber threats. In this chapter, you will get high level view so that you can understand all dimensions of the cybersecurity landscape.

The chapter aims at giving you an insight of both sides that is the end users of the security products as well as the builders of security products. The presentation will focus on providing concise backend insights drawn from direct experiences, while emphasizing comprehensive details from the end user perspective. The majority of the global audience will engage with the platform primarily as end users.

> **Learn more:** For example, one of IBM's Lotus Product categories, that is, email client, or other Office products similar to Word or Excel, ruled before the entry of Microsoft Office products. However, the new features that Microsoft released and the hint or feedback that IBM did not consider on time led to the failure or non-existence of their Office product category. Similarly, cybersecurity is another technology product.

Structure

This chapter encompasses the following key topics:

- Author's experience
- Overview of endpoint security
- Understanding endpoint security
- Architectural overview and the big picture
- Evolution of Microsoft Defender for Endpoint
- Key features and capabilities
- Benefits of Microsoft Defender Endpoint
- Unified portal journey to single portal
- Microsoft billion device benefit in security

Objectives

The objective of this chapter is to provide readers with a clear understanding of the cybersecurity industry's size and scope. It aims to help readers create a comparative framework to analyze cybersecurity alongside other technological areas like **artificial intelligence** (**AI**) and cloud computing. By offering a thorough overview of endpoint security, the chapter prepares readers for deeper exploration into this domain and sets a solid foundation for advanced topics in subsequent sections.

Author's experience

Let us learn about some financial insights from the security business to understand the opportunities in the industry. Microsoft was making around $2 billion in 2018, $3 billion in 2019, $5 billion in 2020, $7 billion in revenue in 2021, and in **2023 it started making close to $20-25 billion revenue** and they are eying toward **$40 billion in 2025**. *Palo Alto* is second in line with earning close to $7 billion from the Security business. If you compare another visionary and leader named CrowdStrike, they managed to make around $400-500 million in revenue.

The following are recent FY 2024 stats for some of the top cybersecurity companies:

Company	Recent revenue (FY 2024)
Palo Alto Networks	$8.0 billion
Cisco	$13.6 billion
Symantec	$3.3 billion
Fortinet	$5.3 billion

Table 1.1: Top cybersecurity companies

Note: Above figures are observed by author during various discussions in the professional experience while working with different security developers so you might not find such crisp year wise figures on public internet.

We will give insights into a thrilling arena of high-tech battles, that is, we will learn more about the digital face-off in the tech world, where security powerhouses are locking horns. Just like in the ring, there is a winner emerging from the heavyweight category!

Let us learn some stats about the Virtual Ring:

- Microsoft's FY21 Digital Defense Report highlighted a staggering 24 trillion daily security signals. Microsoft Defender successfully mitigated approximately 9 billion threats on endpoints. Additionally, it addressed 31 billion identity threats and neutralized 32 billion email threats.
- Microsoft has committed to investing $20 billion over the next five years, starting from 2021.
- In 2023, Microsoft achieved impressive financial success, earning over $20 billion.
- Other major competitors, including Trend Micro, Aqua Security, and Symantec/Broadcom, are actively vying for dominance in the cybersecurity sector.
- The competitive landscape in cybersecurity is dynamic, with ongoing efforts from various companies to achieve excellence and market leadership.

Thoughts

By the way, do you see Google or Amazon somewhere here in the cybersecurity business?

If you just compare the above-mentioned numbers of virtual ring bullet points as layman with other business domains then you can make the assumption about the size of security market and the future opportunity in the security domain lying ahead. After the Cloud and Productivity suite, it is the Microsoft Security products that are making maximum profit for Microsoft. Hiring EVP Charlie Bell from Amazon is another strategic step by Microsoft to keep themself ahead in competition business landscape and showcase serious ness to gain this market share.

Overall, Microsoft is positioning itself strategically to capture a larger share of the cybersecurity market. Their Product Managers have conducted extensive research to enhance security solutions, reflecting a meticulous approach to product development and market positioning. You have made a well-thought-out career choice by selecting the right path and opting for the appropriate vendor and product to enhance your career. Take the time to thoroughly absorb the content of this book to gain valuable experience and build confidence in the exceptional product crafted by the Microsoft Defender Engineering team. It is important to pass information in a concise manner for easy teaching and building confident understanding. Therefore, mind maps will be used to give you a complete overview through images.

Learn more: **Before you go deep into understanding security, please refer to the bell curve released by Microsoft in their FY21 Microsoft Digital Defense report as shown in Figure 1.1:**

The cybersecurity bell curve:
Basic security hygiene still protects against 98% of attacks

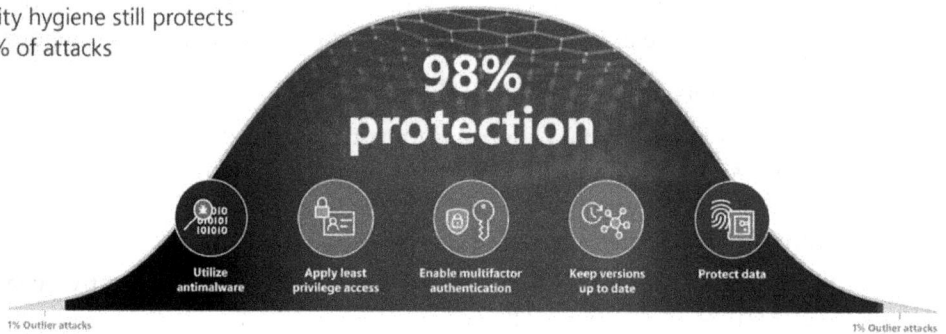

Figure 1.1: Cybersecurity simple protection bell curve [1]

This figure illustrates five key areas where you can effectively protect up to 98% of your IT infrastructure resources without the need for advanced enterprise security solutions.

Overview of endpoint security

Endpoint security is a crucial element of cybersecurity, playing a vital role in protecting organizations from various cyber threats. This book delves into the heart of endpoint security, shedding light on its core principles and how it plays a pivotal role in safeguarding organizations against a multitude of threats. As technology evolves, so do the challenges in securing endpoints, and this text explores these emerging threats and the strategies to counter them effectively. Moreover, it draws a clear distinction between endpoint security and network security, highlighting the key differences between these two vital aspects of cybersecurity. In an era where cyber threats continue to escalate, understanding why endpoint security matters is essential. This book underscores the reasons why organizations must prioritize and invest in robust endpoint security solutions to fortify their defenses in the ever-evolving cyber landscape. Endpoint security is a critical aspect of an organization's cybersecurity strategy. It focuses on protecting individual devices or endpoints, such as laptops, desktops, servers, and mobile devices, from various cyber threats. In this section, we will explore the definition and importance of endpoint security, understand the challenges posed by emerging threats, and distinguish it from network security.

---

1   *Reference: FY21 Microsoft Digital Defense Report*

Microsoft Defender for Endpoint is a key component of the Microsoft 365 Defender architecture and part of the Microsoft 365 Defender platform. It shares data/signals and architecture with the following products:

- **Microsoft Defender for Office365 (MDO)**
- **Microsoft Defender for Cloud Apps (MDA)**
- **Microsoft Defender for Identity (MDI)**
- Microsoft Entra

Defender for Endpoint contains a couple of major functionalities, including:

- Device discovery
- **Threat and vulnerability management (TVM)**
- **Attack surface reduction (ASR)**
- **Next-generation protection (NGP)**
- **Endpoint detection and response (EDR)**
- **Automated investigation and remediation (AIR)**
- **Microsoft threat experts (MTE)**

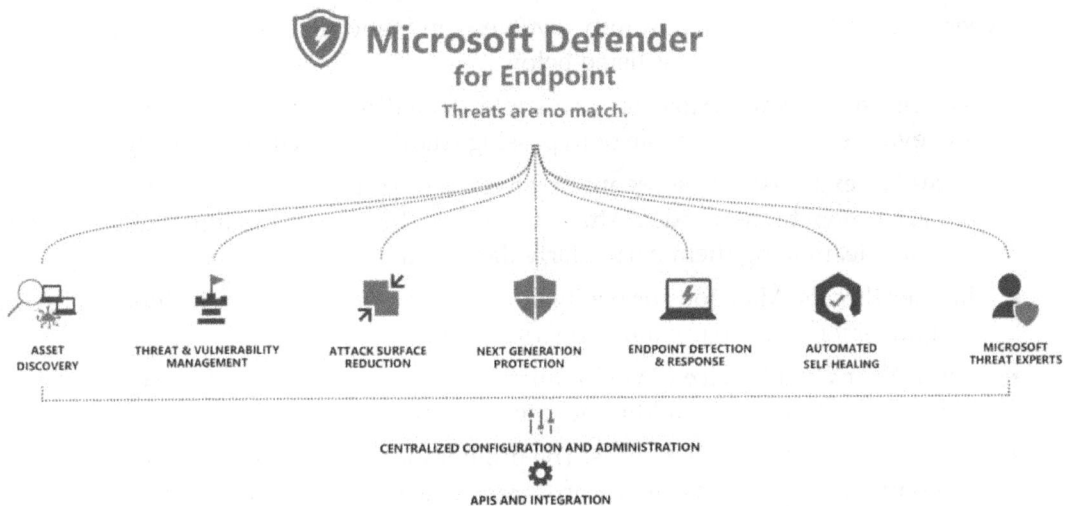

Figure 1.2: *MDE features* [2]

Understanding endpoint security

Endpoint security refers to the practices and technologies used to secure the endpoints within a network from potential cyber threats. These threats include malware, viruses, ransomware, phishing attacks, and other malicious activities. The goal of endpoint security is to safeguard both the data stored on these devices and the devices themselves.

---

[2] *Reference: Microsoft Defender Documentation*

The importance of endpoint security cannot be overstated, especially in today's highly interconnected and digital world. Endpoints are the primary points of access to an organization's sensitive data and systems. Therefore, they represent attractive targets for cybercriminals seeking to infiltrate networks, steal data, or disrupt operations.

Endpoint security extends beyond traditional antivirus protection. It encompasses a range of security measures, including:

- **Anti-malware and antivirus**: Detects and removes malicious software and viruses from endpoints.
- **Firewall protection**: Monitoring and controlling incoming and outgoing network traffic to block unauthorized access.
- **Data loss prevention (DLP)**: Preventing sensitive data from being accessed, transferred, or leaked outside the organization.
- **Encryption**: Protecting data by converting it into a coded format that can only be deciphered with the correct encryption key.
- **Patch management**: Ensuring devices have the latest software updates and security patches applied to address known vulnerabilities and reduce risk. Endpoint security challenges and emerging threats.

The cybersecurity landscape constantly evolves, and endpoint security faces several challenges and emerging threats as listed below:

- **Advanced malware**: Attackers use sophisticated techniques to develop stealthy and evasive malware capable of bypassing traditional security measures.
- **Zero-day exploits**: These are vulnerabilities in software or applications that are not yet known to the vendor. Attackers exploit these vulnerabilities before a patch is available, making them particularly dangerous.
- **Insider threats**: Malicious or negligent actions by employees or insiders can pose a significant risk to an organization's security.
- **Bring Your Own Device (BYOD) policies**: The increasing use of personal devices in the workplace creates additional security challenges.
- **Internet of Things (IoT) devices**: The proliferation of IoT devices adds complexity to endpoint security, as many of these devices may not have robust security features.
- **Ransomware**: Ransomware attacks can encrypt an endpoint's data, making it inaccessible until a ransom is paid to the attackers.

Endpoint security versus network security

While endpoint security and network security are both vital components of cybersecurity, they differ in their focus and scope.

Endpoint security and network security are two pivotal pillars of a robust cybersecurity strategy. While endpoint security centers around safeguarding individual devices, covering everything from operating systems to user data, network security takes a broader approach by securing the entire network infrastructure and communication channels. Both are essential in addressing different dimensions of cybersecurity risks, offering unique advantages in the battle against evolving threats.

Endpoint security

The features of endpoint security are as follows:

- Concentrates on protecting individual devices and endpoints.
- Focuses on securing the devices' operating systems, applications, and user data.
- Addresses risks related to devices being lost, stolen, or compromised.
- Provides granular control and visibility into individual devices' security posture.
- Requires protection even when endpoints are outside the corporate network.

Network security

The features of network security are as follows:

- Concentrates on securing the network infrastructure and communication channels.
- Focuses on filtering and monitoring network traffic to detect and prevent threats.
- Addresses risks associated with unauthorized access and data breaches.
- Provides centralized control and visibility into network-wide security events.
- Protects the network perimeter and internal network segments.

Importance of endpoint security in cyber landscape

In today's cyber landscape, the increasing prevalence of remote work, cloud services, and mobile devices has expanded the attack surface for cyber threats. As a result, endpoint security has become increasingly critical. Here are some reasons why endpoint security matters:

- **Protecting sensitive data**: The term *Endpoints are the primary storage locations for sensitive data* might be misleading. Endpoints are not the primary storage locations but rather access points for data. It would be more accurate to say, *Endpoints are often the points through which sensitive data is accessed or transmitted.*
- **Mitigating insider threats**: Insider threats, intentional or accidental, can lead to data breaches and significant financial losses. Endpoint security solutions extend protection to devices used for remote work, whether they are inside or outside the corporate network.

- **Securing remote work**: With the rise of remote work, employees access corporate data and resources outside the traditional corporate network. Endpoint security provides protection to devices regardless of their location, reducing the risk of data breaches.

- **Combating advanced threats**: Advanced malware and zero-day exploits can bypass traditional security measures. Endpoint security solutions leverage advanced technologies, such as behavioral analysis and ML, to detect and block sophisticated threats.

- **Regulatory compliance**: Many industries are subject to strict regulatory requirements concerning data protection. Endpoint security helps organizations meet regulatory requirements and mitigate the risk of non-compliance penalties.

Architectural overview and the big picture

Microsoft Defender Endpoint boasts a sophisticated architecture that underpins its formidable cybersecurity capabilities. This architecture comprises various components and modules, each with a specific role and interconnected to work harmoniously. What sets it apart is its seamless integration with other Microsoft security products, creating a robust ecosystem for comprehensive threat protection. Moreover, the solution is designed with scalability and performance in mind, ensuring that it can adapt to the evolving demands of modern cybersecurity landscapes without compromising its effectiveness. Microsoft Defender Endpoint is a comprehensive endpoint security solution that provides advanced threat protection, detection, and response capabilities for organizations. In this section, we will dive into the architectural overview of Microsoft Defender Endpoint, exploring its underlying components and modules, how they work together, and their integration with other Microsoft security products. Additionally, we will discuss scalability and performance considerations to ensure seamless deployment and operation.

Understanding the architecture of Microsoft Defender Endpoint

Microsoft Defender Endpoint's architecture is designed to provide multi-layered defense against a wide range of cyber threats. The architecture consists of several key components that collectively secure endpoints and protect organizational assets.

In *Figure 1.3*, you can see we are heavily focusing on the extreme left hand side part that is Endpoint. In this book, we are going to cover in detail the feature and will be using screenshot references of the Microsoft Security portal so that you can relate it while doing your practical.

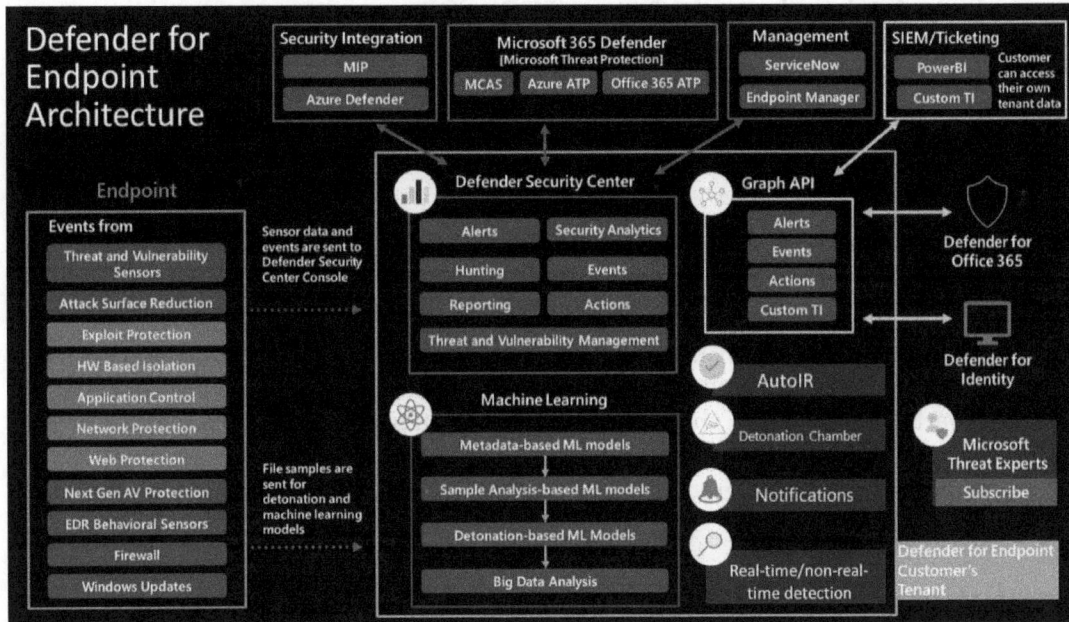

Figure 1.3: Defender architecture [3]

The preceding HLD gives you insight into areas captured to provide you cloud-based protection solutions overview:

- **Endpoint agents**: At the core of the architecture, lightweight agents are installed on individual endpoints, including desktops, laptops, servers, and mobile devices. These agents serve as the first line of defense, continuously monitoring and protecting endpoints from threats.

- **Cloud-based protection**: Microsoft Defender Endpoint leverages the power of the cloud for real-time threat intelligence and analysis. The agents communicate with Microsoft's cloud-based services, which provide up-to-date information about emerging threats and enable faster response times.

- **Threat intelligence and ML**: The cloud-based services incorporate threat intelligence feeds and ML algorithms to identify and block known and unknown threats. This approach enhances the platform's ability to detect zero-day exploits and advanced malware.

Components and modules: Inter-dependability

Microsoft Defender Endpoint comprises several interrelated components and modules, each serving a specific purpose in the overall security ecosystem:

- **Antivirus and antimalware**: This module provides traditional signature-based scanning to detect and remove known malware and viruses from endpoints.

---

3   Ref: **https://blog.ahasayen.com/p1-microsoft-defender-for-endpoint-architecture/**

- **Endpoint detection and response (EDR)**: EDR capabilities enable security teams to investigate and respond to security incidents. It offers advanced behavioral analysis and retrospective investigation to identify and remediate threats.

- **Firewall and network protection**: This module monitors and controls network traffic, preventing unauthorized access and communication with malicious domains.

- **Device control and application guard**: Device control allows administrators to manage peripheral devices' access to endpoints, while Application Guard provides sandboxing capabilities to isolate potentially risky applications.

- **Web protection**: Microsoft Defender Endpoint offers web protection to block access to malicious websites and prevent phishing attacks. Earlier product named SmartScreen is used this functionality and now gradually they have moved toward Web Defense product line with more extensive detection or URL's by implementing more graded URL's that implements more advance techniques for detection.

Evolution from SmartScreen to Web Defense

As the landscape of cyber threats continues to evolve, so must the methods used to defend against them. Microsoft has consistently enhanced its security features to offer more comprehensive protection against web-based threats. This progression is evident in the transition from the original SmartScreen feature to the more robust Web Defense platform. Initially designed to filter out malicious websites, SmartScreen has undergone significant advancements, transforming into a powerful tool that now leverages cutting-edge technologies to safeguard users, which are highlighted as follows:

- **SmartScreen**: Initially, SmartScreen was designed to filter web content and block access to known malicious websites. It provided basic protection against phishing and malware by checking URLs against a database of known threats.

- **Web Defense**: Over time, Microsoft has enhanced this functionality and rebranded it as Web Defense. Web Defense incorporates more advanced techniques for detecting malicious URLs, including:

  o **Machine learning**: Utilizing ML algorithms to identify and block new and emerging threats.

  o **Behavioral analysis**: Analyzing the behavior of websites to detect suspicious activities that may indicate malicious intent.

  o **Integration with browsers**: Extending protection to various browsers, including Microsoft Edge, Chrome, and Firefox, ensuring comprehensive coverage across different platforms.

  o **Real-time updates**: Providing real-time updates to the threat database, ensuring that the latest threats are quickly identified and blocked.

Integration with other Microsoft security products

One of Microsoft Defender Endpoint's strengths lies in its seamless integration with other Microsoft security products, creating a unified and robust security ecosystem. Some key integrations include:

- **Microsoft 365 Security Center**: Microsoft Defender Endpoint is integrated with the Microsoft 365 Security Center, providing a unified portal for security management. This integration allows security teams to have a holistic view of security events and take action from a centralized interface.

- **Microsoft Defender for Office 365**: Integration with Microsoft Defender for Office 365 extends protection beyond endpoints to email and collaboration tools. It helps detect and block phishing emails and malicious attachments, further fortifying the organization's security posture.

- **Microsoft Defender for Identity**: By integrating with Microsoft Defender for Identity, formerly known as Azure Advanced Threat Protection, Microsoft Defender Endpoint gains insights into identity-related threats, such as suspicious sign-in attempts and compromised accounts.

- **Microsoft Defender for Application (MDA)**: This product earlier used to call MCAS and a product category for **cloud access security broker (CASB)** that helps in protecting your organization by monitoring the behaviors of the famous applications.

MDE, MDA, MDI and MDO are the four major pillars on which complete Microsoft Defender is standing.

Scalability and performance considerations

As organizations grow and their endpoint infrastructure expands, ensuring the scalability and performance of security solutions becomes crucial. Microsoft Defender Endpoint addresses these considerations through the following:

- **Cloud-based architecture**: Leveraging cloud-based services enables Microsoft Defender Endpoint to handle massive amounts of data and provide real-time threat intelligence without putting a strain on local infrastructure.

- **Centralized management**: Microsoft 365 Security Center offers centralized management, enabling administrators to deploy security policies, updates, and configurations across all endpoints efficiently.

- **Resource optimization**: The endpoint agents are designed to have a minimal impact on system resources, ensuring that they do not disrupt the performance of user devices. In comparison to competitor's products MDE agent took some more CPU and memory but Defender backend engineering teams are striving to improve such usage to make it most performing agent in the category. During iOS agent development, MDE engineering teams surpassed performance stats beyond the expectation of Apple's team and they showed keen interest in asking details about how the team achieved such enhancements.

- **Automated response**: Microsoft Defender Endpoint incorporates automated response capabilities to handle common security incidents swiftly, reducing the burden on security teams and allowing them to focus on critical tasks.

In conclusion, Microsoft Defender Endpoint's architectural design, integration capabilities, and focus on scalability and performance make it a robust and reliable endpoint security solution for organizations of all sizes. By understanding its architecture and components, organizations can make informed decisions about its deployment and effectively protect their endpoints from a wide range of cyber threats.

Evolution of Microsoft Defender Endpoint

In the ever-changing world of cybersecurity, endpoint protection has become a critical component of any organization's defense strategy. Microsoft Defender Endpoint, originally part of Microsoft's broader security offerings, has evolved significantly over the years to address increasingly sophisticated cyber threats. From its early iterations to the robust, integrated platform it is today, Microsoft Defender Endpoint has continuously adapted to meet the needs of its users. This section explores the historical evolution of Microsoft Defender Endpoint, highlighting key milestones, product enhancements, and how user feedback has shaped its development. Furthermore, we will explore the competitive landscape of endpoint security, examining how Microsoft Defender Endpoint has positioned itself as a leader in this space.

- A historical perspective: Origins of Microsoft Defender Endpoint
- Evolutionary milestones and product enhancements
- Responding to user feedback: Improving the platform
- Competitive landscape and market positioning

Microsoft Defender Endpoint has come a long way in its journey from its humble beginnings to becoming a leading endpoint security solution. In this section, we will explore the historical perspective of Microsoft Defender Endpoint, its evolutionary milestones, product enhancements, and how Microsoft responded to user feedback to improve the platform. Additionally, we will examine its position in the competitive landscape of the endpoint security market.

Origins of Microsoft Defender Endpoint

The roots of Microsoft Defender Endpoint can be traced back to the early days of Microsoft's efforts in providing security solutions to its users. The product started as **Microsoft AntiSpyware** which was a beta released in 2005. It was later renamed to Windows Defender when it was officially released as a part of Windows Vista in 2007. There are more stories behind Antispyware about how they acquired other prevalent companies during that time, but you can consider it as a starting point.

Over the years, Microsoft expanded the capabilities of the tool to cover a broader range of threats, including viruses and other types of malwares. With each iteration, the product evolved and improved, laying the foundation for the more comprehensive and integrated Microsoft Defender Endpoint we know today.

Evolutionary milestones and product enhancements. Below we give you some historical timeline about the product intro and name change in the MDE history:

- **Microsoft Security Essentials**: In 2009, Microsoft introduced Microsoft Security Essentials, a free antivirus solution for consumers. This marked a significant step towards providing basic security protection to a broader user base.

- **Windows Defender**: Integrated into Windows starting with Windows Vista and later improved., Microsoft integrated the security features into the operating system under *Windows Defender*. This integration increased the visibility and accessibility of the security tool to all Windows users.

- **Windows Defender ATP**: The introduction of Windows Defender **Advanced Threat Protection (ATP)** in 2016 marked a shift towards a more advanced and proactive security approach. Windows Defender ATP provided endpoint detection and response capabilities, giving security teams the ability to investigate and respond to threats. Now, Windows Defender ATP has been renamed to Microsoft Defender. Microsoft does not use Widows word in context to security products any more as of 2020, the product has been rebranded and expanded to cover cross-platform environments, not just limited to Windows and now you will find most of parity in between cross Platform OS's.

Responding to user feedback: Improving the platform

Microsoft has been diligent in gathering user feedback and incorporating it into the development and improvement of Microsoft Defender Endpoint. Some key areas where user feedback has driven enhancements include:

- **User experience**: Microsoft has continuously worked on improving the user interface and overall user experience of the platform, making It more intuitive and user-friendly.

- **Performance**: User feedback regarding the impact of security tools on system performance has led to optimization efforts to ensure that Microsoft Defender Endpoint remains lightweight and efficient. It is always on radar or on top priority while writing down the code as the community already shared lot of feedback of high CPU usages that has been fixed over the time but according to product development experience point of view it is iterative and continuous process as every day many ADO git **pull and merge (PR/MR)** requests are getting into the MDE agent code base. It is by considering the fact to have in regard to the change happening around bigger ecosystem of Microsoft world in respect to XDR integration that is Azure Sentinel.

- **Threat intelligence and detection**: Microsoft actively collects telemetry data and feedback from users to enhance the platform's threat intelligence and detection capabilities. This feedback loop allows for quicker responses to emerging threats.

Competitive landscape and market positioning

The endpoint security market is highly competitive, with several established players and new entrants vying for market share. Microsoft Defender Endpoint competes with a range of endpoint security solutions from various vendors, each offering unique set of features and capabilities.

Microsoft's strategic advantage lies in its deep integration with other Microsoft products and services, such as Microsoft 365 and Azure. This integration provides a cohesive security ecosystem for organizations already invested in Microsoft's suite of tools, making the adoption of Microsoft Defender Endpoint a natural choice.

Additionally, Microsoft's extensive user base, spanning millions of devices globally (Billion+ Windows OS device telemetry), provides the company with a wealth of data and telemetry that can be leveraged to enhance threat intelligence and improve the platform's effectiveness.

As the threat landscape continues to evolve, Microsoft remains committed to evolving Microsoft Defender Endpoint to stay ahead of emerging threats and meet the ever-changing security needs of organizations worldwide. Its position as a prominent player in the endpoint security market is a testament to its dedication to providing robust and reliable security solutions to its customers.

Key features and capabilities

Microsoft Defender Endpoint offers a comprehensive suite of security features. It delivers real-time protection that encompasses antivirus, firewalls, and more. Advanced threat detection and response capabilities equip it to identify and counter evolving threats effectively. With its **endpoint detection and response (EDR)** capabilities, it offers a granular approach to threat monitoring and mitigation. Furthermore, the integration of behavioral analysis and machine learning enhances its ability to detect anomalous activities. To top it off, robust security management and reporting features provide valuable insights into your security posture and facilitate informed decision-making. Microsoft Defender Endpoint offers a comprehensive suite of features and capabilities designed to protect endpoints from a wide range of cyber threats. In this section, we will explore the key features that make Microsoft Defender Endpoint a robust and reliable endpoint security solution.

Real-time protection: Antivirus, firewall, and beyond

The following are the areas for real-time protection that you can configure and manage through good, featured security product:

- **Antivirus protection**: Microsoft Defender Endpoint employs signature-based scanning and heuristic analysis to detect and block known malware, viruses, and other malicious software in real-time.

- **Firewall protection**: The integrated firewall monitors and controls incoming and outgoing network traffic to prevent unauthorized access and block malicious connections.

- **Intrusion prevention system (IPS)**: IPS capabilities detect and block known attack patterns and exploit attempt to protect endpoints from known vulnerabilities.

- **Secure web browsing**: Microsoft Defender Endpoint provides web protection to block access to malicious websites and protect users from phishing attempts.

Advanced threat detection and response

Security companies build advanced threat detection and response capabilities through the following areas:

- **Behavioral analysis**: Microsoft Defender Endpoint uses behavioral analysis to detect suspicious activities and anomalies on endpoints. By monitoring unusual behavior, it can identify potential zero-day exploits and advanced threats.

- **ML**: The platform leverages ML algorithms to analyze vast amounts of data and telemetry, enabling it to improve threat detection and stay ahead of emerging threats.

- **Threat intelligence**: Microsoft Defender Endpoint is integrated with Microsoft's cloud-based threat intelligence services, which provide real-time information about known threats, enabling faster response times and proactive protection.

Endpoint detection and response capabilities

EDR capabilities can be built using the following areas:

- **Incident investigation**: Microsoft Defender Endpoint offers EDR capabilities, allowing security teams to investigate security incidents, understand the root cause of the attack, and identify affected endpoints.

- **Endpoint isolation**: In the event of a suspected compromise, security teams can isolate affected endpoints from the network to prevent further spread of the threat.

- **Threat hunting**: EDR features enable proactive threat hunting, allowing security analysts to search for potential threats across the organization's endpoints.

Behavioral analysis and ML integration

Security companies build behavioral analysis through ML capabilities and heavily relies on the following areas:

- **Behavior monitoring**: Microsoft Defender Endpoint continuously monitors endpoint behavior, looking for deviations from normal patterns. This proactive approach helps detect new and unknown threats.

- **Anomaly detection**: Behavioral analysis helps identify anomalies that might indicate a breach or suspicious activity, such as unusual file access or network communication.

- **ML models**: The platform utilizes ML models to analyze and identify patterns indicative of malicious behavior. These models continuously learn from new data to improve accuracy.

Security management and reporting features

Security product companies build security management features for **Security Operation Center (SOC)** teams and bring the following features on the web interfaces:

- **Centralized management**: Microsoft 365 Security Center provides a unified portal for security management, allowing administrators to view and manage security settings and incidents across all endpoints.

- **Security policy management**: Administrators can configure and deploy security policies to endpoints, ensuring consistent protection and compliance with organizational security standards.

- **Reporting and insights**: Microsoft Defender Endpoint offers comprehensive reporting and insights into security events, allowing organizations to monitor their security posture and identify areas for improvement.

Benefits of Microsoft Defender Endpoint

Microsoft Defender Endpoint offers numerous benefits. It significantly improves threat detection and response times, ensuring that potential risks are identified and dealt with swiftly. The enhanced endpoint protection and risk mitigation features provide robust security, safeguarding your systems from various threats. The platform simplifies security management and deployment, making it easier for organizations to protect their digital assets. Moreover, Microsoft Defender Endpoint is cost-efficient and scalable, making it a viable solution for organizations of all sizes. Microsoft Defender Endpoint offers a wide range of benefits to organizations seeking a robust and comprehensive endpoint security solution.

Improved threat detection and response times

Security companies improve **mean time to detect (MTTD)** and **mean time to resolve (MTTR)** by implementing the following technologies:

- **Advanced threat detection**: Microsoft Defender Endpoint leverages behavioral analysis and machine learning to detect advanced and sophisticated threats that traditional signature-based antivirus solutions may miss.

- **Real-time threat intelligence**: By integrating with Microsoft's loud-based threat intelligence services, the platform receives real-time updates about emerging threats, enabling faster response times to new attack vectors.

- **Endpoint detection and response (EDR)**: The EDR capabilities of Microsoft Defender Endpoint provide security teams with detailed insights into security incidents, allowing them to investigate and respond promptly to potential threats.

Enhanced endpoint protection and risk mitigation

There are more areas to cover, and security vendors are continuously covering the latest protecting and mitigation techniques, such as:

- **Zero-day exploit detection**: Microsoft Defender Endpoint's behavioral analysis and machine learning models enable the identification of zero-day exploits and unknown threats, mitigating risks associated with unpatched vulnerabilities.

- **Ransomware protection**: The platform includes features to protect against ransomware attacks, preventing unauthorized encryption of critical data and minimizing the impact of such attacks on the organization.

- **Application control**: Microsoft Defender Endpoint allows administrators to control which applications can run on endpoints, reducing the risk of unauthorized or potentially malicious software execution.

Simplified security management and deployment

The following are the features for simplified security management and deployment:

- **Centralized management**: Microsoft 365 Security Center provides a unified portal for managing security settings and incidents across all endpoints, streamlining security operations.

- **Easy deployment**: Microsoft Defender Endpoint's lightweight agents and cloud-based architecture facilitate seamless deployment and reduce the impact on endpoint performance.

- **Automatic updates**: The platform automatically updates its threat intelligence and protection mechanisms, ensuring endpoints are always equipped with the latest security measures.

- **Integration with Microsoft Ecosystem**: For organizations using other Microsoft products like Microsoft 365 and Azure, the integration of Microsoft Defender Endpoint with these services offers a cohesive and streamlined security ecosystem.

Cost-efficiency and scalability for organizations

Security companies are bringing unified portals to meet the requirements of cost-efficiency and scalability by doing the following:

- **Cost-effective solution**: Microsoft Defender Endpoint's inclusion in Microsoft 365 licensing can lead to cost savings for organizations already invested in Microsoft's productivity suite. There are multiple licensing options provided by them so you can choose from them.

  Microsoft Defender for Endpoint Plan 1 (MDE P1) has been included in **Microsoft 365 E3** and **Microsoft 365 A3** plans since January 2022. This integration ensures that organizations can benefit from advanced endpoint security without additional licensing costs.

Reference: https://techcommunity.microsoft.com/t5/microsoft-defender-for-end-point/microsoft-defender-for-endpoint-plan-1-now-included-in-m365-e3/ba-p/3060639.

- **Single solution for multiple threats**: The platform's multi-layered defense approach consolidates various security features into a single solution, reducing the need for multiple standalone security products.
- **Scalability**: Microsoft Defender Endpoint's cloud-based architecture allows it to scale effortlessly to protect endpoints across organizations of all sizes, from small businesses to large enterprises.
- **Minimal resource impact**: The lightweight endpoint agents have minimal resource requirements, ensuring that endpoint performance remains unaffected while maintaining robust security.

Unified portal journey to single portal

Microsoft Defender Endpoint has embraced a unified portal approach for security management, streamlining the user experience and providing a centralized hub for security operations. In this section, we will explore the journey towards a single portal, the benefits it offers, the integration with Microsoft 365 Security Center, and the improvements in user experience and interface design.

Move towards Unified Security Management

In the past, organizations often managed their security solutions through separate consoles and interfaces. This siloed approach could lead to inefficiencies, increased complexity, and difficulties in correlating security events across different tools. Recognizing these challenges, Microsoft embarked on a journey toward a unified portal for security management.

Microsoft Defender Endpoint became an integral part of this vision, with Microsoft's commitment to integrating security products and services into a centralized platform. This move aims to simplify security management, provide consistent visibility across all security events, and enable security teams to respond to threats more effectively.

Benefits of a single portal approach

Adopting a single portal to manage all security products provides several key advantages, such as:

- **Centralized visibility**: A unified portal offers comprehensive visibility into all security events, incidents, and alerts across endpoints, emails, identities, and cloud services. This centralized view enables security teams to detect and respond to threats more quickly and effectively.

- **Simplified workflows**: Managing security through unified portal streamlines workflows, reducing the time and effort required to perform security-related tasks. Administrators can apply consistent policies and settings, ensuring a more coherent security posture.

- **Enhanced collaboration**: A centralized portal fosters better collaboration between security teams, allowing them to work together seamlessly and share critical insights to respond to complex security incidents effectively.

Integration with Microsoft 365 Security Center

Microsoft Defender Endpoint is tightly integrated with the Microsoft 365 Security Center, which serves as the unified portal for security management across the Microsoft Ecosystem. The integration brings various security products and services together, including Microsoft Defender for Office 365 and Microsoft Defender for Identity, offering unified experience.

User experience and interface improvements

The journey towards a single portal has also focused on enhancing the user experience and interface design to empower security teams with intuitive tools and actionable insights. The key improvements include:

- **Unified dashboard**: The unified dashboard presents a consolidated view of security events, incidents, and threats across endpoints and other Microsoft security services. This dashboard provides at-a-glance visibility into an organization's security posture.

- **Interactive threat analytics**: The portal offers interactive threat analytics, enabling security analysts to investigate incidents, trace attack chains, and understand the scope and impact of security events easily.

- **Incident response workflows**: Microsoft 365 Security Center facilitates incident response workflows, guiding security teams through the steps required to investigate and remediate security incidents effectively.

- **Actionable recommendations**: The portal provides actionable recommendations and insights based on threat intelligence and best practices, helping security teams make informed decisions and improve their security strategies.

Microsoft billion device benefit in security

Microsoft Defender Endpoint leverages the massive user base of Microsoft's products and services to provide a unique advantage in the security market. In this section, we will explore how Microsoft harnesses the power of its user base to strengthen security through insights from real-world data and telemetry. We will also discuss how collective intelligence contributes to a more robust security posture and the ethical and privacy considerations involved in data usage.

Leveraging the power of Microsoft's massive user base

Microsoft's products, such as Windows, Office 365, and Azure, are used by billions of devices worldwide. This extensive user base generates a vast amount of security-related data and telemetry. Microsoft collects anonymized data and insights from these devices, creating a wealth of information about the ever-evolving threat landscape.

Insights from real-world data and telemetry

The data collected from Microsoft's massive user base provides invaluable insights into real-world cyber threats and attack patterns. By analyzing this data, Microsoft gains a deep understanding of various attack techniques, malware behavior, and emerging threats. This knowledge enables Microsoft to improve its threat intelligence and adapt its security solutions to address the latest threats effectively.

Strengthening security posture through collective intelligence

Microsoft Defender Endpoint leverages collective intelligence to enhance its threat detection and response capabilities. Some key aspects include:

- **Behavior-based analysis**: Collective intelligence allows Microsoft Defender Endpoint to identify new attack techniques and behaviors based on data from diverse sources, making it more resilient against zero-day exploits and unknown threats.

- **ML and AI**: The large-scale data allows ML models to be trained on a wide range of real-world scenarios, leading to more accurate threat detection and fewer false positives.

- **Rapid response**: With collective intelligence, Microsoft can quickly detect and respond to emerging threats, proactively protecting all endpoints in its user base.

Ethical and privacy considerations in data usage

While leveraging collective intelligence is beneficial for improving security, Microsoft is committed to maintaining the highest ethical standards and safeguarding user privacy. The following principles guide Microsoft's approach:

- **Anonymization**: The data collected is anonymized and stripped of **personally identifiable information** (**PII**) to protect user privacy. Internally in Microsoft, we refer scrubbed and un scrubbed data terms and MD Data platform team manages the access as per the security boundaries set by team as per the data category.

- **User consent**: Microsoft ensures that users are informed about data collection and gives them the option to provide consent.

- **Data protection and encryption**: Collected data is securely stored and transmitted using encryption to prevent unauthorized access.

- **Compliance with regulations**: Microsoft adheres to relevant data protection laws and regulations to ensure responsible data handling practices.

Conclusion

Endpoint security is a cornerstone of modern cybersecurity, and Microsoft Defender Endpoint stands as a stalwart solution. By tapping into collective intelligence and analyzing real-world data, it fortifies threat intelligence and response times, all while respecting user trust and privacy. With real-time protection, advanced threat detection, and robust endpoint response features, it offers a multi-layered defense against evolving cyber threats.

Additionally, its seamless integration with the Microsoft Ecosystem ensures that organizations benefit from cost-efficient, scalable, and streamlined security management. This chapter has provided a thorough overview of endpoint security fundamentals and explored the evolution, features, and organizational advantages of Microsoft Defender Endpoint. This chapter provided an in-depth understanding of endpoint security fundamentals and introduced Microsoft Defender Endpoint's evolution, features, and organizational benefits. The next chapter will explore further into technical aspects, covering configuration, deployment, and optimization best practices.

CHAPTER 2
Understanding Endpoint Security Fundamentals

Introduction

In this chapter, we will go into the fundamental concepts of endpoint security. We will explore the ever-evolving threat landscape, uncover common challenges faced in endpoint security, emphasize the significance of effective endpoint protection, and provide insights into best practices that organizations can adopt to mitigate risks. Additionally, we will examine the paradigm shift from traditional to proactive security measures and explore into the renowned MITRE ATT&CK framework and its coverage within the context of Microsoft Defender Endpoint.

Indirectly, there are many learning aspects involved like understanding the state of cybercrime like economy and services, ransomware, extortion, phishing, malicious emails, malware, malicious domains and associated adversarial machine learning. Nation-state threats, supply chain, **Internet of Things (IoT)** and **Operational Technology (OT)** security are other major items in the security picture. Broadly, all such items are handled by mentioned four security products.

Structure

The chapter discusses the following topics:

- Categorization of endpoint security
- Endpoint security threat landscape
- Common endpoint security challenges
- Importance of endpoint protection
- Endpoint security best practices
- Understanding MITRE and MDE portal coverage

Objectives

The objective of this chapter to give insights into the significance of endpoint protection within the broader cybersecurity landscape. It aims to explore the critical role endpoints play in defending against evolving threats, emphasizing the impact of breaches on organizations, regulatory compliance requirements, and the imperative for ensuring business continuity. Additionally, the chapter seeks to address common challenges faced in endpoint security, such as insider threats, **Bring Your Own Device** (**BYOD**), patch management, and data leakage. By highlighting best practices, including layered defense strategies, user training, and regular security audits, it aims to equip readers with the knowledge needed to navigate these challenges effectively and build resilient endpoint security strategies. Moreover, it introduces proactive security approaches and technologies like **Endpoint Detection and Response** (**EDR**), illustrating the journey towards a more proactive and intelligence-driven security posture. The chapter concludes with insights into MITRE ATT&CK framework and Microsoft Defender Endpoint coverage, empowering readers with enhanced security intelligence.

Categorization of endpoint security

There are many solutions available in market that helps you to mitigate security but to better understand the high-level categorization then you will find either in device, network, application or identities.

Broadly, endpoint security is categorized into:

- Device
- Network
- Application
- Identities

Refer to the following figure:

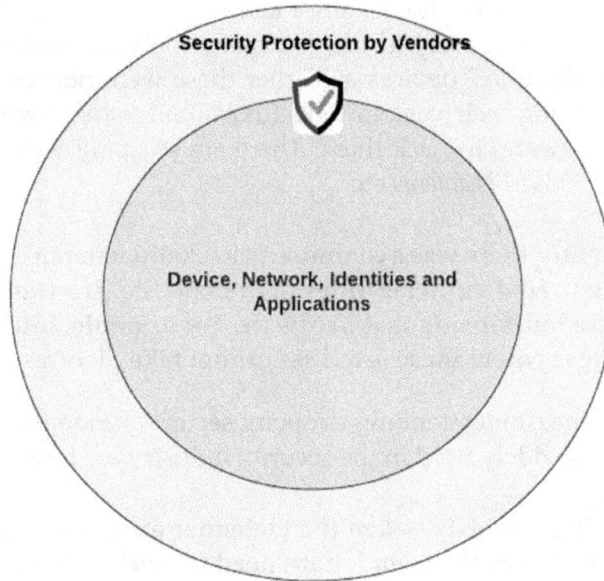

Figure 2.1: Endpoint security product categories

The categories are discussed as follows:

- **Devices**: Endpoint agents primarily protect various types of devices. The following are the key asset types to monitor which include:
  - Bare-metal physical machines
  - Virtual machines
  - Cloud-based virtual machines or instances
  - Containers
  - IoT
- **Network**: Behavioral monitoring is another component where endpoint agents continuously track the activities and forward the telemetry to cloud solutions to take required actions. Defender Agent performs behavior monitoring and helps protect against these threats.
- **Application**: The **Cloud Access Security Broker** (**CASB**) category helps in giving coverage in this area.
- **Identities**: This category includes tools like Microsoft Entra AAD are covered under this. It can help you to protect yourself from identity hijacking and further infiltration into the environment. Microsoft Entra is a comprehensive suite of identity services, incorporating products such as **Active Directory** (**AD**), **Azure Active Directory** (**AAD**), and other related tools.

IoT edge devices may not be large or complex. However, security companies do have their investment by considering the future aspects of the growing market, like fridges, ACs or similar appliances used in home, office and corporate environments etc. But these days Black Hat hackers are actively leveraging many tools and techniques to enter into organization through these IoT devices as earlier these were not focused or prioritized so hackers started building their custom tools (tools built using Raspberry PI or similar custom developed hardware) to hack them. There are so many well attacks that can be done on *Wifi routers, TV, Wi-Fi cameras* etc.

Informational: Recently, there was a community hackathon organized where security hackers were trying to find vulnerabilities in the satellite firmware and understand the logical code base built inside that hardware. For example, internationally, there are high-security areas where these satellites cannot take pictures, etc.

Before you dive deep into understanding endpoint security fundamentals, here is a list of words or terminologies widely used in the security industry as shown in *Table 2.1*.

Informational: During Covid-19, when the Defender team was scaling too fast and onboarding many members, the team felt the need for such a glossary. They created a long list for them but as of now, it is good enough for you to understand the domain.

S.No.	Domain	Full form
1	EDR	Endpoint detection and response
2	EPP	Endpoint protection platform
3	MDR	Managed detection and response
4	SOC	Security operation center
5	SIEM	Security information and event management
6	XDR	Extended detection and response
7	SAST	Static application security testing
8	DAST	Dynamic application security testing
9	CASB	Cloud access security broker
10	TVM	Threat and vulnerability management
11	AIR	Automated investigation and response
12	WAF	Web application firewall
13	ATT&CK	Adversarial tactics, techniques, and common knowledge
14	MITRE	MITRE is organization name
15	HUMOR	Human operated ransomware

Table 2.1: Terminologies or full form of words

Categorized view in rows in relation to each other: We have grouped together certain security roles/activities together for your better understanding. *Figure 2.2* gives insight into the Security Research Profile:

Security Research	ThreatIntel	Advanced Hunting
Malware Analysis	Dynamic MBA	Static MBA
MITRE		

Figure 2.2: *Security research profile*

Figure 2.3 talks about various endpoint security areas from endpoint detection, response to managed detection response and various testing techniques:

EDR	EPP	MDR
SOC	SIEM	XDR
Penetration	SAST	DAST
CASB	TVM	AIR
API Security	WAF	

Figure 2.3: *Endpoint security areas*

With *Table 2.2*, we understand some application security-related terminologies:

S.No.	Domain	Full form
1	DNS	Domain name system
2	DoS	Denial of service
3	DDoS	Distributed denial of service
4	VPN	Virtual private network
5	IoT	Internet of Things
6	AI	Artificial intelligence
7	ML	Machine learning
8	SOCaaS	Security operations center as a service
9	IAM	Identity and access management
10	LDAP	Lightweight Directory Access Protocol
11	RDP	Remote desktop protocol
12	RCE	Remote code execution

S.No.	Domain	Full form
13	XSS	Cross-site scripting
14	CSRF	Cross-site request forgery
15	JWT	JSON Web Token
16	API	Application programming interface
17	**Secure Sockets Layer (SSL)**	Secure Sockets Layer

Table 2.2: Application security terminologies

Table 2.3 helps us understand other security terminologies used:

Term	Description
Endpoint security	Protecting individual devices in a network.
Malware	Malicious software designed to harm endpoints.
Antivirus	Software to detect and remove malware.
Firewall	Network security system that filters traffic.
Intrusion detection system	Monitors network for suspicious activities.
Intrusion prevention system	Blocks malicious activities on a network.
Encryption	Data protection through code transformation.
Vulnerability assessment	Identifying weaknesses in endpoint security.
Patch management	Keeping software updated to prevent vulnerabilities.
Zero-day exploit	Attacks on software vulnerabilities before patches.
Phishing	Deceptive emails to trick users into actions.
Ransomware	Encrypts data until ransom is paid.
Data loss prevention	Safeguarding sensitive data from leakage.
Endpoint detection and response (EDR)	Monitoring and responding to endpoint threats.
Behavioral analytics	Analyzing user behavior for threat detection.
Sandboxing	Isolating and testing potentially harmful code.
Two-factor authentication	Requires two methods for user authentication.
Secure boot	Ensuring only authorized software starts at boot.
Mobile device management	Managing security on mobile devices.
Application whitelisting	Allowing only approved apps to run on endpoints.
URL filtering	Blocking or allowing URLs based on a policy.

Term	Description
Device control	Managing and controlling devices connected to a network.
Host-based Intrusion Detection System (HIDS)	Monitors endpoint activities for intrusions.
User and Entity Behavior Analytics (UEBA)	Analyzing user and entity behavior for threats.
Secure Socket Layer (SSL)	Encrypts data transferred between user and server.
Virtual Private Network (VPN)	Secures internet connection with encryption.
Multi-factor authentication (MFA)	Uses multiple methods for user authentication.
Biometric authentication	Using unique biological traits for authentication.
Remote wipe	Removing data from a lost or stolen device.
File integrity monitoring	Monitoring and detecting unauthorized file changes.
Privilege management	Assigning and controlling user permissions.
Data classification	Categorizing data based on sensitivity.
Device encryption	Encrypting data stored on devices.
Application control	Controlling which applications can run.
Incident response	Plan to manage and mitigate security incidents.
Network access control	Regulating access to network resources.
Port control	Controlling which ports are open on devices.
SIEM	Centralized log management and analysis.
Next-generation antivirus	Advanced antivirus solutions with enhanced features.
Botnet	A network of infected computers controlled by an attacker.
Command and control (C&C) servers	Servers used to send commands to malware.
Insider threat	Threats from individuals within the organization.
Advanced persistent threat (APT)	Long-term targeted cyberattacks.
Exploit	Taking advantage of a software vulnerability.
Social engineering	Manipulating individuals to gain information.
Brute force attack	Attempting to guess passwords or keys.
Rootkit	Malicious software that gains root access.

Term	Description
Logic bomb	Malware activated by specific conditions.
Payload	Malicious action carried out by malware.
Trojan horse	Malware disguised as legitimate software.
Backdoor	Unauthorized access to a system.
Bot	Automated software performing tasks.

Table 2.3: General security terminologies

Endpoint security threat landscape

The endpoint security landscape encompasses various dynamic aspects, which are outlined as follows:

- **The evolving threat landscape**: This involves understanding the dynamic and diverse nature of threats that target endpoints.

- **Attack vectors**: It relates to exploring the various ways cybercriminals exploit vulnerabilities to compromise endpoints.

- **Zero-day exploits**: Here, we delve into the concept of zero-day vulnerabilities and how they can be used as potent weapons by attackers.

- **Advanced persistent threats (APTs) and advanced malware**: We will uncover the **tactics, techniques, and procedures (TTPs)** employed by APTs and the role of advanced malware.

Evolving threat landscape

In today's interconnected digital landscape, endpoint devices are at the forefront of cyberattacks. The threat landscape is dynamic, with adversaries continually evolving their tactics to exploit vulnerabilities and gain unauthorized access to sensitive data. From malware and ransomware to phishing and insider threats, the range of potential dangers is vast and ever-expanding.

Attack vectors

Attackers utilize a variety of vectors to target endpoints, including malicious email attachments, compromised websites, and infected removable media. Social engineering techniques are employed to manipulate users into taking actions that compromise security. Understanding these vectors is essential for implementing effective countermeasures.

Zero-day exploits

A zero-day exploit is a cyberattack that targets an undisclosed vulnerability in software before a patch is available. These exploits can have devastating consequences, as attackers can exploit the vulnerability undetected. Endpoint security must account for these threats and provide proactive defense mechanisms.

Advanced persistent threats and advanced malware

APTs represent sophisticated and well-funded adversaries that engage in long-term campaigns to breach specific targets. They often employ advanced malware that is specifically designed to evade traditional security measures. Detecting and mitigating APTs requires a comprehensive and proactive security approach.

There are many identified APT groups across the world. The ones identified in China are listed in *Table 2.4*:

Activity group name	Other names	Country of origin	Industries targeted
MANGANESE	APT5, Keyhole Panda	China	Communications infrastructure, defense industrial base, software/technology
ZIRCONIUM	APT31, China	China	Government agencies and services, diplomatic organizations, economic organizations
HAFNIUM		China	Higher education, defense industrial base, think tanks, NGOs, law firms, medical research
NICKEL	APT15, Vixen Panda	China	Government agencies and services diplomatic organizations
CHROMIUM	ControlX	China	Energy communications infrastructure, education, government agencies and services
GADOLINIUM	APT40	China	Maritime, healthcare, higher education, regional government organizations

Table 2.4: APT group name and references

The following are the various APT groups from China those who are involved in various malicious activities:

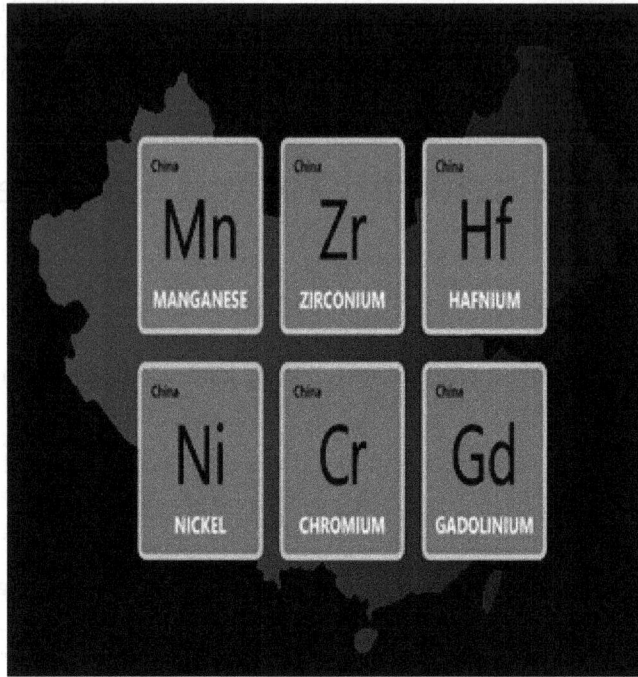

Figure 2.4: APT group related to China[1]

The ones identified in China are listed in *Table 2.5:*

Activity group name	Other names	Country of origin	Industries targeted
PHOSPHORUS	Houseblend Tortoise Shell	Iran	Diplomatic and nuclear policy communities, academics, and journalists
CURIUM	Houseblend Tortoise Shell	Iran	US military and defense contractors, IT services, and Middle Eastern governments
RUBIDIUM	Fox Kitten Parasite	Iran	Israeli logistics companies, IT services, and defense

Table 2.5: APT groups related to Iran

The following are the various APT groups from Iran those who are involved in various malicious activities:

---

1   FY21 Microsoft Digital Defense Report

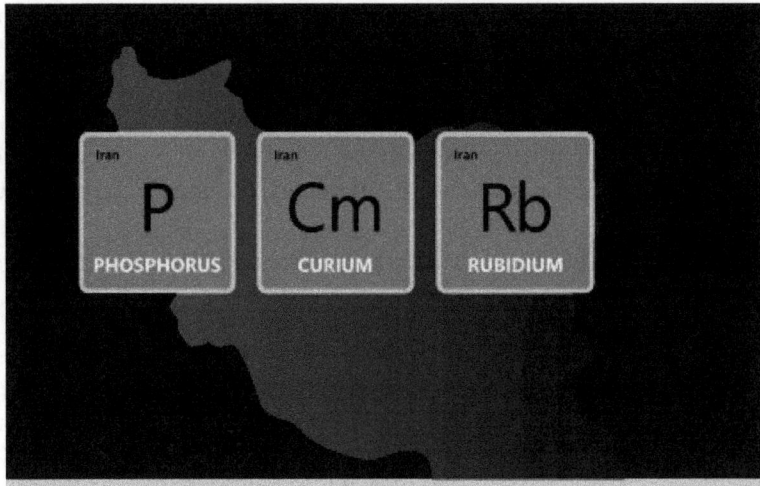

Figure 2.5: APT groups in Iran[2]

Common endpoint security challenges

There are many general and common challenges that as security engineer you will encounter on day-to-day basis and are listed as follows:

Insider threats

Insider threats, whether malicious or unintentional, pose a significant risk to endpoint security. Employees with access to sensitive data can intentionally or inadvertently compromise security, underscoring the need for robust access controls and monitoring mechanisms.

Bring Your Own Device and remote work

The proliferation of **Bring Your Own Device (BYOD)** policies and remote work arrangements introduces challenges in securing endpoints beyond the corporate network perimeter. Protecting endpoints in diverse environments while ensuring data integrity and confidentiality is a complex task.

Patch management

Timely software updates and patch management are critical to preventing the exploits of known vulnerabilities. However, patching can be challenging, especially in large organizations, as delays can leave endpoints exposed to attacks.

---

2   FY21 Microsoft Digital Defense Report

Operating system vendor or application software provider releases new Patches as per their predefined cycle and as an end user (company). It should be your priority to deploy such an upgrade. Linux OS vendors like Red Hat, openSUSE, and Ubuntu have their release cycle and similarly, platforms like Kubernetes and web servers have their own. Microsoft Defender's TVM feature gives you the capability to manage patches across the cross platform operating system and insights directly from the Microsoft Security Portal.

> **Note: Whenever we are referring to Microsoft Security Portal, we are referring to https://security.microsoft.com web portal.**

> **Learn more: There was a one of the version of virus named Petya that created the issues and troubled one of the biggest shipping companies named Maerks. This forced them to shut down their operations for a few days. It was estimated that it cost $10 billion in revenue to companies impacted by such malware.**

Data leakage and loss

Endpoints often store sensitive data, making them targets for data exfiltration. Unauthorized access, whether due to a breach or insider threat, can lead to data leakage, financial losses, and reputational damage.

Importance of endpoint protection

Endpoint protection forms a fundamental pillar of any organization's cybersecurity strategy. With the ever-evolving nature of cyber threats, protecting endpoints such as laptops, desktops, servers, and mobile devices has become critical. These devices serve as entry points into an organization's network and are often targeted by malicious actors seeking to exploit vulnerabilities. Without robust endpoint protection, the organization's sensitive data, intellectual property, and operational continuity are at constant risk of compromise.

Endpoint protection not only shields individual devices from various forms of malware, ransomware, and phishing attacks but also plays a vital role in ensuring regulatory compliance. Industries across the globe are governed by strict data protection standards, and failure to meet these standards can lead to severe financial penalties and reputational damage. Moreover, with the rise of remote work, securing endpoints has gained even greater importance, as employees now connect to organizational networks from diverse locations, often using personal devices.

A strong endpoint protection strategy provides centralized management, enabling IT administrators to monitor, enforce, and update security policies across the organization's device landscape efficiently. By mitigating risks, enhancing productivity, and supporting uninterrupted business operations, endpoint protection serves as a cost-effective investment that safeguards the organization's present and future against the financial and reputational impacts of cyberattacks.

Critical role of endpoints

Endpoints, including laptops, desktops, and mobile devices, are the entry and exit points for data traffic. Securing these endpoints is paramount, as compromise can lead to lateral movement within the network and potential data breaches.

Impact of breaches

Endpoint breaches can have far-reaching consequences, including financial losses, regulatory fines, and damage to an organization's reputation. Recovering from a breach can be expensive and time-consuming, highlighting the importance of prevention. There was a data breach hacking incident that happened on 14th August 2023 to **Discord.io,** a community-based collaboration platform. The famous community-based collaboration solution was hacked yesterday, prompting the team to cease operations temporarily to prevent further damage. They communicated the incident and their decision to their subscriber base through a post by the Admin on their Discord.io page. The breach occurred due to hackers exploiting vulnerabilities on their website, leading to unauthorized access to their user database. Discord.io actively addressed the situation by rewriting their website's code to eliminate vulnerabilities and enhance security. They responsibly managed the incident, including communication with users regarding hack details, subscription refunds, and mitigation plans.

This incident underscores the critical importance of cybersecurity in today's digital landscape. Breaches can not only disrupt operations but also damage a company's reputation and result in legal consequences.

To strengthen your company's security, it is crucial to stay informed about evolving threats. Regularly reviewing resources such as the OWASP Top Ten, which highlights the most critical web application security risks, can help protect your systems. OWASP releases this list annually, providing insights into areas frequently targeted by malicious actors. Implementing measures to mitigate these risks and enabling functionalities to manage them is essential for safeguarding your organization.

Latest Top Ten list: **https://lnkd.in/eKGyQJY**

Other measures that you can take:

- **Security audits**: Conduct routine security audits and penetration testing to identify vulnerabilities before hackers can exploit them.
- **Secure coding practices**: Train your developers in secure coding practices to ensure your software is built with security in mind from the ground up.

- **Stay updated**: Keep your software, operating systems, and third-party libraries up to date with the latest security patches.
- **User education**: Educate your employees about cybersecurity best practices to minimize the risk of human errors leading to breaches.
- **Incident response plan**: Develop a comprehensive incident response plan to effectively address any security breaches that may occur.

Security testing using **Static Application Security Testing (SAST)**, **Dynamic Application Security Testing** (**DAST**) and a well-mature DevSecOps workflow using Aqua Security, MS Defender for Cloud, Wiz.io etc. kind of solutions can help you to have mature software release process.

Your company's security is paramount, and we must remain vigilant in safeguarding our digital assets. Let us learn from incidents like this and work together to fortify our online presence.

Regulatory compliance

Many industries are subject to stringent data protection regulations that require robust endpoint security measures. Non-compliance can result in severe penalties, making effective endpoint protection essential for meeting regulatory requirements.

Business continuity

Unsecured endpoints can disrupt business operations, leading to downtime, loss of productivity, and revenue. Ensuring the availability and integrity of endpoints is crucial for maintaining business continuity.

Endpoint security best practices

Always follow the recommended practices and endpoint security also has such best practices that you as engineer can follow.

Layered defense

A layered defense strategy involves implementing multiple security measures to create overlapping layers of protection. This approach reduces the likelihood of a successful attack by requiring adversaries to overcome multiple obstacles.

User training and awareness

Educating users about security risks, social engineering tactics, and safe online behavior is a fundamental defense against threats. By enhancing user awareness, organizations can prevent many attacks from succeeding.

Least privilege principle

The principle of least privilege dictates that users should only have the minimum level of access necessary to perform their tasks. Limiting user privileges reduces the potential attack surface and the impact of a breach.

Regular security audits

Frequent security audits and assessments help identify vulnerabilities, misconfigurations, and areas for improvement. Regular reviews of security controls and practices are essential for maintaining a strong security posture.

In the following pages, we will delve deeper into the transition from traditional to proactive security measures and explore how Microsoft Defender Endpoint aligns with the MITRE ATT&CK framework to provide comprehensive protection against a wide range of threats.

Navigating endpoint security challenges

Understanding and addressing common endpoint security challenges is paramount to establishing a strong security foundation. Insider threats, BYOD and remote work complexities, patch management intricacies, and data leakage risks demand proactive and comprehensive solutions. By implementing effective strategies to counter these challenges, organizations can enhance their overall security posture and minimize the potential impact of security incidents.

As we proceed, the subsequent pages will delve into the critical importance of endpoint protection and explore best practices that organizations can adopt to ensure robust security measures for their endpoints.

Safeguarding the core of operations

In conclusion, understanding the importance of endpoint protection is pivotal in establishing a holistic security strategy. Recognizing the critical role endpoints play, grasping the potential consequences of breaches, adhering to regulatory compliance requirements, and safeguarding business continuity all underscore the necessity of robust endpoint security measures. By effectively securing endpoints, organizations can ensure the integrity of their operations, data, and reputation, and bolster their ability to thrive in an increasingly digital and interconnected world.

In the next pages, we will explore actionable best practices for endpoint security, empowering organizations to take proactive steps towards safeguarding their endpoints and strengthening their overall security posture.

Building a resilient endpoint security strategy

In conclusion, adhering to endpoint security best practices is a cornerstone of establishing a robust and resilient security strategy. A layered defense approach, coupled with user training and awareness, the principle of least privilege, and regular security audits, forms a formidable defense against the ever-evolving threat landscape. By proactively implementing these practices, organizations can bolster their endpoint security posture, mitigate risks, and ensure the continued integrity of their digital operations.

In the subsequent pages, we will embark on a journey that traces the evolution from traditional security measures to proactive security approaches, shedding light on how organizations can transition from reactive to anticipatory endpoint security strategies.

- **Traditional security approaches**: It involves understanding the limitations of traditional reactive security measures and signature-based detection.
- **Proactive security**: This explores the transition towards proactive security strategies, including behavior-based analysis, ML, and threat hunting.
- **Endpoint detection and response**: We will discuss how EDR capabilities contribute to a more proactive and comprehensive security approach.

In an era marked by relentless cyber threats, the evolution of endpoint security from traditional to proactive measures represents a paradigm shift in fortifying digital landscapes. This transition is driven by a deep-seated understanding of the inadequacies of reactive approaches and the imperative to remain one step ahead of cyber adversaries.

Traditional security approaches

Traditional security measures often relied on reactive tactics, where threats were countered after they had infiltrated the system. Signature-based detection, the cornerstone of many traditional approaches, aimed to identify known threats by comparing them to a database of signatures. However, this method struggled to keep pace with the sheer volume and rapid mutation of modern malware. As attackers advanced, traditional approaches found themselves constrained by the limitations of predefined patterns.

Proactive security

The emergence of proactive security strategies represents a departure from the limitations of traditional models. Proactive measures anticipate threats before they manifest, relying on a constellation of advanced techniques to identify and counteract potential risks. Behavior-based analysis monitors the activities of endpoints, identifying anomalous behaviors that might indicate a breach. ML algorithms sift through vast data sets to recognize patterns that may indicate malicious activity. Threat hunting, a human-driven process, involves actively seeking out indicators of compromise to identify hidden threats.

Endpoint detection and response

At the forefront of proactive security is the concept of EDR. It encompasses a suite of technologies and practices that enable real-time monitoring, threat detection, and rapid response. EDR platforms provide an enhanced view into endpoint activities, allowing security teams to trace the paths of threats and isolate compromised systems. By facilitating swift response to emerging threats, EDR contributes to a more proactive and comprehensive security approach, helping organizations identify and mitigate risks before they escalate.

Pioneering the proactive security frontier

In conclusion, the journey from traditional to proactive security marks a fundamental transformation in how organizations approach endpoint security. Acknowledging the limitations of reactive approaches, the industry has shifted towards anticipating and countering threats before they breach defenses. Proactive security leverages innovative technologies, behavioral analysis, and human expertise to detect and respond to threats in real-time. The advent of EDR underscores the commitment to proactive security, providing a multifaceted approach to safeguarding endpoints.

As we delve deeper into the technical aspects of Microsoft Defender Endpoint in the subsequent pages, we will unravel how these proactive strategies manifest in a comprehensive and powerful solution that fortifies endpoints against an array of cyber threats.

Understanding MITRE and MDE portal coverage

The MITRE framework, renowned in security, provides a comprehensive taxonomy of TTPs utilized by adversaries during cyberattacks. It serves as a valuable resource for security professionals, offering insights into various threat actors' behaviors and aiding in the development of robust defense strategies. MDE portal has built in functionality to show case security incidents in relation to MITRE format, such as:

- **Introduction to MITRE ATT&CK**: It involves exploring the MITRE ATT&CK framework, a comprehensive knowledge base of adversary tactics and techniques.
- **Microsoft Defender Endpoint coverage**: It relates to understanding how Microsoft Defender Endpoint aligns with and addresses various MITRE ATT&CK techniques.
- **Threat intelligence and analytics**: Here, we discussing how MITRE ATT&CK provides actionable insights for threat detection, analysis, and response.

As the threat landscape continues to evolve, understanding and countering adversaries' tactics and techniques is pivotal in building effective defense mechanisms. The MITRE ATT&CK framework serves as a beacon of knowledge, shedding light on the intricacies of adversary behaviors. Let us explore how this framework, coupled with **Microsoft Defender Endpoint (MDE)**, forms a powerful alliance in safeguarding endpoint security.

Introduction to MITRE ATT&CK

The MITRE ATT&CK framework is a treasure trove of insights into the strategies, tactics, and techniques employed by adversaries across different stages of an attack. By categorizing adversary behaviors, ATT&CK provides a structured approach to understanding their methodologies. ATT&CK encompasses a wealth of knowledge, empowering security teams to anticipate, detect, and respond to threats with heightened precision.

Microsoft Defender Endpoint coverage

Microsoft Defender Endpoint aligns seamlessly with the MITRE ATT&CK framework, bridging the gap between knowledge and implementation. It actively addresses and counters various techniques outlined in ATT&CK. This alignment enables Microsoft Defender Endpoint to provide robust protection against a wide spectrum of threats, ranging from initial access to exfiltration. By synergizing the insights from MITRE ATT&CK with the capabilities of Microsoft Defender Endpoint, organizations can enhance their threat detection and response capabilities.

Threat intelligence and analytics

MITRE ATT&CK's significance extends beyond a mere catalog of adversary tactics. It serves as a foundation for threat intelligence and analytics. The framework aids in identifying patterns and behaviors indicative of malicious activity. By leveraging this intelligence, security teams can proactively analyze and assess potential threats, rapidly identifying anomalies that might otherwise evade detection. This analytical approach elevates an organization's ability to respond effectively to emerging threats, mitigating risks and minimizing potential damage.

Empowering security intelligence

In essence, the synergy between the MITRE ATT&CK framework and Microsoft Defender Endpoint signifies a fusion of knowledge and action, resulting in an elevated security posture. By embracing ATT&CK, organizations gain a deeper understanding of adversary behavior, empowering them with insights to anticipate and mitigate threats.

In the subsequent chapters in the book that covers MDE solution functionality we will give insight into the technical mechanics of Microsoft Defender Endpoint, unveiling its functionalities, features, and configuration strategies. By comprehending how Microsoft Defender Endpoint aligns with the principles of the MITRE ATT&CK framework, organizations can harness a comprehensive security solution that is primed to protect endpoints from a multitude of cyber threats.

Conclusion

In this chapter, we given insights into the fundamental principles of endpoint security. We examined the ever-evolving threat landscape, identified common challenges, and emphasized the critical importance of effective endpoint protection. By understanding best practices, the journey from reactive to proactive security, and the significance of the MITRE ATT&CK framework within the context of Microsoft Defender Endpoint, organizations are better equipped to establish a robust security foundation.

In the subsequent chapter, we will take a comprehensive look at the technical aspects of Microsoft Defender Endpoint, including its configuration, deployment, and optimization strategies for maximizing its effectiveness.

Join our book's Discord space

Join the book's Discord Workspace for Latest updates, Offers, Tech happenings around the world, New Release and Sessions with the Authors:

https://discord.bpbonline.com

CHAPTER 3

Deploying Microsoft Defender Endpoint

Introduction

This chapter provides a comprehensive guide to the deployment and installation of **Microsoft Defender for Endpoint (MDE)** within an organization. It covers the various architectural approaches, system requirements, and installation procedures to ensure successful implementation.

The chapter begins by exploring the different deployment architectures available, including cloud-native, co-managed, on-premises, and custom-built deployment Script architecture. It emphasizes the importance of thorough preparation, highlighting key considerations such as understanding organizational needs, defining deployment goals, allocating resources, fostering communication and collaboration, and clearly defining roles and responsibilities.

The chapter then gives insight into the system requirements and prerequisites for MDE, covering hardware, licensing, and supported operating system requirements. This information is crucial for ensuring that the target environment is compatible and can accommodate the successful installation and operation of the solution.

Finally, the chapter provides a detailed overview of the various deployment methods, including the Microsoft Security Web Portal, Microsoft Endpoint Configuration Manager, Active Directory Group Policy, manual installation, and MDM/Microsoft Intune. It also highlights the important Defender binaries that are essential for the proper functioning of the solution.

Structure

This chapter covers the following points:

- Deployment preparation
- System requirements and prerequisites
- MDE (Agents) installation

Objectives

The primary objective of this chapter is to provide a comprehensive guide for the successful deployment and installation of MDE within an organization. By the end of this chapter, readers will have a thorough understanding of the various deployment architectures, system requirements, and installation methods, enabling them to make informed decisions and implement MDE effectively in their respective environments.

By achieving these objectives, readers will be well-prepared to embark on the MDE deployment journey, confident in their ability to navigate the process and implement a robust endpoint security solution that safeguards their organization's assets against advanced threats.

Deployment preparation

Before embarking on the journey of deploying MDE, meticulous preparation is essential. This section outlines the crucial steps and considerations to ensure a smooth and successful deployment process. Effective preparation sets the stage for a robust security infrastructure that can safeguard your endpoints from emerging threats.

There are five broad areas that you need to prepare for deployment:

- Prepare for deployment
- Assign roles and permissions
- Identify your architecture
- Onboard devices
- Configure capability

The following figure shows the MDE agent deployment planning and implementation stages:

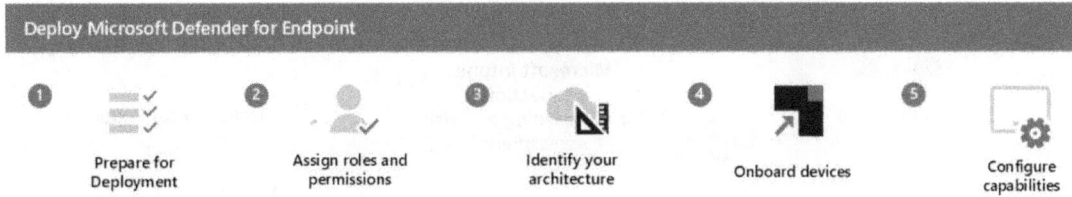

Figure 3.1: MDE deployment stages

The following are the implementation stages for MDE agent deployment:

1. **Set up Microsoft Defender for Endpoint deployment**: This step focuses on getting your environment ready for deployment.

2. **Assign roles and permissions**: Identify and assign roles and permissions to view and manage Defender for Endpoint.

3. **Identify your architecture and choose deployment method**: Identify your architecture and the deployment method that best suits your organization.

4. **Onboard devices**: Assess and onboard your devices to Defender for Endpoint.

5. **Configure capabilities**: You are now ready to configure Defender for Endpoint security capabilities to protect your devices.

The second major thing before you start your deployment is to review your requirement and choose the right deployment architecture.

Choosing the architecture

Microsoft supports different deployment architectures for MDE to manage devices, such as:

- Cloud-native
- Co-management
- On-premises
- Script and evaluation

Let us discuss them.

Cloud-native architecture

The following figure shows **High Level Diagram (HLD)** of cloud-native deployment architecture where Microsoft Intune is integrated with Defender for Endpoint:

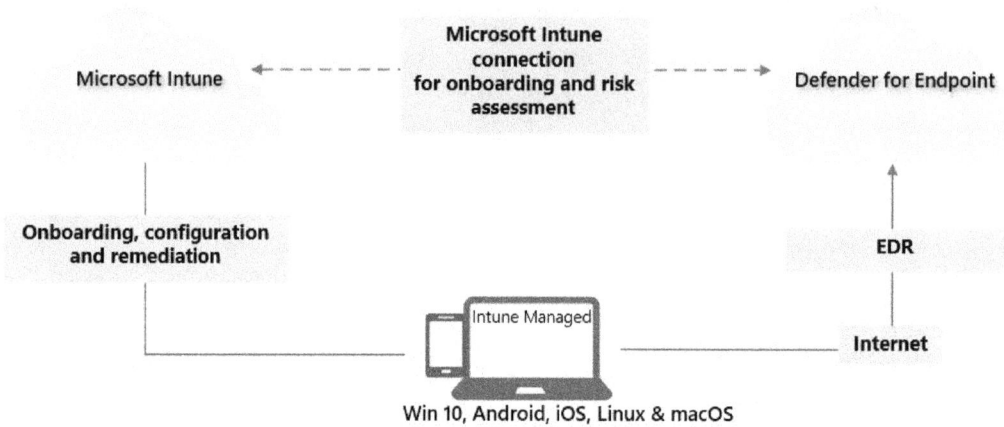

Figure 3.2: Cloud-native deployment architecture HLD

Co-managed architecture

Here, additional ConfigMgr is also introduced to manage or to do the deployment along with Intune and MDE, as shown in the following figure:

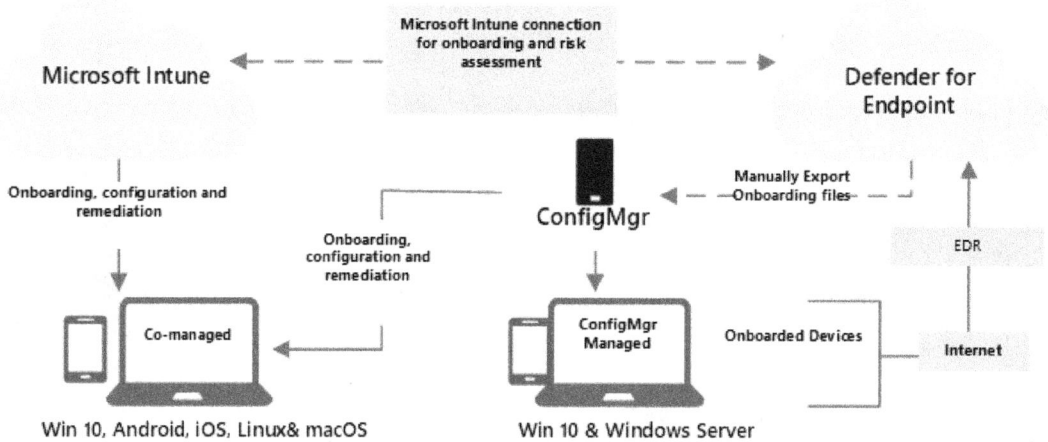

Figure 3.3: Co-managed deployment architecture HLD

On-premises architecture

On-premises deployment architecture with ConfigMgr and without Intune is leveraged for the deployment management, as shown in the following figure:

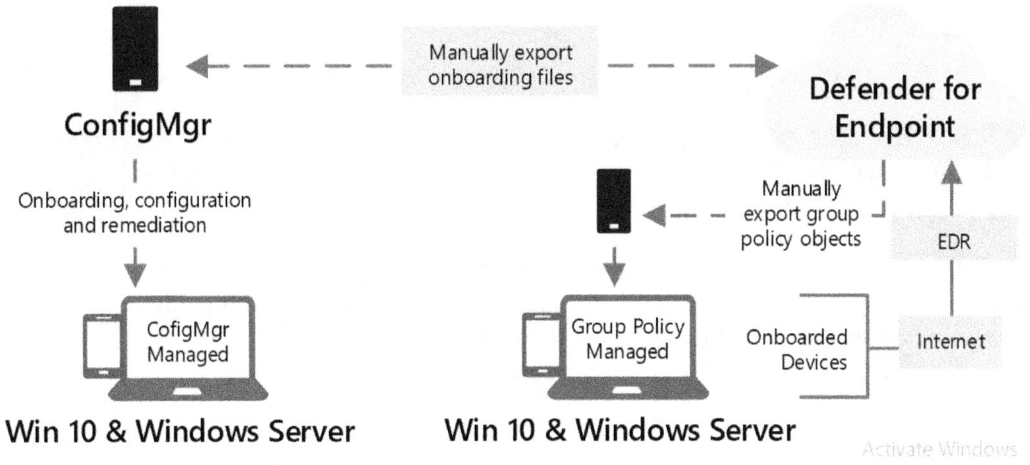

Figure 3.4: *On-premises deployment architecture HLD*

Custom deployment script evaluation architecture

This deployment strategy might be mostly used in automated deployment with your custom scripts or deployment tools like Ansible, Octopus, Puppet, Bash or PowerShell script, etc. It is the simplest and most straight forward way to deploy the agent, as shown in the following figure:

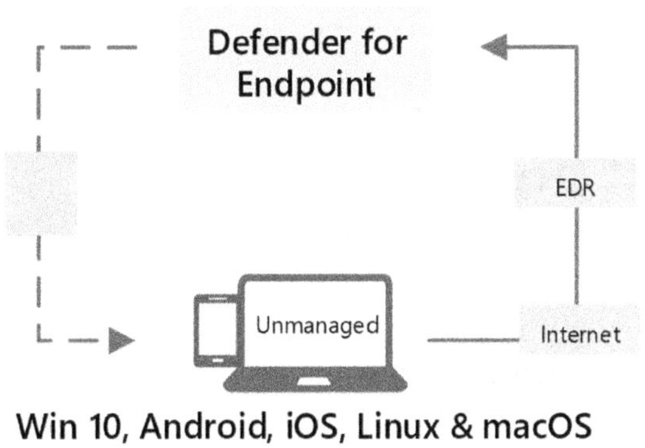

Figure 3.5: *Script evaluation architecture HLD*

Note: In this chapter, we will be focusing on onboard devices as this topic gives core installation steps and the different alternative that you will have for the deployment. In the next chapter, i.e., configure MDE we will touch down on assign role and permission and other various configuration capabilities.

Pre-requisites

The following is a list of pre-requisites required to deploy Defender for Endpoint:

- You are a global admin
- You meet the minimum requirements
- You have a full inventory of your environment

The following table provides a starting point to gather information and ensure your environment is deeply understood by stakeholders, which will help identify potential dependencies and/or changes required in technologies or processes:

Item	Description
Endpoint count	Total count of endpoints by operating system.
Server count	Total count of servers by operating system version.
Management engine	Management engine name and version (for example, System Center Configuration Manager Current Branch 1803).
CDOC distribution	High level CDOC structure (for example, Tier 1 outsourced to Contoso, Tier 2 and Tier 3 in-house distributed across Europe and Asia).
Security information and event (SIEM)	SIEM technology in use.

Table 3.1: Customer setup understanding for deployment planning

Importance of preparation

Preparing for the deployment of MDE is akin to laying the foundation of a strong fortress. Without a solid foundation, the entire structure is vulnerable to cracks and breaches. The same principle applies to endpoint security. Adequate deployment preparation minimizes the risk of deployment hiccups, enhances efficiency, and allows for the full utilization of the solution's capabilities.

Understanding organizational needs

A successful deployment starts with a clear understanding of your organization's security needs. Conduct a comprehensive assessment of your existing security measures, potential vulnerabilities, and threat landscape. Identify critical assets, user behaviors, and potential entry points for threats. This understanding forms the basis for tailoring your deployment strategy to fit your unique requirements.

In the landscape of deploying MDE, comprehending the specific security needs of your organization is paramount. This phase acts as a compass, guiding the deployment strategy towards aligning with your organization's unique security challenges and goals.

- **Assessment of current security landscape**: Begin by conducting an in-depth assessment of your current security measures. This involves scrutinizing existing security solutions, policies, and practices. Identify any gaps, vulnerabilities, or potential entry points for malicious actors. This understanding provides a realistic view of your organization's security posture.

- **Threat landscape analysis**: Analyze the threat landscape relevant to your industry and business vertical. This analysis provides insight into potential risks and aids in prioritizing security measures. It also enables you to anticipate threats and align your deployment to address these risks proactively.

- **Critical asset identification**: Determine the critical assets within your organization. These assets can range from sensitive customer data to intellectual property. Understanding what needs the highest protection enables a focused deployment approach. MDE can then be tailored to guard these vital assets effectively.

- **User behavior patterns**: Study user behavior patterns within your organization. Understanding how users interact with endpoints and data helps in designing policies that accommodate these behaviors without compromising security.

- **Regulatory compliance**: Factor in any regulatory compliance requirements pertinent to your industry. Depending on your geographical location and sector, you might need to adhere to specific regulations. Ensure that your deployment aligns with these compliance needs, reducing the risk of non-compliance penalties.

- **Business objectives and growth plans**: Consider the broader business objectives and growth plans of your organization. If you are expanding, your security measures should be scalable. If entering new markets, your endpoint security might need to adapt to regional threats.

By dissecting these aspects, you forge a blueprint for your MDE deployment. This blueprint is rooted in an acute understanding of your organization's security landscape, enabling you to build a resilient security infrastructure that caters to your unique needs and ensures the protection of your digital assets.

This content offers a detailed explanation of the importance of understanding organizational needs when deploying MDE.

Defining deployment goals

Set clear objectives for your MDE deployment by determining your primary focus areas. Concentrate on malware prevention, incident response, and vulnerability management. By defining these goals, you ensure that the deployment aligns seamlessly with your organization's overall security strategy.

A successful deployment of MDE begins with a clear sense of purpose. Defining specific deployment goals not only provides a roadmap but also ensures that your implementation aligns with your organization's overarching security strategy.

Let us understand the deployment goals:

- **Focused security objectives**: Identify your primary security objectives. Whether they are enhancing malware prevention, strengthening incident response capabilities, or improving vulnerability management. You need to clearly define these goals to drive the direction of your deployment efforts.

- **Risk reduction targets**: Gauge the level of risk reduction you intend to achieve through MDE. This could involve reducing the number of successful cyberattacks, mitigating data breaches, or minimizing the impact of security incidents.

- **Visibility and monitoring**: Ensure your deployment goals include enhanced visibility and monitoring capabilities. Gain real-time insights into endpoint activities to detect and respond to threats swiftly.

- **Resource optimization**: Defining goals also involve optimizing resource allocation. Streamline resource utilization by centralizing security management. Identify areas where efficiency gains can be made.

- **Alignment with security strategy**: Ensure that your deployment goals are in harmony with your organization's broader security strategy. If your strategy emphasizes proactive threat hunting, your deployment might focus on advanced detection and response capabilities.

- **Incident response enhancement**: If incident response is a priority, your goals might involve minimizing the time taken to detect and mitigate security incidents. This enhances your organization's ability to swiftly counter emerging threats.

- **User education and training**: Consider whether your deployment goals encompass user education and training. If so, your focus might be on empowering employees to identify and report potential security threats.

Informational: You can leverage Microsoft provided course and training for your engineers to gain initial understanding and it is available at https://learn.microsoft. com/en-us/training/modules/m365-introduction-defender-endpoint/

- **Metrics and key performance indicators (KPIs)**: Establish metrics (*Total machines onboarded etc.*) and KPIs (*Critical vulnerability indicators etc.*) to measure the success of your deployment. Whether it is the reduction in the number of successful phishing attacks or the increase in endpoint visibility, clear metrics guide your progress.

- **Adaptability**: If your organization is growing, your deployment goals might involve creating an adaptable security infrastructure. This ensures that your endpoint security solution can accommodate expansion without compromising effectiveness.

- **Continuous improvement**: Lastly, consider if your deployment goals extend to continuous improvement. This involves refining your security measures based on insights gained from ongoing monitoring and analysis.

By meticulously defining your deployment goals, you lay a solid foundation for your MDE implementation. These goals drive the configuration, policies, and strategies that will be employed, ultimately culminating in a security infrastructure tailored to safeguard your organization's digital assets.

Resource allocation

Ensure you have the necessary resources in terms of personnel, hardware, and software for successful deployment. Designate a dedicated team responsible for the deployment process. This team should include experts in security, network administration, and system management. Allocate appropriate time and budget to the deployment, considering potential training requirements as well.

Deploying MDE demands a judicious allocation of resources, ensuring that your implementation is not only effective but also efficiently managed. Proper resource allocation contributes to a streamlined deployment process and sets the stage for a robust security infrastructure.

The following is the resource allocation planning:

- **Dedicated deployment team**: Start by assembling a dedicated team responsible for the deployment process. This team should comprise experts from various domains, including security, network administration, system management, and possibly user training.

> **Informational: It can be one Senior Engineer (8+ years) leading the efforts along with one or more early to mid-level engineers (2 to 5 years) to assist in deployment and troubleshooting. It is assumed that Senior Engineer will be having good understanding of automation, network, IT architecture, system administration experience. In case you have thousands (like 10K+) of devices isolated in different network requirement then you might need 2+ assisting engineer in implementation and deployment troubleshooting. Usually, Indian outsourcing companies are deploying 1+2 engineer team for big international deployment.**

- **Expertise and skillsets**: Assess the skills and expertise of team members to allocate tasks accordingly. Having individuals with specialized knowledge can expedite decision-making and troubleshooting during the deployment.

> **Informational: Try to have senior engineers with automation capabilities so that he/she can think of automated deployment as you may encounter multiple situations where you need to automate some tasks.**

- **Time commitment**: Allocate sufficient time for the deployment process. Rushing through implementation can lead to oversights and mistakes. Consider potential disruptions that might arise during deployment and ensure that the allocated time accounts for these factors.

- **Financial budget**: Determine a budget for the deployment process. This budget should encompass not only the implementation itself but also potential training costs, post-deployment maintenance, and any unforeseen expenses.

- **Software resources**: Ensure that the necessary software resources are available in the form of MDE License, Deployment configuration payload downloaded from MDE web portal.

- **Training and skill enhancement**: Allocate resources for training and skill enhancement. If team members need to acquire new skills to effectively manage MDE, invest in training programs to bridge knowledge gaps.

- **Vendor engagement**: If necessary, allocate resources for engaging with Microsoft or authorized vendors. This might involve seeking assistance during critical stages of deployment or troubleshooting complex issues.

- **Documentation and reporting**: Allocate time for thorough documentation of the deployment process. Proper documentation ensures that the deployment can be replicated, scaled, or troubleshooted effectively in the future.

- **Communication channels**: Establish efficient communication channels among team members. A well-connected team can quickly address challenges and collaborate effectively, reducing delays during the deployment.

- **Backup plans**: Allocate resources for creating contingency plans. Unexpected challenges might arise during deployment. Having backup plans in place ensures that the deployment stays on track despite unforeseen hurdles.

- **Regulatory compliance**: Ensuring adherence to local and international regulations such as GDPR, HIPAA, and others pertinent to the organization. There is the possibility that the organization working in specific domain might need compliance in certain other specific area so as deployment engineer you can also take care for configuration deployment.

Proper resource allocation ensures that your MDE deployment proceeds with the required level of attention, expertise, and preparation. By allocating the necessary resources, you enhance the likelihood of a seamless implementation that strengthens your organization's security posture.

Communication and collaboration

Smooth deployment involves effective communication and collaboration across departments. Engage with stakeholders from IT, security, operations, and management to create a shared understanding of the deployment's impact and benefits. Keep everyone informed about the progress and potential disruptions, fostering a cooperative atmosphere.

Efficient communication and collaboration are the cornerstones of a successful MDE deployment. Establishing clear lines of communication and fostering collaboration among various departments ensures a cohesive and well-coordinated implementation process.

The communication and collaboration item list to consider before deployment is as follows:

- **Shared understanding and awareness**: Effective communication ensures that all relevant stakeholders are aware of the deployment's goals, timelines, and potential impacts. This shared understanding minimizes misunderstandings and keeps everyone aligned.

- **Inter-departmental collaboration**: Collaboration between IT, security, operations, and management departments is essential. Regular cross-departmental meetings and updates prevent silos of information, enabling the seamless exchange of insights and concerns.

- **Risk and impact communication**: Clearly communicate the potential risks and impacts associated with the deployment. This empowers decision-makers to make informed choices and allocate resources accordingly.

- **Communication platforms**: Utilize appropriate communication platforms for updates and discussions. This might involve email chains, virtual meetings, collaborative workspaces, or project management tools.

- **Regular progress updates**: Provide regular updates on the deployment's progress. This keeps stakeholders informed about milestones achieved and any challenges encountered, maintaining transparency throughout the process.

- **Addressing concerns**: Encourage open communication by providing avenues for team members to voice concerns or ask questions. Promptly address these concerns to prevent roadblocks and foster a positive atmosphere.

- **Change management**: If the deployment involves significant changes for end-users, ensure effective change management. Transparent communication about changes and potential disruptions eases user adoption.

- **Adaptability and flexibility**: Maintain flexibility in your communication approach. Adapt to the preferences and schedules of different teams to facilitate effective communication.

- **Crisis communication**: Establish a protocol for crisis communication. In the event of unexpected issues or delays, ensure that there is a designated point of contact responsible for communicating updates.

- **Lessons learned**: After deployment, conduct a post-mortem discussion to discuss lessons learned. This allows you to identify communication gaps and areas for improvement in future deployments.

Incorporating robust communication and collaboration practices into your deployment strategy enhances team cohesion, prevents misunderstandings, and ensures a smooth Microsoft Defender Endpoint implementation. By fostering an environment of open dialogue, you lay the groundwork for a successful deployment journey.

Defining roles and responsibilities

Clearly define the roles and responsibilities of each team member involved in the deployment process. Identify who will handle tasks such as system configuration, integration, testing, and user training. Assigning specific roles ensures a structured approach and avoids confusion during critical stages.

In the complex landscape of deploying MDE, clarity in roles and responsibilities is paramount. Clearly defining the tasks and duties of each team member involved in the deployment process ensures coordinated and efficient implementation.

Role clarification

Before deployment we should have clarity with the roles that will be participating in the deployment of the product. The following are the roles:

- **Security architect**: The security architect takes charge of designing the overall security framework for the deployment. This includes creating security policies, defining access controls, and ensuring alignment with industry best practices.

- **Network administrator**: Responsible for configuring network settings and ensuring seamless communication between endpoints and security components. The network administrator ensures that the deployment does not disrupt network operations.

- **System administrator**: This role involves setting up the necessary server infrastructure and ensuring proper integration with existing systems. The system administrator also manages software updates and compatibility issues.

- **Endpoint security specialist**: Focused on configuring and fine-tuning MDE security policies. This role involves selecting appropriate settings for real-time protection, behavior monitoring, and threat detection.

Responsibilities breakdown

As part of the deployment planning responsibilities should be broken down for better management among teams or members.

The following is the responsibility list for deployment management:

- **Deployment planning and strategy**: The security architect takes the lead in planning the deployment strategy. They collaborate with other team members to ensure that the deployment aligns with security objectives.

- **Hardware and software configuration**: System administrators handle the configuration of hardware and software resources required for MDE. This involves setting up servers and ensuring compatibility.

- **Policy configuration**: The endpoint security specialist configures security policies based on the organization's security needs. They define parameters for malware detection, firewall rules, and vulnerability scans.

- **Integration and testing**: The network administrator focuses on integrating MDE with existing security infrastructure. This role also involves testing the deployment's compatibility and identifying any potential conflicts.

- **User training and support**: System administrators and endpoint security specialists conduct user training sessions. They educate users about the new security measures and provide support for any issues that arise.

- **Monitoring and reporting**: The network administrator and endpoint security specialist are responsible for monitoring the deployment's performance and generating reports on security incidents and threat detection.

Collaborative approach

A successful deployment happens through better collaboration among different parties so it should be kept in mind during planning.

The following are the general guidelines around collaboration:

- **Regular communication**: Collaborative success relies on regular communication. Team members should have a clear line of communication to discuss progress, challenges, and changes in deployment requirements.

- **Flexibility and adaptability**: Roles might need to evolve as the deployment progresses. Flexibility ensures that adjustments can be made swiftly to address emerging needs.

- **Cross-functional training**: Encourage cross-functional training to broaden team members' skill sets. This facilitates smoother collaboration and enables team members to step into each other's roles if needed.

Defining roles and responsibilities is not just about assigning tasks; it is about fostering collaboration, leveraging strengths, and streamlining efforts. With well-defined roles, your Microsoft Defender Endpoint deployment gains the clarity and structure necessary for successful implementation.

System requirements and prerequisites

Before deploying MDE, it is important to ensure that your systems meet the necessary requirements and prerequisites. This includes verifying that your devices are running a supported operating system, have the necessary hardware specifications, and meet the licensing, browser, and network requirements.

The following are the system requirements:

- Supported operating systems
- Hardware requirements
- Licensing requirements
- Browser requirements

MDE supports a range of Windows operating systems, including:

- Windows 11 Enterprise, Education, Pro, and Pro-education
- Windows 10 Enterprise, Enterprise LTSC 2016 (or later), Enterprise IoT, Education, Pro, and Pro-education
- Windows 8.1 Enterprise and Pro
- and Windows 7 SP1 Enterprise and Pro

MDE also supports various versions of Windows Server, including:

- Windows Server 2008 R2 SP1
- Windows Server 2012 R2
- Windows Server 2016
- Windows Server version 1803 or later
- Windows Server 2019 and later

It is recommended to install the latest available security patches for any operating system.

Hardware requirements

The minimum hardware requirements for MDE on Windows devices are the same as the requirements for the operating system itself. This means that the hardware requirements are not in addition to the requirements for the operating system. The minimum requirements include at least:

- Two cores (four preferred)
- At least 1 GB of memory (4 GB preferred)
- Network connectivity

Licensing requirements

There are licenses available to cater for the need as per the category. For example, Microsoft has multiple offerings and specially designed for the US Government. Some of them are as follows:

- **Govt Community Cloud (GCC)**
- **Govt Community Cloud High (GCC High)**

- **Department of Defense (DoD)**
- Commercial (publicly available). We will discuss this throughout the book.

GCC is a basic version and preferred for small to medium US Gov Organizations and GCC High contains full fledge feature with more certifications and preferred for bigger US Govt organizations.

> **Note: Commercial and other Gov offering mostly remains in parity and parity SLA is 90 days. New features first come in Commercial and then to Other.**

MDE requires one of several Microsoft volume licensing offers. These include:

- Windows 10 Enterprise E5
- Windows 10 Education A5
- Microsoft 365 E5 (which includes Windows 10 Enterprise E5)
- Microsoft 365 A5, Microsoft 365 E5 Security, or Microsoft 365 A5 Security

It is important to note that MDE Plan 1 and Plan 2 (standalone or as part of other Microsoft 365 plans) do not include server licenses. To onboard servers to those plans, you will need either Microsoft Defender for Cloud or Microsoft Defender for Business servers.

Browser requirements

Access to MDE is done through a browser. The supported browsers include Microsoft Edge and Google Chrome. While other browsers might work, these are the only ones that are officially supported.

The following are the prerequisites:

- Network connectivity
- Software dependencies

Let us discuss them:

- **Network connectivity**: MDE requires network connectivity to function properly. This includes connectivity to the internet as well as connectivity to internal resources such as **Active Directory Domain Services** (**AD DS**) and other security infrastructure components. It is important to ensure that your network infrastructure can support the traffic generated by MDE.
- **Software dependencies**: MDE Windows Desktop or Servers has several software dependencies that must be installed before deployment. These include the latest version of the .NET Framework and the latest version of the Visual C++ Redistributable Package. Additionally, certain features of MDE may require additional software components such as PowerShell or SQL Server.

Similarly, other cross-platform supported OS have their own dependency requirements.

In summary, before deploying MDE it is important to verify that your systems meet the necessary system requirements and prerequisites. This includes ensuring that your devices are running a supported operating system, have the necessary hardware specifications, meet the licensing requirements, can access MDE through a supported browser, have network connectivity, and have all necessary software dependencies installed.

Supported OS by Defender

The scope of MDE's protection extends across a wide range of operating systems, including Windows variants like Windows 11, Windows 10, and Windows Server editions. Additionally, MDE caters to cross-platform security, extending its coverage to Linux, macOS, iOS, and Android environments.

Windows Flavors

The following are the supported OS List as of Sept/2023 for MDE agent deployment:

- Windows 11
- Windows 10
- Windows 10 Enterprise (WVD Multi Session)
- Windows Server 2022
- Windows Server 2019
- Windows Server 2016

Cross-platform OS

After mid-2021, most of the parity features are available on cross-platform OS and the following are the supported OS:

- Linux
- macOS
- iOS
- Android

MDE (Agent) installation

After ensuring that your systems meet the necessary requirements and prerequisites, the next step in deploying MDE is to install the software. This can be done through several methods, including using the following:

- Microsoft Security Web Portal
- Microsoft Endpoint Manager
- Active Directory Group Policy

- Microsoft Intune
- Manually installing the software on individual devices

Informational: Azure Arc is one more Microsoft service that can be leveraged for multi-vendor or multi-cloud onboarding/deployments.

On the Microsoft Security Web Portal (a.k.a. MDE Portal) under **Settings | Endpoint | Onboarding** settings you will be able to find the following five options for the deployment:

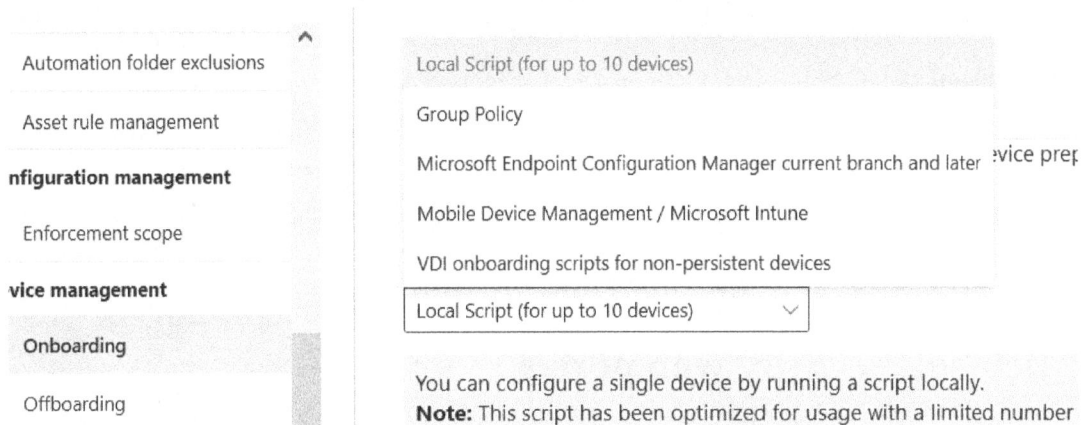

Automation folder exclusions	Local Script (for up to 10 devices)
Asset rule management	Group Policy
nfiguration management	Microsoft Endpoint Configuration Manager current branch and later :vice prep
Enforcement scope	Mobile Device Management / Microsoft Intune
vice management	VDI onboarding scripts for non-persistent devices
Onboarding	Local Script (for up to 10 devices) ⌄
Offboarding	You can configure a single device by running a script locally. **Note:** This script has been optimized for usage with a limited number

Figure 3.6: Agent deployment script download option on MDE portal

Installation methods

The following are the installation/deployment options available for MDE agent and configuration:

1. Microsoft Security Web Portal
2. Microsoft Endpoint Configuration Manager
3. Group Policy
4. Manual Installation
5. MDM/Microsoft Intune

The following figure is the mind map for the installation option available to you in graphical format:

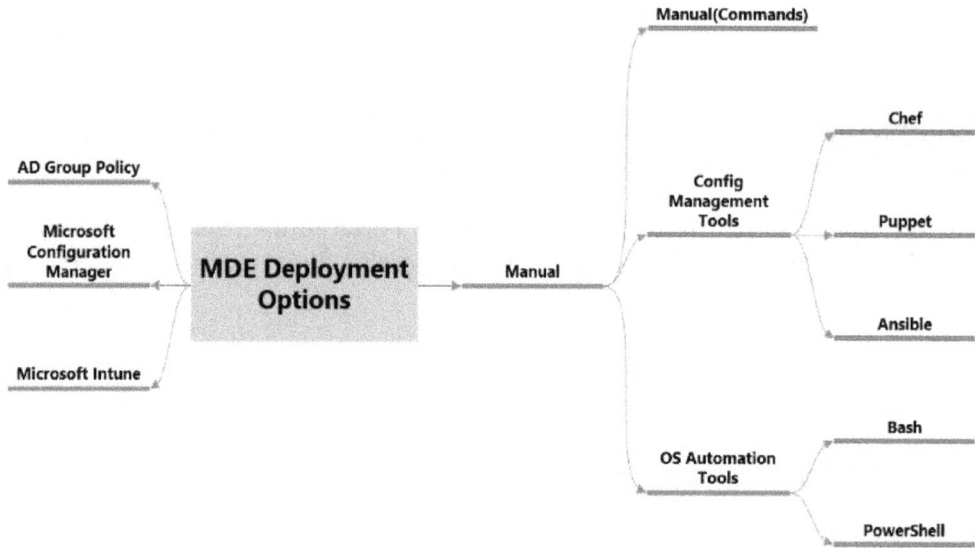

Figure 3.7: MDE deployment option mind map

Microsoft security web portal

Microsoft security web portal is also known as **MDE Portal** or **Security Portal** or **Security Console** or **M365D Security Portal** and accessible on **https://security.microsoft.com/**. This is the most basic option to start with onboarding the devices and it is more covered in the Manual deployment step. We are going to cover this option in *Chapter 6, Monitoring and Alerting with Defender SOC, Chapter 7, Defender SOC Investigating Threats*, and *Chapter 8, Responding to Threats with Defender SOC*.

The following figure is a screenshot of security web portal home page for reference for better understanding in case you do not have access on the portal, and you can see Menu bar option is available on left hand side for selection:

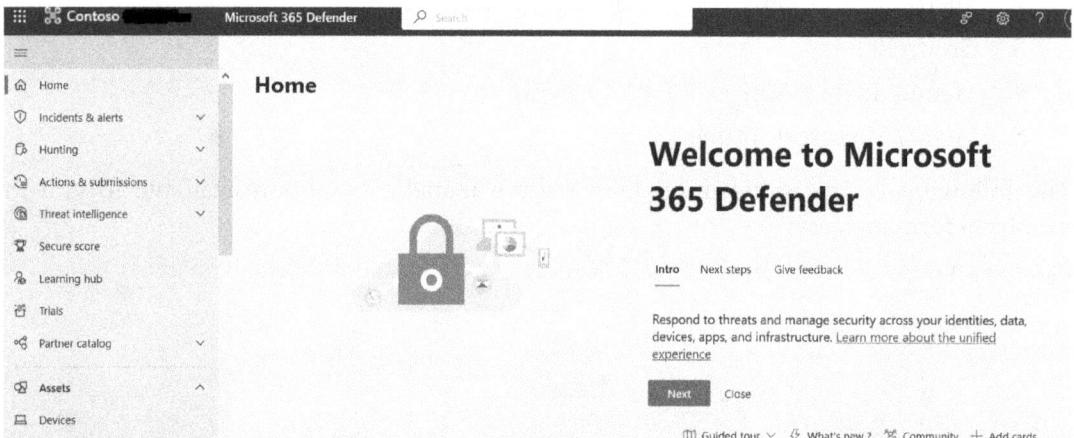

Figure 3.8: MDE security web portal home page

Note: Now MDE security portal is also known as Microsoft Defender XDR portal, as now Azure Sentinel is also integrated with the product.

Microsoft endpoint configuration manager

Second, another way to install MDE is through the Microsoft Endpoint Configuration Manager. This method is recommended for organizations that are already using Microsoft Intune or Configuration Manager to manage their devices. To install MDE using the Microsoft Endpoint Manager, you will need to create a device configuration profile and assign it to your devices. The profile will include the settings necessary to install and configure MDE on your devices.

The following figure shows the deployment architecture using endpoint configuration manager in co-management option:

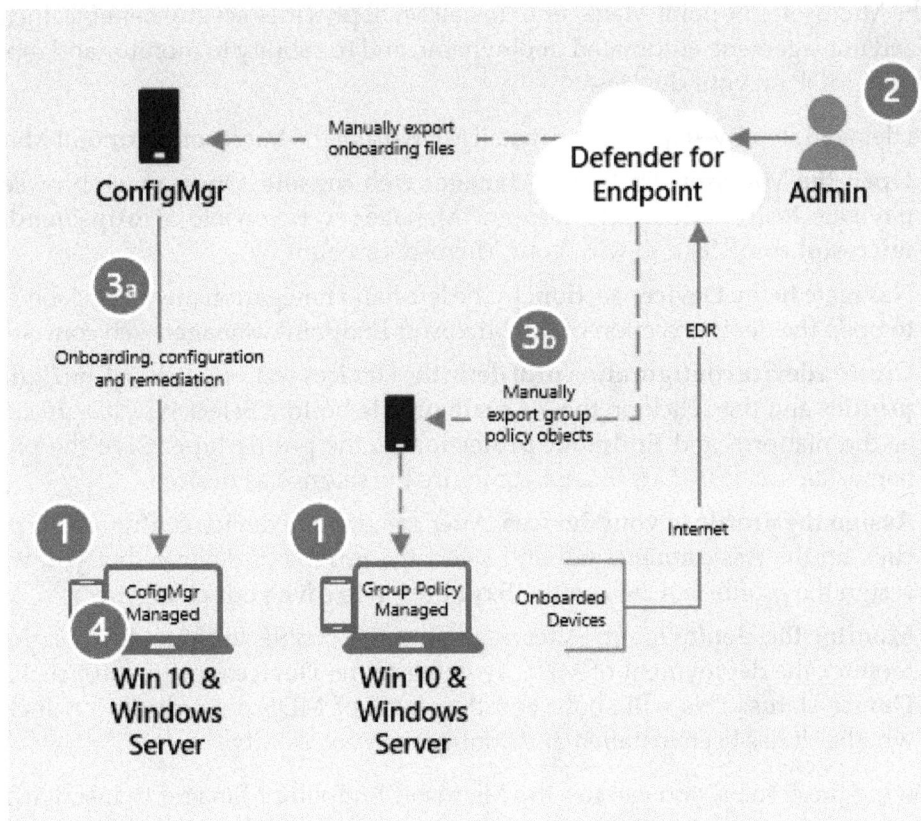

Figure 3.9: *Microsoft Endpoint Configuration Manager based deployment architecture HLD*[1]

---

1   Source: https://download.microsoft.com/download/5/6/0/5609001f-b8ae-412f-89eb-643976f6b79c/
     mde-deployment-strategy.vsdx

> **Note: Using above link you can download complete MS Visio that has all deployment option available with their Architecture diagrams captured in this book.**

Microsoft Endpoint Manager is a unified management platform that provides a centralized solution for managing and securing devices, applications, and data. One way to install MDE is through the Microsoft Endpoint Manager. This method is recommended for organizations that are already using Microsoft Intune or Configuration Manager to manage their devices.

To install MDE using the Microsoft Endpoint Manager, you will need to create a device configuration profile and assign it to your devices. The profile will include the settings necessary to install and configure MDE on your devices. Once the profile is assigned, the Microsoft Endpoint Manager will automatically deploy MDE to the target devices and configure the necessary settings.

Using the Microsoft Endpoint Manager to install MDE provides several benefits, including centralized management, automated deployment, and the ability to monitor and report on the status of MDE on your devices.

Here is a detailed step-by-step guide to install MDE using the Microsoft Endpoint Manager:

1. **Open the Microsoft Endpoint Manager web console**: Open a web browser and navigate to the Microsoft Endpoint Manager web console at **https://endpoint. microsoft.com/**. Sign in with your Microsoft account.

2. **Navigate to the Devices section**: In the left-hand navigation menu, click on *Devices* to open the devices section of the Microsoft Endpoint Manager web console.

3. **Create a device configuration profile**: In the **Devices** section, click on **Configuration profiles** and then click on the + **Create profile** button. Select *Windows 10 and later* as the platform and **Endpoint protection** as the profile type. Give the profile a name, such as *Install MDE,* and configure the settings as desired.

4. **Assign the profile to your devices**: After creating the device configuration profile, click on the **Assignments** tab and select the groups of devices that you want to assign the profile to. Click on the **Save** button to save your changes.

5. **Monitor the deployment**: After assigning the profile to your devices, you can monitor the deployment of MDE by going to the **Devices** section and clicking on **Device status**. This will show you the status of MDE on each device, including whether it has been installed and configured successfully.

By following these steps, you can use the Microsoft Endpoint Manager to install MDE on multiple devices in your organization.

Active Directory Group Policy

Another way to install MDE is through Group Policy. This method is recommended for organizations that are using AD DS to manage their devices. To install MDE using Group Policy, you will need to create a **Group Policy Object** (GPO) and link it to the **Appropriate Organizational Unit** (OU) in your AD DS environment. The GPO will include the settings necessary to install and configure MDE on your devices.

Here is a step-by-step guide to install MDE using Group Policy:

1. **Create a GPO**: Open the **Group Policy Management Console** (GPMC) on a domain controller or a computer with the **Remote Server Administration Tools (RSAT)** installed. Right-click on the appropriate OU and select **Create a GPO in this domain and Link it here…**. Give the GPO a name, such as *Install MDE*.

2. **Edit the GPO**: Right-click on the newly created GPO and select **Edit…**. This will open the Group Policy Management Editor.

3. **Configure the GPO**: In the Group Policy Management Editor, navigate to **Computer Configuration | Policies | Administrative Templates | Windows Components | Windows Defender Antivirus**. Double-click on the setting **Turn off Windows Defender Antivirus** and set it to **Disabled**. This will ensure that Windows Defender Antivirus is enabled on the target devices.

4. **Download the MDE installation package**: Download the MDE installation package from the Microsoft website and save it to a network share that is accessible by the target devices.

5. **Create a startup script**: Create a startup script that will run the MDE installation package on the target devices. The script should check if MDE is already installed and, if not, run the installation package. Save the script to a network share that is accessible by the target devices.

6. **Configure the GPO to run the startup script**: In the Group Policy Management Editor, navigate to **Computer Configuration | Policies | Windows Settings | Scripts (Startup/Shutdown)**. Double-click on **Startup** and click on the **Add…** button. Browse to the location of the startup script and select it.

7. **Link the GPO**: Link the GPO to the appropriate OU in your AD DS environment. This will ensure that the GPO is applied to all devices in that OU.

8. **Test the GPO**: On a test device, run `gpupdate/force` to force an update of Group Policy. Verify that MDE is installed and configured correctly.

By following these steps, you can use Group Policy to install MDE on multiple devices in your organization.

In the following figure, you will see the PowerShell script on windows system after unzip of the file that usually carry Onboarding steps as Sensor Agent is already installed and it just activates and configures Sensor to send data to correct tenant on security portal. You can open this PowerShell script and can see what exactly it is doing, and each package is custom for each independent customer and onboarding script from one organization cannot be used for other as otherwise it will wrongly onboard your device to other customer.

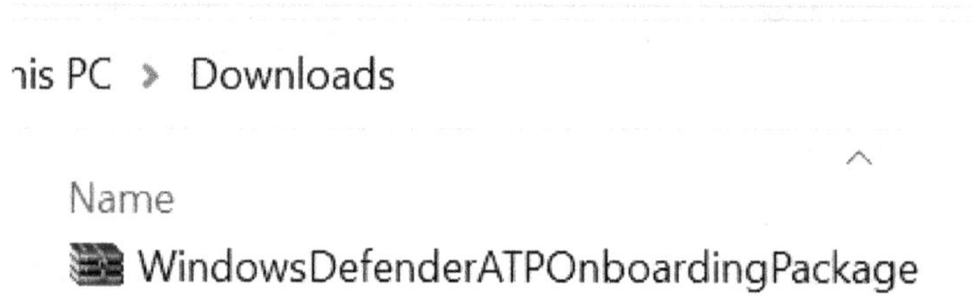

iis PC > Downloads

Name

WindowsDefenderATPOnboardingPackage

Figure 3.10: MDE Agent package name

The following figure is the script extracted from the above zip file that helps in activation or configuration of the sensor agent:

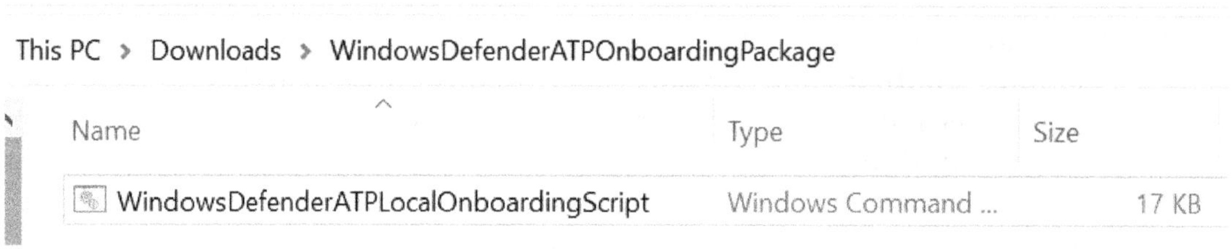

This PC > Downloads > WindowsDefenderATPOnboardingPackage

Name	Type	Size
WindowsDefenderATPLocalOnboardingScript	Windows Command ...	17 KB

Figure 3.11: MDE Agent installation script name under package

The following is the example of a few lines out from the PowerShell script:

```
echo Starting the service, if not already running
echo.
sc query "SENSE" | find /i "RUNNING" >NUL 2>&1
if %ERRORLEVEL% EQU 0 GOTO RUNNING

net start sense > %TMP%\senseTmp.txt 2>&1
if %ERRORLEVEL% NEQ 0 (
    echo Microsoft Defender for Endpoint Service has not started yet
    GOTO WAIT_FOR_THE_SERVICE_TO_START
)
goto SUCCEEDED
```

```
:RUNNING
set "runningOutput=The Microsoft Defender for Endpoint Service is already
running!"
echo %runningOutput%
echo.
eventcreate /l Application /so WDATPOnboarding /t Information /id 10 /d
"%runningOutput%" >NUL 2>&1
GOTO WAIT_FOR_THE_SERVICE_TO_START
```

Manual installation

If you are unable to use either of the above methods, you can manually install MDE on individual devices. This method is not recommended for large-scale deployments as it can be time-consuming and difficult to manage. To manually install MDE, you will need to download the installation package from the Microsoft website and run it on each device. You will then need to manually configure the settings for MDE on each device.

> **Information: You can download Onboarding/Offboarding Scripts (PowerShell or Bash) from Defender Security Portal for individual platform.**
>
> **You can follow the given menu bars to download the onboarding/offboarding script:**
>
> **Settings | Endpoints | Onboarding/Offboarding**

It does not mean you have to execute the downloaded onboarding script directly by logging in to that server, but you can use OS automation to perform such installation and configuration steps. The following *Figure 3.12* depicts such deployment push from central computer and your DevOps engineer can push MDE binaries/agent and configuration to your destination OS and it can be any supported OS i.e., Windows, Linux and macOS.

Onboarding script

The following figure has been created for readers to understand how to deploy agent through central VM or server and you can leverage Ansible or PowerShell/Bash scripts for such automation:

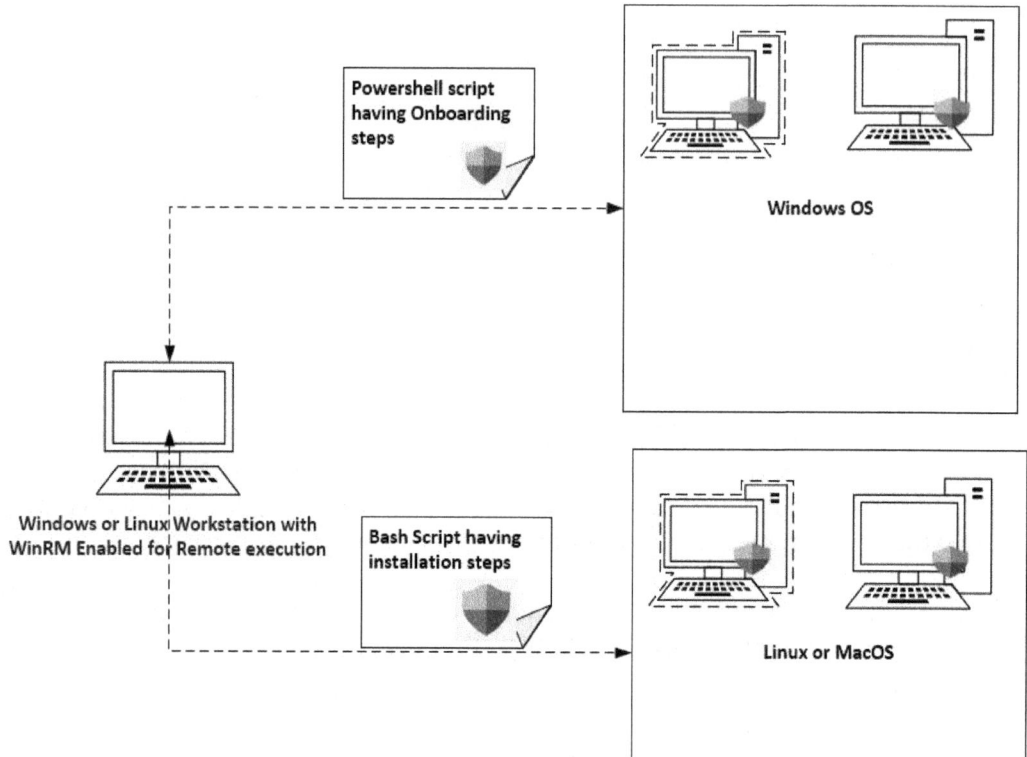

Figure 3.12: Agent deployment using script from central server

Yes, MDE can also be installed using automation tools such as Ansible, Puppet and Chef and such examples are available on Microsoft Defender page.

Ansible/Puppet/Chef

Ansible/Puppet/Chef are an open-source automation tool that can be used to automate the installation and configuration of software on multiple devices, as shown in the following figure:

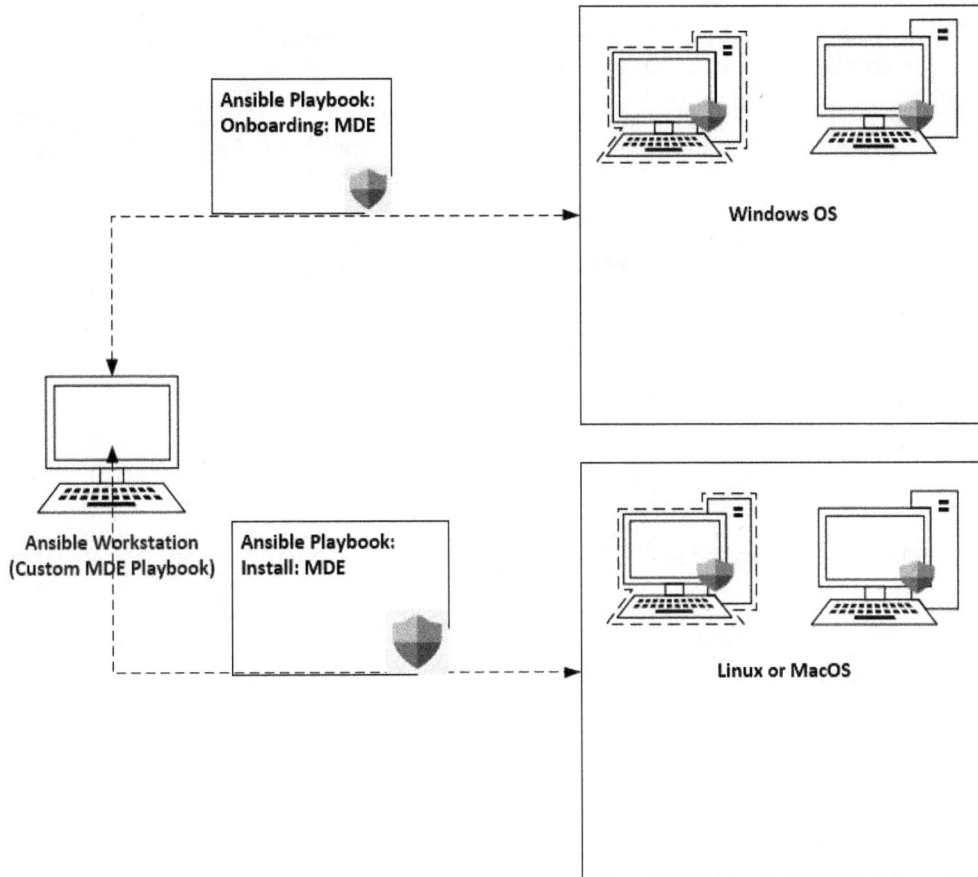

Figure 3.13: Agent deployment using Ansible from central server

Here is an example of how you can use Ansible to install MDE on Windows devices:

```
---
- name: Install Microsoft Defender for Endpoint
  hosts: windows
  tasks:
    - name: Download MDE installation package
      win_get_url:
        url: "https://download.microsoft.com/download/latest_version_of_
mde_setup.exe"  # Change to the correct URL for the latest MDE setup
        dest: C:\Temp\MDESetup.exe

    - name: Install MDE
      win_package:
```

```
          path: C:\Temp\MDESetup.exe
          product_id: "{XXXXXXXX-XXXX-XXXX-XXXX-XXXXXXXXXXXX}"  # Replace
with the actual product ID for MDE
          state: present
          arguments: "/quiet /norestart"  # Optional: Silent install with no
restart


    - name: Configure MDE settings (Enable Defender)
      win_regedit:
        path: HKLM:\SOFTWARE\Policies\Microsoft\Windows Defender
        name: DisableAntiSpyware
        data: 0
        type: dword


    - name: Start Microsoft Defender Antivirus service
      win_service:
        name: WinDefend
        state: started
        start_mode: auto


    - name: Ensure the Microsoft Defender Antivirus service is running
      win_service:
        name: WinDefend
        state: started
        start_mode: auto
```

This Ansible playbook will download the MDE installation package from the Microsoft website, install it on the target devices, and configure the necessary settings. You can customize this playbook to meet your specific needs and requirements.

You need Ansible binary installed on your machine from where you would like to push these changes.

Here you can find details about how you can push packages and configuration files through ansible:

```
# ansible-playbook -I <inventory-file> <playbook.yaml>
```

Output:

```
<You will see the installation logs on your screen about the steps that you
have configured inside the playbook>
```

Ansible documentation gives a good overview about how to install and configure ansible so that you can run the playbooks. Ansible is based on Python, so you need to install concerned python and ansible package on your machine.

Ansible supports both push and pull based deployment model but as of now to keep things simple you can use push-based approach to install packages on N number of servers. You can group the servers in your inventory file so that you can run against environments, regions etc.

The following is an example of inventory file containing device IP or name categorized into groups that **ansible-playbook** command will use: **inventory.ini**

```
[Dev]
X.X.X.X
[Prod]
Xyz.production.domain.com
Yed.production.domain.com
```

Make sure you modify the **ansible.cfg** file to configure required connection or login settings. Usually, on Linux OS it is available under **/etc/ansible/ansible.cfg** but you can place this file in same folder from where you are executing it and then the local file will override the file of default location.

Ansible runs on both Linux and Windows system and even you can use it on macOS as during Cross Platform Lab builds, we heavily used Ansible to Scale Mac VM's and it showed pretty guide results. We even used Chef but my recommendation is to use Ansible.

In summary, there are several methods for installing MDE, including using the Microsoft Endpoint Manager, Group Policy, or manually installing the software on individual devices. The method you choose will depend on your organization's existing infrastructure and management tools.

MDM/Microsoft Intune

Microsoft Intune (Microsoft's MDM) is a cloud-based service that focuses on **Mobile Device Management** (MDM) and **Mobile Application Management** (MAM). It integrates with other Microsoft services and products that focus on endpoint management, including Endpoint Configuration Manager for on-premises endpoint management and Windows Server, Windows Autopilot for modern OS deployment and provisioning, and Endpoint analytics for visibility and reporting on end user experiences[1].

Microsoft Intune allows you to manage devices, users, and apps from a single console (*Accessible from Azure Cloud portal as well*). You can use it to enforce compliance policies, protect data, and provide secure access to company resources. Microsoft Intune also integrates with Microsoft Entra a.k.a **Azure Active Directory** (**Azure AD**) to provide identity and access management capabilities.

Intune supports a wide range of devices, including:

- iOS/iPadOS
- Android
- Windows
- macOS

You can use it to manage both organization-owned and personal devices. Microsoft Intune provides a range of features for managing devices, including device enrollment, device configuration, device compliance, and device actions.

In summary, Microsoft Intune is a powerful tool for managing mobile devices and applications. It integrates with other Microsoft services and products to provide a comprehensive solution for endpoint management.

Microsoft has enabled the feature on both Microsoft Intune and Microsoft Defender Security Portal for the integration and by just enabling the feature on web portals both can fetch below mentioned information to onboard devices.

Information: When Microsoft Intune and Microsoft Defender Security portal are integrated, they can fetch a variety of device and inventory information to onboard devices effectively. Here is what they can fetch:

1. **Device information: This includes details like device name, model, operating system version, and hardware specifications.**
2. **Compliance status: Information about whether the device complies with the organization's security policies and configurations.**
3. **Risk level: An assessment of the device's security posture, identifying potential vulnerabilities or threats.**
4. **Application inventory: A list of installed applications on the device, helping to identify unauthorized or potentially harmful software.**
5. **Security baseline: Details about the security settings and configurations applied to the device, ensuring they meet organizational standards.**
6. **User information: Information about the device owner or primary user, which can be useful for tracking and managing access.**

The following figure is the screenshot taken from Microsoft Security web portal to enable Intune integration and it is available under **Settings | Endpoints | Advanced Features**.

The following figure showcases Microsoft Security web portal's sub options available in Settings menu and how you can enable the Microsoft Intune integration with the MDE web portal:

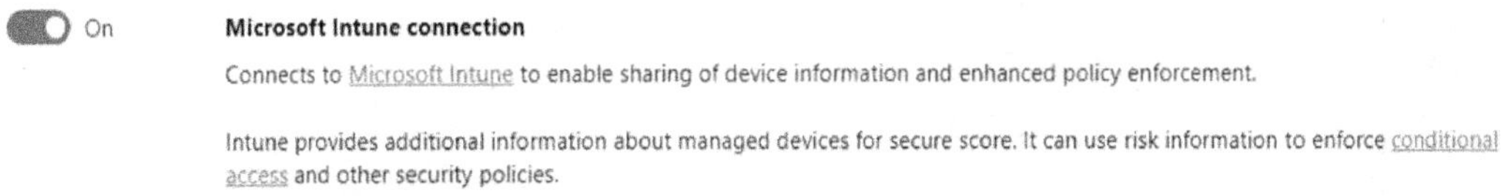

On **Microsoft Intune connection**

Connects to Microsoft Intune to enable sharing of device information and enhanced policy enforcement.

Intune provides additional information about managed devices for secure score. It can use risk information to enforce conditional access and other security policies.

Figure 3.14: MDE Settings | Endpoint page on web portal

The following figure showcases Microsoft Intune Web Portal home page that you can from either from Azure web portal or directly from Intune page:

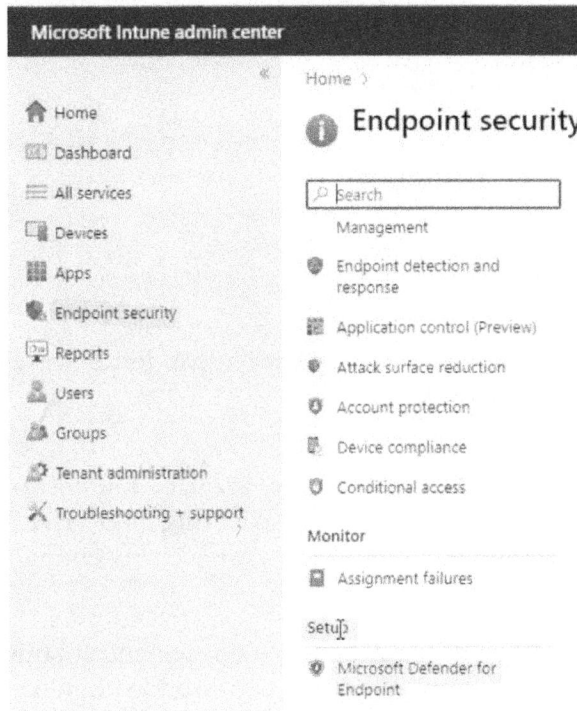

Figure 3.15: Microsoft Intune Admin center homepage

Once you enable Microsoft Intune option from MS Security web portal then you will see status *Connection Status* to enabled on the MS Intune web console on the Azure.

The following figure showcases a screenshot taken from Intune page showcasing the MDE configuration that you can customize from Intune page itself:

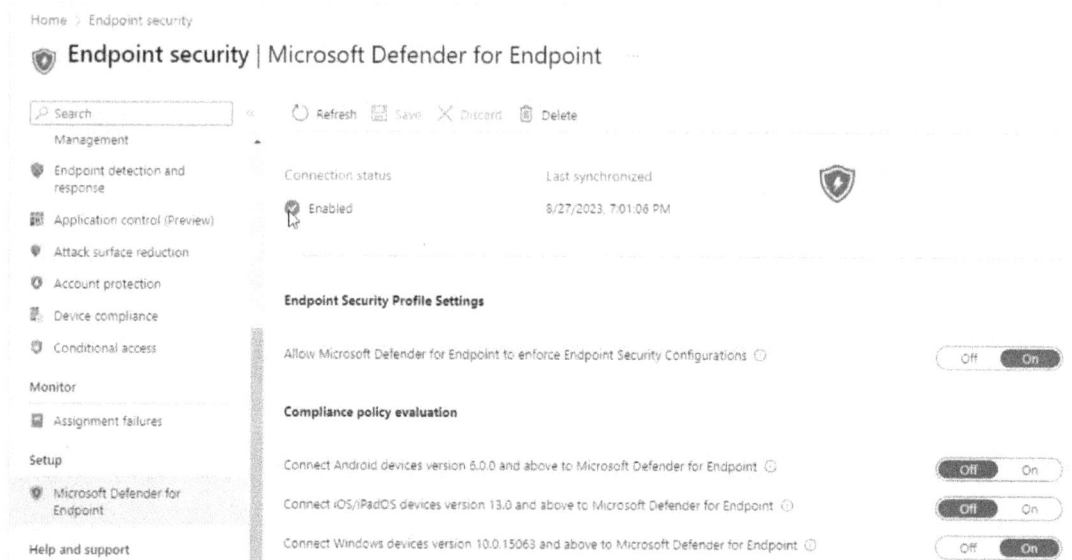

Figure 3.16: Microsoft Intune Admin center page to customize MDE settings

Information: Leverage Azure Security Center for Endpoint Security on Azure Resources like VM, databases etc.

Note: Keep in mind that MDE and Azure Security Endpoint both are different products as of now and in this book, we are covering only MDE not Azure Security, but in small doses will build clarity on the Azure security endpoints as well as those are mostly related to the Cloud Workload.

Azure Security Center is a cloud-based security management and threat protection service that provides security posture management for your workloads in Azure, on-premises, and in other clouds. It can help you to automatically identify the use of a number of popular anti-malware solutions for your virtual machines and report the endpoint protection running status and make recommendations.

By leveraging Azure Security Center for endpoint security, you can gain visibility into the security posture of your endpoints and receive recommendations for improving their security. Azure Security Center uses a built-in Azure Policy initiative in audit-only mode (the Azure Security Benchmark) as well as Azure Monitor logs and other Azure security solutions like Microsoft Cloud App Security to provide you with tailored recommendations (hardening tasks). Strengthening your security posture can be achieved by implementing these recommendations.

In summary, Azure Security Center provides a powerful tool for monitoring and improving the endpoint security of your workloads. By integrating with other Azure security solutions, it provides a comprehensive view of your organization's security posture and helps you to take proactive steps to improve it.

> **Information: Mostly such policies are controlled through Azure Management subscription as mostly bigger companies are composed of so many organizations like Microsoft is having C+AI (Cloud and AI) as separate org and Windows is part of E+D (Experience and Devices), Security is part of MPS and earlier it was part of SCIM and so on and you as security admin can design such policies for Org, Department and subset of cloud VM instances.**

Important Defender binaries

The following table shows the important processes or files that you will see after the installation on your system:

Process	Path	Comment
	Windows 11, Windows 10, Windows Server 2022 and Windows Server 2019	
MpCmdRun.exe	C:\Program Files\Windows Defender	Microsoft Defender Antivirus command-line utility
MpDlpCmd.exe	C:\Program Files\Windows Defender	Microsoft Endpoint DLP command-line utility
MsMpEng.exe	C:\Program Files\Windows Defender	Microsoft Defender Antivirus service executable
ConfigSecurityPolicy.exe	C:\Program Files\Windows Defender	Microsoft Security Client Policy Configuration Tool
NisSrv.exe	C:\Program Files\Windows Defender	Microsoft Defender Antivirus Network Realtime Inspection
MsSense.exe	C:\Program Files\Windows Defender Advanced Threat Protection	Microsoft Defender for Endpoint service executable
SenseCnCProxy.exe	C:\Program Files\Windows Defender Advanced Threat Protection	Microsoft Defender for Endpoint communication module
SenseIR.exe	C:\Program Files\Windows Defender Advanced Threat Protection	Microsoft Defender for Endpoint Sense IR (Incident response) module

Process	Path	Comment
SenseCE.exe	C:\Program Files\Windows Defender Advanced Threat Protection\Classification	Microsoft Defender for Endpoint Sense CE (Classification engine) module
SenseSampleUploader. exe	C:\Program Files\Windows Defender Advanced Threat Protection	Microsoft Defender for Endpoint Sample Upload module
SenseNdr.exe	C:\Program Files\Windows Defender Advanced Threat Protection	Microsoft Defender for Endpoint Sense NDR (Network Detection and Response) module
SenseSC.exe	C:\Program Files\Windows Defender Advanced Threat Protection	Microsoft Defender for Endpoint Sense SC (Screenshot Capture) module
SenseCM.exe	C:\Program Files\Windows Defender Advanced Threat Protection	Microsoft Defender for Endpoint Sense CM (Configuration Management)
	Windows Server 2016 and Windows Server 2012 R2 (Unified Agent)	
MsSense.exe	C:\Program Files\Windows Defender Advanced Threat Protection	Microsoft Defender for Endpoint service executable
SenseCnCProxy.exe	C:\Program Files\Windows Defender Advanced Threat Protection	Microsoft Defender for Endpoint communication module
SenseIR.exe	C:\Program Files\Windows Defender Advanced Threat Protection	Microsoft Defender for Endpoint Sense IR (Incident Response) module
SenseSampleUploader. exe	C:\Program Files\Windows Defender Advanced Threat Protection	Microsoft Defender for Endpoint Sample Upload module
SenseCM.exe	C:\Program Files\Windows Defender Advanced Threat Protection	Microsoft Defender for Endpoint Sense CM (Configuration Management)
MpCmdRun.exe	C:\Program Files\Windows Defender	Microsoft Defender Antivirus command-line utility
MsMpEng.exe	C:\Program Files\Windows Defender	Microsoft Defender Antivirus service executable

Process	Path	Comment
ConfigSecurityPolicy. exe	C:\Program Files\Windows Defender	Microsoft Security Client Policy Configuration Tool
NisSrv.exe	C:\Program Files\Windows Defender	Microsoft Defender Antivirus Network Realtime Inspection
	Windows 8.1 and Windows Server 2016 (MMA Based)	
MonitoringHost.exe	C:\Program Files\Microsoft Monitoring Agent\Agent	Microsoft Monitoring Agent Service Host Process
HealthService.exe	C:\Program Files\Microsoft Monitoring Agent\Agent	Microsoft Monitoring Agent Service
TestCloudConnection. exe	C:\Program Files\Microsoft Monitoring Agent\Agent	Microsoft Monitoring Agent Cloud Connection Test utility
MpCmdRun.exe	C:\Program Files\Windows Defender	Microsoft Defender Antivirus command-line utility
MsMpEng.exe	C:\Program Files\Windows Defender	Microsoft Defender Antivirus service executable
ConfigSecurityPolicy. exe	C:\Program Files\Windows Defender	Microsoft Security Client Policy Configuration Tool
NisSrv.exe	C:\Program Files\Windows Defender	Microsoft Defender Antivirus Network Realtime Inspection

Table 3.2: Important Windows OS binaries for security

Conclusion

In this chapter, we embarked on a journey through the intricate landscape of deployment preparation for Microsoft Defender. We explored different architectural choices, such as Cloud Native, Co-Managed, On-Premises, and Script Evaluation architectures, and their implications. Understanding the significance of preparation was highlighted through aspects like comprehending organizational needs, defining deployment goals, allocating resources, and fostering effective communication and collaboration. Role clarification and responsibilities breakdown were emphasized to ensure a collaborative approach to deployment, setting the stage for a smooth implementation process.

Moving forward, the chapter gives insights into system requirements and prerequisites, ensuring that your deployment foundation is solid. Hardware, licensing, browser compatibility, and supported operating systems were meticulously discussed to provide a comprehensive overview. The various installation methods, from Microsoft Security web portal and Microsoft Endpoint Configuration Manager to Active Directory Group Policy and manual installations, were outlined to cater to diverse deployment scenarios. We also shed light on the importance of key Defender binaries, equipping you with the knowledge to make informed decisions regarding your deployment journey.

In the next chapter, we are doing this to cover the configuration of the agent so that you can manage as per your requirement, and it covers Windows and cross platform OS's.

Join our book's Discord space

Join the book's Discord Workspace for Latest updates, Offers, Tech happenings around the world, New Release and Sessions with the Authors:

https://discord.bpbonline.com

CHAPTER 4
Configuring Microsoft Defender Endpoint

Introduction

In the ever-evolving landscape of cybersecurity, the proper configuration of defense mechanisms is paramount. This chapter gives insights into the intricacies of configuring **Microsoft Defender for Endpoint (MDE)**, an indispensable tool in fortifying an organization's digital perimeters. Broadly categorized into two essential domains, this chapter embarks on a journey that unravels the nuances of MDE configuration, offering insights into both Defender web portal and Endpoint Agent settings. By exploring these categories, we equip ourselves with the knowledge and strategies required to optimize MDE's capabilities and tailor its protection to the unique needs of our organization. As we navigate through Defender Web Portal Configuration and delve into Endpoint Agent Configuration, we will uncover the keys to establishing a robust security infrastructure that guards against the ever-evolving threats that permeate the digital realm.

The following are the areas of web portal configuration:

• **Endpoint Detection and Response (EDR)**
• **Threat and Vulnerability Management (TVM)**
• **Microsoft Defender Antivirus capabilities**
Note: Earlier it was referred as Next Generation Protection (NGP) and later rebranded as Microsoft Defender Antivirus or Microsoft Defender Antivirus capabilities.

• **Attack surface reduction (ASR)**
• **Auto investigation and remediation (AIR)**
• Agent Proxy configuration so that onboarded devices can work properly in isolated environment.

Table 4.1: *Areas of web portal configuration*

Structure

This chapter is divided into two categories that touch on the above configuration settings:

- Defender web portal configuration
- Permissions
- Role-based access control
- MDE agent configuration
- Proxy services and URLs
- Important configuration
- Important commands

Objectives

This chapter serves as a comprehensive guide to configuring and managing Microsoft Defender, covering a wide array of topics essential for effective implementation. It begins with an exploration of Defender web portal configuration, providing insights into optimizing settings for optimal security. Advanced features of endpoints are discussed, offering readers a deeper understanding of the capabilities available to enhance protection. License information is outlined, ensuring clarity on licensing requirements and usage. The Secure Score feature is highlighted, showcasing its significance in assessing and improving overall security posture.

Permissions are thoroughly examined, emphasizing the importance of granular control over access to safeguard sensitive data and resources. The chapter proceeds to elucidate Microsoft Defender Endpoint settings, offering readers insights into maximizing the effectiveness of Defender within their environment. Configuration of the MDE agent is detailed, along with guidelines for establishing robust endpoint security policies across various platforms, including MacOS, Windows, and Linux systems. Additionally, optional sections cover Azure Sentinel integration and proxy services, providing readers with a holistic view of security infrastructure. By the chapter's conclusion, readers will have gained practical knowledge and valuable insights to effectively deploy and manage Microsoft Defender Antivirus within their organizations.

We will be covering all points about the configuration from the Web Portal and Endpoint agent point of view.

First, in this chapter, we will focus on Defender web portal configuration.

Defender web portal configuration

The MDE portal offers a comprehensive array of navigation options to configure and manage resources effectively. These options span across various functionalities, including incidents and alerts, threat intelligence, Secure Score, Learning Hub, and more. This user-friendly interface empowers security professionals to navigate seamlessly and tailor their configuration to the organization's specific needs.

Five pivotal menus along with other inside the security web portal are accessible for configuration within the MDE portal. These encompass Security Center, Microsoft 365 Defender, Endpoints, Email & Collaboration, and Device Discovery. Each area offers granular control over settings and strategies to fortify an organization's security posture.

The following are the five broad areas that you can configure from the MDE portal and we will touch briefly on a few of them as we will be covering those features in detail in the subsequent chapters:

• Security Center
• Microsoft 365 Defender
• Endpoints
• Email & Collaboration
• Device Discovery

Table 4.2: MDE security web portal menu bars (Focused in the book)

Now, the following are the representation of the Navigation option in different formats (*Graphical Web Portal Navigation, Textual and Mind map diagram*) that will help you understand this information to build your mind map while exploring security options on the web portal:

- **Navigation screenshot from the portal**: MDE is a licensed product and not available freely for learning so those who do not have access to MDE web portal, we have captured screenshot references for you so that you can easily relate our references while you read the chapters. Refer to the following figure:

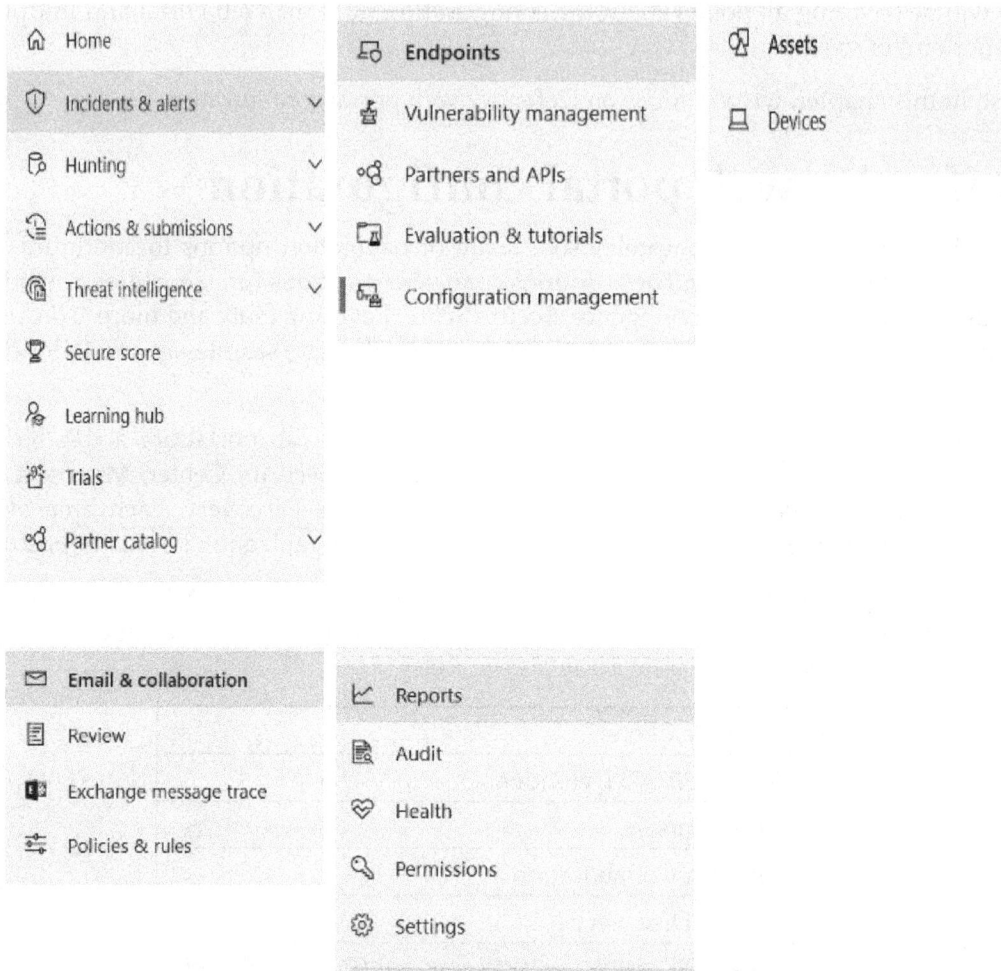

Figure 4.1: MDE web portal

- **Navigation mind map**: You will find the navigation options on the MDE portal to configure resources through our specially designed Mind maps for our readers, as shown in the following figure:

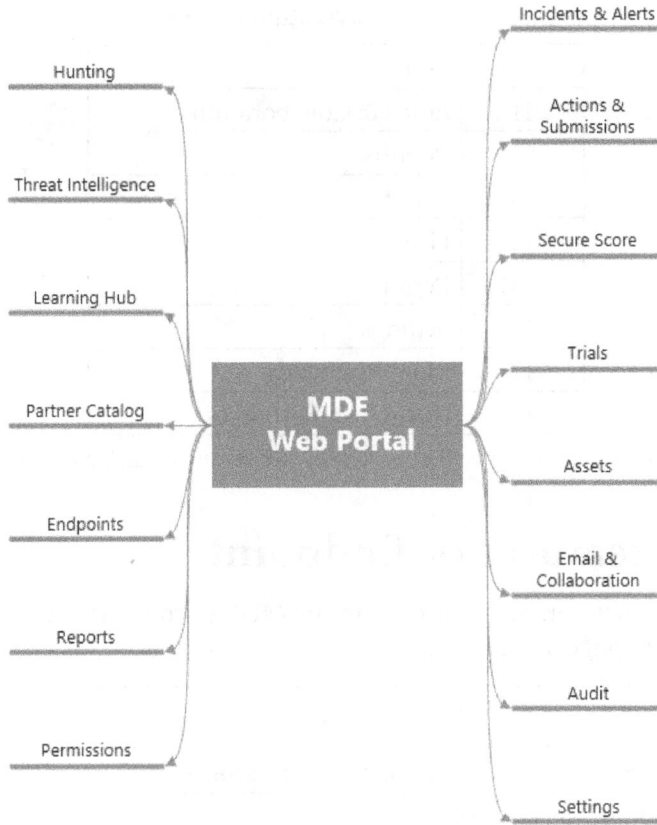

Figure 4.2: MDE security web portal navigation menus

- **Navigation in text**: The following table shows the navigation menus that you will see after you login into MDE web portal:

S.No.	Navigation menus
1	Incidents &alerts
2	Hunting
3	Actions & Submissions
4	Threat Intelligence
5	Secure Score
6	Learning Hub
7	Trials
8	Partner Catalog
9	Assets

S.No.	Navigation menus
10	Endpoints
11	Email & Collaboration
12	Reports
13	Audit
14	Health
15	Permissions
16	Settings
17	More Resources
18	Customize Resources

Table 4.3: MDE menu bar options on security web portal (available on left hand side)

Advanced features of Endpoint

Advanced features that you can control from the MDE portal under **Settings** | **Endpoints** | **Advanced feature** page, are given as follows:

S.No	Feature name	Default status
1	Restrict correlation to within scoped device groups	ON
2	Enable EDR in block mode	ON
3	Automatically resolve alerts	ON
4	Allow or block file	OFF
5	Hide potential duplicate device records	ON
6	Custom network indicators	ON
7	Tamper protection	ON
8	Show user details	ON
9	Skype for business integration	OFF
10	Office 365 Threat Intelligence connection	OFF
11	Microsoft Defender for Cloud Apps	OFF
12	Web content filtering	OFF
13	Device discovery	OFF
14	Download quarantined files	ON
15	Live Response	OFF
16	Live Response for Servers	OFF

S.No	Feature name	Default status
17	Live Response unsigned script execution	OFF
18	Share endpoint alerts with Microsoft Compliance Center	OFF
19	Microsoft Intune connection	OFF
20	Authenticated telemetry	OFF
21	Preview features	OFF
22	Endpoint Attack Notifications	ON

Table 4.4: Endpoint Advance features configuration options available under Settings pagecaption

License information page

As a security Administrator or concerned person for the MDE, many a time you would like to see the License information that your organization is using. To get such information from the MDE portal, navigate to the following location:

Settings | Endpoint | Licenses

The following figure shows the screenshot to showcase License information of a MDE on web portal:

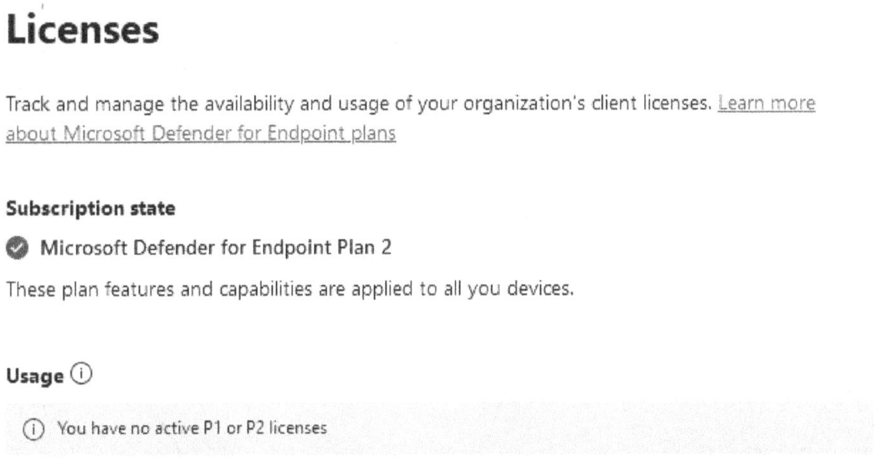

Licenses

Track and manage the availability and usage of your organization's client licenses. Learn more about Microsoft Defender for Endpoint plans

Subscription state

✅ Microsoft Defender for Endpoint Plan 2

These plan features and capabilities are applied to all you devices.

Usage ⓘ

ⓘ You have no active P1 or P2 licenses

Figure 4.3: License page showcasing subscription details

Secure score feature

Microsoft Defender for Endpoint's Secure Score feature is a valuable tool that empowers organizations to enhance their security posture and mitigate risks effectively. Secure

Score provides a clear and concise assessment of an organization's security configuration, offering actionable insights to improve overall security. By analyzing security settings and comparing them to recommended best practices, it helps organizations identify and address vulnerabilities. This feature enables security teams to prioritize their efforts and make data-driven decisions to bolster defenses, ultimately safeguarding their digital environment against evolving cyber threats. Secure Score is a fundamental component of Microsoft Defender for Endpoint, aligning security efforts with industry standards and best practices to ensure a robust defense strategy.

Few examples of activities happened that increased the Secure Score of your organization are given as follows.

Example one is shown in the following figure:

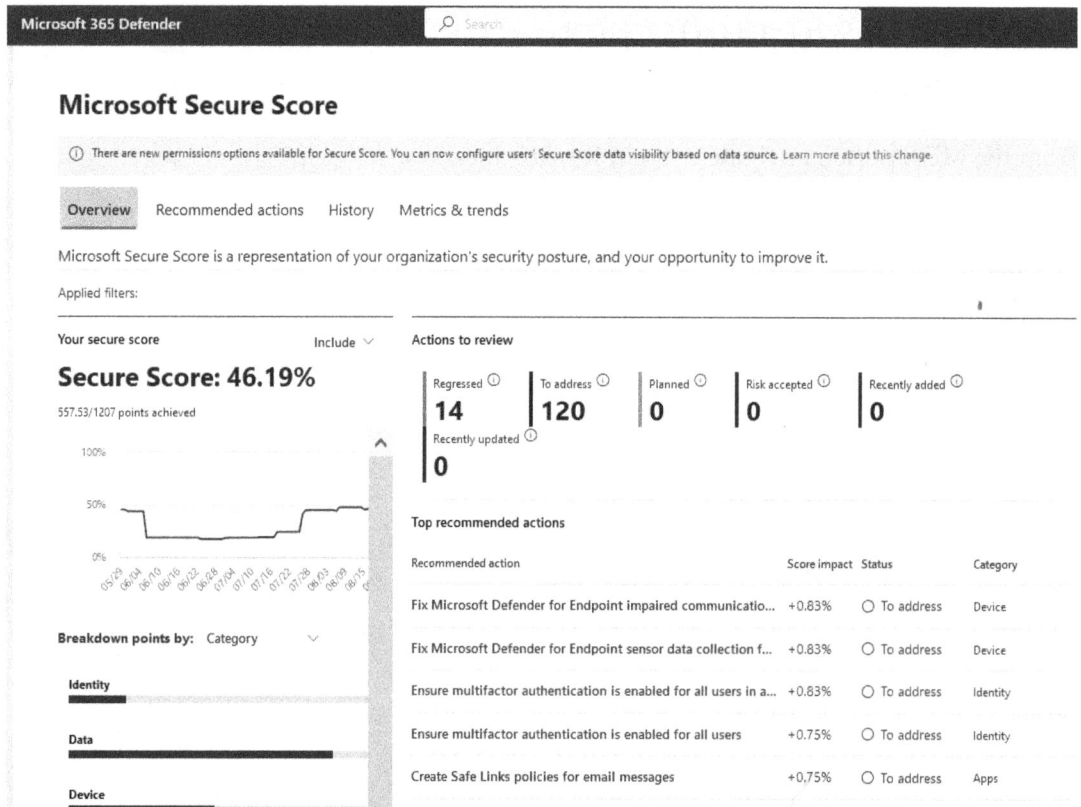

Figure 4.4: Secure Score page on MDE web portal

The following figure shows the second example:

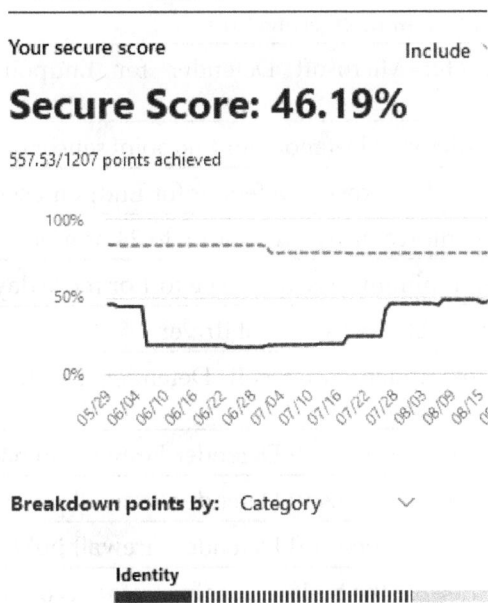

Figure 4.5: Secure Score coverage page

The following figure shows example three:

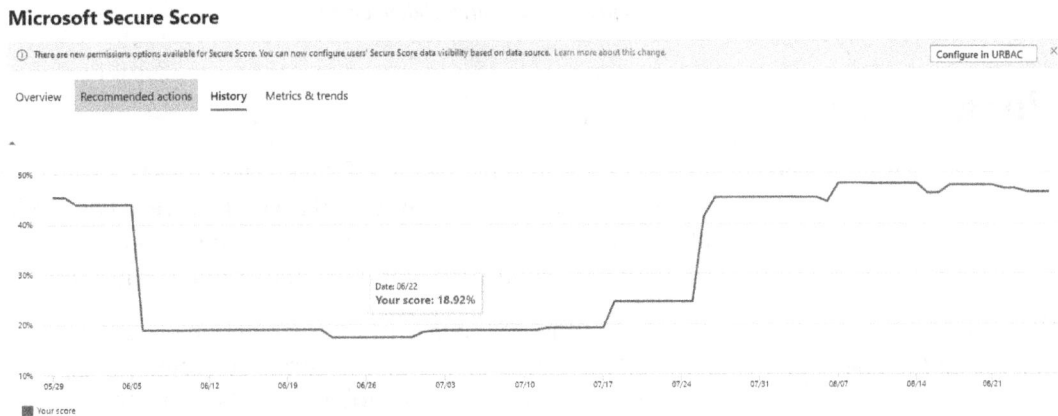

Figure 4.6: Secure Score coverage or strengeth increase/decrease insight widget on page

Activity

The following table shows the activity transaction and how it gained the points over time by enabling certain product feature:

Activity transaction	Category
2.67 points gained for turn on tamper protection	Device
1.67 points gained for fix Microsoft Defender for Endpoint impaired communications	Device
1.67 points gained for fix Microsoft Defender for Endpoint sensor data collection	Device
1.67 points gained for turn on Microsoft Defender for Endpoint sensor	Device
1.67 points gained for set enforce password history to 24 or more password(s)	Device
1.67 points gained for set minimum password age to 1 or more day(s)	Device
2.67 points regressed for disable SMBv1 client driver	Device
5.00 points regressed for update Microsoft Defender for Endpoint core components	Device
3.00 points regressed for secure Microsoft Defender Firewall domain profile	Device
3.00 points regressed for secure Microsoft Defender Firewall private profile	Device
3.00 points regressed for secure Microsoft Defender Firewall public profile	Device
2.67 points regressed for disable the built-in administrator account	Device
+3.00 points score change because ensure modern authentication for exchange online is enabled has become relevant	Apps
+3.00 points score change because ensure MailTips are enabled for end users has become relevant	Apps

Table 4.5: Secure score activities shown on page

Permissions

In cybersecurity, control and access are paramount. Microsoft Defender takes this seriously with its robust permissions and **role-based access control** (**RBAC**) features. The RBAC features described are generally correct, but the details about specific methods and role descriptions may not fully align with Microsoft's current offerings or documentation.

With permissions, you can designate who can perform specific actions, keeping your security protocols intact. Meanwhile, RBAC enables you to structure roles within your cybersecurity teams, from local security operations to global experts. This ensures that every member has a designated sphere of influence and responsibility, contributing to a well-organized and efficient defense.

In a landscape where precision and control matter, Microsoft Defender's permissions and RBAC are your allies, elevating your security posture and creating a structured defense that is second to none.

Role-based access control

Microsoft recommends using the concept of *least privileges*. Defender for Endpoint leverages built-in roles within Azure Active Directory:

- Security administrator
- Security analyst
- Endpoint administrator
- Infrastructure administrator
- Business owner/stakeholder

Microsoft recommends utilizing **Privileged Identity Management** (**PIM**) to effectively oversee roles, ensuring added auditing, control, and access reviews for individuals with directory permissions. Within Defender for Endpoint, there are two methods for managing permissions:

- **Basic permissions management**: This approach involves setting permissions to either full access or read-only. Users possessing Global Administrator or Security Administrator roles in Azure Active Directory are granted full access. In contrast, the Security reader role offers read-only access without permission to view machines or device inventory.
- **RBAC**: It provides a more granular level of permissions by allowing the definition of roles, assignment of Azure AD user groups to these roles, and granting access to specific device groups. For further details, refer to the guide on managing portal access through role-based access control.

Understanding cyber defense operations center structure

The following table example aims to delineate the structure of your Cyber Defense Operations Center within your environment. This aids in discerning the necessary RBAC structure needed for your specific environment.

Tier	SOC team	Description
Tier 1	Local security operations team / IT team	This team primarily handles triaging and investigating alerts within their specific geographic location. They escalate incidents to Tier 2 when active remediation is needed.
Tier 2	Regional security operations team	This team possesses visibility into all devices within their region and executes remedial actions as required.
Tier 3	Global security operations team	Comprising security experts, this team holds authorization to view all devices and perform necessary actions from the portal.

Table 4.6: SOC team tiered representation

In the following figure, we have captured Role creation screenshot for reference: We are showing example to create custom role for Local regional SOC team that will have only **Read Only (RO)** permissions on all resources managed by MDE. We choose India as country and Delhi as local office site so this role is for local Delhi, India SOC team that can perform RO roles in this location.

> **Note: Under Permission and roles page you will get options to create custom role. The following page does not have any role available and that is the reason you cannot see any role on the page and just get started message is displayed on the same page. Once you will create a role that message will go away.**

The following page can be reached under **Permission** menu bar available on main MDE security web portal (below left-hand side). The steps for the same are:

1. Press on **Create custom role**:

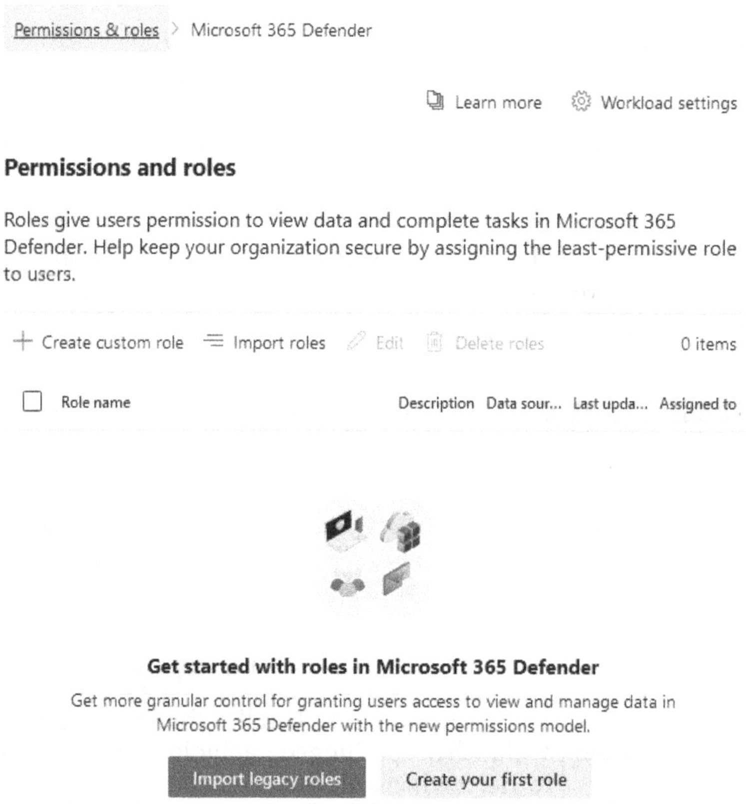

Permissions & roles > Microsoft 365 Defender

🖥 Learn more   ⚙ Workload settings

Permissions and roles

Roles give users permission to view data and complete tasks in Microsoft 365 Defender. Help keep your organization secure by assigning the least-permissive role to users.

+ Create custom role   ≡ Import roles   ✎ Edit   🗑 Delete roles   0 items

□ Role name   Description Data sour... Last upda... Assigned to

Get started with roles in Microsoft 365 Defender

Get more granular control for granting users access to view and manage data in Microsoft 365 Defender with the new permissions model.

Import legacy roles   Create your first role

Figure 4.7: Permission and roles page during role creation

2. Fill in the basic information about the role, as shown in the following figure, so that your peers can understand its purpose and try to follow the naming convention defined by your team:

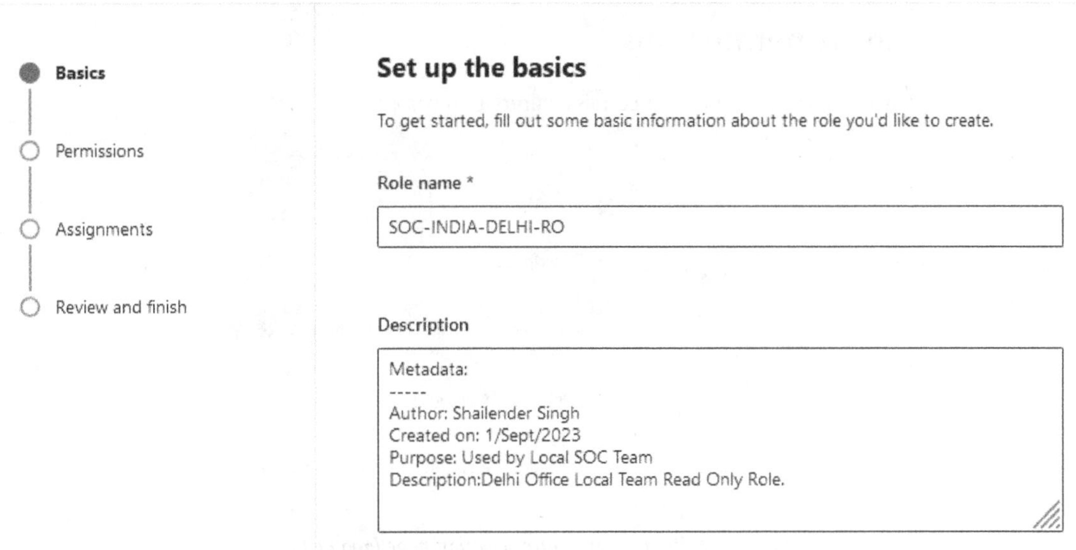

Figure 4.8: *Basic role name and description page*

3. Choose the permission as per your requirement; we are choosing Read Only as this role is only for RO activities, as shown in the following figure:

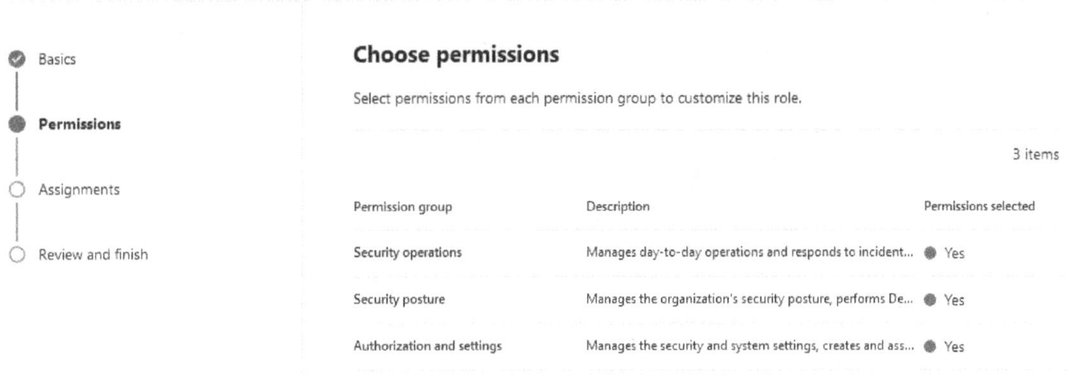

Figure 4.9: *Permission selection page*

There are three permissions groups for the role:

*   Security operations
*   Security posture
*   Authorization and settings

The following figure is a screenshot show casing three important security administration groups that contains the permissions:

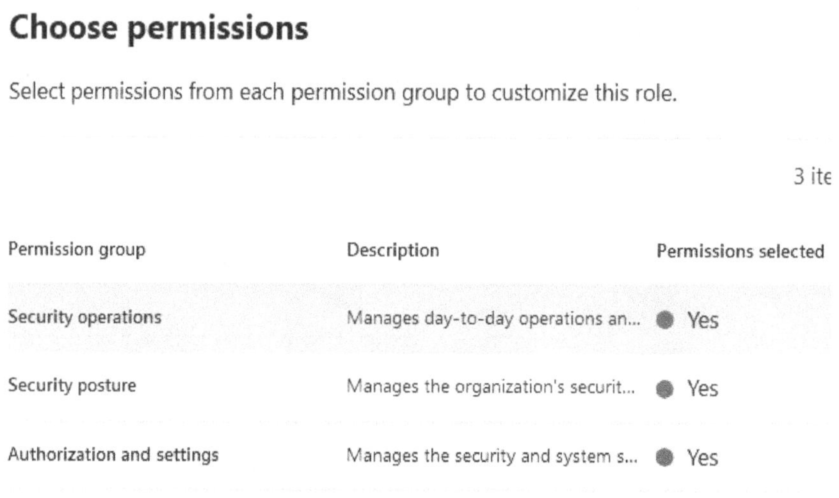

Choose permissions

Select permissions from each permission group to customize this role.

3 ite

Permission group	Description	Permissions selected
Security operations	Manages day-to-day operations an...	● Yes
Security posture	Manages the organization's securit...	● Yes
Authorization and settings	Manages the security and system s...	● Yes

Figure 4.10: Permission group selection page (zoomed in)

- **Security operations**: Assign required permissions to group members who can response to incidents and advisories.

    Refer to the following figure:

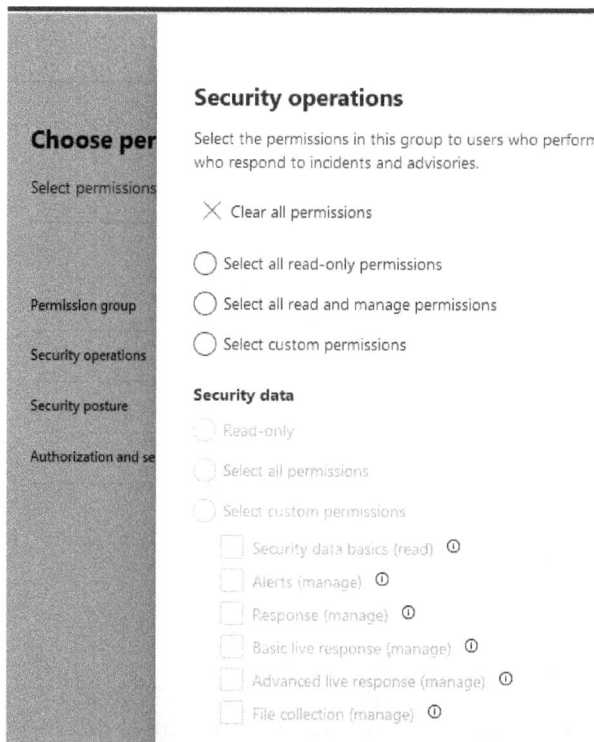

Figure 4.11: Security operations permission selection page

- **Security posture**: You can choose the permissions as per your requirement for the users who need to take actions on the security track remediation tasks, exceptions and on TVM. There are prefilled permissions or your ease that you can choose.

As part of the role creation, you can assign users and data sources and the following figure is just a captured screenshot for reader's reference.

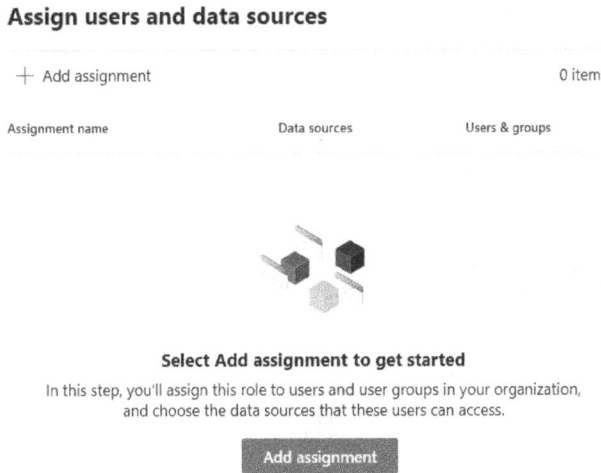

Figure 4.12: Assign users and data sources page

- **Authorization and settings**: Choose the required permissions for the users who to need to control settings and create and assign roles. Refer to the following figure:

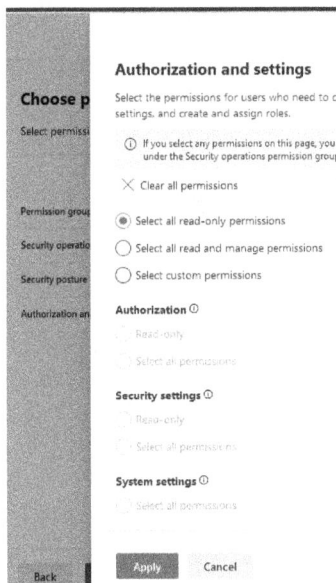

Figure 4.13: Authorization and settings page

The following are the permission options available under second permission group i.e., **Security Posture** for the selection.

1. **Assign users to the roles**: Once you have selected the required permissions and settings for the role then you can assign users to this role and even later you can assign users to it. Refer to the following figure:

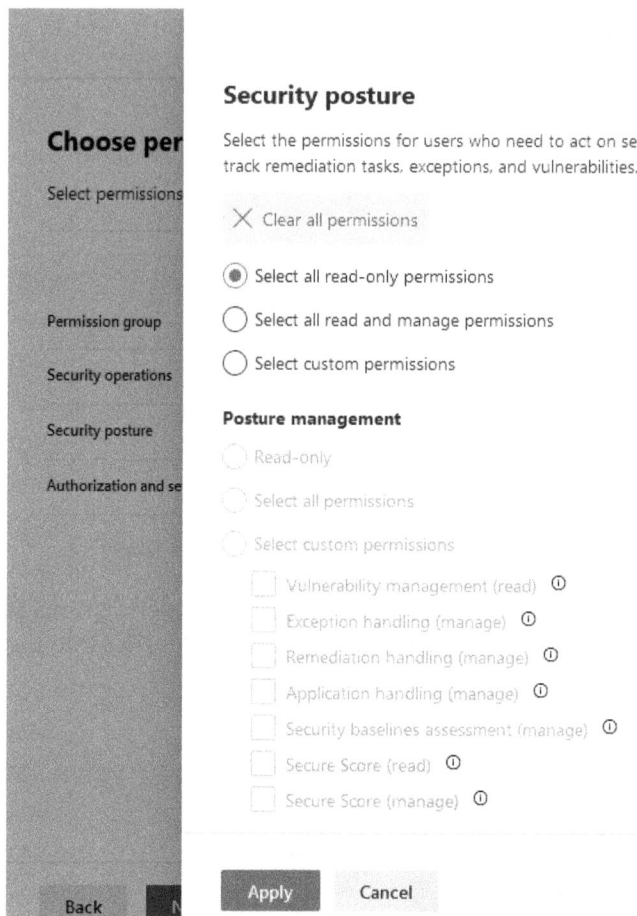

Figure 4.14: Security Posture Permission selection page

2. **Press on add assignment**: There are multiple security data sources that you can choose on which this role can act. By default, all data sources are selected and in case you would like to control the access to specific Microsoft security data sources then you can choose the specific option. Give an easily identifiable name to the assignment. Try to create some standard in your organization for easy human identification so that just by reading the assignment SOC analyst can understand the purpose of the role. Refer to the following figure that show case data source selection:

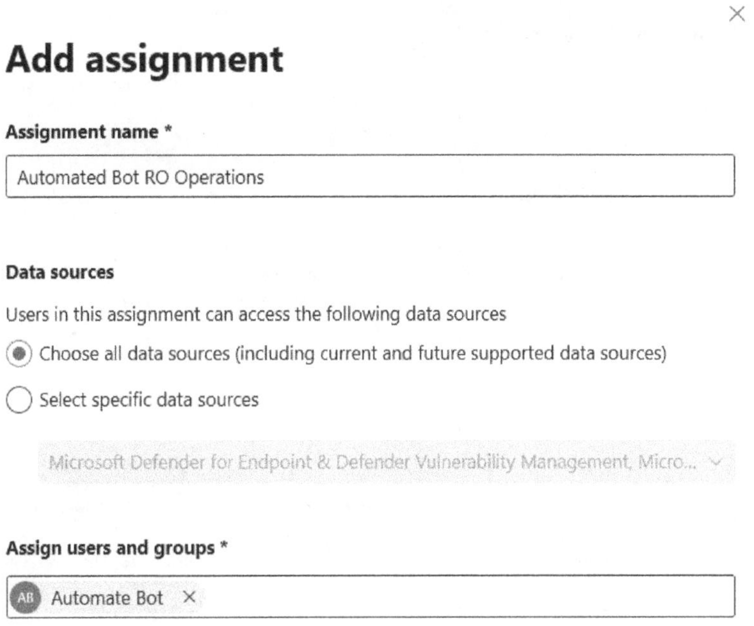

×

Add assignment

Assignment name *

Automated Bot RO Operations

Data sources

Users in this assignment can access the following data sources

⦿ Choose all data sources (including current and future supported data sources)

◯ Select specific data sources

Microsoft Defender for Endpoint & Defender Vulnerability Management, Micro... ⌄

Assign users and groups *

ᴬᴮ Automate Bot ✕

Figure 4.15: Data source assignment page to the role

3. **Select users**: Within the same assignment page or have to choose the users for the assignment. Refer to the following figure:

Assign users and data sources

╋ Add assignment   1 item

Assignment name	Data sources	Users & groups
Automated Bot RO Operations ⋮	All Scopes	1 users

Figure 4.16: Assign users and data sources page

4. **Final review screen during new role creation**: Review and finish are the final screen that you have overview before finally provisioning the role. Even though it can be deleted, edited later as well, as shown in the following figure:

Review and finish

Basics

Role name

SOC-INDIA-DELHI-RO

Description

Metadata: ----- Author: Shailender Singh Created on: 1/Sept/2023 Purpose: Used by Local SOC Team Description:Delhi Office Local Team Read Only Role.

Edit name and description

Permissions   ✎

Permission group	Description	Permissions selected
Security operations	Manages day-to-day operati...	● Yes
Security posture	Manages the organization's ...	● Yes
Authorization and settings	Manages the security and sy...	● Yes

Figure 4.17: Final review or confirmation page before role creation

5. After successfully creation, it will show the creation message, as shown in the following figure:

✅ **SOC-INDIA-DELHI-RO role was created**

Next steps

View & edit roles
Activate workloads

Learn more about Microsoft 365 Defender RBAC

Figure 4.18: Message showing successful role creation

6. After successful creation, you can see new custom role available under **Permissions** tab, as shown in the following figure:

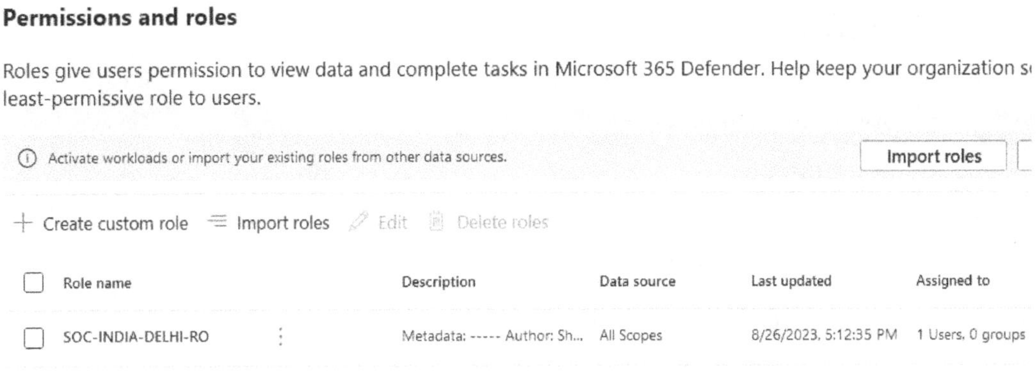

Permissions and roles

Roles give users permission to view data and complete tasks in Microsoft 365 Defender. Help keep your organization s‹ least-permissive role to users.

ⓘ Activate workloads or import your existing roles from other data sources. | Import roles |

+ Create custom role   ≡ Import roles   ✎ Edit   🗑 Delete roles

	Role name	Description	Data source	Last updated	Assigned to
☐	SOC-INDIA-DELHI-RO ⋮	Metadata: ----- Author: Sh...	All Scopes	8/26/2023, 5:12:35 PM	1 Users, 0 groups

Figure 4.19: Permission and roles page view (after role creation)

Microsoft 365 Defender settings

The following are the configuration options available under settings page on MDE web portal:

Topic	Description
General settings	Adjust or modify the previously defined general settings established during onboarding.
Permissions	Administer access to the portal using RBAC alongside device grouping.
APIs	Activate integration for threat intelligence and SIEM.
Rules	Set up rules for suppressing and automating certain actions.
Device management	Initiate the onboarding and offboarding processes for devices.
Network assessments	Designate devices for regular scanning and inclusion in the device inventory.

Table 4.7: Configuration options under the MDE settings page

You can customize the given settings from the security portal. The account tab contains the information about your Tenant and Org ids that are used to onboard your devices.

You can follow these steps under **Settings | Microsoft 365 Defender | Permissions and roles**.

- **General**:
  - ○ Account
  - ○ Email notification
  - ○ Alert service settings

- o   Permission and roles
- o   Streaming API
- **Rules**:
  - o   Asset rule management
  - o   Alert tuning
- **Automation**:
  - o   MDO automation settings

Streaming API

Configure direct export of events from Microsoft 365 Defender to Azure Storage and/ or Azure Event Hub. Configure new Streaming API settings, to forward Microsoft 365 Defender events to Azure Storage and/or Event Hub.

There are a total of 12 event types, categorized into alerts (two) and devices (ten), mentioned as follows:

- AlertInfo, AlertEvidence
- DeviceInfo
- DeviceNetworkInfo
- DeviceProcessEvents
- DeviceNetworkEvents
- DeviceFileEvents
- DeviceRegistryEvents
- DeviceLogonEvents
- DeviceImageLoadEvents
- DeviceEvents
- DeviceFileCertificateInfo

MDE agent configuration

First, we will discuss endpoint security policies and configuration. This includes how to create and manage policies for different operating systems, including macOS, Windows, and Linux. We will also cover how to configure real-time protection settings to ensure that your devices are protected against threats in real-time.

Second, in this chapter, we will learn how to manage endpoint security policies and configurations for macOS, Windows, and Linux devices. We will cover how to customize real-time protection settings, antivirus, malware protection, and endpoint firewall configurations.

Next, we will explore customizing antivirus and malware protection. This includes how to configure scan settings, manage exclusions, and set up notifications for detected threats. We will also discuss how to manage quarantine and remediation actions for detected threats.

Finally, we will cover endpoint firewall and network protection configuration. This includes how to configure firewall rules to control network traffic, set up intrusion prevention and detection, and manage network protection settings.

By the end of this chapter, you will have a solid understanding of how to configure Microsoft Defender Endpoint to protect your devices against threats. You will be able to customize your security settings to meet the needs of your organization and ensure that your devices are protected against the latest threats.

Endpoint security policies and configuration

Microsoft Defender for Endpoint provides a range of security policies and configurations to help you manage the security of your devices. These policies allow you to control various aspects of endpoint security, including antivirus, firewall, and EDR settings.

Antivirus policies can help security admins focus on managing the discrete group of antivirus settings for managed devices. Antivirus policy includes several profiles, each containing only the settings that are relevant for Microsoft Defender for Endpoint antivirus for macOS and Windows devices or the user experience in the Windows Security app on Windows devices.

EDR policies allow you to manage the EDR settings and onboard devices to Microsoft Defender for Endpoint. These policies provide you with the ability to configure EDR settings, such as enabling or disabling EDR, configuring advanced features, and setting up notifications.

Firewall policies allow you to manage the firewall settings on your devices. These policies provide you with the ability to configure firewall rules, set up intrusion prevention and detection, and manage network protection settings.

In addition to these policies, Microsoft Defender for Endpoint also provides support for managing security settings on non-managed clients through its integration with Microsoft Intune. This allows you to enforce fundamental security policy on non-managed clients, including antivirus, firewall, and EDR policies.

Overall, Microsoft Defender for Endpoint provides a comprehensive set of security policies and configurations to help you manage the security of your devices.

To configure Microsoft Defender for Endpoint policies, you can use the Microsoft Endpoint Manager admin center or the Microsoft 365 Defender portal. Here are the steps to configure policies in the Microsoft Endpoint Manager admin center:

1. **Go to the Microsoft Endpoint Manager admin center**: Go to the Microsoft Endpoint Manager admin center and sign in.

2. **Create a device configuration policy**: In the Microsoft Endpoint Manager admin center, create a device configuration policy using the **Microsoft Defender for Endpoint** profile type or Microsoft Defender Antivirus profile type. Please note that non-Windows devices require an installation package that must be downloaded from the Microsoft Defender Security Center[1].

3. **Configure policy settings**: Configure the policy settings according to your needs. You can configure settings for antivirus, firewall, and EDR.

4. **Assign the policy**: Assign the policy to the devices or groups of devices that you want to apply the policy to.

You can also use the Microsoft 365 Defender portal to configure settings for Defender for Endpoint and perform tasks such as taking response actions on detected threats. To do this, you need to have appropriate permissions assigned.

macOS, Windows and Linux policies

MDE is a security solution that protects devices running on Windows, Linux, and macOS operating systems. The MDE agent can be configured to meet the specific needs of your organization. Here are some details on the configuration settings of the MDE agent for each operating system.

> **Note: Actual Configuration examples are given at the end of this chapter so just first understand the high-level steps.**

Windows policies

On Windows devices, MDE can be configured using Group Policy, Microsoft Endpoint Configuration Manager, or other management tools. You can use these tools to create and deploy a device configuration profile that includes the settings necessary to install and configure MDE on your devices. Some of the settings that can be configured include real-time protection, cloud-delivered protection, and exclusion lists.

Here is a detailed step-by-step guide to configure the MDE agent on Windows devices after installation:

1. **Open the Windows Security app**: On the Windows device, open the **Start** menu and search for **Windows Security**. Click on the app to open it.

2. **Navigate to the Virus & threat protection section**: In the Windows Security app, click on the **Virus & threat protection** tab to open the virus and threat protection settings.

3. **Configure real-time protection**: In the **Virus & threat protection** section, click on the **Manage settings** link under the **Virus & threat protection settings** heading.

This will open the real-time protection settings. Here, you can enable or disable real-time protection, configure cloud-delivered protection, and set up automatic sample submission.

4. **Configure exclusion lists**: In the **Virus & threat protection** section, click on the **Manage settings link** under the Exclusions heading. This will open the exclusion settings. Here, you can add or remove files, folders, file types, or processes from being scanned by MDE.

5. **Configure notifications**: In the **Virus & threat protection** section, click on the **Change notification settings link**. This will open the notification settings. Here, you can enable or disable notifications for various events, such as when a threat is detected or when a scan is completed.

Here are some more technical details on how to configure the MDE agent on Windows devices after installation:

- **Real-time protection**: Real-time protection can be enabled or disabled by modifying the DisableRealtimeMonitoring registry value under the `HKEY_LOCAL_MACHINE\SOFTWARE\Policies\Microsoft\Windows` Defender\Real-time protection key. Setting the value to 1 will disable real-time protection, while setting it to 0 will enable it.

- **Cloud-delivered protection**: Cloud-delivered protection can be enabled or disabled by modifying the SpynetReporting registry value under the `HKEY_LOCAL_MACHINE\SOFTWARE\Policies\Microsoft\Windows` Defender\Spynet key. Setting the value to 0 will disable cloud-delivered protection while setting it to 1 or 2 will enable it.

- **Exclusion lists**: Exclusion lists can be configured by modifying the Exclusions registry key under the `HKEY_LOCAL_MACHINE\SOFTWARE\Policies\Microsoft\Windows` Defender key. The key contains several subkeys, including Extensions, Paths, and Processes, which can be used to exclude specific file types, file paths, and processes from being scanned by MDE.

- **Notifications**: Notifications can be enabled or disabled by modifying the DisableNotifications registry value under the `HKEY_LOCAL_MACHINE\SOFTWARE\Policies\Microsoft\Windows` Defender key. Setting the value to 1 will disable notifications while setting it to 0 will enable them.

Here are the steps to download the onboarding package for Windows from the Microsoft Defender Security Center:

1. **Go to the Microsoft 365 Defender portal**: Go to the Microsoft 365 Defender portal and sign in.

2. **Navigate to the Onboarding page**: In the navigation pane, choose Settings | Endpoints, and then under Device management, choose Onboarding.

3. **Select Windows 10 and 11**: Select Windows 10 and 11, and then, in the Deployment method section, choose Local script.

4. **Download the onboarding package**: Select **Download onboarding package**. We recommend that you save the onboarding package to a removable drive.

There is different package for **Virtual Desktop Infrastructure (VDIs)**. Here are the steps to download the VDI package for non-persistent (VDI) devices from the Microsoft Defender Security Center:

1. **Go to the Microsoft 365 Defender portal**: Go to the [Microsoft 365 Defender portal] and sign in.

2. **Navigate to the Onboarding page**: In the navigation pane, select **Settings | Endpoints | Device management | Onboarding**.

3. **Select the operating system**: Select the operating system you want to onboard.

4. **Select VDI onboarding scripts**: In the **Deployment method** field, select **VDI onboarding scripts for non-persistent endpoints**.

5. **Download the package**: Click **Download package** and save the .zip file.

After downloading the VDI package, you can follow the instructions provided in the Microsoft Learn documentation to onboard your non-persistent VDI devices to Microsoft Defender for Business.

After downloading the onboarding package, you can follow the instructions provided in the Microsoft Learn documentation to onboard your Windows devices to Microsoft Defender for Business.

Linux policies

Linux devices under MDE management can utilize a configuration profile, deployed via the preferred management tool. This profile, typically a `.json` file, comprises entries marked by keys (representing preference names) and their corresponding values. These entries cater to various preferences such as real-time protection, on-demand scanning, and exclusion lists.

- Real-time protection
- On-demand scanning
- Exclusion lists

Here are the steps to download the onboarding package for Linux from the Microsoft Defender Security Center:

1. **Access Microsoft 365 Defender portal**: Go to the [Microsoft 365 Defender portal] and sign in.

2. **Open the Onboarding page**: In the navigation pane, choose **Settings | Endpoints**, and then under **Device management**, choose **Onboarding**.

3. **Select Linux**: Select **Linux**, and then, in the **Deployment method** section, choose **Local script**.

4. **Download/Get the onboarding package**: Select **Download onboarding package**. We recommend that you save the onboarding package to a removable drive.

After downloading the onboarding package, you can follow the instructions provided in the (Microsoft Learn documentation) to onboard your Linux devices to Microsoft Defender for Business:

1. **Create a configuration file**: Create a configuration file for the MDE agent. The configuration file is a **.json** file that contains entries identified by a key, followed by a value. The key denotes the name of the preference, while the value depends on the nature of the preference.

2. **Configure real-time protection**: To enable or disable real-time protection, add an entry to the configuration file with the key **real_time_protection_enabled** and set the value to true or false, respectively.

3. **Configure exclusion lists**: To configure exclusion lists, add an entry to the configuration file with the key exclusions. The value should be an object that contains one or more of the following keys: files, folders, extensions, and processes. Each key should have an array of strings as its value, where each string represents an item to be excluded from scanning.

4. **Apply the configuration**: To apply the configuration, copy the configuration file to the **/etc/opt/microsoft/mdatp/** directory on your Ubuntu Linux server and restart the MDE agent using the command **sudo systemctl restart mdatp**.

By following these steps, you can configure the MDE agent on Ubuntu Linux servers to meet your specific needs and requirements.

You can also push similar configuration using the Ansible.

One way to upload a pre-configured **.json** file for the MDE agent on Linux servers is to use a configuration management tool such as Ansible. Ansible is an open-source automation tool that can be used to automate the deployment and configuration of software on multiple devices.

Here is an example of how you can use Ansible to upload a pre-configured **.json** file for the MDE agent on Linux servers:

```
- name: Configure MDE agent on Linux servers
  hosts: linux_servers
  tasks:
    - name: Copy MDE configuration file
      copy:
        src: /path/to/mde_config.json
        dest: /etc/opt/microsoft/mdatp/mde_config.json
        owner: root
```

```
      group: root
      mode: '0644'


  - name: Restart MDE agent
    service:
      name: mdatp
      state: restarted
```

This Ansible playbook will copy the pre-configured **.json** file from the specified source path to the **/etc/opt/microsoft/mdatp/** directory on the target Linux servers. It will then restart the MDE agent to apply the new configuration.

Before running this playbook, you should ensure that the **.json** file contains all of the required values and is properly formatted. You can use a JSON validator tool to verify that the file is valid.

Here is an example of a **.json** configuration file for the MDE agent on Linux servers:

```
{
    "real_time_protection_enabled": true,
    "cloud_protection_level": "high",
    "exclusions": {
        "files": ["/path/to/file1", "/path/to/file2"],
        "folders": ["/path/to/folder1", "/path/to/folder2"],
        "extensions": [".ext1", ".ext2"],
        "processes": ["process1", "process2"]
    },
    "scheduled_scan": {
        "day": 1,
        "time": "02:00",
        "type": "quick"
    }
}
```

This **.json** file includes several configuration options for the MDE agent, including enabling real-time protection, setting the cloud protection level, configuring exclusion lists, and scheduling a scan. You can customize this file to meet your specific needs and requirements.

macOS policies

On macOS devices, MDE can be managed through a configuration profile that is deployed using one of several management tools. The configuration profile is a **.plist** file that consists of entries identified by a key (which denotes the name of the preference), followed by a value, which depends on the nature of the preference Some of the preferences that can be configured include real-time protection, on-demand scanning, and exclusion lists.

Here is an example of a **.plist** configuration file for the MDE agent on macOS devices:

```xml
<?xml version="1.0" encoding="UTF-8"?>
<!DOCTYPE plist PUBLIC "-//Apple//DTD PLIST 1.0//EN"
        "http://www.apple.com/DTDs/PropertyList-1.0.dtd">
<plist version="1.0">
<dict>
    <key>RealTimeProtectionEnabled</key>
    <true/>
    <key>CloudProtectionLevel</key>
    <string>high</string>
    <key>Exclusions</key>
    <dict>
        <key>Files</key>
        <array>
            <string>/path/to/file1</string>
            <string>/path/to/file2</string>
        </array>
        <key>Folders</key>
        <array>
            <string>/FOLDER_PATH1</string>
            <string>/FOLDER_PATH2</string>
        </array>
        <key>Extensions</key>
        <array>
            <string>.extX</string>
            <string>.extY</string>
        </array>
        <key>Processes</key>
```

```
        <array>
            <string>processX</string>
            <string>processY</string>
        </array>
    </dict>
    <key>ScheduledScanDay</key>
    <integer>1</integer>
    <key>ScheduledScanTime</key>
    <string>12:00</string>
    <key>ScheduledScanType</key>
    <string>quick</string>
</dict>
</plist>
```

Let us understand:

- The **.plist** file contains various MDE agent configurations such as activating real-time protection, defining cloud protection levels, managing exclusion lists, and scheduling scans. Customization of this file is possible to align with specific preferences and needs.

- To deploy the **.plist** configuration file for the MDE agent on macOS devices, it should be located in the **/Library/Preferences/com.microsoft.wdav.plist** directory. Employing tools like **scp** or **rsync** allows file transfer to the intended macOS device, while configuration management tools like Ansible or Puppet enable automated deployment.

- Once the **.plist** file is transferred, the MDE agent must be restarted for the modifications to take effect. This can be achieved by executing a command on the targeted macOS device:

  ```
  # sudo launchctl unload /Library/LaunchDaemons/com.microsoft.wdav.plist

  # sudo launchctl load /Library/LaunchDaemons/com.microsoft.wdav.plist
  ```

Apart from employing a **.plist** file, another method to configure MDE on macOS devices involves using the defaults command. This command enables the reading and writing of values in **.plist** files directly through the command line interface. For instance, to activate real-time protection, execute the command:

```
#sudo    defaults    write    /Library/Preferences/com.microsoft.wdav.plist
RealTimeProtectionEnabled -bool true.
```

Incorporating a new security solution into an existing security framework is a vital aspect of its deployment. Seamless integration ensures the new solution aligns harmoniously with the current security tools and processes, bolstering the organization's overall security stance. Various integration methods can be employed to achieve this synergy.

One approach involves leveraging open standards and APIs to foster interoperability among diverse security tools. This exchange of data enables collaborative efforts among these tools, culminating in a unified view of the organization's security landscape. Additionally, adopting a centralized management platform streamlines the administration and oversight of multiple security tools from a singular interface, streamlining operations and enhancing efficiency.

Moreover, integration with existing IT and business processes is pivotal. This integration spans across identity and access management systems, network infrastructure, and other pivotal systems, allowing the new solution to harness established protocols and controls for augmented security measures. Ultimately, the effective integration of a new security solution hinges on open standards, centralized management platforms, and harmonious integration with existing IT and business processes.

Proxy services and URLs

To ensure the portal and agent operate seamlessly, it is crucial to enable specific URLs in your firewall settings. The following are the essential details about these URLs:

- **Reference**: You can access the latest Excel sheets containing comprehensive URL details from the following link. It is organized into two main sections, as show in the following figure:

Spreadsheet of domains list	Description
Microsoft Defender for Endpoint URL list for commercial customers	Spreadsheet of specific DNS records for service locations, geographic locations, and OS for commercial customers. Download the spreadsheet here. ⬈
Microsoft Defender for Endpoint URL list for Gov/GCC/DoD	Spreadsheet of specific DNS records for service locations, geographic locations, and OS for Gov/GCC/DoD customers. Download the spreadsheet here. ⬈

Figure 4.20: Spredsheet reference page[1]

---

1   Source: https://learn.microsoft.com/en-us/microsoft-365/security/defender-endpoint/produc-tion-deployment?view=o365-worldwide#proxy-service-urls

Proxy configuration through GPO

In case direct traffic is not allowed and you have a proxy in place, then please follow the process captured in the following URL to add Proxy details through GPO policies:

**https://learn.microsoft.com/en-us/microsoft-365/security/defender-endpoint/
production-deployment?view=o365-worldwide**

Important configuration

MDE has many important configurations, but agent mode settings are super important as it helps running agent in active or passive mode.

Comparing active, passive, and disabled mode

The following table describes what to expect when Microsoft Defender Antivirus is in active mode, passive mode, or disabled:

Mode	Actions taken
Active mode	In active mode, Microsoft Defender Antivirus serves as the primary antivirus application on the device. It conducts file scans, resolves detected threats, and logs these in security reports and the Windows Security app.
Passive mode	In passive mode, Microsoft Defender Antivirus is not the primary antivirus application. It conducts file scans and reports identified threats, but it does not remediate them.
Disabled/uninstalled	When disabled or uninstalled, Microsoft Defender Antivirus stops functioning. It does not perform file scans or resolve threats. Disabling or uninstalling is generally discouraged for maintaining device security.

Table 4.8: MDE agent mode configuration with meaning

Important commands

We give a reference of Get-MpComputerStatus and **mdatp** command output status with an available argument option for a quick overview of how the output looks like. You can execute the below commands on your device to check your configuration.

Get-MpComputerStatus

Use PowerShell to check the status of Microsoft Defender Antivirus, as shown in the following steps:

1. Select the **Start** menu, and begin typing `PowerShell`. Then, open Windows PowerShell in the results.

2. Type Get-MpComputerStatus.

3. In the list of results, look at the **AMRunningMode** row:

   - **Normal** means Microsoft Defender Antivirus is running in active mode.

   - **Passive mode** means Microsoft Defender Antivirus running but is not the primary antivirus/antimalware product on your device. Passive mode is only available for devices that are onboarded to Microsoft Defender for Endpoint and that meet certain requirements. To learn more, see Requirements for Microsoft Defender Antivirus to run in passive mode.

   - EDR block mode means Microsoft Defender Antivirus is running and EDR in block mode, a capability in Microsoft Defender for Endpoint, is enabled. Check the **ForceDefenderPassiveMode** registry key. If its value is 0, it is running in normal mode; otherwise, it is running in passive mode.

   - SxS **passive mode** means Microsoft Defender Antivirus is running alongside another antivirus/antimalware product, and limited periodic scanning is used.

The following is the Get-MpComputerStatus output:

```
AMEngineVersion                : 1.1.18100.6
AMProductVersion               : 4.18.2107.4
AMRunning                      : True
AMServiceEnabled               : True
AMServiceVersion               : 4.18.2107.4
AntispywareEnabled             : True
AntispywareSignatureAge        : 0
AntispywareSignatureLastUpdated : 7/31/2023 4:55:06 PM
AntispywareSignatureVersion    : 1.355.221.0
AntivirusEnabled               : True
AntivirusSignatureAge          : 0
AntivirusSignatureLastUpdated  : 7/31/2023 4:55:05 PM
AntivirusSignatureVersion      : 1.355.221.0
BehaviorMonitorEnabled         : True
ComputerID                     : ABCD1234-5678-90EF-1234-567890ABCDEF
ComputerState                  : 0
FullScanAge                    : 4294967295
```

```
FullScanEndTime                    : 12/31/1600 5:00:00 PM
FullScanStartTime                  : 12/31/1600 5:00:00 PM
IoavProtectionEnabled              : True
IsTamperProtected                  : False
LastFullScanSource                 : 0
LastQuickScanSource                : 0
NISEnabled                         : True
QuickScanAge                       : 0
QuickScanEndTime                   : 7/31/2023 6:24:55 PM
QuickScanStartTime                 : 7/31/2023 6:24:20 PM
RealTimeProtectionEnabled          : True
RealTimeProtectionSignatureAge : 0
RealTimeProtectionSignatureLastUpdated : 7/31/2023 6:23:54 PM
RealTimeProtectionSignatureVersion : 1.355.221.0
PSComputerName                     :
```

Linux 'mdatp' commands

Here is a cheat sheet of commonly used **mdatp** commands for MDE on Linux:

- Cancel an ongoing on-demand scan: `mdatp scan cancel`
- Request a security intelligence update: `mdatp definitions update`
- Print the full protection history: `mdatp threat list`
- Get threat details: `mdatp threat get --id [threat-id]`
- List all quarantined files: `mdatp threat quarantine list`
- Remove all files from the quarantine: `mdatp threat quarantine remove-all`
- Turn on/off real-time protection: `mdatp config real-time-protection --value [enabled|disabled]`
- Add/remove an antivirus exclusion for a file extension: `mdatp exclusion extension [add|remove] --name [extension]`
- Add/remove an antivirus exclusion for a file: `mdatp exclusion file [add|remove] --path [path-to-file]`
- Add/remove an antivirus exclusion for a directory: `mdatp exclusion folder [add|remove] --path [path-to-directory]`
- Add/remove an antivirus exclusion for a process: `mdatp exclusion process [add|remove] --path [path-to-process]` or `mdatp exclusion process [add|remove] --name [process-name]`

- List all antivirus exclusions: `mdatp exclusion list`
- Check the product's health: `mdatp health`
- Scan a path: `mdatp scan custom --path [path]`
- Do a quick scan: `mdatp scan quick`
- Do a full scan: `mdatp scan full`
- Turn on/off cloud protection: `mdatp config cloud --value [enabled|disabled]`
- Turn on/off product diagnostics: `mdatp config cloud-diagnostic --value [enabled|disabled]`
- Turn on/off automatic sample submission: `mdatp config cloud-automatic-sample-submission --value [enabled|disabled]`

Conclusion

Throughout this chapter, we discussed the myriad configurations and advanced functionalities of Microsoft Defender, shaping a robust landscape for endpoint security. Our journey commenced with a foundational introduction, laying the groundwork for a comprehensive understanding of subsequent sections. From the detailed exploration of the Defender web portal configuration, covering pivotal elements that serve as the epicenter for security operations, to the thorough investigation of advanced features encompassing licensing insights, Secure Score intricacies, and permission intricacies, we have equipped you to leverage the full potential of your Defender deployment.

Exploring further, we navigated through Microsoft 365 Defender settings, meticulous MDE Agent configurations, and the intricacies of endpoint security policies. Our detailed examination of policies tailored for macOS, Windows, and Linux ensures a holistic understanding of fine-tuning endpoint security across diverse platforms. For those venturing into Azure Sentinel integration, we provided a comprehensive overview. We also explored the significance of proxy services and URLs, offering insights into their configuration through GPO for establishing a secure and streamlined network environment. Crucial considerations in configuration, including a comparative analysis of active, passive, and disabled modes, were highlighted. To cap it off, we furnished you with essential commands to monitor Microsoft Defender Antivirus status in both Windows and Linux environments.

In next chapter, we will cover general endpoint detection and response in respect to **security operation center** (**SOC**) in detail. It will provide a comprehensive overview of EDR, in the context of modern cybersecurity. It will explore the key domains and functionalities of EDR, emphasizing its proactive defense capabilities.

Join our book's Discord space

Join the book's Discord Workspace for Latest updates, Offers, Tech happenings around the world, New Release and Sessions with the Authors:

https://discord.bpbonline.com

CHAPTER 5

General EDR with Respect to SOC

Introduction

Endpoint Detection and Response (EDR), also known as **Endpoint Detection and Threat Response (EDTR)**, represents a pivotal cybersecurity technology designed to incessantly monitor end-user devices. Its primary function is to identify and counter cyber threats, including ransomware and malware. *Anton Chuvakin*, acknowledged by *Gartner*, coined the word EDR. However, it was corrected to indicate that *Chuvakin* did not coin the term, as a solution that meticulously records and analyze behaviors at the endpoint system level. Employing diverse data analytics techniques scrutinizes suspicious system activities, furnishing contextual information, thwarting malicious endeavors, and presenting remedial recommendations to reinstate affected systems. EDR security solutions capture endpoint and workload activities and events, offering crucial visibility to security teams, revealing otherwise undetected incidents. Essential to an EDR solution is continuous, comprehensive visibility into real-time endpoint activities. It should encompass advanced capabilities in threat detection, investigation, and response, facilitating incident data search, alert triage, validation of suspicious activities, proactive threat hunting, and detection and containment of malicious activities.

EDR technology combines extensive visibility across endpoints with **Indicators of Attack (IOAs)** and utilizes behavioral analytics, analyzing real-time billions of events to detect potential suspicious behavior automatically. By interpreting individual events within larger sequences, EDR tools employ security logic derived from threat intelligence. If a series of events aligns with a known IOA, the EDR tool flags the activity as malicious, triggering an automatic detection alert.

Structure

In this chapter, we will cover the following topics:

- Understanding endpoint detection and response
- Difference between EPP and EDR
- Understanding XDR
- MDE as EDR solution
- Microsoft EDR architecture
- Data loss and prevention overview
- Overview of SOC

Objectives

The objective of this chapter is to provide a comprehensive overview of EDR, in the context of modern cybersecurity. We will explore the key domains and functionalities of EDR, emphasizing its proactive defense capabilities and its role in countering the ever-evolving threat landscape. By understanding the differences between EDR and **Endpoint Protection Platform** (**EPP**), readers will gain insights into how EDR forms a dynamic shield against modern threats.

Furthermore, we will explore the benefits of EDR, offering a detailed look at its role in disrupting the cyberattack kill chain and its relation to **Extended Detection and Response** (**XDR**). The chapter will focus on **Microsoft Defender for Endpoint** (**MDE**) as an EDR solution, highlighting its architectures and integration with the broader Microsoft 365 Defender suite. Readers will also gain insights into MDE Agent security logging and **Data Loss Prevention** (**DLP**), ensuring a comprehensive understanding of how EDR fits into an organization's security operations. Lastly, the chapter will provide an overview of the **Security Operations Center** (**SOC**) and the role of **Microsoft Threat Experts** (**MTE**) in enhancing SOC capabilities.

Understanding endpoint detection and response

Before exploring EDR, it is important to understand the following terminologies to get an idea about how EDR fits in the bigger picture. The following figure simplifies the terminologies:

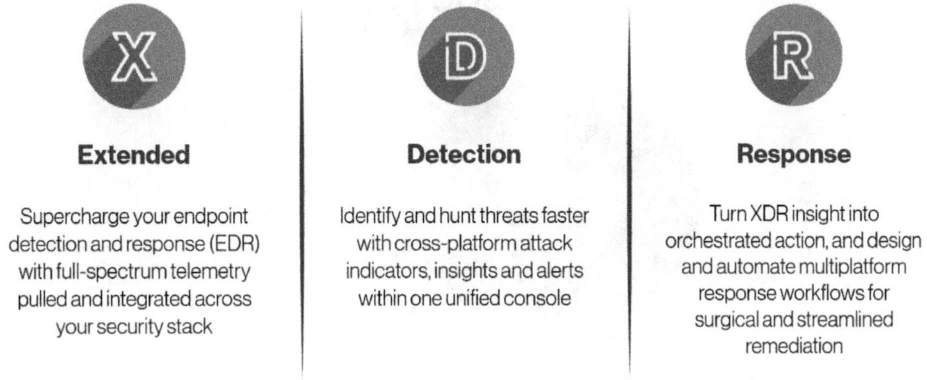

Extended

Supercharge your endpoint detection and response (EDR) with full-spectrum telemetry pulled and integrated across your security stack

Detection

Identify and hunt threats faster with cross-platform attack indicators, insights and alerts within one unified console

Response

Turn XDR insight into orchestrated action, and design and automate multiplatform response workflows for surgical and streamlined remediation

Figure 5.1: *EDR meaning*

The field of cybersecurity is filled with various terminologies and acronyms. Here are some additional terms related to EDR, **Managed Detection and Response** (**MDR**), XDR, **Security Information and Event Management** (**SIEM**), and related concepts:

- **Network detection and response (NDR)**: NDR solutions focus on monitoring network traffic to detect and respond to threats. They complement EDR by providing visibility into network-level threats and anomalies.

- **Endpoint detection and threat hunting (EDT)**: EDT combines EDR capabilities with proactive threat hunting to actively seek out and identify advanced threats on endpoints.

- **SOC**: A SOC is a centralized facility responsible for monitoring, detecting, responding to, and mitigating security incidents in an organization.

- **Incident Response (IR)**: IR is the process of reacting to and managing a security incident, such as a breach, with the goal of minimizing damage and reducing recovery time and costs.

- **Security orchestration, automation, and response (SOAR)**: SOAR platforms automate and orchestrate security processes, including IR, to improve the efficiency and effectiveness of security operations.

Key domains around EDR

Beside EDR, there are other terms revolving around it, and most of them are captured in the following *Figure 5.2*. Throughout this book, we will be using these terms, along with their references and definition.

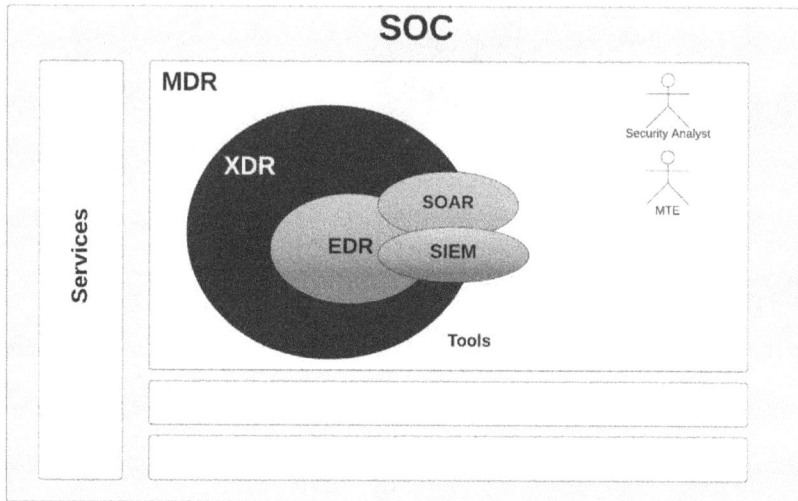

Figure 5.2: SOC, MDR, XDR, EDR, SOAR and SIEM big picture

Informational: The following are references for MDR and one of the opensource EDR agent initiatives:

- **https://www.zielbox.com/security: Zielbox is a company that provides managed security services along with other important IT infrastructure services, in respect to MDE and DevSecOps. In case you would like to get MDE installation and configuration services with automation and best practices then you can approach them for the implementation.**

- **https://www.openedr.com/: There were some initative to write Open Source EDR solution but it seems it got defunct in between (Just a reference but it seems it is not actively getting developed).**

The following figure represents the key words/terminologies used around endpoint security and we put together all such words to build readers understanding:

Figure 5.3: Keywords or domains in endpoint security

Shielding against modern threats in the face of an increasingly complex and diverse threat landscape, cybersecurity strategies have undergone a profound transformation. Among the arsenal of defensive measures, EDR has emerged as a critical paradigm shift, offering organizations a proactive and comprehensive approach to safeguarding their digital assets. This chapter provides an in-depth overview of EDR, exploring its significance, key functionalities, benefits, and its role in modern cybersecurity.

Difference between EPP and EDR

EPP and **EDR** are both crucial components of an endpoint security strategy, but they serve different purposes, as mentioned henceforth:

- EPP refers to a collection of endpoint security tools, like antivirus, data encryption, and **Data Loss and Prevention** (**DLP**). These work collectively on an endpoint device to identify and halt security threats, including file-based malware attacks and malicious activities. Besides detection and prevention, its primary objective is to preempt cyberattacks before they occur. While EPP primarily focuses on prevention and detection of known threats (e.g., file-based malware, known vulnerabilities), it typically does not offer as robust investigation and response capabilities as EDR. EPP solutions usually focus on preventing attacks before they can execute, whereas EDR is more concerned with detecting and responding to threats that have bypassed these preventive measures.

- **EDR**, on the other hand, is a type of security solution that provides real-time visibility into endpoint activities. This is done by detecting malicious behavior, monitoring and recording endpoint data, and responding to threats EDR solutions can detect and respond to threats that your EPP and other security tools did not catch. EDR is designed to detect and respond to threats. However, it is important to clarify that while EDR provides real-time visibility and can detect threats missed by EPP, it often works in conjunction with EPP rather than as a standalone solution.

While some modern security solutions integrate features of both EPP and EDR, they are often distinct solutions with different core functionalities. Organizations typically use them together rather than choosing one over the other.

Proactive defense strategy

EDR is a cybersecurity solution designed to protect an organization's digital endpoints, which includes devices like laptops, desktops, servers, and mobile devices. Unlike traditional security measures that primarily focus on preventing external threats from breaching the perimeter, EDR adopts a proactive stance by monitoring, detecting, investigating, and responding to threats that occur within the endpoints themselves. This shift in approach acknowledges the reality that breaches can and do occur, necessitating the ability to swiftly identify and mitigate threats within the organization's internal environment.

The following figure shows various activities that the security team performs as part of proactive defense strategy:

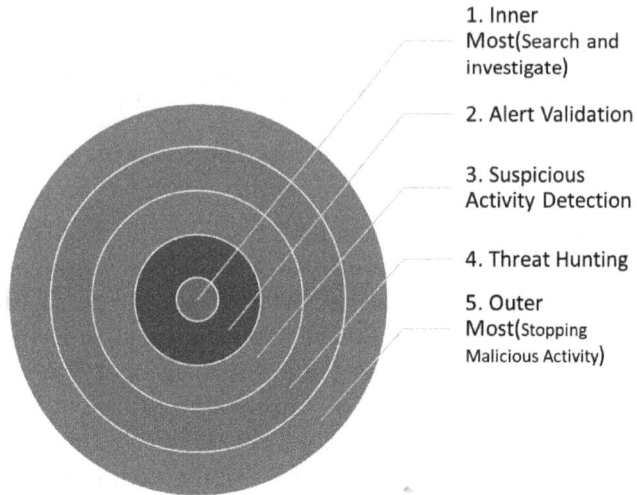

1. Inner Most(Search and investigate)

2. Alert Validation

3. Suspicious Activity Detection

4. Threat Hunting

5. Outer Most(Stopping Malicious Activity)

Figure 5.4: Order of EDR detection through information collection and response

Key functionalities of EDR

EDR offers a range of functionalities that collectively create a robust security posture, such as:

- **Real-time monitoring and visibility**: EDR solutions provide continuous monitoring of endpoints, collecting data on activities, events, and behaviors. This real-time visibility allows security teams to detect anomalies and potential threats as they unfold.

- **Threat detection and analysis**: EDR employs sophisticated algorithms and machine learning to identify patterns indicative of cyber threats. This includes spotting unusual behaviors, unauthorized access attempts, and suspicious activities.

- **Incident investigation and response**: When a potential threat is detected, EDR facilitates thorough incident investigations. It enables security analysts to trace the origin of the threat, analyze attack vectors, and determine the scope of impact.

- **Automated and manual response**: EDR solutions offer the ability to respond to threats in various ways. This includes automated actions, such as isolating compromised endpoints, blocking malicious processes, and even initiating predefined response playbooks. Manual intervention is also possible for nuanced situations.

- **Forensic analysis**: EDR tools often include features for detailed forensic analysis. Security teams can recreate the sequence of events leading up to a breach, aiding in understanding the nature of the attack and planning future prevention strategies.

Benefits of EDR

The adoption of EDR brings several advantages to organizations. The following are some of them:

- **Early threat detection**: EDR's strength is often in detecting threats once they have begun to manifest, rather than solely at the earliest stages. Early threat detection is more a characteristic of proactive security measures combined with threat intelligence.

- **Rapid IR**: The ability to respond swiftly and decisively to threats minimizes the window of vulnerability and reduces potential damage.

- **Enhanced visibility**: Real-time monitoring and granular visibility into endpoint activities provide insights that support decision-making.

- **Improved investigation**: EDR's forensic capabilities enhance incident investigations, allowing organizations to understand attack methods and vulnerabilities better.

- **Reduced dwell time**: The time between a breach and its detection, known as **dwell time**, is significantly reduced with EDR, limiting attackers' ability to move laterally within the network.

A contemporary SOC is a dynamic, intelligence-driven entity that embraces a strategic approach to threat defense by proactively integrating security processes into the early stages of deployment. In this context, the conventional approach of assigning standalone technologies and processes to individual security analysts falls short due to the influx of data from diverse sources. The evolution demands a holistic perspective from security professionals, urging them to collaborate and leverage shared insights across various platforms and domains for more impactful responses.

In light of these changes, the deployment and execution of the Microsoft 365 Defender platform necessitate meticulous planning in conjunction with the SOC team. This collaboration ensures the optimal management of day-to-day operations and the lifecycle of the Microsoft 365 Defender service itself. This content explores several concepts that outline strategies for effectively operationalizing and seamlessly integrating Microsoft 365 Defender. These strategies encompass both new and existing personnel, processes, and technologies, forming the foundation for a forward-looking security operations approach.

Understanding Cyber Attack Kill Chain

There are multiple kill chain models adopted in the market and Cyber Kill Chain is one among them which has seven stages. Understanding the Cyber Attack Kill Chain is essential as it helps in comprehending how EDR, particularly through solutions like MDE, can provide insights at various stages of an attack.

The Cyber Attack Kill Chain is a structured framework that describes the stages involved in a typical cyberattack. Understanding this framework is crucial for organizations and cybersecurity professionals as it helps in identifying and mitigating threats effectively. Here is a brief introduction to the Cyber Attack Kill Chain and its stages.

The Cyber Attack Kill Chain is a concept developed to analyze and counteract cyber threats systematically. The Cyber Attack Kill Chain traditionally includes the cleanup phase, but its importance can vary based on the model used and this stage may or may not be part of attack stage. It breaks down a cyberattack into a series of stages, each representing a critical step in the attacker's strategy. By dissecting an attack into these stages, organizations can develop proactive defense measures and IR strategies to protect their assets and data.

The following figure represents how the kill chain starts from Reconnaissance and ends at action on the objective:

Note: You can ignore the text in small font as the high-level heading gives you the hint about the stage.

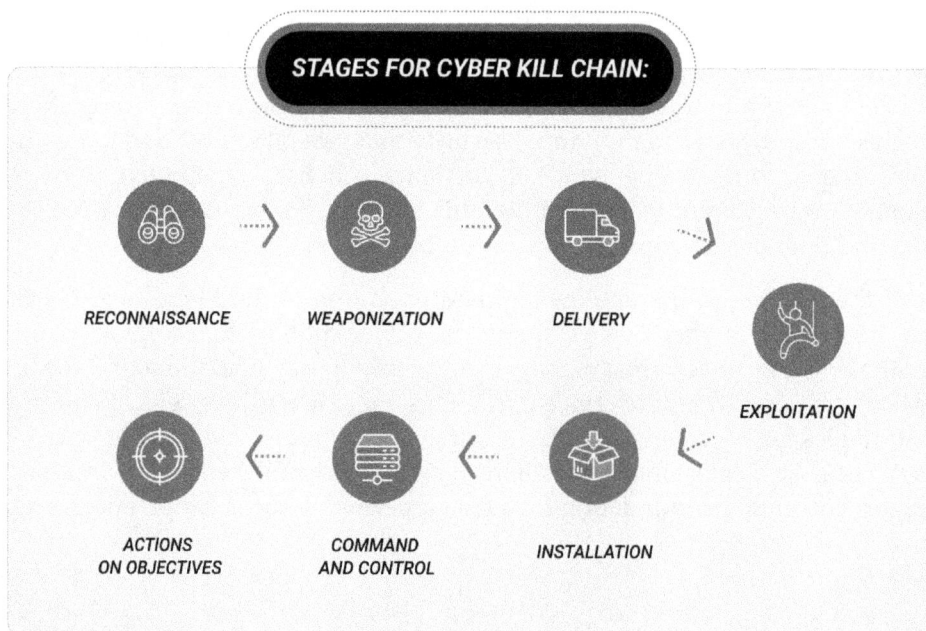

Figure 5.5: Cyber Kill Chain steps

The following are the stages of the Cyber Attack Kill Chain:

- **Reconnaissance**: Attackers gather information about the target, such as vulnerabilities, network architecture, and potential entry points.

- **Intrusion (weaponization and delivery)**: Malicious code or exploits are weaponized and delivered to the target, often through phishing emails, malicious websites, or compromised software.

- **Exploitation**: The attacker exploits vulnerabilities in the target's systems or applications to gain access.

- **Privilege escalation (installation, persistence)**: Once inside, the attacker seeks to elevate privileges, establish persistence, and maintain control over the compromised system.

- **Command and control (C2C)**: Attackers establish communication channels with the compromised system to send commands and receive data. This phase allows them to control the target.

- **Lateral movement**: Attackers move laterally within the network, seeking additional targets or sensitive data. They may exploit vulnerabilities in connected systems.

- **Action and objective (data exfiltration)**: The attacker's primary goal is realized, which could include data theft, system disruption, or other malicious actions.

- **Cleanup**: After achieving their objectives, attackers attempt to cover their tracks, delete logs, and erase any evidence of their presence. The stage labeled "Cleanup" is not universally included in every model of the Kill Chain. Some models end with the "Action" phase.

By understanding these stages, organizations can develop defenses and monitoring capabilities at each phase of the Kill Chain, making it more challenging for attackers to succeed. This proactive approach enables organizations to detect, respond to, and recover from cyberattacks more effectively, ultimately enhancing their overall cybersecurity posture.

The following figure is just another representation of Cyber Attack Kill Chain:

Figure 5.6: Cyber Attack Kill Chain

Understanding XDR

XDR is a cybersecurity technology that provides a holistic approach to threat detection and response. It should be noted that XDR is not exclusively SaaS-based; some XDR solutions may be deployed on-premises or in hybrid environments. It was coined by *Nir Zuk*, the CTO of *Palo Alto Network*, in 2018. XDR breaks down traditional security silos to deliver detection and response across all data sources. It operates as a **Software as a Service** (**SaaS**) solution, streamlining security through the integration of various security products and data. XDR serves to monitor an enterprise's technological landscape, encompassing endpoint devices, firewalls, cloud systems, and select third-party applications. Its comprehensive approach amalgamates prevention, detection, investigation, and response capabilities. By offering enhanced visibility, analytical insights, correlated incident alerts, and automated responses, XDR significantly bolsters data security while countering diverse threats. Leveraging AI, it continually monitors suspicious activities, enabling automated responses and mitigation against potential attacks.

Note: Asserting distinctiveness: NDR + SOAR + SIEM not equals to XDR

The following figure shows the distinct difference among security product categories:

Figure 5.7: *Clarity among different security product categories*[1]

Earlier XDR was much talked, or some features were present inside the Security and Azure Sentinel web portal separately but now Microsoft has brought up XDR as an independent solution in its offering by stitching together existing security solutions from its portfolio, as shown in the following figure:

---

1   Source: **https://www.crowdstrike.com/wp-content/uploads/2021/12/crowdstrike-what-is-xdr-info-graphic.pdf**

Extended detection and response (XDR)			

	Microsoft 365 Defender	Azure Defender	Azure Sentinel
Mcrosoft extended detection and response (XDR) solutions deliver intelligent, automated and integrated security across domains. This in turn help defender's connect seemingly disparate alerts and get ahead of attackers.	Microsoft 365 Defender deliver XDR capabilities for identities, endpoints, cloud apps, email and document. Its built-in self-healing technology fully automates remediation more than 70% of the time. It combines: •Microsoft Defender for Endpoint •Microsoft Defender for Office 365 •Microsoft Defender for Identities •Microsoft Cloud App Security •Azure AD Identity Protection	Delivers XDR left capabilities to protect multi-cloud and hybrid workloads including virtual machine databases, containers, IoT, and more It combines: • Azure Defender for Servers • Azure Defender for IoT • Azure Defender for SQL	To gain visibility across your entire environment and include data from other security solutions such as firewall and existing security tools connect Microsoft Defender to Azure Sentinel, Microsoft's cloud native SIEM. Azure Sentinel is deeply integrated with Microsoft Defender so you can integrate your XDR data in only a few clicks and combine it with all your security data from across your entire enterprise

Figure 5.8: *MD XDR service coverage*

MDE as EDR solution

Several EDR solutions have gained prominence in the cybersecurity landscape. Few notable contenders are mentioned in the following list:

- **MDE**: MDE provides an array of advanced features. It seamlessly integrates with Microsoft 365 security solutions, bolstering threat detection and response capabilities. Its powerful behavioral analytics and machine learning algorithms enhance real-time monitoring, enabling organizations to identify and respond to threats swiftly. MDE, now known as Microsoft Defender for Endpoint (*formerly Microsoft Defender ATP*), integrates with the broader Microsoft 365 security suite. It got **renamed from ATP to MDE in September 2020**. It is accurate to say it offers advanced threat detection and response capabilities through behavioral analytics and machine learning.

- **CrowdStrike Falcon**: Falcon offers a cloud-native EDR platform that delivers comprehensive visibility across endpoints. Its lightweight agent architecture ensures minimal impact on system performance. Falcon leverages AI-driven threat intelligence to provide real-time protection and advanced threat hunting capabilities.

- **Carbon Black by VMware (Now part of Broadcom security suite)**: Carbon Black by VMware offers strong EDR features and integration with other security tools.

- **FireEye Endpoint Security**: Renowned for its threat intelligence and malware analysis capabilities.

- **Symantec Endpoint Security**: Provides comprehensive EDR features and is known for its antivirus heritage.
- **McAfee MVISION EDR:** Offers a broad range of endpoint security capabilities and integration with the McAfee ecosystem.
- **Trend Micro Apex One**: Known for its threat detection and response features along with protection against modern threats.
- **Cisco Secure Endpoint (formerly AMP for Endpoints)**: Provides strong EDR features and integration with Cisco's security portfolio.
- **Palo Alto Networks Cortex XDR**: Offers EDR capabilities along with threat prevention and network security features.
- **SentinelOne**: Known for its AI-driven EDR and automated threat response capabilities.

The following are ten more top EDRs:

- **Cybereason EDR**
- FortiEDR by Fortinet
- Kaspersky Endpoint Security
- CylancePROTECT by BlackBerry
- ESET Endpoint Security
- Sophos Intercept X
- IBM Security QRadar
- F-Secure Rapid Detection and Response
- Symantec (NortonLifeLock) Norton 360 for Business
- Bitdefender GravityZone

Microsoft EDR architecture

Understanding architecture about how things are stitched together is important for deep insight and the following figure shows the **high level diagram (HLD)** of complete solution as well major component inside the EDR agent.

M365D EDR integration overview

The following figure showcases MDE components and the workflow of how agents authenticate and report back to MDE portal:

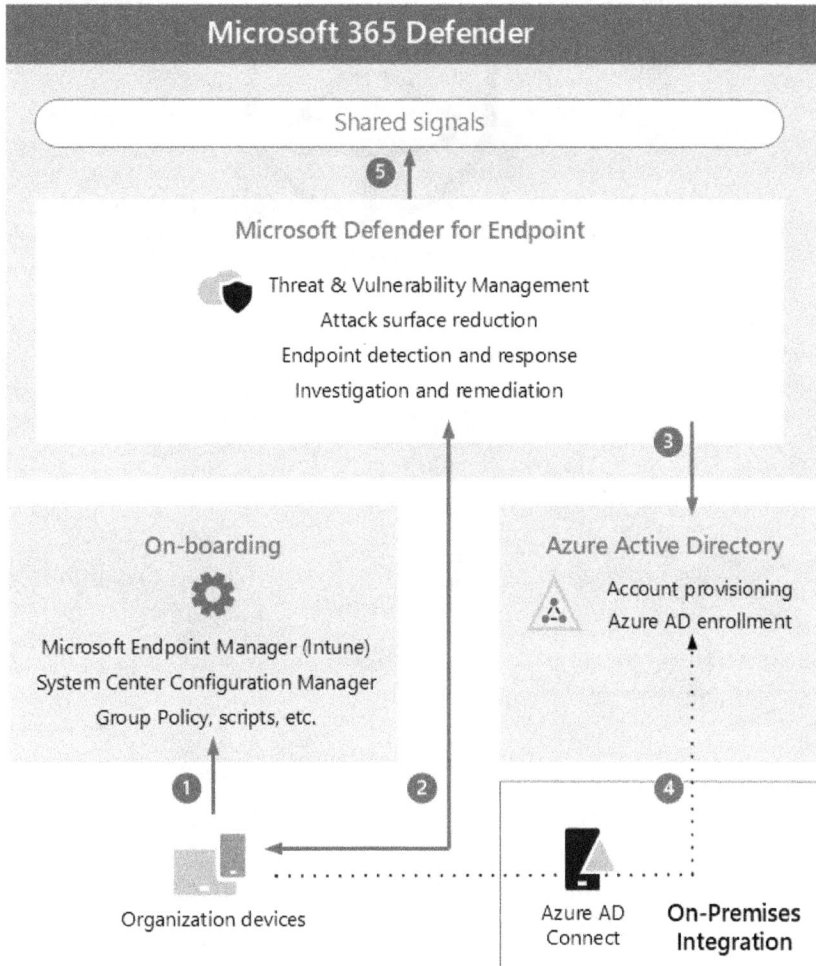

Figure 5.9: *MDE product component overview showcasing integration*

EDR/sense agent architecture with binaries

The following figure provides information about how EDR (sense) agent leverages in built binaries packaged as part of Windows installation and communicates back with Microsoft Defender backend services hosted on the cloud:

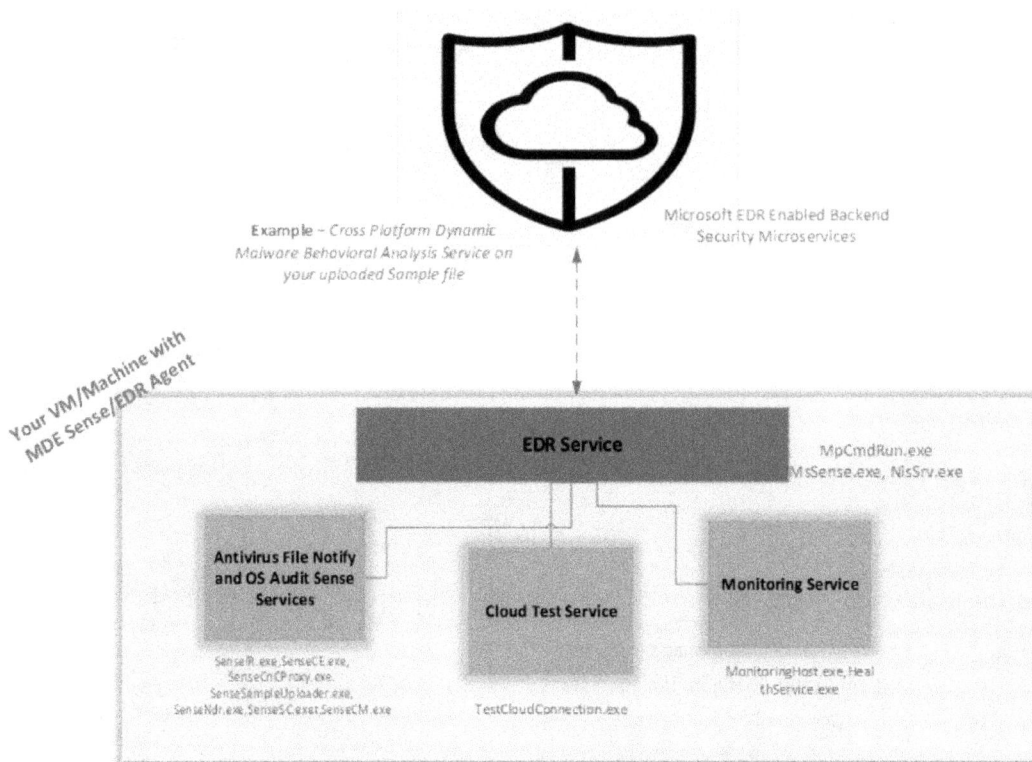

Figure 5.10: MDE agent in built binaries and internal services

MDE agent security logging functionality insight: This block gives information about the logging technology inbuilt in the Linux endpoint agent.

AuditD to eBPF migration of agent for logging

Recently, assistance was provided to a SOC analyst in deploying the Defender Agent and resolving issues with MDE agent deployment. During this process, a crucial decision was documented wherein the MDE team opted to transition from the AuditD agent to eBPF.

Informational:
- **New ebpf usage from Microsoft documentation.**
- **URL: https://learn.microsoft.com/en-us/microsoft-365/security/defender-endpoint/linux-support-ebpf?view=o365-worldwide**

The following figure shows the output of **mdatp health** on Linux system showing usage of **ebpf** module:

```
[leonid@lliansky-rh86 WD.Client.Linux.eBPF]$ mdatp health
healthy                                  : true
health_issues                            : []
licensed                                 : true
engine_version                           : "1.1.20300.5"
app_version                              : "101.23052.0003"
org_id                                   : "d7c7c745-195f-4223-9c7a-99fb420fd000"
log_level                                : "info"
machine_guid                             : "47adefa8-81d1-004c-93fe-3f9643f55bbb"
release_ring                             : "InsiderFast"
product_expiration                       : Mar 03, 2024 at 01:22:05 AM
cloud_enabled                            : true
cloud_automatic_sample_submission_consent : "safe"
cloud_diagnostic_enabled                 : false
passive_mode_enabled                     : true
behavior_monitoring                      : "disabled"
real_time_protection_enabled             : false
real_time_protection_available           : true
real_time_protection_subsystem           : "fanotify"
supplementary_events_subsystem           : "ebpf"
tamper_protection                        : "disabled"
automatic_definition_update_enabled      : true
definitions_updated                      : Jun 27, 2023 at 12:12:32 PM
definitions_updated_minutes_ago          : 201
definitions_version                      : "1.391.2822.0"
definitions_status                       : "up_to_date"
edr_early_preview_enabled                : "disabled"
edr_device_tags                          : [{"key":"AzureResourceId","value":"/subscriptions/d6bcccc5-9989-473a-b97b-7673583721a1/resourceGroups/L
LIANSKY-DEV_GROUP/providers/Microsoft.Compute/virtualMachines/lliansky-rh86"},{"key":"SecurityWorkspaceId","value":"d6bcccc5-9989-473a-b97b-767358372
1a1"}]
edr_group_ids                            : ""
edr_configuration_version                : "30.199999.main.2023.06.25.03-0EAC4F0E4598DC411437E7E492EC4123BEB231758BDB834E59EA8FF25EE8F904"
edr_machine_id                           : "fea3df12bd644617682b750a9fd24a4f90a6216f"
conflicting_applications                 : []
network_protection_status                : "stopped"
network_protection_enforcement_level     : "disabled"
troubleshooting_mode                     : false
[leonid@lliansky-rh86 WD.Client.Linux.eBPF]$
```

Figure 5.11: Example of mdatp health output on Linux showing ebpf usage

The command to enable eBPF on Linux is:

```
# sudo mdatp config ebpf-supplementary-event-provider --value [enabled/
disabled]
```

Microsoft is replacing the auditd agent with eBPF in MDE on Linux for several reasons, such as:

- **System stability and performance**: eBPF helps with system stability and improves CPU and memory utilization and reduces disk usage. The eBPF sensor uses capabilities of the Linux kernel without requiring the use of a kernel module, which helps increase system stability.

- **Reduced log noise**: eBPF reduces system-wide auditd-related log noise.

- **Optimized event rules**: eBPF optimizes system-wide event rules, reducing the possibility of conflicts between applications.

- **Improved event rate throughput**: eBPF improves event rate throughput and reduces memory footprint.

Microsoft Defender for Endpoint on Linux has switched from using AuditD to **extended Berkeley Packet Filter (eBPF)** as the primary event provider. This change was implemented to improve system stability, performance, and reduce overhead.

The eBPF sensor is automatically enabled for all customers by default on agent versions 101.23082.0006 and later. If eBPF is not supported on a specific kernel, the system will automatically switch back to AuditD. Please note that auditd will be removed in future versions.

Data loss and prevention overview

DLP stands as a security measure designed to detect and mitigate unsafe or inappropriate sharing, transfer, or utilization of sensitive data. This solution assists organizations in monitoring and safeguarding sensitive information spread across on-premises systems, cloud-based platforms, and endpoint devices.

MDE and DLP

Endpoint DLP *applies to non-server-based OS like Windows 10/11 and macOS*. DLP policies are created by your information protection and governance team. Each DLP policy defines what elements within a data set to look for, like sensitive information types or labels, and how to protect this data.

For example, a DLP policy can look for personal data like a passport number. The DLP policy includes a condition that triggers the policy to take action, such as when a passport number is shared with people outside your organization. The action the policy takes can be configured as well. Options range from simply reporting the action to admins, warning users, or even preventing the data from being shared.

Endpoint DLP extends the activity monitoring and protection capabilities of DLP to sensitive items that are physically stored on windows 10, 11 and macOS. Once devices are onboarded into the Microsoft Purview solution, the information about what users are doing with sensitive items is made visible in activity explorer of the solution and you can enforce protective actions on those items via DLP policies.

Importance of MDA and Microsoft Purview in DLP

Microsoft Defender for Apps (MDA) is a part of the Microsoft Defender suite that provides security for applications. It helps protect against threats, vulnerabilities, and misconfigurations in applications and provides certain DLP features. However, it is totally separate from Microsoft Purview in terms of DLP features and has its own DLP engine that can auto block file access on certain filters or can auto attach labels as per defined filters on the security web portal.

Microsoft Purview constitutes a suite of solutions focused on data governance, risk assessment, and compliance, aiming to assist organizations in governing, protecting, and managing their complete data infrastructure. These integrated solutions aim to tackle the growing challenges of remote connectivity, data dispersion across organizations, and the evolving landscape of IT management roles. Azure Purview was officially announced on September 28, 2021, but the rebranding and merging of Azure Purview and Microsoft 365 compliance services into Microsoft Purview occurred in 2022.

Microsoft Purview merges the capabilities of Azure Purview and Microsoft 365 compliance services under a unified brand. Together, these solutions help organizations to execute the following:

- Enhance visibility into data assets spanning your organization
- Facilitate access to your data, security, and risk management solutions
- Securely manage and oversee sensitive data across various clouds, applications, and endpoints
- Address comprehensive data risks and regulatory compliance throughout the data lifecycle
- Enable your organization to govern, protect, and manage data in innovative and holistic manners

While both MDA and Purview are integral parts of Microsoft's security and data governance solutions, they serve different purposes and function independently. **Microsoft Defender for Cloud Apps (MDA)** and Purview (Microsoft Purview) do have integration points, particularly around the application of sensitivity labels and data governance. MDA can use labels from Purview for file protection and governance.

However, MDA can automatically apply sensitivity labels from Microsoft Purview Information Protection. These labels will be applied to files as a file policy governance action, and depending on the label configuration, can apply encryption for additional protection. You can also investigate files by filtering for the applied sensitivity label within the Defender for Cloud Apps portal. This shows that while MDA and Purview may not directly interact, they can work together within the larger Microsoft security ecosystem to enhance data protection.

In a landscape where cyber threats grow increasingly sophisticated, EDR solutions have become a necessity for organizations striving to protect their digital assets. Solutions, like MDE and CrowdStrike Falcon, exemplify the transformational impact of EDR in fortifying endpoint security. By embracing the proactive approach of EDR, organizations can bolster their defenses, detect emerging threats, and respond effectively to safeguard their operations in the digital realm.

Overview of SOC

A SOC is a centralized unit within an organization dedicated to monitoring, detecting, and responding to cybersecurity threats and incidents. It serves as the frontline defense against a wide range of cyberattacks, including malware infections, data breaches, and network intrusions. The primary goal of a SOC is to ensure the confidentiality, integrity, and availability of an organization's digital assets and data. SOC teams use advanced tools, technologies, and processes to continuously analyze security data, identify vulnerabilities, and respond swiftly to security incidents. By maintaining a proactive and vigilant stance, a SOC plays a pivotal role in safeguarding an organization's digital infrastructure, mitigating risks, and minimizing the impact of cyber threats.

SOC responsibilities

Provided in the following figure is a list of key functions typically performed by a well-organized and efficient SOC:

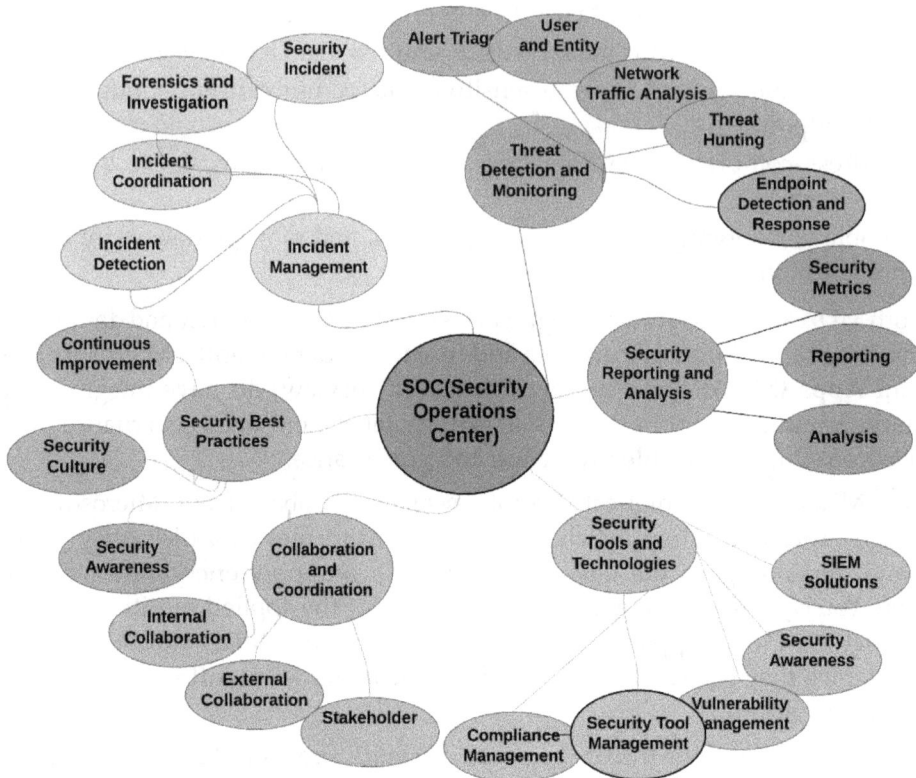

Figure 5.12: SOC Mind Map

Note: Security orchestration, automation, and response (SOAR) is another widely used terminology in the security domain, which play a critical role in automating and orchestrating SOC operations. MDE or Microsoft product already have such functionality inbuilt and as XDR and Copilot are gaining momentum so not sure if it will become a direct feature inside the security products and even some of the folks in recent RSA event talking that SOAR is dead so keep this topic on your list to review back.

The following are the activities performed by SOC team:

- **Threat monitoring**: Continuously monitor the organization's network, systems, and applications for signs of security threats and anomalies.

- **Incident detection**: Detect and identify security incidents, including breaches, malware infections, and unauthorized access.

- **Alert triage**: Prioritize and classify security alerts based on severity and relevance to focus on the most critical threats.

- **Vulnerability management**: Identify and assess vulnerabilities in the organization's IT infrastructure and applications, and coordinate the patching process.

- **Security IR**: Develop and implement IR plans to address security incidents promptly, minimize damage, and recover systems.
- **SIEM**: Deploy and maintain SIEM solutions to collect, correlate, and analyze security data from various sources.
- **Threat intelligence**: Collect, analyze, and incorporate threat intelligence to understand emerging threats and vulnerabilities relevant to the organization.
- **Security reporting and analysis**: Generate reports on security incidents, trends, and performance metrics to inform decision-makers and stakeholders.
- **Forensics and investigation**: Conduct forensic analysis of security incidents to determine the extent of the breach, the tactics used, and the impact on the organization.
- **User and entity behavior analytics (UEBA)**: Employ analytics to detect abnormal user and system behavior, potentially indicating insider threats or compromised accounts.
- **Network traffic analysis**: Monitor network traffic patterns for suspicious activities, such as data exfiltration or unusual access patterns.
- **EDR**: Manage EDR solutions to monitor, investigate, and respond to security threats on endpoints.
- **Security awareness training**: Educate employees and stakeholders about security best practices to reduce the risk of social engineering attacks.
- **Threat hunting**: Proactively search for hidden threats and vulnerabilities within the organization's network and systems.
- **Security architecture review**: Assess the organization's security architecture and recommend improvements to enhance resilience against threats.
- **Compliance management**: Ensure adherence to regulatory and compliance requirements by monitoring and reporting on security controls.
- **Incident coordination**: Collaborate with internal and external stakeholders, such as law enforcement, vendors, and IR teams, during security incidents.
- **Security tool management**: Maintain and update security tools and technologies, such as firewalls, IDS/IPS, and antivirus software.
- **Security awareness**: Promote a security-conscious culture within the organization and conduct training sessions for employees.
- **Continuous improvement**: Regularly review and enhance SOC processes, procedures, and tools to adapt to evolving threats and technologies.

A well-functioning SOC is a critical component of an organization's cybersecurity posture, helping to detect and respond to threats effectively and minimize the potential impact of security incidents.

Microsoft threat experts and SOC

MTE is a managed threat hunting service within **Microsoft Defender Advanced Threat Protection (ATP)** that provides SOCs with expert-level oversight and analysis. This service helps SOCs to ensure that critical threats in their unique environments are identified, investigated, and resolved. It includes two capabilities: targeted attack notifications and experts on demand. The targeted attack notifications provide special insights and analysis to help identify the most critical threats, so SOCs can respond to them quickly. The experts on demand feature allows SOCs to consult with Microsoft's threat experts on relevant detections and adversaries. This service is not an IR service, but it can engage with your own IR team to address issues that require an IR. In terms of SOC operations, this service can significantly enhance the ability of SOCs to detect, prioritize, and triage potential cyberattacks.

The following figure gives key insight of MTE service:

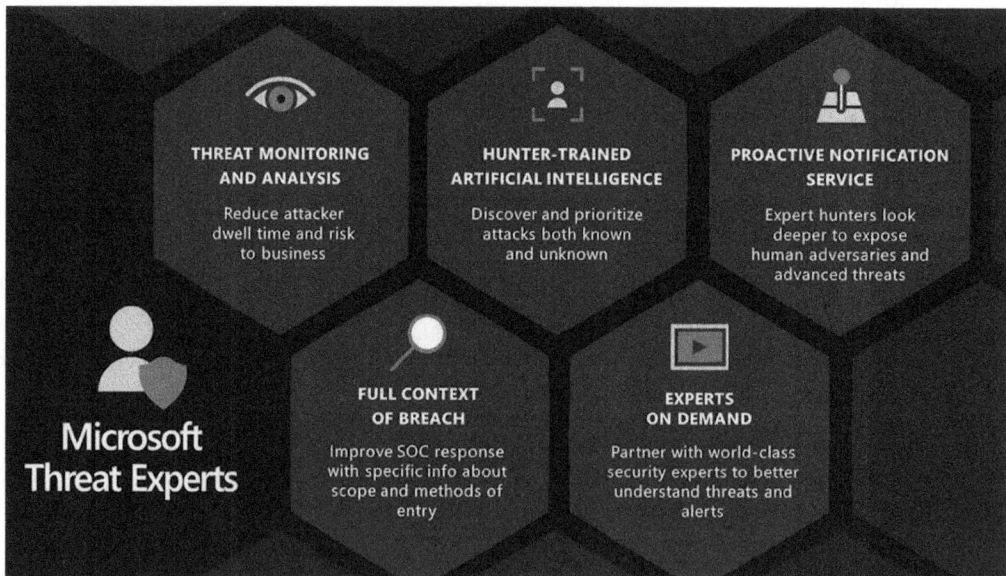

Figure 5.13: MTE service features

MTE, a managed threat hunting service within MDE, provides several key features that augment security operations capabilities, such as:

- **Focused attack alerts (TAN)**: These notifications are customized for organizations, promptly delivering crucial details about significant threats in their network, such as the breach timeline, extent of the breach, and intrusion techniques.

- **On-demand expertise**: In situations where a threat surpasses the SOC's investigation capacity or requires further actionable insights, security experts offer technical guidance concerning pertinent detections and adversaries. Additionally, a smooth transition to Microsoft IR services is facilitated if a complete IR is warranted.

- **Threat monitoring and analysis**: This reduces attacker dwell time and risk to business.

- **Hunter-trained AI**: This helps discover and prioritize both known and unknown attacks.

- **Identifying important risks**: This helps SOCs maximize time and energy.

- **Additional clarification on alerts**: This includes root cause or scope of the incident.

- **Clarity into suspicious machine behavior**: This includes recommended next steps if faced with an advanced attacker.

- **Determine risk and protection**: This is regarding threat actors, campaigns, or emerging attacker techniques.

- **Seamless transition to Microsoft IR services**: This is necessary for MTE to move the incident into Microsoft IR service for better attention

If your organization is already a MDE customer, you can use for MTE automated notification through the Microsoft 365 Defender portal.

You can use the following steps to use automated notifications through the Microsoft 365 Defender portal:

1. In MDE web portal, go to **Settings | General | Advanced features | Endpoint Attack Notifications**.

2. As shown in *Figure 5.14*, click **Apply**:

Microsoft Threat Experts - Targeted Attack Notifications

Collaborate with Microsoft Threat Experts to help monitor and analyze suspicious cybersecurity activities in your organization.

Apply

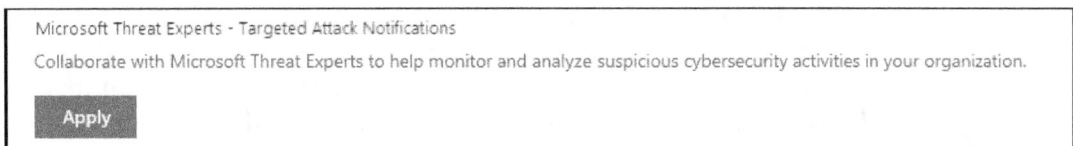

Figure 5.14: Enable MTE service for your account

3. Add your name and email address so that Microsoft can get back to you on your application, as shown in *Figure 5.15*:

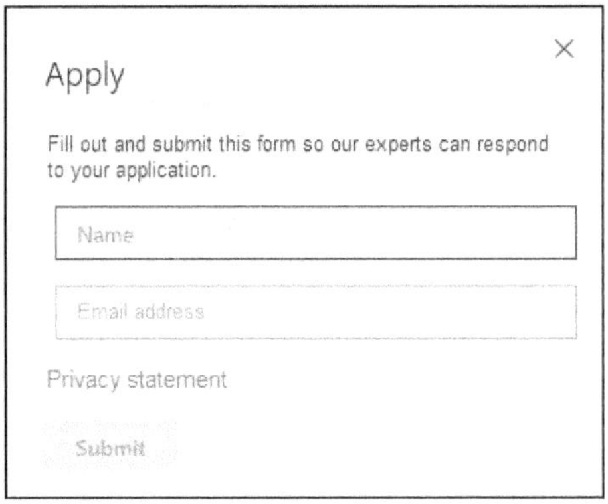

Apply ×

Fill out and submit this form so our experts can respond to your application.

Name

Email address

Privacy statement

Submit

Figure 5.15: Enable MTE service (sub step)

4. Read the privacy statement, then click **Submit** when you are done. You will receive a welcome email once your application is approved.

5. When accepted, you will receive a welcome email, and you will see the **Apply** button change to a toggle that is "on". In case you want to take yourself out of the Endpoint Attack Notifications service, slide the toggle "off" and click **Save preferences** at the bottom of the page.

6. You will see the Endpoint Attack Notifications from Microsoft Defender Experts

7. You can receive TAN from MD Experts through the following medium:

   a. The MDE web portal's **Incidents** page

   b. The MDE web portal's **Alerts** dashboard

   c. OData alerting API and REST API

   d. DeviceAlertEvents table in Advanced hunting

   e. Your email, if you choose to configure it

To receive Endpoint Attack Notifications through email, create an email notification rule.

Conclusion

This chapter has provided a comprehensive overview of EDR, emphasizing its significance as a dynamic shield against modern threats. We have explored the key domains and functionalities of EDR, differentiating it from EPP and highlighting the benefits of EDR in maintaining a proactive defense strategy. By understanding the cyberattack kill chain and the concept of XDR, readers are better equipped to grasp the role of EDR in today's cybersecurity landscape. We have also introduced MDE as an EDR solution, outlined its architectures, and discussed its integration within the Microsoft 365 Defender suite. Furthermore, we have examined the agent security logging functionality, DLP, and the role of EDR within a SOC.

With this foundational knowledge, readers are now well-prepared to delve into the technical aspects of EDR, its deployment, configuration, and best practices, as explored in the subsequent chapters of this book. By understanding the principles and objectives outlined in this chapter, organizations can harness the capabilities of EDR solutions like MDE to bolster their cybersecurity defenses and proactively counter emerging threats.

In the next chapter, we are going to cover MDE SOC monitoring and alerting so that SOC team can configure monitoring on **Key Performance Indicator (KPI)** factor to alert SOC members.

CHAPTER 6

Monitoring and Alerting with Defender SOC

Introduction

This chapter will give you insight into the importance of endpoint security monitoring and reporting within a **Security Operations Center** (**SOC**). It will discuss the significance of monitoring and analyzing security events and how these insights contribute to a robust security posture.

Endpoint security analytics and reporting are essential components of managing the security of your organization's endpoints. MDE offers powerful tools and features to help you monitor and analyze security events effectively.

Structure

In this chapter, we will cover the following topics:

- Guide for monitoring
- Monitoring security posture

Objectives

In this chapter, we would like to provide insight into the security event monitoring on the MDE portal and alerting options available for SOC analyst on which they can act in timely manner before any major incident. This chapter will also provide you with reference screenshots from the MDE portal for users who do not have access to the MDE portal. These screenshots will help you get insight into reports, like overall security report, device health report, vulnerable device and many such reports. You will also gain insight into configuring alerting for the real time threat alerts.

Guide for monitoring

A step-by-step guide to achieve your goal from monitoring to reporting is mentioned as follows:

1. **Access the MDE portal**: Log in to your MDE account. You have to make sure that you have required permission on the portal to access.

2. **Navigate to the security center**: In the Microsoft 365 Defender portal, locate the Security Center or a similar section dedicated to security analytics and reporting.

3. **Define your reporting goals**: Determine what you want to achieve with your security analytics and reporting. Whether it is monitoring user activity, investigating specific incidents, or ensuring regulatory compliance, having clear goals is crucial.

4. **Configure data collection**: MDE allows you to collect a wide range of data from your endpoints, such as telemetry, security events, and threat intelligence. Configure the data collection settings based on your reporting goals.

5. **Create custom queries**: Use MDE's query-building Advanced hunting options to create custom queries tailored to your specific reporting needs. These queries can help you filter and analyze security data effectively.

6. **Set up scheduled reports**: Schedule regular reports to keep stakeholders informed. You can configure these reports to be delivered via email or saved in a centralized location for easy access.

7. **Monitor security events in real-time**: Leverage MDE's real-time monitoring capabilities to keep a constant eye on security events as they occur. You can set up alerts for specific events or anomalies.

8. **Investigate security incidents**: If a security incident occurs, MDE offers in-depth investigation tools. You can access detailed data, review historical information, and identify the scope and impact of the incident.

9. **Generate compliance reports**: For regulatory compliance purposes, MDE provides templates and tools for generating compliance reports. These reports can help you demonstrate adherence to industry-specific regulations.

10. **Collaborate with SOC teams**: Foster collaboration between different teams within your SOC. Share insights, reports, and findings to ensure a unified approach to endpoint security.

11. **Continuously refine your security strategy**: Regularly review the data, reports, and analytics to adapt your security strategy to emerging threats. Use the insights gained to improve your overall security posture.

12. **Stay informed about threat intelligence**: Keep an eye on threat intelligence sources within the MDE portal. Threat intelligence reports can provide valuable insights into current threat trends and indicators.

Endpoint security analytics and reporting within MDE empower organizations to monitor, respond to, and recover from security incidents effectively. By following these steps and utilizing the tools available, your organization can maintain a robust security posture, address emerging threats, and demonstrate regulatory compliance.

Providing insights into potential security incidents

One of MDE's primary strengths lies in its ability to provide SOC teams with insights into potential security incidents. These insights go beyond mere alerts and offer context and actionable data for incident investigation. MDE facilitates this through the following processes:

1. **Incident prioritization**: MDE uses its threat intelligence and behavior analytics to prioritize alerts. It ensures that SOC teams focus on the most critical incidents first, reducing response times for high priority threats.

2. **Timeline of events**: For each security alert, MDE provides a detailed timeline of events leading up to the incident. This chronological view assists SOC analysts in understanding how the threat manifested, helping them make informed decisions during investigation.

3. **Actionable data**: MDE arms SOC teams with the data they need to respond effectively. This includes information on compromised devices, the scope of the attack, and recommended remediation actions. The platform empowers analysts to take swift and well-informed steps to mitigate threats.

4. **Automation of routine tasks**: MDE automates repetitive tasks, such as isolating compromised devices or collecting forensic data. This automation accelerates the investigative process, allowing SOC teams to work more efficiently.

Real-time threat detection and analysis in MDE

Realtime threat detection and analysis are vital components of a proactive defense strategy within the MDE platform. By following these steps and leveraging the real-time capabilities provided by MDE, your SOC can swiftly identify and respond to security threats as they occur, minimizing potential damage and ensuring a robust security posture.

To utilize real-time threat detection features effectively, it is essential to:

1. **Enable and configure real-time alerts**: Customize alert thresholds and notification settings to ensure immediate awareness of potential threats. Tailor these settings to align with your organization's risk tolerance and operational requirements.

2. **Leverage Automated Investigation and Response (AIR)**: Enable AIR to automatically investigate alerts and take appropriate remediation actions. This reduces the burden on SOC analysts and speeds up the response time.

3. **Utilize threat intelligence**: Integrate global threat intelligence feeds to stay informed about emerging threats and vulnerabilities. This helps in contextualizing alerts and understanding their potential impact.

4. **Monitor endpoint behaviors continuously**: Use MDE's behavioral analytics to detect unusual activity patterns that might indicate malicious behavior. Continuously monitoring endpoints allows for the early detection of stealthy attacks.

5. **Conduct regular threat hunts**: Engage in proactive threat hunting exercises using MDE's advanced hunting capabilities. This involves querying collected data for signs of potential threats that might have evaded automatic detection mechanisms.

The following are the real-world scenarios and examples:

- **Example 1: Detecting ransomware in progress**:
  - **Scenario**: An employee opens an email attachment that contains a ransomware payload.
  - **Real-time detection**: MDE identifies malicious activity based on the file's behavior and triggers an alert.
  - **Response**: AIR isolates the affected device, preventing the ransomware from spreading. Simultaneously, a SOC analyst receives a detailed investigation report, allowing for rapid assessment and remediation.

- **Example 2: Identifying unauthorized access attempts**:
  - **Scenario**: A suspicious login attempts from an unfamiliar IP address targets multiple endpoints within a short timeframe.
  - **Real-time detection**: MDE's behavioral analytics flags the activity as anomalous and sends an alert.
  - **Response**: The SOC team utilizes MDE's threat intelligence integration to determine if the IP is associated with known threat actors and takes immediate steps to block the IP and investigate affected endpoints.

Monitoring security posture

The following options are available under the Reports page on the MDE web portal. You can gain insights into your environment and leverage this area for monitoring the status of your organization corresponding to multiple factors. These options are covered in the next section.

Security key performance indicator

In usual IT infrastructure resource monitoring, we usually identify **key performance indicators** (**KPIs**) and monitor them. Similarly, in security monitoring, we identify KPIs in form of key security events that we monitor to create alerts, and if required, can attach such alerts to incidents so that the required action can be taken. So, to provide an insight into such KPI's, in the next section there are various screenshots to provide you an understanding of KPI's for security monitoring.

Informative report screenshots

Let us explore the options provided by a web portal. *Figure 6.1* shows the MDE portal under each category for your reference. Once you click on the **Reports** page, then you will find the following options to explore more:

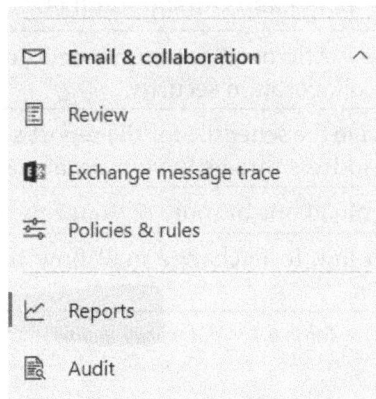

Figure 6.1: Report menu location on MDE portal

The following table shows the menus and sub menus available on MDE portal:

General (2)	
Security report	View information about security trends and track the protection status of your identities, data, devices, apps, and infrastructure.
Query resources	Review how your hunting queries consume resources and understand how to prevent throttling due to excessive use.

Endpoints (8)	
Threat protection	See details about the security detections and alerts in your organization.
Device health	Monitor device health, antivirus software status, operating system platform, and Windows 10 if applicable.
Vulnerable devices	View information about the vulnerable devices in your organization, including their exposure to vulnerabilities by severity level, exploitability, age, and more.
Monthly security summary	View a monthly executive report that shows a snapshot of your organization's protection state and the work that was done to prevent and respond to cyberthreats.
Web protection	Get information about the web activity and web threats detected within your organization.
Firewall	View connections blocked by your firewall including related devices, why they were blocked, and which ports were used
Device control	This report shows your organization's media usage data.
Attack surface reduction rules	View information about detections, misconfiguration, and suggested exclusions in your environment.
Email and collaboration (4)	
Email and collaboration reports	Review Microsoft recommended actions to help improve email and collaboration security.
Manage schedules	Manage the schedule for the report's security teams use to mitigate and address threats to your organization.
Reports for download	Download one or more of your reports.
Exchange mail flow reports	Deep link to Exchange mail flow report in the Exchange admin center.

Table 6.1: MDE portal menus

Security report

A security report can be accessed to observe trends in security and monitor the safeguarding status of your identities, data, devices, applications, and infrastructure.

An example of ASR rule report under security report area is shown in the following figure. ASR is **On** but configured with audit only mode.

ASR rule configuration

ASR rules are on in audit only

Deploy standard attack surface reduction (ASR) rules to proactively stop common attacks.

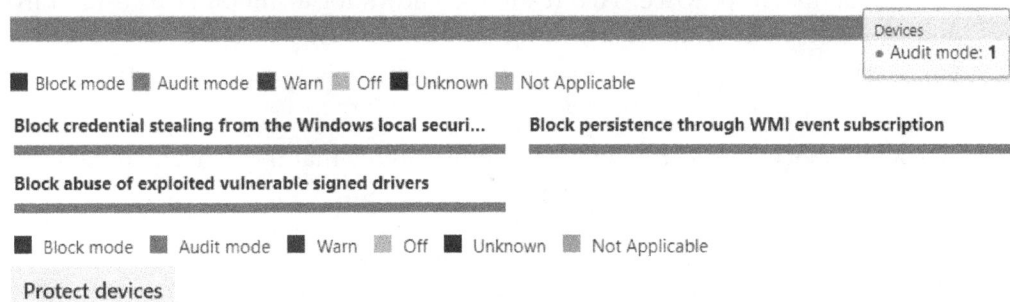

Devices
• Audit mode: 1

■ Block mode ■ Audit mode ■ Warn ▨ Off ■ Unknown ▨ Not Applicable

Block credential stealing from the Windows local securi... **Block persistence through WMI event subscription**

Block abuse of exploited vulnerable signed drivers

■ Block mode ■ Audit mode ■ Warn ▨ Off ■ Unknown ▨ Not Applicable

Protect devices

100% of devices are not blocking detections

Set ASR rules to block detections for better protection.

Block executable content from email client and webmail **Block all Office applications from creating child processes**

Block Office applications from creating executable cont... **Block Office applications from injecting code into other...**

Block JavaScript or VBScript from launching downloade... **Block execution of potentially obfuscated scripts**

■ Block mode ▨ Audit mode ■ Warn ▨ Off ■ Unknown ▨ Not Applicable

View configuration   Add exclusions

Figure 6.2: ASR report under security report

Implications of Audit Mode in ASR

When **attack surface reduction (ASR)** rules in MDE are set to *audit only mode*, it means that while the ASR rules will monitor and log potentially harmful activities, they will not block or prevent these activities from occurring. This configuration allows security teams to:

- **Assess impact without disruption**: Evaluate the potential impact of ASR rules on user productivity and application compatibility. By observing which activities would have been blocked, teams can adjust rules to minimize false positives and avoid unnecessary disruptions.

- **Gather insights for fine-tuning**: Collect valuable data on suspicious activities. This information helps in fine-tuning ASR rules to better align with the organization's threat landscape and operational needs.

- **Improve rule accuracy**: Use the insights gathered during the audit phase to refine and enhance the accuracy of ASR rules. This iterative process ensures that when the rules are enforced, they effectively block real threats while minimizing false positives.

- **Prepare for enforcement**: Establish a clearer understanding of what enforcement might look like in practice. This readiness allows for a smoother transition from audit to enforcement mode, ensuring that the security measures are robust and effective.

As shown in the following figure, you can see two different security report for **Device compliance** and **Device with active malware**. It highlights that the concerned data is not available, otherwise it would have shown related insights.

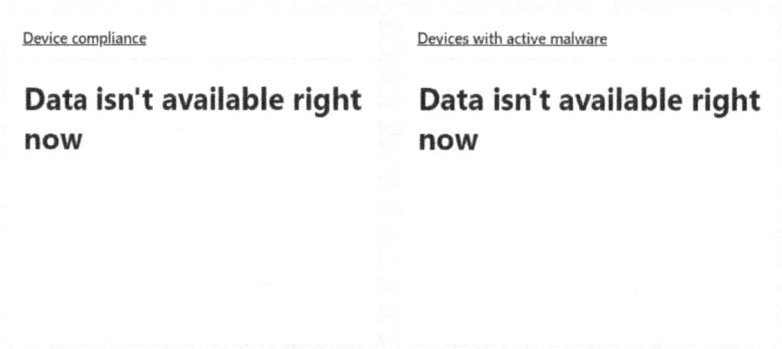

Device compliance

Data isn't available right now

Devices with active malware

Data isn't available right now

Figure 6.3: Device related report highlight on security report page.

In the following figure, the window shows the Web threat detection over time. On the Y axis, it shows the number of detection and currently it is set to 0 and X axis shows the DD/MM format. This covers Custom Indicators, Tech Support Scan, Untrusted URL's etc.

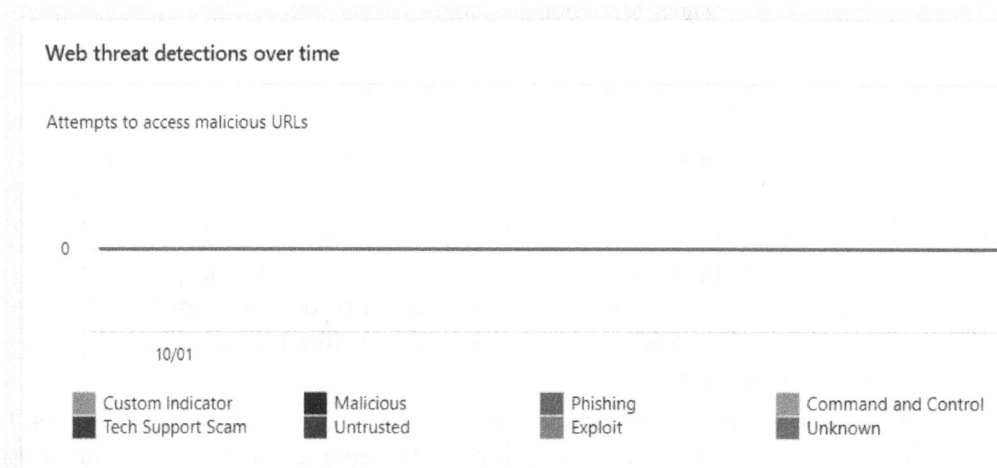

Web threat detections over time

Attempts to access malicious URLs

0

10/01

| ■ Custom Indicator | ■ Malicious | ■ Phishing | ■ Command and Control |
| ■ Tech Support Scan | ■ Untrusted | ■ Exploit | ■ Unknown |

Figure 6.4: Web threat detection over time window

Threat protection

The following figure shows various detection sources by creation date, by unresolved alerts etc. You can also see details about the security detections and alerts in your organization.

Detection source of all alerts by creation date

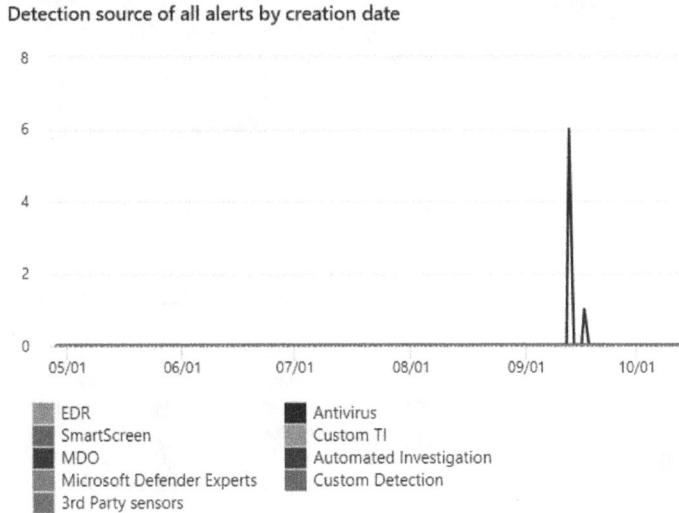

Figure 6.5: Detection source of all alerts by creation date

In the following figure, the window highlights detection sources of unresolved alerts. You can see sources like Antivirus, EDR solution, SmartScreen, Custom Threat Intel sources, Microsoft Defender for Office etc. on the X axis legend.

Detection source of currently unresolved alerts

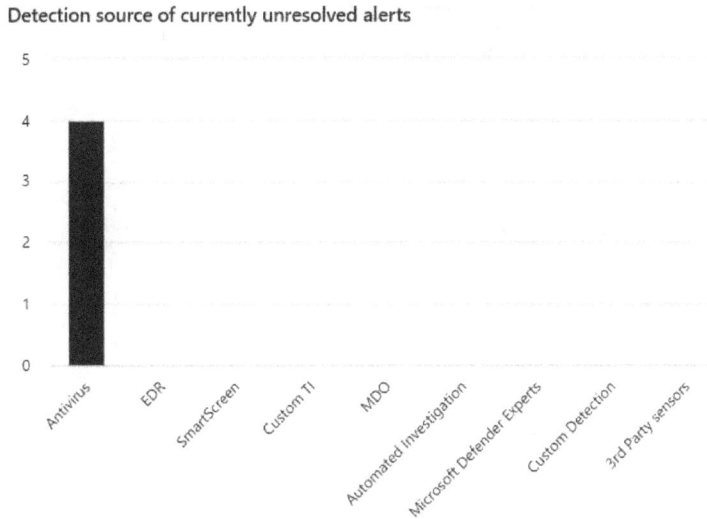

Figure 6.6: Detection source of currently unresolved alerts window

As shown in the following figure, the window shows categorization of threat alerts by creation date:

Threat categories of all alerts by creation date

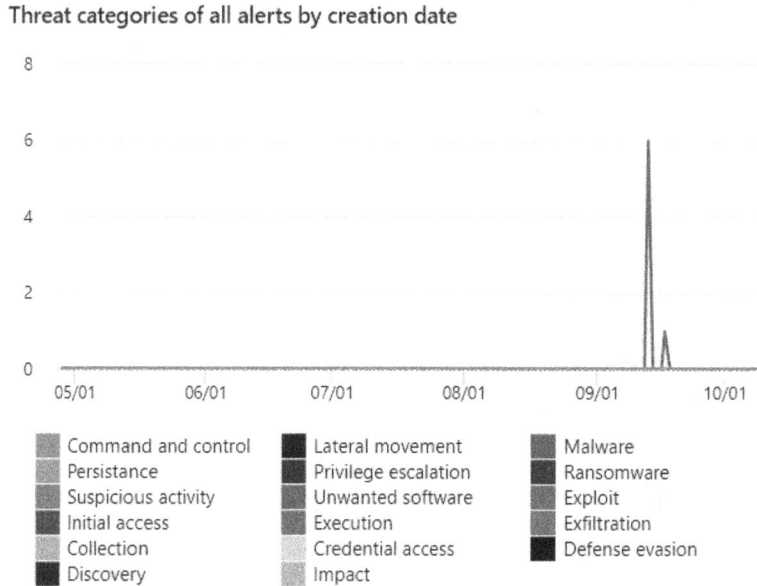

Figure 6.7: *Threat categories of all alerts by creation date*

In the following figure, the window shows threat categories of currently unresolved alerts and on X axis it highlights various categories like Malware, C2C, Lateral movement, Phishing etc.:

Threat categories of currently unresolved alerts

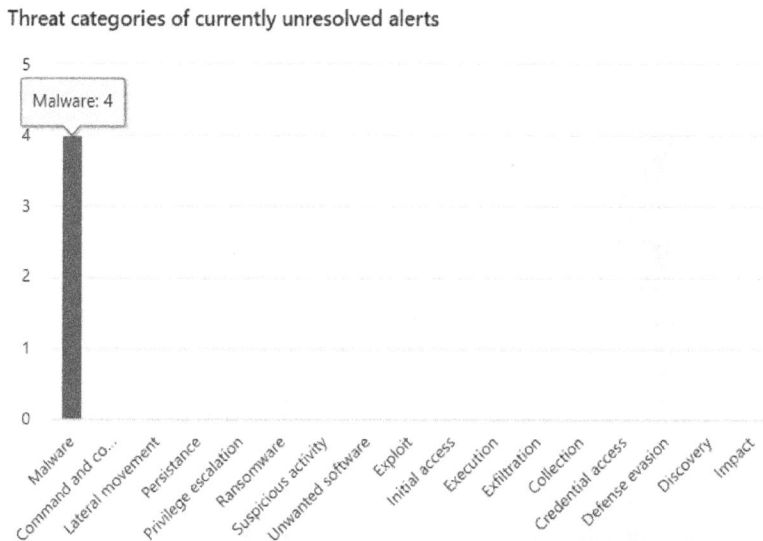

Figure 6.8: *Threat categories of currently unresolved alerts*

Severity of all alerts by creation date window highlight on the page can be seen in the following figure:

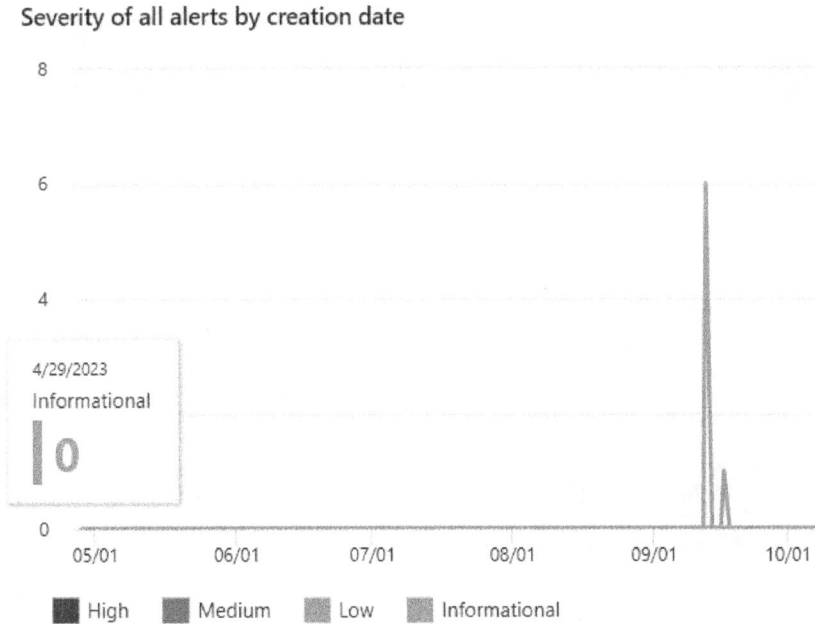

Figure 6.9: Severity of all alerts by creation date

The severity of currently unresolved alerts window on the page can be seen in the following figure:

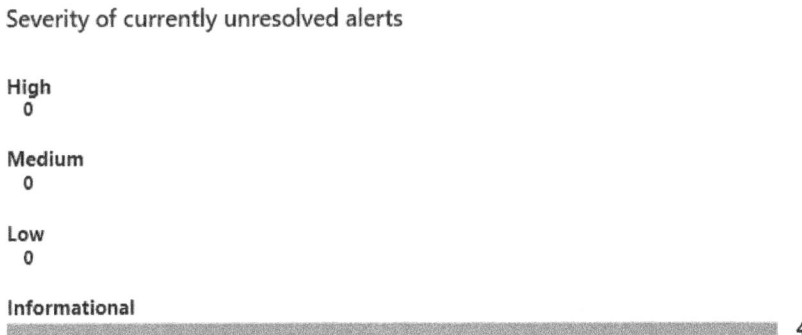

Figure 6.10: Severity of currently unresolved alerts

The following figure shows the status of all alerts by creation date:

Status of all alerts by creation date

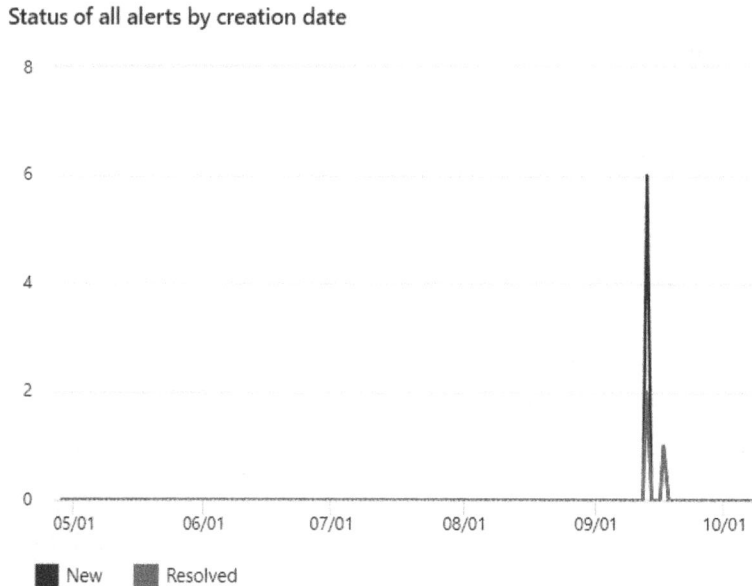

Figure 6.11: Status of all alerts by creation date

The following figure shows the classification of alerts by classification date. It can classify **False Positives** (**FPs**) that is a major problem in any monitoring solution.

Classification of alerts by classification date

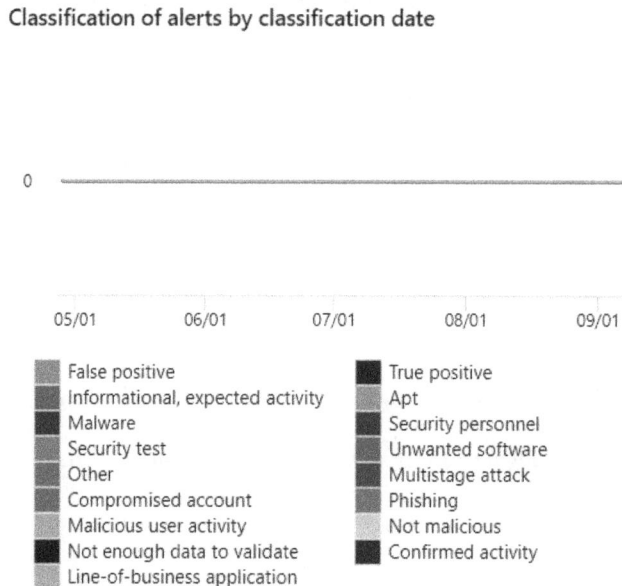

Figure 6.12: Classification of alerts by classification date

The following figure shows the status of current unresolved alerts:

Status of currently unresolved alerts

New
━━ 4

In progress
0

Figure 6.13: Window showing status of current unresolved alerts

There is a possibility that the MDE portal will not find the relevant data due to multiple valid reasons and you might see message as shown in the following figure:

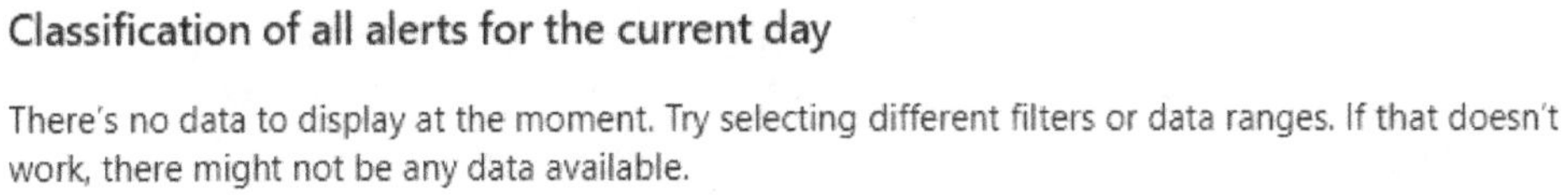

Classification of all alerts for the current day

There's no data to display at the moment. Try selecting different filters or data ranges. If that doesn't work, there might not be any data available.

Figure 6.14: Alert for no data due to either filter issue or no data

Device health

This section will help MDE Portal users to monitor device health, antivirus software status, operating system platform, and Windows 10 version status.

The following check the health status of devices:

- Sensor health and OS
- MDE antivirus health

The following figure shows Agent (Sensor Agent) health status of all the registered devices on the MDE portal:

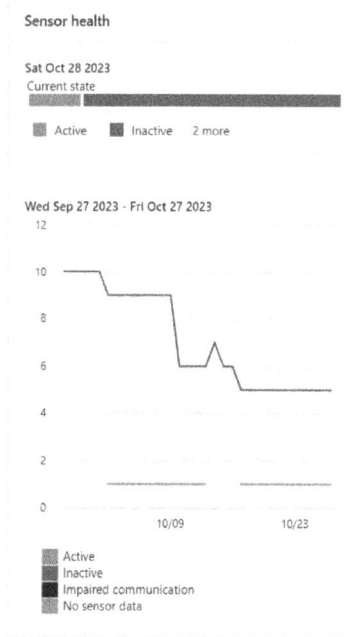

Figure 6.15: *Agent (sensor) health status*

The following figure shows the different types of OS with platform registered on the MDE portal:

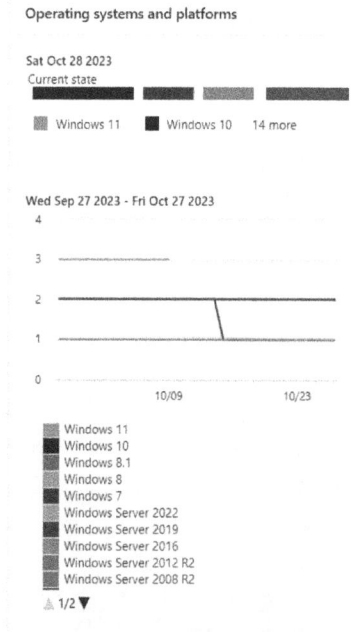

Figure 6.16: *OS and platforms window registration status*

The following figure highlights Windows with its version registered on the portal:

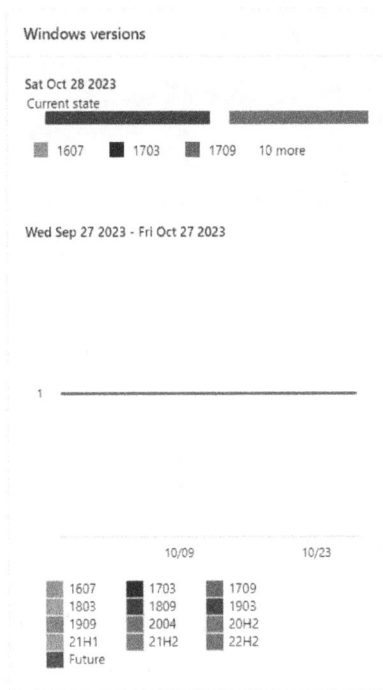

Figure 6.17: *Window showing windows OS version registered on the portal*

The widget demonstrating device health on the report page is shown in the following figure:

Figure 6.18: *Device health widget*

The following figure shows an AV (MDE Antivirus) engine version:

Antivirus engine version

Last updated Oct 28, 2023 2:26 AM

Windows devices

1.1.23090.2007

1

Linux devices
No data found

Mac devices
No data found

View full report

Figure 6.19: AV engine version

The following figure shows the widget demonstrating AV security intelligence and platform versions:

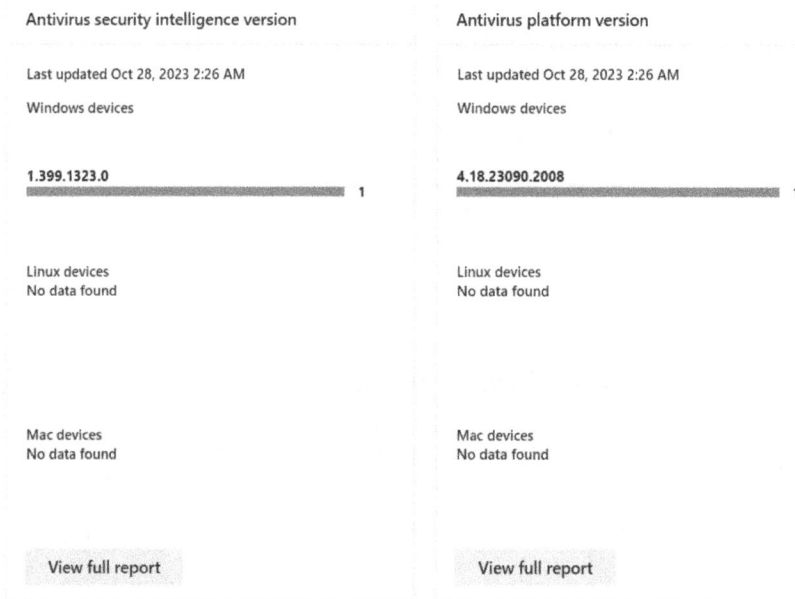

Antivirus security intelligence version

Last updated Oct 28, 2023 2:26 AM

Windows devices

1.399.1323.0

1

Linux devices
No data found

Mac devices
No data found

View full report

Antivirus platform version

Last updated Oct 28, 2023 2:26 AM

Windows devices

4.18.23090.2008

1

Linux devices
No data found

Mac devices
No data found

View full report

Figure 6.20: AV security intelligence and platform version

The following figure shows AV engine updates available for registered devices:

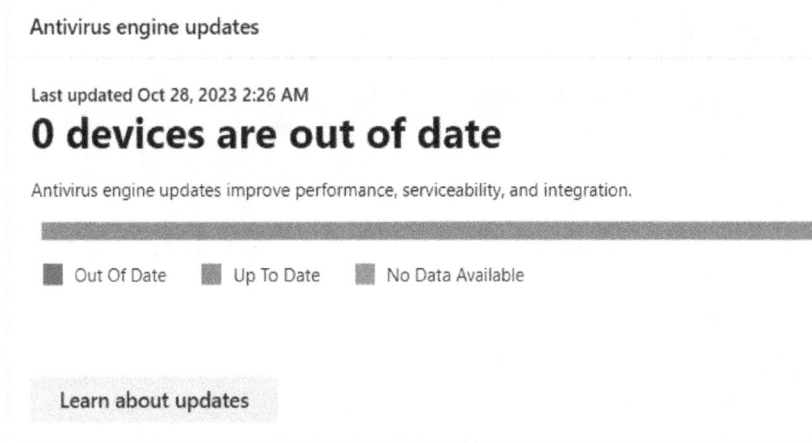

Antivirus engine updates

Last updated Oct 28, 2023 2:26 AM

0 devices are out of date

Antivirus engine updates improve performance, serviceability, and integration.

■ Out Of Date   ■ Up To Date   ■ No Data Available

Learn about updates

Figure 6.21: AV engine updates for devices widget

The following figure shows security intelligence udpates avaialble for devices:

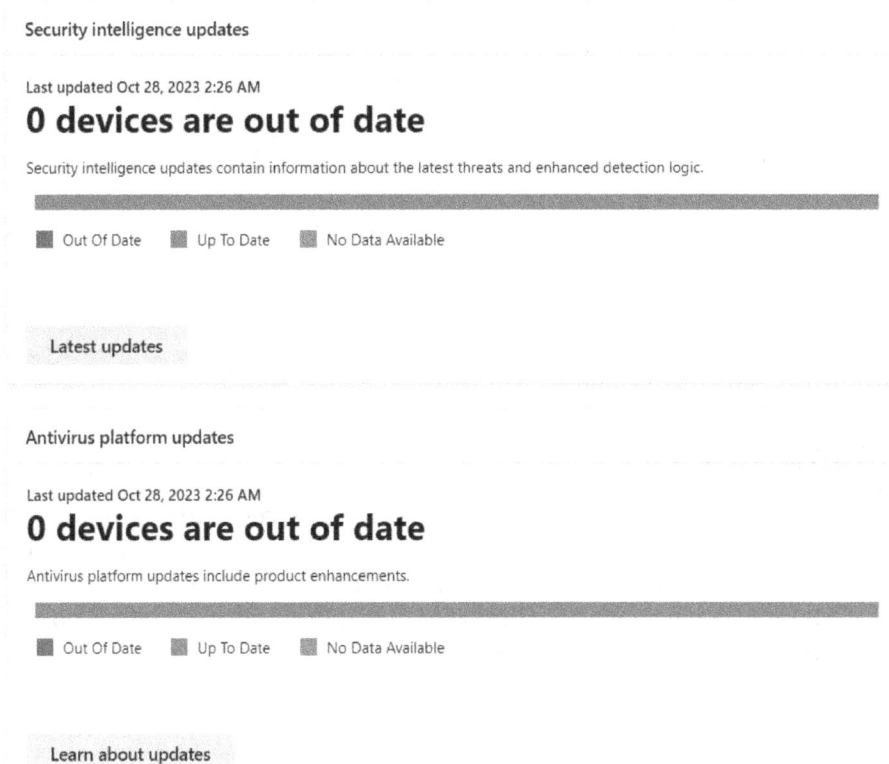

Security intelligence updates

Last updated Oct 28, 2023 2:26 AM

0 devices are out of date

Security intelligence updates contain information about the latest threats and enhanced detection logic.

■ Out Of Date   ■ Up To Date   ■ No Data Available

Latest updates

Antivirus platform updates

Last updated Oct 28, 2023 2:26 AM

0 devices are out of date

Antivirus platform updates include product enhancements.

■ Out Of Date   ■ Up To Date   ■ No Data Available

Learn about updates

Figure 6.22: Security intelligence updates widget

The following figure shows the recent AV scan results of Quick and Full scan reports:

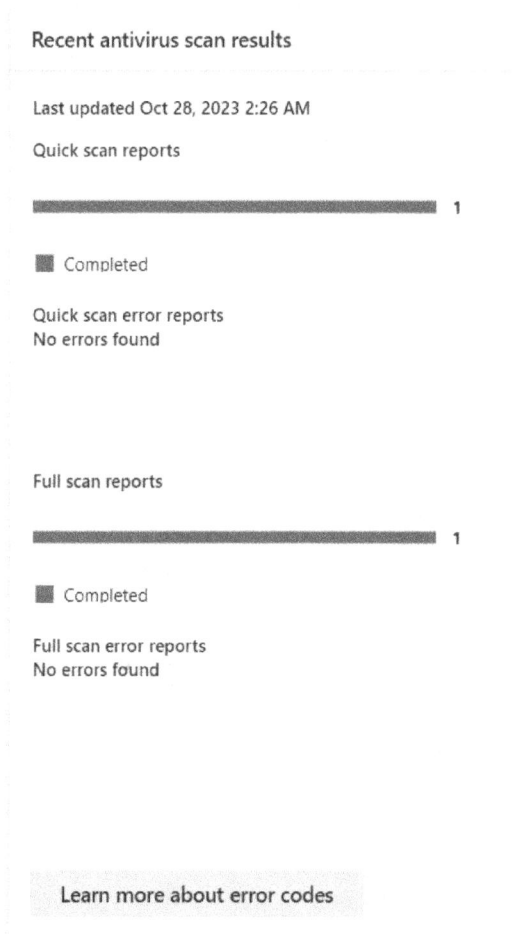

Recent antivirus scan results

Last updated Oct 28, 2023 2:26 AM

Quick scan reports

1

■ Completed

Quick scan error reports
No errors found

Full scan reports

1

■ Completed

Full scan error reports
No errors found

Learn more about error codes

Figure 6.23: *AV engine version availability widget*

Vulnerable devices

Explore detailed insights regarding the vulnerable devices within your organization through the MDE Portal's Vulnerable Devices section. Gain visibility into various aspects such as the severity level of vulnerabilities, their exploitability, age of the vulnerabilities, and more. This comprehensive view allows for a deeper understanding of potential risks and aids in crafting effective mitigation strategies

The following figure shows vulnerable devices in the organization with severity level over the time:

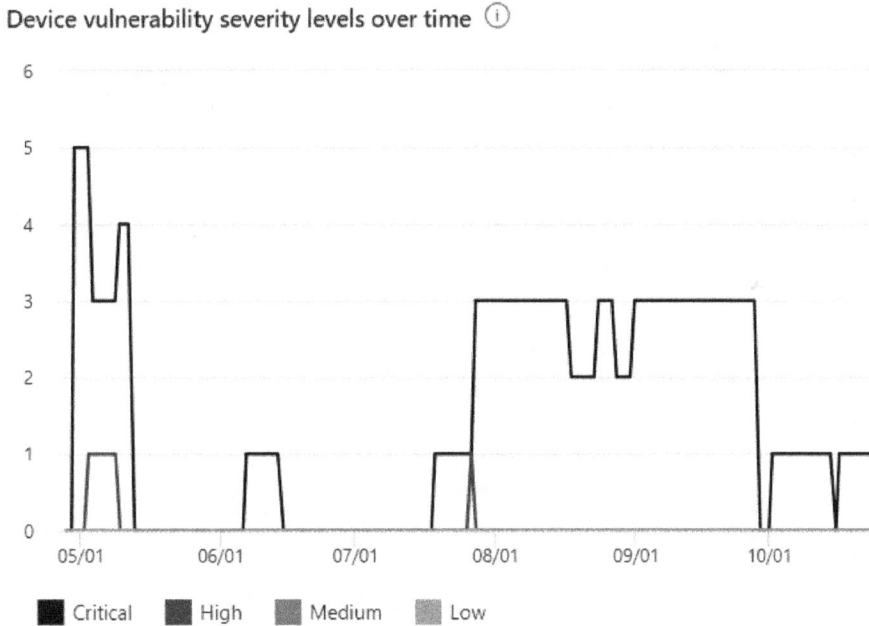

Figure 6.24: Device vulnerability severity levels over time widget

The following figure shows the different severity levels defined by MDE portal:

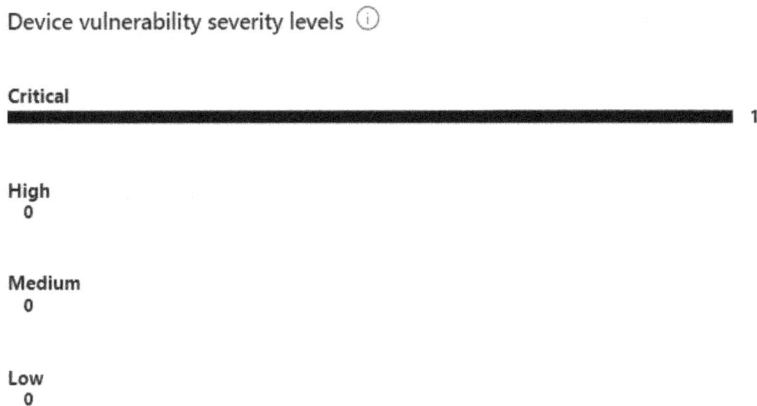

Figure 6.25: Different severity levels available on MDE portal

The following figure shows the exploits available over the time:

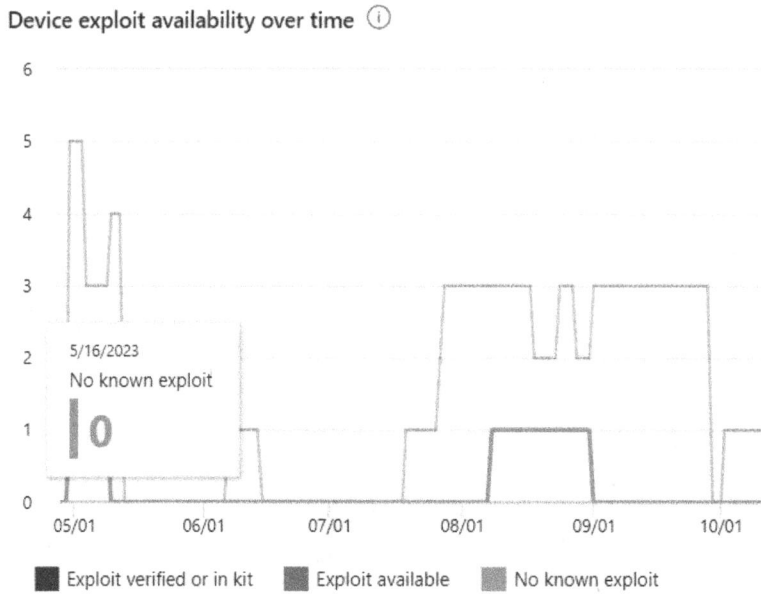

Figure 6.26: Device exploit availability over time widget

The following figure shows device vulnerability age over time:

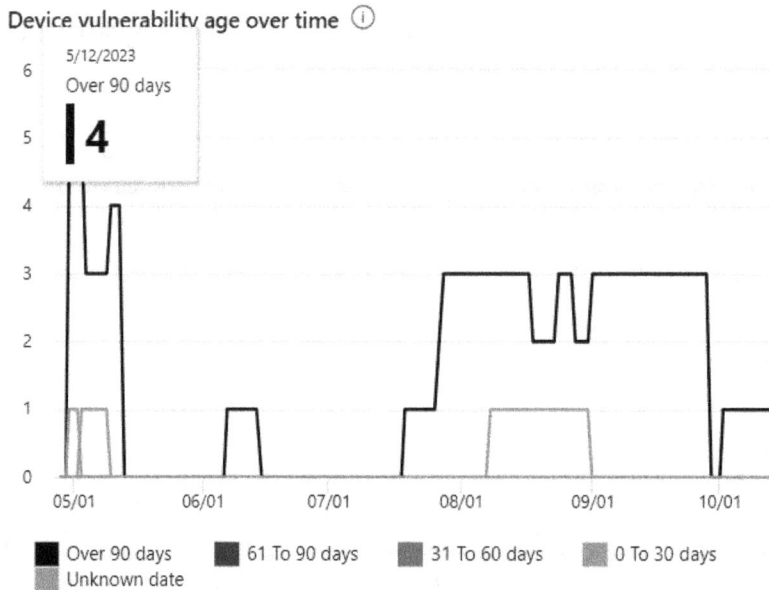

Figure 6.27: Device vulnerable age over time widget

The following figure shows the vulnerability by age for devices:

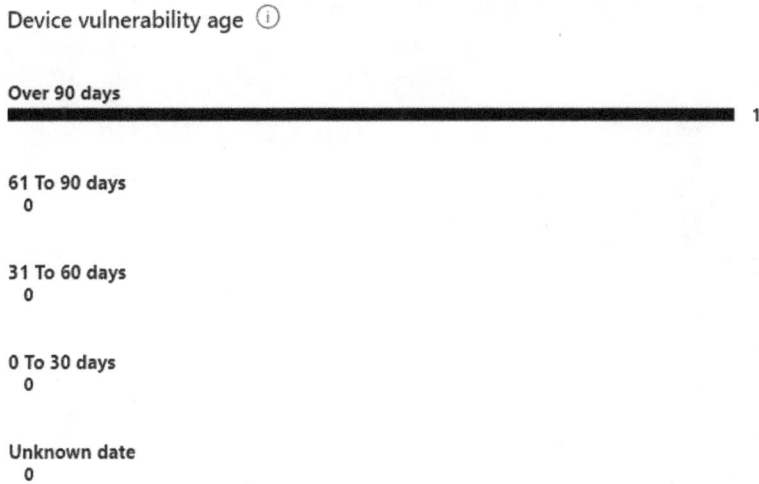

Device vulnerability age ⓘ

Over 90 days
━━━ 1

61 To 90 days
0

31 To 60 days
0

0 To 30 days
0

Unknown date
0

Figure 6.28: Device vulnerable age widget

The following figure shows the Vulnerable devices by operating system and platform over time:

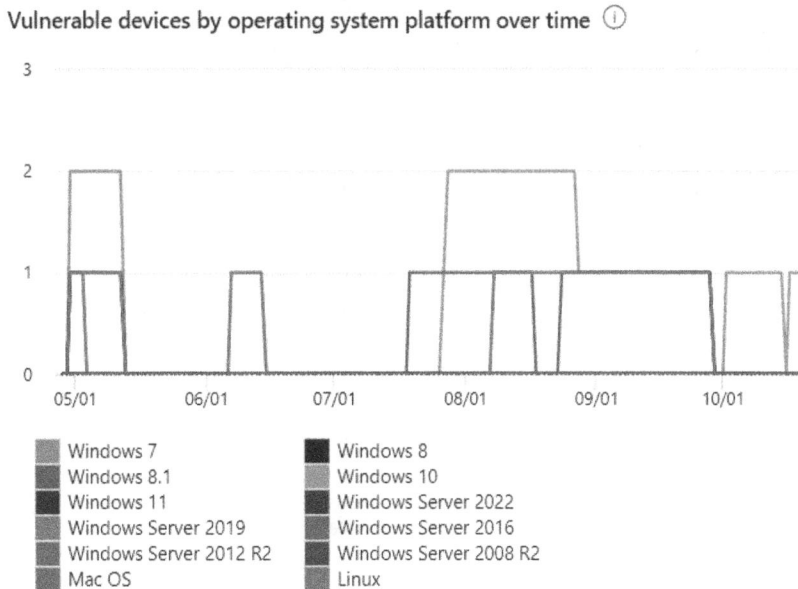

Vulnerable devices by operating system platform over time ⓘ

▪ Windows 7	▪ Windows 8
▪ Windows 8.1	▪ Windows 10
▪ Windows 11	▪ Windows Server 2022
▪ Windows Server 2019	▪ Windows Server 2016
▪ Windows Server 2012 R2	▪ Windows Server 2008 R2
▪ Mac OS	▪ Linux

Figure 6.29: Vulnerable devices by OS and Platform over time widget

The following figure shows Vulnerable devices by operating system platform:

Vulnerable devices by operating system platform ⓘ

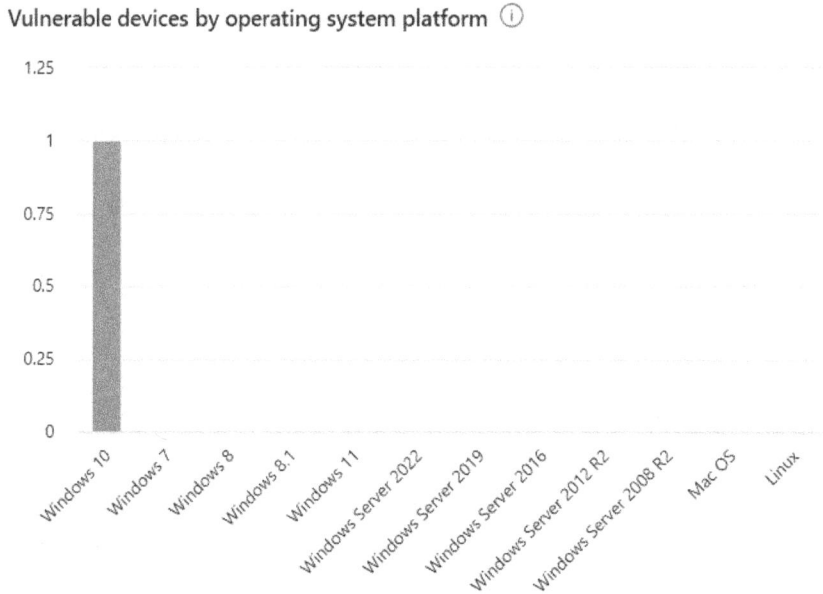

Figure 6.30: Total vulnerable devices by OS

The following figure shows vulnerable devices by Windows 10 and 11 versions over time:

Vulnerable devices by Windows 10 & 11 version over time ⓘ

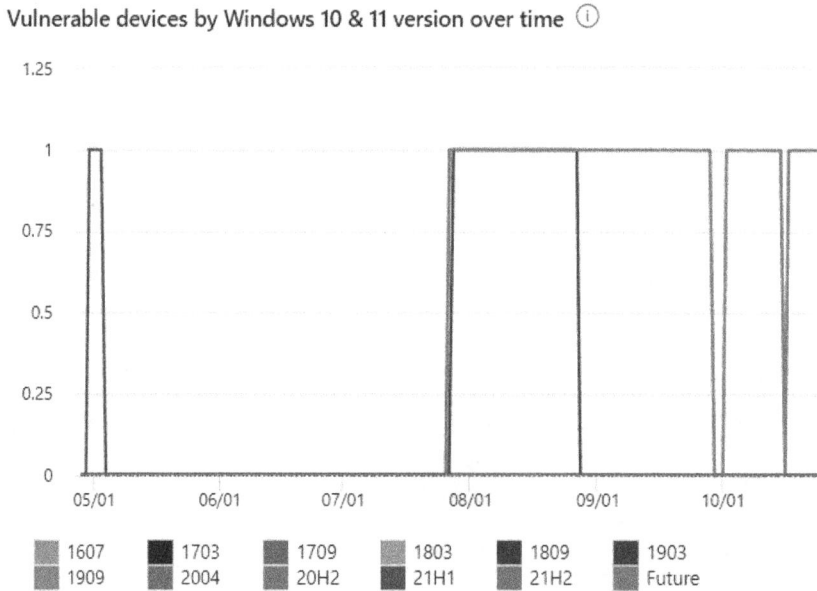

Figure 6.31: Vulnerable devices by Windows over time

An example of the total vulnerable devices by Windows 10 and 11 version in your organization are shown in the following figure:

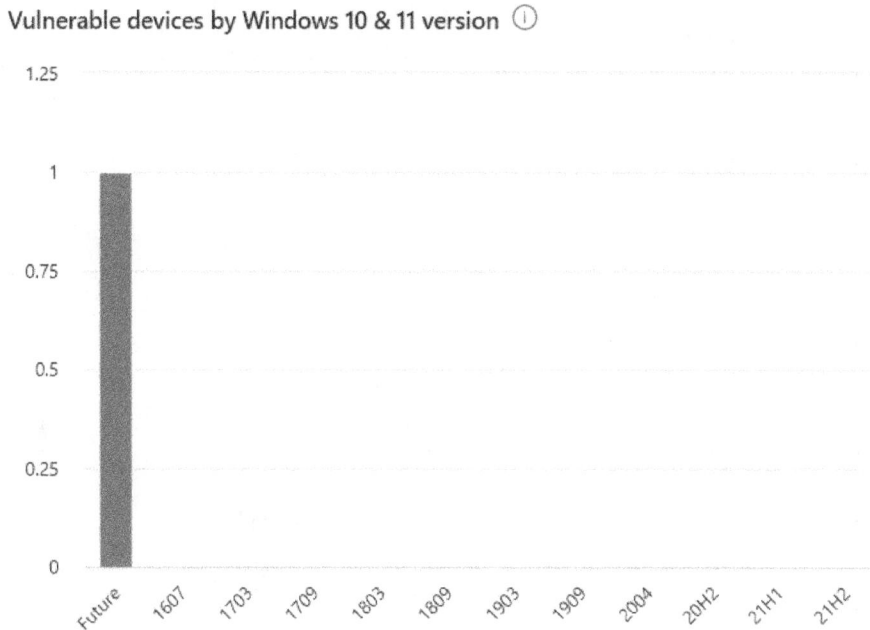

Figure 6.32: Total vulnerable devices by Windows widget

Monthly security summary

Access a detailed monthly executive report providing a concise overview of your organization's security posture. This report offers a snapshot of the protection status, highlighting efforts undertaken to prevent and respond to cyber threats effectively. It encapsulates key metrics, incident summaries, threat intelligence updates, and proactive measures implemented during the month. This comprehensive summary aids in informed decision-making, facilitates strategic planning, and ensures continuous enhancement of your organization's security resilience. The following figure gives you monthly security summary:

Monthly Security Summary

28 October 2023 6:23:35 pm
Report is for the last 30 days: 28 September 2023 to 28 October 2023

Summary   ...

A snapshot of your organization's protection state powered by Microsoft Defender
for Endpoint. This report shows how well your organization is prepared to prevent
and respond to cyberthreats.

Your secure score is 49.51% and it improved by 3.36% from last month.It is 2.96%
higher than other organizations of a similar size.1 devices were onboarded this
month.0 URLs were blocked across 0 restricted categories.There have been 0
resolved incidents and 0 resolved alerts this month.

Figure 6.33: Monthly security summary widget

The following figure showcases the score and hints about protection:

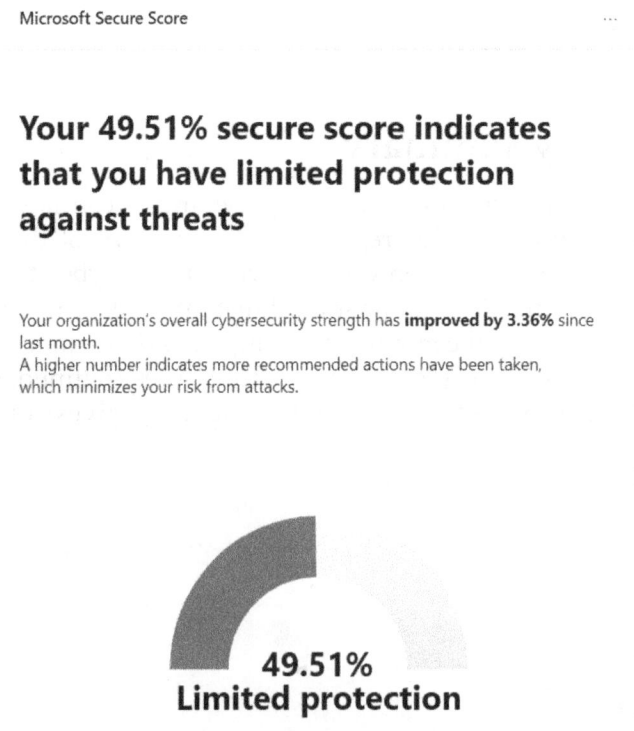

Microsoft Secure Score   ...

Your 49.51% secure score indicates that you have limited protection against threats

Your organization's overall cybersecurity strength has **improved by 3.36%** since
last month.
A higher number indicates more recommended actions have been taken,
which minimizes your risk from attacks.

49.51%
Limited protection

Figure 6.34: Secure score widget

Secure score features are used by Microsoft to showcase strength or posture of security in comparison to other organizations. The following figure shows the secure score comparison with other organization:

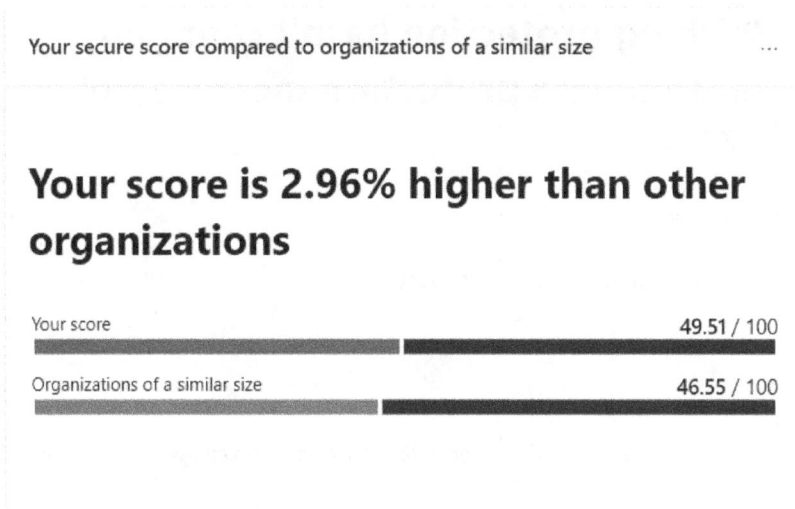

Your secure score compared to organizations of a similar size ...

Your score is 2.96% higher than other organizations

Your score 49.51 / 100

Organizations of a similar size 46.55 / 100

Figure 6.35: Secure score widget

The following figure shows the total devices registered/onboarded on MDE portal:

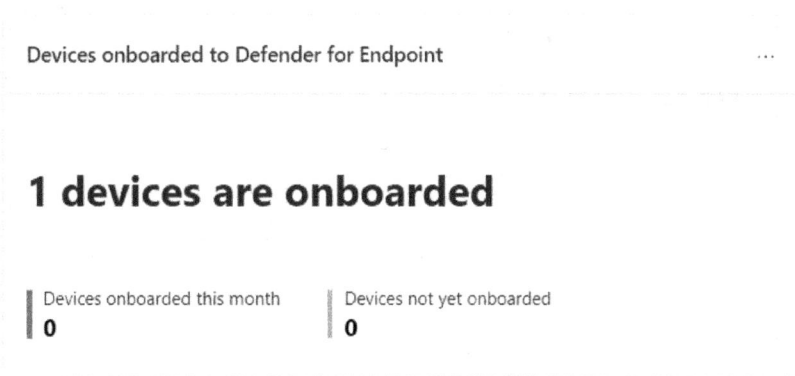

Devices onboarded to Defender for Endpoint ...

1 devices are onboarded

Devices onboarded this month | Devices not yet onboarded
0 | 0

Figure 6.36: Total devices registered on MDE Portal

The widget, in the following figure, shows the increase/decrease of threats. The ransomware protection increased by 5.75%.

Protection against specific types of threats   ...

Phishing protection hasn't changed Ransomware protection increased by 5.75%

Attack name	Your score
Phishing protection	**59.14%** (0%)
Ransomware protection	**42.44%** (+5.75%)

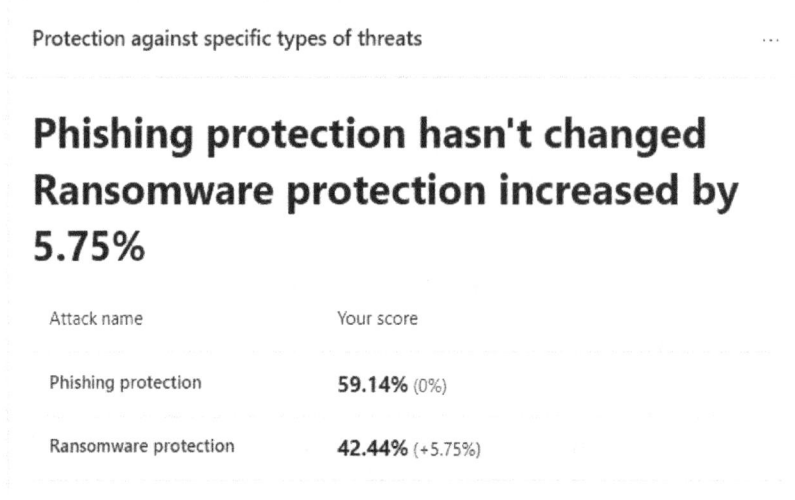

Figure 6.37: *Change in threat detection percentage*

The following figure shows 0 urls blocked as part of web content filtering:

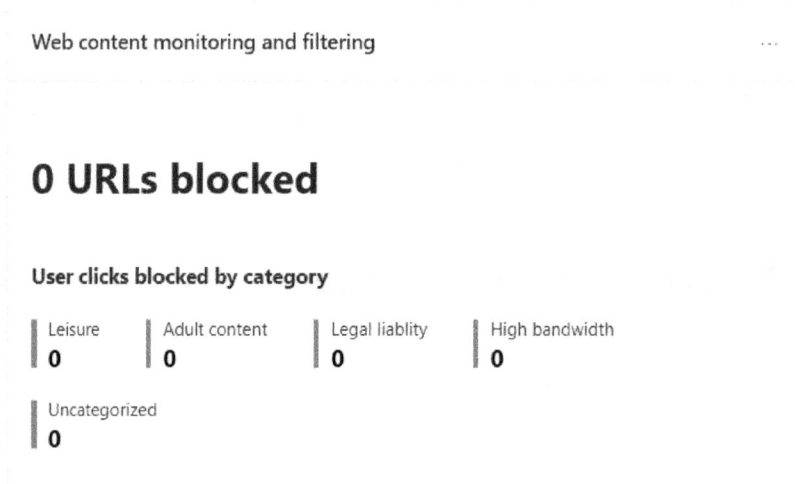

Web content monitoring and filtering   ...

0 URLs blocked

User clicks blocked by category

Leisure	Adult content	Legal liablity	High bandwidth
0	**0**	**0**	**0**

Uncategorized
0

Figure 6.38: *Web content filtering widget*

The following figure shows 0 incidents and 0 alerts for malicious activities:

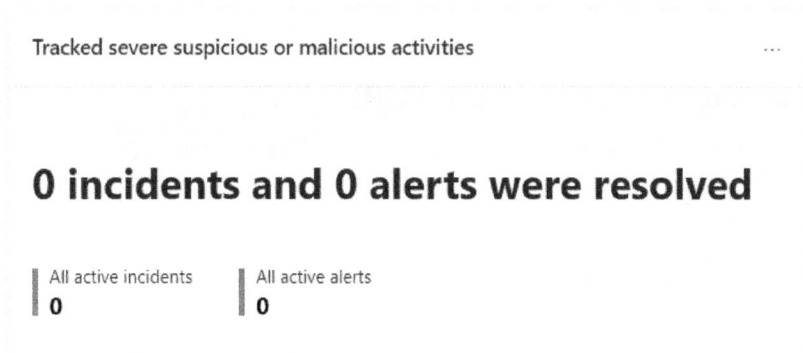

Tracked severe suspicious or malicious activities   ...

0 incidents and 0 alerts were resolved

All active incidents   All active alerts
0   0

Figure 6.39: *Malicious activity widget*

Web protection

Access comprehensive insights into web activity and threats detected within your organization's network. This includes detailed information about browsing patterns, potential security risks, and any malicious activities identified on websites accessed by your employees. By leveraging this data, you can proactively monitor and protect your organization's digital assets, ensuring a secure browsing experience for all users while mitigating potential cyber threats.

The following figure shows web threat detection over time:

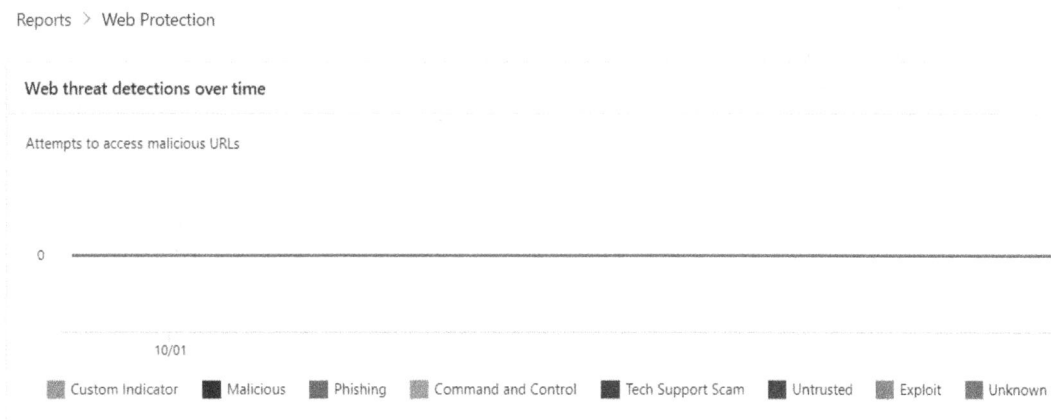

Reports > Web Protection

Web threat detections over time

Attempts to access malicious URLs

0

10/01

Custom Indicator   Malicious   Phishing   Command and Control   Tech Support Scam   Untrusted   Exploit   Unknown

Figure 6.40: *Web threat detections over time*

Overall, the summary of identified web threats is shown in the following figure:

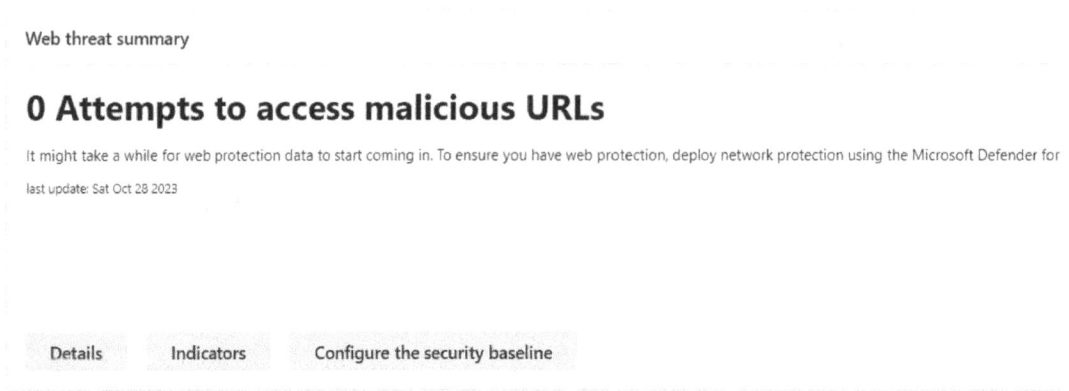

Web threat summary

0 Attempts to access malicious URLs

It might take a while for web protection data to start coming in. To ensure you have web protection, deploy network protection using the Microsoft Defender for

last update: Sat Oct 28 2023

Details   Indicators   Configure the security baseline

Figure 6.41: Web threat summary widget

The following figure shows the change in access required for specific web categories. For example, you can see a decrease in web requests for High Bandwidth and Leisure usage sites:

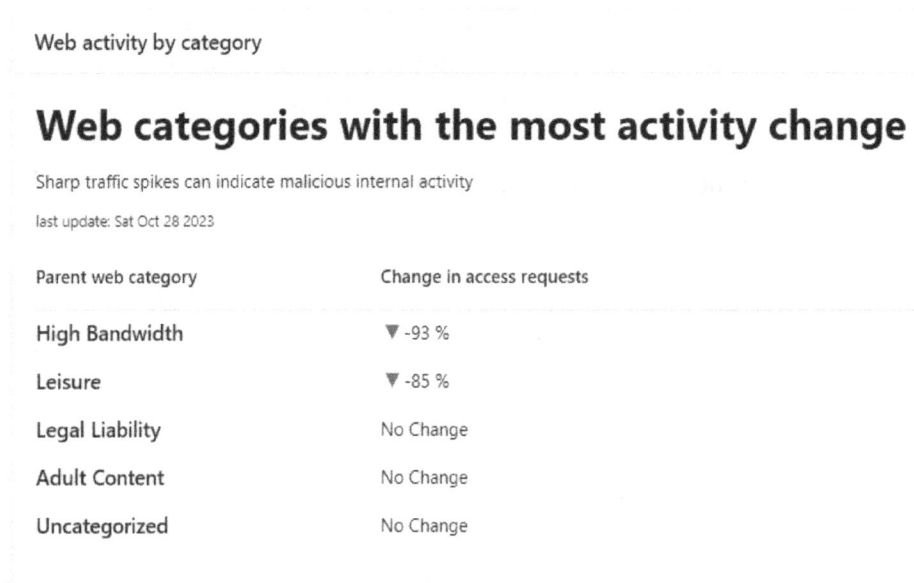

Web activity by category

Web categories with the most activity change

Sharp traffic spikes can indicate malicious internal activity

last update: Sat Oct 28 2023

Parent web category	Change in access requests
High Bandwidth	▼ -93 %
Leisure	▼ -85 %
Legal Liability	No Change
Adult Content	No Change
Uncategorized	No Change

Figure 6.42: Web activity by category widget

The following figure shows the percentage of categories used in total web requests and web activity summary that has been observed with 33 web requests in the High Bandwidth and Leisure categories:

Web activity summary

33 web requests

Total number of requests for web content in all URLs

last update: Sat Oct 28 2023

Requests

High Bandwidth ▪ Leisure ▪ Legal Liability ▪ Adult Content ▪ Uncategorized

Details   Policies

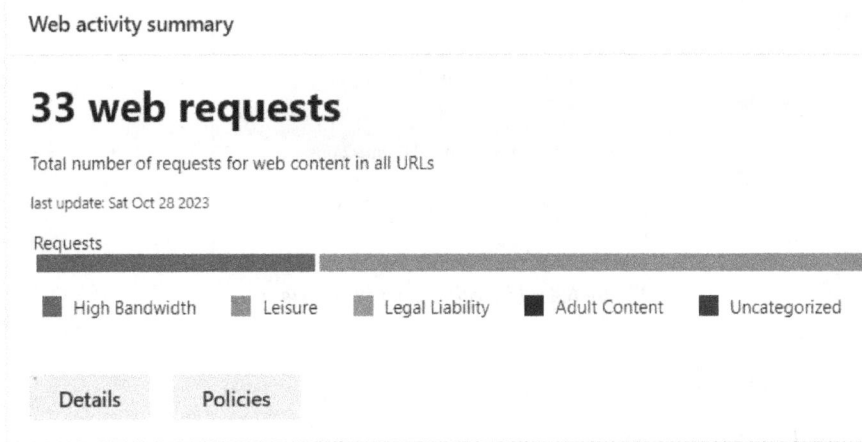

Figure 6.43: Web activity summary widget

The following figure shows web content filtering summary that indicates in case an URL block happened in certain pre-configured category:

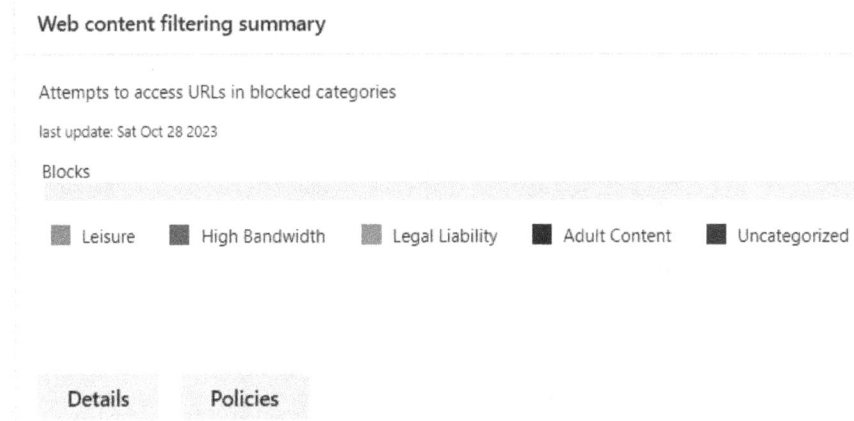

Web content filtering summary

Attempts to access URLs in blocked categories

last update: Sat Oct 28 2023

Blocks

Leisure ▪ High Bandwidth ▪ Legal Liability ▪ Adult Content ▪ Uncategorized

Details   Policies

Figure 6.44: Web content filtering summary widget

Firewall

MDE portal helps you in reporting Firewall Inbound and Outbound alerts, view connections blocked by your firewall, including related devices, the reason for being blocked, and the ports used.

The following figure shows the firewall widget in the reports section with a heading of Firewall Blocked Inbound Connections. However, it does not have any such reported incident, so it is just an empty widget.

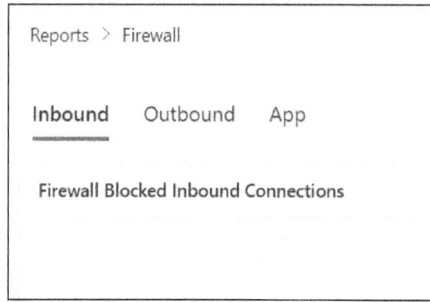

Figure 6.45: Firewall widget in reports section

Device control

Device control on MDE portal gives control to manage external devices, like USB, etc. In the following figure, the report shows your organization's media usage data:

The following figure shows USB mount and unmount events along with Plug and Play device activity, reporting that in total the USB got attached/detached around 9 times on some specific days:

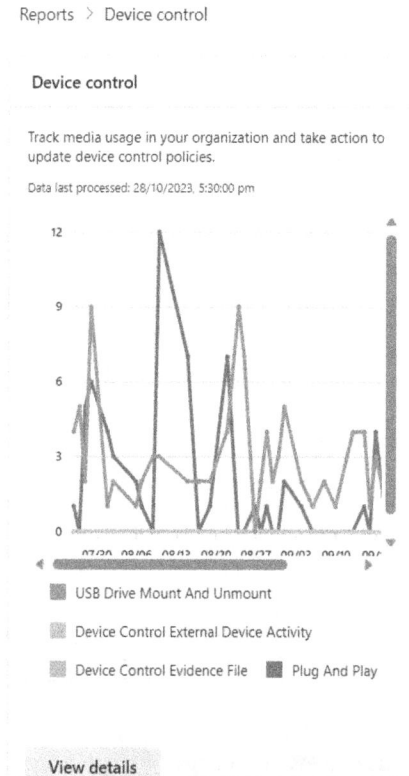

Figure 6.46: Device control widget showcasing media tracking

ASR rules

In this book, we have covered **attack surface reduction** (**ASR**) in detail in *Chapter 14, Practical Configuration Examples and Case Studies* and the following widget gives information about detections, misconfiguration, and suggested exclusions in your environment.

The following figure shows the under **Reports** menu for ASR rule showcasing audited and blocked alerts:

Reports > Attack surface reduction rules

Detections   Configuration   Add exclusions

Review possible breach activity detected by attack surface reduction rules on your devices. Learn more abou

Filters: Rules: **All**   ✕   Date: **9/28/2023-10/28/2023**   ✕   Select rules: **Any**   ▽ Add filter

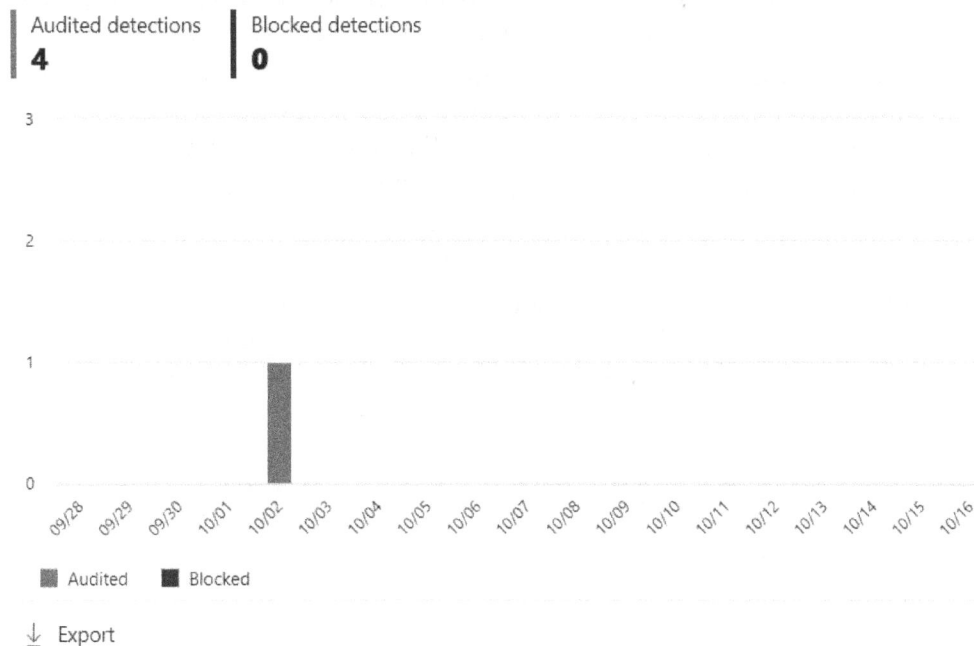

Audited detections | Blocked detections
4 | **0**

■ Audited   ■ Blocked

↓ Export

Figure 6.47: ASR report showing audited and blocked alerts

Alert settings on MDE portal

There are multiple ways to create alerts on the MDE web portal as more security copilot features with advanced functionality are getting integrated to create, update, attach, and close incidents on the portal. To provide a quick glimpse of manual incident creation on the web portal, we have covered it in the following sections, as without license you cannot access the security portal or the alert configuration page. Additionally, to benefit our readers we have added such learning references in the *Configure alerts through setting page* section to build their understanding.

Detecting and alerting on real-time threats

MDE stands as a stalwart sentinel, equipped with a range of capabilities designed to swiftly detect an alert on emerging threats. This section delves into the prowess of MDE in real-time threat detection and how it provides insights into potential security incidents.

MDE's real-time threat detection capabilities are founded on a bedrock of continuous monitoring, advanced analytics, and ML. The platform excels in its ability to identify and alert on threats as they occur, reducing the dwell time of malicious actors within an organization's network. Here is how MDE achieves this:

1. **Behavior-based analysis**: MDE employs behavior-based analysis to scrutinize the actions of files, applications, and processes on endpoints. It monitors suspicious or anomalous behavior and generates alerts when such activity is detected.

2. **ML algorithms**: Advanced ML algorithms within MDE are trained to recognize patterns associated with known malware and emerging threats. This enables the platform to spot previously unseen threats based on their behavioral attributes.

3. **Cloud-powered threat intelligence**: MDE harnesses the power of the cloud to access real-time threat intelligence. This cloud connection allows it to stay updated with the latest threat indicators, further enhancing its detection capabilities.

4. **Custom indicators of compromise**: Security teams can create custom **Indicators Of Compromise (IoCs)**, such as known malware signatures or network patterns, to trigger alerts when encountered. This flexibility allows organizations to tailor their real-time threat detection to specific threats relevant to their environment.

Configure alerts through the settings page

MDE portal provides options to customize alerting rules through IOC, as shown in the following figure:

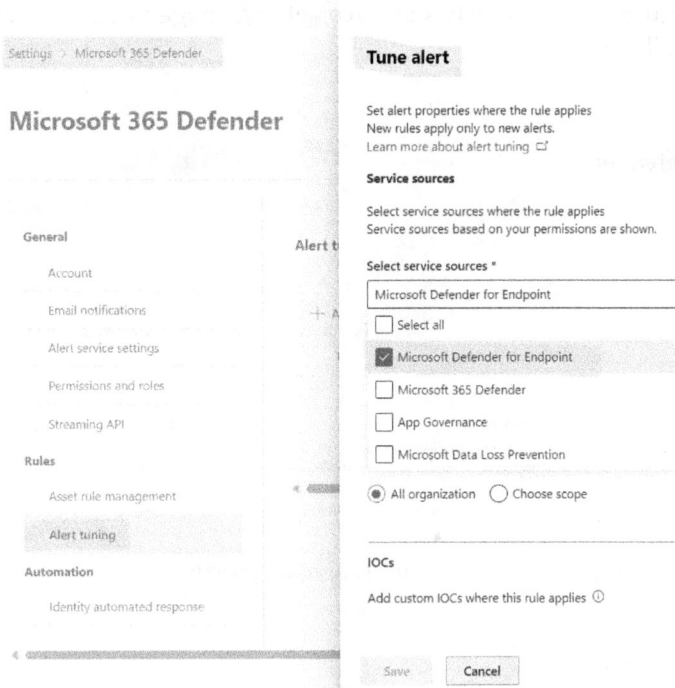

Figure 6.48: *Alert tuning rule*

The following figure shows the next step for the **Alert tuning**:

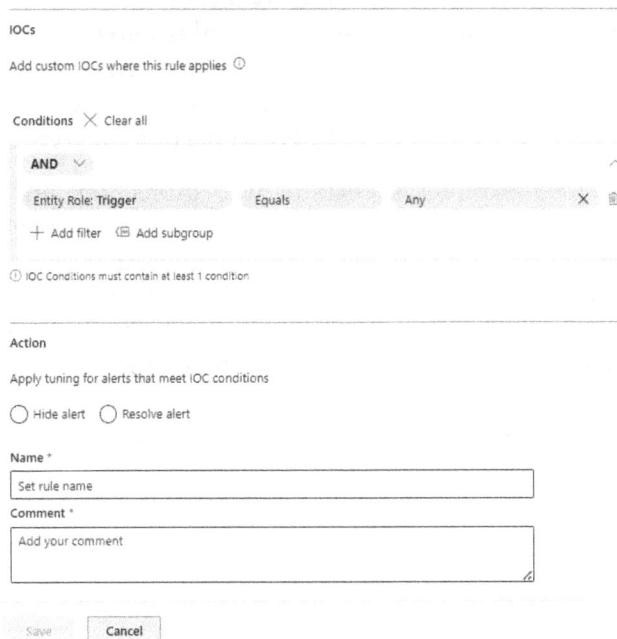

Figure 6.49: *Indicator of compromise condition*

The following figure shows the **Alert service settings** page to choose between only high-impact alerts or all alerts:

Settings > Microsoft 365 Defender

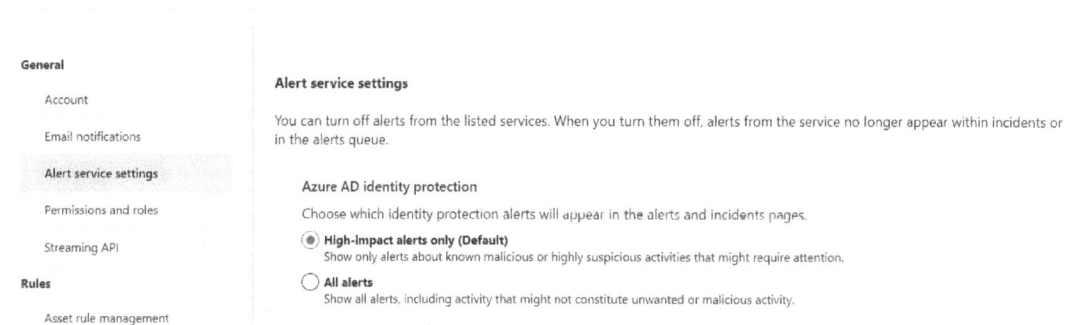

Microsoft 365 Defender

General

    Account

    Email notifications

    Alert service settings

    Permissions and roles

    Streaming API

Rules

    Asset rule management

Alert service settings

You can turn off alerts from the listed services. When you turn them off, alerts from the service no longer appear within incidents or in the alerts queue.

Azure AD identity protection

Choose which identity protection alerts will appear in the alerts and incidents pages.

◉ **High-Impact alerts only (Default)**
Show only alerts about known malicious or highly suspicious activities that might require attention.

◯ **All alerts**
Show all alerts, including activity that might not constitute unwanted or malicious activity.

Figure 6.50: *MDE setting page showing alerts service setting*

Conclusion

Chapter 5, General EDR with Respect to SOC, culminates with a comprehensive overview of the monitoring and alerting capabilities integrated within MDE. This chapter meticulously covers a step-by-step guide for endpoint security analytics and reporting, and details the process of detecting real-time threats, providing insights into potential security incidents, and monitoring the security posture through reports. KPIs and informative report screenshots augment the understanding of security reports, including threat protection, device health, vulnerable devices, and summaries on a monthly basis.

Furthermore, the chapter explores aspects of web protection, firewall configurations, device control, and ASR rules, elucidating their roles in the context of endpoint security. An example illustrating alert creation offers practical insights into leveraging MDE's robust alerting system, empowering security teams to proactively address potential threats and maintain a resilient security infrastructure. In next chapter, we are going to cover MDE SOC Investigation Threats that will help to build understanding about how to investigate through MDE portal.

CHAPTER 7

Defender SOC Investigating Threats

Introduction

In today's ever-evolving digital landscape, organizations face an array of cyber threats that can jeopardize their valuable data, infrastructure, and even their reputation. As the frequency and sophistication of cyberattacks continue to rise, the role of a **Security Operations Center** (**SOC**) in safeguarding an organization's digital assets has become critical. One of the pivotal functions within a SOC is threat investigation, a process that plays a critical role in identifying, mitigating, and responding to security incidents. This chapter will explore threat investigation and its vital significance in contemporary cybersecurity and will give insights about various types of threats, advantages of using MDE as a solution, identification methods and many more things.

Structure

In this chapter, we will cover the following topics:

- Threat investigation in SOC
- MDE SOC feature integration
- Incident investigation workflow
- Data collection and analysis
- Advanced hunting

Objectives

This chapter is aimed at offering a concise overview of threat investigation's paramount importance within a SOC. It underscores the urgency of threat investigation by elucidating its pivotal role in swiftly identifying, mitigating, and responding to security threats, ultimately reducing potential damage and fortifying an organization's security posture. The integration of **Microsoft Defender for Endpoint (MDE)** into SOC workflows is highlighted, emphasizing the advantages it brings to the realm of threat investigation.

The chapter further explores MDE's capabilities in real-time threat detection, detailing its potential to detect and alert on security threats and provide insights into potential security incidents. It also provides an overview of the workflow SOC analysts typically follow during security incident investigations, outlining the essential steps involved. Advanced threat-hunting techniques are examined, focusing on the proactive measures SOC analysts can employ, alongside a discussion of the role of threat intelligence and behavioral analysis in threat hunting.

Data collection and analysis within MDE are addressed, elucidating how essential data is collected and stored for effective threat investigations. The chapter also outlines methods for identifying threats within MDE and the significance of prioritizing responses based on severity and potential impact. By the end of this chapter, readers will have a clear understanding of the vital role threat investigation plays in SOC operations.

Threat investigation in SOC

A SOC serves as an organization's watchtower, monitoring network traffic and endpoint activities to detect and respond to security threats. Threat investigation within a SOC involves the meticulous examination of suspicious activities or anomalies, which could indicate a security incident. This process is crucial for several reasons.

First and foremost, it is a reactive approach to cybersecurity. Instead of merely relying on preventive measures, threat investigation focuses on identifying potential threats and follows detection, focus on analyzing and responding to the detected threats and vulnerabilities in real-time or near-real-time. This proactive stance allows a SOC to react swiftly, often before significant damage occurs, reducing the impact and potential losses for the organization.

Furthermore, a SOC is tasked with the responsibility of ensuring the continuity of operations and protecting sensitive information. Threat investigation is the front line of defense in this endeavor, helping organizations maintain the confidentiality, integrity, and availability of their data and systems. By identifying and addressing threats promptly, a SOC can thwart malicious actors and minimize the damage inflicted by cyberattacks.

In essence, threat investigation is a pivotal function within a SOC, serving as the bridge between proactive security measures and responsive incident handling. It allows organizations to detect, analyze, and mitigate potential threats swiftly, which is essential for maintaining a robust security posture in the face of an ever-changing threat landscape.

MDE SOC feature integration

MDE offers a comprehensive suite of tools designed to seamlessly integrate with SOC workflows, bolstering the capabilities of security teams and enhancing their threat investigation procedures. In this section, we will explore the tight integration of MDE within SOC environments and highlight the advantages it brings to the table.

Seamless integration with SOC workflows

MDE has been meticulously engineered to align with the workflow of modern SOC teams. Its integration capabilities allow SOC analysts to incorporate MDE into their daily routines with ease. From incident detection to in-depth threat investigation, MDE provides a unified platform that harmonizes various security functions. Here is how it seamlessly integrates into SOC workflows:

- **Real-time threat visibility**: MDE offers real-time visibility into the security posture of endpoints. SOC teams can access a centralized dashboard to monitor alerts, incidents, and threat indicators. This consolidated view ensures that analysts can quickly identify potential security issues.

- **Actionable insights**: MDE employs advanced analytics and machine learning to provide SOC analysts with actionable insights. It helps prioritize threats, allowing teams to focus their efforts on the most critical issues, thus increasing efficiency.

- **Threat intelligence**: Integration with threat intelligence services ensures that SOC analysts have access to up-to-date information about emerging threats. This empowers them to make informed decisions when investigating potential incidents.

- **Automated response**: MDE's automation capabilities enable SOC teams to respond swiftly to threats. Automated investigation and response play a vital role in reducing the time it takes to mitigate security incidents.

Advantages of using MDE

The advantages of incorporating MDE into SOC threat investigation processes are manifold. Some of them are:

- **Enhanced visibility**: MDE provides a granular view of endpoints, enhancing visibility into their security status. SOC teams can drill down into details, such as device health, network connections, and running processes, for a comprehensive understanding of potential threats.

- **Rapid investigation**: The platform offers the tools and data necessary for expedited threat investigation. Analysts can swiftly determine the scope and impact of an incident and take necessary actions to contain it.

- **Streamlined incident response**: MDE streamlines incident response through automation and orchestration. It assists SOC teams in isolating compromised devices, remediating vulnerabilities, and eradicating threats.

- **Threat hunting**: Advanced threat-hunting techniques are facilitated by MDE, empowering SOC analysts to proactively seek out threats that may not trigger traditional alerts. This proactive approach is essential for identifying and mitigating emerging threats.

- **Integration with Microsoft Ecosystem**: MDE's compatibility with other Microsoft security products creates a holistic security environment. Integration with Microsoft 365 Defender and Azure Sentinel, among others, offers a cohesive and robust security solution for SOC teams.

Incident investigation workflow

Incident investigation is a critical process within a SOC that aims to identify, understand, and mitigate security incidents effectively. SOC analysts follow a well-structured workflow to ensure a comprehensive and efficient investigation. Here, we outline the typical steps and processes involved in the incident investigation workflow:

- **Alert triage**: The investigation journey begins with the reception of security alerts generated by various security tools and systems. The SOC analyst's first task is to triage these alerts, determining their validity and severity. Alerts are categorized based on their priority, and the most critical ones are investigated first.

- **Alert enrichment**: Once an alert is selected for investigation, SOC analysts enrich it by gathering additional contextual information. This may include data about the affected systems, user accounts, network traffic, or any other relevant details. The goal is to understand the broader context of the alert.

- **Identification and classification**: After gathering contextual data, the SOC analyst aims to identify the type and nature of the incident. It is also important to identify and classify a malware infection, a network breach, a data leak, or another form of security compromise that requires immediate attention. Classification helps in selecting the appropriate investigative approach.

- **Scope determination**: The next step involves defining the scope of the incident. Analysts must identify all affected systems, users, and data to understand the extent of the compromise fully. This step helps in isolating the incident and preventing its further spread.

- **Data collection and analysis**: With the scope determined, SOC analysts proceed to collect relevant data for in-depth analysis. This may include log files, system snapshots, memory dumps, or any other artifacts related to the incident. Advanced tools, like EDR solutions, are invaluable for collecting and analyzing forensic data.

- **Timeline reconstruction**: One of the key aspects of incident investigation is creating a timeline of events leading up to and following the incident. A chronological view of activities helps analysts understand how the breach occurred and its potential impact.

- **Threat actor attribution**: In some cases, analysts attempt to attribute the incident to a specific threat actor or group. This requires advanced threat intelligence and often involves collaboration with external agencies or threat intelligence providers.

- **Evidence preservation**: Proper evidence preservation is vital for legal and compliance reasons. SOC analysts ensure that all evidence is securely stored to maintain its integrity for potential legal actions or further investigations.

- **Incident report and documentation**: As the investigation progresses, analysts maintain detailed records of their findings and actions taken. This documentation is crucial for reporting, compliance, and knowledge sharing.

- **Remediation and recovery**: Based on the investigation's findings, SOC analysts work on mitigating the incident. This may involve cleaning malware, removing compromised accounts, patching vulnerabilities, or enhancing security controls to prevent similar incidents in the future. Remediation and recovery should generally be part of the post-incident phase, not necessarily during the investigation phase. Investigation focuses on identifying and analyzing the incident, while remediation is a subsequent phase after understanding the incident's scope and impact.

- **Post-incident review**: Once the incident is under control, SOC teams conduct a post-incident review to assess the effectiveness of their response and identify areas for improvement. Lessons learned from the investigation are integrated into security practices to enhance the organization's overall security posture. The post-incident review is indeed conducted after the incident is contained, but it is often an ongoing process that begins as soon as the initial investigation is complete and remediation efforts are underway. It should be emphasized that the review happens as part of the overall incident management process rather than after the incident is entirely under control.

- **Reporting and communication** While communication with stakeholders is crucial, it is typically more structured and formalized once an incident is confirmed rather than throughout the entire investigation process. Communication strategies are often more focused during specific phases of the incident management process.

Note: Chapter 13, Future Ahead with AI and LLM, covers more advanced insight of Microsoft Security Copilot features that automates the mentioned steps to reduce down time for investigation.

Data collection and analysis

One of the cornerstones of effective threat investigation within a SOC is the comprehensive collection and analysis of endpoint security data. MDE plays a pivotal role in this process by seamlessly gathering, storing, and making this data accessible for thorough analysis.

Data collection by Microsoft Defender for Endpoint

MDE is designed to operate at the endpoint level, allowing it to gather an extensive range of endpoint security data. This data collection process operates silently and efficiently, without disrupting end-user activities. The key components of data collection include:

- **Endpoint agents**: MDE agents are deployed on all managed endpoints. These agents continuously collect information about system activities, user behaviors, and network traffic.
- **Telemetry and logs**: MDE captures extensive telemetry and log data, including information about file executions, network connections, registry changes, and security events. This data is crucial for identifying suspicious activities and potential threats.
- **Sensor-based technology**: MDE relies on sensors placed at different vantage points across the endpoint. These sensors monitor and collect data on various activities, such as file access, system calls, and process behaviors.
- **Cloud integration**: MDE integrates seamlessly with the Microsoft security cloud. This cloud-based architecture allows for real-time data uploads, analysis, and centralized storage.

Unifying SIEM and XDR

MDE team has added new features on the MDE web portal and they have integrated the Microsoft Sentinel. They announced this integration in Nov 2023, Ignite and the feature Go Alive. With this feature you need not go to Azure Sentinel and you can leverage your Sentinel investment directly from the MDE Security portal.

All logs from Sentinel will be directly available on the portal and you can leverage the Advanced Hunting feature of MDE portal on the Sentinel data.

The following are the three sub-menus that MDE portal users are going to get under Microsoft Sentinel main menu that they can find on left hand side along with other Menus:

- Threat management
- Configuration management
- Configuration

You are going to get some of the amazing features like Threat Intelligence, MITRE ATT&CK, Notebooks, Hunting, Workbooks etc.

> **Note: I specifically watched the session recording and captured the following notes for the readers for the new features:**
> - **You can watch complete feature discussed in MS Ignite on Security Nija session available at https://www.youtube.com/watch?v=S5ISlCRtDIc.**
> - **In case, you are not having required license that you will not see above option available to you on web portal.**
> - **In case, the feature is not GA even in such conditions the above option will not be available as we are specifically bringing this option to you from the Ignite session.**

The following figure is taken from Ninja session for the new feature:

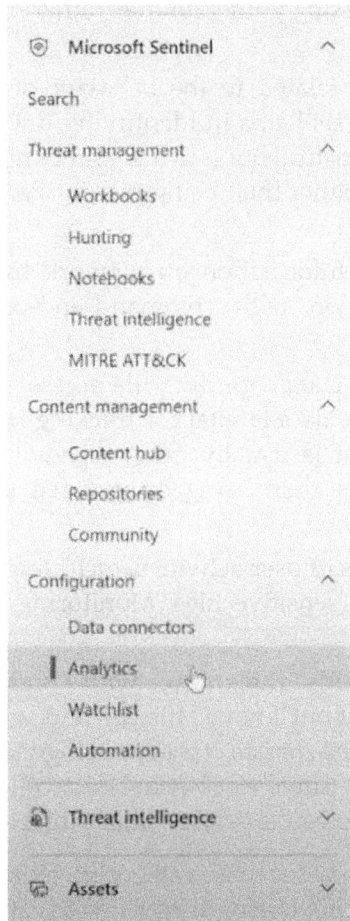

Figure 7.1: Newly integrated Microsoft Sentinel menu bar option in web portal

Essential data for threat investigation

When it comes to threat investigation, certain types of data are essential for analysts to make informed decisions and respond effectively to security incidents. The critical data categories include:

- **Alert data**: This includes data related to alerts generated by MDE based on suspicious activities. Analysts rely on these alerts as starting points for further investigation.

- **Incident data**: Information about identified security incidents, including the timeline of activities, affected endpoints, and the severity of the incident.

- **Endpoint configuration data**: Details on the configuration of individual endpoints, including installed applications, user accounts, and system settings. This information helps analysts understand the attack surface. While endpoint configuration data is important, it is often more useful for understanding the attack surface and assessing vulnerabilities rather than directly for ongoing threat investigation.

- **Behavioral data**: Data related to the behavior of endpoints, applications, and users. Behavioral analysis helps in identifying deviations from normal patterns. Behavioral data can be critical but is usually more relevant for detecting anomalies and potential threats, rather than being categorized as essential data for incident response.

- **Network traffic data**: Information on network traffic patterns, including data transfers, communication with command-and-control servers, and unusual network behaviors.

- **File and registry data**: Data regarding file access, execution, and changes to the Windows Registry. This data is vital for tracking malicious activities. Behavioral data can be critical but is usually more relevant for detecting anomalies and potential threats, rather than being categorized as essential data for incident response.

- **User activity logs**: Logs of user activities, including login/logout events, account changes, and access to sensitive files. Monitoring user behavior is essential for detecting insider threats.

- **Threat intelligence feeds**: Integration with threat intelligence feeds provides updated information about known threats and attack indicators, aiding in the identification of potential threats. Threat intelligence feeds are crucial for context but are not typically classified as essential data collected during an investigation. They provide additional context rather than direct investigative data.

Data collection by MDE encompasses these categories, making it a comprehensive source for SOC analysts to draw insights during threat investigation. With the ability to access real-time data and historical records, analysts can retrace the steps of potential threats, identify vulnerabilities, and proactively respond to security incidents.

Reporting and documentation

In the intricate landscape of threat investigation, thorough reporting and documentation play a pivotal role in the efficacy of a SOC. Properly documented findings and comprehensive reports not only aid in understanding the incident but also facilitate informed decision-making, resource allocation, and future prevention. MDE acknowledges the significance of this aspect and offers robust reporting capabilities to empower SOC teams.

Importance of thorough reporting and documentation

There are many benefits of reporting and documentation during threat investigation while performing SOC analyst role. Some of them are:

- **Understanding the incident**: Detailed documentation is the foundation of comprehending a security incident. By documenting every phase of an investigation, from initial detection to final resolution, SOC teams can gain an in-depth understanding of the incident. This knowledge is essential for assessing its impact and devising an effective response strategy.

- **Legal and compliance requirements**: In many industries, compliance mandates require organizations to maintain comprehensive records of security incidents and responses. Proper documentation ensures that organizations are in compliance with these legal obligations, reducing the risk of regulatory penalties.

- **Continuous improvement**: Well-documented incidents provide a wealth of data that can be used for post-incident analysis. SOC teams can assess what worked and what didn't, enabling them to continuously refine their incident response procedures and enhance their cybersecurity posture.

- **Communication**: Security incidents often require communication with various stakeholders, including senior management, legal teams, and external partners. Accurate and well-structured reports facilitate effective communication, allowing stakeholders to understand the situation and make informed decisions.

MDE's reporting capabilities for SOC teams

MDE empowers SOC teams with a suite of reporting capabilities to support thorough documentation and reporting in threat investigations. Some of these are as follows:

- **Customizable reports**: MDE allows SOC analysts to generate reports that are tailored to the specific needs of the organization. Reports can be customized to include relevant information, such as incident details, affected endpoints, user accounts, and mitigation actions.

- **Centralized reporting**: The platform provides a centralized location for creating and storing incident reports. This simplifies access and retrieval, ensuring that reports are readily available for reference or sharing with stakeholders.

- **Export and sharing**: Reports can be easily exported in various formats, such as PDF or CSV, for sharing with different teams or individuals. This flexibility in sharing helps in disseminating information to those who need it.

- **Real-time reporting**: MDE offers real-time reporting capabilities, allowing SOC teams to track the progress of an incident as it unfolds. This immediate visibility is invaluable for monitoring the incident response and adapting strategies as needed.

- **Historical data**: MDE retains historical data related to incidents and investigations, creating a valuable resource for trend analysis, threat intelligence, and the development of proactive security measures.

Challenges and best practices

Effective threat investigation within a SOC is both a science and an art, often fraught with challenges. In this section, we will explore some of the common hurdles faced during threat investigations and present best practices and tips to overcome these challenges, optimizing the SOC's ability to safeguard the organization's digital landscape.

Challenges faced during threat investigation

Each security incident is unique, and SOC analyst faces the following challenges while performing their duties:

- **Complexity of threats**: The ever-evolving threat landscape presents SOC teams with increasingly sophisticated and complex threats. These threats may employ advanced tactics, making detection and investigation more challenging.

- **Alert fatigue**: An overwhelming number of alerts can lead to alert fatigue within SOC teams. Sorting through alerts and prioritizing them is a significant challenge, as not all alerts represent actual security incidents.

- **Data overload**: The abundance of security data generated by various tools can be overwhelming. Analyzing this data efficiently to detect anomalies and threats is a persistent challenge.

- **Resource constraints**: SOC teams often face resource constraints, both in terms of personnel and technology. Limited resources can hinder their ability to investigate and respond to threats effectively.

- **Incident attribution**: Tracing threats back to their source, a process known as attribution, can be elusive. Determining the origin of an attack is often complex and time-consuming.

Best practices and tips for effective investigations

To overcome challenges new tools and practices are getting followed in the industry. Some of them are mentioned as follows:

- **Threat intelligence integration**: Integrate threat intelligence feeds into your investigation process. This enables SOC teams to stay updated on the latest threats, tactics, and vulnerabilities, enhancing their detection and response capabilities.

- **Automated alert triage**: Implement automated alert triage systems that prioritize alerts based on predefined criteria. This reduces the burden of alert fatigue and allows analysts to focus on high-priority incidents.

- **Advanced analytics**: Leverage advanced analytics and ML to identify anomalies and potential threats within the vast volume of data. These technologies can help in the early detection of threats.

- **Collaboration and training**: Promote collaboration between SOC analysts, other security teams, and external partners. Regular training and tabletop exercises ensure that the team is well-prepared for real incidents.

- **Case management**: Use case management systems to organize and document investigations. A structured approach helps in maintaining a consistent and organized record of each incident.

- **Incident playbooks**: Develop incident response playbooks that provide step-by-step guidance for handling different types of incidents. These playbooks can expedite response times and reduce errors.

- **Resource scaling**: Implement flexible resource scaling strategies that allow the SOC to adapt to the evolving threat landscape. This may involve hiring additional personnel during peak periods or using cloud-based security solutions.

- **Threat attribution caution**: Exercise caution when attempting threat attribution. Attribution is a challenging task and can be unreliable. Focus on response and mitigation rather than solely seeking to attribute an incident.

- **Continuous improvement**: Continuously review and refine your investigation processes. Learn from each incident and use the knowledge gained to enhance your security posture.

Advanced hunting

Advanced hunting is a feature on MDE portal that gives you the query language power to explore security event log world. MDE provides prebuilt in house and community-built queries on the web interface for quick investigation for most common attacks and you can save your own queries for future reference. Microsoft has launched Security Copilot feature that gives you more advanced possibility with this technique and you can find more details in *Chapter 13, Future Ahead with AI and LLM*.

Investigation through **Kusto Query Language** (KQL) is one way and second more advanced version is through the Windows events logged into the devices and long list of EventID's are available on Microsoft site. The following are some of the samples for your reference. The following figure is an example of one reported incident and gives an overview and other related information for through investigation to help SOC Analyst:

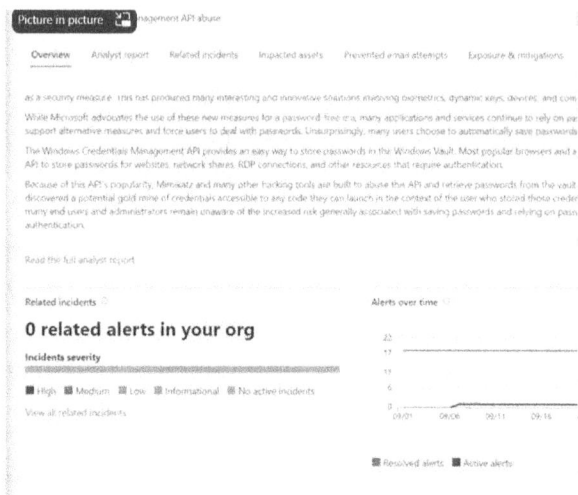

Figure 7.2: Example of reported Incident on MDE web portal

Recently, the defender team has also added guided hunting option, as shown in the following figure:

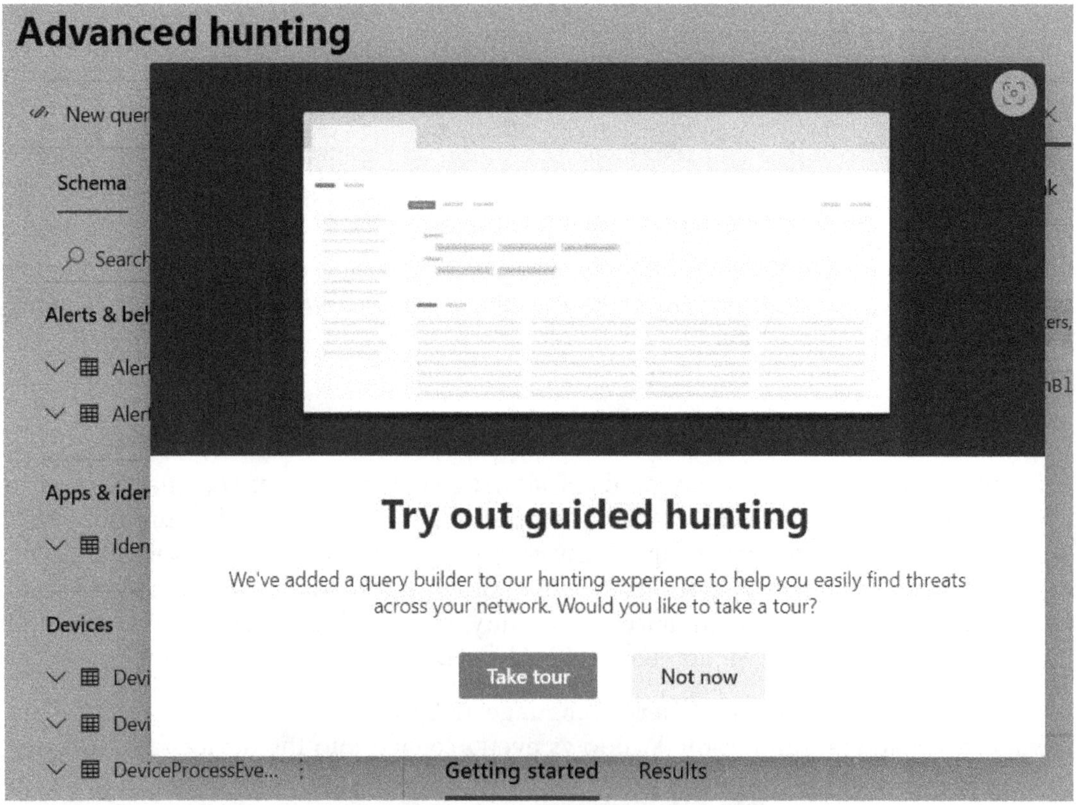

Figure 7.3: Advanced hunting trial page pop up

The following is a subsequent figure taken while creating a new query on an advanced hunting page:

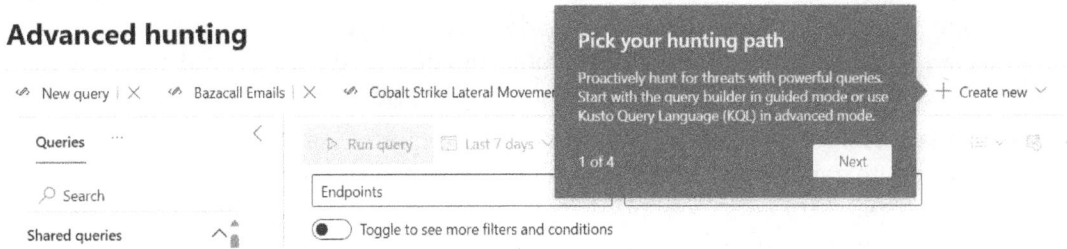

Advanced hunting

Figure 7.4: *Advanced hunting query interface*

Advanced threat-hunting techniques

Advanced threat-hunting techniques go beyond basic incident response and require a deep understanding of security principles. Here, we dig into some of these advanced techniques employed by SOC analysts:

- **Threat intelligence integration**: Proactive threat hunting is significantly enhanced when SOC teams incorporate threat intelligence feeds into their workflow. Threat intelligence provides up-to-date information on emerging threats, attacker tactics, and known indicators of compromise. Analysts can leverage this intelligence to search for signs of known attack patterns and vulnerabilities.

- **Behavioral analysis**: Understanding the behavior of systems and users is fundamental to advanced threat hunting. SOC analysts analyze normal behavior patterns within an organization to identify deviations that may indicate malicious activity. This may involve examining network traffic, system logs, user activities, and application behaviors.

- **Anomaly detection**: Advanced threat hunters use anomaly detection techniques to identify deviations from established baselines. This can include sudden surges in network traffic, unusual file access patterns, or unexpected spikes in system resource usage. Anomalies can signal potential threats or vulnerabilities.

- **YARA rules and indicators of compromise**: Threat hunters create custom YARA rules and **indicators of compromise (IoCs)** to identify specific patterns or artifacts associated with known threats. These rules can be applied to search across systems, networks, and endpoints for signs of compromise. YARA rules offer a high level of flexibility in threat detection. YARA rules are used to identify patterns and are particularly effective for malware detection, but IoCs are more general and can be used across various detection methods, not just YARA rules.

- **Threat-hunting platforms**: Specialized threat-hunting platforms and tools enable SOC analysts to streamline their investigations. These platforms often incorporate machine learning and advanced analytics to aid in pattern recognition and anomaly detection. They provide a centralized environment for creating and executing complex threat-hunting queries. Not all threat-hunting platforms incorporate machine learning or advanced analytics. Some may offer basic query and reporting capabilities without advanced analytics. As of now MDE directly doesn't provide any anomaly detection function on the portal, but they refer it as Advanced hunting due to the fact that they provide you the KQL for hunting.

- **Data correlation**: Advanced threat hunting requires analyzing data from multiple sources to gain a comprehensive view of potential threats. SOC analysts correlate data from endpoints, network traffic, and logs to identify patterns that may be indicative of a sophisticated attack.

- **User and entity behavior analytics**: **User and entity behavior analytics (UEBA)** solutions focus on monitoring and analyzing user and entity behaviors to identify suspicious or malicious activities. By building behavioral profiles of users and systems, analysts can detect insider threats and external attacks that blend with legitimate user actions.

- **Threat emulation and red-teaming**: Threat hunters often emulate threat actor behavior through red-teaming exercises. By simulating real-world attacks, SOC analysts can identify weaknesses in security controls and enhance detection and response capabilities.

- **Cloud and IoT threat hunting**: As organizations adopt cloud services and the **Internet of Things (IoT)**, threat hunting extends to these environments. Analysts search for cloud misconfigurations, suspicious IoT device activities, and potential cloud-based threats. Cloud and IoT threat hunting is more complex and not just limited to misconfigurations and suspicious activities. It often involves specific tools and techniques tailored to the unique nature of cloud environments and IoT devices.

- **Collaboration and continuous learning**: Advanced threat hunters engage in collaboration with colleagues, external threat-sharing communities, and industry peers. Continuous learning and knowledge sharing are essential for staying ahead of evolving threats.

Troubleshooting with Windows event viewer

SOC Analyst leverages Windows OS Event Viewer functionality to troubleshoot threats and uses **attack surface reduction (ASR)** custom event view:

XML for attack surface reduction rule events

The following query is used to identify EventID 1121/1122/5007 on a specific event path:

```
<QueryList>
  <Query Id="0" Path="Microsoft-Windows-Windows Defender/Operational">
```

```
    <Select Path="Microsoft-Windows-Windows Defender/Operational">*[Sys-
tem[(EventID=1121 or EventID=1122 or EventID=5007)]]</Select>

    <Select Path="Microsoft-Windows-Windows Defender/WHC">*[System[(Even-
tID=1121 or EventID=1122 or EventID=5007)]]</Select>

  </Query>
</QueryList>
```

Note: Event IDs 1121, 1122, and 5007 are not standard ASR event IDs. The specific IDs used for ASR events may differ and should be verified for accuracy.

- **Event ID 1121: This event indicates the blocking of disallowed operations. It is typically logged when certain actions are prevented by security policies, such as attack surface reduction rules.**

- **Event ID 1122: This event signifies the auditing of operations for review and analysis. It is logged when actions are monitored but not necessarily blocked, allowing administrators to review potentially risky behaviors without immediately stopping them.**

- **Event ID 5007: This event is related to Windows Defender and indicates that a configuration change has been made to Windows Defender settings. It helps in tracking changes to security settings, ensuring that any modifications are logged for security auditing purposes.**

XML for exploit protection events

The following query leverages to identify exploit protection events:

```
<QueryList>
  <Query Id="0" Path="Microsoft-Windows-Security-Mitigations/KernelMode">
    <Select Path="Microsoft-Windows-Security-Mitigations/KernelMode">*[Sys-
tem[Provider[@Name='Microsoft-Windows-Security-Mitigations' or @Name='Mi-
crosoft-Windows-WER-Diag' or @Name='Microsoft-Windows-Win32k' or @
Name='Win32k'] and ( (EventID &gt;= 1 and EventID &lt;= 24)  or EventID=5
or EventID=260)]]</Select>
    <Select Path="Microsoft-Windows-Win32k/Concurrency">*[System[Provider[@
Name='Microsoft-Windows-Security-Mitigations' or @Name='Microsoft-Win-
dows-WER-Diag' or @Name='Microsoft-Windows-Win32k' or @Name='Win32k'] and
( (EventID &gt;= 1 and EventID &lt;= 24)  or EventID=5 or EventID=260)]]</
Select>
    <Select Path="Microsoft-Windows-Win32k/Contention">*[System[Provider[@
Name='Microsoft-Windows-Security-Mitigations' or @Name='Microsoft-Win-
dows-WER-Diag' or @Name='Microsoft-Windows-Win32k' or @Name='Win32k'] and
( (EventID &gt;= 1 and EventID &lt;= 24)  or EventID=5 or EventID=260)]]</
Select>
    <Select Path="Microsoft-Windows-Win32k/Messages">*[System[Provider[@
```

```
Name='Microsoft-Windows-Security-Mitigations' or @Name='Microsoft-Win-
dows-WER-Diag' or @Name='Microsoft-Windows-Win32k' or @Name='Win32k'] and
( (EventID &gt;= 1 and EventID &lt;= 24)  or EventID=5 or EventID=260)]]</
Select>

    <Select Path="Microsoft-Windows-Win32k/Operational">*[System[Provider[@
Name='Microsoft-Windows-Security-Mitigations' or @Name='Microsoft-Win-
dows-WER-Diag' or @Name='Microsoft-Windows-Win32k' or @Name='Win32k'] and
( (EventID &gt;= 1 and EventID &lt;= 24)  or EventID=5 or EventID=260)]]</
Select>

    <Select Path="Microsoft-Windows-Win32k/Power">*[System[Provider[@
Name='Microsoft-Windows-Security-Mitigations' or @Name='Microsoft-Win-
dows-WER-Diag' or @Name='Microsoft-Windows-Win32k' or @Name='Win32k'] and
( (EventID &gt;= 1 and EventID &lt;= 24)  or EventID=5 or EventID=260)]]</
Select>

    <Select Path="Microsoft-Windows-Win32k/Render">*[System[Provider[@
Name='Microsoft-Windows-Security-Mitigations' or @Name='Microsoft-Win-
dows-WER-Diag' or @Name='Microsoft-Windows-Win32k' or @Name='Win32k'] and
( (EventID &gt;= 1 and EventID &lt;= 24)  or EventID=5 or EventID=260)]]</
Select>

    <Select Path="Microsoft-Windows-Win32k/Tracing">*[System[Provider[@
Name='Microsoft-Windows-Security-Mitigations' or @Name='Microsoft-Win-
dows-WER-Diag' or @Name='Microsoft-Windows-Win32k' or @Name='Win32k'] and
( (EventID &gt;= 1 and EventID &lt;= 24)  or EventID=5 or EventID=260)]]</
Select>

    <Select Path="Microsoft-Windows-Win32k/UIPI">*[System[Provider[@
Name='Microsoft-Windows-Security-Mitigations' or @Name='Microsoft-Win-
dows-WER-Diag' or @Name='Microsoft-Windows-Win32k' or @Name='Win32k'] and
( (EventID &gt;= 1 and EventID &lt;= 24)  or EventID=5 or EventID=260)]]</
Select>

    <Select Path="System">*[System[Provider[@Name='Microsoft-Windows-Secu-
rity-Mitigations' or @Name='Microsoft-Windows-WER-Diag' or @Name='Micro-
soft-Windows-Win32k' or @Name='Win32k'] and ( (EventID &gt;= 1 and EventID
&lt;= 24)  or EventID=5 or EventID=260)]]</Select>

    <Select Path="Microsoft-Windows-Security-Mitigations/UserMode">*[Sys-
tem[Provider[@Name='Microsoft-Windows-Security-Mitigations' or @Name='Mi-
crosoft-Windows-WER-Diag' or @Name='Microsoft-Windows-Win32k' or @
Name='Win32k'] and ( (EventID &gt;= 1 and EventID &lt;= 24)  or EventID=5
or EventID=260)]]</Select>

  </Query>
</QueryList>
```

Note: The query provided includes a mix of event paths and IDs that may not correspond correctly to exploit protection events. The exact Event IDs and paths should be verified against Microsoft's official documentation.

XML for network protection events

The following query is used for network protection events:

```
<QueryList>
 <Query Id="0" Path="Microsoft-Windows-Windows Defender/Operational">
  <Select Path="Microsoft-Windows-Windows Defender/Operational">*[System[(EventID=1125 or EventID=1126 or EventID=5007)]]</Select>
  <Select Path="Microsoft-Windows-Windows Defender/WHC">*[System[(EventID=1125 or EventID=1126 or EventID=5007)]]</Select>
 </Query>
</QueryList>
```

Note: Event IDs 1125 and 1126 are specific to network protection but should be checked for accuracy. The exact event paths and IDs should be verified.

Exploit protection event codes

Microsoft security team has published various exploit protection event codes that can be used to identify various threats through Widows Event viewer tool. The following table showcases some of the event codes:

Provider/source	Event ID	Description
Security-Mitigations	1	ACG audit
Security-Mitigations	2	ACG enforce
Security-Mitigations	3	Don't allow child processes audit
Security-Mitigations	4	Don't allow child processes block
Security-Mitigations	5	Block low integrity images audit
Security-Mitigations	6	Block low integrity images block
Security-Mitigations	7	Block remote images audit
Security-Mitigations	8	Block remote images block
Security-Mitigations	9	Disable win32k system calls audit
Security-Mitigations	10	Disable win32k system calls block
Security-Mitigations	11	Code integrity guard audit

Provider/source	Event ID	Description
Security-Mitigations	12	Code integrity guard block
Security-Mitigations	13	EAF audit
Security-Mitigations	14	EAF enforce
Security-Mitigations	15	EAF+ audit
Security-Mitigations	16	EAF+ enforce
Security-Mitigations	17	IAF audit
Security-Mitigations	18	IAF enforce
Security-Mitigations	19	ROP StackPivot audit
Security-Mitigations	20	ROP StackPivot enforces
Security-Mitigations	21	ROP CallerCheck audit
Security-Mitigations	22	ROP CallerCheck enforces
Security-Mitigations	23	ROP SimExec audit
Security-Mitigations	24	ROP SimExec enforces
WER-Diagnostics	5	CFG Block
Win32K	260	Untrusted Font

Table 7.1: Exploit protection OS event codes

Note: The event codes listed should be checked against the latest Microsoft security documentation for accuracy, as they may change or be updated but as per our experience those rarely get change as many security administrators keep these id's into their monitoring system.

Rule name and rule GUID

Microsoft security team has published Rule name and unique Group UID for specific types of event, as shown in the following table:

Rule name	Rule GUID
Block abuse of exploited vulnerable signed drivers	56a863a9-875e-4185-98a7-b882c64b5ce5
Block Adobe Reader from creating child processes	7674ba52-37eb-4a4f-a9a1-f0f9a1619a2c
Block all Office applications from creating child processes	d4f940ab-401b-4efc-aadc-ad5f3c50688a

Rule name	Rule GUID
Block credential stealing from the Windows local security authority subsystem (lsass.exe)	9e6c4e1f-7d60-472f-ba1a-a39ef669e4b2
Block executable content from email client and webmail	be9ba2d9-53ea-4cdc-84e5-9b1eeee46550
Block executable files from running unless they meet a prevalence, age, or trusted list criterion	01443614-cd74-433a-b99e-2ecdc07bfc25
Block execution of potentially obfuscated scripts	5beb7efe-fd9a-4556-801d-275e5ffc04cc
Block JavaScript or VBScript from launching downloaded executable content	d3e037e1-3eb8-44c8-a917-57927947596d
Block Office applications from creating executable content	3b576869-a4ec-4529-8536-b80a7769e899
Block Office applications from injecting code into other processes	75668c1f-73b5-4cf0-bb93-3ecf5cb7cc84
Block Office communication application from creating child processes	26190899-1602-49e8-8b27-eb1d0a1ce869
Block persistence through WMI event subscription * File and folder exclusions not supported	e6db77e5-3df2-4cf1-b95a-636979351e5b
Block process creations originating from PSExec and WMI commands	d1e49aac-8f56-4280-b9ba-993a6d77406c
Block untrusted and unsigned processes that run from USB	b2b3f03d-6a65-4f7b-a9c7-1c7ef74a9ba4
Block Win32 API calls from Office macros	92e97fa1-2edf-4476-bdd6-9dd0b4dddc7b
Use advanced protection against ransomware	c1db55ab-c21a-4637-bb3f-a12568109d35

Table 7.2: Event rule name and unique group ID

Note: We request you to cross verify these GUID's from Microsoft website before integrating into your system.

Advanced hunting using KQL

You can use advanced hunting in three different forms. The following are the three options available on advanced hunting page to leverage the functionality:

- Schema
- Functions
- Queries

For example, Microsoft security team has provided options to leverage community created queries to hunt in your organization and such queries can be opened up from same MDE web portal.

Community based advanced hunting queries example

The following figure showcases the community advanced hunting query grouping on security web portal:

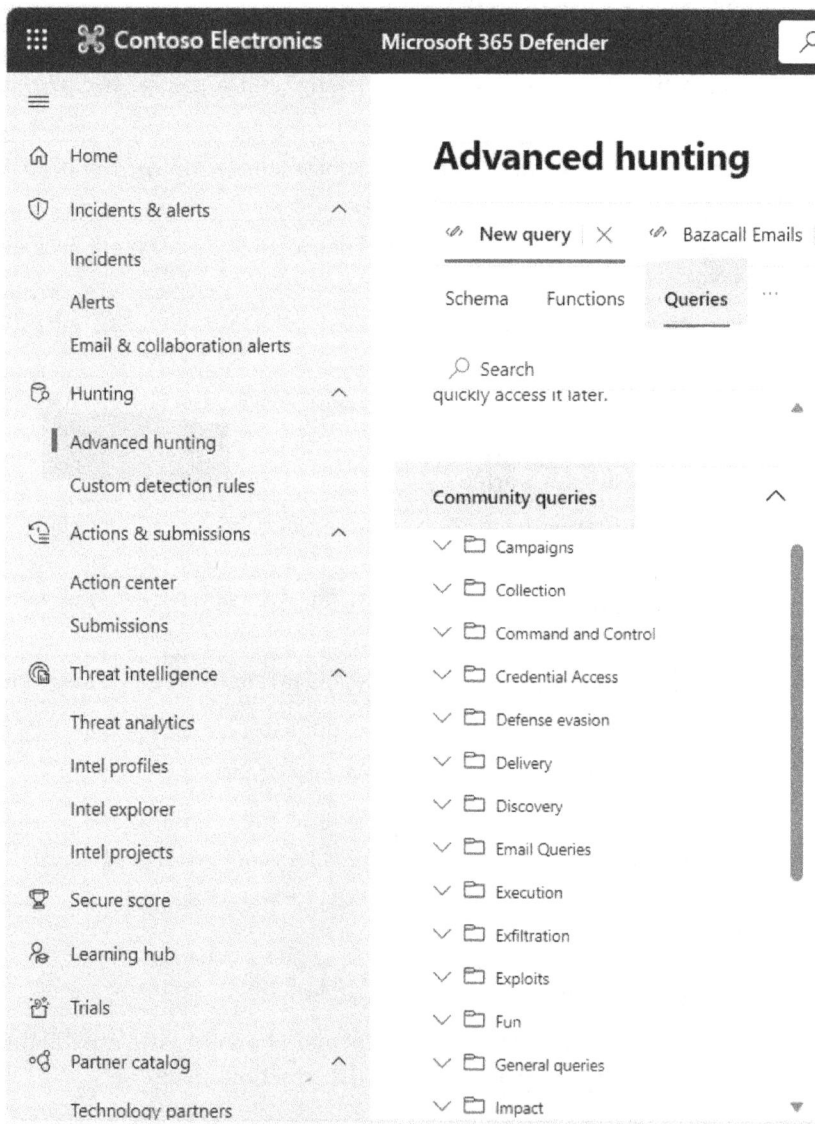

Figure 7.5: Advanced hunting menu bar MDE web portal

The following figure is an example of schema for **Advanced hunting**:

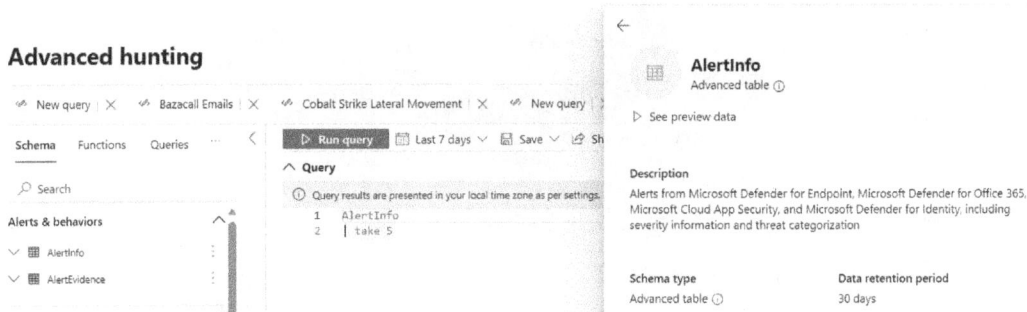

Figure 7.6: Advanced hunting Schema interface on web portal

The following figure is an example of query for advanced hunting. There are multiple options available on the query interface. You can click on shared queries or your own saved queries and directly run or open in query editor for further editing.

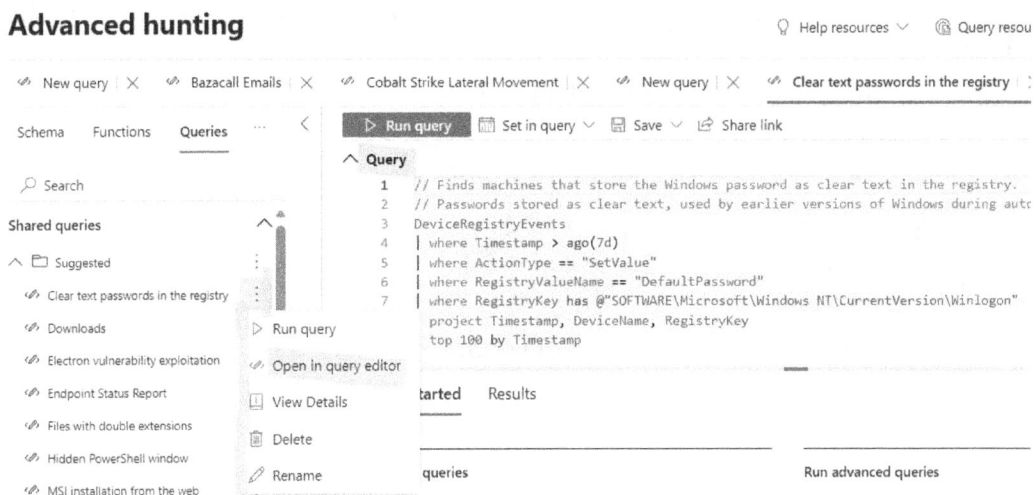

Figure 7.7: Advanced hunting editor example

Share results: SOC analysts usually run the query and share the same query in team or for documentation for various purpose.

The following figure shows the query link sharing reference:

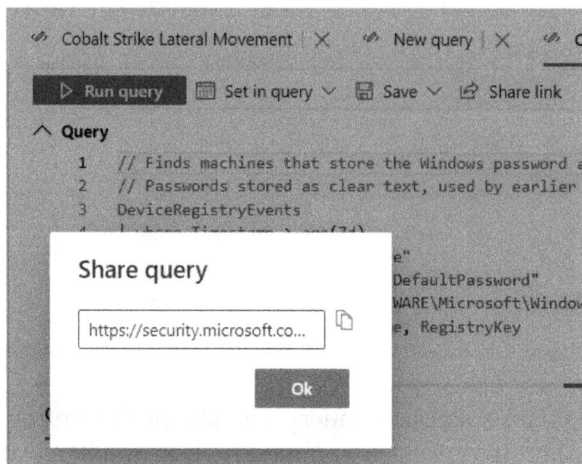

Figure 7.8: Query link sharing reference

Here are random 20 KQL queries references that you can use for advanced hunting in Microsoft Defender:

- **List all devices with recent threat detection**:

```
DeviceEvents
| where Timestamp > ago(7d)
| where ActionType == "Alert"
| summarize ThreatCount=count() by DeviceId
| project DeviceId, ThreatCount
```

The following figure is an example from the portal:

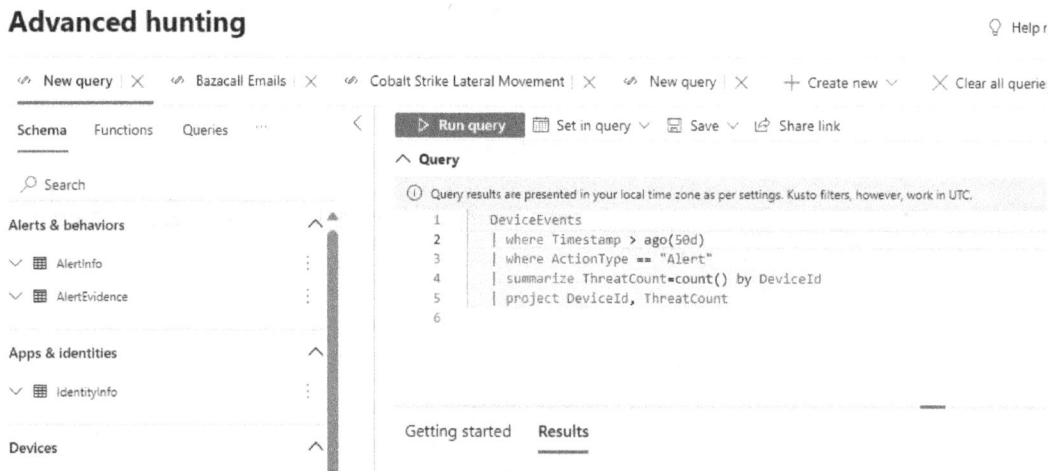

Figure 7.9: Just another Advanced hunting query example

- **Identify unusual process execution**:

```
DeviceProcessEvents
| where Timestamp > ago(1d)
| summarize Count=count() by ProcessCommandLine
| order by Count desc
```

The following figure is an example from the portal:

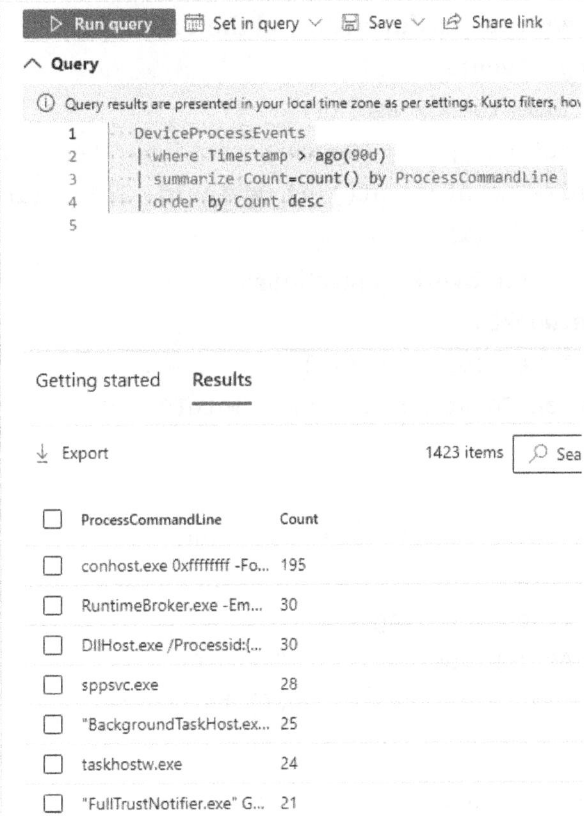

Figure 7.10: Query with Result example

- **List devices with disabled real-time protection**:

```
DeviceInfo
| where RealTimeProtectionEnabled == "False"
| project DeviceName, OSVersion, LastSeen, ProjectInfo = "Your-ProjectInfoHere"
```

- **Identify devices with multiple malware detections**:

```
DeviceEvents
| where Timestamp > ago(7d)
```

```
| where ActionType == "Alert" and Category == "Malware"
| summarize ThreatCount=count() by DeviceId
| where ThreatCount > 1
```

- **Find devices with disabled firewall**:

```
DeviceInfo
| where FirewallEnabled == "False"
```

- **List devices with successful credential theft attempt**s:

```
DeviceLogonEvents
| where Timestamp > ago(1d)
| where ActionType == "LogonSuccess" and LogonType == "3"
| summarize Count=count() by DeviceId, InitiatingProcessFileName,
AccountName
```

- **Identify unusual network connections**:

```
DeviceNetworkEvents
| where Timestamp > ago(1d)
| summarize Count=count() by RemoteIP, LocalPort, RemotePort,
Protocol
| order by Count desc
```

- **List all devices with recent exploit detection**:

```
DeviceEvents
| where Timestamp > ago(7d)
| where ActionType == "Alert" and Category == "Exploit"
| summarize ThreatCount=count() by DeviceId
| project DeviceId, ThreatCount
```

- **Identify devices with disabled auto-update**:

```
DeviceInfo
| where AutoUpdateSettingsEnabled == "False"
```

- **List devices with frequent failed logon attempts**:

```
DeviceLogonEvents
| where Timestamp > ago(1d)
| where ActionType == "LogonFailure"
| summarize Count=count() by DeviceId, InitiatingProcessFile-
Name, AccountName
| order by Count desc
```

- **Identify devices with unusual registry changes**:

```
DeviceRegistryEvents
| where Timestamp > ago(1d)
| summarize Count=count() by RegistryKey
| order by Count desc
```

- **List devices with suspicious Powershell activity**:

```
DeviceProcessEvents
| where Timestamp > ago(1d)
| where ProcessCommandLine has "powershell.exe"
| extend CommandLineLower = tolower(ProcessCommandLine)
| where CommandLineLower has_any ("-enc", "-nop", "-w hidden", "iex", "invoke-expression", "downloadstring", "bypass")
| summarize Count=count() by DeviceId, ProcessCommandLine, AccountName, InitiatingProcessFileName
| order by Count desc
```

- **Identify devices with multiple suspicious script block executions**:

```
DeviceProcessEvents
| where Timestamp > ago(1d)
| where ProcessCommandLine has "ScriptBlock" and ProcessCommandLine has "powershell.exe"
| summarize ThreatCount=count() by DeviceId, InitiatingProcessCommandLine
| where ThreatCount > 1
```

- **Find devices with disabled AMSI protection**:

```
DeviceInfo
| where AmsiProtectionEnabled == "False"
```

- **List devices with frequent service creation events**:

```
DeviceProcessEvents
| where Timestamp > ago(1d)
| where ActionType == "ServiceCreation"
| summarize Count=count() by DeviceId, InitiatingProcessCommandLine
| order by Count desc
```

- **Identify devices with disabled credential guard**:

```
DeviceInfo
| where CredentialGuardEnabled == "False"
```

- **List devices with successful lateral movement attempts**:

```
DeviceNetworkEvents
| where Timestamp > ago(1d)
| where ActionType == "NetworkConnection"
| summarize Count=count() by DeviceId, RemoteIP, RemotePort,
InitiatingProcessCommandLine
| order by Count desc
```

- **Identify devices with frequent failed script block execution**:

```
DeviceProcessEvents
| where Timestamp > ago(1d)
| where ActionType == "ScriptBlock"
| summarize Count=count() by DeviceId, InitiatingProcessCommand-
Line
| where Count > 10
```

- **List devices with disabled bitlocker encryption**:

```
DeviceInfo
| where BitLockerEnabled == "False"
```

- **Identify devices with frequent execution of unsigned code**:

```
DeviceProcessEvents
| where Timestamp > ago(1d)
| where ActionType == "ImageLoad" and IsSignerTrusted == "False"
| summarize Count=count() by DeviceId, InitiatingProcessCommand-
Line, ImageFileName
| order by Count desc
```

These queries can help you uncover more insights and potential security threats within your Microsoft Defender environment. You need to adjust the time frame and other parameters as needed for your specific investigation and monitoring requirements.

Microsoft security copilot

Microsoft Security Copilot is another newly launched security product under same Defender umberalla. IT heavily leverages LLM in co relating various security events and signals. You are highly interested in learning about the new features introduced by AI/ML. We understand your enthusiasm and we will give complete insight into *Chapter 13, Future Ahead with AI and LLM,* that will extensively cover all advanced hunting features introduced by it. We kept this note here as we would like to keep Security Copilot in notes while covering threat investigation techniques as MDE product is evolving at fast pace and turning into advanced product enabled with Copilot capabilities.

Conclusion

This chapter has been an insightful exploration into the vital role threat investigation plays within a SOC. Beginning with an introduction to network attack vectors and various threat landscapes impacting backend IT infrastructures, applications, and services, the chapter navigated through the crucial elements of understanding and categorizing network threats.

The integration of MDE into SOC workflows was highlighted, emphasizing the advantages it offers in incident investigation workflows, efficient data collection, and threat identification and prioritization. The significance of thorough reporting and documentation, along with challenges faced during threat investigations, was discussed, followed by best practices for effective investigations.

Moreover, the chapter explored advanced threat-hunting techniques, including troubleshooting with Windows Event Viewer, utilizing XML for attack surface reduction rule events, and employing KQL for advanced hunting purposes. These sections provided valuable insights into leveraging specific tools and methods to enhance threat investigation capabilities within the SOC.

In next chapter, we are going to cover how SOC analysts responds to threats that will help you to gain insight about the way of working in that role.

Join our book's Discord space

Join the book's Discord Workspace for Latest updates, Offers, Tech happenings around the world, New Release and Sessions with the Authors:

https://discord.bpbonline.com

CHAPTER 8

Responding to Threats with Defender SOC

Introduction

The cyber world presents a multitude of threats, ranging from the subtle and stealthy to the overt and aggressive. To safeguard against these adversaries, **Security Operations Centers** (**SOCs**) play a pivotal role. These hubs of cybersecurity expertise are tasked with the formidable responsibility of identifying, responding to, and mitigating security incidents. The efficiency and effectiveness of a SOC can determine the outcome of security breaches, making it essential for organizations to equip their SOC teams with advanced tools, strategies, and knowledge.

This chapter immerses us into the dynamic realm of incident response and recovery. It navigates through the essential components that make up a SOC's rapid response arsenal. It encompasses vital aspects, such as regulatory compliance, the Live Response feature (*a feature available on MDE portal to isolate a onboarded device from network and run command on infected device during incident*), effective security incident management, and the unique power of Microsoft Threat Modelling tools. By the end of this journey, you will gain comprehensive insights into the procedures, techniques, and tools that enable SOCs to respond swiftly and effectively to a wide array of security threats while ensuring compliance with the ever-evolving regulatory landscape.

Structure

In this chapter, we will cover the following:

- Regulatory compliance considerations
- Incident response and mitigation
- Managing security incident response and recovery
- Responding to threats

Objectives

The objective of the chapter is to equip readers with a deep understanding of incident response and recovery strategies within a SOC setting. This chapter aims to explore the significance of regulatory compliance, emphasizing the measures necessary to align with industry-specific regulations and legal frameworks. Next, we take a closer look at the Live Response feature—a vital tool for real-time incident handling. We discuss its capabilities, practical applications, and best practices. Additionally, we address the comprehensive process of managing security incidents, covering containment, eradication, recovery, and lessons learned. Throughout, we highlight the importance of effective coordination among team members and departments during incident response. Lastly, we underscore the value of Threat Model Diagrams in expediting threat understanding and response within the SOC environment. Microsoft do have tool named **Microsoft Threat Modeling Tool** through which you can create Threat Model Diagrams.

By the end of this chapter, readers will possess the knowledge and insights needed to respond effectively to security incidents, ensure regulatory compliance, and harness advanced tools and techniques to fortify their organization's security posture.

Regulatory compliance considerations

In a SOC environment, regulatory compliance plays a pivotal role in shaping security practices and incident response protocols. Compliance requirements are not one-size-fits-all; they are specific to industries and geographic regions. This section will explore the critical importance of regulatory compliance considerations within a SOC, highlighting the following key aspects:

- **Industry-specific regulations**: Different industries have their own unique regulatory requirements. Whether it is healthcare (HIPAA), finance (PCI DSS), or critical infrastructure (NIST), organizations operating in these sectors must comply with industry-specific regulations.
- **Legal frameworks**: Beyond industry regulations, legal frameworks at the national and international levels can impact a SOC's operations. This section will explore how laws like the **Digital Protection Data Protection Bill 2022** (of *India*), **General**

Data Protection Regulation (GDPR), the **California Consumer Privacy Act** (**CCPA**), and others influence data protection and privacy practices within a SOC.

- **Compliance audits and assessments**: SOC teams often undergo compliance audits and assessments to ensure they are meeting the necessary regulatory standards. This section will detail the process of preparing for and undergoing these audits, including documentation, evidence collection, and reporting.

- **Penalties and consequences**: Understanding the consequences of non-compliance is vital. We will discuss the potential penalties, fines, and legal actions that can result from failing to adhere to regulatory requirements. This serves as a strong motivator for organizations to prioritize compliance.

- **Adaptive compliance strategies**: The landscape of regulatory compliance is constantly evolving. SOC teams must adapt to changes in regulations and compliance standards. We will provide insights into building adaptive compliance strategies that can withstand regulatory shifts.

By comprehensively addressing these aspects, this section equips SOC practitioners with the knowledge and strategies required to navigate the complex terrain of regulatory compliance while handling security incident. It emphasizes that compliance is not just a checkbox but a fundamental component of a resilient and secure SOC.

Incident response and mitigation

In the complex landscape of cybersecurity, incidents are inevitable. Whether it is a malware infection, a data breach, or a targeted cyberattack, organizations must be well-prepared to respond swiftly and effectively. **Microsoft Defender for Endpoint** (**MDE**) plays a crucial role in incident response and provides a robust platform for mitigating and containing security incidents.

Features of MDE in incident response

MDE offers a comprehensive set of tools and features that support incident response efforts in respect to devices, including the following as the features listed (like real-time alerts and incident dashboards) are accurate for Microsoft Defender for Endpoint. The platform should be contextualized as part of a broader suite of security tools and not as a standalone solution for all SOC needs as **Microsoft Defender for Identities** (**MDI**), **Microsoft Defender for Application** (**MDA**) etc. are separate product and SOC team separately manages incidents for such platform on the respective portals:

- **Real-time alerts**: MDE continuously monitors endpoint activities and provides real-time alerts when suspicious behavior is detected. This proactive approach allows security teams to identify potential incidents as they unfold.

- **Incident dashboard**: MDE offers an incident dashboard that provides a centralized view of ongoing security incidents. This dashboard displays relevant information, such as affected endpoints, users, and the severity of the incident.

- **Incident investigation**: SOC analysts can use MDE to conduct in-depth investigations into security incidents. The platform provides detailed insights into the **tactics, techniques, and procedures (TTPs)** employed by attackers.

- **Automated playbooks**: MDE supports the creation and execution of automated playbooks for incident response. These playbooks help streamline response activities and reduce manual intervention.

- **Response actions**: Security teams can initiate response actions directly from MDE, such as isolating compromised endpoints, blocking malicious processes, and collecting forensic data.

- **Threat intelligence integration**: MDE integrates with threat intelligence feeds to provide additional context for security incidents. Analysts can correlate incident data with known **indicators of compromise (IOCs)** to better understand the threat. While MDE does integrate with threat intelligence feeds, the effectiveness of this integration depends on the quality and relevance of the threat intelligence sources used.

- **Reporting and documentation**: MDE facilitates the generation of incident reports, which are crucial for documenting the incident, the response actions taken, and the lessons learned for future prevention.

Steps to mitigate and contain security incidents

Mitigating and containing security incidents is a multi-step process, and MDE aligns with these best practices to ensure a robust response:

- **Identification**: The first step is to identify and verify the security incident. MDE helps by providing real-time alerts, detailed incident information, and context.

- **Containment**: Once identified, the incident must be contained to prevent it from spreading further. MDE allows for the isolation of compromised endpoints and the blocking of malicious processes or network traffic.

- **Eradication**: After containment, security teams work to eradicate the root cause of the incident. This may involve removing malware, closing vulnerabilities, or securing compromised accounts.

Note: It often requires additional tools and manual intervention as MDE does not have all such feature directly available on the portal.

- **Recovery**: Organizations must return to normal operations as swiftly as possible. MDE helps by facilitating recovery efforts, such as system restoration and data cleanup.

Note: It often requires additional tools and manual intervention as MDE does not have all such feature directly available on the portal.

- **Lessons learned**: Incident response is not complete without a post-incident analysis. MDE supports the documentation of lessons learned, helping organizations improve their security posture.
- **Threat intelligence integration**: Continuous threat intelligence feeds and integration with MDE ensures that organizations are informed about emerging threats and can adapt their incident response strategies accordingly.

Note: MDE does integrate with threat intelligence feeds, but continuous threat intelligence and its application might involve additional tools and services beyond MDE.

Case management in MDE

MDE offers robust case management features that empower SOC teams to create, manage, and track security cases seamlessly.

Features of case management

MDE's case management features provide SOC analysts with a structured and organized approach to handling security incidents. These features include:

- **Case creation**: MDE allows analysts to create new cases to document and investigate security incidents. When an alert or potential threat is identified, it can be converted into a case for further investigation. This initiates a formalized process to assess, contain, and resolve the incident.
- **Incident enrichment**: Within a case, analysts can enrich the incident with additional context and information. This includes details such as the affected endpoints, user accounts, potential IOCs, and the severity of the incident. This rich data helps in understanding the scope and impact of the security event.
- **Collaborative workflow**: MDE's case management fosters collaboration among SOC team members. Multiple analysts can work on the same case simultaneously, sharing insights, findings, and investigation progress. The collaborative approach enhances efficiency and leverages the expertise of the entire team.

Note: Absence of role-based access control and versioning.

- **Task assignment**: Assigning tasks within a case allows for the delegation of responsibilities. Analysts can distribute specific investigative actions, such as collecting forensic data, reviewing logs, or communicating with affected users.

Task assignments streamline the workflow and ensure that critical actions are not overlooked.

Note: It is not fully featured task management solution and comes with limited feature for tracking of task progress and deadlines.

- **Timeline and audit trail**: MDE maintains a comprehensive timeline and audit trail within each case. This feature tracks every action taken by analysts, from the initial case creation to resolution. It provides a chronological record of all activities, fostering transparency and accountability.

- **Evidence collection**: MDE enables the collection of forensic evidence directly within the case. Analysts can gather relevant data, such as memory dumps, file artifacts, or registry keys, to support the investigation. This centralized evidence repository simplifies access and analysis.

Note: While MDE provides some capability for evidence collection, it is generally part of a broader forensic toolkit, and the scope of evidence collection might be limited compared to specialized forensic tools.

- **Status tracking**: Throughout the incident investigation, the case's status can be updated to reflect its progress. Cases can be categorized as *open, in-progress,* or *closed*. This helps in tracking and managing the incident lifecycle.

- **Reporting and documentation**: MDE facilitates the generation of incident reports directly from the case. These reports are invaluable for documenting the incident, detailing the response actions taken, and recording findings for future reference.

Managing security incident response and recovery

This section is a critical component of a robust SOC strategy, focusing on the processes and procedures involved in effectively managing security incidents, with a strong emphasis on coordinated responses and recovery. The following key areas will be explored:

- **Incident response framework**: Begin by introducing the incident response framework, which serves as the foundation for managing security incidents. Discuss the key phases of an incident response, which typically include identification, containment, eradication, recovery, and lessons learned.

- **Coordination and communication**: Emphasize the importance of effective coordination and communication during incident response. Highlight the need for seamless collaboration among SOC team members, IT departments, legal teams, and other stakeholders. Discuss the role of a centralized incident commander in ensuring that responses are well-coordinated.

- **Incident classification and prioritization**: Detail how security incidents are classified and prioritized. Explain the criteria used to assess the severity and potential impact of each incident, guiding the allocation of resources and response efforts.

- **Containment and eradication**: Describe the steps involved in containing and eradicating security threats. Highlight the importance of swift containment to prevent further damage. Discuss various methods, tools, and best practices used for threat eradication.

- **Recovery and restoration**: Address the recovery phase, focusing on how to restore affected systems and services to their normal state. Explain the importance of monitoring and validation to ensure that threats are entirely eradicated, and systems are secure.

- **Lessons learned and continuous improvement**: Discuss the significance of conducting post-incident reviews and documenting lessons learned. Emphasize how these insights can be used to improve incident response processes, refine security policies, and enhance the overall security posture.

- **Automation and tools**: Highlight the role of automation and specialized incident response tools in streamlining response efforts. Explain how automation can reduce response times and enhance efficiency during incident management.

- **Legal and compliance considerations**: Touch upon the legal and compliance aspects of incident response. Explain how compliance requirements, such as reporting to regulatory bodies, impact the incident response process.

Responding to threats

MDE portal gives good summary of identified threats on the portal under *Threat intelligence* page and once you click on one of the *Latest threats* then it redirects page that gives good summary of Analytic Report, impacted assets, related incidents and good summary of incident is provided so that you can take effective actions on the incident.

The following figure showcases **Threat analytics** and summary of threats like **Ransome** and **Phishing** attempt happened in the organization:

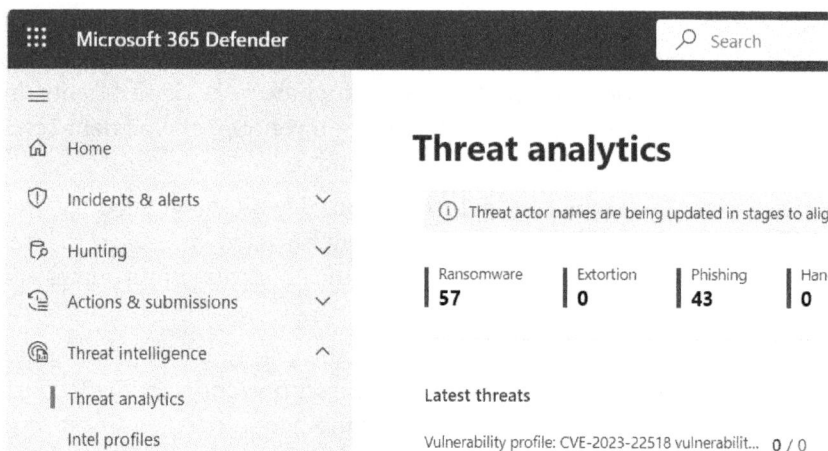

Figure 8.1: Threat analytics features under Threat intelligence

Each page covers the following information on the page that helps in easy navigation and provides insight into the overall impact:

- Overview
- Analyst report
- Related incidents
- Impacted assets
- Endpoint exposure
- Recommended actions

A brief insight of each page under Threat analytics is provided as follows. This is an important page that helps SOC analyst in reviewing in situation of incident analysis.

- **Overview page**: The overview page gives the incident summary for better understanding that also helps in saving many analyst hours, as shown in the following figure:

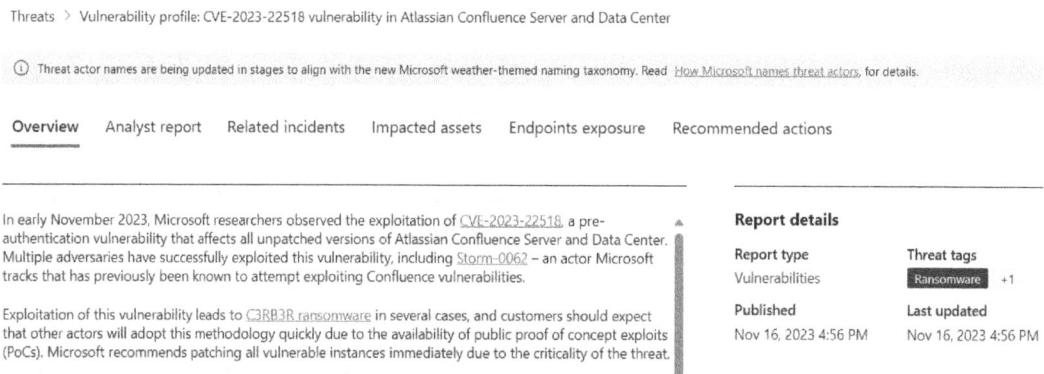

Figure 8.2: Threat analytics overview page

- **Executive summary**: This page rephrases the summary for executive reference, as shown in the following figure:

Overview   **Analyst report**   Related incidents   Impacted assets   Endpoints exposure   Recommended actions

Executive summary

In early November 2023, Microsoft researchers observed the exploitation of CVE-2023-22518, a pre-authentication vulnerability that affects all unpatched versions of Atlassian Confluence Server and Data Center. Multiple adversaries have successfully exploited this vulnerability, including Storm-0062 – an actor Microsoft tracks that has previously been known to attempt exploiting Confluence vulnerabilities.

Exploitation of this vulnerability leads to C3RB3R ransomware in several cases, and customers should expect that other actors will adopt this methodology quickly due to the availability of public proof of concept exploits (PoCs). Microsoft recommends patching all vulnerable instances immediately due to the criticality of the threat.

Microsoft Defender for Endpoint detects malicious activities associated with this vulnerability and Microsoft Defender Antivirus protects and remediates files, like web shells and ransomware payloads, dropped in these attacks. Organizations can use scanning tools like Microsoft External Surface Attack Management (EASM) to help identify vulnerable web-facing assets. Organizations should quickly triage the referenced alerts to determine and scope impact, and investigate if the attacks spread within the organization. Refer to Microsoft's report on ransomware as a service (RaaS) for a holistic security guide on defending against ransomware.

Figure 8.3: Threat analytics analyst report for execute summary

- **Impacted assets**: This page gives references for the impacted devices, users and email inboxes with alerts over time, as shown in the following figure:

Overview   Analyst report   Related incidents   **Impacted assets**   Endpoints exposure   Recommended actions

Devices with alerts over time ⓘ	Users with alerts over time ⓘ	Mailboxes with alerts over time ⓘ
No data available	No data available	No data available
No data to display	No data to display	No data to display
▪ Devices with active alerts ▪ Devices with resolved alerts	▪ Users with active alerts ▪ Users with resolved alerts	▪ Mailboxes with active alerts ▪ Mailboxes with resolved alerts

Apps with alerts over time ⓘ	Cloud resources with alerts over time ⓘ
No data available	No data available

Figure 8.4: Threat analytics impacted assets

- **Recommended actions**: This page gives required recommendation that SOC analyst can take to remediate and avoid future occurrences for such incident. It also gives you the tracking option under Status column, as shown in the following figure:

Overview   Analyst report   Related incidents   Impacted assets   Endpoints exposure   **Recommended actions**

Perform these actions to address this threat and improve your overall posture. For a broader assessment and more recommended actions, view your secure score.

ⓘ There are new permissions options available for Secure Score. You can now configure users' Secure Score data visibility based on data source.   Learn more about this change.   **Configure in URBAC**

↓ Export   3 items   🔍 Search   ⅀ Filter ≡ (

	Rank	Recommended action	Score impact	Points achieved	Status	Regressed	Have license?	Category
☐	11	Use advanced protection against ransomware	+0.84%	0/9	○ To address	No	Yes	Device
☐	18	Block executable files from running unless they meet a prevalei	+0.84%	0/9	○ To address	No	Yes	Device
☐	109	Enable cloud-delivered protection	+0.75%	8/8	✓ Completed	No	Yes	Device

Figure 8.5: Threat analytics recommendations for action

New options have been recently added in form on the Threat intelligence page to gain more insight into the various threat actors and you can gain more insight before responding on the incident, shown as follows:

- Intel Profiles
- Intel Explorer
- Intel Projects

The following figure shows multistage incident identification and tagging:

Multi-stage incident involving Execution & Lateral movement on multiple endpoints reported by multiple sources

Chain Event Detection   ContosoHotels   SecCxpNinja

↺ Open incident page   ✎ Manage incident

Incident details   ∧

Status	Active
Assigned to	bebischo@microsoft.com
Severity	▮▮▮ High
Incident ID	8812
Classification	Not set
	Set status and classification
Categories	Execution
	Persistence
	Defense evasion
	Credential access
	Discovery
	Lateral movement
Activity time	First Sep 30, 2022, 2:52:29 AM
	Last · Sep 30, 2022, 3:25:25 AM

Impacted entities   ∧

Machine	Risk level	Exposure level
🖥 adfs01	▮▮▮ High	⚠ High

Figure 8.6: Multistage incident identification and tagging

The following figure is another screenshot available on portal that shows the actions that you can take on the alert:

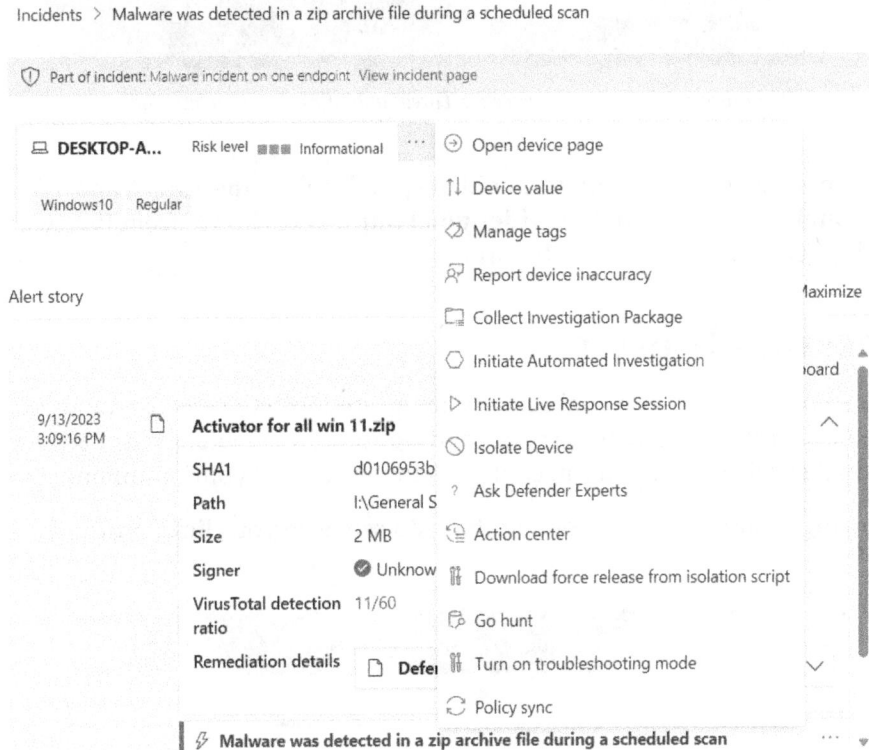

Figure 8.7: Menus showing option that can be taken on device

The following figure gives more options available for beginners to take further action:

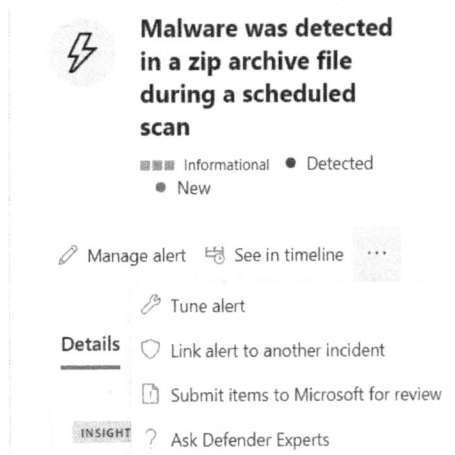

Figure 8.8: More menu or actions available for SOC analyst on web portal

Analyst report reference: The following figure showcases the website with a Microsoft article that gives the latest information about the all the pages covered above:

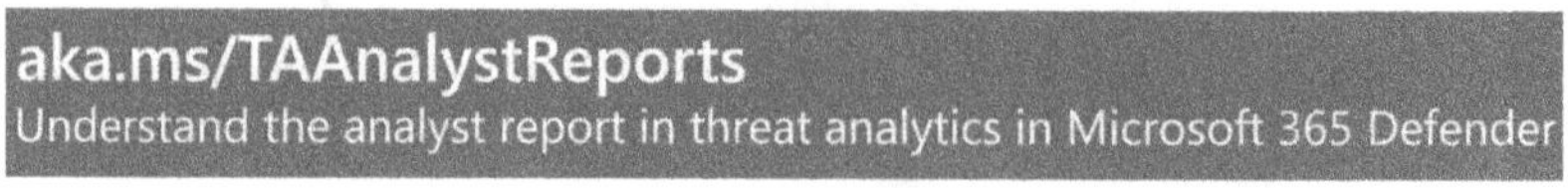

aka.ms/TAAnalystReports
Understand the analyst report in threat analytics in Microsoft 365 Defender

Figure 8.9: Website reference for Threat analytics menu understanding

Note: In case you would like to avoid responding on the threat and like to take professional help then portal provides good options to choose from the available 1st and 3rd party services on the web portal.

Professional services

MDE portal provides professional services integrated into the web portal to manage and respond on security alerts with partners and option is available under **Partner catalog** | **Professional services**, and you can configure things are per your requirements.

The following figure shows the content that you see once you click on the menu:

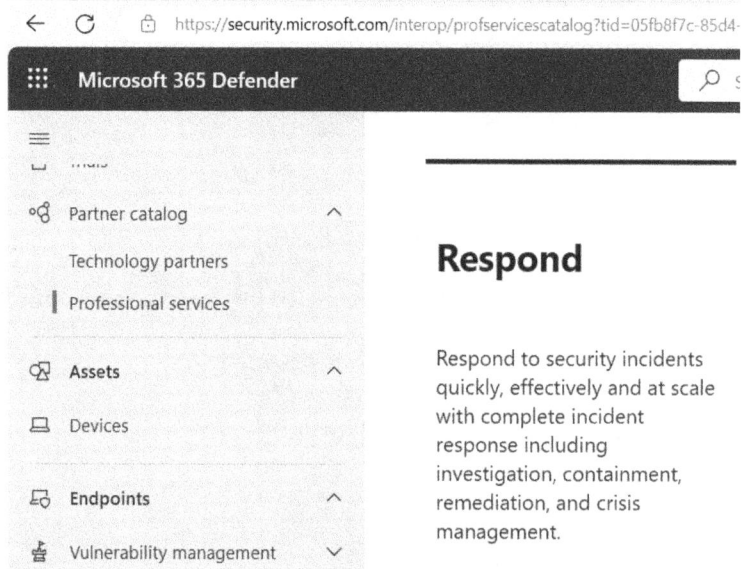

Figure 8.10: Professional services page

Microsoft also supports and enables vendor to participate in responding to threat and some of such service provider options are listed on the page for selection.

Respond services: The following *Figures 8.10* and *8.11* show the first or third-party services listed on the response page:

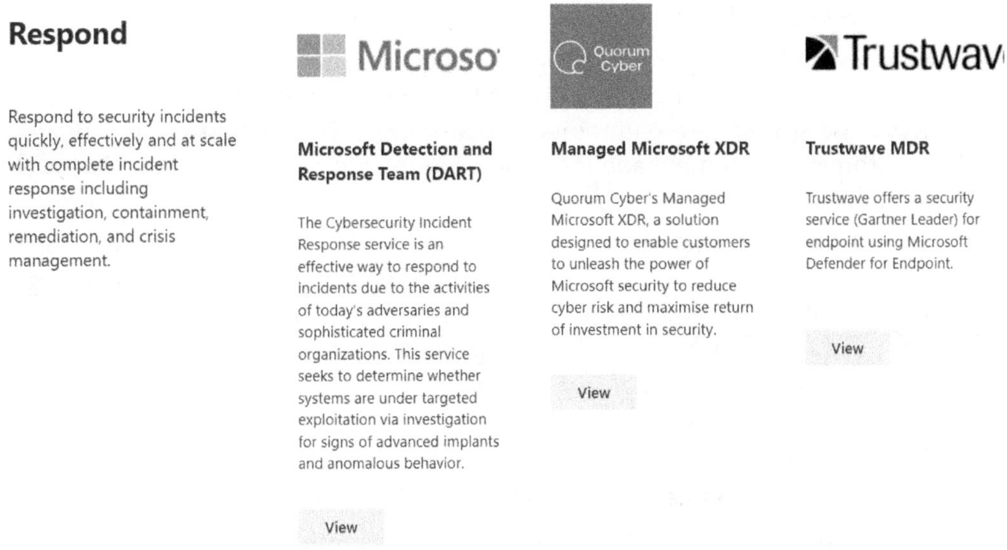

Respend

Respond to security incidents quickly, effectively and at scale with complete incident response including investigation, containment, remediation, and crisis management.

Microsoft Detection and Response Team (DART)

The Cybersecurity Incident Response service is an effective way to respond to incidents due to the activities of today's adversaries and sophisticated criminal organizations. This service seeks to determine whether systems are under targeted exploitation via investigation for signs of advanced implants and anomalous behavior.

View

Managed Microsoft XDR

Quorum Cyber's Managed Microsoft XDR, a solution designed to enable customers to unleash the power of Microsoft security to reduce cyber risk and maximise return of investment in security.

View

Trustwave MDR

Trustwave offers a security service (Gartner Leader) for endpoint using Microsoft Defender for Endpoint.

View

Figure 8.11: Vendor option for incident response

Active Remediation

Red Canary security experts respond to remediate threats on your endpoints, 24x7. Requires Red Canary MDR for Microsoft.

View

Onevinn DFIR

Onevinn DFIR, Digital Defense and Incident Response team, when you are having a breach and you need urgent assistance to gain back control of your IT Environment.

View

Cloud Security Operations Center

We monitor your Microsoft Security Solutions 24/7, respond to threats on your behalf and work closely with your IT to continuously improve your security posture.

View

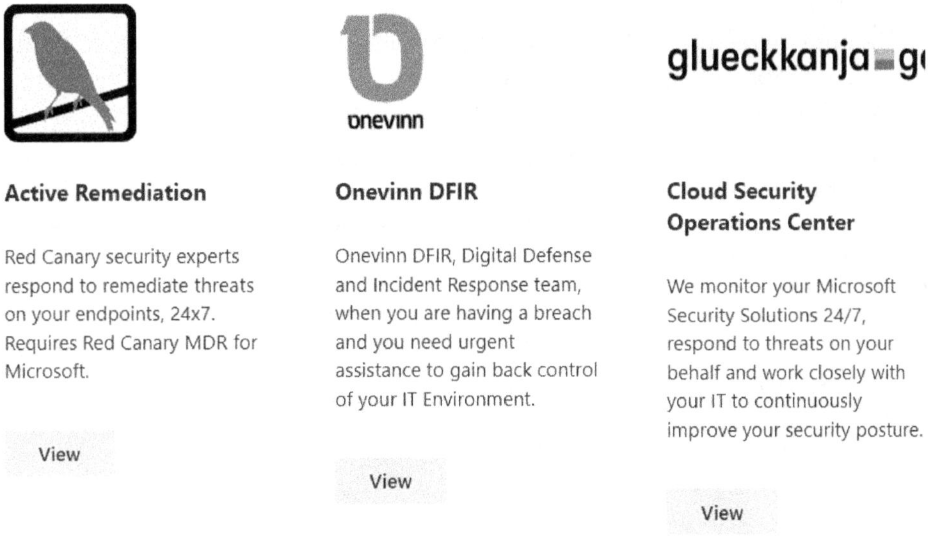

Figure 8.12: Vendor option for incident response

Live response feature

This section is a critical component in the arsenal of tools available to incident responders within a SOC and will provide a comprehensive understanding of the Live Response feature, emphasizing its significance in real-time response to security incidents and its practical applications.

The following key points will be covered for live response:

- **Overview of live response**: To begin, we will introduce the Live Response feature and explain its core functionality. Live Response allows SOC analysts to remotely access and investigate endpoints in real-time. This capability is invaluable for rapid threat containment and incident response. Please refer *Figure 8.14* about how to initiate live response.

- **Capabilities and use cases**: We will explore the specific capabilities of Live Response, such as file retrieval, memory analysis, process inspection, and registry checks. Real-world use cases will be explored, showcasing how Live Response can be applied to gather crucial data during live security incidents.

- **Benefits for incident response**: Highlight the advantages of Live Response in incident response scenarios. Its ability to collect live data from endpoints enables analysts to make informed decisions swiftly. Discuss how it aids in reducing incident response times and limiting potential damage.

- **Best practices and workflows**: Provide insights into best practices for utilizing Live Response effectively. Discuss workflow recommendations for SOC teams, including when and how to use the feature, as well as procedures for data collection and analysis.

- **Remote investigation techniques**: Explain the techniques involved in remote investigations using Live Response. This may include memory forensics, artifact collection, and analyzing live system data to identify threats and vulnerabilities.

- **Integration with other SOC tools**: Highlight how Live Response can be integrated with other security tools commonly used in a SOC environment. This interoperability enhances the capabilities of incident responders and allows for a more holistic approach to security.

You can click on 3 dots (**...**) as shown in the following figure on the concerned incident page on the concerned device name and can **Initiate Live Response Session** and other similar actions, as shown in the following figure:

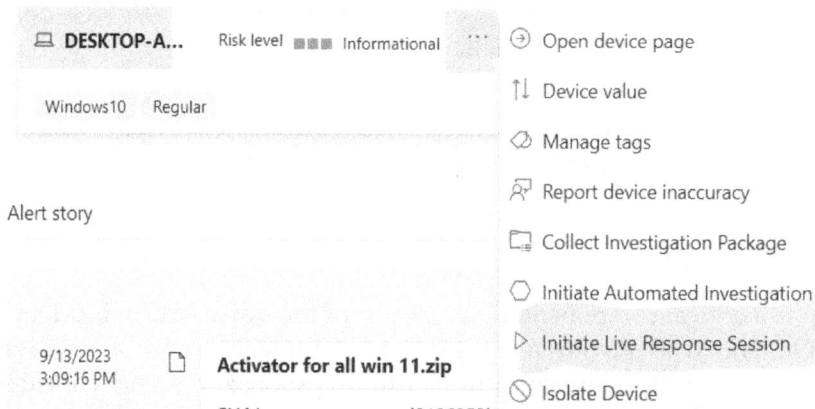

Figure 8.13: *Live Response Session selection option on the onboarded device*

Device summary page (*Figure 8.14*) gives you all the important insight that as security engineer you should be aware of. It gives **key performance indicator** (**KPI**) like Vulnerabilities Count categorizing them into critical and high, Last scan time, OS version, Domain name etc., of the device in concern to security risk and exposure level, as shown in the following figure:

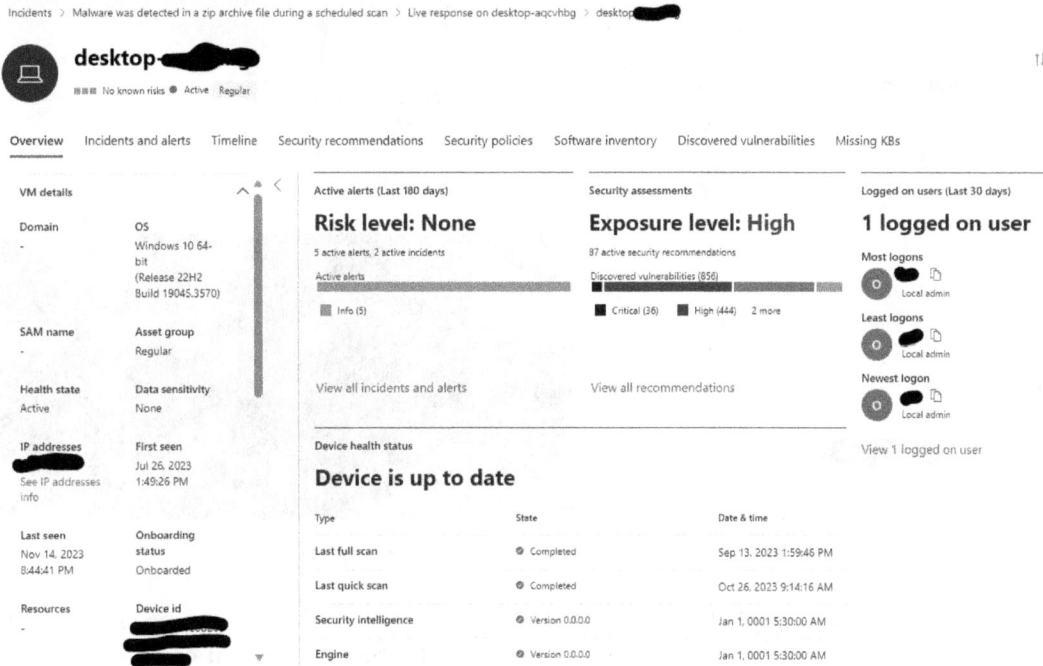

Figure 8.14: Device summary page

When you select the live response option that will show you progress of it, as shown in the following:

Live Response

Loading...

Figure 8.15: Live Response progress indicator during option selection

- **Live response on device page**: In a moment, a page will open a session to the device so that you can run the required command as part of incident management. Live log analysis, some troubleshooting steps or removal of some binary etc., are visible, as depicted in the following figure:

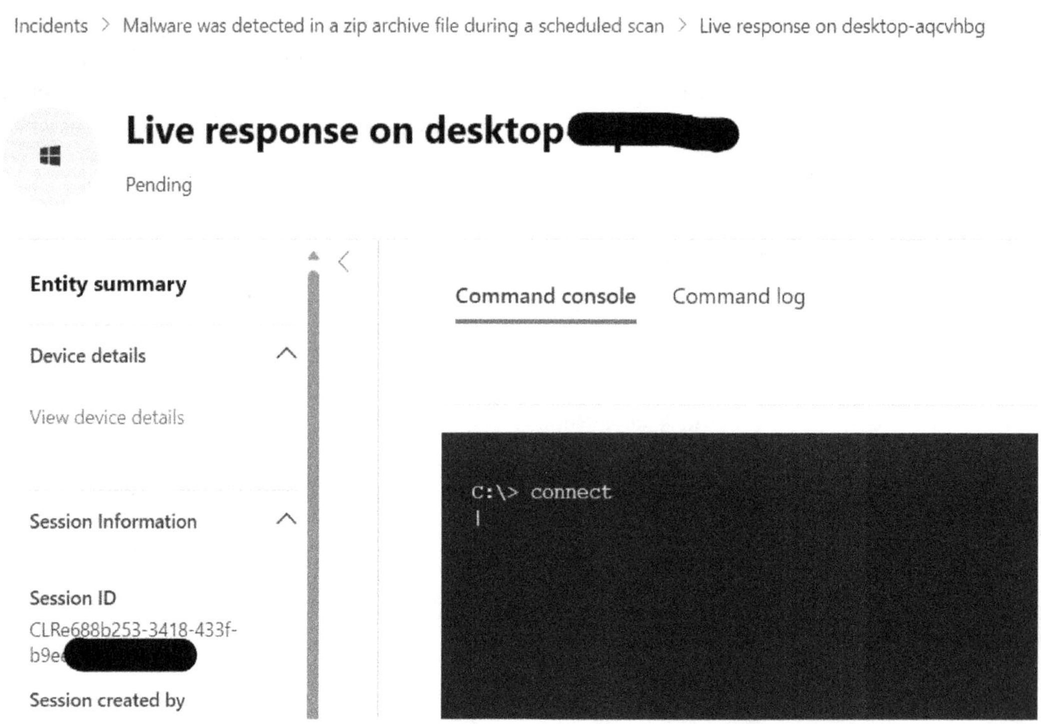

Incidents > Malware was detected in a zip archive file during a scheduled scan > Live response on desktop-aqcvhbg

Live response on desktop

Pending

Entity summary		Command console Command log
Device details	∧	
View device details		
		`C:\> connect`
Session Information	∧	
Session ID		
CLRe688b253-3418-433f-b9e		
Session created by		

Figure 8.16: OS command prompt provided during live response

You can upload the scripts to the effected device to take further action, as shown in the following figure. It gives you the serial port console that means you cannot just copy/paste on the session or command prompt so the web portal gives you the option to upload file/script that you can run during live session:

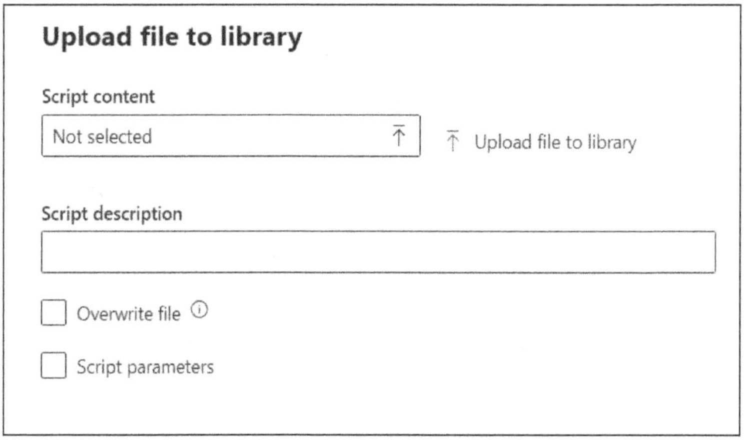

Upload file to library

Script content

| Not selected | ↑ |

↑ Upload file to library

Script description

☐ Overwrite file ⓘ

☐ Script parameters

Figure 8.17: Page providing option to upload some script

Automated investigation

Automated investigation is another feature on MDE web portal that is much useful for SOC analyst and saves hours in troubleshooting the security incident. The following steps will help you in running an automated investigation:

1. You can also **Initiate Automated Investigation** in case you would like handover investigation to MDE intelligence, and it will give summary at the end, as shown in the following figure:

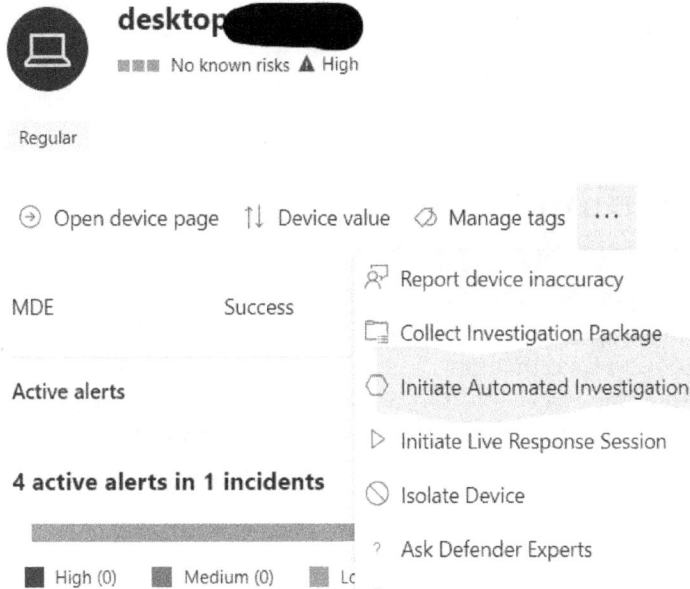

Figure 8.18: Menu showing to initiate AI action on device

2. Once you start an automated investigation, you can find such details under the Incident and Alerts page, as shown in the following figure:

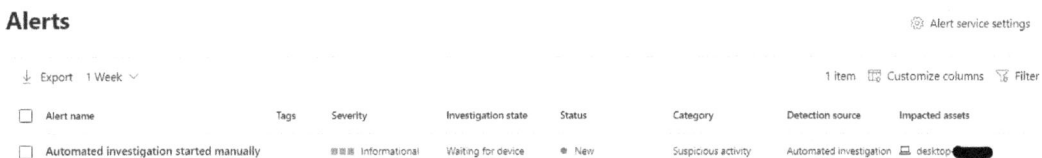

Figure 8.19: Alert window showing AI action taken on the window

3. Collect the investigation package, as shown in the following figure:

Collect investigation package from desktop

This action will gather information about the device. Once completed, you can download and view the package.

Comment:

Confirm   Close

Figure 8.20: Collect investigation page example

Device isolation

Once SOC engineer detects the threat, most of the time they isolate the device. This means that the device will get disconnected from the network to avoid further impact in your environment through specific VM instance. However, during troubleshooting many times the engineer needs access to that machine to transfer some scripts for troubleshooting and needs the event logs back from effected or isolated machine to SOC engineer machine. So, MDE portal gives you such option where you can keep Outlook, Skype and MS Teams traffic open so that they can communicate with the machine.

Isolate device

Once you click on the device to isolate, then it will show you the following page that you can leverage to put comment for reference. The following figure shows a screenshot from the Portal, giving you the same option during the step when you would like to isolate the machine from the network:

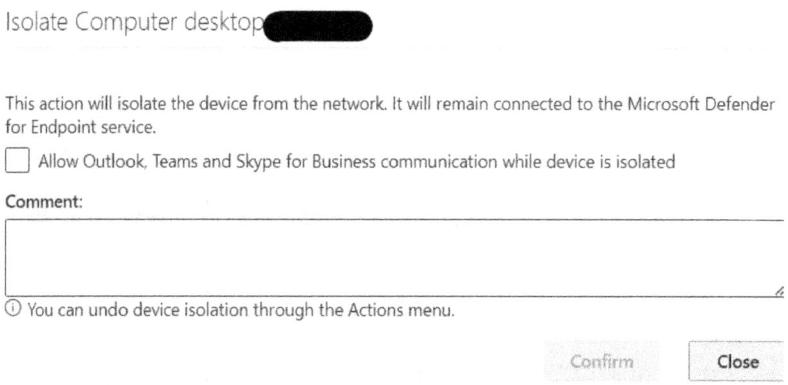

Isolate Computer desktop

This action will isolate the device from the network. It will remain connected to the Microsoft Defender for Endpoint service.

☐ Allow Outlook, Teams and Skype for Business communication while device is isolated

Comment:

ⓘ You can undo device isolation through the Actions menu.

Confirm   Close

Figure 8.21: Device isolation window

Microsoft Defender Expert option during live response

Microsoft Threat Expert aka MTE feature selection is available on the web portal.

> **Informational: Microsoft Threat Expert services are not available by default to all MDE users. They require a subscription to the Microsoft 365 E5 plan, which provides access to the Microsoft Defender Advanced Threat Protection (ATP) security service. Additionally, MDE users need to have MDE Plan 2 licensed and enabled on eligible devices.**

Microsoft Threat Expert services consist of two components:

- **Experts on demand:** This is a service that allows customers to consult with Microsoft threat experts on relevant detections and adversaries.
- **Targeted attack notifications**: This service provides proactive hunting, prioritization, and alerts that are tailored to organizations.

> **Note: If you are interested in using Microsoft Threat Expert services, you can apply through the Windows Defender Security Center or contact your account team or Microsoft representative for more information.**

The following figure showcases the page showing MTE submission option so that MTE professional can jump in to help with security incident:

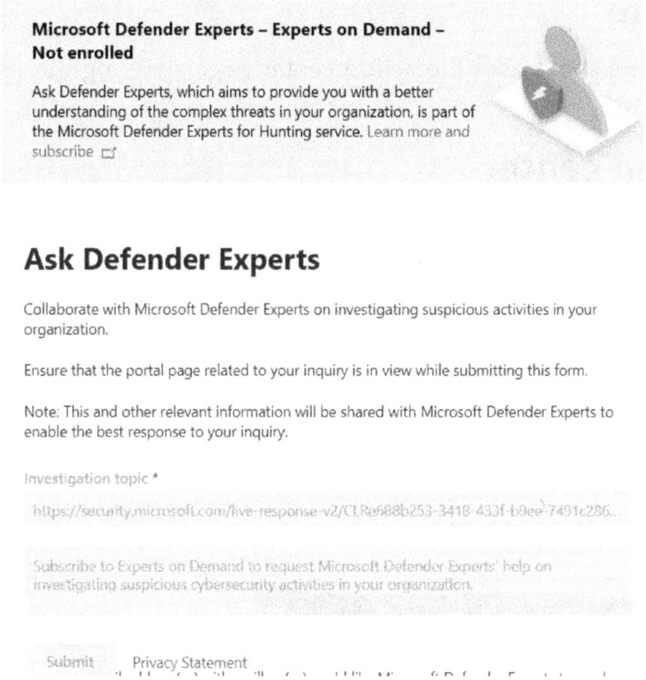

Figure 8.22: Microsoft Threat Expert service usage page

Device value option

Device value is another important labelling feature given on the MDE web portal so that you can define the criticality of the device, as shown in the following figure:

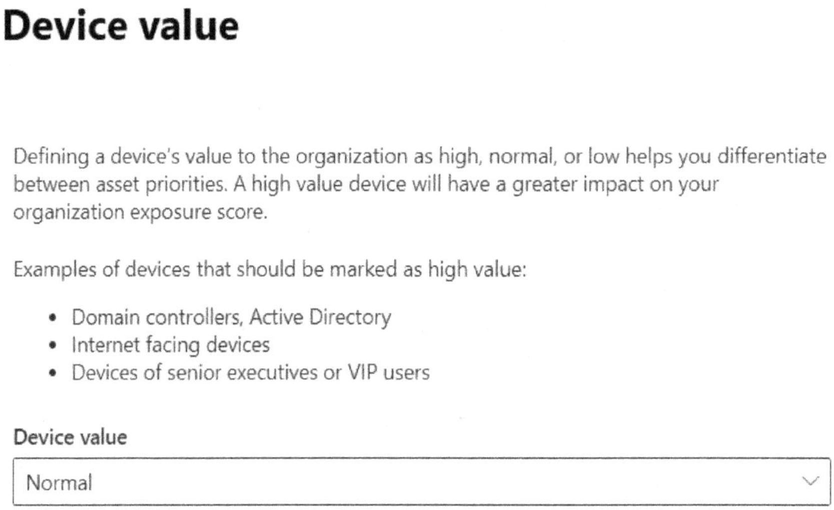

Device value

Defining a device's value to the organization as high, normal, or low helps you differentiate between asset priorities. A high value device will have a greater impact on your organization exposure score.

Examples of devices that should be marked as high value:

- Domain controllers, Active Directory
- Internet facing devices
- Devices of senior executives or VIP users

Device value

Normal	⌄

Figure 8.23: Device value selection page

Action centre

The following figure showcases the action center page showing the option available for your brief overview:

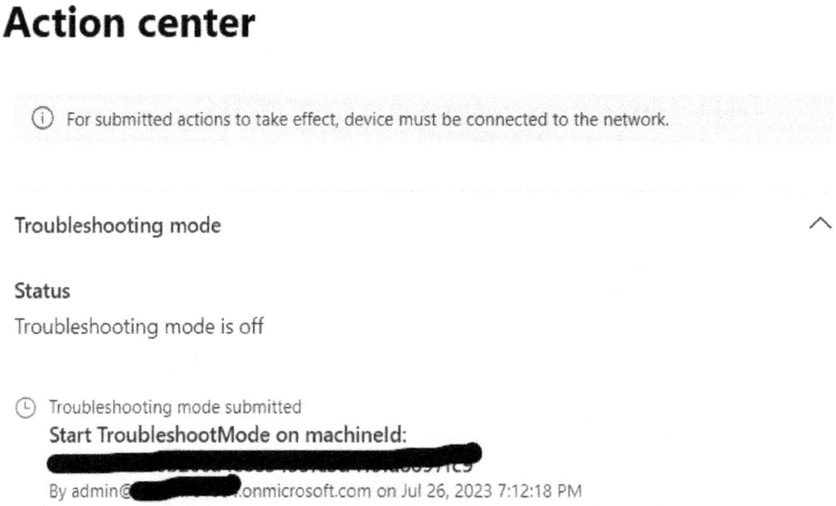

Action center

ⓘ For submitted actions to take effect, device must be connected to the network.

Troubleshooting mode ⌃

Status
Troubleshooting mode is off

🕐 Troubleshooting mode submitted
Start TroubleshootMode on machineId:

By admin@███████onmicrosoft.com on Jul 26, 2023 7:12:18 PM

Figure 8.24: Action center page

Conclusion

In conclusion, the chapter has provided a comprehensive overview of crucial aspects of incident response and recovery within a SOC. Throughout this chapter, we explored the multifaceted dimensions of threat response, ranging from regulatory compliance considerations to advanced incident response tools and methodologies.

We began by emphasizing the significance of regulatory compliance within a SOC setting, underlining the importance of adhering to industry-specific regulations and legal frameworks. Compliance is not just a legal requirement; it is a fundamental aspect of securing an organization's digital assets and maintaining trust.

Next, we explored the Live Response feature, an invaluable tool for incident responders. We uncovered its capabilities, practical applications, and best practices, highlighting how it empowers SOC teams to respond in real-time to evolving security incidents.

Managing security incident response and recovery processes was another critical focal point. We discussed the various phases of incident response, including containment, eradication, and recovery, emphasizing the importance of coordination and communication among team members and departments to ensure a swift and effective response.

This chapter equips readers with the knowledge and tools necessary to respond to security incidents effectively, ensure regulatory compliance, and harness advanced techniques to enhance their organization's security posture. By mastering the skills presented in this chapter, SOC teams are better prepared to face the ever-evolving landscape of cybersecurity threats and challenges.

In next chapter, you will learn about the endpoint vulnerability management that give insight about the industry fundamentals behind the CVE and related items around it.

Join our book's Discord space

Join the book's Discord Workspace for Latest updates, Offers, Tech happenings around the world, New Release and Sessions with the Authors:

https://discord.bpbonline.com

CHAPTER 9

Endpoint Vulnerability Management

Introduction

Reducing cyber risk requires comprehensive risk-based vulnerability management to identify, assess, remediate, and track all your biggest vulnerabilities across your most critical assets, all in a single solution.

Defender Vulnerability Management delivers asset visibility, intelligent assessments, and built-in remediation tools for Windows, macOS, Linux, Android, iOS, and network devices. Leveraging Microsoft threat intelligence, breach likelihood predictions, business contexts, and devices assessments, Defender Vulnerability Management rapidly and continuously prioritizes the biggest vulnerabilities on your most critical assets and provides security recommendations to mitigate risk.

> **Note:** Microsoft Defender Vulnerability Management (MD VM) and Threat Vulnerability Management (TVM) are two separate things but are very much similar but in this chapter, we might interchangeably use it in our context. TVM is a top-level umbrella term whereas MD VM is Microsoft's implementation of it. CVE stands for Common Vulnerabilities and Exposures.

The following figure gives you key services or the core functionality of the **Microsoft Defender Vulnerability Management** (MD VM) feature on the MDE product:

Figure 9.1: *MD TVM coverage overview*

Structure

In this chapter, we will cover the following topics:

- Principles of MDE TVM
- Risk management
- TVM principles
- Understanding critical vulnerabilities
- General CVE understanding
- Web portal TVM menu

Objectives

The ultimate objective of a threat and vulnerability management solution is to prevent security incidents from happening in the first place, because when they happen, it will cost you time, effort, money and even your customer's trust.

One effective method to deter attacks and handle incidents involves proactively avoiding their occurrence. Achieving this involves fortifying your assets and bolstering your overall security stance. The initial step entails obtaining comprehensive visibility into all assets and evaluating them for vulnerabilities and misconfigurations. While on-site options are available, the hurdle lies in gaining oversight and management over remote assets beyond the confines of your on-site network. The statement that cloud-based solutions excel at managing remote assets may oversimplify the complexities involved in securing remote assets compared to on-premises solutions.

Principle of MDE TVM

The philosophy of MDE TVM is based on the following three key principles:

- Continuous discovery
- Threat and business intelligent prioritization
- Automated remediation

The following figure is the graphical representation of TVM service offering by MDE:

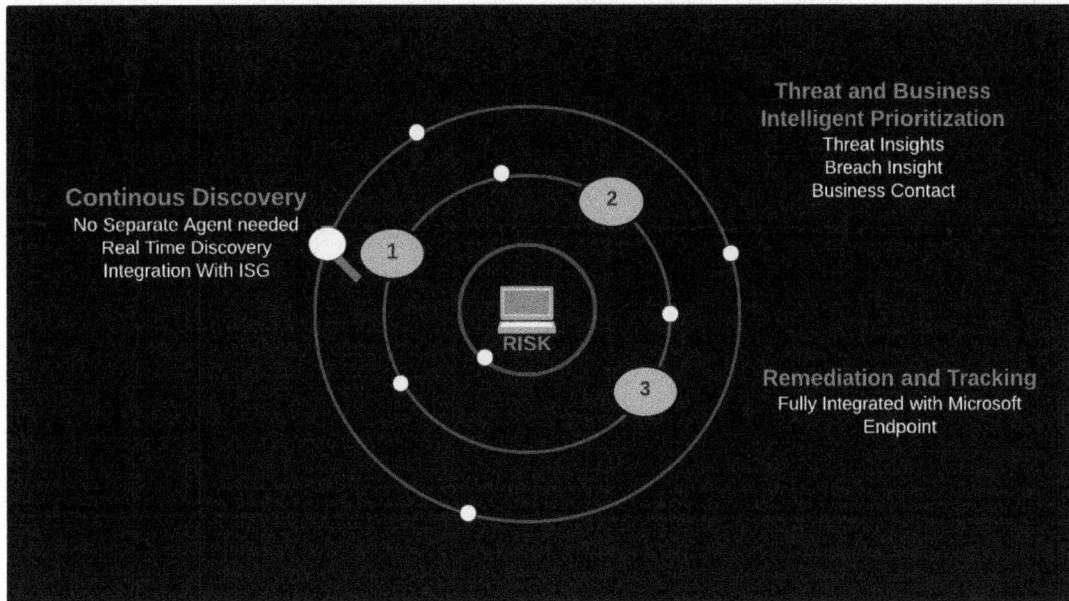

Figure 9.2: TVM overview or TVM service offering

The following is a brief overview of MDE **Vulnerability Management** (**VM**) features:

- **Continuous discovery**: MDE TVM provides continuous asset discovery and monitoring to identify vulnerabilities in real-time. This helps organizations stay up to date with the latest vulnerabilities and take proactive measures to mitigate risks.

- **Threat and business intelligent prioritization**: MDE TVM leverages Microsoft threat intelligence, breach likelihood predictions, business contexts, and device assessments to prioritize vulnerabilities based on the threat landscape and detections in your organization. This helps organizations focus on the most critical vulnerabilities and take remediation actions accordingly.

- **Automated compensation**: MDE TVM provides built-in remediation tools for Windows, macOS, Linux, Android, iOS, and network devices. This helps organizations seamlessly remediate vulnerabilities and track progress. MDE TVM also provides security recommendations to mitigate risk and reduce cyber security risk across the organization.

Risk management

Risk-based vulnerability management is an approach that prioritizes addressing security vulnerabilities based on their potential impact on an organization's operations and assets. Instead of treating all vulnerabilities equally, this method involves evaluating and managing vulnerabilities by considering their likelihood of being exploited and the potential harm they could cause.

Risk management is at the centre stage and is all about identifying weaknesses (vulnerabilities) and understanding how they can be exploited (threats). With that information, you can focus on which vulnerabilities have the most impact and the likelihood of occurrence (risk level).

Risk sits in between the following:

- Threat
- Asset
- Vulnerability

The following figure shows the Venn diagram represents the Threat, Asset and Vulnerability and highlights the Risky area that should get covered in security products:

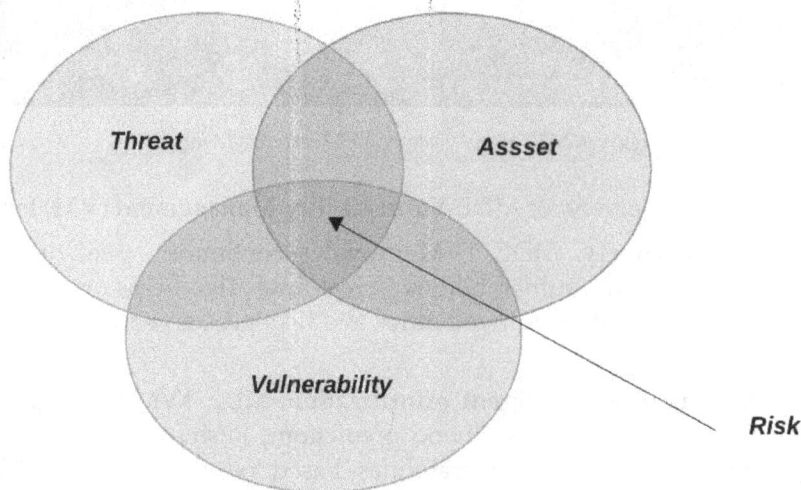

Figure 9.3: Risk sitting among Asset, Threat and Vulnerability representation through Venn Diagram

Important:

- **It helps you discover vulnerabilities using the built-in Windows OS sensors, thus without the need of deploying additional agents or to rely on periodic (network) scans.**

- **TVM feature on MDE Portal was announced around March 2019 and continuously more improvements are getting under this feature.**

- **Microsoft Defender Vulnerability Management uses the same signals in Defender for Endpoint's endpoint protection to scan and detect vulnerabilities.**

Risk based TVM lifecycle

The following are the key steps in risk-based vulnerability management:

1. **Vulnerability assessment**: Identifying and evaluating vulnerabilities within systems, networks, or applications. This involves using tools and techniques to scan for weaknesses.

2. **Risk assessment**: Analyzing the vulnerabilities discovered in the assessment phase to determine their potential impact on the organization if exploited. Factors considered might include the ease of exploit, potential damage, and likelihood of an attack.

3. **Prioritization**: Ranking vulnerabilities based on their risk level. High-risk vulnerabilities that are easier to exploit or could cause significant damage are given priority for immediate remediation.

4. **Mitigation and remediation**: Addressing high-priority vulnerabilities by applying patches, updates, configuration changes, or implementing other security measures to reduce the risk of exploitation.

5. **Continuous monitoring**: Regularly reviewing and reassessing vulnerabilities to adapt to evolving threats and changes in the IT environment. This ensures ongoing protection against emerging risks.

By focusing on high-risk vulnerabilities first and aligning remediation efforts with the organization's specific risk tolerance and business objectives, risk-based vulnerability management aims to maximize the effectiveness of security measures while efficiently utilizing resources.

The following figure shows the TVM Lifecyle that provides an overview of various TVM stages:

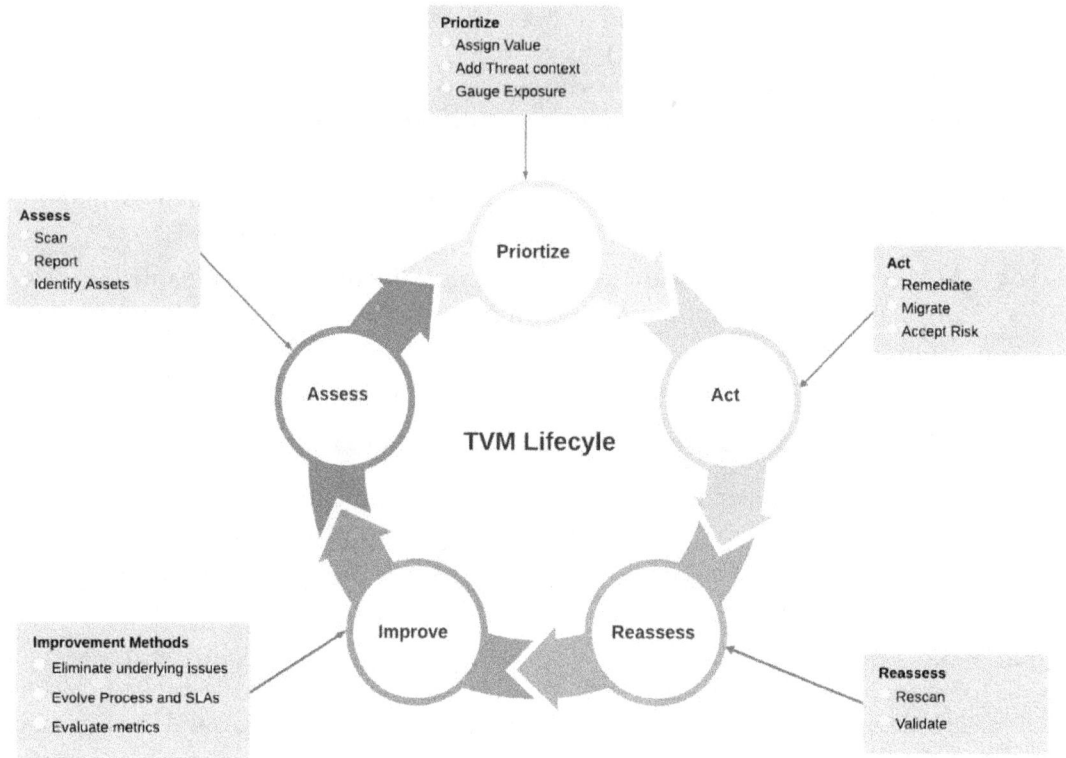

Figure 9.4: TVM Lifecycle

Responsibility of risk management

The following are the two profiles that manage and track vulnerabilities, and the IT administrators responsible for carrying out the remediation activities (patching systems):

- Security administrators (SOC members)
- IT administrators (DevOps, DevSecOps, Sysadmins etc.)

TVM principles

We will cover the TVM principle in detail.

Continuous asset discovery and monitoring

MD Vulnerability Management has built-in and agentless scanners continuously monitor and detect risk in your organization even when devices are not connected to the corporate network.

Consolidated inventories provide a real-time view of your organization's software applications, digital certificates, hardware and firmware, and browser extensions to help you monitor and assess all your organization's assets.

Defender Vulnerability Management delivers asset visibility, intelligent assessments, and built-in remediation tools for Windows, macOS, Linux, Android, iOS, and network devices. Leveraging Microsoft threat intelligence, breach likelihood predictions, business contexts, and devices assessments, Defender Vulnerability Management rapidly and continuously prioritizes the biggest vulnerabilities on your most critical assets and provides security recommendations to mitigate risk. This is shown in the following figure:

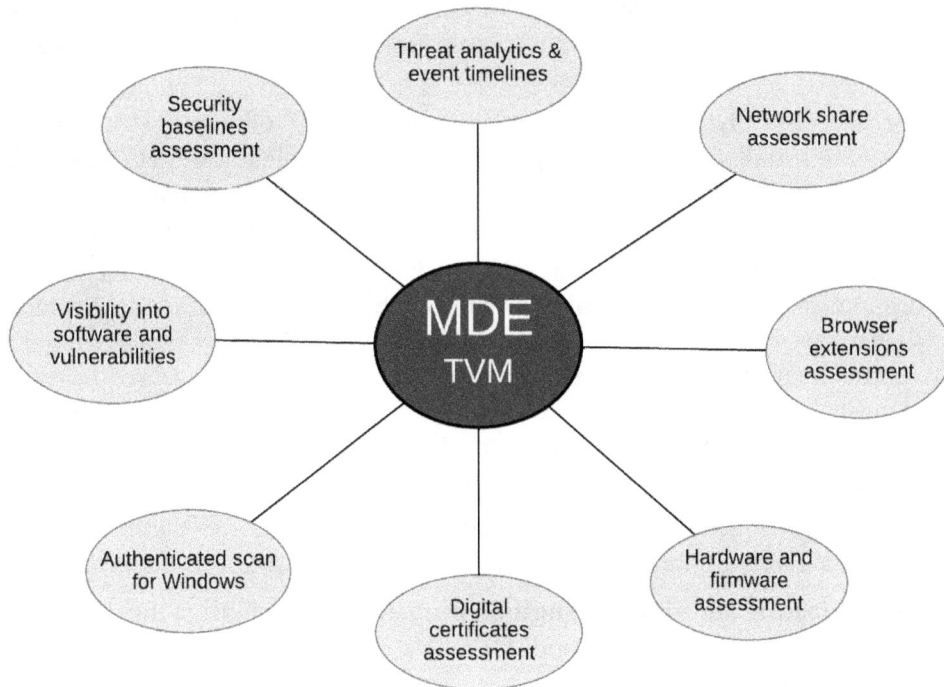

Figure 9.5: *MDE TVM Features*

Advanced vulnerability and configuration assessment tools help you understand and assess your cyber exposure, including:

- **Security baselines assessment**: Create customizable baseline profiles to measure risk compliance against established benchmarks, such as, **Center for Internet Security (CIS)** and **Security Technical Implementation Guides (STIG)**.

- **Visibility into software and vulnerabilities**: Get a view of the organization's software inventory, and software changes like installations, uninstalls, and patches.

- **Network share assessment**: Assess vulnerable internal network shares configuration with actionable security recommendations.

- **Authenticated scan for Windows**: Scan unmanaged Windows devices regularly for software vulnerabilities by providing Microsoft Defender Vulnerability Management with credentials to remotely access the devices.

- **Limitations**: This authenticated scanning is specifically designed for Windows devices and may not be applicable to non-Windows devices. Ensure that credentials and remote access permissions are correctly configured to facilitate the scan process.

- **Threat analytics and event timelines**: Use event timelines, and entity-level vulnerability assessments to understand and prioritize vulnerabilities.

- **Browser extensions assessment**: View a list of the browser extensions installed across different browsers in your organization. View information on an extension's permissions and associated risk levels.

  For example, there are many organizations those who put strict control on software installation on your laptop, but they completely forget the installation management of extensions that can expose the endpoints to threat actors so having this kind of features gives you better control for such software management.

- **Digital certificates assessment**: View a list of certificates installed across your organization in a single central certificate inventory page. Identify certificates before they expire and detect potential vulnerabilities due to weak signature algorithms. All the certificates do have expiry date set and MDE uses the value to alert for the expiration. Digital certificates assessment detects weak signature algorithms by analyzing the cryptographic hash algorithms used in the certificates1. Here is how it works:

  o **Identifying hash algorithms**: The assessment identifies the hash algorithms used in the digital certificates, such as SHA-1, SHA-256, or MD52.

  o **Evaluating algorithm strength**: It evaluates the strength of these algorithms3. Algorithms like SHA-1 and MD5 are considered weak and vulnerable to attacks4.

  o **Detecting vulnerabilities**: By detecting the use of weak algorithms, the assessment highlights potential vulnerabilities that could be exploited by attackers to forge or tamper with certificates.

- **Hardware and firmware assessment**: View a list of known hardware and firmware in your organization organized by system models, processors, and BIOS. Each view includes details such as the name of the vendor, number of weaknesses, threats insights, and the number of exposed devices.

There are two types of discovery available in MDE for TVM, as shown in the following figure:

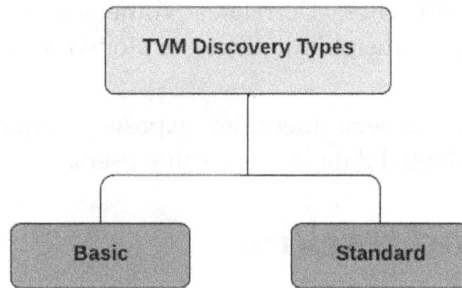

Figure 9.6: MDE TVM Discovery Type

The following figure shows the MDE TVM devices overview that support discovery of unmanaged devices like Network Devices and IoT devices available in network like SmartTV:

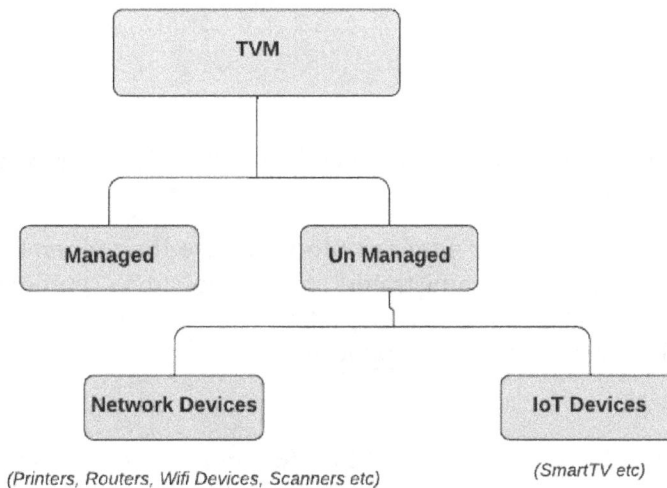

Figure 9.7: MDE TVM Device Coverage Overview

Risk-based intelligent prioritization

Defender Vulnerability Management leverage Microsoft's threat intelligence, breach likelihood predictions, business contexts, and device assessments to quickly prioritize the biggest vulnerabilities in your organization. A single view of prioritized recommendations from multiple security feeds, along with critical details including related CVEs and exposed devices, helps you quickly remediate the biggest vulnerabilities on your most critical assets. Risk-based intelligent prioritization helps in handling the following area:

- **Focuses on emerging threats**: Dynamically aligns the prioritization of security recommendations with vulnerabilities currently being exploited in the wild and emerging threats that pose the highest risk.

- **Pinpoints active breaches**: Correlates vulnerability management and EDR insights to prioritize vulnerabilities being exploited in an active breach within the organization.

- **Protects high-value assets**: Identifies exposed devices with business-critical applications, confidential data, or high-value users.

Remediation and tracking

To remediate vulnerabilities, MDE TVM provides built-in remediation tools for the following:

- Windows
- macOS
- Linux
- Android
- iOS
- Network devices

MDE TVM also provides security recommendations to mitigate risk and reduce cyber security risk across the organization.

To request remediation, security administrators can use the vulnerability management capabilities to request IT administrators to remediate a vulnerability from the Recommendation pages to Intune. Security admins can fill out the form, including what they are requesting remediation for, applicable device groups, priority, due date, and optional notes.

> Note: The Service Level Agreement (SLA) for remediation requests in Microsoft Defender Vulnerability Management (TVM) typically ensures that remediation tasks are addressed within a specific timeframe. However, the exact SLA can vary based on the organization's internal processes and the priority level assigned to the request.
>
> For high-priority requests, the SLA might specify a shorter timeframe, such as 24 to 48 hours, while lower-priority requests might have a longer timeframe, such as 7 to 10 business days.

You can find this option under **Web Portal** | **Endpoints** | **Vulnerability Management** | **Remediation**

The following is just a screenshot that we captured here for reference to showcase Remediation feature availability on the security portal:

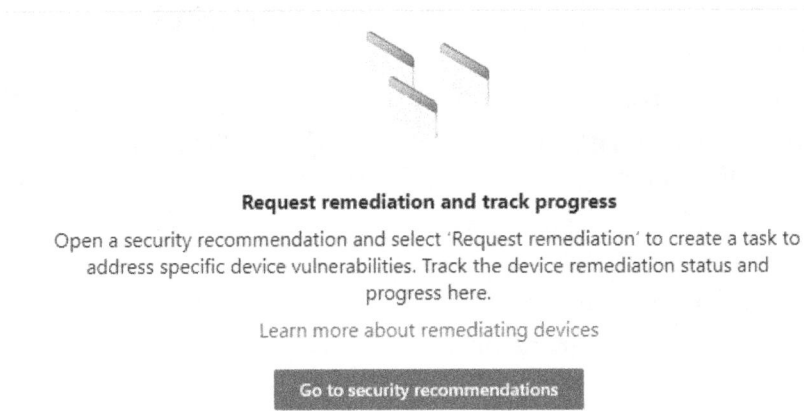

Request remediation and track progress

Open a security recommendation and select 'Request remediation' to create a task to address specific device vulnerabilities. Track the device remediation status and progress here.

Learn more about remediating devices

Go to security recommendations

Figure 9.8: MDE TVM page to request remediation through portal

When you click on **Go to security recommendation** button, it will show recommendations as shown in the following figure. You can get further details and the same page also shows remediation activities:

Security recommendations

Fil

↓ Export   84 items   🔍 Search   ⛃ Filte

Filters: Status: **Active +1** ✕

	Threats	Exposed devices		Remediation type	Remediation activities	Impact ⓘ	T.
5	⚙ 🐞	1 / 1		Software update	0	▼ 81.40	+
	⚙ 🐞	1 / 1		Software update	0	▼ 74.00	+
	⚙ 🐞	1 / 1		Software update	0	▼ 64.80	+

Figure 9.9: Requested Remediation Status page on web portal

To track remediation progress, security administrators can go to the **Remediation page** in **Microsoft Defender Vulnerability Management** (**MDE TVM**) to view the status of their remediation request. The Remediation page provides a comprehensive view of all remediation activities and their status. The page contains the following columns:

- **Recommendation**: This column displays the name of the recommendation that requires remediation.
- **Remediation activity**: This column displays the remediation activity ID.
- **Status**: This column displays the status of the remediation activity. The status can be one of the following: **Not started, In progress, Completed**, or **Failed**.
- **Assigned to:** This column displays the user or group that is assigned to remediate the vulnerability.
- **Due date**: This column displays the due date for the remediation activity.
- **Last updated**: This column displays the date and time when the remediation activity was last updated.

When a remediation activity is completed, the status column is updated to **Completed**. If a remediation activity fails, the status column is updated to **Failed**.

The following figure shows a MDE web portal security recommendations page showcasing active recommendations:

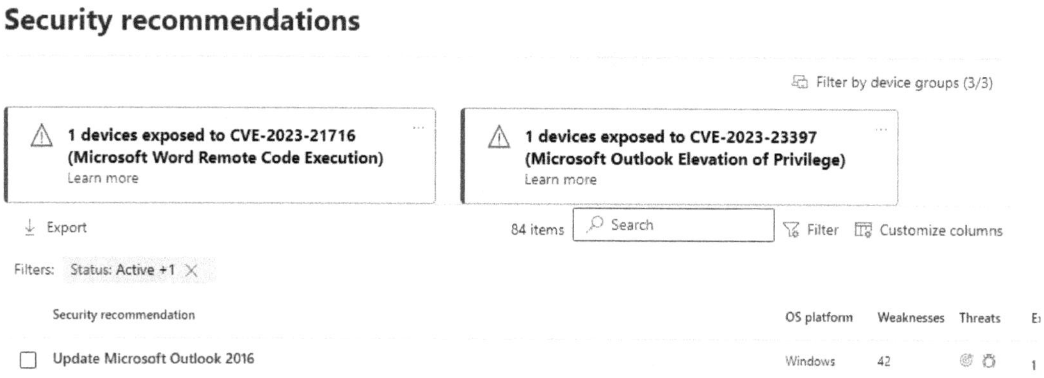

Security recommendations

Figure 9.10: Security recommendation on web portal for a device

Submitting a remediation request creates a remediation activity item within vulnerability management, which can be used for monitoring the remediation progress for this recommendation. This will not trigger remediation or apply any changes to devices. Notify your IT Administrator about the new request and have them log into Intune to approve or reject the request and start a package deployment.

The following figure shows an example of security recommendation showing remediation required and you can click button to request it:

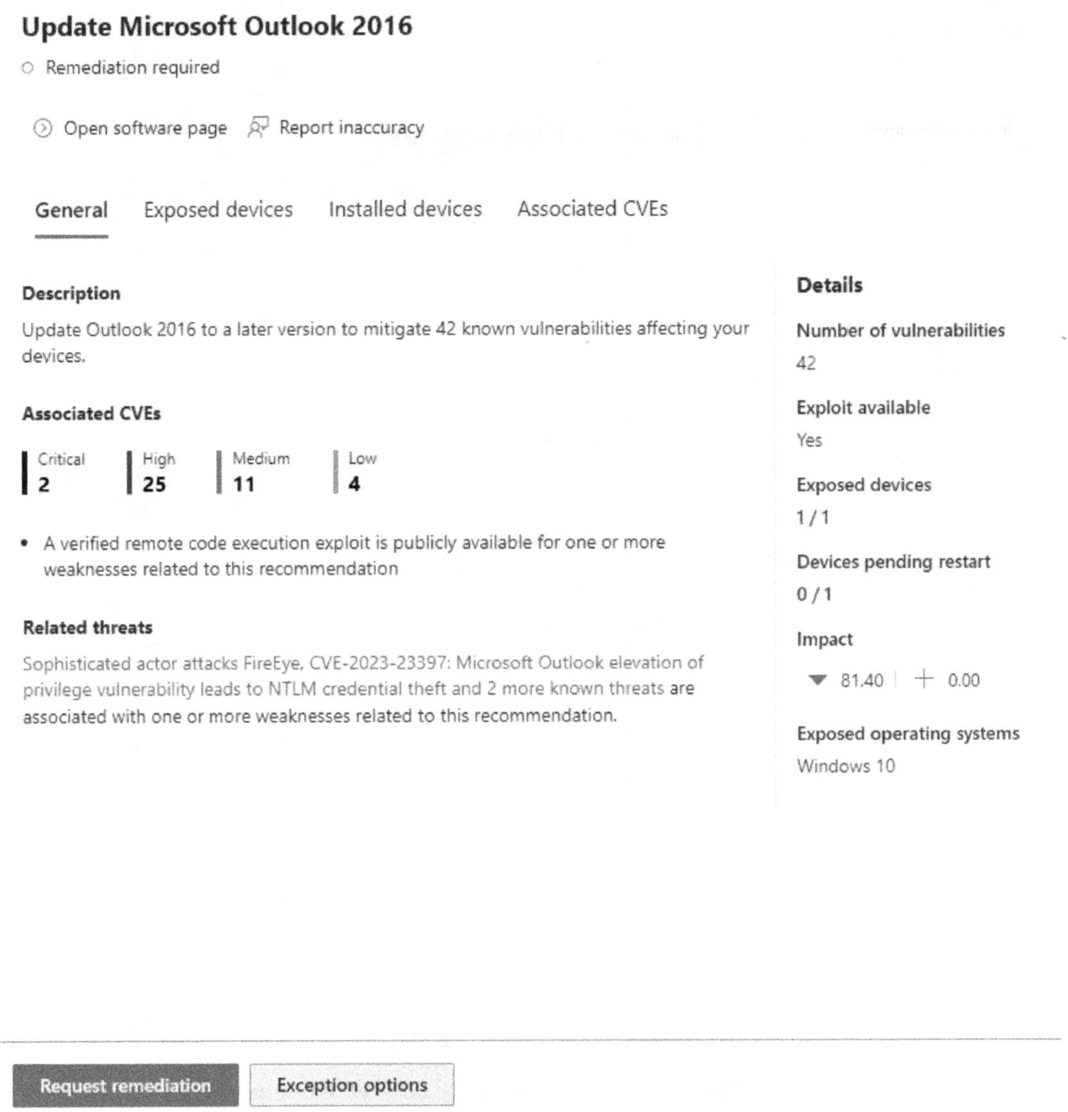

Update Microsoft Outlook 2016

○ Remediation required

⊙ Open software page   ⅊ Report inaccuracy

General   Exposed devices   Installed devices   Associated CVEs

Description

Update Outlook 2016 to a later version to mitigate 42 known vulnerabilities affecting your devices.

Associated CVEs

| Critical | High | Medium | Low |
| 2 | 25 | 11 | 4 |

- A verified remote code execution exploit is publicly available for one or more weaknesses related to this recommendation

Related threats

Sophisticated actor attacks FireEye, CVE-2023-23397: Microsoft Outlook elevation of privilege vulnerability leads to NTLM credential theft and 2 more known threats are associated with one or more weaknesses related to this recommendation.

Details

Number of vulnerabilities

42

Exploit available

Yes

Exposed devices

1 / 1

Devices pending restart

0 / 1

Impact

▼ 81.40 | ＋ 0.00

Exposed operating systems

Windows 10

Request remediation   Exception options

Figure 9.11: Active Vulnerability Metadata

Remediation request workflow

The following figures walk us through the remediation request workflow:

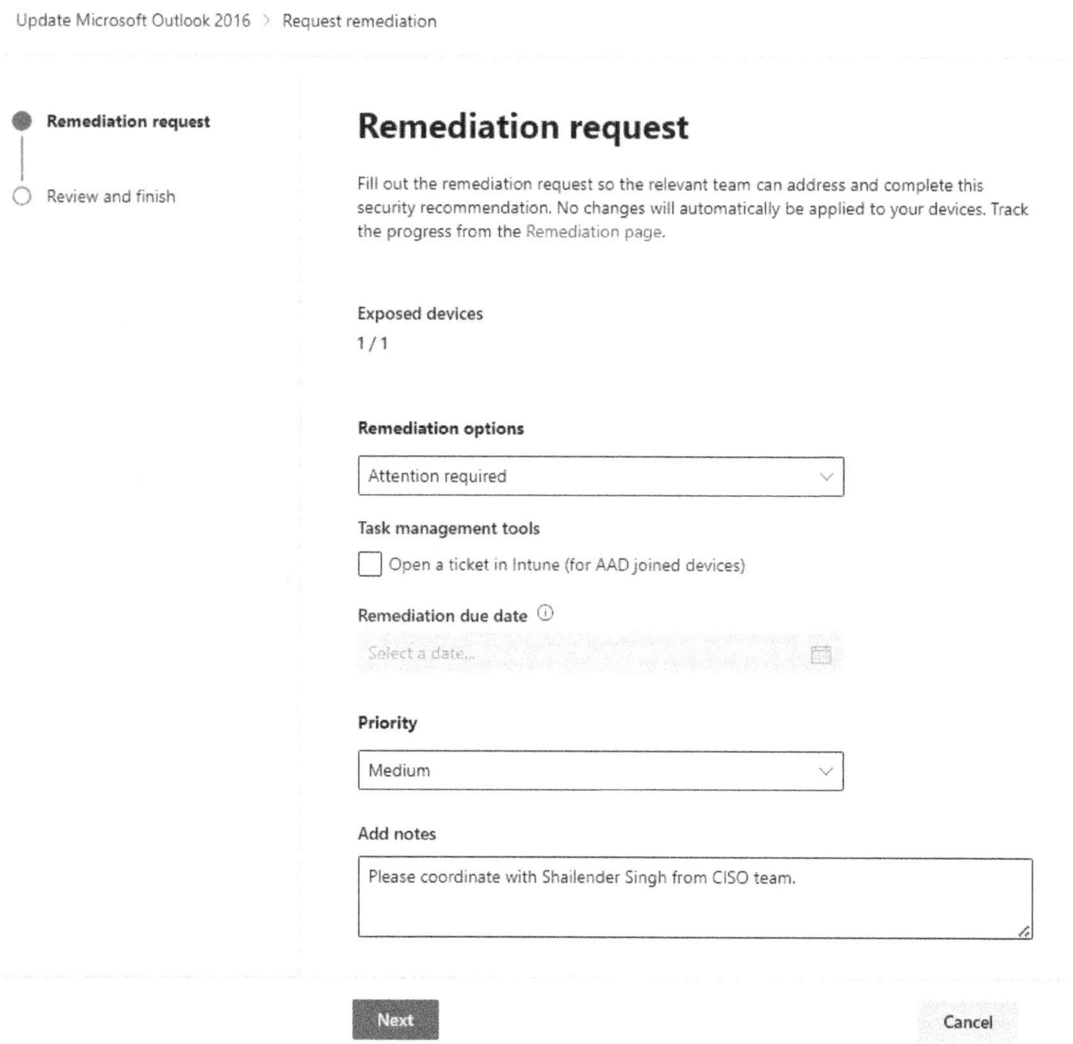

Update Microsoft Outlook 2016 > Request remediation

Remediation request

Review and finish

Remediation request

Fill out the remediation request so the relevant team can address and complete this security recommendation. No changes will automatically be applied to your devices. Track the progress from the Remediation page.

Exposed devices
1 / 1

Remediation options

| Attention required | ∨ |

Task management tools

☐ Open a ticket in Intune (for AAD joined devices)

Remediation due date ⓘ

| Select a date... | 🛗 |

Priority

| Medium | ∨ |

Add notes

| Please coordinate with Shailender Singh from CISO team. |

[Next]   Cancel

Figure 9.12: MDE page to request to remediate on web portal

The following figure after requesting the remediation on the web portal:

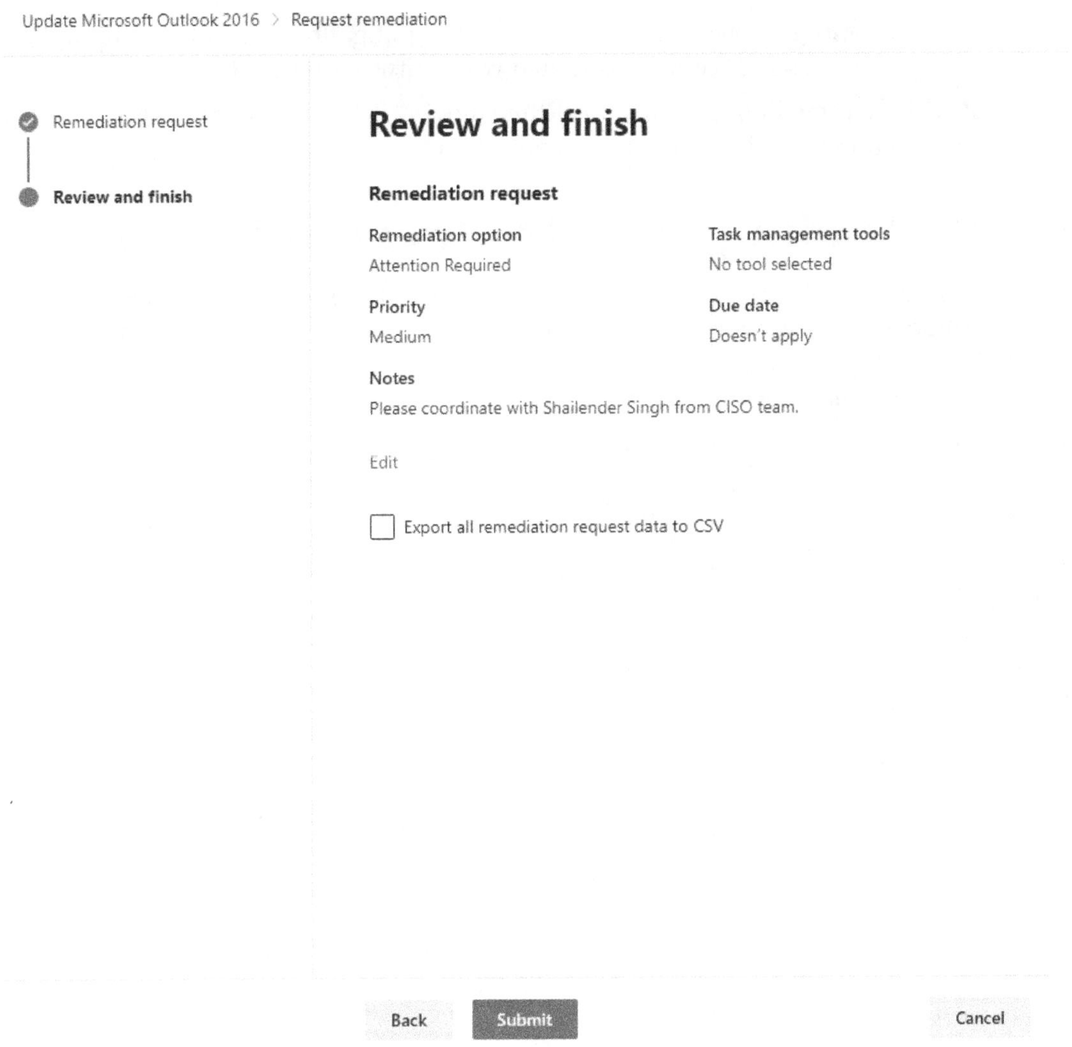

Update Microsoft Outlook 2016 〉 Request remediation

Remediation request

Review and finish

Review and finish

Remediation request

Remediation option	**Task management tools**
Attention Required	No tool selected
Priority	**Due date**
Medium	Doesn't apply

Notes

Please coordinate with Shailender Singh from CISO team.

Edit

☐ Export all remediation request data to CSV

Back   Submit   Cancel

Figure 9.13: Request remediation review page before submission

To track remediation progress, security administrators can go to the Remediation page to view the status of their remediation request. They can also select remediation options to triage and track the remediation tasks and select exception options and track active exceptions.

Enable security administrators and IT administrators to collaborate and seamlessly remediate issues with built-in workflows and the following are the coverage area:

- **Remediation requests sent to IT**: Create a remediation task in Microsoft Intune from a specific security recommendation.

- **Block vulnerable applications**: Mitigate risk with the ability to block vulnerable applications for specific device groups.

- **Alternate mitigations**: Gain insights on other mitigations, such as configuration changes that can reduce risk associated with software vulnerabilities.

- **Real-time remediation status**: Real-time monitoring of the status and progress of remediation activities across the organization.

Understanding critical vulnerabilities

There are so many vulnerabilities disclosed but you must identify the exploited one and need to mitigate in case those are available in your environment. Such vulnerabilities should be your top priority as SOC or IT administrator engineer that your security team should be worried about most.

The following figure is the pictorial representation of critical vulnerability understanding:

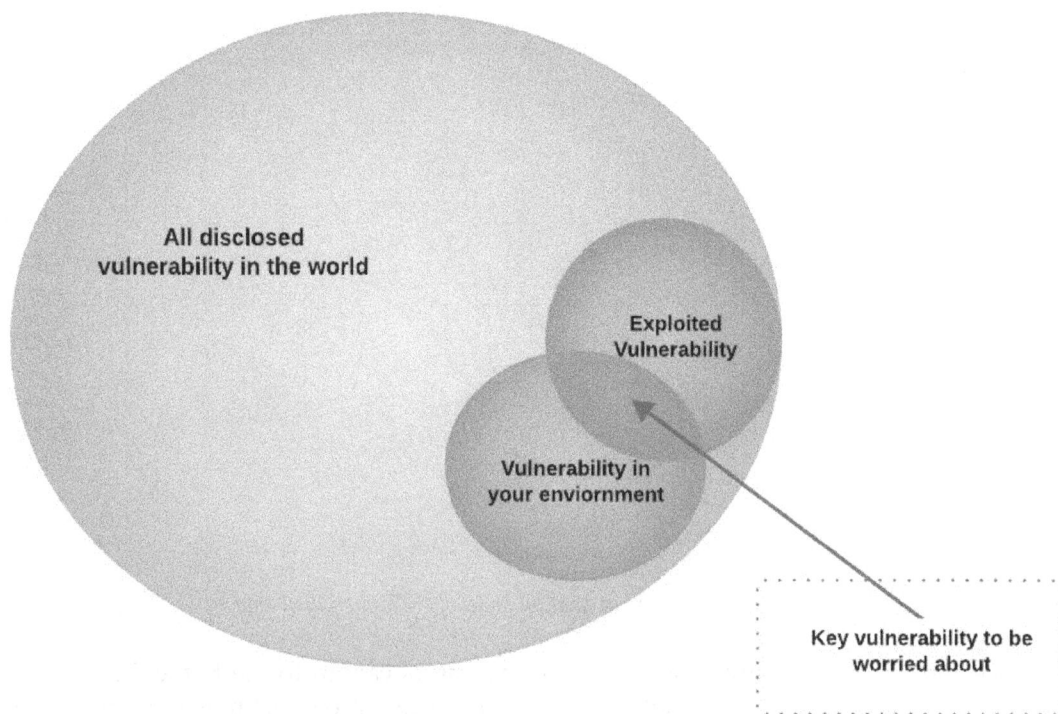

Figure 9.14: Critical vulnerability understanding in haystack

General CVE understanding

CVE is a publicly disclosed and standardized list of known cybersecurity vulnerabilities found in software, hardware, or firmware. Each CVE entry is assigned a unique identifier, description, and details of the vulnerability, allowing for easy reference and tracking across different cybersecurity databases and tools. This standardized naming system assists in information sharing, making it easier for security practitioners, organizations, and vendors to identify, discuss, and mitigate known security vulnerabilities across various systems and software.

Most of the security vendors that deal in CVE or TVM, they fetch this information from CVE API's and feed into their system and similarly MDE team also perform same level of scrapping or CVE fetch through API and feed into backend systems.

CVE high level crawler's workflow

Crawlers are the software that automatically scraps or pull web contents as per your custom requirement. Security companies use such general approach to scrap CVE websites to pull latest CVE information and inserts back such content inside their backed database so that their software's can parse as per requirement and can function as expected.

The following figure is just a general CVE crawler workflow captured to show you end to end cycle:

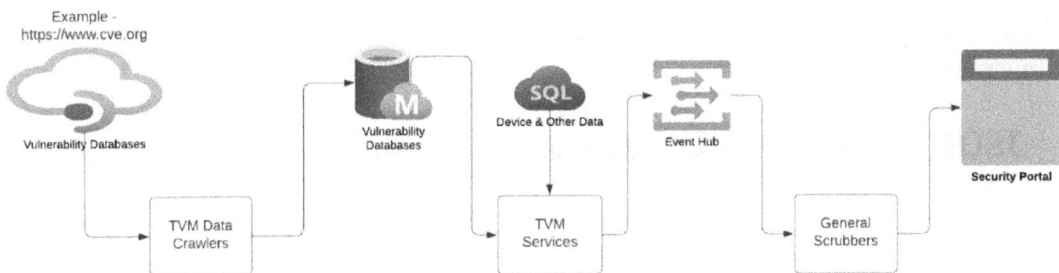

Figure 9.15: General crawler workflow used by security companies for CVE

CVE JSON structure

It is very important to understand the structure of CVE for easy understanding. The following figure provide important details that will give you 100% confidence in managing the CVE in your environment irrespective of product used:

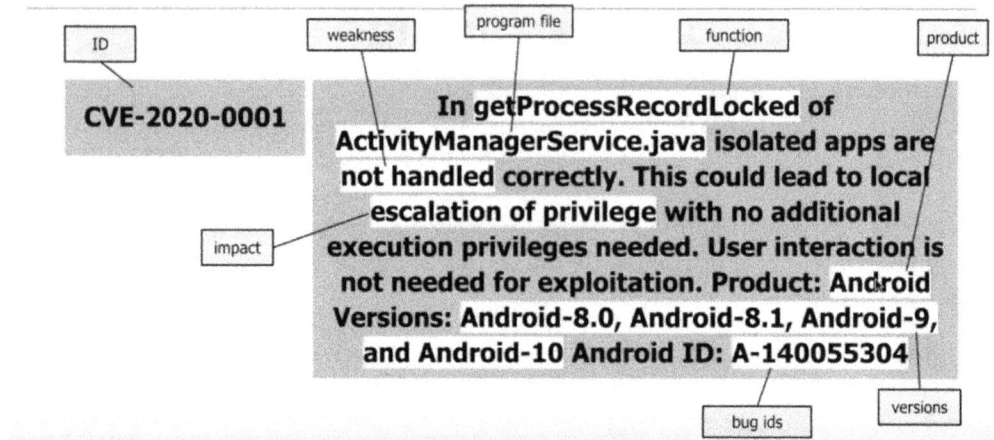

Figure 9.16: CVE with details

Informational:

- **YouTube: https://youtu.be/YWZECqzRI7M?si=JvYdxly0WzmsFE-8**
- **GitHub Repo: https://github.com/CVEProject/cve-schema**

In case you are more interested, you can more read on **https://www.cve.org/**.

CVE JSON field understanding

The following figure is the pictorial representation of CVE JSON that MDE parses internally while publishing on the portal:

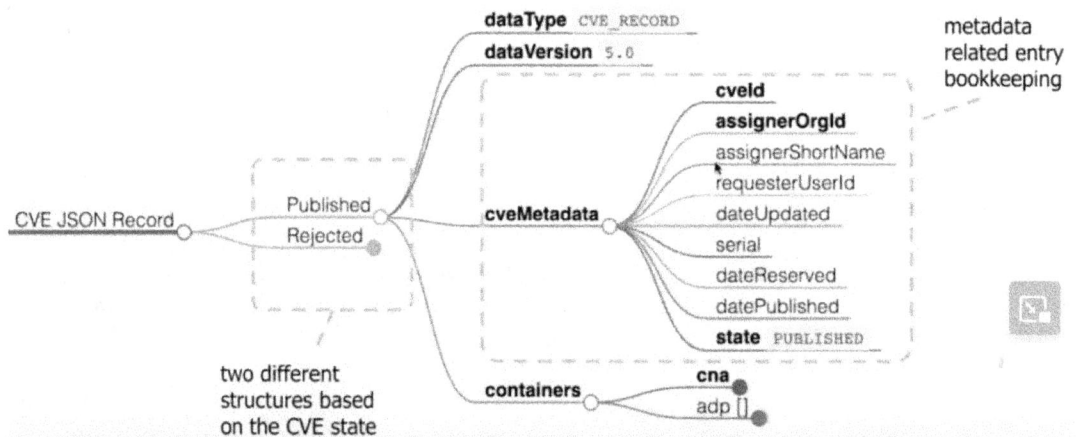

Figure 9.17: CVE JSON Record details

CNA field

CVE Numbering Authorities (CAN) that includes vendor, researcher, opensource, hosted services, bug bounty provider etc., and the following figure shows the fields filled by them:

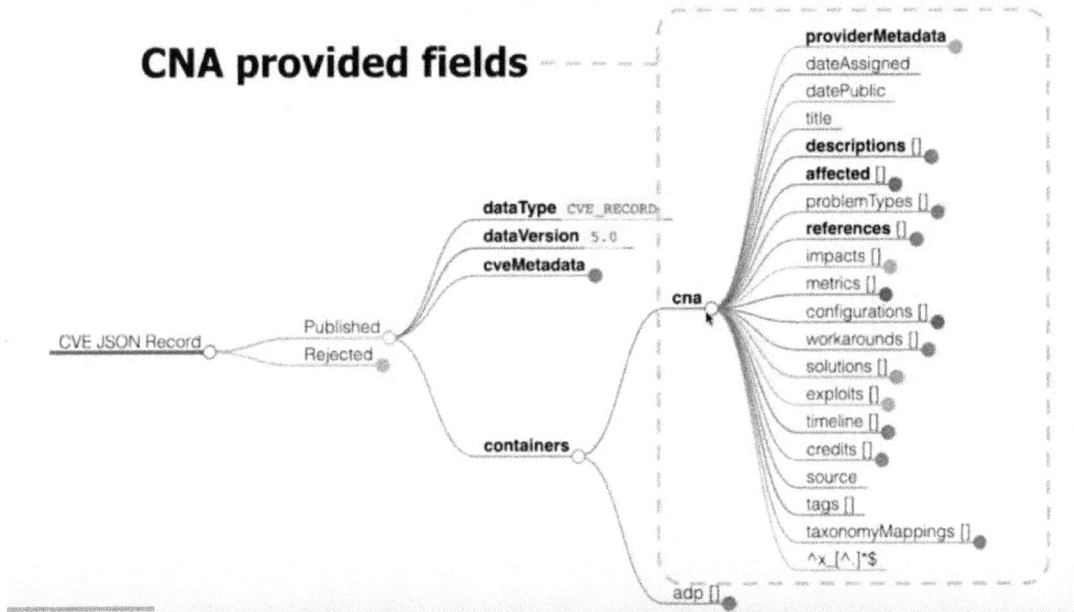

Figure 9.18: CAN fields in the JSON

Minium information in record

CVE holds the following mentioned minimum information before publishing it on CVE website that is publicly available and leverage by the security companies and all fetch from this source:

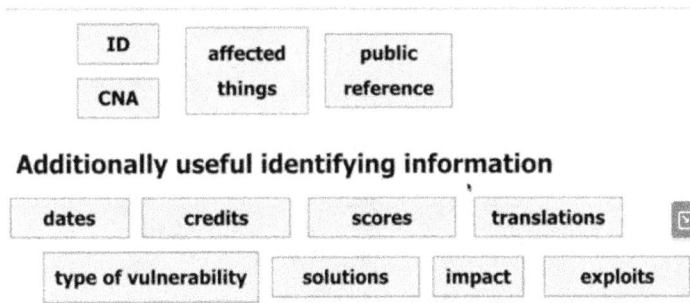

Figure 9.19: CVE required or optional fields

New ADP provided fields

Further, **Application Delivery Platforms** (**ADP**) can add more fields, as shown in the following figure:

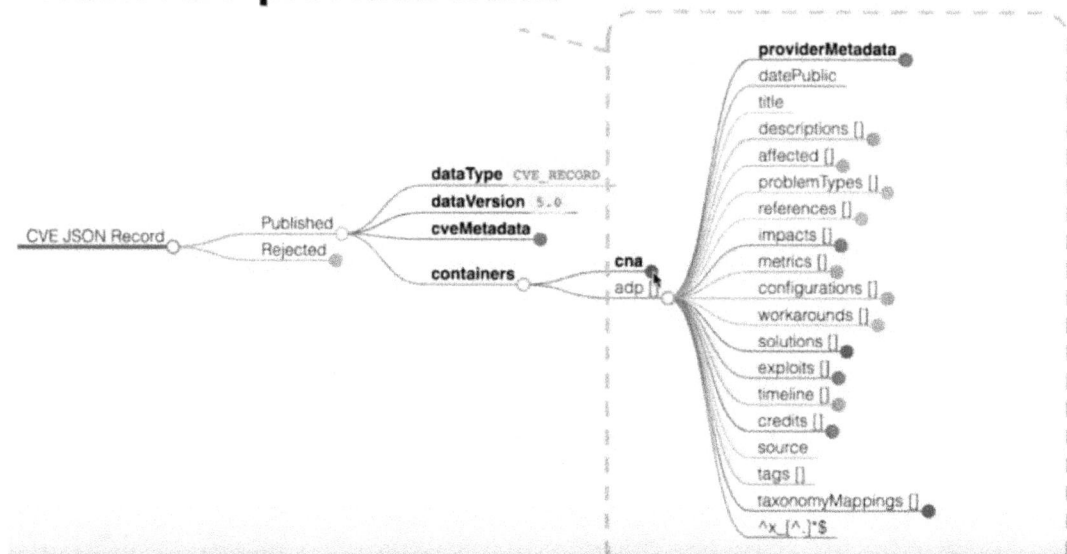

Figure 9.20: ADP Provided fields

Common vulnerabilities and exposure detection logic

Similar to the software evidence, we show the detection logic we applied on a device in order to state that it is vulnerable. It is applicable for all devices supported and onboarded on the MDE portal. It can be Server, Desktop and Mobile Device. Below is the example of Windows Desktop OS.

To see the detection logic, follow the given steps:

1. Select a device from the Device inventory page.
2. Select **Discovered vulnerabilities** from the device page.
3. Select the vulnerability you want to investigate.

A flyout will open and the Detection logic section shows the detection logic and source, as shown in the following figure:

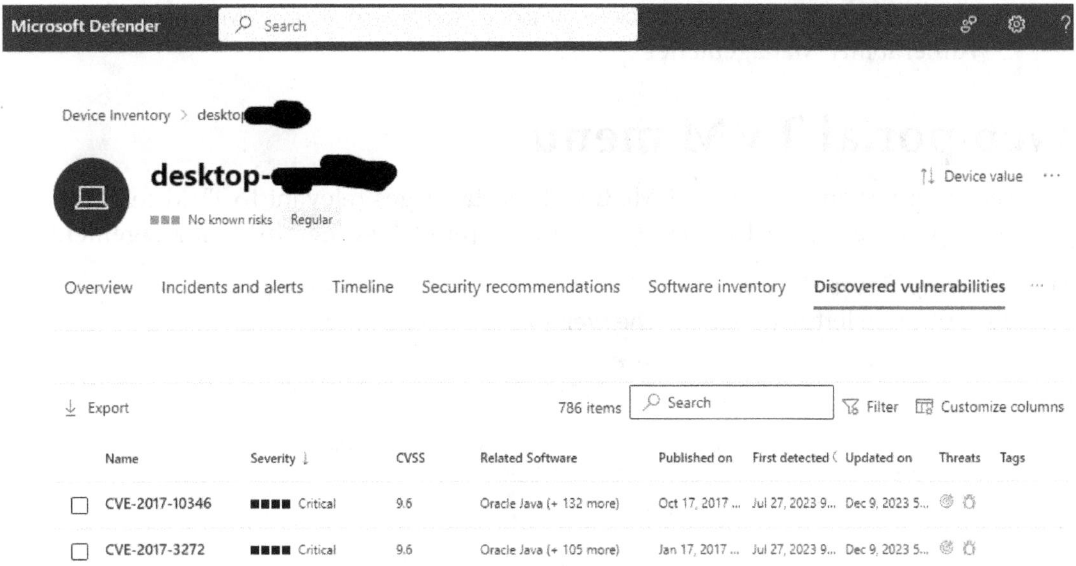

Figure 9.21: CVE shown on a device in MDE web portal

The *OS Feature* category is also shown in relevant scenarios. This is when a CVE would affect devices that run a vulnerable OS if a specific OS component is enabled. For example, if Windows Server 2019 or Windows Server 2022 has vulnerability in its DNS component we will only attach this CVE to the Windows Server 2019 and Windows Server 2022 devices with the DNS capability enabled in their OS.

Note: However, it is important to note that not all vulnerabilities are limited to devices with specific features enabled. Some CVEs may affect broader categories of devices, depending on the nature of the vulnerability. For instance, a vulnerability in the core operating system itself would apply to all devices running that OS, irrespective of the specific features or components enabled.

Report inaccuracy

Report a false positive when you see any vague, inaccurate, or incomplete information. You can also report on security recommendations that have already been remediated.

You can follow the given steps:

1. Open the **Common Vulnerabilities and Exposures** (**CVE**) on the Weaknesses page.
2. Select **Report inaccuracy** and a flyout pane will open.
3. From the flyout pane, choose an issue to report.
4. Fill in the requested details about the inaccuracy. This will vary depending on the issue you are reporting.

5. Select **Submit**. Your feedback is immediately sent to the Microsoft Defender Vulnerability Management experts.

Web portal TVM menu

This section gives an overview of MDE web portal pages relevant to TVM features and you can explore each page by clicking under: **Endpoint** | **Vulnerability management**.

The following figure showcases the TVM Menus/feature on the web portal and you will find this option in left hand side of the web page:

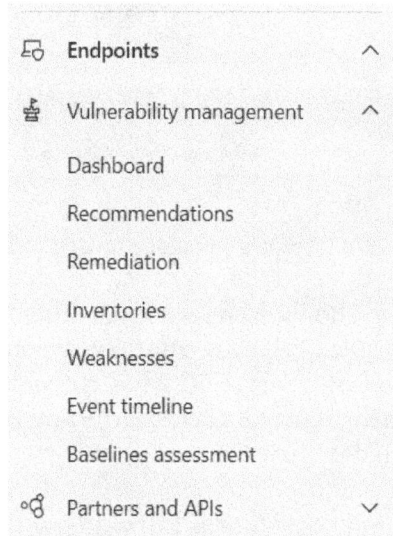

Figure 9.22: MDE VM Menu on web portal

Navigation pane

Navigation options available on MDE web portal for TVM are available in the following table:

Area	Description
Dashboard	Get a high-level view of the organization exposure score, threat awareness, Microsoft Secure Score for Devices, expiring certificates (*in case of expired certificate it will remove encryption feature, someone else can impersonate etc.*), device exposure distribution, top security recommendations, top vulnerable software, top remediation activities, and top exposed device data.

Area	Description
Recommendations	See the list of security recommendations and related threat information. When you select an item from the list, a flyout panel opens with vulnerability details, a link to open the software page, and remediation and exception options. You can also open a ticket in Intune if your devices are joined through Azure Active Directory and you have enabled your Intune connections in Defender for Endpoint. **Note: Microsoft collects telemetry across different OS and CVE and leverages machine learning workflows to calculates mostly exploited CVE and then alert such items on the portal.**
Remediation	See remediation activities you have created and recommendation exceptions.
Inventories	Discover and assess all your organization's assets in a single view.
Weaknesses	See the list of CVEs in your organization.
Event timeline	View events that may impact your organization's risk. It will highlight all identified events on the list.
Baselines assessment	Monitor security baseline compliance and identify changes in real-time.

Table 9.1: TVM navigation options on MDE web portal

Dashboard

Once you click on the TVM Dashboard page, the following figure shows some of the first few insights you will get from the page. It will highlight exposure score of the managed devices using the categorization factor defined in terms of low to high and similarly it also highlights MDE Configuration score for each supported components like Application, OS, Network, Account and Security controls.

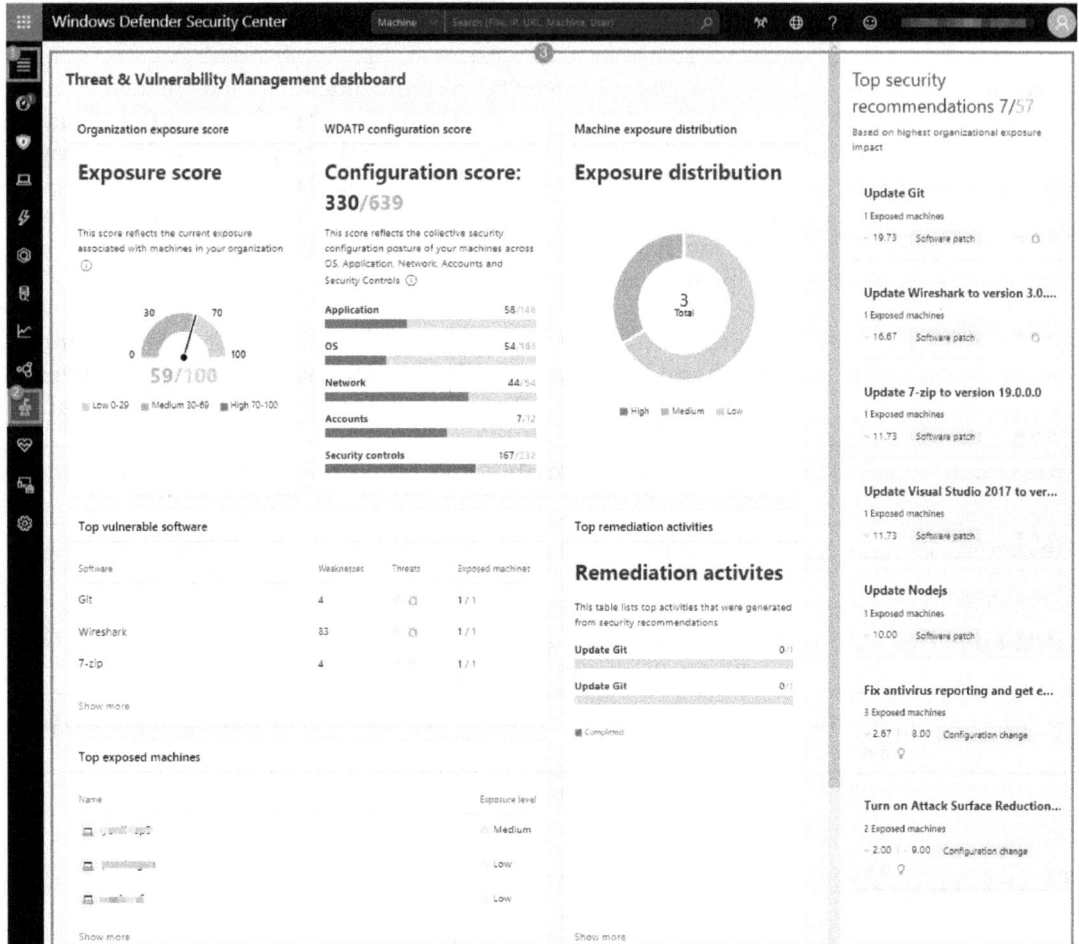

Figure 9.23: MDE TVM dashboard main page

In the following figure, you can see the continuation of widget shown on the dashboard:

Top vulnerable software

Software	OS platform	Weaknesses	Threats	Exposed devices	
Outlook 2016	Windows	42	⊚ ⓞ	1 / 1	
Office 2016	Windows	119	⊚ ⓞ	1 / 1	
Jre	Windows	359	⊚ ⓞ	1 / 1	

Show more

Top exposed devices

Name	Security recommendations	Discovered vulnerabilities	Exposure level
desktop-aqcvhbg	82	824	⚠ High

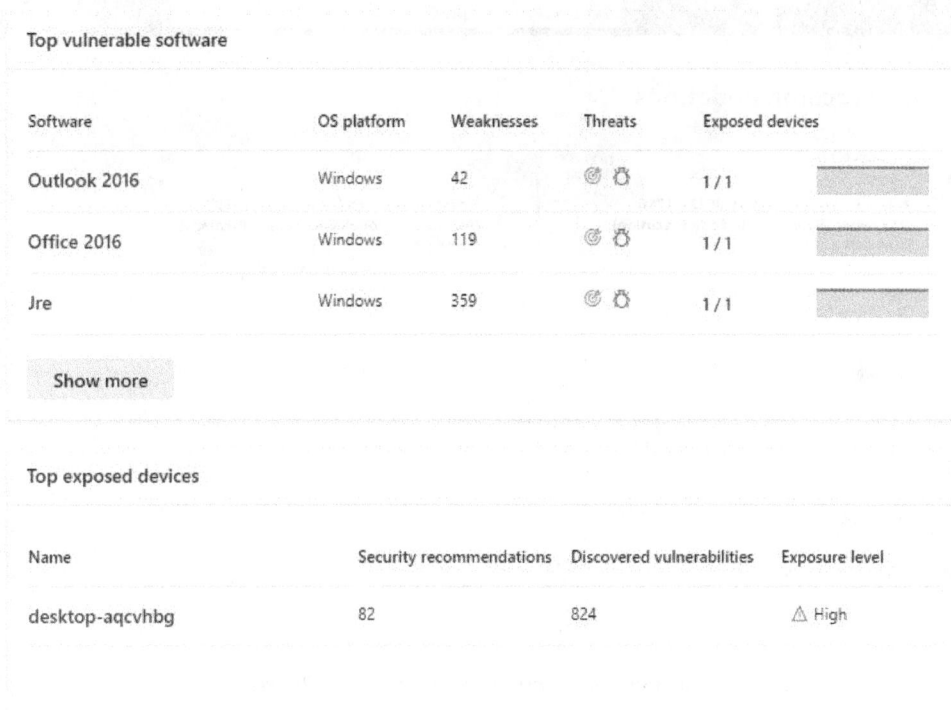

Figure 9.24: MDE TVM dashboard widgets

The following figure is a reference of expiring server certificate on TVM dashboard:

Expiring server certificates

0 certificates expire w...

■ Expired ■ Expires In 30 Days 2 more

View all

Figure 9.25: TVM dashboard widget for server certificate expiry

Security recommendation

The following figure shows the security recommendation page showing key highlights and complete list in tabular form, and you can click and get more insight into each recommendation:

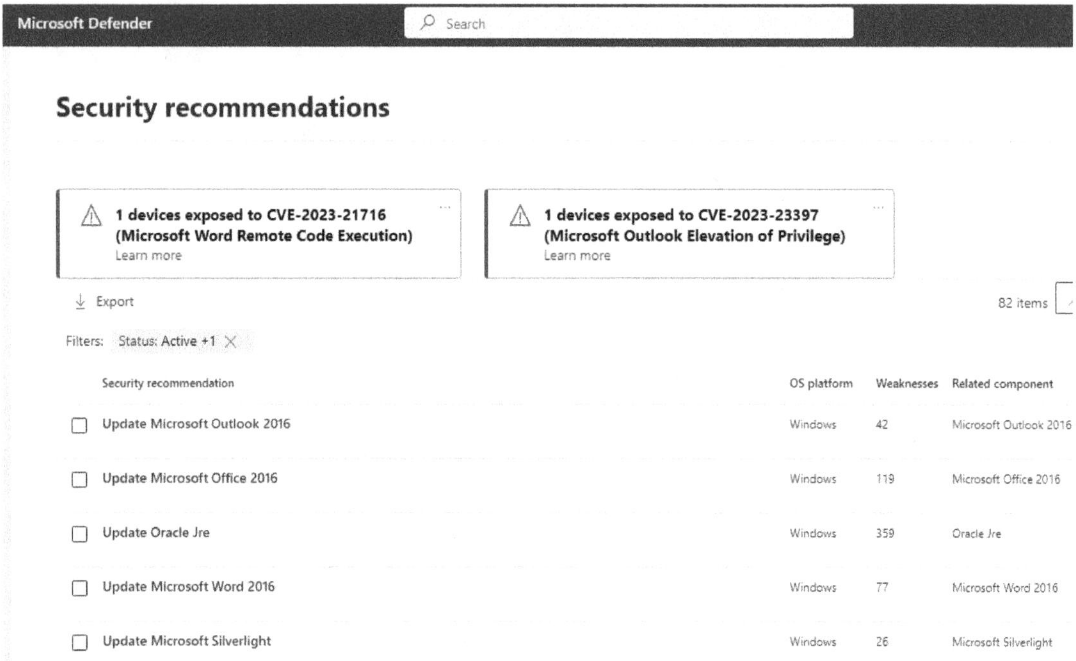

Figure 9.26: Security recommendation page on MDE web portal

Breach and threat insights

View any related breach and threat insights in the **Threats** column when the icons are colored red.

> **Note: Always prioritize recommendations that are associated with ongoing threats. These recommendations are marked with the threat insight icon and breach insight icon marked above in red triangle form. SOC specialist should take such alert on high priority and should map them against the incident P1-P6 priority and should take actions accordingly and in worst case device can be taken out from the network.**

The breach insights icon is highlighted if there is a vulnerability found in your organization.

The threat insights icon is highlighted if there are associated exploits in the vulnerability found in your organization. Hovering over the icon shows whether the threat is a part of an exploit kit or connected to specific advanced persistent campaigns or activity groups. When available, there is a link to a Threat Analytics report with zero-day exploitation news, disclosures, or related security advisories.

Gain vulnerability insights

If you select a CVE, a flyout panel will open with more information such as the vulnerability description, details and threat insights. For each CVE, you can see a list of the exposed devices and the software affected.

When a security recommendation is available you can select **Go to the related security recommendation** for details on how to remediate the vulnerability.

Recommendations for a CVE are often to remediate the vulnerability through a security update for the related software. However, some CVEs would not have a security update available. This might apply to all the related software for a CVE or just a subset, for example, a software vendor might decide not to fix the issue on a particular vulnerable version.

When a security update is only available for some of the related software, the CVE will have the tag **Some updates available**. Once there is at least one update available, you will have the option to go to the related security recommendation.

If there is no security update available, the CVE will have the tag **No security update**. There will be no option to go to the related security recommendation as software that does not have a security update available is excluded from the Security recommendations page.

> Note: Security recommendations only include devices and software packages that have security updates available.

The information on security update availability is also visible in the *Update availability* column on the **Exposed devices** and **Related software** tabs.

Unsupported software management

A CVE for software that is not currently supported by vulnerability management still appears in the Weaknesses page. Because the software is not supported, only limited data will be available.

Exposed device information will not be available for CVEs with unsupported software. Filter by unsupported software by selecting the **Not available** option in the **Exposed devices** section.

Remediation

Remediations are the solution offered to the underline identified problem. We have already covered remediation earlier in the chapter so just keep it as placeholder for your reference.

The following figure shows Remediation web portal page of MDE TVM:

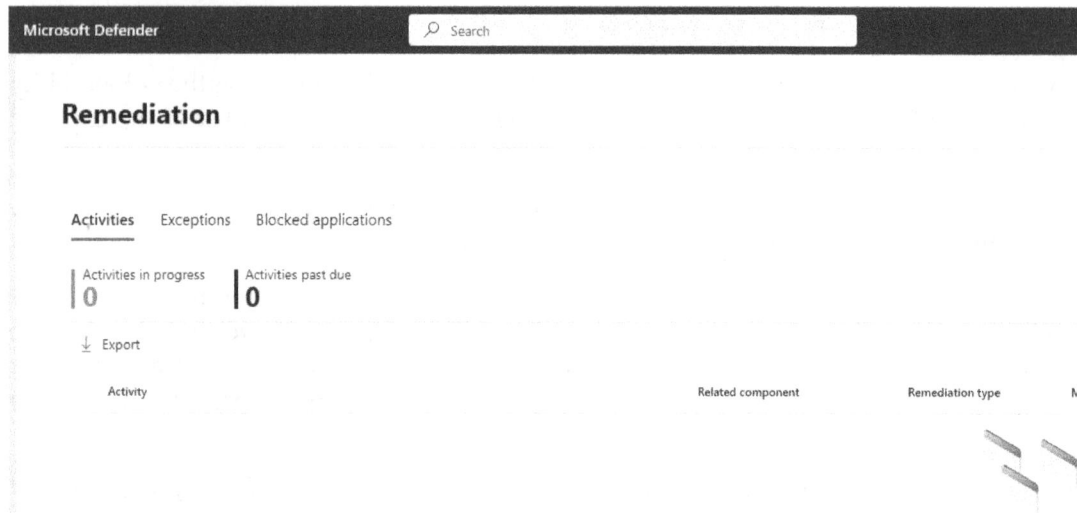

Figure 9.27: MDE TVM Remediation page

Inventories

Inventory page contains important information about the following:

- Software
- Browser extension
- Certificates
- Hardware and firmware

Software

Software inventory listed installed on the devices in your environment, as shown in the following figure:

Microsoft Defender		○ Search			

Inventories

Software   Browser extensions   Certificates   Hardware & Firmware

Software
29

↓ Export   29 ite

Filters: Product Code (CPE): Available ✕

	Name	OS platform	Vendor	Weaknesses	Threats	Exposed device
☐	Outlook 2016	Windows	Microsoft	42	⊘ ⊘	1 / 1
☐	Office 2016	Windows	Microsoft	119	⊘ ⊘	1 / 1
☐	Jre	Windows	Oracle	359	⊘ ⊘	1 / 1
☐	Word 2016	Windows	Microsoft	77	⊘ ⊘	1 / 1
☐	Silverlight	Windows	Microsoft	26	⊘ ⊘	1 / 1
☐	Excel 2016	Windows	Microsoft	129	⊘ ⊘	1 / 1
☐	Vlc Media Player	Windows	Videolan	31	⊘ ⊘	1 / 1

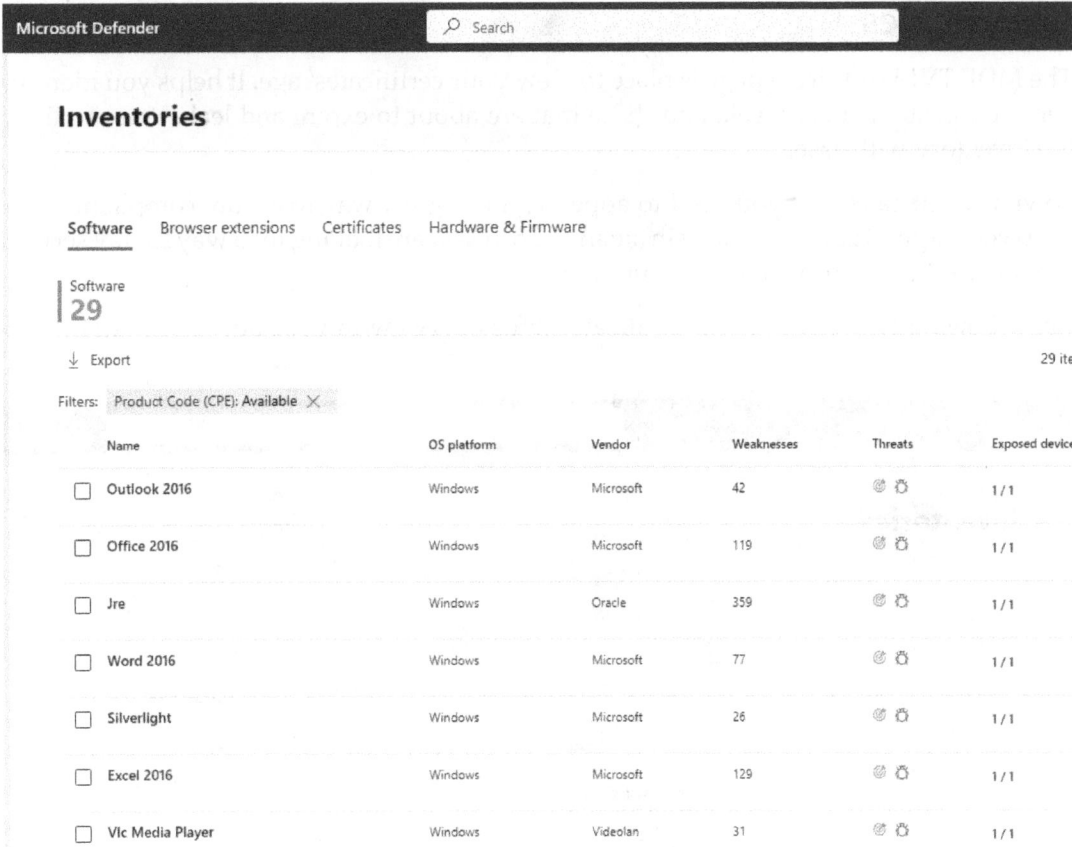

Figure 9.28: Software inventory list for the device

Browser extensions page

The following figure show browser extension page options under inventories page:

Inventories

🖻 Filter by device groups (3/3)

Software   **Browser extensions**   Certificates   Hardware & Firmware

↓ Export   0 items   ○ Search   ⊽ Filter   ▦ Customize columns

Name	Browser	OS platform	Permission risk ⓘ	Requested per...	Devices with extension on ↓	Installed devices

Figure 9.29: Browser extension page

Certificates

The MDE TVM certificate page is place to view your certificates' age. It helps you identify such certificate that are weak, and those that are about to expire and leak. You can filter the inventory with ease.

To view certificates that you need to appease, it is a great way to ensure compliance and keep your organization's security in alliance. So, if you are looking for a way to stay secure, the MDE TVM certificate page is your cure.

The following figure shows the certificate status overview in your devices on MDE web portal:

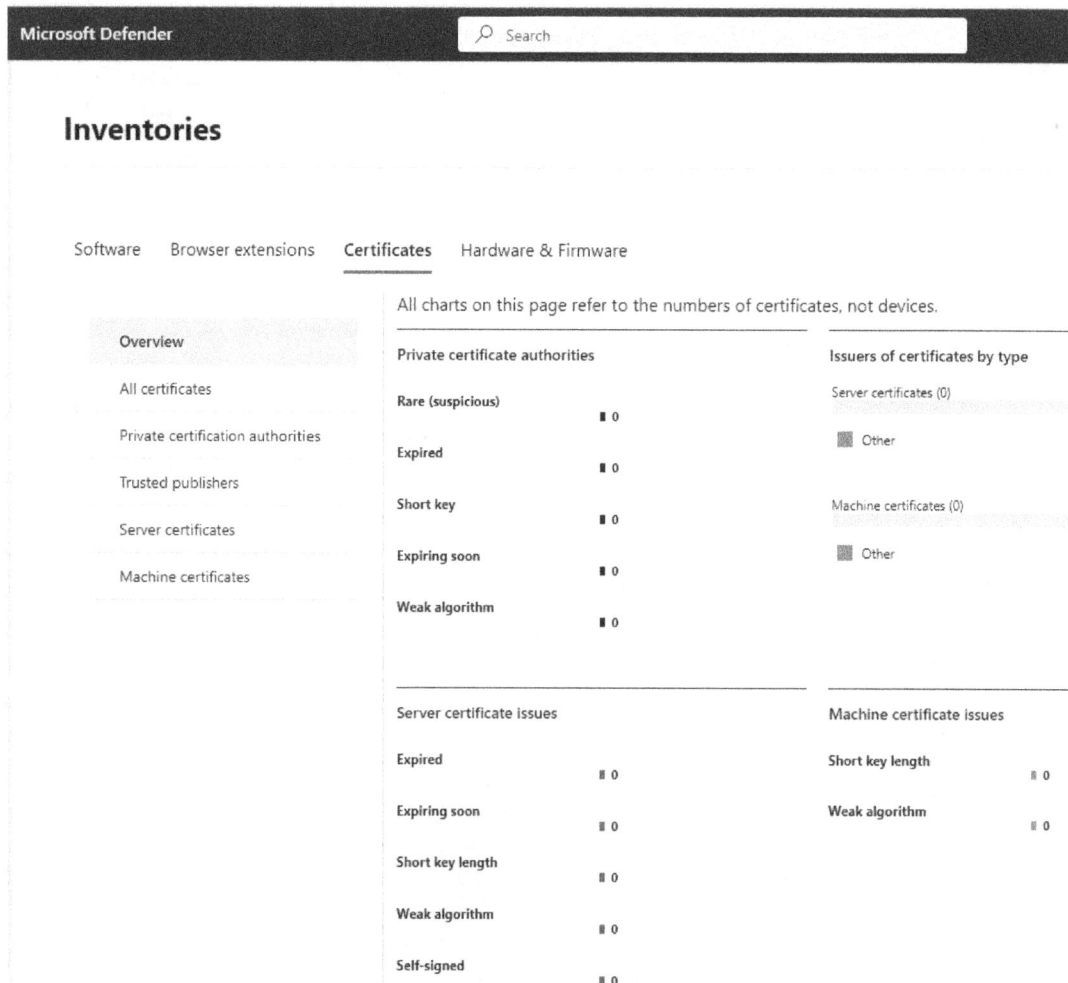

Figure 9.30: Certificate status page

Hardware and firmware

MDE supports few limited vendor firmware upgrades from the web portal and there are prerequisite steps before proceeding. Each vendor has their own mechanism to support so read the documentation before proceeding. For an example, firmware Upgrade on Air feature on Zebra devices are available and detailed steps are documented on Defender site etc.

The following figure is a screenshot of **Hardware & Firmware** page:

| Software | Browser extensions | Certificates | **Hardware & Firmware** |

Figure 9.31: Hardware & Firmware page under inventories on web portal

Weaknesses

Weakness page shows all the CVEs available in your environment. Remediate the vulnerabilities in exposed devices to reduce the risk to your assets and organization. If the **Exposed Devices** column shows zero, that means you are not at risk.

The **Weaknesses** page lists the software vulnerabilities your devices are exposed to by listing the CVE ID. You can also view the severity, **Common Vulnerability Scoring System** (**CVSS**) rating, prevalence in your organization, corresponding breach, threat insights, and more.

Navigate to the Weaknesses page, Access the Weaknesses page a few different ways.

Navigation menu

Select **Weaknesses** from the **Vulnerability management** navigation menu in the Microsoft 365 Defender portal to open the list of CVEs.

The following steps show the vulnerabilities in global search:

1. Go to the global search drop-down menu.
2. Select **Vulnerability** and key in CVE ID that you are looking for, for example *CVE-2018-5568*, then select the search icon. The **Weaknesses** page opens with the CVE information that you are looking for.

3. Select the CVE to open a flyout panel with more information, including the vulnerability description, details, threat insights, and exposed devices.

To see the rest of the vulnerabilities in the **Weaknesses** page, type CVE, then select search. The following figure shows the first page of weakness page:

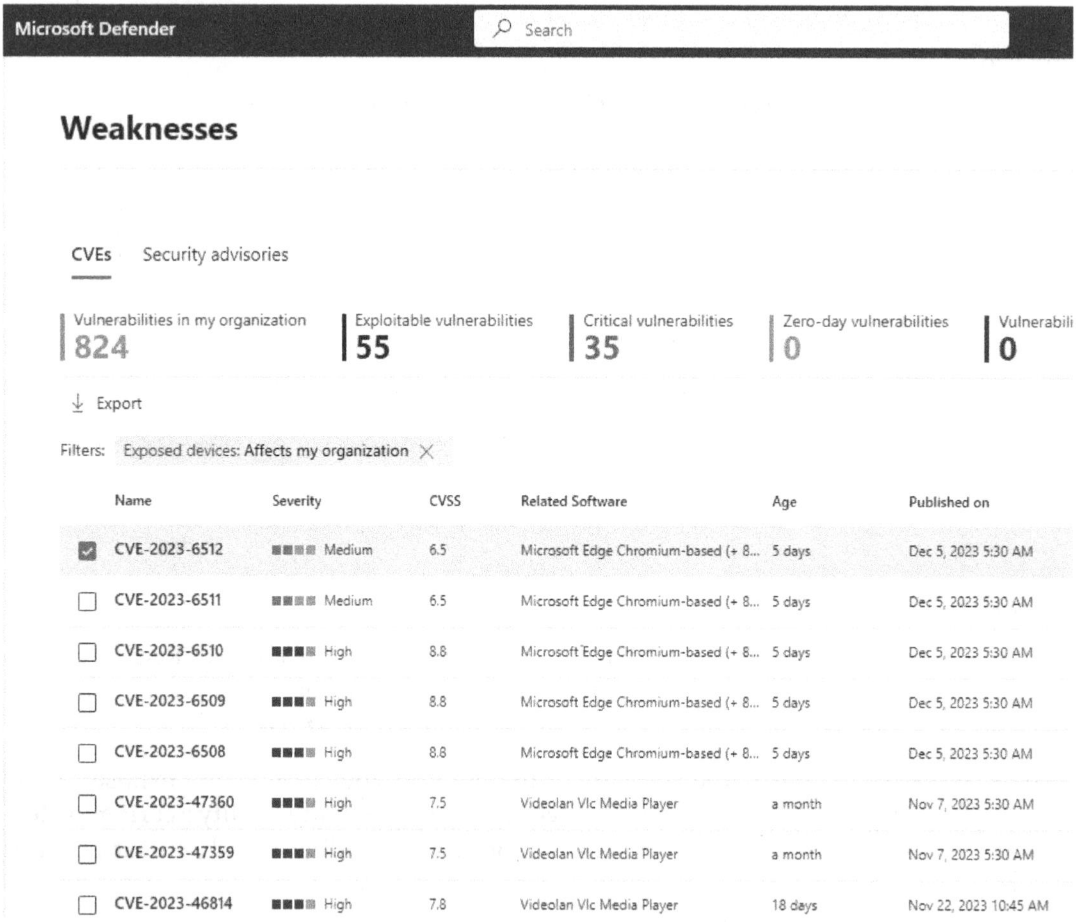

Figure 9.32: TVM Weaknesses page on MDE web portal

Once you click on any one of the CVE then it gives a complete overview, as shown in the following figure:

CVE-2023-6512

ⓢ Open vulnerability page   𝆕 Report inaccuracy

Vulnerability details   Exposed devices   Related software

ⓘ **Legal Notice** The vulnerability data provided and shown as part of your Microsoft Defender for Endpoint (MDE) services is made available

Vulnerability description

This vulnerability affects the following vendors: Fedora, Google, Microsoft. To view more details about this vulnerability please visit the vendor website.

Threat insights

Public	**Verified**
No	No
Exploit kits	**Type**
No	Not available
Reference	
Not available	

Security updates status

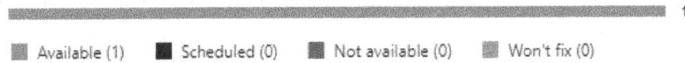

━━━━━━━━━━━━━━━━━━━━━━━━━━━━━━━━ 1

▦ Available (1)   ■ Scheduled (0)   ▦ Not available (0)   ▦ Won't fix (0)

Vulnerability details

Vulnerability name
CVE-2023-6512

Severity
■■■▦ Medium

CVSS
6.5 (Ibm)

CVSS Version
3

Published on
Dec 5, 2023 5:30 AM

First detected
Dec 6, 2023 7:48 AM

Updated on
Dec 10, 2023 3:45 AM

Age
5 days

Go to related security recommendation

Figure 9.33: CVE detail page

Event timeline

The event timeline page shows important events related to vulnerabilities impacting your devices, as shown in the following figure:

Event timeline

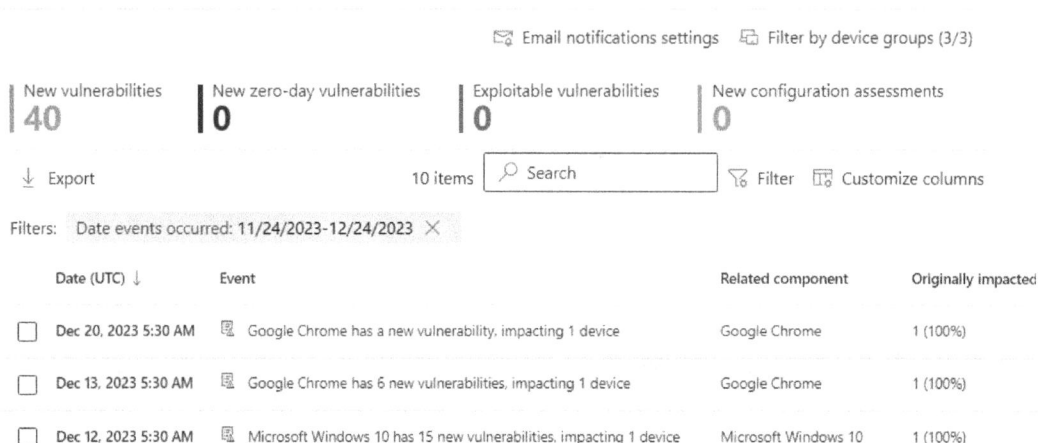

☒ Email notifications settings   ⎙ Filter by device groups (3/3)

New vulnerabilities	New zero-day vulnerabilities	Exploitable vulnerabilities	New configuration assessments
40	0	0	0

⬇ Export   10 items   🔍 Search   ⅄ Filter   ⬚ Customize columns

Filters: Date events occurred: 11/24/2023-12/24/2023 ✕

Date (UTC) ↓	Event	Related component	Originally impacted
☐ Dec 20, 2023 5:30 AM	🔳 Google Chrome has a new vulnerability, impacting 1 device	Google Chrome	1 (100%)
☐ Dec 13, 2023 5:30 AM	🔳 Google Chrome has 6 new vulnerabilities, impacting 1 device	Google Chrome	1 (100%)
☐ Dec 12, 2023 5:30 AM	🔳 Microsoft Windows 10 has 15 new vulnerabilities, impacting 1 device	Microsoft Windows 10	1 (100%)

Figure 9.34: Vulnerabilities identified in the environment with timeline

Baseline assessment

The security baselines assessment feature helps you to continuously monitor your organization's security baselines compliance and identify changes in real-time. A security baseline profile is a customized profile (*Only out from the provided list on the portal*) that you can create to assess and monitor endpoints in your organization against industry security benchmarks. When you create a security baseline profile, you are creating a template that consists of multiple device configuration settings and a base benchmark to compare against. Security baselines provide support for **Center for Internet Security (CIS)** benchmarks for Windows 10, Windows 11, and Windows Server 2008 R2 and later versions, helping organizations adhere to industry-recognized security standards .

Additionally, the **Security Technical Implementation Guides** (**STIG**) benchmarks are supported not only for Windows 10 and Windows Server 2019 but may also cover other versions or systems. This broader coverage ensures that various systems within your organization can be assessed and monitored for compliance with stringent security standards.

The following figure provides a baseline profiles created on MDE web portal:

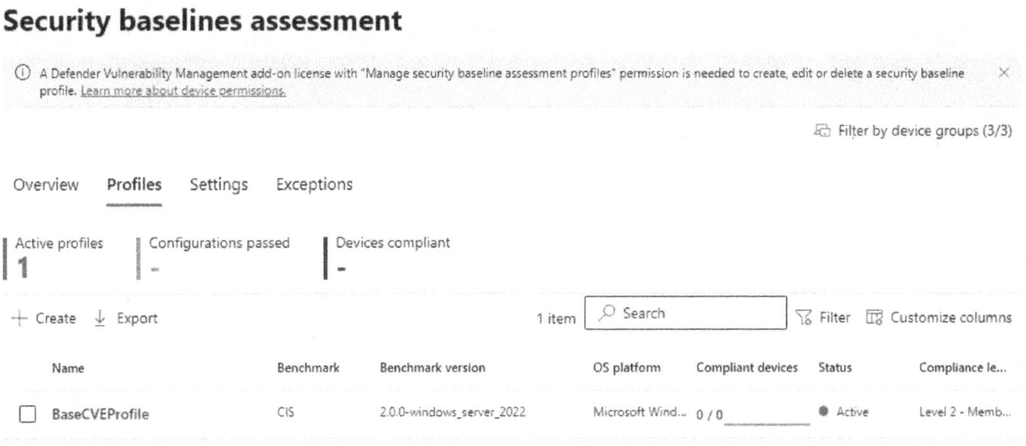

Security baselines assessment

ⓘ A Defender Vulnerability Management add-on license with "Manage security baseline assessment profiles" permission is needed to create, edit or delete a security baseline ✕
profile. Learn more about device permissions.

🗗 Filter by device groups (3/3)

Overview   **Profiles**   Settings   Exceptions

Active profiles	Configurations passed	Devices compliant
1	-	-

＋ Create   ⭳ Export   1 item   🔍 Search   ⅂⊽ Filter   🖽 Customize columns

	Name	Benchmark	Benchmark version	OS platform	Compliant devices	Status	Compliance le...
☐	BaseCVEProfile	CIS	2.0.0-windows_server_2022	Microsoft Wind...	0 / 0	● Active	Level 2 - Memb...

Figure 9.35: CVE baseline profile list managed by administrator

Example of profile creation steps

In the following figure, we have captured the steps for baseline profile creation on the security web portal page:

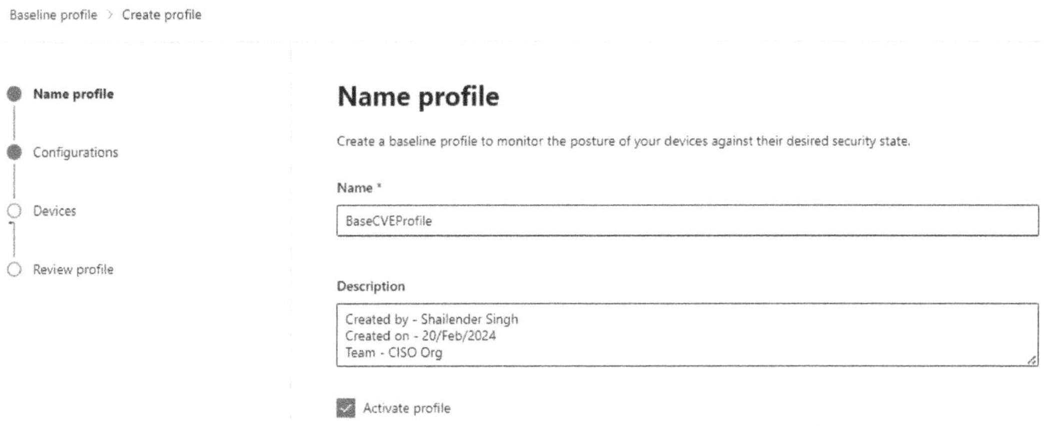

Baseline profile ＞ Create profile

● **Name profile**

● Configurations

○ Devices

○ Review profile

Name profile

Create a baseline profile to monitor the posture of your devices against their desired security state.

Name *

BaseCVEProfile

Description

Created by - Shailender Singh Created on - 20/Feb/2024 Team - CISO Org

☑ Activate profile

Figure 9.36: New Baseline profile creation step page

Note: A Defender Vulnerability Management add-on license with Manage security baseline assessment profiles permission is needed to create, edit or delete a security baseline profile.

In the following configuration selection page, please select the Windows OS version for which you would like to create baseline profile:

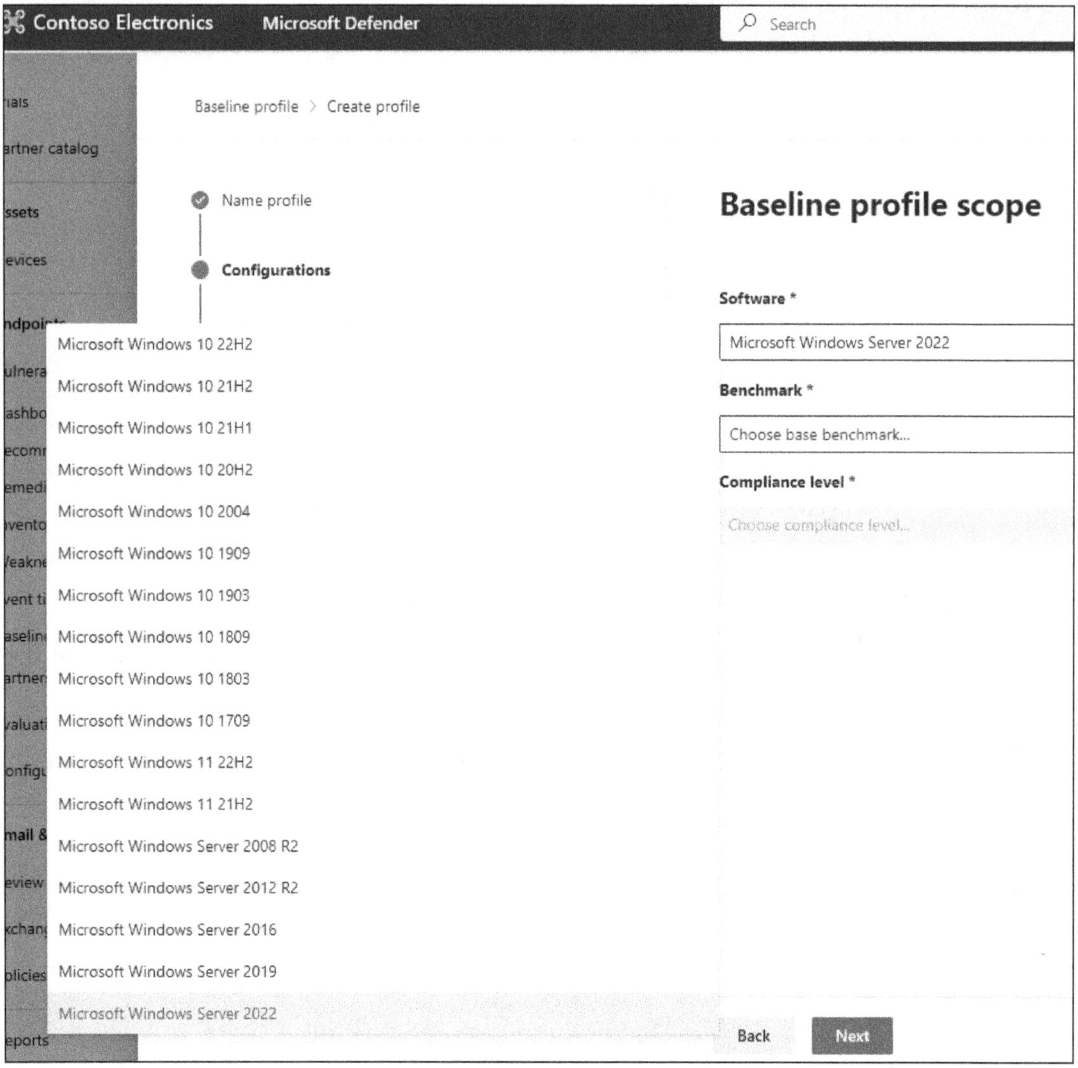

Figure 9.37: Profile creation page continuation

CIS is an organization that creates the benchmarks for various OS and Platform that you can check against for comparison and as part of baseline profile creation you have to choose one of them, as shown in the following figure:

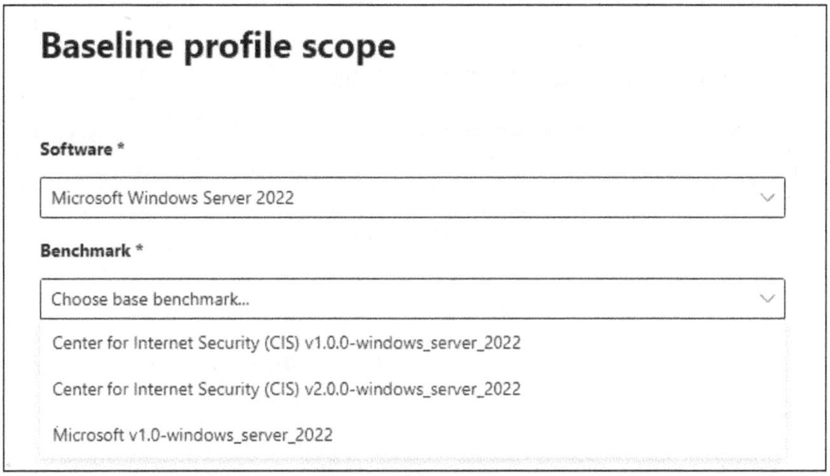

Figure 9.38: CIS Baselines to choose

The following figure shows the continuation of profile creation:

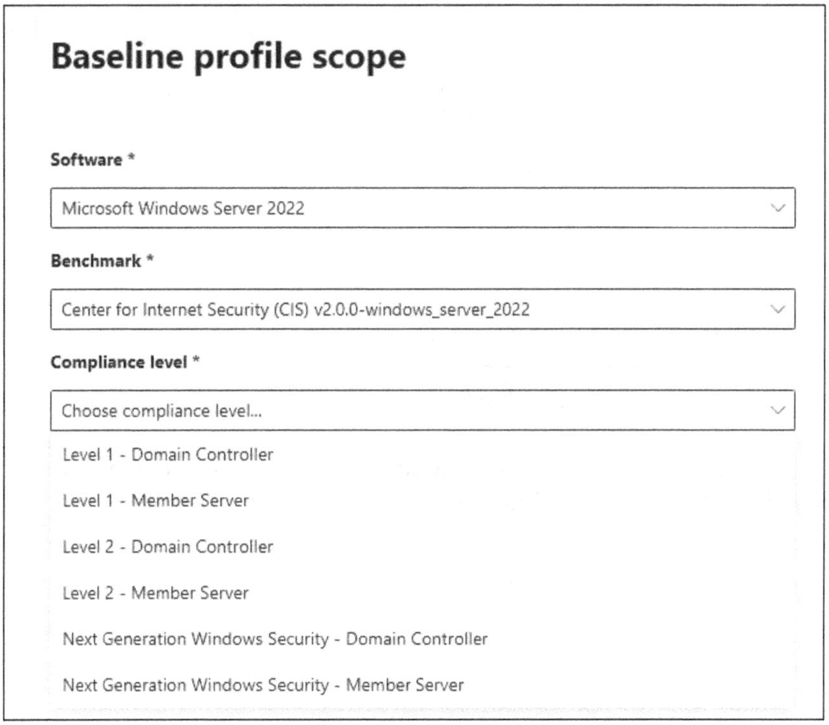

Figure 9.39: Compliance level reference

The following figure shows the continuation of profile creation and you can choose specific area of the OS configuration:

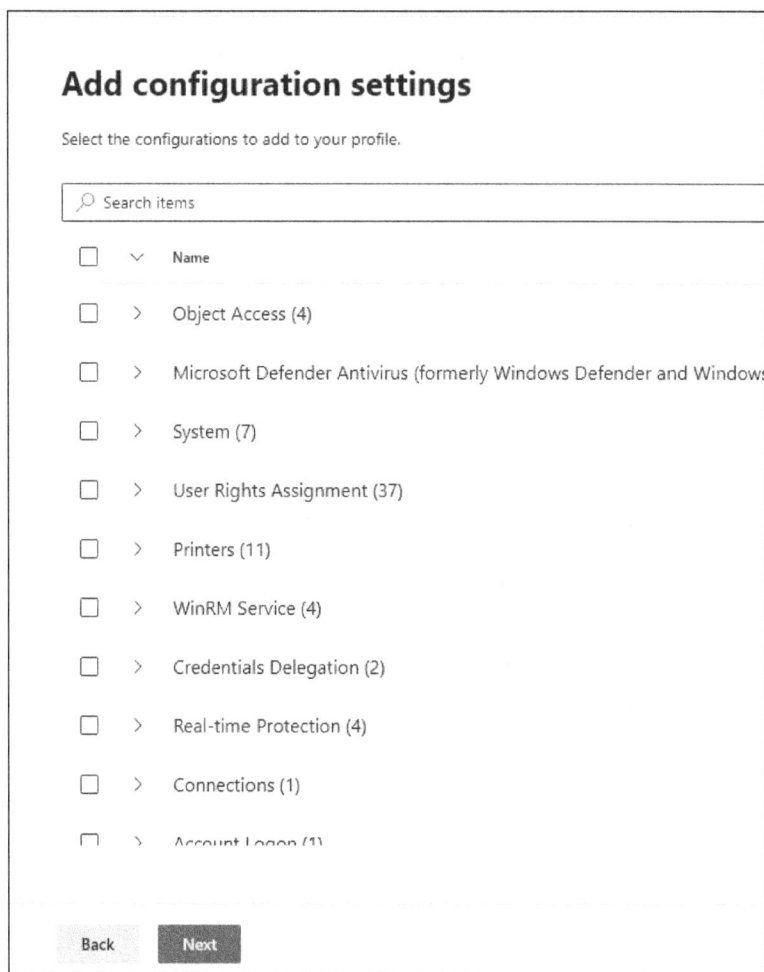

Add configuration settings

Select the configurations to add to your profile.

🔎 Search items

		Name
☐	>	Object Access (4)
☐	>	Microsoft Defender Antivirus (formerly Windows Defender and Windows
☐	>	System (7)
☐	>	User Rights Assignment (37)
☐	>	Printers (11)
☐	>	WinRM Service (4)
☐	>	Credentials Delegation (2)
☐	>	Real-time Protection (4)
☐	>	Connections (1)
☐	>	Account Logon (1)

Back Next

Figure 9.40: *Baseline Profile configuration settings page*

The following figure is an example of how to choose some of the configuration settings that you would like to add in baseline profile for the WinRM Service:

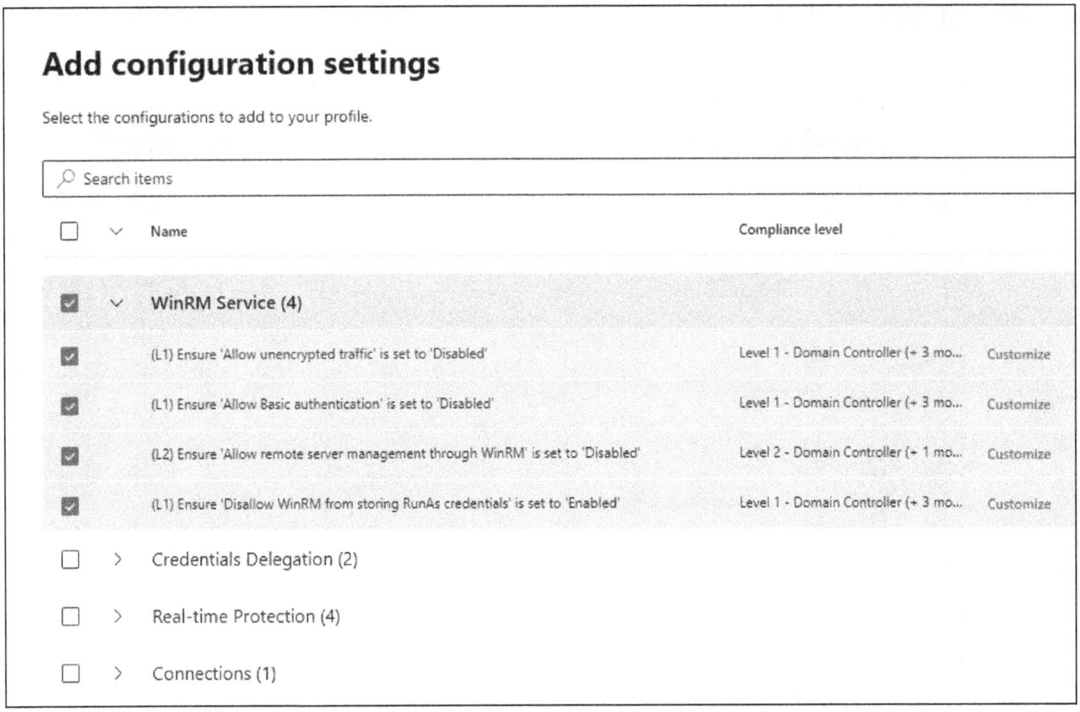

Figure 9.41: Showcasing WinRM service selection for profile

The following figure shows the device selection page that you would like to compare against for baseline profile comparision:

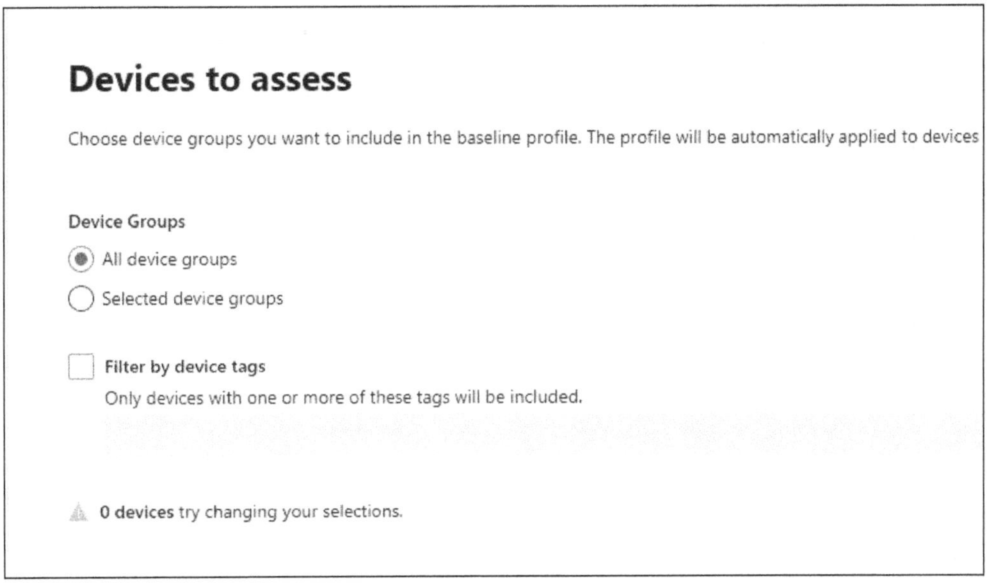

Figure 9.42: Device filter or selection page during profile creation

The following figure shows the final review page before creating the profile on web portal:

Review profile

Review the profile settings before creating it.

⚠ Your profile doesn't include any devices to assess at the moment.

Rule name

Name	BaseCVEProfile
Status	Enabled

Edit Rule name

Configurations

Software	Microsoft Windows Server 2022
Benchmark	CIS 2.0.0-windows_server_2022
Compliance	Level 2 - Member Server
Selected configurations	4 configurations selected
Customized configurations	0 customized configurations

Edit Configurations

Devices

Device groups	All device groups

Back   Submit

Figure 9.43: Profile review page before creation

The following figure shows the final confirmation of creation:

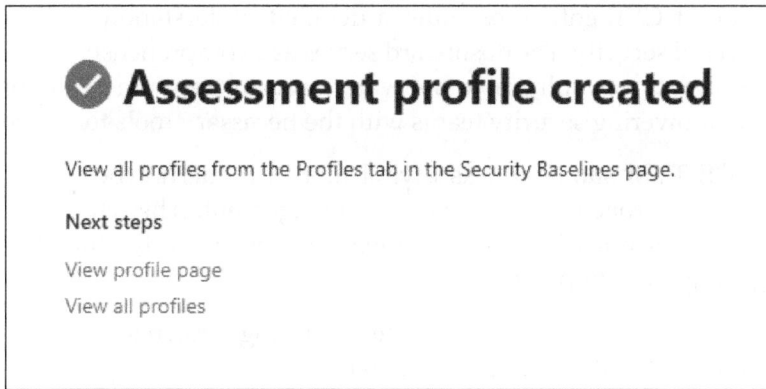

Figure 9.44: *Profile creation status shown during creation*

Once created, you can see the profile listed on the assessment page, as shown in the following figure:

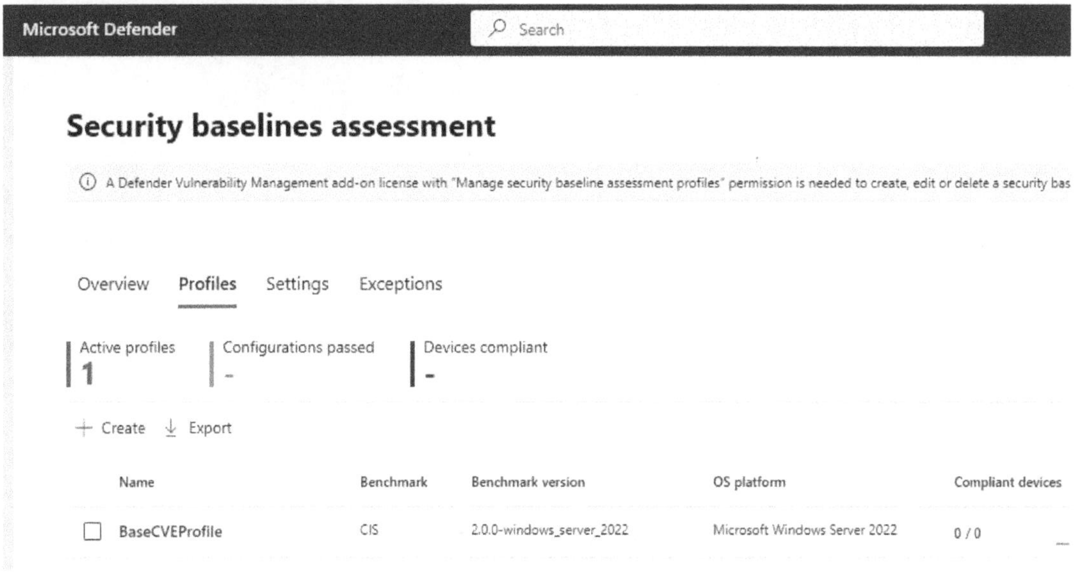

Figure 9.45: *Available profiles for assessment on MDE portal for TVM*

Conclusion

In conclusion, our exploration of MDE TVM reveals a robust framework designed to enhance digital security. We have examined how MDE TVM's risk-based lifecycle approach integrates continuous asset discovery, intelligent risk prioritization, and effective remediation processes. The platform's user-friendly interface allows for swift identification of vulnerabilities and insightful threat analysis, aiding informed decision-making.

The incorporation of CVE entries provides a detailed understanding of vulnerabilities, strengthening overall security. The dashboard serves as a comprehensive command center, presenting critical data on vulnerable software, security recommendations, and event timelines, thus empowering security teams with the necessary tools for strategic action.

In summary, MDE TVM stands out as a vital tool in modern cybersecurity, offering a detailed and agile approach to vulnerability management. This chapter highlights its significance in safeguarding digital environments against emerging threats, emphasizing its role in enhancing security practices.

MDE TVM is designed to support diverse operating systems, including those not specifically highlighted in the upcoming chapter.

In the next chapter, we are going to cover more specific details around cross-platform endpoint security that talks about macOS, Android, Linux along with Windows protection feature that really makes MDE a great product from OS coverage point of view.

Join our book's Discord space

Join the book's Discord Workspace for Latest updates, Offers, Tech happenings around the world, New Release and Sessions with the Authors:

https://discord.bpbonline.com

CHAPTER 10

Cross-platform Endpoint Security

Introduction

Cross Platform, also internally known as **XPlatform** in Defender team achieved so many milestones in 2020-2023. It delivered so many **generally available (GA)** products, features and services offering to strengthen the Microsoft Defender portfolio and recognized by industry indicated by numbers in terms of revenue growth. It has taken all leader and visionary positions in the Forester and gained much more score in MITRE attack technique coverage ranking. It is much ahead of its competitors and has taken the front seat on terms of all growth numbers. We have already covered much about cross-platform support, but this chapter is unique because you are going to learn about how Microsoft built such great cross-platform features with some timeline references to gain confidence about the freshness of the future and the maturity level lying ahead in the future.

The following is the representation of MDE features developed for multiple supported operating system so that you can gauge the feature development parity by the MDE team for all OS along with cross platform.

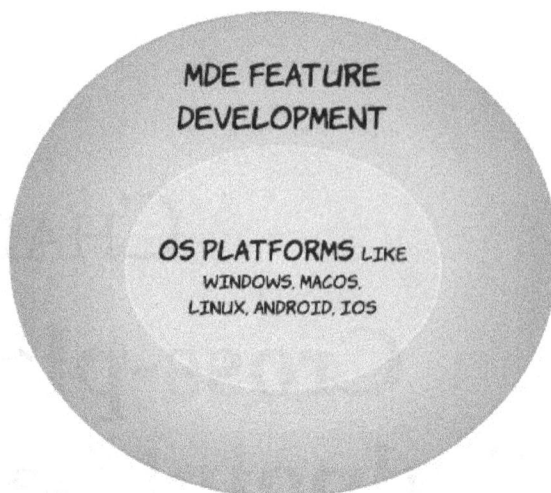

Figure 10.1: *General feature development by MDE team for cross platform OS*

MDE cross platform covers the following **operating system** (**OS**) platforms to provide 100% coverage on mostly used operating system available in the world. Either it is Desktop or Server category OS or in mobile device category in form of iOS and Android.

The following are the desktop or server-based OS:

- Windows
- Linux
- macOS

The following are mobile-based OS:

- iOS/iPad
- Android

Structure

In this chapter, we will cover the following topics:

- Author's experience in Defender MDE Cross Platform team
- MDE backend platform virtualization insight
- Apple's licensing restriction and COGS management
- Public macOS datacenters
- Security or cross-platform technologies
- MBA of Zip file (XPlode)
- Public MBA vendors available in market

- Clean or historical samples
- Security research
- Native engine support in cross platform
- NE general availability and Bit Defender replacement
- Microsoft software release and cycles
- Microsoft mobile threat defense cross-platform solutions
- Create app configuration policies for MTD
- Microsoft Tunnel and VPN for cross platform
- Microsoft cloud native protection platform

Objectives

We have multiple objectives that we would like to cover in this chapter. First, we would like to show you the development efforts that went into building a strong solution, and which will gain insight and confidence on the product features.

Then, you will also gain some insight into the technologies used to strengthen the Defender for Endpoint for cross-platform operating systems. You will get to know about the macOS, Android and Linux virtualization exposure through the experience that author went through in his journey in the team.

Another objective is to bring you the clarity about all the Microsoft security products that we have as of now or some of the product those are going to come in coming days due to the AI/ML advancement in the security domain in form of Microsoft Copilot solution.

Author's experience in Defender Cross Platform team

As the first **Site Reliability Engineer** (**SRE**) in Defender India team in Hyderabad R&D center was educational. He participated in the journey of development of backend platform and the teams initial primary focus was to build the Cross Platform **Malware Behavioral Analysis** (**MBA**) backend infrastructure at scale to reduce down the False Positive on malware detection by running thousands of malware analysis a day. Before the author joined the team, the developers were already working on the solution and were performing MBA on Mac Pros and the defender team hired SRE Engineers to meet the scale requirement. The team successfully delivered production ready platform in around a year that used to perform MBA on macOS, Android, Linux and iOS.

The following figure shows the high-level product categories and organization of cross-platform area.

Note: It is mostly covered under M365D I MDE I Cross Platform OS Platforms. In this chapter, we will share insights from author's experience working in this area.

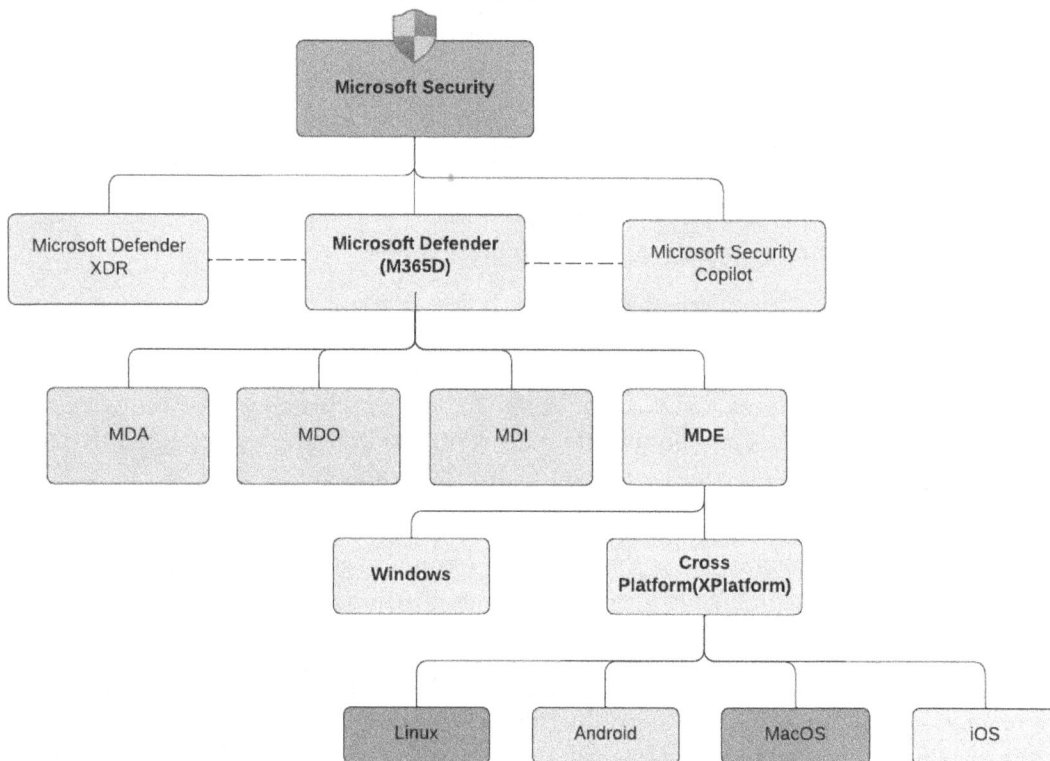

Figure 10.2: Hierarchical structure of cross platform products in Microsoft Security

Author's journey in MDE R&D team

If you get the gist out from the author's experience, then you will realize that you have understood about how actually a **software as a service (SaaS)** based antivirus or behavioral monitoring based security solution works in the cloud. You will learn about the following terminologies:

- **Malware Behavioral Analysis (MBA)** (Internally in MDE team a.k.a. **Detonation**)
- Static and dynamic analysis
- Clean sample and historical samples
- MBA of Zip file (Internally in MDE team a.k.a. **XPlode**)
- Geolocation requirements
- **Endpoint Protection Platform (EPP)**—mainly focused on Antimalware
- Security Researchers

Practically, Defender was playing in the EPP space and was trying to build strong proactive protection for their customer by warming up their system by sampling millions of unknown files and stored signatures in their backend system to reduce down the prediction time.

The team had targets to complete the analysis of around 35 million files, categorizing them as clean or malicious through the platform they built. Microsoft already had a similar setup for the Windows platform but did not have this capability for cross-platform operating systems. So, it was a fresh journey for the team to implement and build similar workflow pipelines to perform such automation at scale.

This included using the latest and greatest technologies available at that time. Many machine learning workflows were implemented to strengthen the verdict given by the backend system.

Cross platform backend OS virtualization stack

The MDE cross platform SRE team was doing the system engineering work that only a few engineers in the security domain have been playing around. This helped to analyze samples at scale level.

For example, you will hardly find the system engineers scaling macOS or Android virtual machines in a similar fashion as how the industry was using the Virtual Hypervisors to scale the Windows or Linux OS's. It was a great learning experience to scale ,macOS and Android infrastructure on the fly, where platform was supposed to run malicious activities, clean the setup and automatically bring up a new instance on the fly to handle MBA coming from complex workflows in defender system.

MDE backend platform virtualization insight

Android virtualization was altogether another insightful experience where the team decided to use Azure Nested virtualization to spin up Android VM. Android is a Linux OS so all the famous hypervisors were available to the team and team used their own in-house Microsoft Hypervisor to run the Android compute. Microsoft Hypervisor is not as great as VMware hypervisor is but in-house solution was meeting teams requirement.

> **Informational: In recent days, Apple brought up its own Hypervisor to support such Virtualization requirement and opened the possibilities to try native solution.**

Apple's licensing restriction and COGS management

The team learned about the license limitations implemented by Apple for the virtualization of macOS. Apple wanted to sell more hardware and was not interested in supporting the running of more than two VMs, even when CPU and memory were available.

This experience led to a drop in the usage of Apple's Mac Pro hardware. As a result, the team decided to buy cheaper Mac Minis to perform backend sample MBA activities as that saved our cost on the hardware used to run the MBA.

Through this decision, the team reduced the **Cost of Operating Goods and Services** (**COGS**).

Apple macOS hardware and datacenter

There is no Emulator for Mac hardware and if you are playing in Cross Platform domain and developing for iOS and macOS then you have to test products on Apple hardware and same team did in Defender data center builds and procured Apple hardware during cross-platform development journey. In the following sections, you will see various hardware range and some public reference of similar datacenter labs that team built for Defender Org.

Apple Mac Minis

We used to run detonation at scale on this hardware range at scale to meet our internal MBA requirement and all cross-platform macOS products were tested on both Intel and M1 ARM chips and primarily we used this hardware range for our scale planning as there were millions of samples files for Mac platform those were not analyzed by Microsoft team as MDE leverages internally built database to give verdict about malicious files.

The following figure showcases the Mac Mini hardware as many of you might have not seen this hardware as it gives you the over view of specification of the hardware where we primarily leveraged the thunderbolt and Ethernet ports:

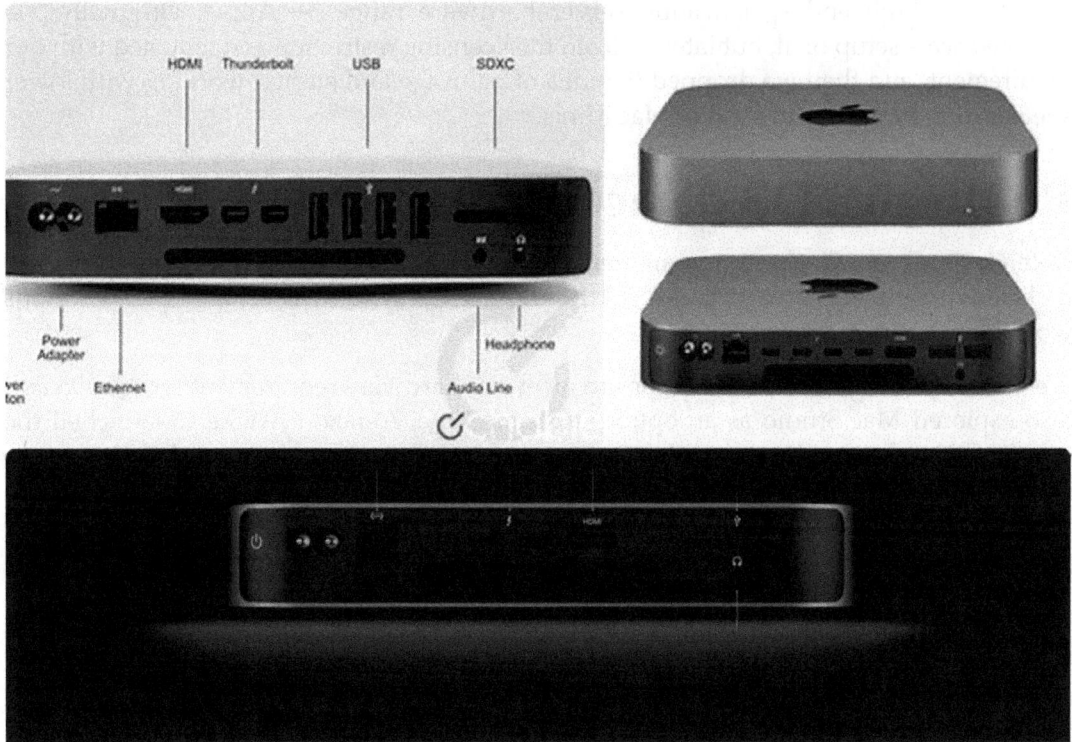

Figure 10.3: *Apple Mac Mini hardware*[1]

Apple Mac Pros

The following is the reference of Apple's Mac Pro Old Generation and New Generation hardware reference and team started running MBA on the following old generation hardware and then we switched to Mac Mini to save cost:

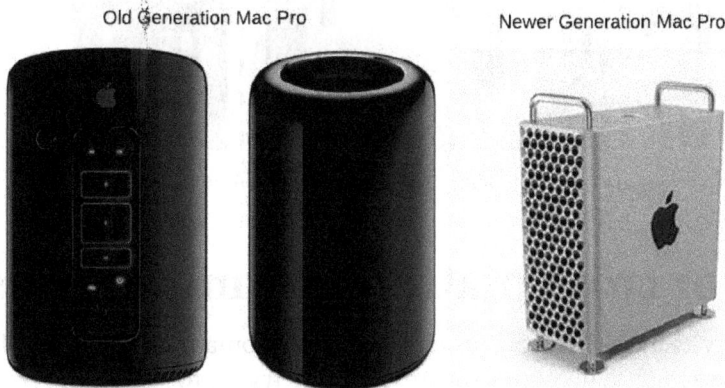

Figure 10.4: *Apple Mac Pro Hardware reference for reader*

Mac Pro is high end specification server hardware range by Apple. Originally, we explored scale setup on it, but later realized the licensing restriction and matched with our requirement, and then we dropped the idea of its usage and started working with lower specification hardware in form of Mac Minis.

Public macOS datacenters

Defender's Cross Platform requirement was unique, and we were doing proactive malicious activities to protect the world through the backend R&D using backend various workflows.

We were exploring third party options to meet our hardware requirement for macOS and also explored Mac Studio as an option. At same time, Amazon AWS also launched the macOS EC2 instances. However, due to the nature of malicious activity work that we were doing to test the un analyzed files, we were not in position to leverage these vendors due to security and compliance requirements so we ended up building our own labs in multiple geographical regions to meet regional and governmental compliance requirement.

Our setup was very similar to some of the commonly known public vendor, as shown in the following figure:

Figure 10.5: Mac Mini Datacenter reference from internet

Security or cross platform terminologies

There are so many technical jargons used in security domain and learning these words will help you to use them with correct context. We are trying to highlight very few among those that we used to use on daily basis while building cross-platform scale infrastructure.

Detonation or MBA

Malware behavior analysis in security involves examining the actions and activities of malicious software to understand its functionality, capabilities, and potential impact on a system or network. This analysis is crucial for cybersecurity professionals to develop effective detection and mitigation strategies against various forms of malware.

The following figures shows that MBA and Detonation are the same:

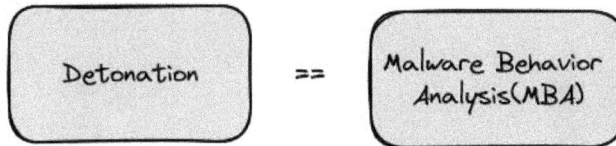

Figure 10.6: *MBA and Detonation are same*

In any MBA workflow, usually, the sources shown in the following figure are used by any security vendor:

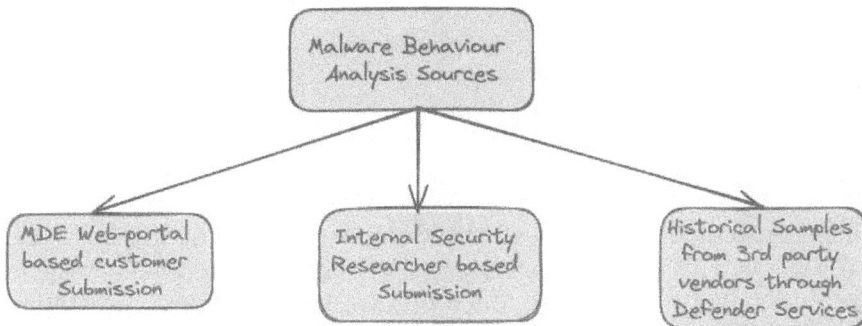

Figure 10.7: *Defender backend team supports 3 different sources to submit samples*

Here is an overview of how malware behavior analysis is conducted in security.

Dynamic analysis

The following items describe what happens in dynamic Malware Behavior Analysis:

- **Execution in a controlled environment**: Malware samples are executed in a controlled environment, such as a sandbox or virtual machine, to observe their behavior without risking the actual system's integrity.
- **Behavior monitoring**: Analysts monitor the malware's activities in real-time, observing actions like file modifications, network communications, registry changes, and attempts to evade detection.
- **Traffic and communication analysis**: Malware often communicates with command-and-control servers. Analysts monitor this communication to understand the

information being transmitted, potentially identifying the malware's purpose and its origin.

The following figure showcases or just represent high level understanding of automated dynamic malware behavior analysis by any security vendor in their own datacenters:

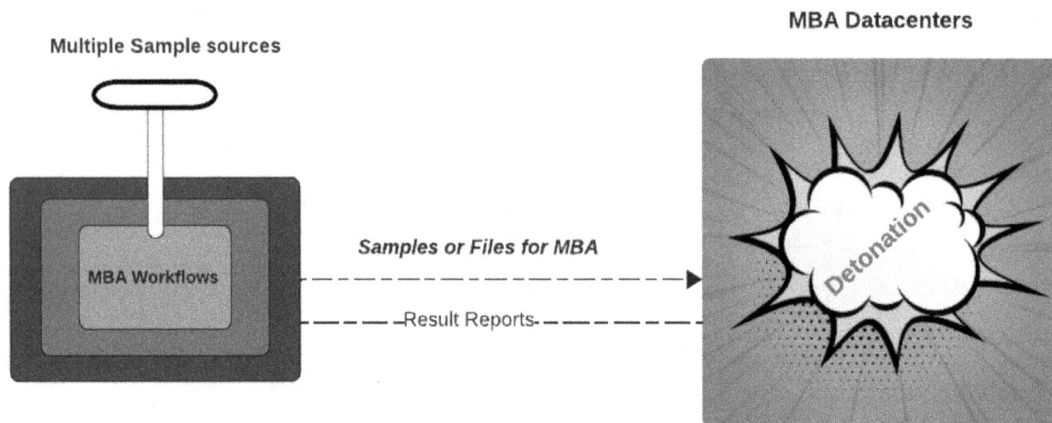

Figure 10.8: Sample submission representation for dynamic MBA

Static analysis

The following items describe what happens in Static Malware Behavior Analysis:

- **Code inspection**: Examining the code and structure of the malware without executing it. This includes examining file headers, embedded strings, and other attributes to identify potential functionalities or known signatures.

- **Malware profiling**: Building a profile of the malware based on static indicators, like file hashes, specific file paths, or registry keys it modifies, to aid in detection across systems.

Comparison of static vs. dynamic MBA

The following table differentiate in between Static and Dynamic MBA:

Area of comparison	Static malware analysis	Dynamic malware analysis
Method	Analyzes malware without execution, examining code and attributes.	Observes malware behavior during execution in a controlled environment.
Execution	Does not execute the malware; focuses on the file's structure.	Executes malware to observe its behavior, interactions, and impact.

Area of comparison	Static malware analysis	Dynamic malware analysis
Detection capability	Limited ability to detect evasive or polymorphic malware.	Often more effective in detecting complex, evasive malware variants.
Resource requirement	Less resource-intensive; suitable for large-scale scanning.	More resource-demanding due to real-time observation and monitoring.
Speed of analysis	Faster analysis compared to dynamic methods.	Slower analysis due to real-time monitoring and behavioral observation.
Threat visibility	Offers insights based on static attributes like file signatures.	Provides insights into real-time behavior, including network activities.
Interaction with environment	No interaction with the malware; low risk of triggering malicious actions.	Interaction can trigger malware actions; higher risk but controlled.
Complexity	Relatively simpler analysis approach based on code inspection.	Involves more complex analysis due to dynamic behavior observation.

Table 10.1: Static vs. dynamic MBA

Behavioural patterns and anomalies

The following items describe behavioral patterns and anomalies detection methods:

- **Baseline creation**: Establishing a baseline of normal behavior for systems or applications to detect deviations caused by malware.
- **Anomaly detection**: Identifying deviations from the established baseline, such as unusual network traffic, unauthorized access attempts, or unexpected file modifications, signaling potential malware presence.

Reporting and mitigation

The following points talks about reporting and mitigation by Security research team:

- **Reporting findings**: Documenting observed behaviors, patterns, and **indicators of compromise (IOCs)** for further analysis or sharing with security communities.
- **Mitigation strategies**: Developing and implementing security measures and countermeasures based on the behavior analysis to prevent, contain, or eradicate the malware.

Behavioral analysis allows security experts to gain insights into the intent and capabilities of malware, enabling them to enhance security measures, develop effective threat intelligence, and create more robust defenses against evolving cyber threats.

MBA of Zip file (XPlode)

Xplode in MBA domain referred to unzip of the sample files to submit before the MBA. Most of the company perform unzip of deep zipped files and usually it done till 255 subfolders as that is the max limit of any OS. Once unzipped then each file is further submitted to same MBA workflow as similar to normal sample files.

> **Note: Technically, you cannot just run MBA on zip file as it contains multiple files so as vendor companies need to extract individual file and then forward it further MBA workflow as end goal is to analyze the single file not the zip file and that is the reason to build a separate service to extract file from zip.**

The following figure represent the MBA of zipped file:

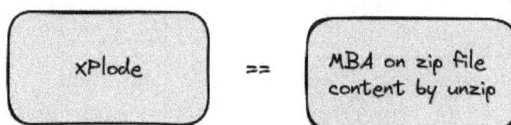

Figure 10.9: *MBA of zip file referred as XPlode in Defender team*

It was just one another variant of the MacOS lab that we built to perform MBA of samples Development of new cross-platform XPlode service.

Windows and cross-platform MBAs are performed separately due to the fact that earlier Microsoft Defender windows service was unable to unzip macOS DMZ package and cross-platform team built a new service from scratch to handle this scenario.

The following figure is just logical representation of MBA of zipped file:

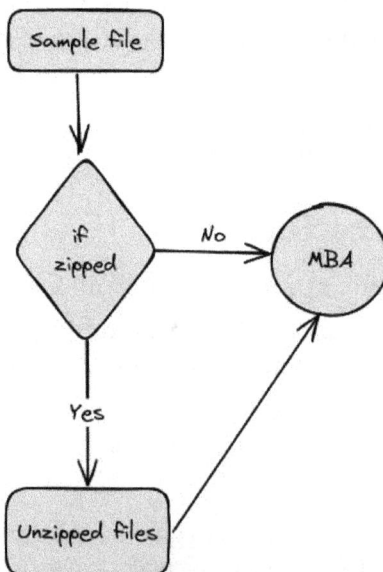

Figure 10.10: *Logical flow how ideally anyone will be doing MBA of zipped file*

Public MBA vendors available in market

Joe Sandbox detects and analyzes potential malicious files and URLs on Windows, Android, Mac OS, and Linux for suspicious activities. It performs deep malware analysis and generates comprehensive and detailed analysis reports. Their SaaS solution gives you access to the Community and Enterprise Edition of Joe Sandbox Cloud. It allows you to run a maximum of 15 analyses/month, five analyses/day on Windows, Linux and Android with limited analysis output. In case, you would like to setup same system internally for your own requirement that you can buy license to run MBA in your own setup and you do not require Cloud SaaS Version.

Public MBA vendor URL reference: **https://www.joesandbox.com/#mac**

The following figure is the sample reference of JoeSandbox cloud console that can also be used to run MBA:

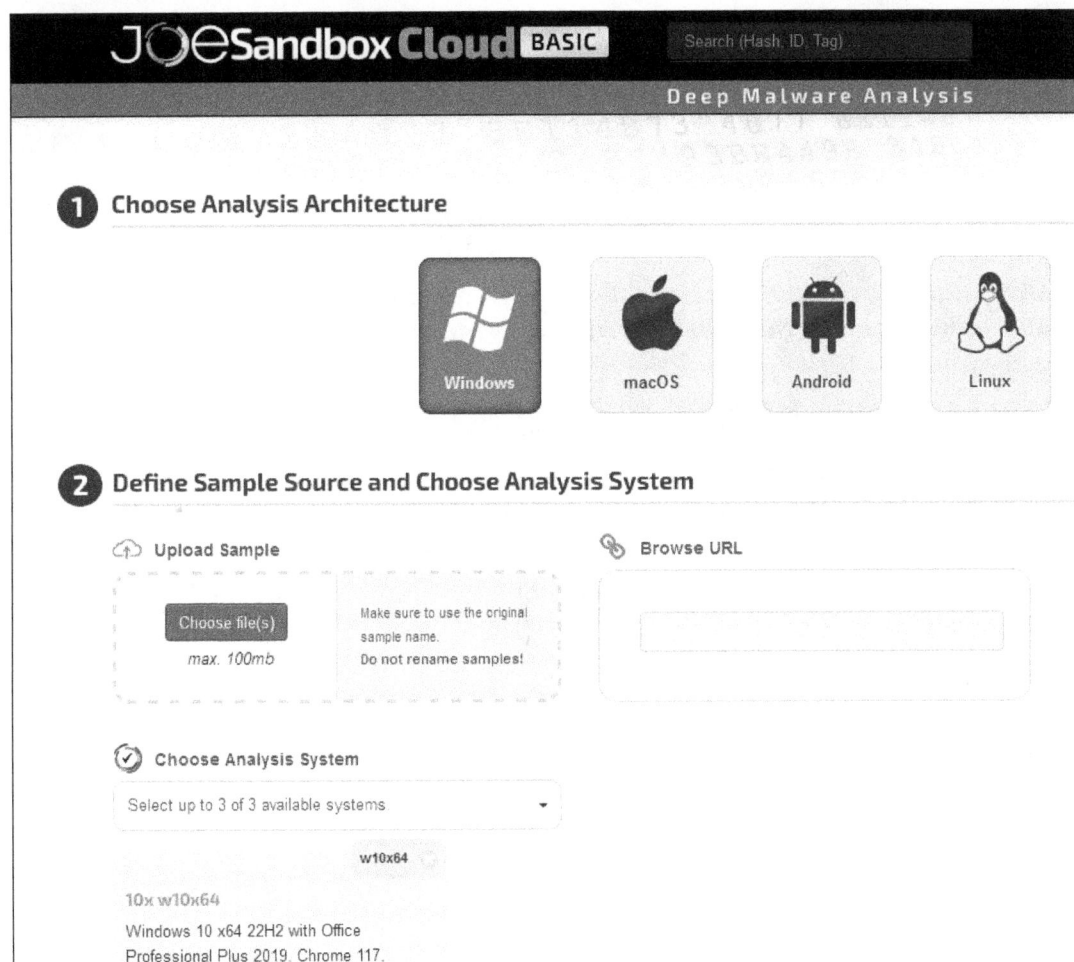

Figure 10.11: JoeSandbox web portal interface

The following figure is a continuation of sample submission page:

3 **Live Interaction**

Live Interaction
☐ Use Live Interaction

4 **Settings**

☐ Comments   🕐 Execution / Run Time

///.

30 sec   120 ⌄   500 sec

Show Advanced Settings

ⓘ Your complete sample and analysis will be published on this website and accessible to anyone (including a download of the sample, screenshots etc). Upgrade to Cloud Pro to get a private account

5 **Accept Terms and Conditions**

☐ I have read and understood and agree to the Terms and Conditions. If and to the extent I use Joe Sandbox Cloud Basic services on behalf of or for the benefit of a private business or a government agency or instrumentality ('Entity'), I agree to the Terms and Conditions on behalf of such Entity and I confirm to be authorized to bind such Entity to the Terms and Conditions.

☐ I have read and understood and agree to the Data Protection Policy

Analyze with Joe Sandbox

Figure 10.12: JoeSandbox web portal submission page reference

Informational: MDE customer gets the same feature to upload and test the dynamic MBA of files through MDE web portal.

Geo location MBA support

The specimens designated for detonation originate from various contributors and varied origins. They can be set off automatically, upon request, or on an impromptu basis by Researchers within their laboratory environments (sandbox).

The following figure is just a representation of Geo location specific MBA performed in Defender labs:

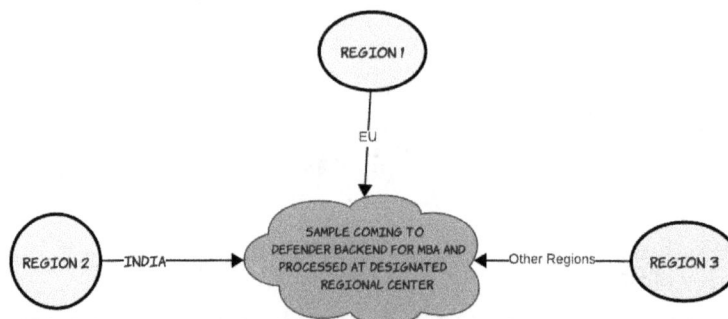

REGION 1

EU

REGION 2 —INDIA→ SAMPLE COMING TO DEFENDER BACKEND FOR MBA AND PROCESSED AT DESIGNATED REGIONAL CENTER ←Other Regions— REGION 3

Figure 10.13: Defender supports Geo specific compliance requirement in MBA

Note: Currently there is no such regional requirement for India but in coming days you might see introduction into defender support due to the fact of new Data Law approved by India and no such regional support available for EU but you might see such support available on MDE platform.

Given the multitude of sources and Microsoft's dedication to safeguarding customer privacy and security, it is crucial to ensure compliance with geo-location requirements. This becomes imperative as our cross-platform offerings reach and serve customers worldwide. It is vital to integrate regional business and customer forecasts into our geo-location strategy.

It is important to highlight that enabling detonation in a particular region demands prior planning, allocation of resources, and time.

The following figure represents the three different types of MBA supported on MDE platform:

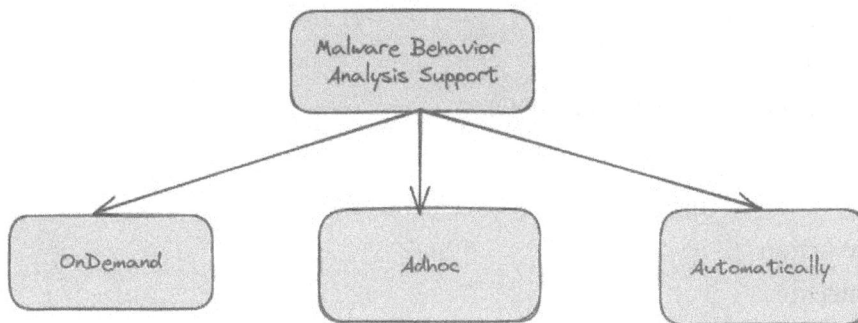

Figure 10.14: Different types of support available to submit sample for MBA

Clean or historical samples

In the context of malware behavioral analysis, a *clean sample* refers to a benign or non-malicious piece of software that serves as a baseline or reference for comparison. Security researchers and analysts use clean samples to understand and establish the normal or expected behavior of a software application or system. By studying the behavior of clean samples, analysts can identify deviations or anomalies that may indicate the presence of malicious activity.

The process typically involves running the clean sample in a controlled environment, known as a **sandbox**, and observing its interactions with the system. This allows analysts to create a behavioral profile of the clean sample, documenting the legitimate actions and operations it performs during execution.

Once the baseline behavior is established, security analysts can use it as a point of reference when analyzing suspicious or potentially malicious samples. Comparing the behavior of unknown or potentially harmful samples to the clean sample's behavior helps in detecting and understanding malicious activities, such as unauthorized access, data exfiltration, or attempts to exploit vulnerabilities.

Security research

Security research is a critical field dedicated to uncovering vulnerabilities, developing safeguards, and advancing the overall security of systems and networks. Researchers in this domain continuously explore new threats, devise innovative defensive techniques, and contribute to the creation of robust security protocols. This work is essential for protecting sensitive data, ensuring the integrity of digital infrastructures, and fostering trust in technology. By staying ahead of cybercriminals and understanding the ever-evolving landscape of security threats, security research plays a pivotal role in maintaining a safe and secure digital world.

Security profiles are around the following areas:

- Security audit
- Hacking
- **Security operation center (SOC)**
- Research

So, if you look into security research, it covers the following areas:

- Prediction
- Detection
- Analyze
- Continuous learning through MITER
- SOC
- Threat Intel management

Native engine support in cross-platform

Previously, Microsoft primarily focused on Windows and had internally created their antivirus software for the Windows operating system. However, under *Satya Nadella's* leadership and the strategic shift to develop applications across all platforms, they faced a gap in capabilities for non-Windows OS (cross-platform) and mobile devices. To address this, as part of their strategic approach, they collaborated with Bit Defender, either through partnerships or licensing agreements. This led to the launch of their security client agents embedding Bit Defender's AV engine within their solution.

However, this approach was considered temporary. Eventually, Microsoft developed its own cross platform security engine with nearly identical features. This proprietary engine, referred to internally as the **native engine** (**NE**), replaced the previously embedded software. During this transition, customers might have observed both engines available in their mdatp health command status.

> **Informational: Libmpengine.so is a library that you can find in agent code that has native engine capability.**

The initial version of the MDATP solution utilized the OEM Bit Defender Scan Software Development Kit. Subsequently, they introduced EDR capabilities, which transitioned toward the MDATP Side by Side solution. Their objective was to substitute the Bit Defender Scan Engine with the Microsoft Native Engine, marking the evolution to MDATP V2.

The **Microsoft Defender for Endpoint** (**MDE**) agent encompasses various components, each operating independently with separate release cycles. Defender offers functionalities to manage the release of each component, providing customers with similar control over these features.

The following are the three Client Agent Software pieces bundled in the Agent:

- Native Engine Code (Antimalware/EPP)
- MDE Agent (AM + EDR Agents)
- Malware Signatures

The Defender Cross Platform team explored all dimensions to build a strong EDR product. They managed the interaction between EDR and EPP binaries effectively through Inter Process Communication constructs of the programming. This approach enhanced the efficiency during such communications.

The same feature is utilized during device isolation for incident troubleshooting on identified devices. Scripts are configured on each respective OS to manage moving in and out of the network during these incidents.

We have already covered this feature in *Chapter 2, Understanding Endpoint Security Fundamentals,* but kept here in reference as this feature got developed in Cross Platform Defender team.

The following figure is a reference of inter communication in between EDR and EPP agents:

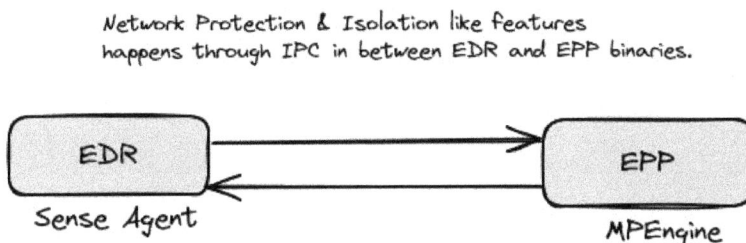

Figure 10.15: EDR and EPP direct communication representation

The following command returns various different library versions used in the Agent:

```
# Get-MpComputerStatus
AMEngineVersion                    : 1.1.18100.6
AMProductVersion                   : 4.18.2107.4
AMRunning                          : True
AMServiceEnabled                   : True
AMServiceVersion                   : 4.18.2107.4
AntispywareEnabled                 : True
AntispywareSignatureAge            : 0
AntispywareSignatureLastUpdated    : 7/31/2023 4:55:06 PM
AntispywareSignatureVersion        : 1.355.221.0
```

NE general availability and Bit Defender replacement

MDE has a native engine that provides security intelligence updates and product updates to keep the devices up-to-date with the latest technology and features needed to protect against new malware and attack techniques. The native engine replaces the Bitdefender engine that was used in the past in your agent binary. The platform and engine versions are updated monthly, and the latest versions can be viewed on the Microsoft Defender Antivirus security intelligence and product updates page.

> **Information: In Mid of 2022 Microsoft Team replaced Bit Defender with Native Engine in both Linux and macOS.**

Microsoft software release and cycles

Microsoft defender actively contributing and releasing so many products and services in the market and the following are some early day time lines when the team was actively working on Private and Public preview of the whole product and then many small features on top of the product and services are continuously getting launched. Few Defenders Product General Availability Dates for Public are mentioned in the following table for your reference.

MDE product release timeline

The following are the MDE product release timeline:

Product	General availability date
Microsoft Defender for Endpoint (formerly Defender ATP)	April 2019
Microsoft Defender for Identity (formerly Azure ATP)	June 2019
Microsoft Defender for Office 365 (formerly Office 365 ATP)	February 2020
Microsoft Defender for Endpoint on Android	June 2020
Microsoft Defender for Endpoint on iOS	June 2020
Microsoft Defender for macOS	June 2020
Microsoft Defender for Linux	June 2021

Table 10.2: MDE product release timeline

You will see the following mentioned release terminologies in many announcements and Ring-X terminology is much used internally and private, public preview and GA terminologies are more used for mass communication.

Release rings

Ring terminologies are more for internal teams for discussion during planning and management of work with tech and non tech audience in respect to developer, system engineers, management and org leadership as accordingly product manager and program managers drive the work and it keeps aligned toward the business goal to achieve the epic(Big chunk of work or objective) completion.

The release rings internally used by Defender team before releasing it publicly are shown in the following table:

Release terminology	Description
Ring-0	Initial release to a select group for validation/testing.
Ring-1	Expanded release to a broader internal audience.
Ring-2	Further expanded release to a wider set of users.
General Availability	Full release available to the public or all users.

Table 10.3: Internal release rings used by Defender team

Release stages

You will see the following terminologies in all Microsoft release announcements. This applies to Azure Cloud service releases as well as any other product and service releases announced by Microsoft. Throughout all internal teams, they follow the same terminology and practices. These terminologies and practices have been consistently followed for many years.

These release stages give indication for the internal test teams on the expectation on work receivable and delivery of the test results to next level team so that leadership can communicate new features in advance with confidence to internal and external community.

The following are the release stages leveraged by Microsoft Defender team:

Stage	Audience
Pre-Dogfood	Internal product team
Dogfood	Microsoft Employees
Insider-Slow and Fast	Internal selected groups
Private Preview	Invited external users
Public Preview	External users
GA (Go Live)	External users

Table 10.4: Release stage references used by Microsoft

Microsoft mobile threat defense cross platform solution

Microsoft Defender for Endpoint on Android and iOS is their **Mobile Threat Defense Solution (MTD)**. Typically, companies are proactive in protecting PCs from vulnerabilities and attack while mobile devices often go unmonitored and unprotected. Where mobile platforms have built-in protection such as app isolation and vetted consumer app stores, these platforms remain vulnerable to web-based or other sophisticated attacks. As more employees use devices for work and to access sensitive information, it is imperative that companies deploy an MTD solution to protect devices and your resources from increasingly sophisticated attacks on mobiles.

The following figure represents the different category of devices in MTD:

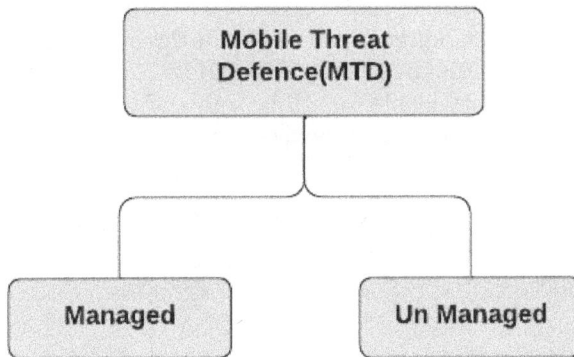

Figure 10.16: Device categorization in MTD

Key capabilities

Microsoft Defender for Endpoint on Android and iOS provide the following key capabilities:

Capability	Description
Web protection	Anti-phishing, blocking unsafe network connections, and support for custom indicators.
Malware protection (Android-only)	Scanning for malicious apps.
Jailbreak Detection (iOS-only)	Detection of jailbroken devices.
Microsoft Defender Vulnerability Management (MDVM)	Vulnerability assessment of onboarded mobile devices. Includes OS and apps vulnerabilities assessment for both Android and iOS. Visit this **page** to learn more about Microsoft Defender Vulnerability Management in Microsoft Defender for Endpoint.
Network protection	Protection against rogue Wi-Fi related threats and rogue certificates; ability to allow list the root CA and private root CA certificates in Intune; establish trust with endpoints.
Unified alerting	Alerts from all platforms in the unified M365 security console.
Conditional access, conditional launch	Blocking risky devices from accessing corporate resources. Defender for Endpoint risk signals can also be added to app protection policies (MAM).

Capability	Description
Privacy controls	Configure privacy in the threat reports by controlling the data sent by Microsoft Defender for Endpoint. Privacy controls are available for admin and end users. It's there for enrolled and unenrolled devices as well.
Integration with Microsoft Tunnel	Integration with Microsoft Tunnel, a VPN gateway solution to enable security and connectivity in a single app. Available on both Android and iOS.

Table 10.5: Android and iOS Defender Agent key capabilities

All these capabilities are available for Microsoft Defender for Endpoint license holders for mobiles.

The following figure shows the defender capabilities for mobile devices:

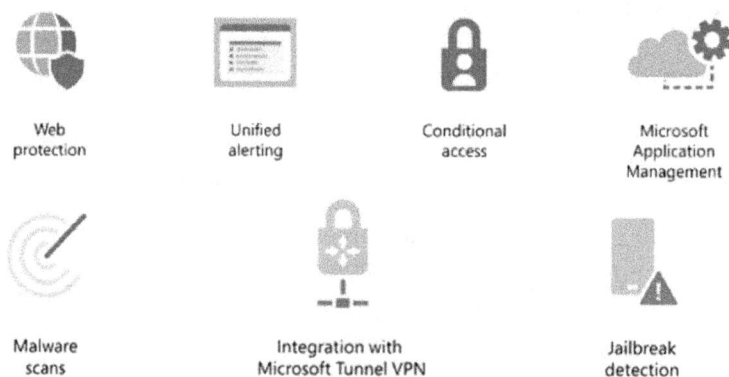

| Web protection | Unified alerting | Conditional access | Microsoft Application Management |
| Malware scans | Integration with Microsoft Tunnel VPN | Jailbreak detection | |

Figure 10.17: Defender capabilities for mobile device

Reference: Configure Microsoft Defender for Endpoint on Android risk signals using App Protection Policies (MAM) https://learn.microsoft.com/en-us/microsoft-365/security/defender-endpoint/android-configure-mam?view=o365-worldwide

Informational: In late 2020 Microsoft team saw hockey stick growth on Android installs and around 70+K installed happened with 25+K onboarding and around 15+K daily active users within short span.

The following figure shows some of the brief examples of the configuration that you need to enable for MTD, but we have already covered such MDE settings in details in *Chapters 4, Configuring Microsoft Defender Endpoint*.

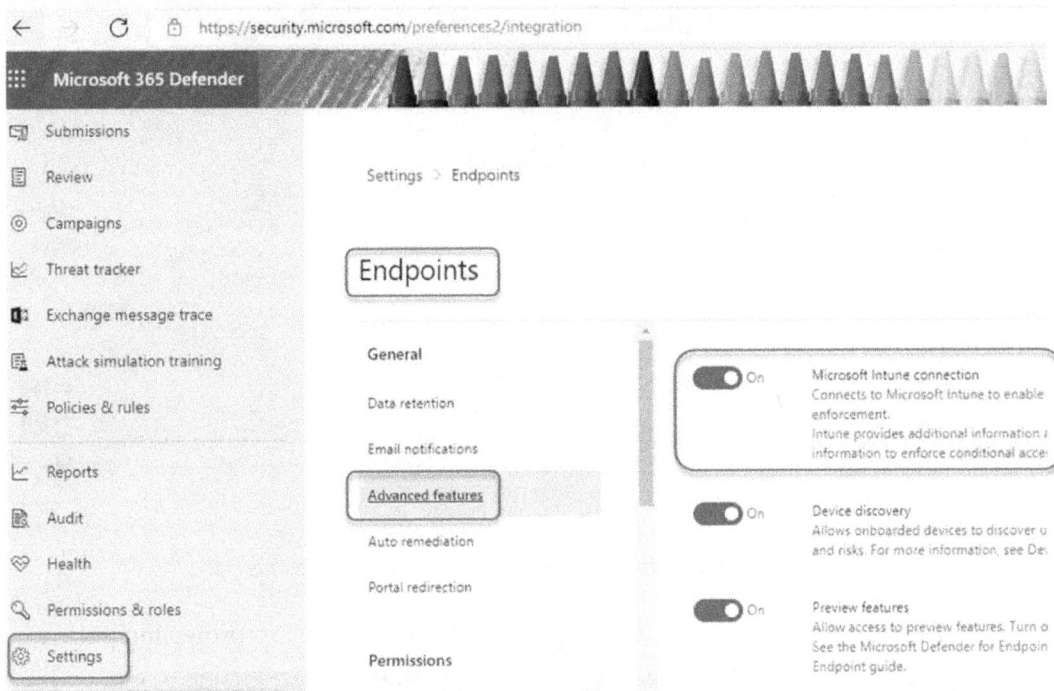

Figure 10.18: MDE web portal Settings page for Intune connection

Intune app protection policy settings

To leverage app protection policies, you need to enable the application protection in MS Intune portal, and we have covered such details in *Chapter 14, Practical Configuration Examples and Case Studies*, and kept it here for quick reference in respect to cross platform work that happened around us.

The following figure shows the Intune reference page showcasing **App Protection policy Settings**:

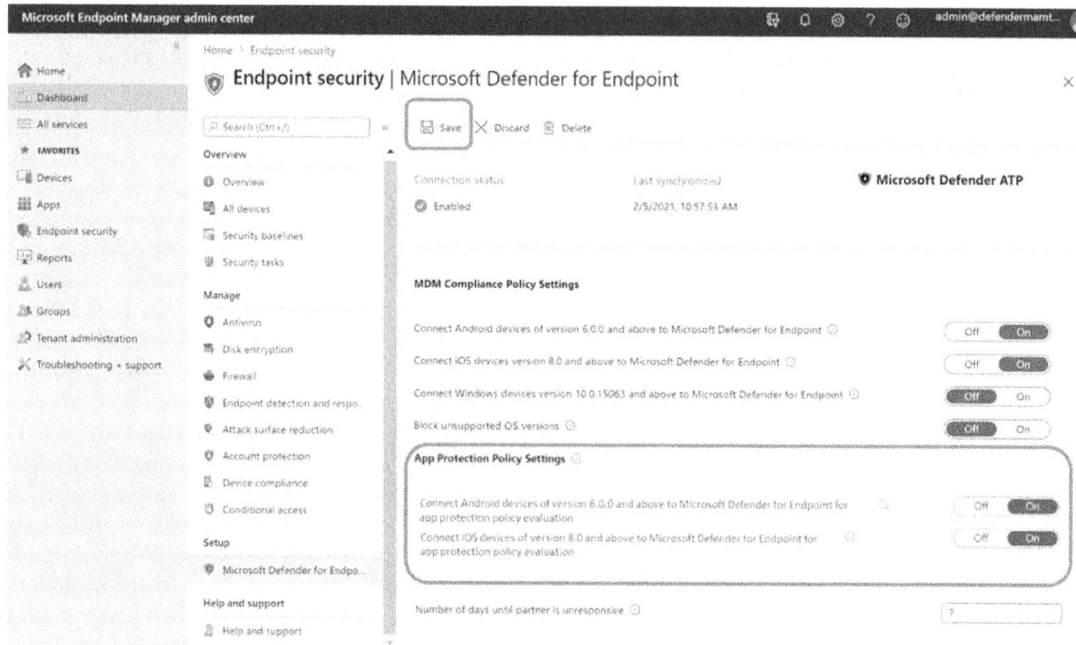

Figure 10.19: App protection policy setting page on Intune web portal

The following figure showcase Untune Apps page representing App protection policies:

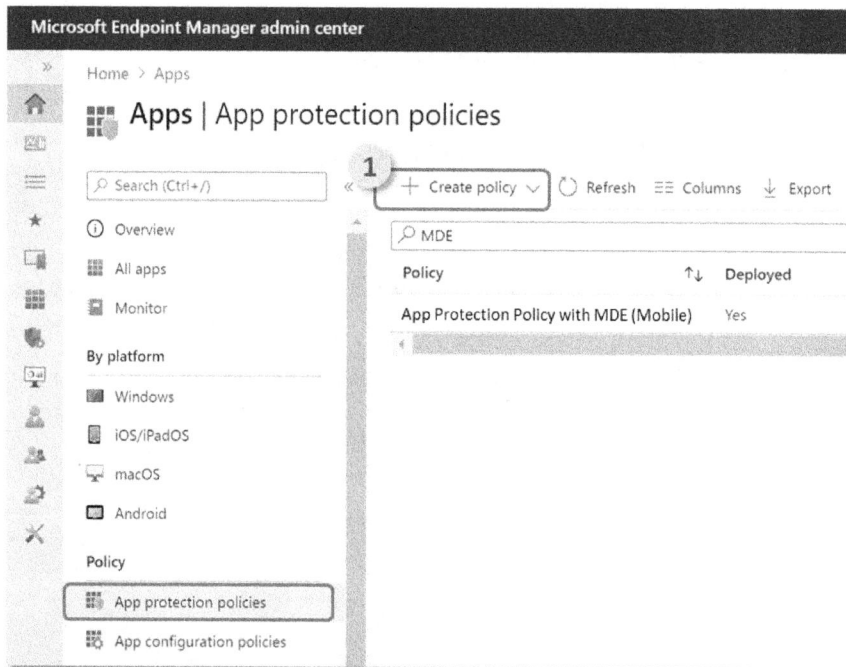

Figure 10.20: Untune Apps page representing App protection policies

MDM, MAM and MTD coverage through security policies

The following figure shows the security policy on Intune portal that provides coverage for MTD. You can more read on Microsoft Intune and MTD documentation about the configuration and we have captured few screenshots for your reference.

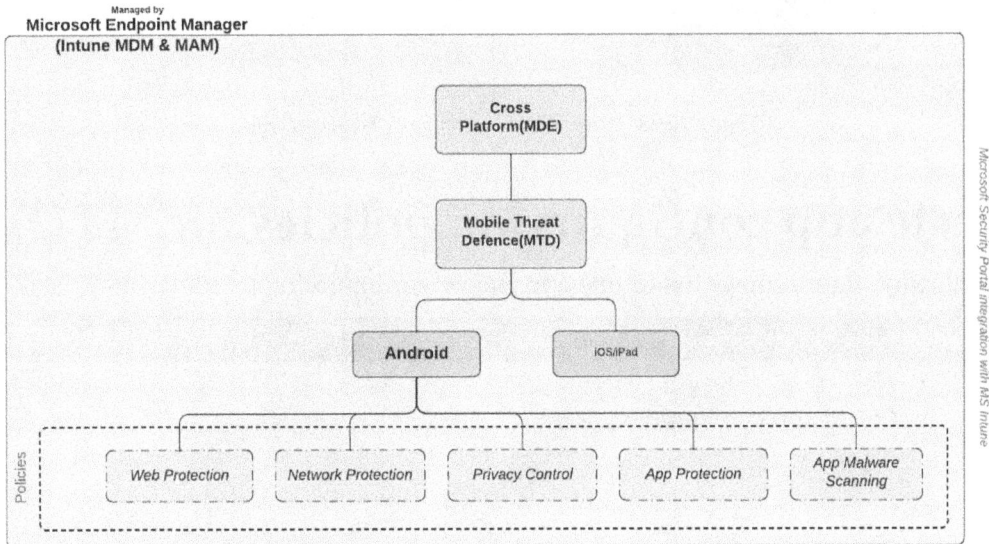

Figure 10.21: Different policies under MTD to manage mobile devices

MD XDR unified portal and android policies

Microsoft Defender XDR is a unified pre and post-breach enterprise defence suite that natively coordinates detection, prevention, investigation, and response across endpoints, identities, email, and applications to provide integrated protection against sophisticated attacks.

The following figure showcase MDE settings web portal page:

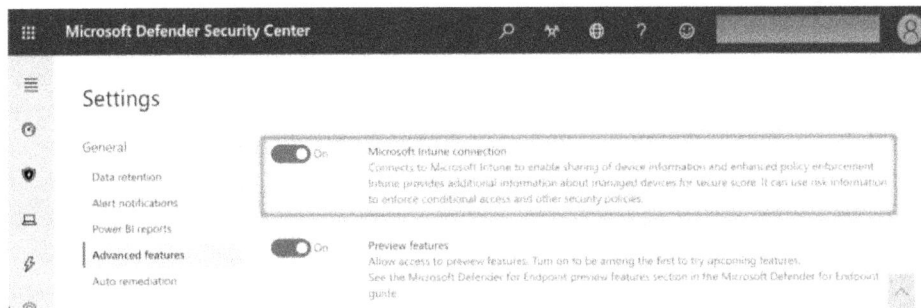

Figure 10.22: MDE settings page reference on web portal

The following figure showcase Intune MDM compliances policy settings:

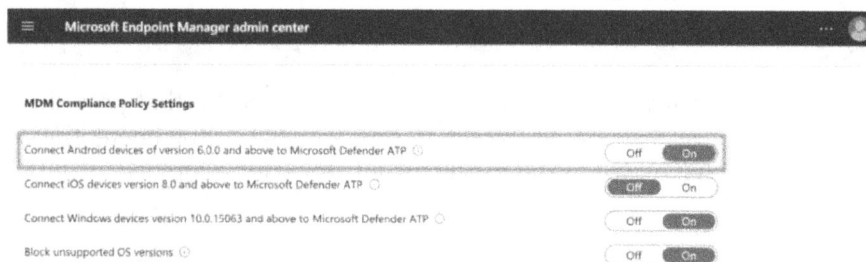

Figure 10.23: *Intune MDM compliance policy settings*

Create app configuration policies for MTD

The following figure shows the Intune application configuration policy creation:

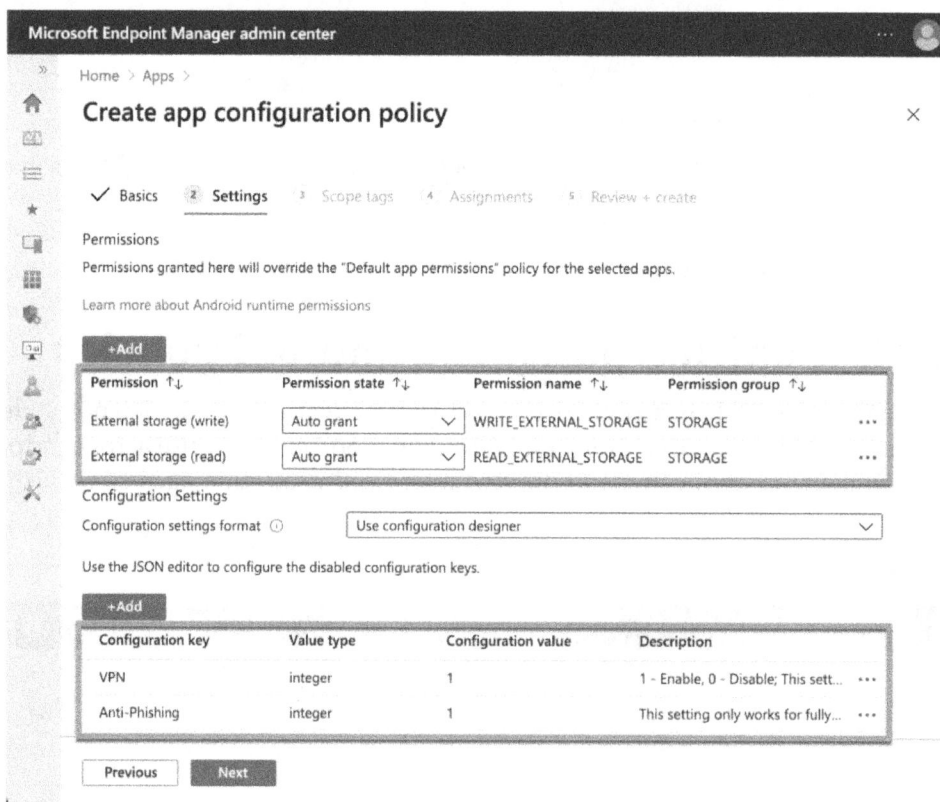

Figure 10.24: *Intune app configuration policy creation page*

The following figure is a continuation of above step:

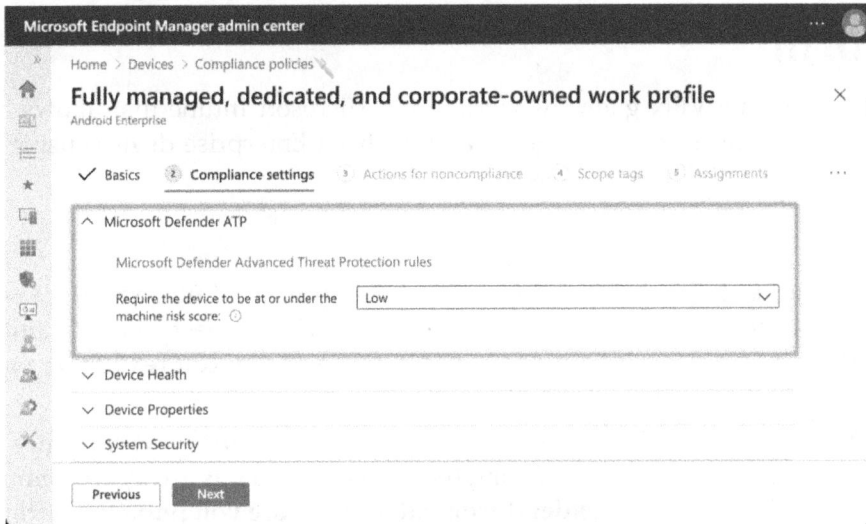

Figure 10.25: Intune App configuration policy creation page

In the following figure, you can see Android MDE app interfaces:

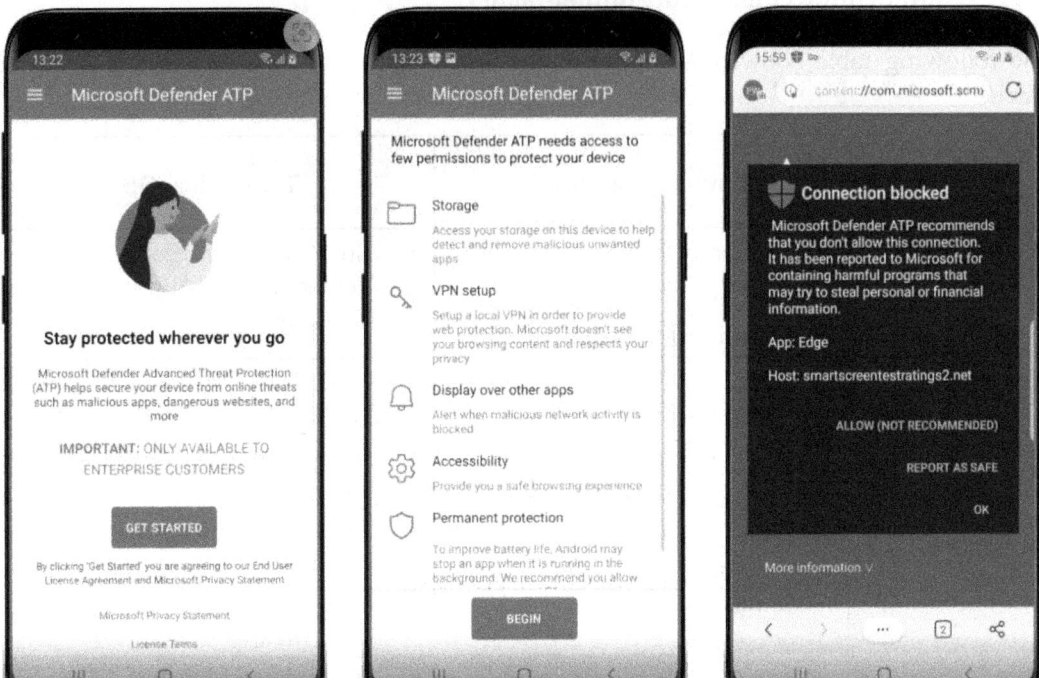

Figure 10.26: MDE app interface on Android

Microsoft Tunnel and VPN for cross-platform

Microsoft Tunnel is a VPN gateway solution for Microsoft Intune that allows access to on-premises resources from iOS/iPadOS and Android Enterprise devices using modern authentication and conditional access.

Note:
- **All these discussions come in Microsoft Intune Management so we just would like to give you brief introduction with respect to MTD and Cross platform team work happened in this area and you can read more on given references to understand better.**
- **As we have highlighted that cross-platform products are currently not in feature parity and there are long list of features so it is always recommended to read Microsoft Defender documentation before you implementation.**
- **For an example Android and iOS has differences in form of Tunnel software installation and device wide VPN is not available for iOS etc and below is the comparison sheet taken from https://learn.microsoft.com/en-us/mem/intune/protect/microsoft-tunnel-mam**

The following table showcase requirements and features for Android and iOS tunnel service:

Requirements and features	Tunnel for android	Tunnel for iOS
Requirements	• Company Portal app (sign-in not required) • Defender for Endpoint app	• No Company Portal app or Defender for Endpoint app requirement

Features	• VPN is provided via the Defender for Endpoint app:
	  o Per App VPN
	  o Device-wide VPN
	• Auto-launch: VPN automatically starts on app launch
		• VPN is provided via Tunnel for MAM SDK for iOS integration
		• Trusted root certificate support for on-premises CA trust
		• Per-App VPN. Tunnel connection is restricted to each targeted app
		• Auto-launch: VPN automatically starts on app launch
		• No device-wide VPN

Table 10.6: Tunnel service requirement and features for MTD supported devices

> **Information: These features are only available on or above Microsoft Intune Plan 2 or Microsoft Intune Suite and you can read more in our license add on chapter to get the high level over.**

Requirement of Tunnel software for MTD

Mobile Device Management (MDM) and **Mobile Application Management (MAM)** are managed through Microsoft Intune. There are scenarios where mobile users want to access corporate resources, and this can only happen after the device is registered to your organization through Microsoft Company Portal.

However, MAM also has scenarios where device registration is not required.

There were complexities involved in design in terms of customer experience as MDE Mobile App, Microsoft Tunnel and Microsoft Company Portal were not connected and were independent products so to simplify this complexity Microsoft Defender Cross Platform team collaborated with Tunnel team to simplify the design and merged Tunnel features into MDE mobile app and now you can run MDE app into Tunnel Only mode and *independent Tunnel app has been discontinued* that lead to simplification of setup as Microsoft goal is to build one Super App instead of multiple Apps in this area.

MAM Tunnel for unregistered devices or for guests

When employing the Microsoft Tunnel VPN Gateway, you have the option to expand its capabilities through the addition of Tunnel for MAM. Tunnel for MAM broadens the functionality of the Microsoft Tunnel VPN gateway to accommodate Android or iOS devices that are not enrolled in Microsoft Intune. This solution enables users to securely access organizational on-premises applications and resources using modern authentication, Single Sign-On, and conditional access, even on a single device that remains unenrolled with Intune. With Tunnel for MAM, users can leverage their personal devices (BYOD) for both work and personal tasks, eliminating the need to grant the organization's IT department control over these devices.

It only applies to the following:
- Android
- iOS/iPadOS

Microsoft Tunnel gateway architecture

Microsoft Company portal app is required to enroll your mobile device in case you would like to join your company corporate network to access concerned company resources like MS Teams, Slack, Web portal, Outlook and many other corporate resources. The following figure shows the Architecture to understand the HLD of overall system for MS Intune Administrator understanding point of view.

The flow starts from the Intune application, setup of VPN infra by Intune Administrators and MDE app installation by user to enroll through Microsoft company portal and get registered on Intune as managed device to get all the managed device benefits.

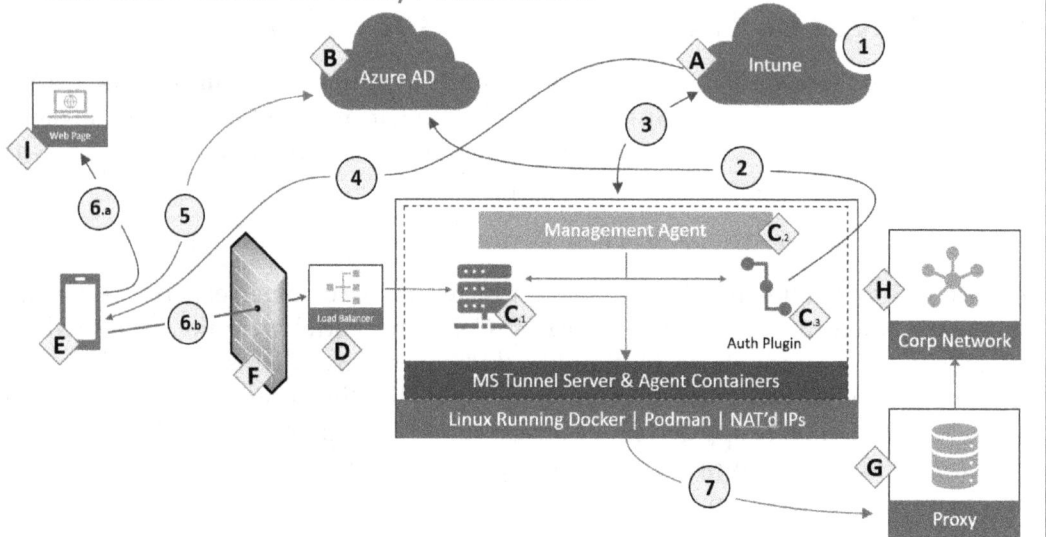

Figure 10.27: Microsoft Tunnel gateway architecture[2]

Microsoft's leadership in the MTD area

Microsoft's focus is more on building XDR, MDR like product categories instead of just selling Antivirus features and you will continue to see changes in feature or app mergers.

> **Note: There were so many bad feedback on Google Play store in this area and it is challenging to manage so many thing in situation of VPN profile activation/ deactivation, app specific VPN usage that complicates the solution management from client side and my recommendation is that Microsoft should keep these features into Alpha or Beta mode instead of hurry to sell them as production ready features as their reputation is on stake and there are high number of frustration shown by end users in terms of performance and authentication issues that directly or indirectly taking down the Microsoft Brand reputation.**

Comprehensive server setup configuration for Intune Administrators

The Microsoft Tunnel Gateway is installed within a container operating on a Linux server, which can either be a physical on-premises device or a virtual machine situated in an

---

2   Reference: https://learn.microsoft.com/en-us/mem/intune/protect/microsoft-tunnel-overview

on-premises or cloud environment. Setting up the Tunnel involves deploying Microsoft Defender for Endpoint as the client app alongside Intune VPN profiles on iOS and Android devices. This configuration allows devices to utilize the tunnel for accessing corporate resources. In scenarios where the tunnel is cloud-hosted, a solution like Azure ExpressRoute becomes necessary to expand the on-premises network into the cloud environment.

Microsoft Tunnel VPN integration for mobile

The general availability of Microsoft Tunnel VPN capabilities unified in the Microsoft Defender for Endpoint app for Android. This unification enables organizations to offer a simplified end user experience with one security app—offering both mobile threat defence (MTD) and the ability to access on-prem resources from their mobile device, while security and IT teams are able to maintain the same admin experiences, they are familiar with.

Existing customers of Microsoft Defender for Endpoint, who are also licensed for Microsoft Tunnel, will see Tunnel Capabilities in the Defender for Endpoint app on Android. Existing Tunnel customers will switch to using the Microsoft Defender for Endpoint app for VPN. They will not see any other changes to Tunnel features, it will simply now appear within the Defender for Endpoint app. IT administrators will be able to continue to use the Microsoft Endpoint Manager admin center to configure both Defender and Tunnel features

The following are the use cases:

- Anti phishing
- Intune (For corporate managed mobile devices)
- Consumer VPN (For individual mobile devices)

Microsoft cloud-native protection platform

There is another Microsoft product gaining momentum around cross-platform and across clouds, including on-premises datacenters. Kubernetes, containers, and DevSecOps practices are on the rise, and container security and IaC should be the highest priority for organizations. Adopting the Shift Left approach ensures that code to cloud activities can be secured through automation.

CNPP brings all such features built-in, allowing you to integrate them with your own setup. It supports multi-cloud environments and a broad range of other setup requirements.

It is not part of MDE but as our goal is to give high level understanding of all the product and services in MDE so that you can build your strong understanding in the security management and hence we captured this topic for your attention. It is toally a new prodcut in early stage and huge pottential to grow in coming days.

You will gain more insight into this topic in next chapter.

Conclusion

In this chapter, I have detailed my extensive journey and experiences with the Defender Cross Platform Team, providing valuable insights into **Microsoft Defender for Endpoint (MDE)**. By the end of this chapter, readers will gain an understanding of the collaboration between Microsoft Office and Azure DevOps engineering teams, and the exploration of cross-platform observability challenges and solutions. They will also learn about the implications of Apple's licensing restrictions on MacOS hardware and datacenters, as well as insights into key security terminologies and behavioral analysis methods like detonation and MBA.

Additionally, readers will comprehend the evolution of Microsoft's Engine from MP to the **Native Engine** (NE) and its General Availability. The chapter covers Microsoft's software release cycles, MDE product timelines, release rings and stages, and MTD solution capabilities. Finally, it provides a brief overview of the Microsoft Tunnel, highlighting its configuration and integration within the mobile environment. This comprehensive overview serves as a knowledge base, offering a nuanced understanding of Microsoft's security solutions and cross-platform endeavors.

In next chapter, we are going to introduce endpoint security for cloud environment and you will learn shift left approach in form of DevSecOps product by Microsoft Security team and will gain insight into container security.

Join our book's Discord space

Join the book's Discord Workspace for Latest updates, Offers, Tech happenings around the world, New Release and Sessions with the Authors:

https://discord.bpbonline.com

CHAPTER 11

Endpoint Security for Cloud Environments

Introduction

Before we understand the endpoint security in cloud, we would like to help you to understand the bigger picture of cloud workload protection and that is beyond endpoint. **Cloud Workload Protection** (CWP) product category covers more than just endpoint and also started covering **Function as a Service (FaaS)** Containers and other cloud services.

Broadcom's Symantec CWP team in 2020 team built and delivered the CWP and was exploring the opportunity to support FaaS like AWS Lamda or Azure Function and was also exploring the *Container Security* market that included *Application Container* (Container images) and the *Container Orchestrator platform* (Kubernetes or OpenShift like platform security) and as on today they also provides container security along with CWP.

A **Cloud Workload Protection Platform** (CWPP) serves as a comprehensive cybersecurity solution designed to safeguard cloud environments within an organization. These platforms provide protection for physical servers, serverless functions, virtual machines, and containers.

With the proliferation of diverse environments, organizations face increased security risks. To effectively mitigate these risks and swiftly respond to active threats, companies require solutions capable of monitoring and safeguarding their multifaceted environments. CWP solutions fulfill this need by providing continuous security monitoring and management for cloud workloads.

CWPPs operate seamlessly to detect and address threats, vulnerabilities, and errors across the aforementioned infrastructure components. They ensure the security of workloads interacting with cloud environments by automatically identifying and remedying security issues in real-time.

The following table illustrates the coverage provided by Microsoft Defender for Cloud as of now.

Category	Services
Compute	Any Server, Azure VMSS, Azure K8s, App Services and unmanaged K8s
Service layer	Defender for DNS, Defender for Key Vault, Defender for Resource Manager, Network Layer V1 and Azure API management.
Database and storage	Defender for Azure Cosmos DB, Defender for Azure SQL Database, Defender for Open-Source Relational Databases, Defender for SQL Servers on Machines. And for Storage like Blob Storage, File Storage is covered.
AWS workload	Amazon EKS, Amazon Ec2, SQL on VM and Unmanaged K8s.
GCP workload	GKE clusters, Google Compute, SQLM on VM and Unmanaged K8s
On-premises workoads	Kubernetes, SQL on VM and serveres.

Table 11.1: Microsoft Defender for Cloud coverage portfolio(with services)

Important: Before you go further, we would like to build some clarity as there are so many things happening in Microsoft Security space and we would like to call out some points for better clarity:

- **Microsoft Defender for Cloud is itself an independent product/Service.**
- **Microsoft cloud native protection platform is subpart of Microsoft Defender for Cloud.**
- **Microsoft Defender Antivirus is recently separated antimalware product and defender team did refactor of their code base and this release happened around November 2023.**
- **Microsoft Defender for Cloud manages multi cloud security and it supports AWS, Azure and GCP Cloud along with a few CI/CD services.**
- **Microsoft Defender for Cloud is separate product than MDE and can still capture or perform activities on the cloud endpoint without any agent and its agentless functionality is integrated with other Microsoft Defender eco system to alert on Microsoft Defender security web portal.**

This chapter will be revolving around Microsoft services to manage Multi and Hybrid cloud resources through Microsoft Security, as shown in the following figure:

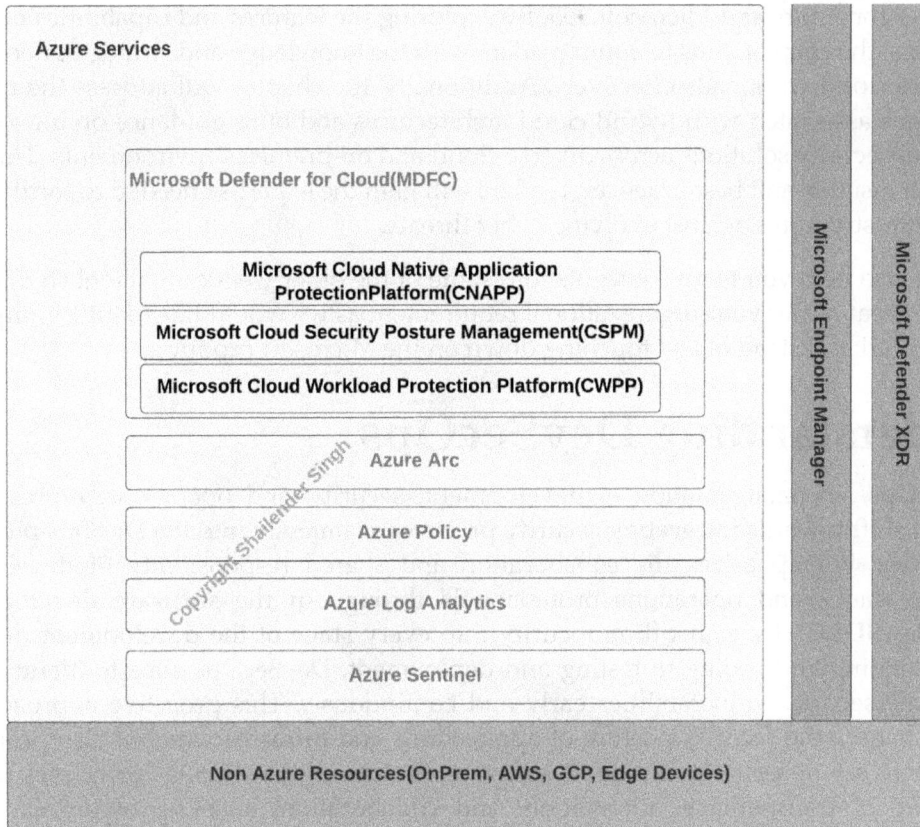

Figure 11.1: Microsoft Defender portfolio showcasing

Structure

In this chapter, we will cover the following topics:

- Understanding DevSecOps
- Understanding security of containers and container platform
- Kubernetes architecture
- Container patform infrastructure security
- Function as a service security
- Microsoft Defender for Cloud
- MCRA architecture for SOC

Objectives

The objective of this chapter is to provide a comprehensive understanding of endpoint security in cloud and container environments, with a focus on leveraging Microsoft

Defender for Azure and Microsoft 365. By exploring the features and capabilities of these platforms, the chapter aims to equip readers with the knowledge and strategies necessary to secure cloud workloads effectively. Additionally, the chapter will address the unique challenges associated with hybrid cloud architectures and offer guidance on integrating endpoint security solutions across diverse cloud and on-premises environments. Through practical insights and best practices, readers will gain the expertise needed to fortify their cloud infrastructures against evolving cyber threats.

We will also help you to give insights into some of the other well-known tool so that you can use them as per your organizational requirement as we would like to give glimpse of overall market instead of just touching down on the Microsoft products.

Understanding DevSecOps

DevSecOps, an amalgamation of development, security, and operations, represents a cultural shift towards integrating security practices seamlessly into the DevOps pipeline. In essence, it emphasizes the collaboration and shared responsibility of developers, security teams, and operations professionals throughout the **software development lifecycle** (**SDLC**). By embedding security into every stage of the development process, from planning and coding to testing and deployment, DevSecOps aims to identify and remediate security vulnerabilities early and continuously. This proactive approach not only enhances the security posture of applications and infrastructure but also promotes faster delivery of secure and reliable software. Embracing DevSecOps principles fosters a culture of transparency, automation, and collaboration, enabling organizations to effectively address security concerns while maintaining agility and innovation in their software delivery practices.

The following figure gives you important stages from Software Development to Software Delivery or Deployment to Production where DevSecOps will come in picture:

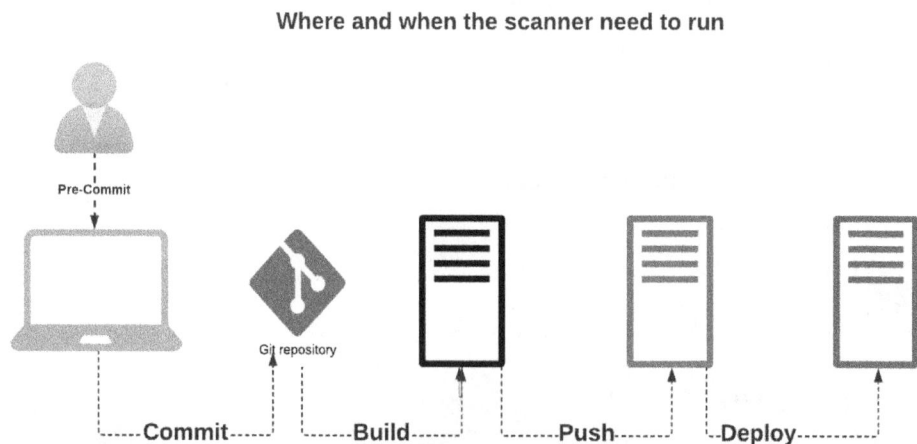

Figure 11.2: Stages in software development to deployment in regard to DevSecOps

Shift left approach

The *shift left* approach in software development and security refers to the practice of integrating security measures and testing earlier in the development process, typically during the initial stages of application design and coding. Traditionally, security testing and measures were implemented towards the end of the development lifecycle, often as a separate phase. However, with the shift left approach, security is moved earlier in the development process, closer to the beginning or *left* side of the development timeline.

The following figure shows the different stages of software from requirement definition to development and from development to deployment and finally the maintenance stage when it runs in production and DevOps recommends to put security from definition:

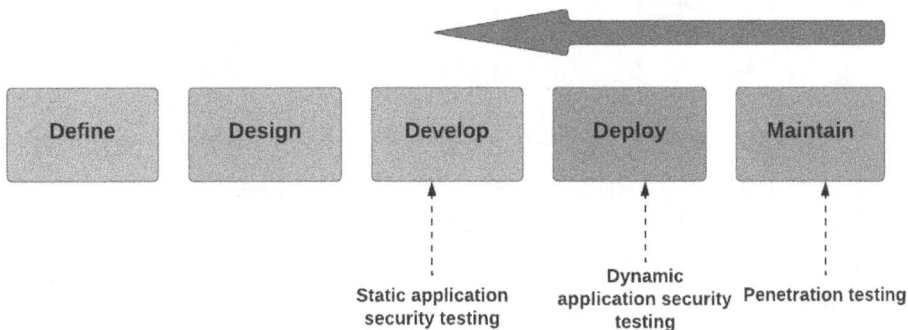

Figure 11.3: Software lifecycle showcasing shift left approach embedding in concerned stage

The shift left approach helps organizations identify and address security vulnerabilities early, ideally during design and coding, preventing costly issues later.

The following are the key aspects:

- **Early integration of security measures**: Security practices like code analysis and testing are part of the development from the start.
- **Continuous security testing**: Ongoing testing to quickly identify and fix vulnerabilities.
- **Automation of security checks**: Automated tools ensure consistent security evaluation.
- **Collaboration between teams**: Developers and security experts work together to address security concerns early.
- **Shift from reactive to proactive security**: Focus on identifying and mitigating risks before they escalate.

Overall, the shift left approach promotes a culture of security awareness and responsibility throughout the development organization, resulting in more secure software products, reduced security risks, and improved time-to-market.

Methodologies

In DevSecOps, various methodologies are employed to integrate security seamlessly into the software development lifecycle.

The following figure showcases three important approaches that security team focus on before applying DevSecOps or Security practices as that helps them in choosing right tools or methodologies:

Methodologies are Based on Approach

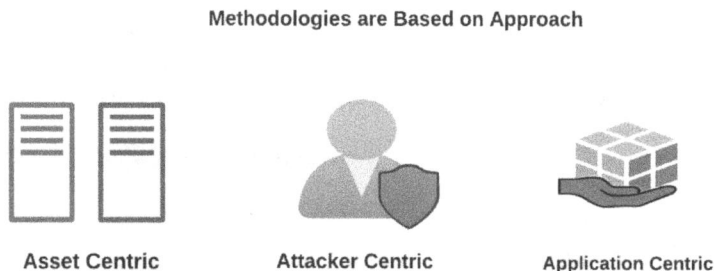

Asset Centric	**Attacker Centric**	**Application Centric**

Figure 11.4: *DevSecOps methodologies applied focusing on approach decided by security team*

Some of the key methodologies include:

- **Continuous integration (CI)**: CI involves the frequent integration of code changes into a shared repository, where automated build and test processes are triggered. Security checks, such as static code analysis and vulnerability scanning, are often incorporated into CI pipelines to identify and address security issues early in the development cycle.

- **Continuous delivery (CD)**: CD extends CI by automating the deployment of code changes to production environments, enabling rapid and reliable releases. Security-focused CD pipelines include additional checks, such as **Dynamic Application Security Testing (DAST)** and penetration testing, to validate the security of applications before they are deployed to production.

- **Infrastructure as code (IaC)**: IaC is a practice that involves managing and provisioning infrastructure resources through code rather than manual processes. By treating infrastructure as code, security configurations can be codified and version-controlled, ensuring consistency and repeatability while reducing the risk of misconfigurations and vulnerabilities.

- **Shift-left security**: Shift-left security involves integrating security practices and controls early in the development process, ideally at the planning and design stages. By addressing security considerations upfront, developers can identify and remediate security issues before they become entrenched in the codebase, reducing the cost and effort required to fix them later in the SDLC.

- **Threat modeling**: Threat modeling is a systematic approach to identifying and mitigating potential security threats and vulnerabilities in software applications.

By analyzing the application's architecture, data flows, and potential attack vectors, developers can prioritize security requirements and implement appropriate controls to mitigate risks effectively.

- **Secure coding practices**: Secure coding practices involve following established guidelines and best practices to write secure and resilient code. Developers should be trained in secure coding principles, such as input validation, authentication, and authorization, to minimize the risk of common security vulnerabilities, such as injection attacks and broken authentication.

By adopting these methodologies and practices, organizations can establish a robust DevSecOps framework that prioritizes security throughout the software development lifecycle, ultimately leading to the delivery of more secure and resilient software products.

Tools categorization

DevSecOps tools encompass a wide range of solutions designed to integrate security practices seamlessly into the software development lifecycle. These tools can be categorized based on their primary function within the DevSecOps pipeline:

Majorly, the tools are divided into following category, as shown in *Figure 11.5*:

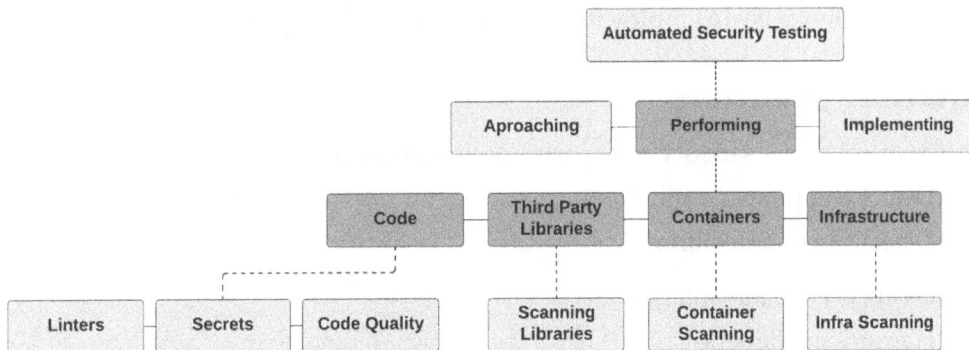

Figure 11.5: High level DevSecOps Automated testing tool categorization

In the following sections we have covered the advantages, compatibility, and trialability information so that you can weigh them as per your requirement and prioritize them accordingly.

Code quality metrics system

The following line items should be considered while focusing on code quality metric system development:

- Makes quality of code visible
- Gives an objective view of the state of the code
- Suggest best practices

The following are advantages:

- Graphical dashboard on code quality
- Gives insight into impact of changes
- The compatibility depends on language

The trialability depends on the following:

- Set up moderately easy
- Configuring
- interpreting results is time-consuming

Third-party libraries scanner

The following items should be focused as part of third-party libraries scanner consideration:

- Alerts about insecure and outdated libraries

The following are the advantages:

- Be actively alerted about insecure and outdated libraries

The trialability depends on:

- Moderately easy to employ in continuous integration pipelines

Container scanners

The scope of container security or scanners are mentioned as follows:

- Detect compliance validations
- Detect out of date libraries

The following are the advantages:

- Hardens containers
- Ensures out of date
- operating system is being noticed

The compatibility depends on **Open Container Initiative** (**OCI**) image format widely supported

The trialability depends on substantial infrastructure requirements choice for a framework.

Infrastructure scanning

The scope of infrastructure scanning software are mentioned as follows:

- Alerts about security misconfigurations
- Scans the running application

The following is the advantage:

- Find security misconfigurations before production

The compatibility depends on the following:

- Most web interfaces can be scanned

The trialability depends on the following:

- Moderately easy to add to pipeline
- Useful scans take a long time

The following are some of the available tools in the market that you can explore. Many good features are hidden behind paid subscription, but some minimal functionality is also offered in free or opensource versions.

The following are the tools for the container security with names:

- SysDig w/ Anchore
- Aqua Security
- Qualys
- Redhat Quay
- JFrog Xray
- Black Duck OpsSight
- Black Duck Hub
- Rapid Nexpose
- Cloud Passage
- TwistLock
- Clair (OpenSource)

The following are the infrastructure scanning tools described in detail:

- **Static application security testing (SAST):**
  - **Tools:**
    - SonarQube
    - Checkmarx
  - **Fortify static code analyzer:** SAST tools analyze source code to identify security vulnerabilities, such as code injection and insecure authentication mechanisms, without executing the application.
- **Dynamic application security testing (DAST):**
  - **Tools:**
    - OWASP ZAP
    - Burp Suite
    - Acunetix

DAST tools assess running applications by sending requests and analyzing responses to identify security vulnerabilities, such as **cross-site scripting** (**XSS**) and SQL injection.

- **Interactive application security testing (IAST)**:
  - Tools:
    - Contrast Security
    - Veracode

IAST tools combine elements of SAST and DAST to provide real-time security analysis during application runtime, offering deeper insights into application behavior and vulnerabilities.

- **Software composition analysis (SCA)**:
  - Tools:
    - WhiteSource
    - Snyk
    - Black Duck

SCA tools identify and manage open-source components and dependencies within applications, detecting known vulnerabilities and license compliance issues.

- **Container security**:
  - Tools:
    - Docker Security Scanning
    - Aqua Security
    - Twistlock

Container security tools provide vulnerability scanning, image signing, and runtime protection for containerized applications, ensuring the integrity and security of container deployments.

- **Infrastructure as code (IaC) security**:
  - Tools:
    - Terraform
    - AWS Config
    - Chef InSpec

IaC security tools assess the security posture of infrastructure code, providing automated checks for misconfigurations, compliance violations, and security best practices.

- **Configuration management:**
  - o **Tools:**
    - Ansible
    - Puppet
    - Chef

Configuration management tools automate the provisioning and configuration of infrastructure components, allowing organizations to enforce security policies and standards consistently.

- **Security information and event management (SIEM):**
  - o **Tools:**
    - Splunk
    - ELK Stack (Elasticsearch, Logstash, Kibana)
    - IBM QRadar

SIEM tools collect, correlate, and analyze security event data from various sources to detect and respond to security incidents in real-time.

- **Continuous integration/continuous delivery (CI/CD) security:**
  - o **Tools:**
    - Jenkins
    - GitLab CI/CD
    - CircleCI

CI/CD security tools integrate security testing and compliance checks into the CI/CD pipeline, enabling automated security validation of code changes and deployments.

- **Security orchestration, automation, and response (SOAR):**
  - o **Tools:**
    - Demisto (now part of Palo Alto Networks)
    - Swimlane
    - Siemplify

SOAR platforms automate incident response processes, orchestrate security workflows, and facilitate collaboration among security teams, improving incident detection and response capabilities.

By leveraging these DevSecOps tools, organizations can enhance their security posture, reduce security risks, and accelerate the delivery of secure and resilient software applications.

Advanced security tools

Well know tools used by security personal for varioius reason and you can pick out of it as per your requirement. The purpose of passing on this tool information will help you to become more advanced in comparison to only SOC analyst activities. Tools like Metasploit and Metagoofil are so strong that you can build your carrier around it and can be leveraged in the penetration testing profile. The following tables shows some of the tools you can add in your DevSecOps pipelines:

Recon/Sub-domain enumeration:	Screenshots:	Web application scanners:	Scanners:
• Massdns	• Webscreenshot.py	• BlackWidow	• Black Duck Hub
• Sublist3r	• CutyCapt	• wpscan	• wpscan
• Amass	• OSINT:	• Burpsuite	• Arachni
• Subfinder	• theHarvester	• Arachni	• Dirsearch
• Dnscan	• GooHak	• Dirsearch	• Gobuster
• Project Sonar	• Whois	• Gobuster	
• AltDNS	• Inurlbr	• wafw00f	
• DNSGen		• WhatWeb	
• spoofcheck.py		• WIG	
• Hunter.io		• WebTech	
• OSINT:		• Nikto	
• theHarvester		• Clusterd	
• GooHak		• CMSMap	
• Whois		• Shocker	
• Metagoofil		• Waybackmachine	
• Inurlbr			
Scanning:	**Exploitation:**	**Brute force:**	**Vuln scans:**
• NMap	• Metasploit	• Hydra	• OpenVAS
• AMap	• NMap scripts	• BruteX	• Yasuo
• Ping			• Vulners script
S3 buckets:	**Sub-domain takeovers:**		
• Slurp	• Subover		
	• Subjagk		
	• Jexboss		

Table 11.2: Security tools names undercategorization

The following are the example and usage of tools in DevSecOps pipeline configured on the Jenkins:

- Linting
- Detect secrets
- Sonar scanner
- Dependency checker
- Scan container
- Nikto
- OWASP ZAP

The following figure showcases the Jenkins pipeline and the stages under it. It also shows time taken to complete the specific stage:

Declarative Checkout SCM	lint	detect new secrets	sonarsca nner	Dependency Check	Build Image	Push to Registry	Launch Sidecar	Scan Container	nikito	OWASP ZAP	Declarative Post Action
8s	4s	3s	2min 59s	2min 30s	16min 4s	30s	1s	22min 9s	10min 9s	2min 6s	1s
8s	4s	3s	2min 59s	2min 30s	16min 4s	30s	1s	22min 9s	10min 9s	2min 6s	1s

Figure 11.6: Example screenshot from Jenkins pipeline showcasing DevSecOps tools implementation

Understanding security of containers and container platform

Container and container platform like **Kubernetes (k8s)** are trending in usage and most of the micro service workload is running on them (around 70% of total workload), so it is more important to cover security of these technologies or platform instead of just covering bare Linux or Windows as only component of the endpoint's discussion.

Throughout in the book, we have talked about Windows, cross-platform and MDE technology. However, this chapter is special and gives extra edge in your learning curve as per latest industry trends that will make you job ready for next generation security implementation on the microservice and **function as a service (FaaS)** world.

So, we would like to give you brief intro of Container and Container Platform so that you can get basic understanding and then continue your learning journey on the endpoint and cloud environment.

> **Note: This chapter does not cover in detail about container and Kubernetes but gives you more security aspects of it so that you understand all the security angle around these technologies.**

Container

A container is a lightweight, standalone, and executable software package that encapsulates an application, its dependencies, and runtime environment. Containers provide a consistent and isolated environment for running applications across different computing environments, such as development, testing, and production environments.

The following are the key characteristics of containers:

- **Isolation**: Containers run independently of each other and share the host operating system's kernel. They provide process-level isolation, ensuring that applications and their dependencies do not interfere with each other.

- **Portability**: Containers are portable and can run consistently across different environments, including physical servers, virtual machines, and cloud platforms. This portability enables developers to build applications once and deploy them anywhere.

- **Efficiency**: Containers are lightweight and consume fewer system resources compared to traditional virtual machines. They achieve efficiency by sharing the host operating system's resources and avoiding the overhead of running multiple guest operating systems.

- **Scalability**: Containers are designed to be scalable, allowing applications to be quickly deployed and scaled up or down to meet changing demands. Container orchestration platforms, such as Kubernetes, provide automated management and scaling of containerized applications.

- **Immutable infrastructure**: Containers are typically created from immutable images, meaning that once created, they remain unchanged throughout their lifecycle. This approach simplifies deployment and ensures consistency across different environments.

Containerization technologies, such as Docker and containerd, have become increasingly popular for building, packaging, and deploying modern applications. They offer developers a flexible and efficient way to develop, deploy, and manage applications in diverse computing environments.

The goal is to highlight security capabilities and improvements as well as security challenges and risks as a result of adoption of the new platform and approach of shipping application containers (rather than application deployment on VMs or bare metal).

There is security tradeoffs involved with adopting new technology. While some of the new capabilities introduced improve security and significantly reduce the risk of compromise - it also makes some of the existing security methods no longer applicable in the new way of application deployment.

Some of the biggest concerns around security in traditional environments are as follows:

- Security policies are dependent on inflexible network parameters - leading to rigid security architectures that cannot adjust to application or infrastructure changes.

- A massive amount of firewall rules needs to be reviewed when the environment changes or new applications are introduced. Typically, these rules are reconciled manually, which can often bring the process to a screeching halt.

- Lack of APIs required to automate security management

Using security policies that use application context instead of relying solely on IP addresses enables engineers to define and include security changes at every phase of the application development and operations lifecycle improving overall security posture while accelerating application delivery.

The biggest shift required with cloud adoption is to be able to move away from highly segmented and inflexible network isolation model relying heavily on border protection in private data centers to flattened cloud networks supporting highly scalable and agile architectures. This is possible only by moving focus from network infrastructure as primary method for security enforcement toward application endpoint protection and requiring applications to secure its communication paths (including databases, messaging, API calls). It is no longer acceptable for application to allow insecure communication to any client that is able to reach application endpoint on the network. Application owners must ensure that only trusted clients are allowed to use application services, and all information transferred over the network must be secured (encrypted) in transit. This applies both for communications happening over public internet and virtual private networks.

Container security

The following are the primary features of the container security product:

- **Registry scanning**: Scans integrated registry for vulnerabilities in the images.
- **Pipeline scanning**: Images are scanned before deploying through pipeline.
- **Container monitoring**: Container run-time security.

Some more features are also integrated in the solution by some of the vendors like Aqua Security:

- Integration with log management tools.
- Profiling of services running in containers
- Hardening policies for containers
- Restrict deployment of containers that do not meet the requirements while in pipeline.

Registry scanning

Registry scanning covers the offline scanning of images available on the Registry as it can help you to proactively pre scanning images before actual deployment and can reduce down the deployment time.

Microsoft Defender for Endpoint can be integrated into your CI/CD pipeline to enhance security and ensure that only scanned and healthy images reach the production environments. Here are the steps to integrate Microsoft Defender for Endpoint into your CI/CD pipeline:

1. **Enable Microsoft Defender for Cloud's**: This will allow the images in your container registries to be scanned for vulnerabilities.

2. **Configure the triggers for an image scan**: There are multiple triggers for an image scan, such as On push, On import and Recently pulled.

3. **Extract scan summary using API**: Scan summaries are available in Microsoft Defender for Cloud dashboards. You can also access them programmatically (through API or PowerShell) using the scan summary ARG query published in Microsoft Defender for Cloud container image scan community GitHub.

Pipeline scanning

Pipeline scanning refers to the concept in which you scan the image before Deployment to the Kubernetes infrastructure through various Validation Webhooks available in the Kubernetes ecosystem or can also be performed during CI/CD phase using tools like Clair, Trivy etc that helps checking the images before actual deployment, but it can increase the deployment time.

Benefits of application container security

The following are the benefits of application container security that an organization can leverage to strengthen their container infrastructure security:

- **Attack surface reduction**: Container technology increases the default security for applications in several ways, such as:
  - Enabling separation of concerns between applications and the host and providing isolation layer between them—restricting application access to the host and radically reducing surface area for host to protect.
  - Enforcing principles of least privilege by running applications in their own root filesystem and using separate user accounts.
  - Mandating resource constraints by using Linux namespaces and cgroups.

- o Limiting access privileges through Linux capabilities model reducing possibility of escalation to a fully privileged root user through application-level vulnerabilities. The following is reference as an example to run process as non-root user:

  - Containers run with a reduced capability set that does not negatively impact on the application and yet improve the overall security system levels and makes running applications more secure by default. This makes it difficult to provoke system level damage during intrusion, even if the intruder manages to escalate to root within a container because the container capabilities are fundamentally restricted.

- o Restricting access by containerized applications to the physical devices on a host, through the use of the device resource control groups (cgroups) mechanism. Containers have no default device access and have to be explicitly granted device access. These restrictions protect a container host kernel and its hardware, whether physical or virtual, from the running applications.

- o Containers use copy-on-write file systems, and any file system changes are only visible within specific container instance—effectively isolating the processes running in independent containers. Any changes made to containers are lost when the container is destroyed and replaced allowing for easy rollback in case of compromise.

- o Core Linux kernel file systems that have to be in the container environment such as **/sys** and other files under **/proc**, come mounted as read-only. This further limit the ability of access, even by privileged container processes, to potentially write to them.

- **Immutable infrastructure lifecycle management**: Application containers promote immutable infrastructure concepts where application images are created and tested as part of software development process and rolled out to production after going through comprehensive testing, but never changed directly in production. This applies both to application changes and to security updates.

  - o Updating application container image is trivial and rolling out updates is done by simply re-spawning containers using updated images.

  - o Risk of updates is reduced by ability to easily rollback to earlier images using image tags

  - o Updated base images can be shared with multiple teams that reduces time and overhead of making security updates.

- o Separation of file system of container images and host makes it trivial for system administrators to update system utilities, packages, and even the kernel of the base hosts.

- o OS upgrade cycles are dramatically reduced and easier to apply therefore, significantly reducing the overall exposure of the infrastructure to attacks.

- o Use of layers make it easy to check OS packages and application dependencies against public **Common Vulnerabilities and Exposures** (**CVE**) lists.

- o Container image represents known good state and make it also easy to roll-back the containers after a compromise.

Kubernetes architecture

Kubernetes is an open-source container orchestration platform that automates the deployment, scaling, and management of containerized applications. Originally developed by Google and now maintained by the **Cloud Native Computing Foundation** (**CNCF**), Kubernetes provides a platform-agnostic framework for managing containerized workloads and services.

The following are the components of Kubernetes architecture that you should keep in mind before building the security around it.

- Primarily, Kubernetes Node (host) security is considered very similar as we manage the security of other VM or machine endpoint.

- Second, Kubernetes is a **platform as a service** (**PaaS**) so there are more components to consider and mostly managed by CNAPP policies.

> **Note: There are many things to discuss around Kubernetes security but that is beyond the scope of this chapter and book and mostly covered under OPA or other security and network policy services and available in public domain.**

The following figure showcases the high-level architecture diagram of Kubernetes to help you to build your understanding on its internal component so that you can plan for security accordingly and it is estimated that 70% IT infrastructure is running on Kubernetes.

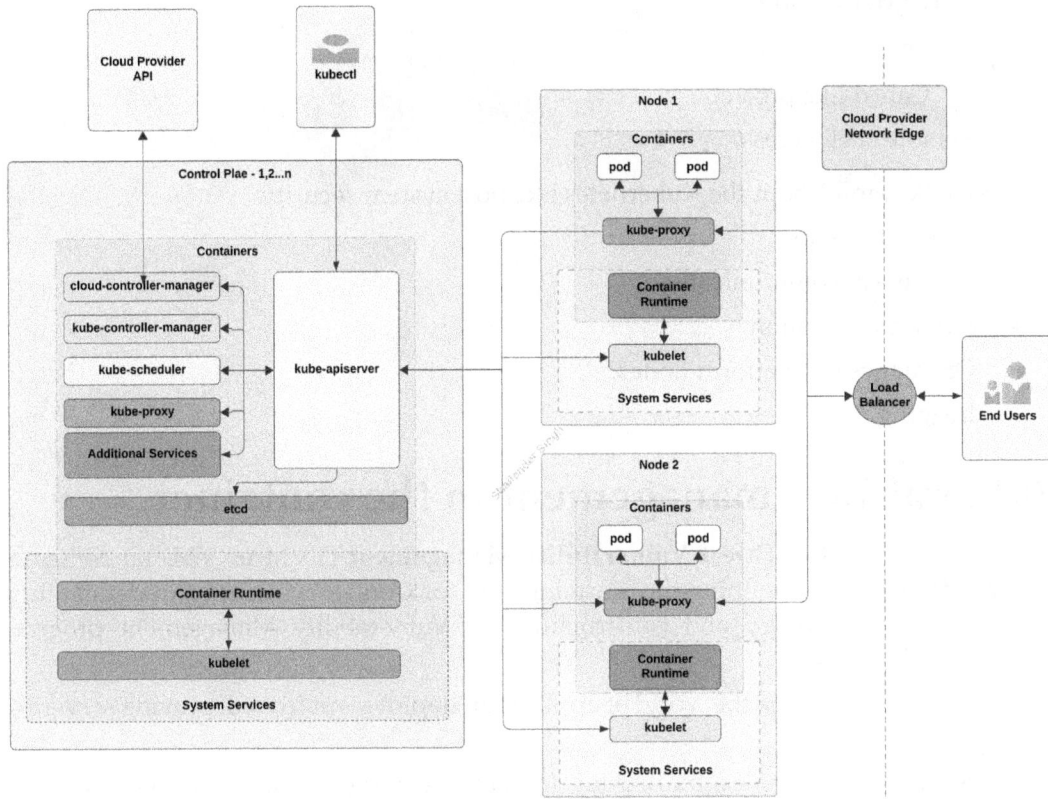

Figure 11.7: *Kubernetes architecture caption*

Container platform infrastructure security

Container platforms are like Kubernetes, Red Hat's OpenShift and any such other platforms.

The following are the resources that should get covered for container platform to strengthen the host or Kubernetes node security:

- Identity and access controls
- Secrets
- Application ports
- Ingress router
- Secure routes
  - o Edge termination
  - o Passthrough termination
  - o Re-encryption termination

- Network isolation
  - o Open vSwitch
  - o Calico-like project
- Remote shell access

This area talks more about the Kubernetes like host system security.

- Security groups
- Secure API communication
- Storage encryption
- OS images for platform nodes
- Logging

Vulnerability management in the container

This section covers the **Threat Vulnerability Management** (**TVM or VM**) on container platform. In parallel to defining the Scanning Tool for Container Security, understanding the Container Technology and constructing the Vulnerability Management program around it is necessary:

- Containers change the world of application deployment from deploying servers to images
- As the containers are built using Images and various team's around are using different registry's such as
  - o Azure Container Registry
  - o Docker Hub (Docker)
  - o Quay (Kubernetes)
  - o Google Container Registry
  - o Amazon ECS

There needs to be a security tool that need to support most of the registries.

- The Images are most flexibly deployed using the pipeline tools, the Security scanner tools needs to support Integration around these automation applications.
- Vulnerability management is mostly processed through API Automation than the scanner webUI. The Security scanner needs to support a robust API.

Note: Microsoft Defender for Cloud also has agentless feature that can find vulnerabilities in the VM's and Containers.

Container security application features

The following are the more granular details of the container security product feature that you can expect from any other vendor:

- Can be integrated with almost every registry around (Amazon ECS, Google Container registry, Docker Hub, quay) and Orchestrators.
- Has the ability to schedule scans around the repositories. Can Scan images at rest. Continuous scan for CVEs.
- Full API integration can be deployed On the Premises (API rate limit can be reached).
- Supports CI/CD pipeline integration with Jenkins and other tools.
- Service network for blog, a network view of all the outgoing connections and their IP's
- Lists the view of ports, UIDs, and many other results for the containers running.
- Micro-segmentation (firewalling between containers).
- Vault support (bridging between containers).
- Solutions for containers where we do not have host access/only container access (CAAS).
- Policies can be set up and enforce the compliance requirements.
- Block unknown images from getting deployed. (Each scan creates a hash of the image)
- Support for windows containers
- Policy around US **National Institute of Standards and Technology** (**NIST**) and governmental standards
- Ability to scan for PII related Info in the images (almost does kind of a DLP scan)
- Ability to implement and execute scripts for image review, Supports UNIX and Power shell.
- Supports triggers and custom script execution on failure events
- Powerful and flexible policy-based restrictions and auditing of execution within a container
- Containers can be deployed with placeholders for secrets. The tool will inject the secrets during deployment.

Function as a service security

As a starting point, the following technologies will be assessed for known threat vectors and protection around these security risks so that their applicability across serverless technologies can be evaluated and prevention/protection plan can be created:

- **Function event-data injection**: At a high level, injection flaws occur when untrusted input is passed directly to workload protection use case an interpreter and eventually gets executed or evaluated. In the context of serverless architectures however, function event-data injections are not strictly limited to direct user input, such as input from a web API call. Most serverless architectures provide a multitude of event sources, which can trigger the execution of a serverless function.

  Examples:

  o Cloud storage events (e.g. AWS S3, Azure Blob Storage, Google Cloud Storage)

  o NoSQL database events (e.g. AWS DynamoDB, Azure CosmosDB)

  o SQL database events Stream processing events (e.g. AWS Kinesis)

  o Code changes and new repository code commits

  o HTTP API calls

  o IoT device telemetry signals

  o Message queue events

  o SMS message notifications, PUSH notifications, Emails, etc.

  Solutions can be:

  o **With the CI/CD pipeline**: A post-deploy lambda function be written to trigger a pentest or a portscan and compare that with the whitelisted policies.

  o **Insecure third-party dependencies**: In the general case, a serverless function should be a small piece of code that performs a single discrete task. Oftentimes, in order to perform this task, serverless functions may be required to depend on third party software packages, open-source libraries and even consume third party remote web services through API calls. Keep in mind that even the most secure serverless function can become vulnerable when importing code from a vulnerable third-party dependency

  o **Broken authentication**: Since serverless architectures promote a microservices-oriented system design, applications assessment use case built for such architectures may oftentimes contain dozens or even hundreds of distinct serverless functions, each with its own specific purpose. These functions are weaved together and orchestrated to form the overall system logic. Some serverless functions may expose public web APIs, while others may serve as some sort of an internal glue between processes or other functions. In addition, some functions may consume events of different source types, such as cloud storage events, NoSQL database events, IoT device telemetry signals or even SMS message notifications. Applying robust authentication schemes, which provide access control and protection to all relevant functions, event types and triggers is a complex undertaking, which may easily go awry if not done carefully.

o **Insecure serverless deployment configuration**: Cloud services in general, and serverless architectures in config assessment use case particular offer many customizations and configuration settings in order to adapt them for each specific need, task or surrounding environment. Some of these configuration settings have critical implications on the overall security posture of the application and should be given attention. The default settings provided by serverless architecture vendors might not always be suitable for your needs.

One extremely common weakness that affects many applications that use cloud-based storage is incorrectly configured cloud storage authentication/authorization. Since one of the recommended best practice designs for serverless architectures is to make functions stateless, many applications built for serverless architectures rely on cloud storage infrastructure to store and persist data between executions.

Common weaknesses in FaaS-based applications

The following are the common weaknesses:

- Over-privileged function permissions and roles
- Inadequate function monitoring and logging prevention of starving of resources. affecting the business. e.g. # of concurrent executions, network
- Excessive or sensitive data logging (sensitive or PII data)
- Insecure application secrets storage
- Denial of service and financial resource exhaustion
- Functions execution flow manipulation
- Improper exception handling and verbose error messages

The following are the two references for AWS FaaS and the points that should get considered as part of their security and same applies for other similar technologies like Azure Functions:

AWS Lambda functions

The following are the items to consider for Lambda function security:

- **Monitoring**: Discovery of functions, details around execution start, end, invoker (user, events etc.)
- **Whitelisting of lambda functions**: Implement a policy that ensures only approved Lambda functions are allowed to execute, reducing the risk of unauthorized or malicious code execution.
- **Detection and response of anomalous behavior**: Look for code injection (monitor, detect, respond)

- **Detection and response of usage of credentials**: Prevent unauthorized or improper usage of keys/secrets
- **Detection of DoS/DDoS attacks**: Triggered using lambda function that results in exhaustion of resources
- **Detection of webhooks**: Results in longer runtime of function or extended use of resources, services or Data.

AWS Fargate

The following are the items that gets considered as part of AWS Fargate security:

- **Vulnerabilities**: Scanning container images for vulnerabilities (Control plane assessment)—**Vulnerabiltiy Assessment (VA)** capability of **Cloud Workload Assessment (CWA)**:
  - o VA capabilities for workloads and containers.
  - o Reporting of vulnerabilities
- **Malware**:
  - o Scanning container images for malware
- Detection of anomalous behavior from containers
- Detection of malware in containers using AV scanner running in privileged container or something similar tech.

Microsoft Defender for Cloud

Microsoft Defender for Cloud constitutes a CNAPP crafted to safeguard cloud-based applications against a spectrum of cyber threats and vulnerabilities. It amalgamates the following functionalities:

- A DevSecOps solution integrating security management into the code level across multicloud and multi-pipeline environments.
- A **Cloud Security Posture Management (CSPM)** solution highlighting actionable insights to pre-empt breaches.
- A **Cloud Workload Protection Platform (CWPP)** equipped with tailored protections for servers, containers, storage, databases, and other workloads.

The following figure gives high level overview of areas covered by Microsoft Defender for Cloud:

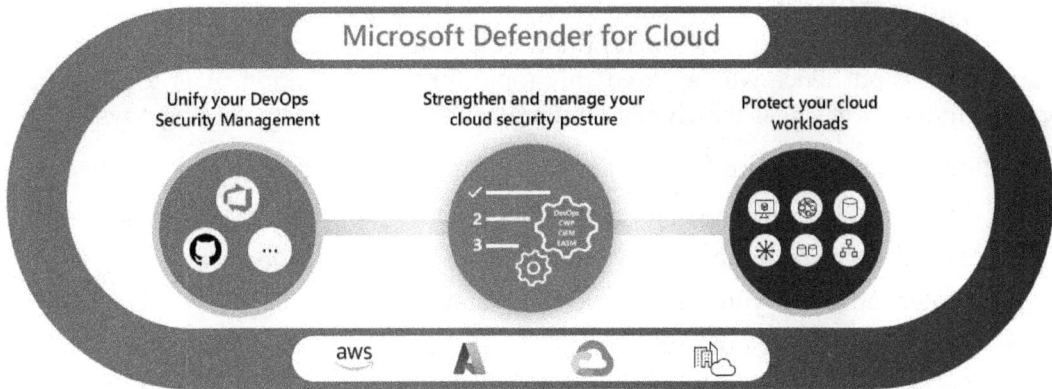

Figure 11.8: Microsoft Defender for Cloud HLD for Coverage overview

Note:

- **When you enable Defender for Cloud, you automatically gain access to Microsoft 365 Defender. Ref: https://learn.microsoft.com/en-us/azure/defender-for-cloud/defender-for-cloud-introduction**

- **Defender for Cloud includes Foundational CSPM capabilities and access to Microsoft Defender XDR for free.**

- **You can add additional paid plans to secure all aspects of your cloud resources.**

- **You can try Defender for Cloud for free for the first 30 days. After 30 days charges begin in accordance with the plans enabled in your environment**

The Microsoft 365 Defender portal aids security teams in probing attacks spanning cloud resources, devices, and identities. Offering a comprehensive view, Microsoft 365 Defender encompasses both suspicious and malicious events unfolding within cloud environments. This is achieved through the correlation of all alerts and incidents, encompassing those originating from the cloud.

Microsoft cloud-native application protection platform

There is one another Microsoft Product gaining momentum around cross platform or across clouds including on-premsis datacenters. It is part of Microsoft Defender for Cloud that we are going to cover in multicloud and hybrid protection support section.

Kubernetes, Containers and DevSecOps practices are on rise and container security, **infrastructure as code** (**IaC**) should be the highest priority of the organization to adapt the Shift Left approach so that *Code to Cloud activities* can be secured through automation and CNPP brings all such features in-built that you can integrate with your own setup as it support Multi cloud and broad range of other setup requirement.

It is not part of MDE but as our goal is to give high level understanding of all the product and services in MDE so that you can build your strong understanding in the security management and hence we captured this topic for your attention. It is totally a new product in the early stages which has a huge potential to grow in coming days.

The following are the comprehensive approaches to manage security across estates:

- Integrated CNAPP capabilities and more in a single portal on a single platform
- Additional capabilities to accelerate cloud-native protection
- Protection across your multicloud data estate
- Protection across your multicloud data estate
- Protection across your multicloud data estate
- Cloud scale and integrated CNAPP

The following figure showcases the areas covered by Microsoft CNAPP:

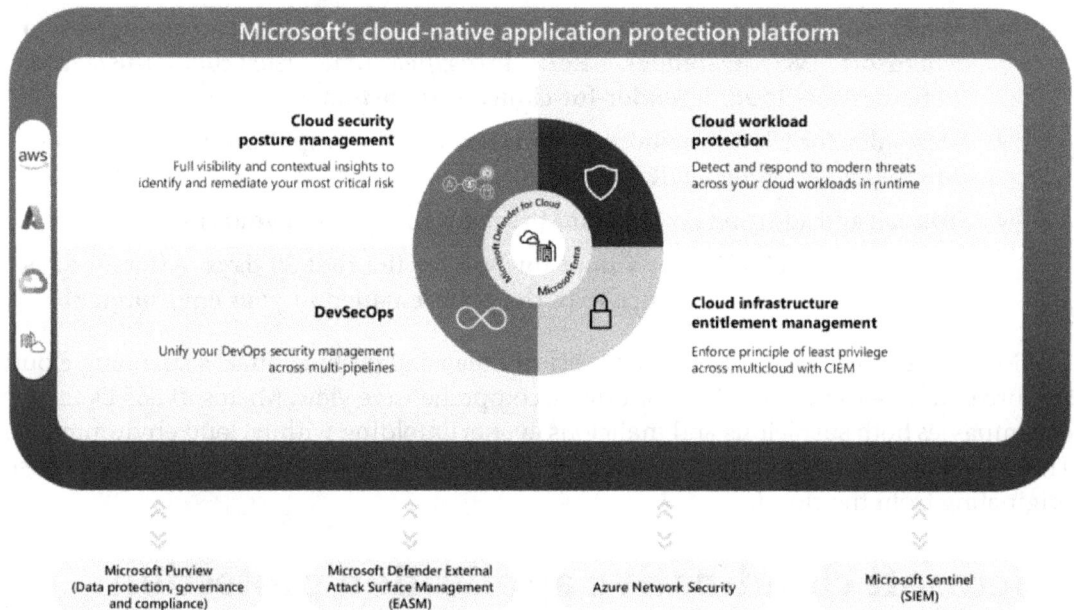

Figure 11.9: Microsoft CNAPP coverage along with Microsoft security products

- **MD for Cloud reference:** *https://www.microsoft.com/en-in/security/business/cloud-security/microsoft-defender-cloud?rtc=1*
- **CNPP reference:** *https://www.microsoft.com/en-us/security/blog/2023/03/22/the-next-wave-of-multicloud-security-with-microsoft-defender-for-cloud-a-cloud-native-application-protection-platform-cnapp/*

Integration with Microsoft Defender XDR

When you enable Defender for Cloud, Defender for Cloud's alerts are automatically integrated into the Microsoft Defender Web Portal. In practice, some integrations might require additional configuration, especially in complex environments or for specific custom use cases.

The integration between Microsoft Defender for Cloud and Microsoft Defender XDR brings your cloud environment into Microsoft Defender XDR. With Defender for Cloud's alerts and cloud correlations integrated into Microsoft Defender XDR, SOC teams can now access all security information from a single interface.

The following are the features of **Microsoft Defender for Cloud** (**MDFC**):

- Security posture monitoring
- Regulatory compliance
- Cyberattack-path analysis
- Cloud Workload protection
- Vulnerability scanning
- DevOps posture visibility
- Infrastructure-as-code security
- Code security guidance
- Secure Cloud Application (DevSecOps)
- Improve Security Posture (CSPM)
- Protect Cloud Workload (CWP)

The following are the last three features of MDFC features described in more details

- **Secure cloud application (DevSecOps)**: Defender for Cloud facilitates the integration of robust security practices at the outset of the software development process, commonly referred to as DevSecOps. It enables the safeguarding of both code management environments and code pipelines while providing consolidated insights into the security stance of the development environment. Empowering security teams, Defender for Cloud facilitates the management of DevOps security across diverse pipeline environments.

  In the present landscape, ensuring the resilience of deployed applications against attacks necessitates vigilance across code, infrastructure, and runtime layers.

- **Improve security posture (CSPM)**: The security of both your cloud and on-premises resources hinges upon accurate configuration and deployment. Recommendations provided by Defender for Cloud outline actionable steps to enhance the security of your environment.

Included within Defender for Cloud are Foundational **Cloud Security Posture Management (CSPM)** capabilities at no additional cost. Furthermore, you can activate advanced CSPM capabilities by enabling the Defender CSPM plan.

- **Protect cloud workload (CWP)**: Adhering to proactive security principles necessitates the adoption of security measures aimed at safeguarding your workloads from potential threats. CWP offer tailored recommendations pertaining to workload security controls, guiding you towards effective protective measures.

  In the event of a threat to your environment, immediate security alerts promptly detail the nature and severity of the threat, enabling you to strategize your response accordingly. Upon identifying a threat within your environment, swift action is imperative to mitigate risks and safeguard your resources.

  Microsoft Defender for Cloud *supports multiple cloud and other CI/CD tools* that can easily be integrated on the console in the Azure portal.

Informational:

- **MDFC currently supported following cloud**
  - **Azure**
  - **AWS Cloud**
  - **GCP Cloud**
- **MDFC currently supports following CI/CD tool for DevSecOps:**
  - **GitHub**
  - **Gitlab**
  - **Azure DevOps**

MDFC screenshot references

It is very important to have a look and feel while reading the MDFC features so we brought screenshot from the MDFC web portal so that you can build your understanding about it. In this section, we have captured some of the screenshot references showcasing supported cloud and supported CI/CD tools on the MDFC Platform.

The following figure is showcasing **Environment settings | Add environment for Amazon Web Services**:

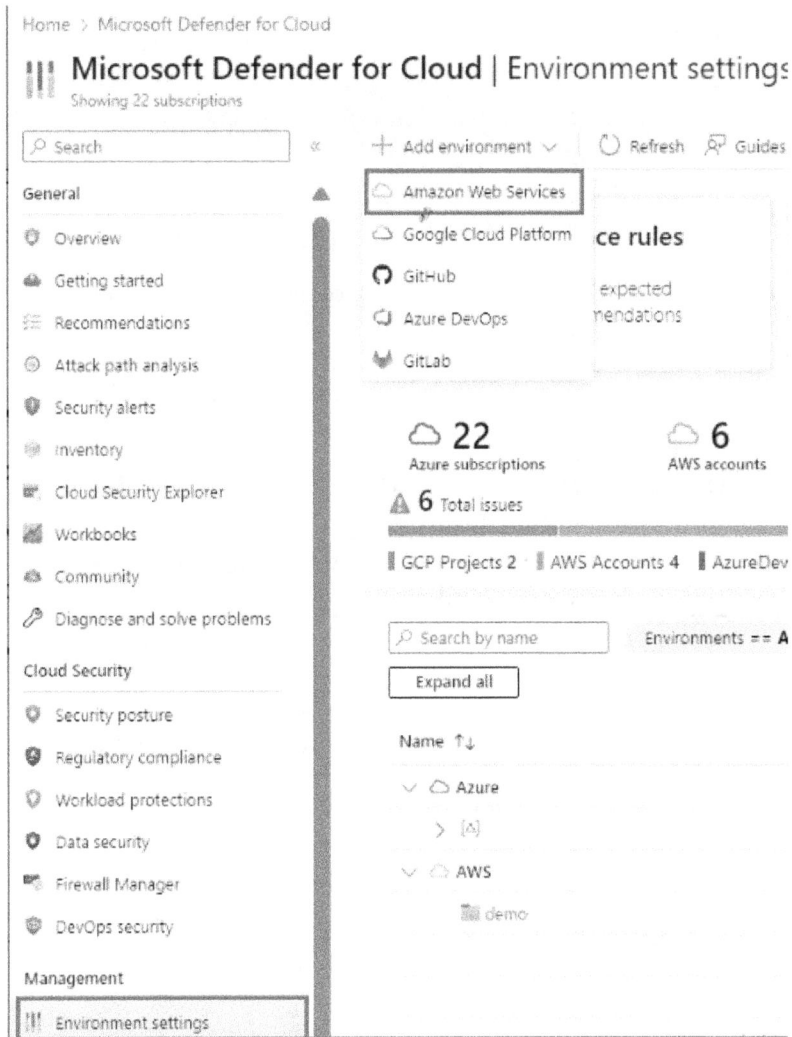

Figure 11.10: MDFC showcasing Environment settings

Informational: You can use the following functionalities of MDFC to integrate other services like:

- **Data sensitivity**
- **Direct onboarding of non-Azure servers with MDE**
- **Connect environment to third party applications.**

The following is the screenshot showcasing widgets of **Data sensitivity**, **Direct onboarding** and other integration on the page:

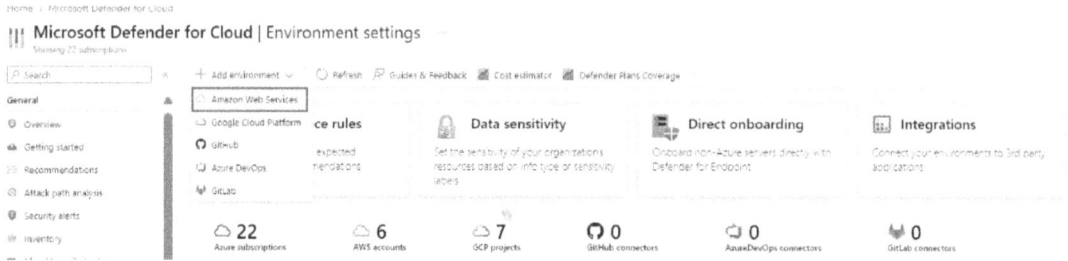

Figure 11.11: MDFC Environment page showcasing Data sensitivity feature etc.

The following table contains the URL references for device onboarding on MDFC:

Cloud onboarding	URL reference
Azure onboarding	**https://learn.microsoft.com/en-us/azure/defender-for-cloud/ connect-azure-subscription**
AWS onboarding	**https://learn.microsoft.com/en-us/azure/defender-for-cloud/ quickstart-onboard-aws**

Table 11.3: Azure and AWS Device onboarding URL's for MDFC

The following *figure* is a screenshot showcasing how to enable Defender Plan like Cloud Security Posture Management from Azure portal under MDFC web page:

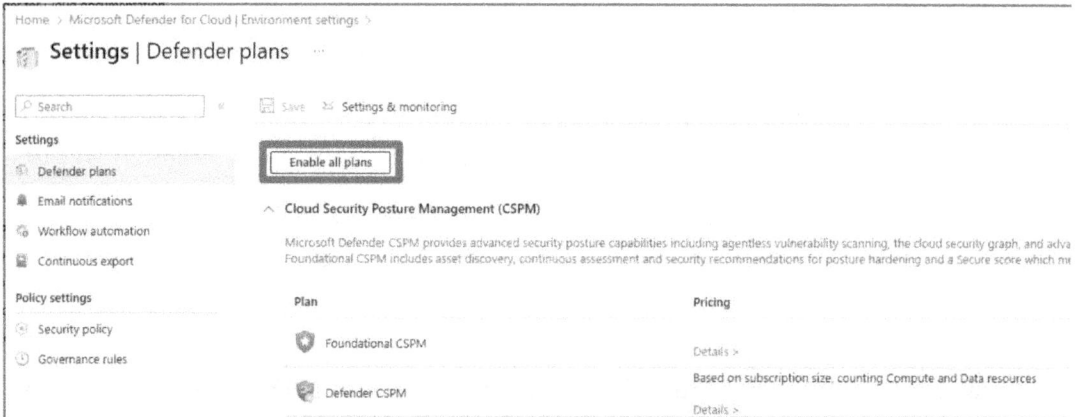

Figure 11.12: MDFC Settings page to choose different plans (CSPM)

The following figure is a screenshot showcasing CWP option to choose under Defender plan:

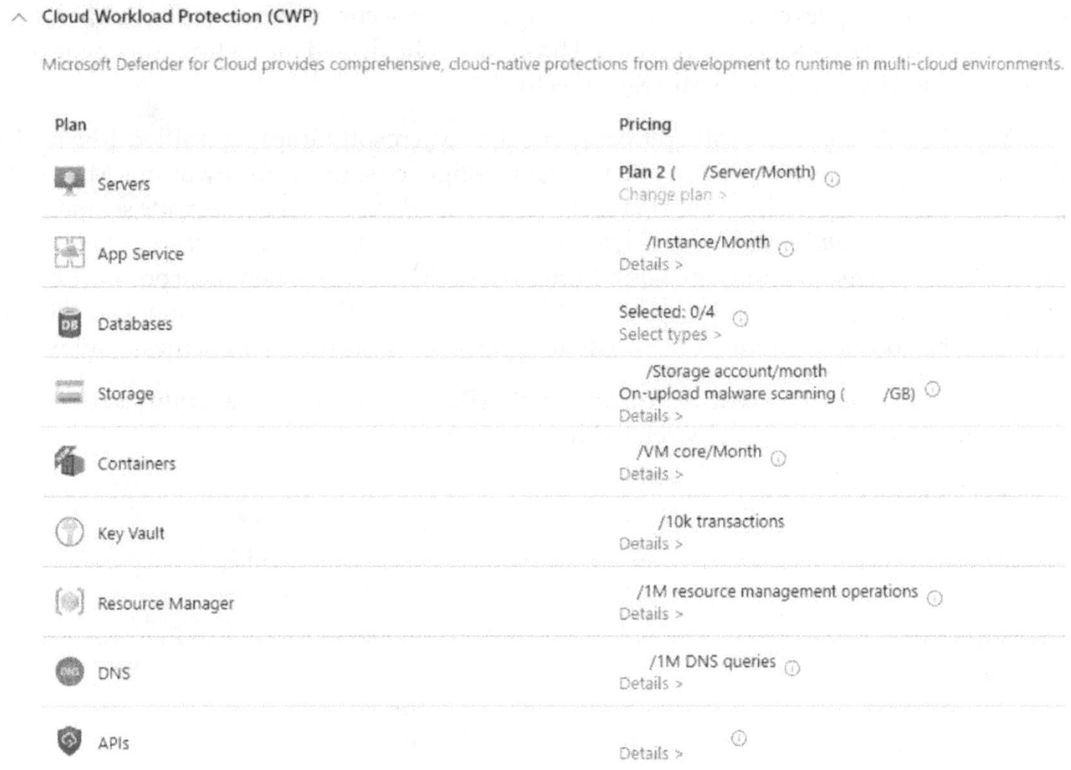

∧ **Cloud Workload Protection (CWP)**

Microsoft Defender for Cloud provides comprehensive, cloud-native protections from development to runtime in multi-cloud environments.

Plan	Pricing
Servers	Plan 2 (　/Server/Month) ⓘ Change plan >
App Service	/Instance/Month ⓘ Details >
Databases	Selected: 0/4 ⓘ Select types >
Storage	/Storage account/month On-upload malware scanning (　/GB) ⓘ Details >
Containers	/VM core/Month ⓘ Details >
Key Vault	/10k transactions Details >
Resource Manager	/1M resource management operations ⓘ Details >
DNS	/1M DNS queries ⓘ Details >
APIs	Details > ⓘ

Figure 11.13: MDFC Settings page to choose different plans (CWP)

Microsoft intelligent security graph API's

Microsoft Graph is a game changer service by Microsoft provided by their Substrate cloud (Microsoft Cloud to serve office service and it is separate than Azure cloud). Microsoft Entra (AAD) their Identity service sits in this cloud and helps in exposing much information to other Microsoft services to expose more contextual and relevant information and same is used by Microsoft Defender for Cloud. It is worth mentioning or referring to the Microsoft Graph and Microsoft Intelligent Security Graph API so that you can go and read more about it.

Many organizations grapple with managing vast amounts of security data and navigating a multitude of security solutions within their infrastructure. This complexity presents a formidable challenge in integrating diverse products and services, requiring significant investment in cost, time, and resources. Such hurdles impede organizations from swiftly detecting and addressing threats in an environment characterized by fast-paced, disruptive attacks.

The integration of security data and systems offers a strategic advantage against contemporary adversaries. At Microsoft, *security offerings leverage the Intelligent Security*

Graph, which *aggregates* extensive threat intelligence and security indicators from Microsoft products, services, and collaborators. Through sophisticated analytics, this platform identifies and counteracts cyberthreats effectively.

The Security API forms an integral component of Microsoft Graph, a unified REST API designed for seamless integration of data and intelligence sourced from various Microsoft products and services. Through Microsoft Graph, *developers can swiftly create solutions by authenticating once and employing a single API call to retrieve or take action on security insights derived from numerous security solutions.* Further benefits emerge when incorporating other Microsoft Graph entities, such as Office 365, Azure Active Directory, Intune, and others, enabling the contextualization of security insights within the broader business context.

The following figure showcase Microsoft Graph API showcasing its availability to so many applications for various security related integration:

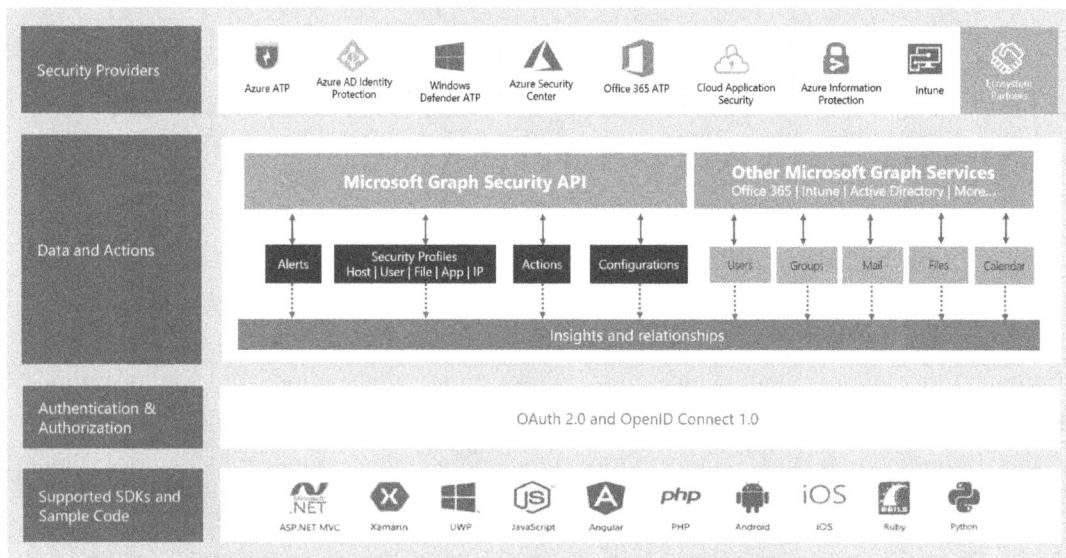

Figure 11.14: Microsoft Graph API availability to different Applications

MCRA architecture for SOC

Microsoft Cloud Resource Architecture (**MCRA**) architecture covers much broader scope than just certain part of the security and gives you full view of the Microsoft security stack and how other security component fits in the whole eco system.

You can see the Defender for Cloud and the coverage under it.

Throughout this book we have talked and differentiated in between Microsoft 365D and Azure security and same you can observe that Azure helps in securing:

- Servers and VM
- Containers
- Azure App Serverless
- Network traffic
- Supported SQL managed services

The following figure is released as part of MCRA for security operations that showcase how different Microsoft product and services are integrated:

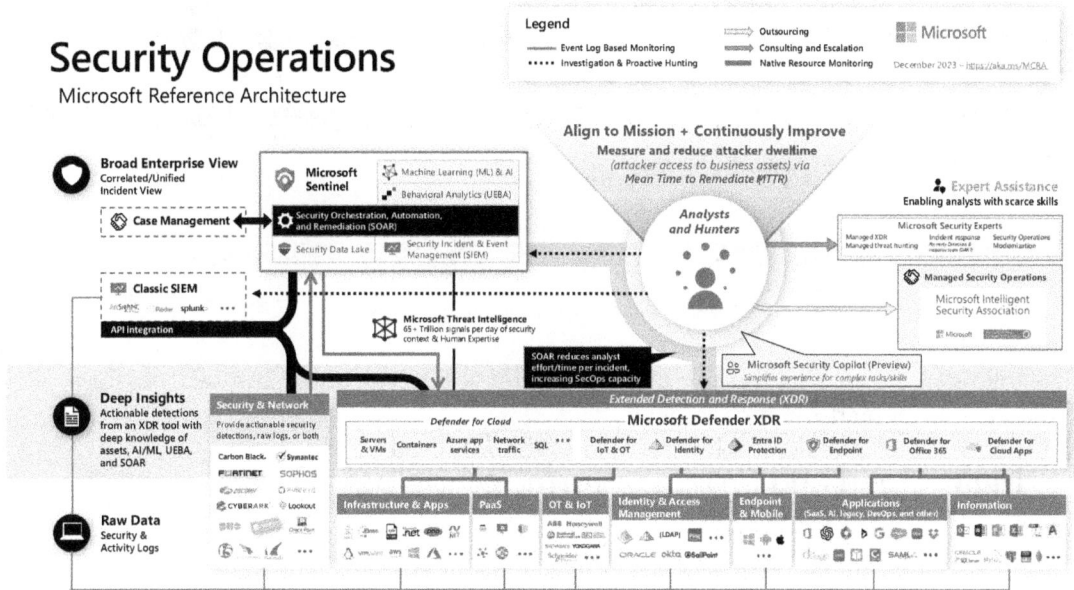

Figure 11.15: MCRA overview

Microsoft cross-cloud and cross platform product overview

As we have covered earlier that Microsoft has breadth and depth in the security domain and same is reflected in the following figure where you can see various Microsoft Security, Compliance and Identity capabilities and their placement.

The following are the capabilities of Microsoft cross-cloud and cross-platform through its various products and services:

- Endpoint and Devices
- **Software as Service (SaaS)**
- Hybrid infrastructure—IaaS, PaaS, On-Premises
- IoT Devices

The following figure shows the MCRA for products around us:

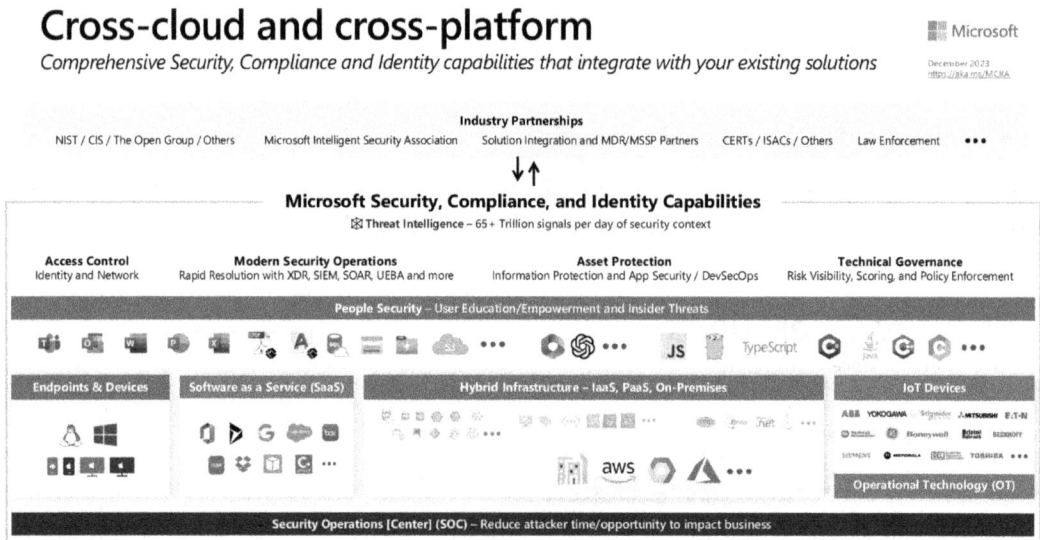

Figure 11.16: MCRA for products around us

The following figure showcases overall Microsoft security product and services for multi-cloud and cross platform technologies:

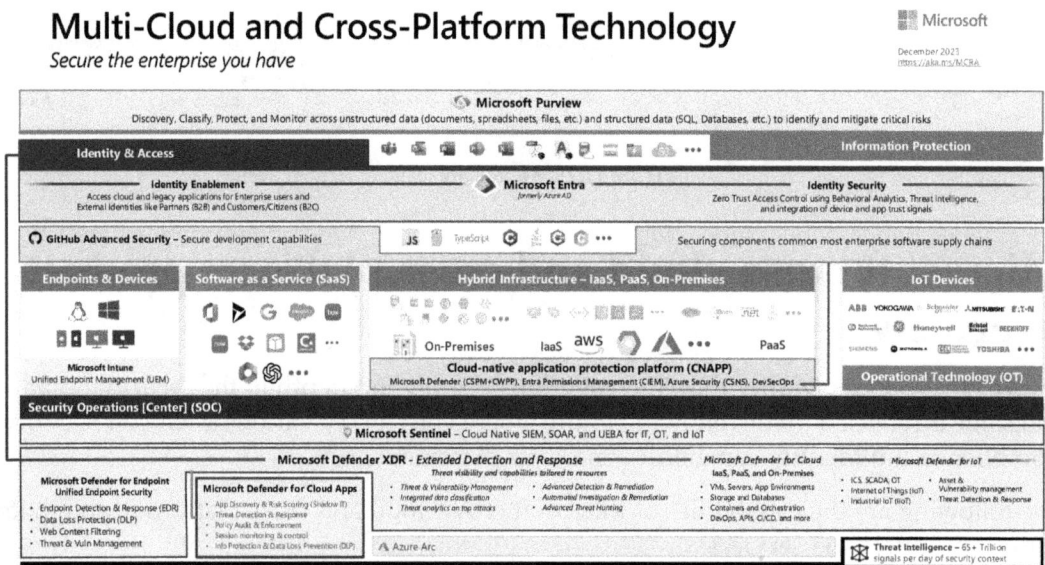

Figure 11.17: MCRA overview (Continued)

MDFC for hybrid integration and protection

Microsoft vision is to build cross platform products, which is reflected in their services, including Azure and Azure Arc is one of such service that helps onboarding of non-Microsoft or non-Azure resources under Azure resources so all benefits of Azure can be leveraged on such non-Azure resources.

Azure Arc

Azure Arc is a bridge that extends the Azure platform to help you build applications and services with the flexibility to run across data centers, at the edge, and in multi-cloud environments. You can install MDE to any cloud vendor or on premises Machine or VM and Azure Arc cloud service provides you with this option to install and configure MDE agent on such platforms. Azure Arc is a cloud service so make sure you have required permissions to connect and configure further steps on the Azure Cloud Web Portal. The following figure shows the Azure Arc infrastructure support page:

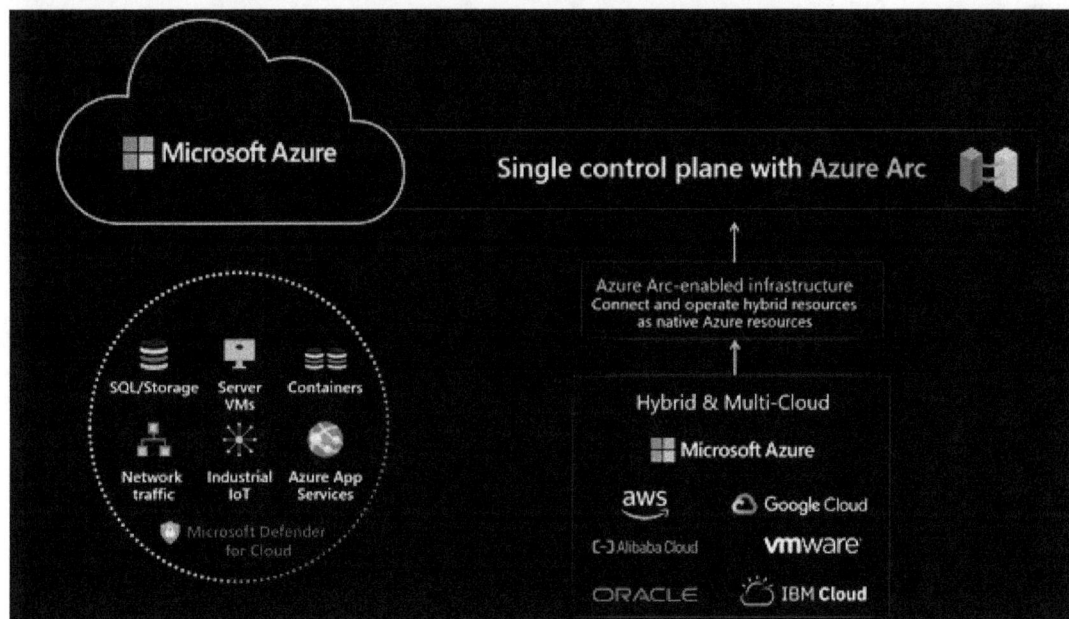

Figure 11.18: Azure Arc infrastructure support

Reference: https://techcommunity.microsoft.com/t5/itops-talk-blog/step-by-step-how-to-connect-aws-machines-to-microsoft-defender/ba-p/3251096

Once you onboard non-Azure resource to Azure then you can leverage all the benefits that other Azure managed services can use in form of the following:

- Centralized Management of Inventory on Azure Web Portal.
- Deployment of Extensions
- Onboarding of VM's to **Microsoft Defender for Cloud (MDFC)**
- Azure Policies

The following figure showcases different devices onboarded into Azure Arc:

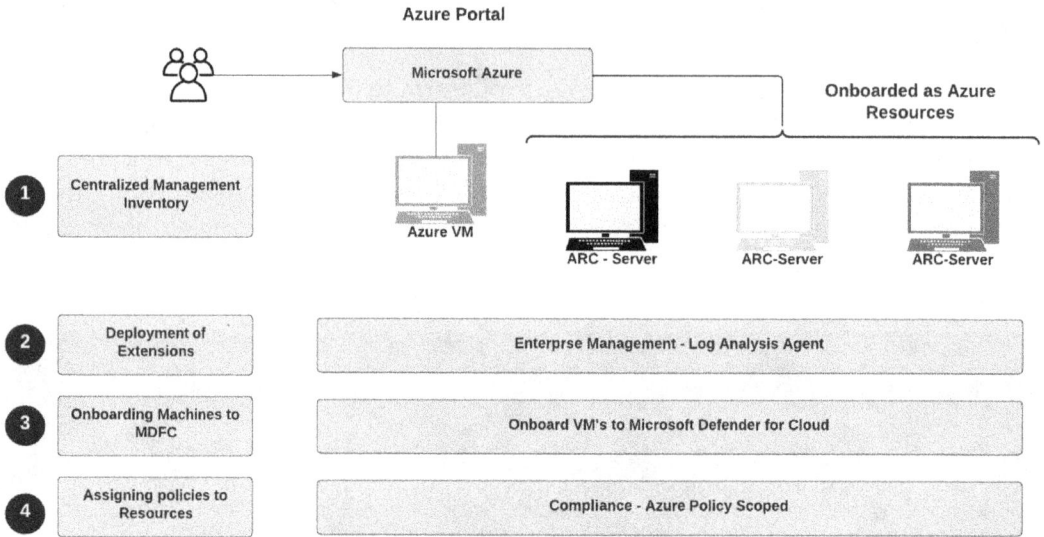

Figure 11.19: Device onboarded under Arc and other security products around it

To manage non-Azure VMs, you must first deploy the Azure Arc agent, so it is registered into ARM. Having this agent and using Azure as the management control plane will also come with a set of new benefits, shown as follows:

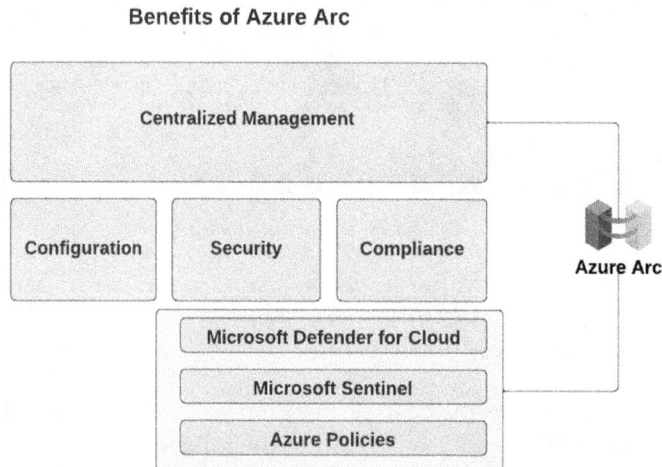

Figure 11.20: Benefits of Azure Arc (Centralized Management)

Onboarding non-Azure servers

After following certain steps on the Azure Portal, you can onboard other cloud or edge devices on the Azure portal and put them in the same. Azure standardized resource groups that other Azure services use to group them together under single location of certain grouping benefits.

The following figure is a reference to showcase non Azure cloud devices onboarding management through Azure portal where azure portal is at the central point:

Azure Arc to onboard non Azure Resources

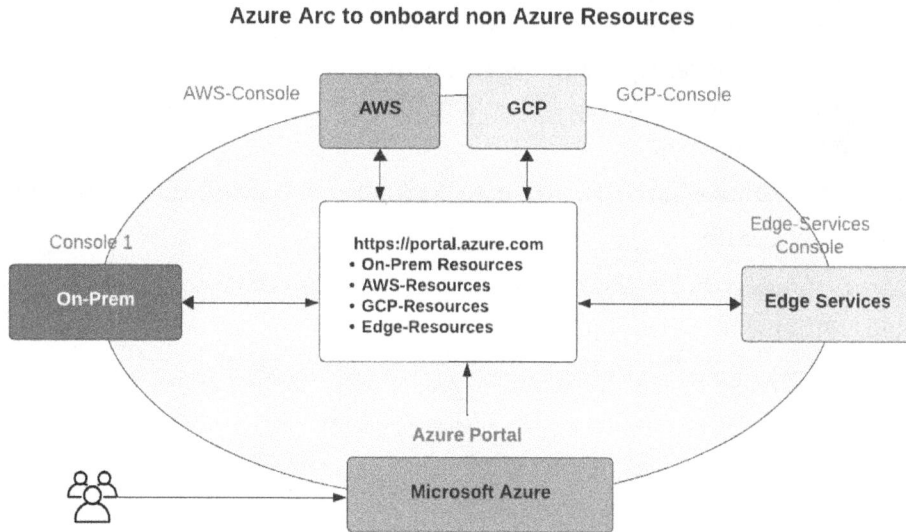

Figure 11.21: Azure Arc showcasing non Azure cloud device onboarding

The following steps provide an overview about how to onboard non Azure Virtual machines on Azure Arc through Azure portal:

1. **Connect hybrid machines to Azure using Azure Arc**: Before you start connecting your machines, review the following requirements:

    - Make sure you have administrator permission on the machines you want to onboard.

    - Administrator permissions are required to install the Connected Machine agent on the machines; on Linux by using the root account, and on Windows as a member of the Local Administrators group.

    - Review the prerequisites available on Azure website and verify that your subscription and resources meet the requirements. You will need to have the **Azure Connected Machine Onboarding** role or the **Contributor** role for the resource group of the machine.

2. **Create a service principal for onboarding**: The Azure Arc service in the Azure portal provides a streamlined way to create a service principal that can be used to connect your hybrid machines to Azure. Following are the steps:

a. In the Azure portal, navigate to Azure Arc, then select **Service principals** in the left menu.

b. Select **Add**.

c. Enter a name for your service principal.

d. Choose whether the service principal will have access to an entire subscription, or only to a specific resource group.

e. Select the subscription (and resource group, if applicable) to which the service principal will have access.

f. In the **Client secret** section, select the duration for which your generated client secret will be in use. You can optionally enter a friendly name of your choice in the **Description** field.

g. In the **Role assignment** section, select **Azure Connected Machine Onboarding**.

h. Select **Create**.

The following figure showcases a reference to create a Service principal account on Azure portal along with the role that you will assign to it:

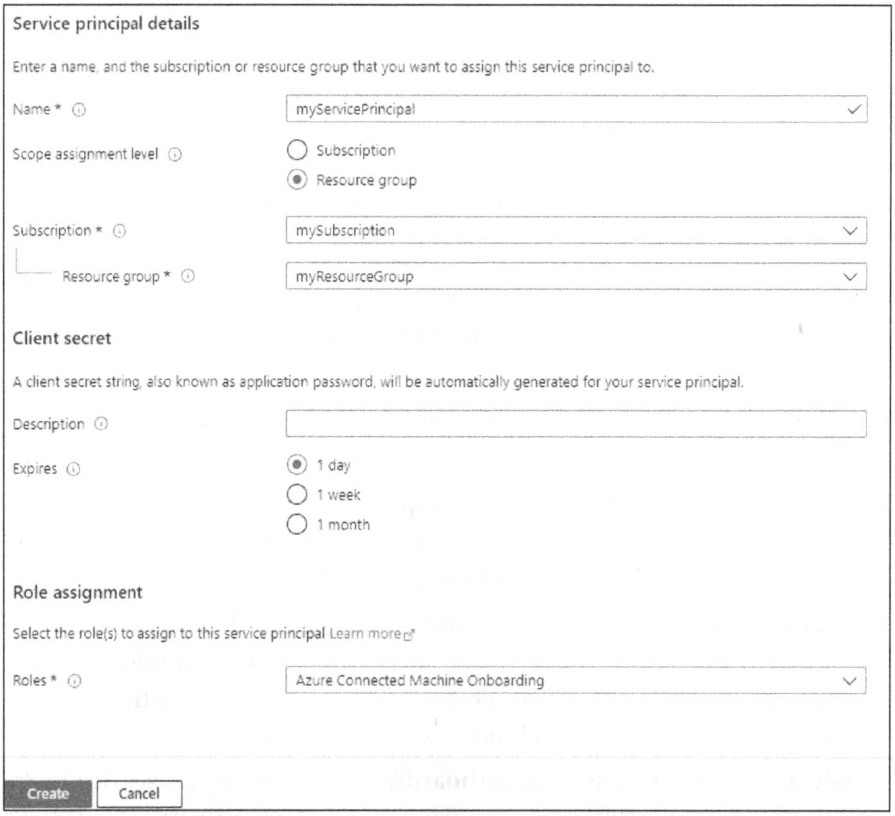

Figure 11.22: Service principal creation for device onboarding on Arc portal

3. **Generate the installation script from the Azure portal**: The script to automate the download and installation, and to establish the connection with Azure Arc, is available from the Azure portal. To complete the process, take the following steps:

   a. From your browser, go to the Azure portal.

   b. On the **Servers—Azure Arc** page, select **Add** at the upper left.

   c. On the **Select a method** page, select the **Add multiple servers** tile, and then select **Generate script**.

   d. On the **Generate script** page, select the subscription and resource group where you want the machine to be managed within Azure. Select an Azure location where the machine metadata will be stored. This location can be the same or different as the resource group's location.

   e. On the **Prerequisites** page, review the information and then select **Next: Resource details**.

   f. On the **Resource details** page, provide the following:

      i. In the **Resource group** drop-down list, select the resource group the machine will be managed from.

      ii. In the **Region** drop-down list, select the Azure region to store the servers metadata.

      iii. In the **Operating system** drop-down list, select the operating system that the script is configured to run on.

      iv. If the machine is communicating through a proxy server to connect to the internet, specify the proxy server IP address or the name and port number that the machine will use to communicate with the proxy server. Using this configuration, the agent communicates through the proxy server using the HTTP protocol. Enter the value in the format `http://<proxyURL>:<proxyport>`.

      v. Select **Next: Authentication**.

   g. On the **Authentication** page, under the **service principal** drop-down list, select **Arc-for-servers**. Then select, **Next: Tags**.

   h. On the **Tags** page, review the default **Physical location tags** suggested and enter a value, or specify one or more **Custom tags** to support your standards.

   i. Select **Next: Download and run script**.

   j. On the **Download and run script** page, review the summary information, and then select **Download**. If you still need to make changes, select **Previous**.

For Windows, you are prompted to save `OnboardingScript.ps1`, and for Linux `OnboardingScript.sh` to your computer.

We have to deploy the above script to corresponding server and that server then will be onboarded to Azure Arc with local administrative permission on windows server and root permission on Linux server.

Onboarding AWS Cloud Windows VM

As you can onboard any machine or VM hosted on any platform so here (**https://techcommunity.microsoft.com/t5/itops-talk-blog/step-by-step-how-to-connect-aws-machines-to-microsoft-defender/ba-p/3251096**) you can find high level steps for installation of MDE agent through Azure Arc.

> **Note: We could have covered more detailed onboarding steps and examples but those can be easily referred to on their website as our goal is to pass on the capabilities and high-level idea about it.**

After onboarding, you will realize that you can take all the benefits of Microsoft Cloud, Security and Compliance stack seamlessly without any differentiation.

The following figure showcases all in one image reflecting categorized on left hand side along with other Microsoft products implementing those areas:

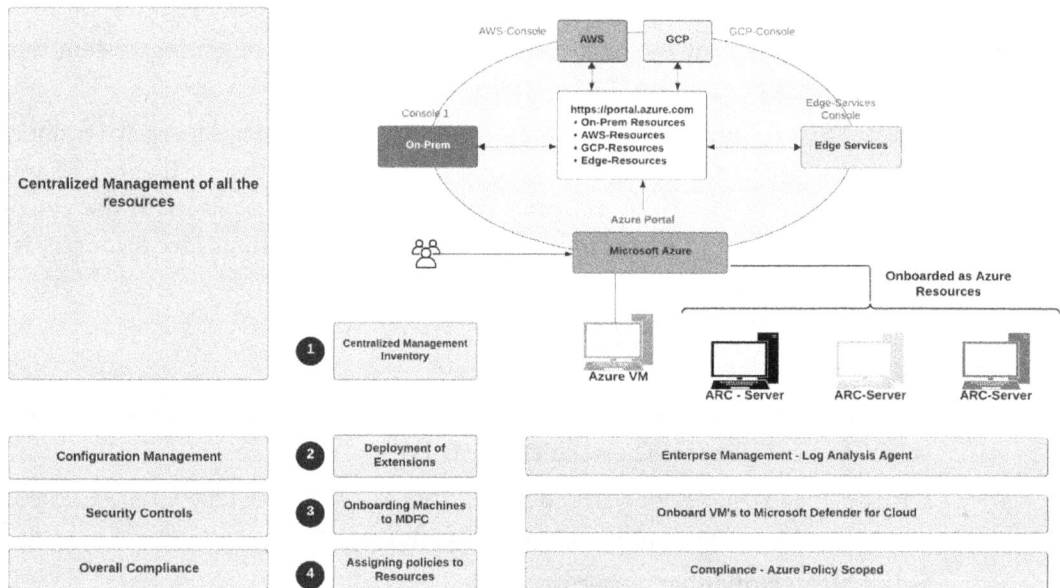

Figure 11.23: Azure Arc onboarding stages

Conclusion

In conclusion, this chapter has provided an in-depth exploration of DevSecOps, highlighting its significance in modern software development practices. By embracing the Shift Left approach, organizations can effectively integrate security measures into the early stages of the software development lifecycle, ensuring proactive threat mitigation. Various methodologies and tools have been discussed, offering insights into enhancing security practices within DevSecOps workflows. The chapter delved into container security, elucidating key concepts such as registry scanning, pipeline scanning, and vulnerability management. Additionally, an understanding of container platforms like Kubernetes was provided, emphasizing the importance of securing containerized environments. Microsoft CNPP and Microsoft Defender for Cloud were presented as robust solutions for safeguarding cloud-based applications and workloads. Furthermore, the integration of security into multi-cloud and hybrid environments through Azure Arc was explored, demonstrating the benefits and steps for onboarding non-Azure servers and AWS Cloud Windows VMs. Overall, this chapter serves as a comprehensive guide to implementing effective security measures in DevSecOps and cloud-native environments, enabling organizations to bolster their defenses against evolving cyber threats.

In next chapter, we are going to cover about how to manage and maintain the MDE from security administrator point of view.

Join our book's Discord space

Join the book's Discord Workspace for Latest updates, Offers, Tech happenings around the world, New Release and Sessions with the Authors:

https://discord.bpbonline.com

CHAPTER 12

Managing and Maintaining Microsoft Defender Endpoint

Introduction

Managing and maintaining Microsoft Defender Endpoint is a comprehensive endeavour that ensures the sustained security and efficiency of your organization's digital infrastructure. This chapter explores the critical aspects of security posture management, leveraging Microsoft **Security Assessment Framework (SAF)** and **Microsoft Cybersecurity Reference Architecture (MCRA)**. These frameworks provide a foundational understanding essential for navigating the broader Microsoft security ecosystem. *MCRA is often part of broader Microsoft security frameworks, but SAF is a specific subset focused more on assessments, not as universally applicable for maturing security best practices.*

We will explore the roles and responsibilities of key executives and the Microsoft technology stack they utilize to uphold security. Additionally, we will examine Microsoft's approach to threat modelling and various threat vectors, offering insights into managing different network configurations in an ideal scenario effectively. By the end of this chapter, you will have a robust grasp of managing Microsoft Defender Endpoint to enhance your organization's security posture.

Structure

In this chapter, we will cover the following topics:

- Management using Microsoft frameworks
- Microsoft cybersecurity reference architecture
- Threat modelling
- Understanding network attack vectors
- Management of MDE
- Using the deception feature

Objectives

The objective of this chapter is to help you build holistic approach in management of security posture of your organization in respect to Microsoft references, frameworks, recommendation and tools and help you build general understanding of the threat vectors, threat modeling and about how you can plan the management of security and MDE by referencing the training material available on Microsoft website.

> **Note: We have already covered in detail the MDE agent installation and upgrades in earlier Chapter 3 and 4 and such activities fall under management and maintenance of the MDE so make sure you have already read contents there.**

Management using Microsoft frameworks

Standards are established guidelines, criteria, or specifications that define how a particular process, product, or service should operate or be implemented. These are commonly accepted and agreed-upon rules that ensure consistency, interoperability, and quality. Standards can be set by industry organizations, government bodies, or international committees to facilitate uniformity, safety, and efficiency across various domains.

A framework is a structured set of guidelines, conventions, and tools that provide a foundation for developing a software application, system, or solution. It offers a pre-defined structure and commonly accepted practices to streamline the development process. Frameworks are designed to address specific challenges and can include libraries, reusable code, and predefined functionalities. They serve as a scaffold that developers can build upon, accelerating the development process and promoting best practices.

Microsoft teams are continuously creating new frameworks to help customers to adopt the best practices and also helps in mapping the tools and techniques to adopt such recommendation. The following are the three major Microsoft Frameworks released by them. SAF and MCRA are released as part of maturing security best practices so that customers can follow and remain aligned as per the framework:

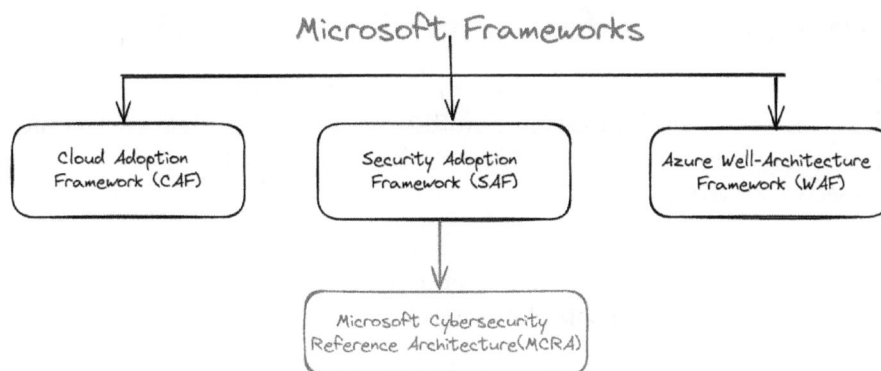

Figure 12.1: Microsoft frameworks leading the fields

Microsoft cybersecurity reference architecture

The MCRA is a component of Microsoft's SAF that describes Microsoft's cybersecurity capabilities and technologies. The MCRA includes diagrams that illustrate how Microsoft security capabilities integrate with Microsoft platforms and third-party platforms like Microsoft 365, Microsoft Azure, ServiceNow, **Salesforce**, **Amazon Web Services** (**AWS**), and **Google Cloud Platform** (**GCP**).

The MCRA includes key information about the following:

- Antipatterns (common mistakes) and best practices
- Guiding rulesets for end-to-end architecture
- Threat trends, and attack patterns
- Mapping Microsoft capabilities to organizational roles
- Overview of mapping Microsoft capabilities to zero trust standards
- Securing privileged access
- Prioritizing using attacker **return on investment** (**ROI**)
- Detailed technical diagrams for Microsoft cybersecurity capabilities, zero trust user access, **security operations** (**SecOps/SOC**), **operational technology** (**OT**), multi-cloud and cross-platform capabilities, Attack chain coverage, Infrastructure and Development security, and security organizational functions.

The MCRA is used as a starting template for security architecture, a comparison reference for security capabilities, a learning tool about Microsoft capabilities and integration investments, and a learning tool about cybersecurity.

Security adoption framework

Microsoft SAF provides guidance for organizations through end-to-end security modernization across a *hybrid of everything* multi-cloud and multi-platform technical estate. It helps organizations to understand and implement the security capabilities included in Microsoft's security portfolio.

The SAF includes the MCRA, which describe Microsoft's cybersecurity capabilities and technologies. The MCRA includes diagrams that illustrate how Microsoft security capabilities integrate with Microsoft platforms and third-party platforms.

Note: SAF includes broader guidelines and tools for security adoption, whereas MCRA specifically details the architecture and technologies for cybersecurity.

The following figure (*Figure 12.2*) is created by SAF/MCRA team to understand various roles and the corresponding responsibilities performed by specific group. Some of the responsibilities are shared in between the adjoining group in the following table:

S.No.	Group	Roles and responsibilities	Comments
1	Business leadership	Security digital transformation	These four roles and responsibility covers almost end to end security stack and these folks leverages various security standards and frameworks released by SAF and MCRA team.
2	Technical leadership	Business and security integration, security strategy, programs and epics	
3	Architects and technical managers	Architecture and policy	
4	Implementation team (Security Administrator/ Engineers and other)	Technical planning, implementation and operations	

Table 12.1: SAF roles and responsibility table

The following figure represents the SAF framework where left hand sides are the roles and in middle are the responsibilities performed by them using the tools leveraged by them on extreme right:

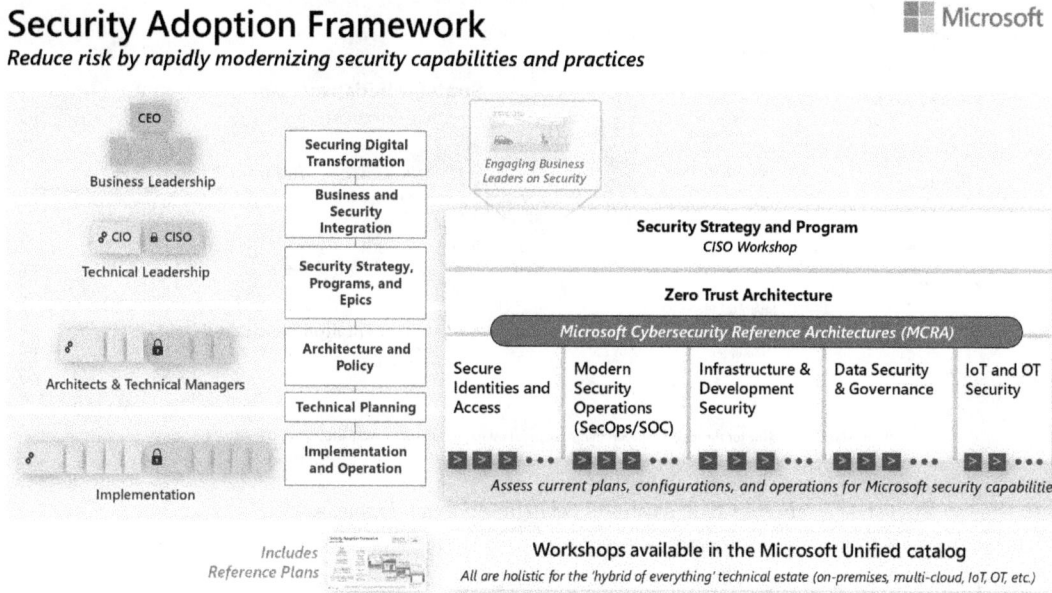

Figure 12.2: Microsoft Security Adoption Framework

SAF also provides resources such as the Microsoft 365 security portfolio, plans for multifactor authentication, security insider reports, and FastTrack for Microsoft 365, which offers expert guidance at no additional cost for the life of your eligible subscription.

In summary, SAF is a comprehensive guide that helps organizations to improve their security posture by leveraging Microsoft's security capabilities.

The following figure shows the high-level responsibilities of different leaders in the hierarchy or security operation management captured in Microsoft Security Adoption Framework reference plan:

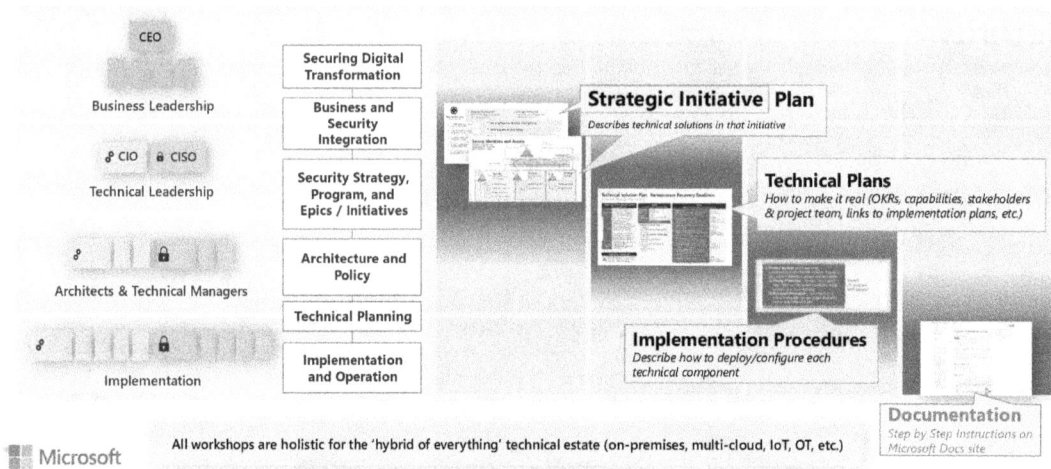

Figure 12.3: *Microsoft Security Adoption Framework[1]*

Ten laws of cybersecurity risk

The following figure shows the laws that are universal in nature and can be linked to any organization:

Figure 12.4: *10 Laws of Cybersecurity Risk*

---

1   Reference: https://learn.microsoft.com/en-us/security/cybersecurity-reference-architecture/mcra

Immutable laws of security

The following figure shows the immutable laws of security also universal in nature and applicable to any organization:

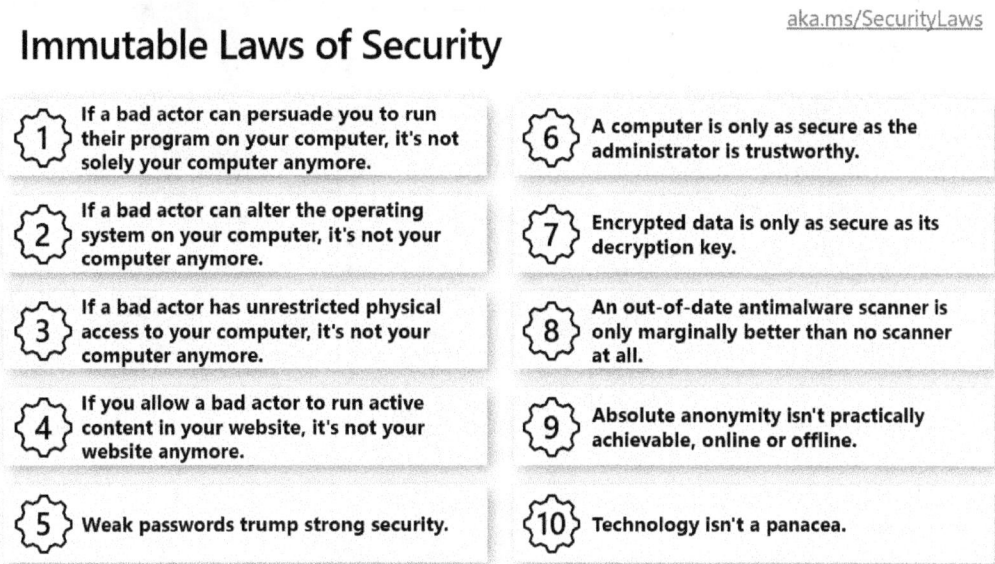

Immutable Laws of Security

aka.ms/SecurityLaws

1. If a bad actor can persuade you to run their program on your computer, it's not solely your computer anymore.

2. If a bad actor can alter the operating system on your computer, it's not your computer anymore.

3. If a bad actor has unrestricted physical access to your computer, it's not your computer anymore.

4. If you allow a bad actor to run active content in your website, it's not your website anymore.

5. Weak passwords trump strong security.

6. A computer is only as secure as the administrator is trustworthy.

7. Encrypted data is only as secure as its decryption key.

8. An out-of-date antimalware scanner is only marginally better than no scanner at all.

9. Absolute anonymity isn't practically achievable, online or offline.

10. Technology isn't a panacea.

Figure 12.5: Immutable Laws of Security

Managing information/cyber risk

Management of cyber risk is owned by many teams from top to bottom and is a shared responsibility and managed by specific subgroups. The following figure depicts how each party interacts with each other in a big enterprise for smooth function of information and cyber risk management.

Some of the top-level owners are:

- Organizational leadership
- Information risk management
- Security leadership
- Technical risk management
- Posture management

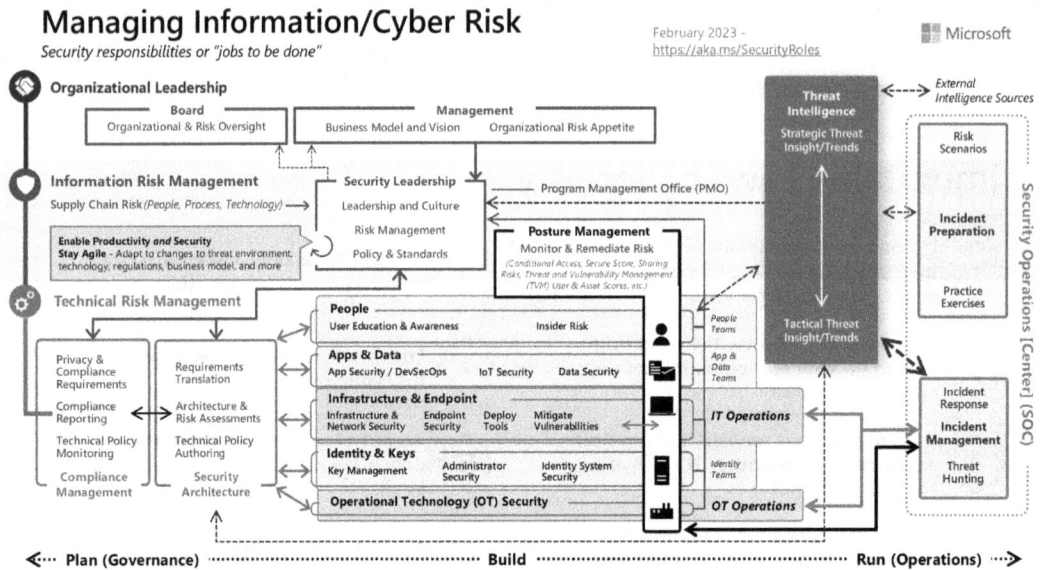

Figure 12.6: *Managing Information/Cyber Risk using different roles*

Note: As we have picked this image from Microsoft website, the font size is hard to adjust on this page. In case it is not visible, please download it from https://aka.ms/ SecurityRoles.

Microsoft security capability mapping

The following figure provides references in the form of the product and service capability that Microsoft is having to manage your cyber risk.

The following are the high level four solution portfolio that Microsoft has in current state and it is ever evolving space and Microsoft is continuously adding more and more product and services in this area. For an example M365D is recently rebranded to XDR, MD Copilot is recently launched and still in Private Preview (*Lunched for selected limited customers only*) and etc.

- Access control
- Security operations
- Security governance
- Asset protection

In this book, we have covered Security Operations portfolio and touched on one of the services under **Microsoft Defender XDR | Microsoft Defender for Endpoint** and also given some brief insight into the Microsoft Security Copilot in next chapter.

The following figure shows the Microsoft security capability mapping:

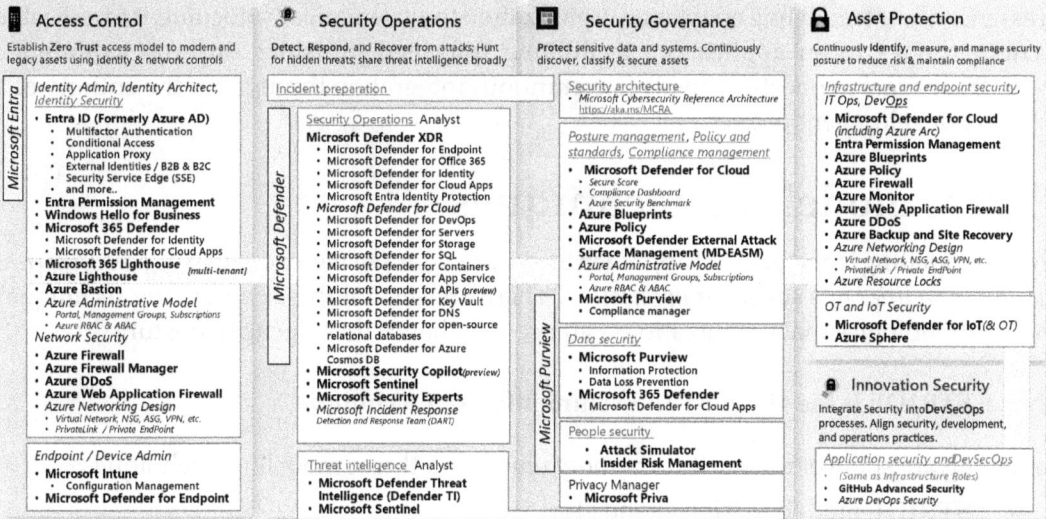

Figure 12.7: *Microsoft security capability mapping*

Threat modelling

Threat modelling is a structured process used to identify security requirements, pinpoint security threats and potential vulnerabilities, and prioritize remediation methods. It works by adopting the perspective of malicious hackers to see how much damage they could do.

> **Note: Threat modelling is not directly associated with MDE; rather, it is a comprehensive exercise conducted by the Security Review team, while security review teams are involved, threat modeling is typically a collaborative process involving various stakeholders like developers, architects, security teams, and infrastructure staff.**

The process typically involves the following four steps:

- Diagram: What are we building?
- Identify threats: What could go wrong?
- Mitigate: What are we doing to defend against threats?
- Validate: Have we acted on each of the previous steps?

Threat modelling can be applied to a wide range of things, including software, applications, systems, networks, distributed systems, Internet of Things (IoT) devices, and business processes. A threat model typically includes a description of the subject to be modelled, assumptions that can be checked or challenged as the threat landscape changes, potential threats to the system, actions that can be taken to mitigate each threat, and a way of validating the model and threats, and verification of success of actions taken.

In essence, threat modeling enables an organization to systematically document foreseeable security threats to an application, facilitating informed decisions on how to mitigate them. Its optimal application involves continuous integration throughout the entirety of a software development project.

Threat modelling techniques

Threat modelling is a structured approach to *identifying, assessing, and mitigating security risks and vulnerabilities in a system or application*. There are several threat modelling techniques and methodologies that organizations can use to enhance their security posture.

Note: STRIDE is the simplest and commonly used technique.

Following are some of the most commonly employed threat modelling techniques:
- **STRIDE model**: STRIDE stands for:
  - Spoofing identity
  - Tampering with data
  - Repudiation
  - Information disclosure
  - Denial of Service
  - Elevation of privilege

Note: The STRIDE model, developed by Microsoft, categorizes threats into these six high-level categories, making it easier to identify potential security issues.

The Microsoft Threat Modelling Tool uses these categories to help users identify potential threats in their applications or systems and analyze their impact. It then provides guidance on how to mitigate these threats, enhancing the security of the application or system. The tool also takes into consideration various aspects of an application's architecture, data flow, and entry points, making it a valuable resource for threat modelling and security analysis.

- **Process for Attack Simulation and Threat Analysis (PASTA)**: PASTA is a risk-centric methodology that guides organizations through threat modelling by considering various aspects of an application's architecture, such as data flow, trust boundaries, and entry points. It encourages the identification of potential attacks and vulnerabilities associated with them.

- **OWASP threat modelling**: The **Open Web Application Security Project** (**OWASP**) provides a comprehensive guide for threat modelling web applications. This method considers assets, entry points, and data flow to identify and assess potential threats.

- **Attack trees**: Attack trees are visual representations of potential attacks with root nodes representing the ultimate goal of an attacker and leaf nodes representing specific attack techniques. This technique helps organizations analyze the possible paths an attacker might take and prioritize defenses accordingly.

- **Attack surface analysis**: This technique involves mapping the exposed attack surface of a system or application. It *identifies entry points, trust boundaries, and potential vulnerabilities within the system*, making it easier to focus on securing these areas.

- **Data flow diagrams (DFD)**: DFDs are used to represent the flow of data within a system. Threat modelling using DFDs focuses on identifying how data moves through the system, which can help pinpoint areas where data might be at risk.

- **Asset-centric modelling**: In asset-centric threat modelling, the emphasis is on identifying and protecting critical assets within a system. This approach is beneficial for organizations that want to prioritize safeguarding their most valuable resources.

- **Adversarial modelling**: This technique involves putting yourself in the shoes of potential adversaries and thinking like them. It helps in considering creative and unexpected attack scenarios.

- **Data-centric model**: In this approach, the focus is on understanding and protecting sensitive data, including how it is processed, stored, and transmitted.

- **Attack surface reduction**: This technique aims to reduce the attack surface by minimizing entry points and trust boundaries. It is a proactive approach to security.

Important: Organizations can choose the threat modelling technique or combination of techniques that best align with their specific needs and the complexity of their systems. The goal is to identify and mitigate potential vulnerabilities before they can be exploited by malicious actors, thereby strengthening security measures.

Importance of Microsoft Threat Models in SOC

Threat modelling tools and diagrams help you in enhancing the effectiveness of a SOC. It focuses on how these documents can be instrumental in helping SOC teams understand and respond to security threats efficiently. Threat model diagrams are predominantly crafted by developers from product or service teams. These diagrams are stored in the organization's knowledge base for future reference. SOC members can tap into this valuable resource to effectively identify entry and exit points of managed solutions, facilitating a rapid identification of gaps during incident response. Without such a resource, comprehending the intricacies during incident management is akin to searching for a needle in a haystack, but with these diagrams, it becomes possible to seamlessly connect all the pieces.

Here is what this section will cover:

- **Introduction to threat modelling**: Begin by providing an overview of what threat modelling is and why it is crucial for security. Explain that it involves identifying, assessing, and mitigating security risks and vulnerabilities.

- **Microsoft threat modelling tools**: Introduce the threat modelling tools provided by Microsoft. Discuss how these tools aid in creating threat models that visualize and document potential threats to an organization's systems and applications.

- **Creating threat model diagrams**: Detail the process of creating threat model diagrams. Explain the key elements typically included in these diagrams, such as assets, threats, vulnerabilities, and countermeasures. Provide insights into how these visual representations help in comprehending complex security scenarios.

- **Use cases in SOC**: Few benefits are as follows:
  o Quickly identify potential threats and vulnerabilities.
  o Understand the relationships between different components of the organization's infrastructure.
  o Prioritize security measures based on threat severity.
  o Communicate security risks and mitigation strategies effectively with stakeholders.

- **Real-world examples**: Provide real-world examples of how threat modelling has been used to detect and respond to security threats. Share case studies or scenarios where threat model diagrams played a critical role in identifying and mitigating risks.

- **Integration with incident response**: Discuss how threat models can seamlessly integrate with incident response processes. Explain how they can serve as references during incident investigations, aiding in the rapid identification of potential attack vectors and vulnerabilities.

- **Benefits of visualization**: Emphasize the benefits of visualizing security threats. This can include quicker decision-making, enhanced collaboration among SOC team members, and improved communication with other departments and stakeholders.

- **Best practices and considerations**: Offer best practices for creating and maintaining threat model diagrams. Discuss considerations for keeping threat models up to date and ensuring their accuracy.

Microsoft Threat Modelling Tool

The Microsoft Threat Modelling Tool primarily employs the STRIDE model to assist users in recognizing and scrutinizing security threats. While it offers basic functionality, providing essential features for creating diagrams and offering necessary icons and editing options to emphasize boundaries and service entities, it serves as a valuable tool. It facilitates constructive discussions between developers and security reviewers, aiding in the identification of weaknesses and the evaluation of the security posture of the reviewed service. Ideally, each service should undergo a revision in the event of any significant changes to the service architecture.

References for download:

https://aka.ms/threatmodelingtool

https://learn.microsoft.com/en-us/azure/security/develop/threat-modeling-tool-releases

After installation, once you open the tool, it will look like the following figure:

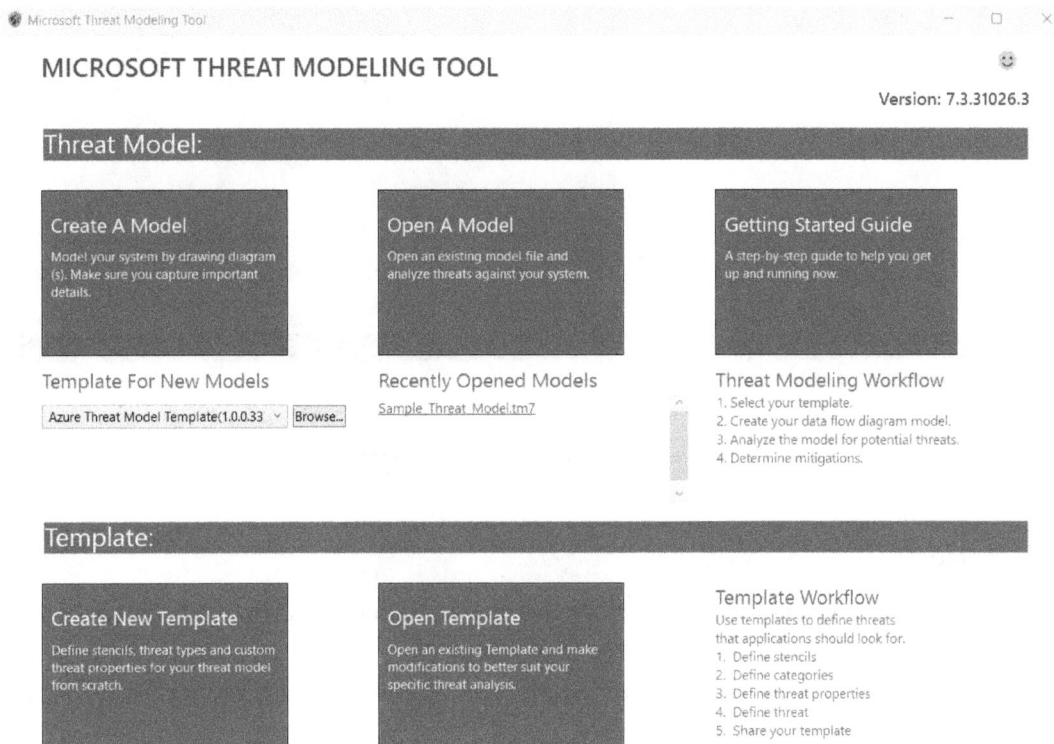

Figure 12.8: Microsoft Threat Modeling Tool home page

Numerous stencils, essentially icons, are available for constructing model diagrams. The tool itself offers specific security tags that can be associated with each vector and service. An illustrative example is provided in the following figure, depicting a general trust boundary that delineates external and internal factors. Internal OS-specific services are deemed secure and are positioned within the trust boundary block.

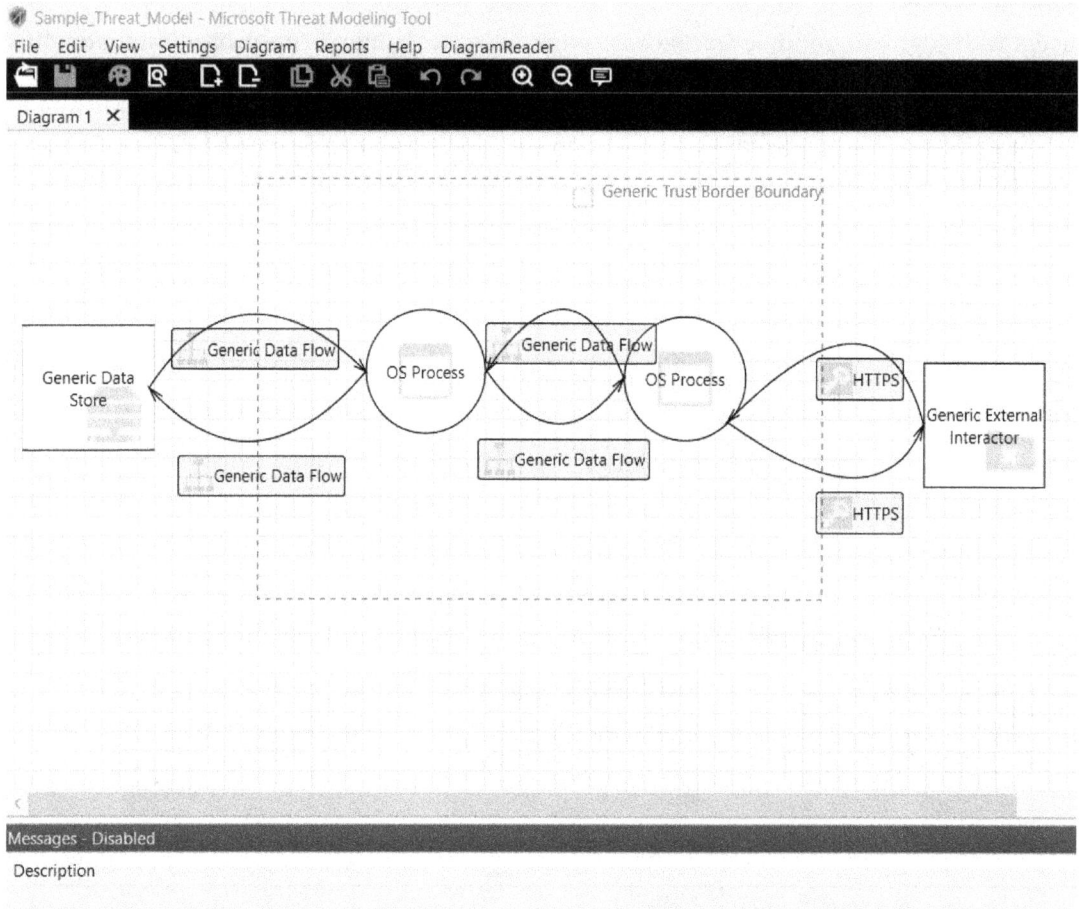

Figure 12.9: Main drawing area of tool

You can attach element properties to each resource that you used on the figure to create extra metadata (extra information).

The following are the two example showcasing metadata or external properties that we can attach to each stencil put on the main drawing area:

- **Example 1**: The following figure showcases the line element properties where we have named it as HTTPS:

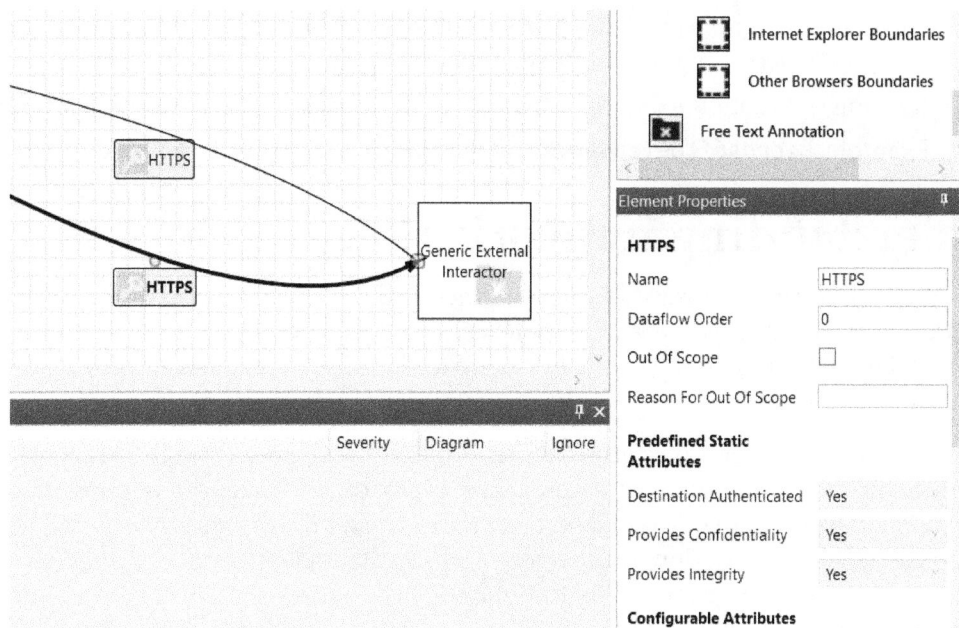

Figure 12.10: Element Properties

- **Example 2**: The following figure showcases square element properties where we have named it as General External Interactor:

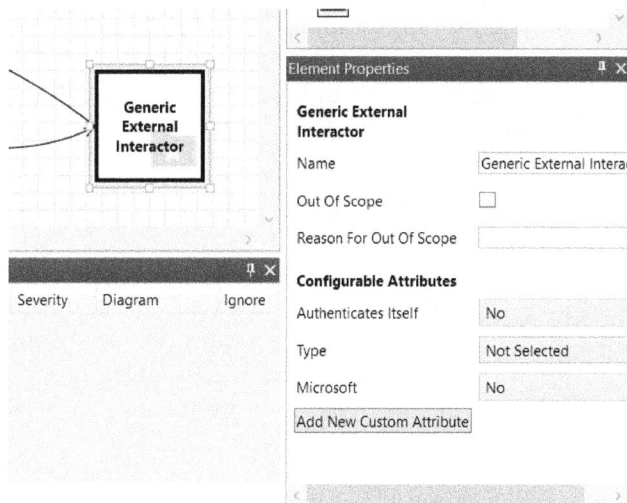

Figure 12.11: External Properties (Continued)

Note: As an SOC analyst, it is crucial to have a readily accessible location reference for any managed service or organizational infrastructure. This ensures efficient document retrieval without unnecessary time wastage. Additionally, your development team should adhere to a standardized naming convention for each document, facilitating quick and easy searches.

The following is an example reference that your team can use to organize such documents, or you can adapt it according to your team's specific standards:

- Naming convention example: `<Product.ServiceName.ReleaseDate.Version>`
- Example: `MicrosoftDefender.XPlatMBAService.27012024.v01`

Understanding network attack vectors

The security industry is progressively embracing the *Zero trust policy*, and Microsoft has already established well-defined policies and philosophies around it. Microsoft's **Azure Active Directory** (**AAD**) policies offer excellent features to assist in bringing and implementing this policy.

Zero trust represents a departure from the traditional network protection-based capabilities, offering a fundamentally different approach. It is essential for security administrators to comprehend various network-based security perimeters. Many organizations still rely on traditional network protection approaches, and zero trust is often seen as a *North Star* goal—a milestone for organizations to enhance their implementation of best-in-breed security solutions and philosophies.

Let us try to first understand network perimeter and the internal and external threat actors with all the techniques that they leverage to attack an organization and MDE software agent or the Microsoft Security eco system components protects from such attacks. We have specially created pictorial representation to cover different network attack types that an attacker can breach to enter your infrastructure and understanding of such areas are crucial as SOC analyst that can help you to build mind map while managing on some incident during reactive time.

Network perimeters for backend IT infra

IT assets are consistently situated within specific networks, with the company's network team frequently discussing traffic movement policies to regulate both internal and external network traffic. These networks are often designated with different names such as corporate network, public or guest network, HR, marketing, engineering, or R&D. However, from an architectural perspective, these networks can be broadly categorized into the following:

- Public
- Web
- Application
- Management networks with controlled access and least privilege principles

This simplification aids in various discussions related to network architecture. The following figure showcase the four different ideal network categorizations along with their interconnectivity:

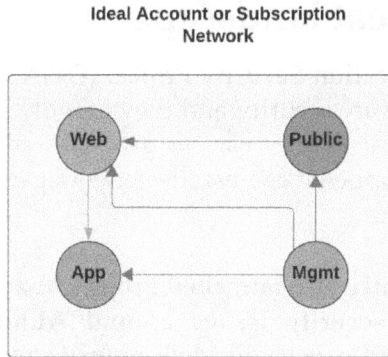

Figure 12.12: Ideal network categorization in an organization

Applications and services under network

Once you have identified the optimal network for deploying your IT infrastructure, adding resources becomes a straightforward process. For instance, network load balancers such as AWS **Elastic Load Balancer (ELB)**, **Application Load Balancer (ALB)**, **Network Load Balancer (NLB)**, Azure Load Balancer, and on-premises LBs like Nginx and HAProxy are typically placed in the public network group. Here, you apply your **web application firewall (WAF)** policies, as this is the initial publicly exposed entity in your network, susceptible to network attacks.

Conversely, databases are placed in the most secure network without direct public network connectivity. Meanwhile, the most powerful assets find their place in the management network, endowed with the capability to access the entire network for executing various automation tasks by your DevOps or system administrators.

The following figure shows four different types of network category and their interaction among them:

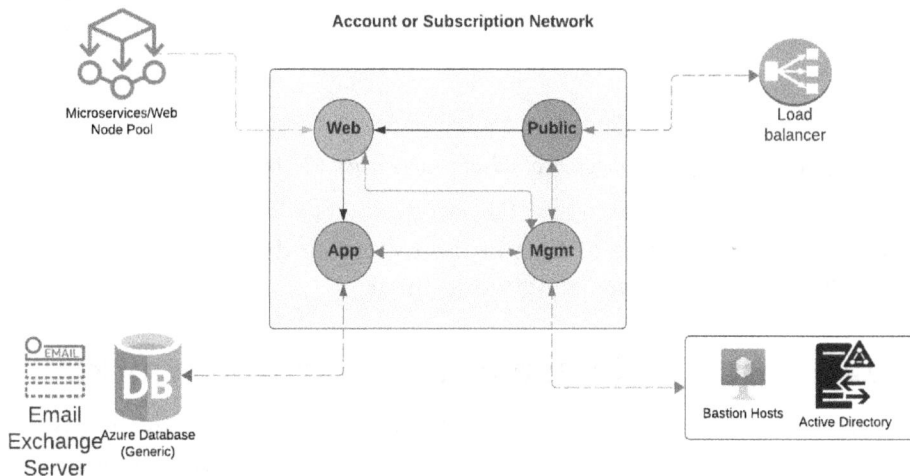

Figure 12.13: Ideal network categorization in an organization along with assets

Understanding threat landscape

The **Open Worldwide Application Security Project (OWASP)** is a nonprofit foundation dedicated to improving software security and they identify and release *top ten developers and web application security list* every year. To give you edge we have organized and categorized such risks and mapped it against the network perimeters so that you can focus on the areas accordingly.

> **Information: OWASP recently also launched Project AI and Security Guide as early community to highlight security issues around AI.https://github.com/OWASP/ www-project-ai-security-and-privacy-guide/blob/main/owaspaiexchange.md**

The following figure is just a high-level overview that covers all vectors:

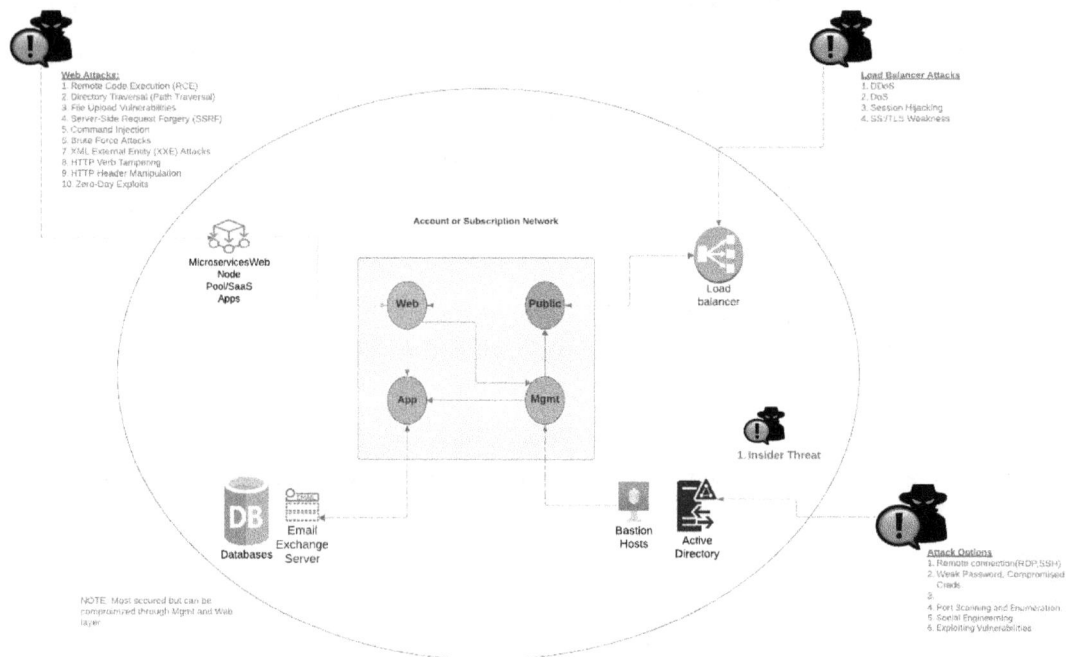

Figure 12.14: High level diagram of threat vectors to your IT infrastructure network

> **Note: You can ignore the size of font in the following diagram. We have captured separate notes for all four types of network threat.**

Ideal traffic flow between environment networks

Once you have established your optimal network design, you proceed to place your IT infrastructure per environment. Additionally, you design your network to facilitate intercommunication between environments, such as Production and Staging, to meet various business requirements. In the following figure, we present an ideal network diagram encompassing all possible combinations and scenarios that may occur within five distinct types of network environments:

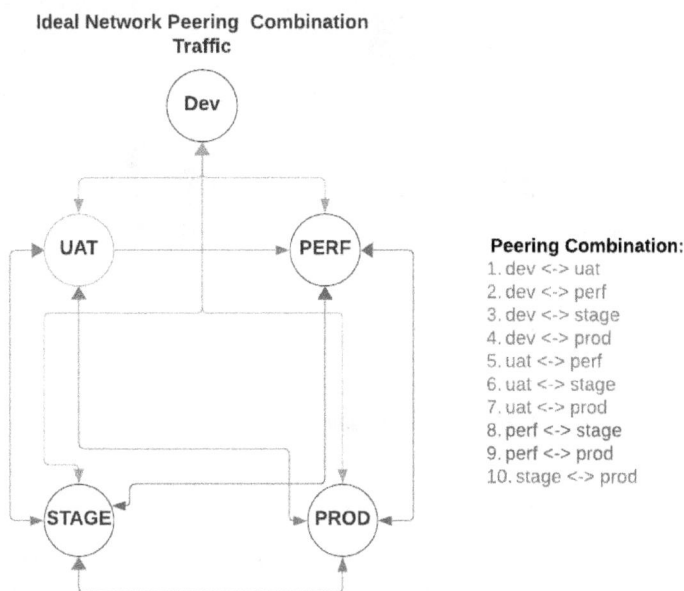

Figure 12.15: Ideal Network Peering Traffic Combination

Types of network threat

We have four types of network threats that you should consider and are captured in the following figures that define the four categories so that you can perform due diligence and do the right protection and detection planning around it.

Types of threat to management network

The management network stands out as the most crucial and pivotal subnetwork within your entire network, wielding supreme powers capable of executing a wide array of actions. A breach into this network could result in significant impacts on your overall network. Typically, IT Administrator machines find their place in this subnet, enabling the execution of various automation actions and access to other subnetworks through bastion points.

A strong recommendation is to implement measures to block **Remote Desktop Protocol (RDP)** and **Secure Shell (SSH)** access to this network from the internet or any public network. Establishing policies that automatically block such traffic is highly advisable for enhanced security.

The following figure showcases different types of threats to your management network:

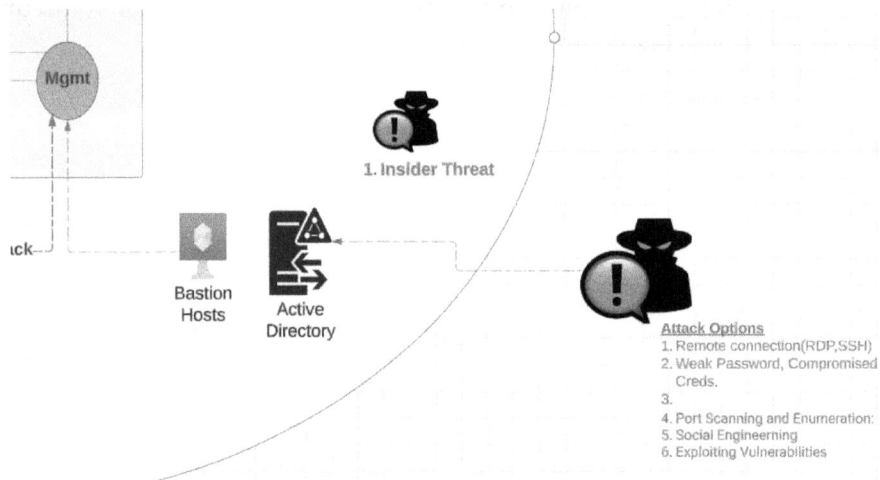

Figure 12.16: Management network attacks

Types of threat to public network

In this area, malicious actors carry out **Distributed Denial of Service (DDoS)** or **Denial of Service (DoS)** attacks to disrupt your services. To safeguard against such threats, it is advisable to activate **web application firewalls (WAF)** services. Many cloud vendors offer managed WAF services. If you manage your own load balancers, you can install and configure tools like *ModSecurity* on Nginx LBs for added protection.

The following figure showcases different types of attacks that can be executed to your Load balancers:

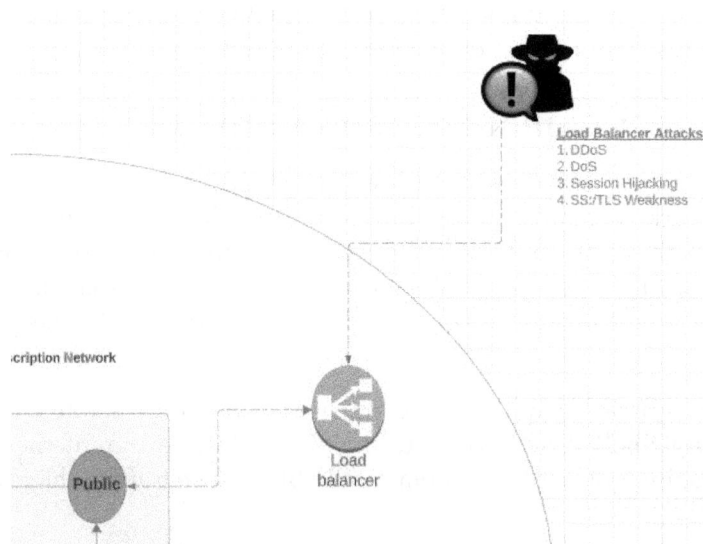

Figure 12.17: Public network attacks

Types of threat to web network

Web attacks are mostly protected by **Microsoft Defender for Application (MDA)** product category (earlier known as MCAS) and a web server administrator and web application developers can play a good role while designing their application from such attacks in case you are not using such managed security products for your application.

The following figure shows the different web network attacks:

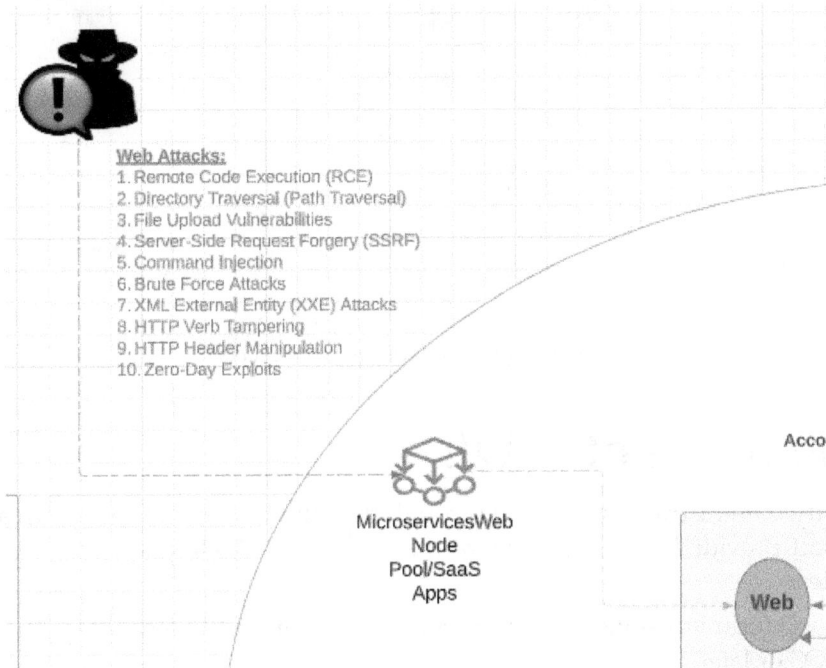

Figure 12.18: Web network attacks

Types of threat to application network

This area is considered as most secure as it is not exposed to any public network and usually, we do not have a security product category that covers this area and usually protected by some other network protection techniques that you leverage for other networks.

The following figure shows the resources or applications deployed under application network and shows the network attack vectors that might lead to unauthorized access to your critical information stored in DB or to central SMTP infrastructure:

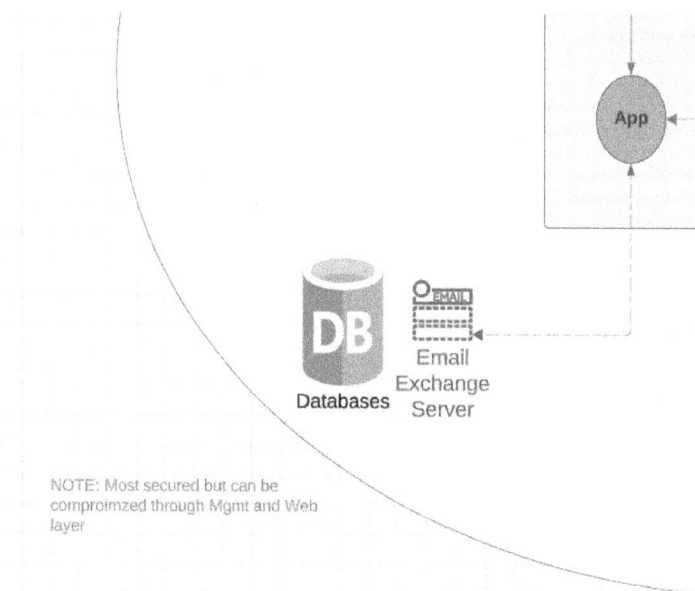

Figure 12.19: Application network attacks

Management of MDE

Each security administrator should go through the following mentioned URL and attend the Microsoft provided free management training for the MDE and it has the following prerequisites:

- Strong technical skills installing, maintaining, and troubleshooting the Windows 10 OS or later

- Strong understanding of computer networking, client security, and application concepts

- Experience using Active Directory Domain Services

Reference: https://learn.microsoft.com/en-us/training/modules/manage-microsoft-defender-endpoint/

Using the deception feature

Deception is a novel addition to Microsoft Defender for Endpoint as a new feature on the MDE web portal. This topic offers a brief summary of this new functionality. It involves the deployment of virtual decoys, such as local accounts/alias and advices/host name, on the devices that have Microsoft Defender for Endpoint assigned to them.

Setup of deception

To set up deception, the first thing you need to do is enable the **Deception** feature in the Advanced setting of Microsoft Defender for Endpoint, as shown in the following figure:

Deception

Manage and deploy lures and decoys to catch attackers in your environment. After you turn this on, go to Rules > Deception rules to run deception campaigns.

Figure 12.20: Toggle button to enable Deception feature on Advanced setting page

Once enabled and configured, you can see newly attached Deception tags to each incident that has signs of such activity. This feature has recently been added in the second half of the 2023. You can explore more about this feature on the following url:

https://derkvanderwoude.medium.com/mde-deception-fe8ba2ae8422

The following figure shows the working Deception tagged screenshot taken from MDE web portal:

		Incident name	Incident Id	Tags			Severity	Categories
☐	⌄	Lateral movement incident on one endpoint	1467	Deception	Production		◼◼◼ High	Lateral movement
☐		Connection attempt over NetBIOS to a deceptive host		Deception	Production		◼◼◼ High	Lateral movement
☐		Connection attempt over SMB to a deceptive host		Deception	Production		◼◼◼ High	Lateral movement
☐		Connection attempt to a deceptive host		Deception	Production		◼◼◼ High	Lateral movement
☐		Remote Desktop session			Production		◼◼◻ Medium	Lateral movement
☐		Connection attempt over RDP to a deceptive host		Deception	Production		◼◼◼ High	Lateral movement

Figure 12.21: Incident with Deception tag on the MDE portal

Credit and reference to Microsoft:

- Most of the diagrams captured in chapter are taken from MCRA and SAF documentation available on Microsoft website.

- We are just re referencing the image of MDE that we captured in this book multiple times so that you can get an idea that this chapter gives you the holistic view of management through the inbuilt features in the MDE product mentioned below in the image.

Conclusion

This chapter covered the introduction and outlines its objectives, followed by an explanation of the **Microsoft Cybersecurity Reference Architecture (MCRA)** and the Security Adoption Framework. It then provides references of the ten Laws of Cybersecurity Risk and the Immutable Laws of Security. The focus shifts to managing information/cyber risk and mapping Microsoft's security capabilities. The importance of Microsoft Threat Model Diagrams during SOC operations is highlighted, along with various threat modeling techniques and tools. The document further explores network attack vectors, network perimeters for backend IT infrastructure, and the applications and services within or hosted on the network. It provides an understanding of the threat landscape and discusses the ideal traffic flow between environment networks. Various types of network threats are examined, including threats to the management network, public network, web network, and application network. The chapter concludes with a discussion on real-time threat detection and analysis with MDE, Microsoft's training on MDE management, and the new deception feature launched in end of 2023 to manage lateral movement, including its setup.

In the next chapter, we are going to give overview of AI and LLM in respect to Microsoft Security Copilot.

Join our book's Discord space

Join the book's Discord Workspace for Latest updates, Offers, Tech happenings around the world, New Release and Sessions with the Authors:

https://discord.bpbonline.com

CHAPTER 13

Future Ahead with AI and LLM

Introduction

This chapter holds special significance for security engineers, whether you are a SOC analyst or a CISO. It will give you deep insight into the general AI/ML and specifically focuses on ML security **large language models (LLM)**. The spotlight is on Microsoft's cutting-edge technologies, including Defender XDR, Microsoft Security Copilot, and **Microsoft Threat Expert (MTE)**. Throughout the chapter, we will unravel the intricacies of these offerings from the Microsoft security team, providing both frontend and backend security insights. Gain a comprehensive understanding of the meticulous work undertaken by the Defender team behind the scenes to deliver security expertise directly to your doorstep through their array of services. Leveraging AI/ML for an extended period, recent advancements in LLM have propelled them to unveil a fully featured product, Microsoft Security Copilot, bringing the accumulated wealth of knowledge and advancements to your organization.

Microsoft Security Copilot is going to be the most advanced and abstract solution over the above vast portfolio of products and services offered by Microsoft and used by Microsoft Customers. As Microsoft teams got the benefits of leveraging both internal and external LLM. They have quickly integrated it with their breadth and depth of product categories.

Microsoft Security Breadth and Depth of Product and service portfolio are shown in the following figure:

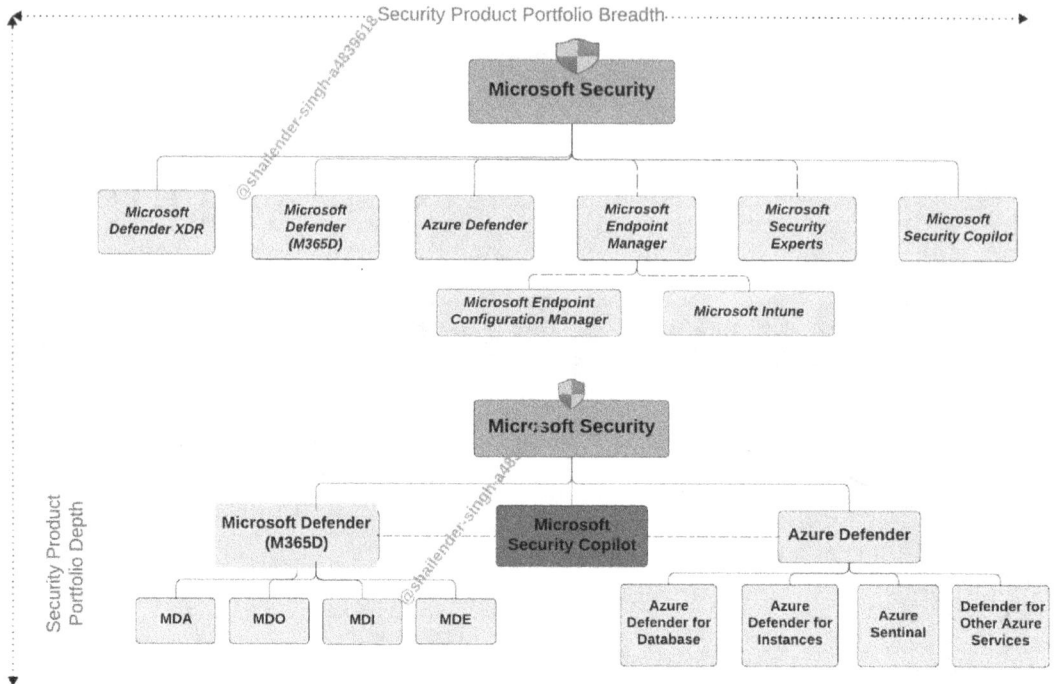

Figure 13.1: Microsoft Security overall portfolio

Structure

In this chapter, we will cover the following topics:

- Security operation capabilities
- Venture capitalist and involvement of business mindset
- Understanding artificial intelligence and machine language
- Understanding large language model
- IT infrastructure related models
- Cybersecurity related models
- Malware categorization as per Microsoft
- Future trends and innovations
- Research enablement
- Microsoft Security Copilot

Objectives

The objective of this chapter is to provide you with a comprehensive understanding of the depth and breadth of Microsoft security services, highlighting the pivotal role of Microsoft Security Copilot as an extensively utilized product in the long term. This tool is designed to significantly reduce the man-hours invested by SOC analysts in their day-to-day responsibilities. Furthermore, it serves as a valuable resource for CISOs, offering a quick summary of the overall health of the organization and detailed insights into any specific escalated incident that has high impact on the organization.

As we explore the future and the latest trends in the security market within the content, our focus will remain aligned with MDE. The chapter will elucidate how Security Copilot revolves around MDE and how MDE SOC engineers can harness its capabilities to streamline various tasks covered throughout this book, including MDE configuration through Security Copilot, SOC activities, monitoring, reporting, alerting, and more.

Security operation capabilities

Microsoft Defender offers a comprehensive suite of capabilities designed to enhance the efficiency and effectiveness of **Security Operations Centers (SOCs)**. Its unified security operations platform integrates cloud-native **Security Information and Event Management (SIEM)** and **Extended Detection and Response (XDR)** capabilities, providing end-to-end protection from prevention to detection and response. With features like AI-powered insights, automated threat intelligence, and incident summaries, Microsoft Defender helps SOC teams prioritize threats, manage exposures proactively, and respond swiftly to security incidents. The platform also supports custom **Security Orchestration, Automation, and Response (SOAR)** playbooks, enabling SOC analysts to streamline workflows and focus on high-value tasks. By breaking down security silos and offering continuous visibility of assets and cyberattack paths, Microsoft Defender empowers security teams to better protect their organizations against evolving threats.

The following figure shows all capabilities of Microsoft Defender Security through its various products and services:

Security Operations Capabilities

Enabling a people-centric function focused rapid remediation of realized risk

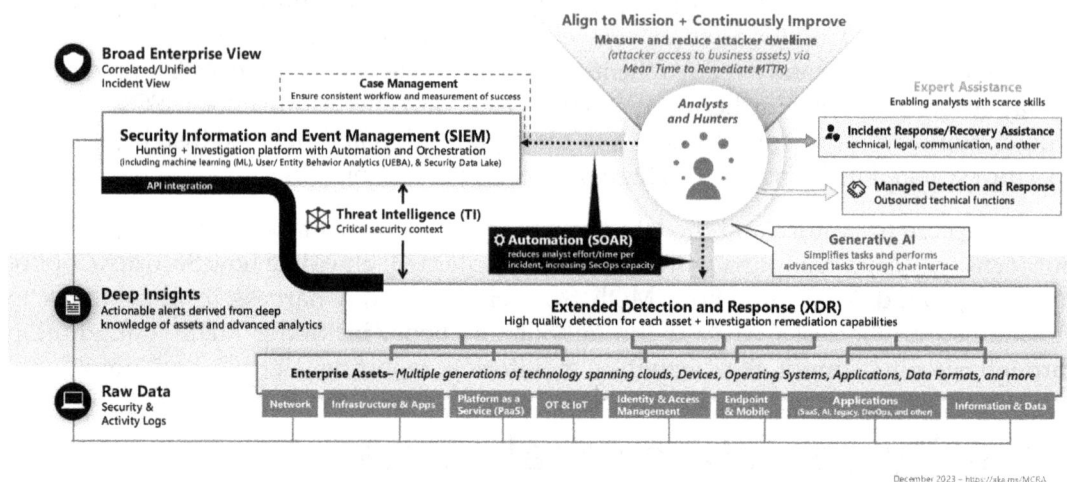

Figure 13.2: Microsoft Security SOC Capabilities

Venture capitalist and involvement of business mindset

There is huge money involved in security business. Security is no more seen just a technology thing and there are businessmen, and venture capitalists who are very actively involved in this market. They are buying and selling companies involved in this segment and it has turned into a big industry in the current situation that stands in the front row with cloud and other major businesses in the world.

The revenue of Microsoft Defender grew from $7 billion in 2020 to around speculative $25 billion in 2023. These numbers highlight the rapid growth and potential of this market. In 2019, Broadcom acquired Symantec, a significant move driven by industry visionaries. Discussions around security industry consolidation are among the major aspirations of key venture capitalists aiming to disrupt this market. Expect more big news in this area in the future.

According to Cybersecurity Ventures, the estimated annual cost of cyber-crime is roughly around these figures, though there might be some variance:

- $6Trillion in 2022
- $8 Trillion in 2023
- $10 Trillion in 2025

The following figure shows the estimated cost of cybercrime in 2025 by Cybersecurity Ventures:

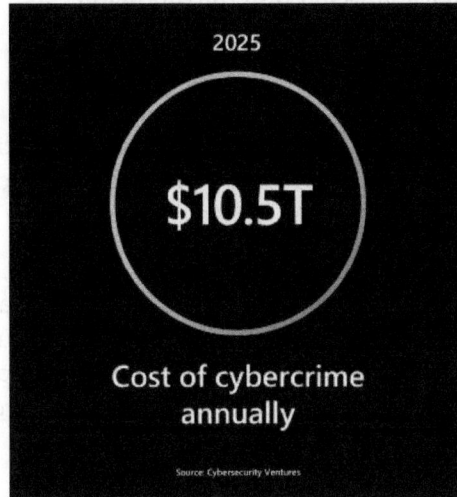

Figure 13.3: *Estimated financial impact of Cybercrime in 2025*[1]

Understanding artificial intelligence and machine language

Artificial intelligence (**AI**) is a broad field of computer science that focuses on creating intelligent machines that can perform tasks that typically require human intelligence, such as visual perception, speech recognition, decision-making, and language translation. AI involves developing algorithms and models that can process and analyze large amounts of data, learn from that data, and make predictions or decisions based on that learning.

Machine learning (**ML**) is a subset of AI that focuses on developing algorithms and models that can learn from data and make predictions or decisions without being explicitly programmed to do so. ML algorithms use statistical techniques to identify patterns and relationships in data and use those patterns to make predictions or decisions about new data.

In other words, AI is a broader field that encompasses many different areas, while ML is a specific subset of AI that focuses on using data to build intelligent systems. AI includes other areas such as robotics, natural language processing, and computer vision, while ML is specifically focused on developing algorithms that can learn from data.

Overall, AI and ML are rapidly growing fields that are transforming many industries and have the potential to solve some of the world's most challenging problems.

---

1   **Sources**: Cybersecurity Ventures

Understanding AI and ML

Learning AI/ML is broadly categorized into the following:

- Supervised
- Unsupervised

Unsupervised learning is progressively moving from **Artificial Narrow Intelligence (ANI)** to **Artificial Superintelligence (ASI)** where currently industry is in between ANI and **Artificial General Intelligence (AGI)** that might require a few or more years to achieve the AGI.

The following figure shows the stages of AI that leaders are categorizing as the release of LLM model by OpenAI in 2022 started the debate in community that we are close in achieving the AGI and throughout all the major innovation happened throughout in 2024 is giving the sign of it and *OpenAI O1 model* released in end of year 2024 or upcoming *O3 model* started giving sign of good reasoning power.

Note: O2 model name is skipped as there is telecom company named O2 in US that might have conflicted with the name so that is the reason they moved from O1 to O3.

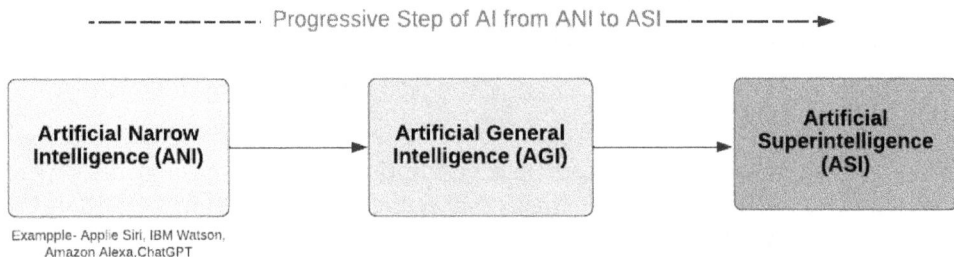

Figure 13.4: AI Stages and North Star of AI field in form of ASI

Introduction of AI/ML in Defender

Microsoft Defender team has been using AI/ML to strengthen its product from long time. The team has been leveraging AI/ML to improve real-time protection against malware and heavily used in EDR backend workflows. Microsoft Defender ATP uses multiple internally built and trained in endpoint grading team at least for SmartScreen service and other different teams might be using more different models and there are automated pipelines that gets auto trigger on schedule or on specific data input event.

Note: Microsoft also do have ML.NET called Threat Learning Component (TLC), which has been the internal machine learning framework used at Microsoft for over ten years, but it is not clear whether it is also used in Defender or not as Defender team mostly using C# code base for most of the development work.

To fortify the existing cloud-delivered automated protection against complex attacks like **Human-operated Ransomware** (**Humor**), Microsoft Defender team developed a cloud-based machine learning system. When queried by a device, it intelligently predicts if it is at risk and typically involving statistical prediction models and risk assessments as part of this intelligence, then leveraging those ML workflows it issues a more aggressive blocking verdict to protect the device, Thwarting an attacker's next steps.

Microsoft Defender for Endpoint customers are already benefitting from ML-driven adaptive protection against human-operated ransomware. The adaptive protection feature works on top of the existing robust cloud protection, which defends against threats through different next-generation technologies. Compared to the existing cloud protection level feature, which relies on admins to manually adjust the cloud protection settings, the adaptive protection is smarter and faster. It can, when queried by a device, automatically ramp the aggressiveness of cloud-delivered blocking verdicts up or down based on real-time machine learning predictions, thus proactively protecting the device. Since the adaptive protection is AI-driven, the risk score given to a device is not only dependent on individual indicators but on a broad swath of patterns and features that the system uses to determine whether an attack is imminent or underway. This leads to protection that is contextual and personalized.

In support of above reference: **https://techcommunity.microsoft.com/blog/microsoftdefenderatpblog/ai-driven-adaptive-protection-in-microsoft-defender-for-endpoint/2966491**

> **Note: Currently servers are excluded from AI-drive adaptive protection features against Humor.**

Understanding large language model

Large Language Model (**LLM**) refers to a type of AI model that is capable of processing and generating natural language at a large scale. LLMs use machine learning algorithms to learn the patterns and structure of human language by processing and analyzing vast amounts of text data.

They can perform a variety of language-related tasks, such as language translation, text summarization, question answering, and chatbot conversations. They are trained on massive datasets of text data, such as books, articles, and websites, to learn the structure and patterns of human language.

Examples of large language models include OpenAI's GPT series, Google's BERT, and Facebook's RoBERTa. These models have been shown to achieve state-of-the-art performance on a variety of language-related tasks and have significantly advanced the field of NLP.

Security Copilot models for LLM

Security Copilot leverages multi model and leverage OpenAI's LLMs models for some GPT areas, alongside internally developed security models trained specifically for security domain, all integrated with Microsoft's global security threat intelligence network. As end users, this information is for your reference only, and you are not required to interact with these areas directly. These managed services are provided by Microsoft, and they are included in the service you pay for. The insight in the following figure will help you understand how Microsoft operates these security models to provide answers through the Security Copilot portal:

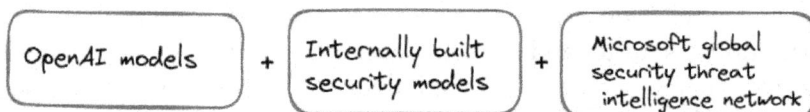

Figure 13.5: LLM Models used by Microsoft security

Building a large language model like Security Copilot involves several steps, which are as follows:

1. **Data collection**: The first step in building a language model is to collect a large corpus of security text data. This data is used to train the model to understand and generate human-like language. In the case of Security Copilot, the data was sourced from various publicly available datasets, internal trillions of security signals flowing from MDE registered devices and from Microsoft global security threat intelligence network through which it participates globally.

2. **Preprocessing**: Once the data is collected, it needs to be preprocessed to remove any irrelevant or redundant information. This involves tasks such as tokenization (splitting the text into individual words), cleaning (removing any unnecessary characters or symbols), and normalization (standardizing the text to a common format).

3. **Model architecture**: The next step is to choose an appropriate model architecture. In the case of Security Copilot, the above-mentioned Model architecture was used, which is combined version of the OpenAI and Microsoft security model architecture. This architecture consists of multiple layers of transformer blocks that can process and generate human-like language.

4. **Training**: Once the model architecture is chosen, the model is trained on the preprocessed security data using a process called **unsupervised learning**. This involves optimizing the model to predict the next word in a sentence given the previous words. The training process typically takes several weeks or months and requires a large amount of computing resources.

5. **Fine-tuning**: After the model is trained, it can be fine-tuned on a specific task, such as Security Copilot chatbot conversations to get a summary of incidents or other contextual security information. This involves further training the model on a smaller dataset that is specific to the task at hand.

6. **Deployment**: Once the model is trained and fine-tuned, it is deployed into the production and there are multiple areas where each independent team works and deploys their own data for an example grading team helps researchers to deploy the graded models for Smart Screen workflows. Overall, building a large language model like Copilot requires a combination of data collection, preprocessing, model architecture selection, training, fine-tuning, and deployment. The process can be complex and time-consuming, but the result is a powerful tool that can understand and generate human-like language.

IT infrastructure related models

Models used in IT infrastructure management can be categorized into various types based on the specific task they are designed to perform. Here are some common categories of models used in IT infrastructure management:

- **Predictive models**: These models use historical data to predict future events or trends in IT infrastructure, such as server downtime or network traffic spikes.

- **Anomaly detection models**: These models use statistical methods to identify abnormal behavior in IT infrastructure, such as unusual traffic patterns or unexpected changes in system performance.

- **Classification models**: These models are used to classify IT infrastructure elements, such as devices, servers, or applications, into different categories based on their characteristics and usage.

- **Clustering models**: These models group IT infrastructure elements together based on their similarities, such as server clusters or network zones.

- **Optimization models**: These models are used to optimize IT infrastructure resources, such as server allocation or network bandwidth, to achieve maximum efficiency and performance.

- **Simulation models**: These models simulate IT infrastructure performance under different conditions, such as peak loads or system failures, to predict how the infrastructure will behave in real-world scenarios.

Cybersecurity related models

In the cybersecurity domain, various AI and machine learning models are employed to detect threats, anomalies, and patterns in data. Here are a few commonly used AI/ML models:

- **Anomaly detection models**:
  - o **Isolation forests**: Identifies anomalies by isolating them in random partitions.
  - o **Autoencoders**: Neural network models that learn to reconstruct input data and detect anomalies in deviations from normal patterns.
  - o **One-class support vector machines (SVM)**: Trains on normal data and identifies deviations as anomalies.
- **Deep learning models**:
  - o **Convolutional neural networks (CNNs)**: Used in image-based threat detection and analysis.
  - o **Recurrent neural networks (RNNs) and long short-term memory (LSTM)**: Useful for sequential data analysis, such as network traffic or logs.
- **NLP models**:
  - o **Bidirectional Encoder Representations from Transformers (BERT)**: Used for text analysis, including analyzing security-related documents, emails, or logs.
  - o **Word embeddings (e.g., Word2Vec, GloVe)**: Represent words in vectors to understand contextual meaning and detect anomalies in text data.
- **Decision trees and random forests**:
  - o **Used for classification and feature importance**: Can be employed to classify threats or determine critical features indicative of cyber-attacks.
- **Generative adversarial networks (GANs)**:
  - o **Used for creating synthetic data**: Helpful in creating diverse datasets for training, which can improve model robustness against attacks.

These models and techniques are applied across various cybersecurity tasks, including intrusion detection, malware analysis, phishing detection, log analysis, and vulnerability assessment, among others. Each model has its strengths and is utilized based on the specific requirements and nature of the cybersecurity problem being addressed.

Building an MDE like supervised ML model

In general, any ML model follows the given release cycle:

1. Prepare your data set
2. Build and train the model on dataset
3. Release the production model

The following figure showcases the AI/ML usual general stages inform of preparing the data for training and then training the security model:

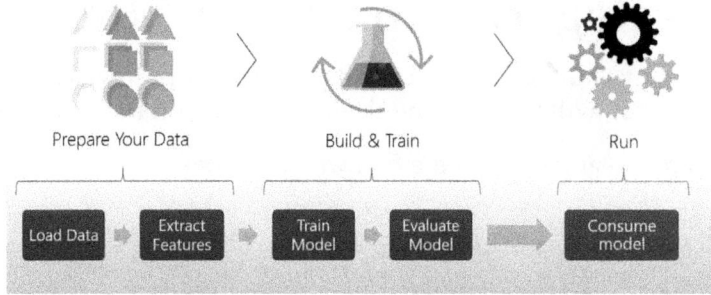

Figure 13.6: AI/ML training model stages

Similarly, the following are the four high level stages that MDE team choose to test and release the security ML models:

- Sample selection
- Feature selection
- Experimentation
- Release to production

The following figure shows implementation of above-mentioned general AI/ML training workflow in Defender for different experimentation.

- **Sample** term is referred to a file that can be clean (without malware) or malware file.
- **Feature selection** – This term is used in AI/ML for factor or dimension selection on the data input to analyze it from different perspective to return diverse result.

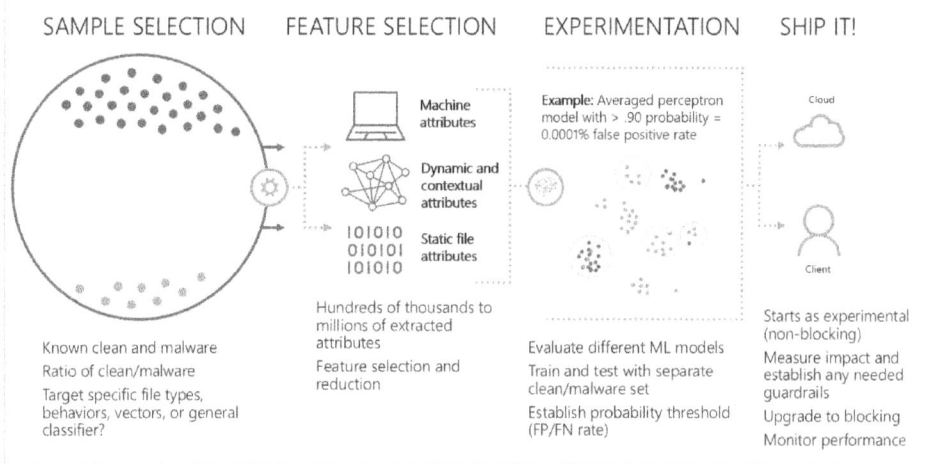

Figure 13.7: Example of running Defender Supervised ML model

Malware categorization as per Microsoft

During analysis of any sample (file), MDE internal ML workflows categorizes files into area and same thing you will see it during security alerting on the MDE portal.

Broadly, the files are categorized into the following:

- Clean
- Unclean

The following figure reflects the graphical representation of sample file categories:

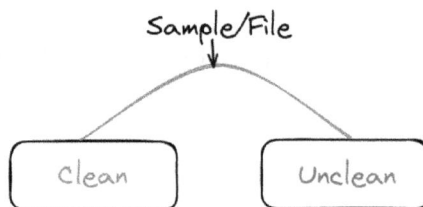

Figure 13.8: Categories of Samples

Unclean files are further categorized into the following:

- Spreading
- Exploit
- Evader
- Banker
- Phishing
- Spyware
- Adware
- Ransomware
- Trojan/Bot

Future trends and innovations

The landscape of threat investigation is in constant evolution as attackers become more sophisticated and technology advances. In this section, we will explore the emerging trends and innovations that are shaping the future of threat investigation. We will also explore how tools like **Microsoft Defender for Endpoint** (**MDE**) are adapting to these trends to stay at the forefront of cybersecurity.

Trends and innovations in threat investigation

The following are the key highlights of the innovation and integration happening to provide better security solution:

- **AI and ML**: AI and machine learning are revolutionizing threat investigation. These technologies enable predictive analytics, anomaly detection, and the automation of routine tasks. By learning from vast datasets, AI can identify and respond to threats more efficiently. *Microsoft Copilot* Product range and the *Microsoft Security Copilot* are going to play the big and major role in threat investigation and day to day work of SOC analysts. Security Copilot is continuously adding new features and brining all the AI and LLM innovation into the security web portal that is making best in breed product that is moving it far away from its competitor and move up in the ladder in Visionary category and due the fact that trillions of signals are flowing into the Microsoft ecosystem so MDE has competitive advantage in comparison to its competitor.

- **Extended detection and response (XDR)**: XDR solutions provide holistic security coverage by integrating various security tools and data sources. This approach enhances the visibility and correlation of security events across an organization, simplifying threat detection and response.

- **Zero trust security**: Zero Trust is a security model where trust is never assumed, and strict identity verification is required from anyone trying to access resources. It minimizes the potential attack surface and emphasizes continuous verification of user and device trustworthiness.

- **Cloud-native security**: As organizations increasingly move their workloads to the cloud, cloud-native security becomes vital. It involves security measures that are specifically designed for cloud environments, including serverless computing and containerization.

- **Threat intelligence sharing**: Collaboration among organizations and threat intelligence sharing is becoming more common. It enables collective defence by allowing organizations to benefit from each other's threat insights, resulting in faster and more accurate threat detection.

- **Quantum-safe cryptography**: With quantum computing on the horizon, quantum-safe cryptography is gaining importance. It ensures that current encryption methods remain secure even in the face of quantum attacks.

MDE and adaptation to future trends

Microsoft Defender for Endpoint is well-positioned to adapt to and leverage these future trends and innovations and the following items highlights such adoption in different feature of MDE:

- **AI and ML**: MDE already utilizes machine learning for threat detection and response. As AI and ML continue to advance, MDE will incorporate more sophisticated algorithms to stay ahead of evolving threats.

- **XDR integration**: MDE is part of Microsoft's XDR strategy, integrating seamlessly with other Microsoft security products. This interconnected approach allows for comprehensive security coverage and improved threat visibility.

Previously, or even till late Q1 of 2022, Microsoft security team did not brand their product as Defender XDR product. However, now, they have independent Microsoft Defender XDR product category, and it signifies how fast this domain is evolving and how quickly Microsoft security team reshuffling things to put them together under right product portfolio.

- **Zero Trust**: Microsoft emphasizes the Zero Trust model through its security solutions, including MDE. By applying strict access controls and continuous verification, MDE supports organizations in implementing Zero Trust security measures.

- **Cloud-native capabilities**: MDE extends its protection to cloud workloads and provides security for cloud-native resources. This adaptability ensures that organizations can confidently embrace cloud technologies without compromising security.

- **Threat intelligence**: MDE leverages Microsoft's extensive threat intelligence network. As threat intelligence sharing becomes more critical, MDE will continue to benefit from Microsoft's insights and collaborative partnerships.

- **Quantum-safe cryptography**: Microsoft invests in research and development of quantum-safe cryptography. As quantum computing advances, MDE will incorporate quantum-resistant encryption methods to maintain the security of endpoint communications.

Future of SOC

Microsoft security team continuously releasing a lot of new products and services, and Microsoft Threat Expert is one of such service that will disrupt the SOC business and will reduce down the SOC headcount in each team and there is possibility to less jobs in outsourcing companies due to this fact. However, as of now this industry is growing by billion-dollar numbers and hopefully it will leave positive signs in the job market instead of any negative outcome, but it is pretty sure you will see lot of improvement through Copilot introduction.

The following *Figure 13.9* depicts how MTE team built whole set of managed security services of existing product category as Microsoft team do have great insight across different customer and they can easily get clues of any major security incident with few click of seconds and can provide support you better to reduce down the **Mean Time to**

Detect (MTTD) and **Mean Time to Resolve (MTTR)**. Reducing MTTR and MTTD helps you by leaps and bound and this is core factor that indirectly decides how many SOC engineers you need to support an outsourced project.

Companies like HCL, TCS and Wipro in India has major chunk of security outsources business where Microsoft Defender is the prevalent and major security product used and there are chances of impact on this business, and you might see reduce down headcount in the SOC analyst staff due to the fact and services provided by MTE and new LLM advancement in upcoming days.

The following figure gives you insight about how MTE Professional services is offered over above existing product and experience of the internal research and engineering teams to solve the customer problem and already integrated with the existing MDE ad SOC solutions:

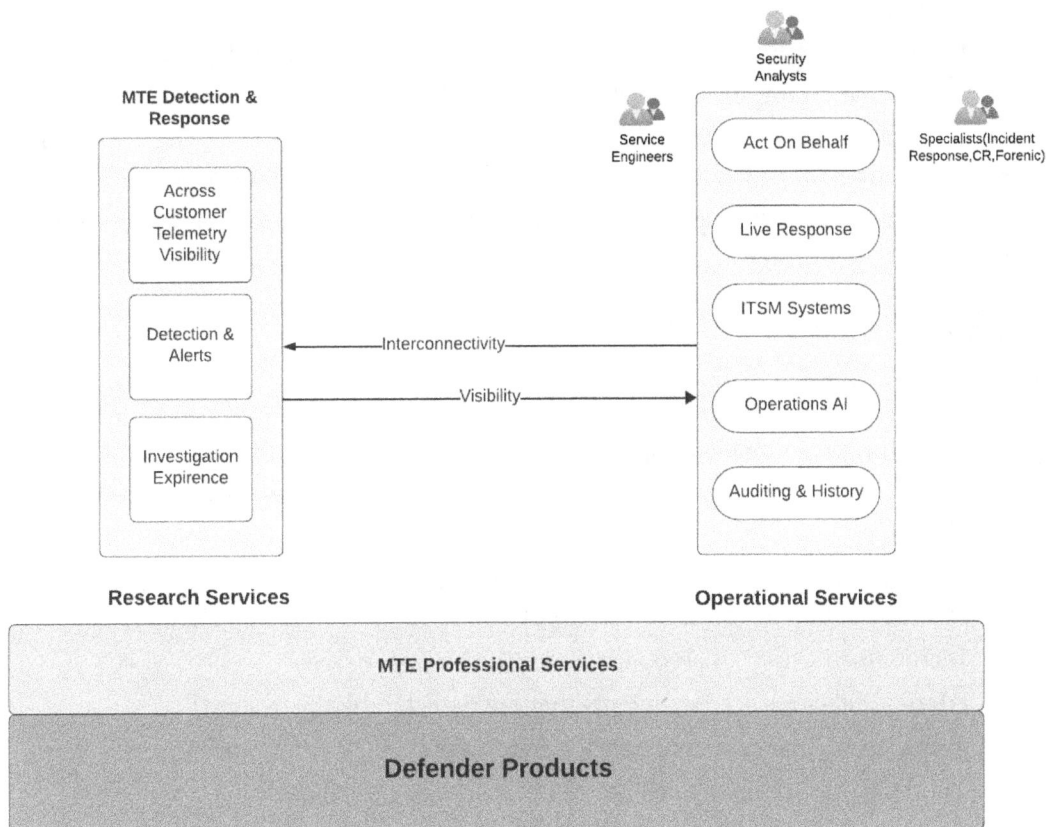

Figure 13.9: Microsoft MTE Professional Service on top of Defender Product

The following are the three categories of MTE offerings that any Defender customer can opt and all are made available through preceding internal integration:

- MTE classic
- MTE starter
- MTE premium

MTE starter

The following are the features supported by MTE Starter:

- **Extend MTE concept**: Extend MTE concept from endpoint to all of Defender.
- **Discover emerging threats**: Leverage unique cloud visibility in Defender to discover emerging / advanced threats.
- **Identity compromise**: Respond to successful phishing or brute force attacks.
- **Device to cloud pivoting**: Connect cloud activity originating from on-premise compromise.
- **Cloud application abuse**: Secure and respond to cloud app attack surface.
- **0365 tenant tampering**: Protect your 0365 tenant from unwanted changes or modifications.
- **Cloud data theft**: Understand scope and scale of potential data breaches.
- **Endpoint compromise**: Expert-enriched Incidents indicating hands-on-keyboard device compromise.

MTE premium

Microsoft Threat Experts (MTE) Premium is a comprehensive security solution that provides 24x7 SOC support and advanced threat protection. It is designed to help organizations build a SOC for the world, providing a unified view of security across all endpoints, email, identities, and cloud services. MTE Premium is a prerequisite for Microsoft Defender for Endpoint.

MTE Premium offers a ticketing system for analysts to work on security-related issues. The system is based on the following concepts:

- **Incidents**: A group of alerts that form the basis of a case.
- **Alerts**: Malicious activity events that are detected by the system.
- **Traps**: Logic that catches activities and raises hits.
- **TrapHits**: Malicious activity events that are detected internally.

MTE Premium also provides raw alerts called **detections**. In addition, it offers **Targeted Alert Notifications (TAN)** to send notifications to customers for events that were missed by automation.

Research enablement

Broadly, the MDE team manages the EPP and EDR product categories, as shown in the following figure, and majority of future feature development happens here. All the new goodies that you are going to get in the upcoming days will come from this sub organization of Microsoft Security Division.

Research enablement: It is internally referenced for the Defender Security research team that enables Defender through various security research performed by humans and through ML workflows trained by Defender ML engineers to learn new insight over data and inputs received from various sources.

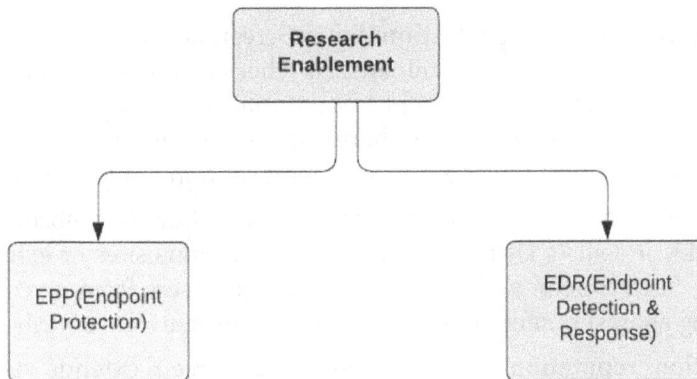

Figure 13.10: Microsoft Security Research Enablement teams

Grading and SmartScreen are both related as grading is a platform that executes multiple ML workflows to train various models to feed input to the Microsoft SmartScreen solution and below we talk in more detail for both services.

Microsoft grading and SmartScreen platform

Microsoft is committed to delivering the best-in-breed security solutions. To achieve this, they continuously improve critical areas that provide the most value to the product, such as URL grading, which attaches security risk metadata. This process plays a crucial role in the broader internet security landscape, delivering value to the entire security ecosystem.

Microsoft SmartScreen is one such internal product. However, with the introduction of more AI and ML tools and techniques, the internal security research and development team has rearchitected and rebuilt a completely new solution from scratch. This new solution is named the Microsoft grading platform for security researchers and currently supports URL grading.

Previously, URL grading was a tedious task involving many manual steps, but the new approach has eradicated these manual processes. The long-term vision is to replace the SmartScreen solution with this newer, more efficient approach.

Grading system automatically ranks the Security ML models that performs better to mark clean or malicious URL in its database and gives flexibility to security researchers or to research enablement team to rank the ML model to get applied as per learnt behavior as per their choice.

Microsoft SmartScreen is a security feature integrated into various Microsoft products, primarily focusing on web browsers like Microsoft Edge and Internet Explorer, as well as in some email clients and the Windows operating system.

Key functions of Microsoft SmartScreen

The following are the four key features of Smart screen service:

- **Phishing and malware protection**: SmartScreen acts as a filter against phishing websites and malicious downloads. It checks websites and files against a continuously updated database of known malicious sites and files. When users attempt to access a potentially harmful site or download a suspicious file, SmartScreen will alert them and recommend caution or block access entirely.

- **URL reputation checks**: It evaluates the reputation of websites by analyzing their URLs. If a site's URL matches known malicious sites or exhibits suspicious behavior, SmartScreen will intervene to prevent users from accessing it, thereby protecting against potential phishing attempts or malware distribution.

- **Application reputation**: In Windows, SmartScreen extends its protection to applications. It checks downloaded executable files against a reputation database to prevent the installation of potentially harmful or unrecognized applications, adding an extra layer of security against malicious software installation.

- **Email protection**: SmartScreen is also integrated into Microsoft's email services, such as Outlook.com and the Outlook desktop application, to help filter out suspicious or malicious email attachments and links, protecting users from phishing attempts and malware spread via email.

Overall, Microsoft SmartScreen acts as a proactive defense mechanism, leveraging a combination of URL and file reputation checks to shield users from potentially harmful content across various Microsoft platforms and applications. Its continuous updates and real-time protection contribute significantly to enhancing cybersecurity for users within the Microsoft ecosystem.

Grading platform functional requirements

The internal grading platform is similar to the workflow management performed by every security company. However, its efficiency largely depends on the internal maturity and how effectively the tools are provided to security researchers and the security engineering team.

The development of the internal grading platform focuses on features that facilitate the grading team, helping researchers efficiently perform their day-to-day tasks. The following are some of the primary functional requirements of the solution:

- ML playgrounds
- Self-service for researchers
- Plug and play auto grading

Features

The features of the product that helps researchers in increasing their productivity by many folds and help them focus on their core research activities in security domain are as follows:

- Unified platform for all grading activity.
- Provides metadata/insights from different sources required by graders for grading.
- Same look and feel across workflows.
- Users can search for data and entities in the platform and view their past grades.

Data on grading platform

Every ML platform need data but to provide a solution to internal researcher's companies need to remain aligned toward the internal data and project context so that they can provide different dimension of same data to different teams to meet their machine learning enabled platform needs and below are the some of the entities that Defender team leveraged to train their machine learning models to help researchers to choose the right model.

The following are the four important items leveraged by the team to build grading like machine learning platform:

- **Entity**: Smallest unit of data, which is individually graded by graders
- **Workset**: Collection of similar entities. Entities can be group based on various attributes
- **Workflow**: Contains worksets of a single business flow
- **Area**: Collection of related workflows

Requirement of grading platform

It is not suddenly built but a lot of frustration experienced by security researchers and development team that lead to the development of this solution. The following are some of the highlights of the requirements:

- Scalable platform to support heavy load customers.
- Role based access (*Support, BO, Grader lead, Grader, Analyst*).

- Self-serve platform which provides Plug and Play capability.
- Search across workflows to provide more data insights.
- Capability to check grading quality and performance.
- Many in-built features (describe in later slides) and still adding.

Microsoft Security Copilot

Microsoft Security Copilot acts as glue between M365Defender and Azure Defender and other threat services (XDR, MTE etc.) by Microsoft and solves a lot of hassle that a SOC analyst spend their time in making a relation in between all the threads or threats around the incident. Please find the following brief overview of the services around Copilot. Microsoft Security Copilot is a generative AI security product that helps defend organizations at machine speed and scale.

Microsoft Security is composed of the following:

- M365 Defender
- Microsoft Security Copilot (Newly launched and in Private Preview)
- Azure Security

The following figure showcases all the Microsoft security products for better understanding:

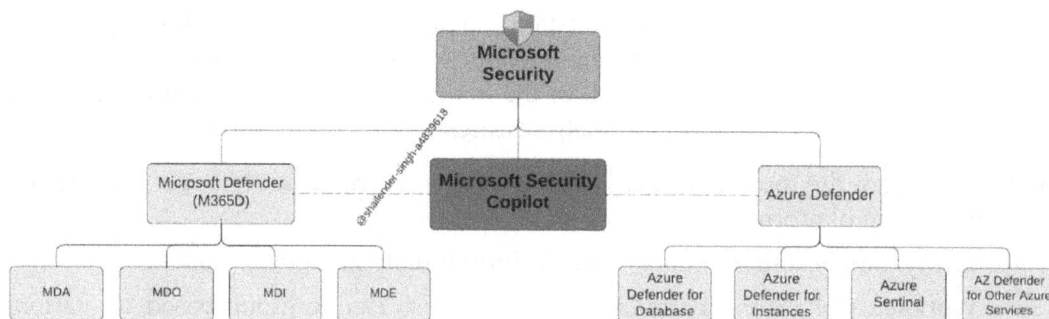

Figure 13.11: Microsoft security product and services portfolio

Microsoft Security Copilot HLD in security ecosystem

It is very important to understand how Microsoft Security Copilot fits into the ecosystem of Microsoft security. The following figure helps you to build the understanding. Microsoft has integrated prompts into its all the major solutions, such as:

- MDE web portal
- Sentinel portal

- Intune portal
- Security Copilot web portal

The following figure showcases the **high level diagram (HLD)** of Microsoft security Copilot workflow:

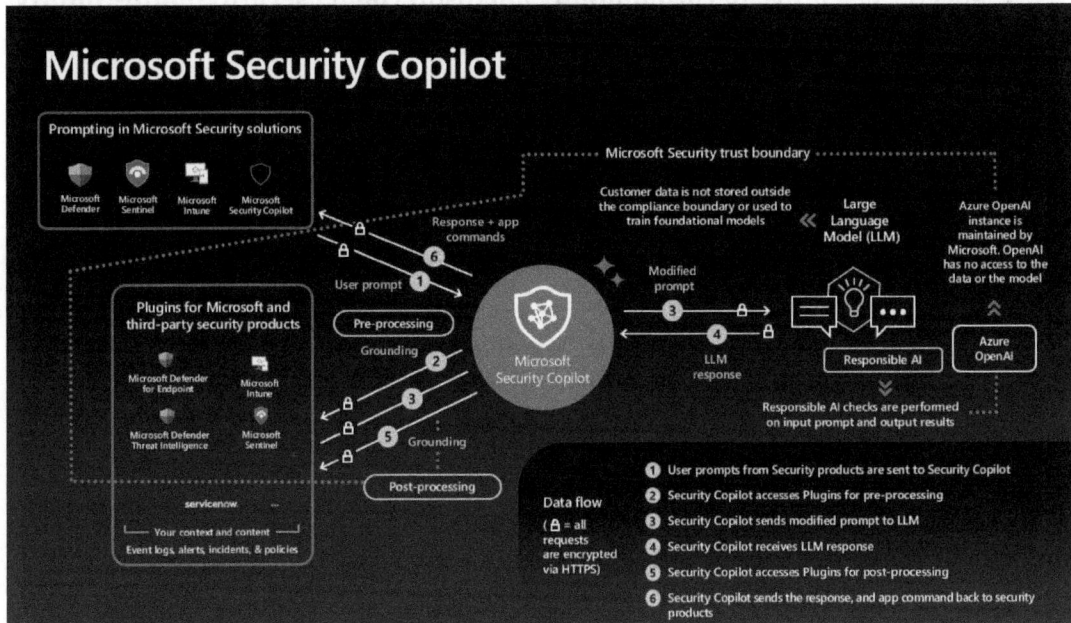

Figure 13.12: Microsoft Security Copilot HLD

OpenAI GPT algorithm and Microsoft CoPilot

Microsoft Security Copilot is an AI-powered security product that enables defenders to move at the speed and scale of AI. It combines the most advanced LLMs from OpenAI with a Microsoft-developed, security-specific model This security-specific model incorporates a growing set of security-specific skills and is informed by Microsoft's unique global threat intelligence and more than 65 trillion daily signals. Security Copilot uses signals and data from other tools to generate guidance that's specific to your organization.

It can help security teams to manage vulnerabilities and emerging cyberthreats, start a guided investigation, and speed up their work with script analysis and query assistance.

Security Copilot is the only security AI product that combines a specialized language model with security-specific capabilities from Microsoft.

It is known that Security Copilot uses a specialized language model and a security-specific model from Microsoft. The security-specific model incorporates a growing set of security-specific skills and is informed by Microsoft's unique global threat intelligence and more than 65 trillion daily signals.

Important Copilot references that you should go through:

- **Microsoft Security Copilot: https://www.microsoft.com/en-us/security/business/ai-machine-learning/microsoft-security-copilot**
- **Introducing Microsoft Security Copilot: end-to-end defense at the speed ... https://techcommunity.microsoft.com/t5/security-multi-country/introducing-microsoft-security-copilot-end-to-end-defense-at-the/td-p/3808220**
- **What is Security Copilot: https://microsoft.github.io/PartnerResources/skilling/microsoft-security-academy/microsoft-security-copilot**
- **Introducing Microsoft Security Copilot: Empowering defenders at the ...https://blogs.microsoft.com/blog/2023/03/28/introducing-microsoft-security-copilot-empowering-defenders-at-the-speed-of-ai/**

  https://youtu.be/g1HoXNoP3V0
- **Titanium integration example: Microsoft Copilot & Tanium | ODFP306 – YouTube - https://www.youtube.com/watch?v=2mL9iDr_lUY**

License and costing

Microsoft Security Copilot delivers natural language insights and guidance to increase the efficiency and capabilities of security operations teams.

Few notes for Security Copilot are as follows:

- The service is available to enterprise and education customers.
- The current price is *$30 per user per month*. It is available as an add-on or part of higher-tier plans like Microsoft 365 E5 or Defender for Endpoint Plan 2. It is typically sold as an additional service with a separate cost structure.

Note: Please cross-verify the latest costing or licensing information as it might change over time.

Benefits of Security Copilot

The following are the benefits of Microsoft Security Copilot:

- Reduced response time
- Comprehensive threat coverage
- Cost savings
- Advanced analytics and reporting

Security Copilot features on MDE web portal

The new features introduced in the Microsoft Security Copilot on the Microsoft Defender portal are as follows:

- **Summarize incidents quickly**: Security Copilot can summarize an incident for you, providing an overview of the attack, the assets involved, and the timeline of the attack.
- **Guided responses**: Security Copilot provides guided responses to help security teams approach solutions and mitigation for any incident
- **Analyze scripts and codes**: Security Copilot can analyze scripts and codes, helping security teams understand attacks immediately.
- **Generate KQL queries**: Security Copilot can generate KQL queries to help security teams hunt for threats with ease.
- **Create incident reports**: Security Copilot can create incident reports within the portal.
- **Integration with Microsoft 365 Defender**: Security Copilot is embedded in Microsoft 365 Defender, enabling security teams to tackle attack investigations in a timely manner with ease and precision.

Security Copilot feature and interface examples

As of today, Security Copilot is not publicly available and is in Private Preview for selected customers. However, to help reader of this book we have captured the screenshots from the recordings to get early expertise into the product but there are possibility of some minor changes due to customer feedback loop.

Manage security plugin

Security Copilot gives you the option to integrate only selected products as per your requirement or security policy and any time you can enable and disable such plugins through Manage Plugins page, as shown in the following figure:

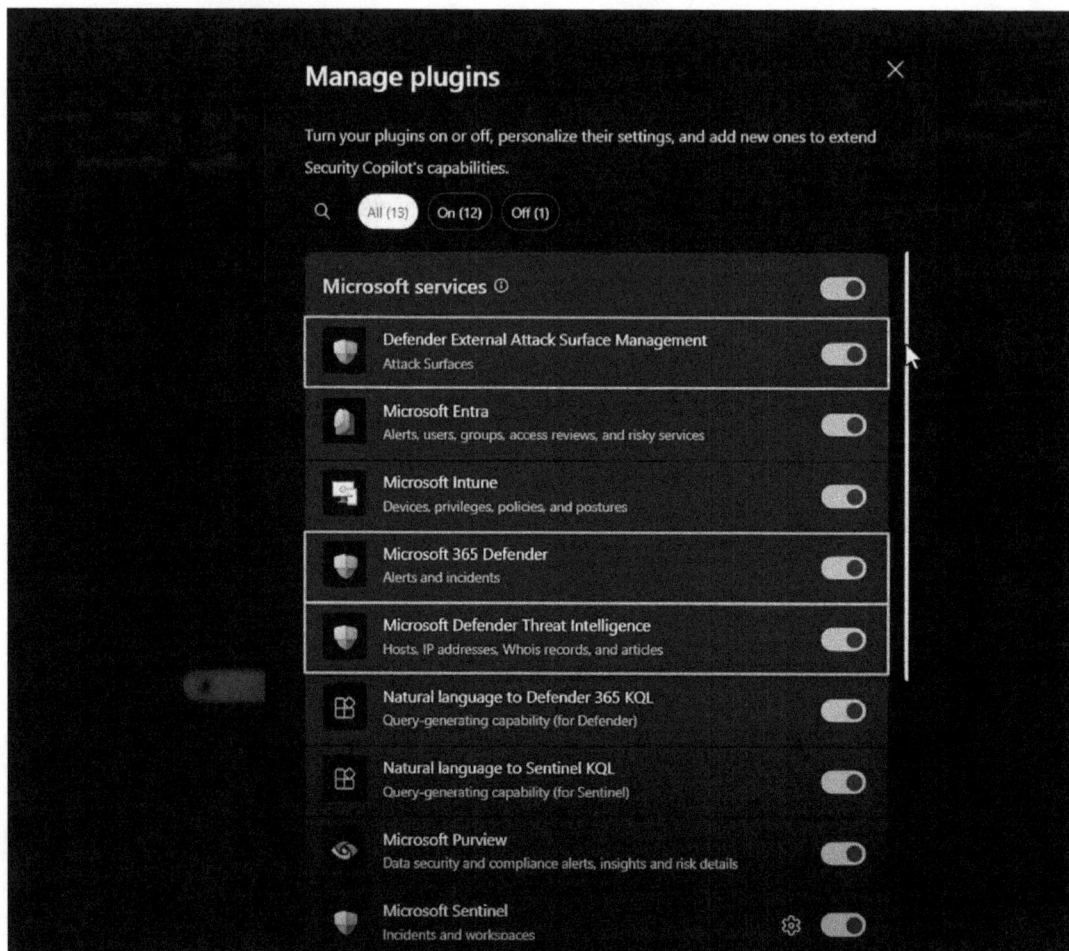

Figure 13.13: Security Copilot to enable only specific services to integrate with it

Reference of the recording: **https://youtu.be/0lg_derTkaM**

Script reverse engineering by Security Copilot

It has capability to summarize the script to give insight without reading and understanding the script logic to help you quickly by giving logic insight in case some hidden malicious code is embedded inside the program logic.

The following figure shows the explanation of script through LLM on the Copilot portal:

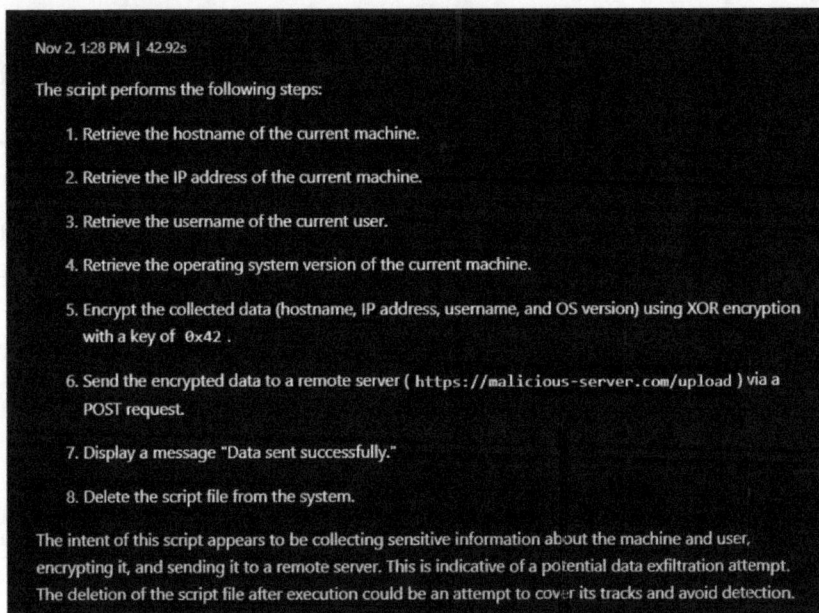

Nov 2, 1:28 PM | 42.92s

The script performs the following steps:

1. Retrieve the hostname of the current machine.

2. Retrieve the IP address of the current machine.

3. Retrieve the username of the current user.

4. Retrieve the operating system version of the current machine.

5. Encrypt the collected data (hostname, IP address, username, and OS version) using XOR encryption with a key of `0x42`.

6. Send the encrypted data to a remote server (`https://malicious-server.com/upload`) via a POST request.

7. Display a message "Data sent successfully."

8. Delete the script file from the system.

The intent of this script appears to be collecting sensitive information about the machine and user, encrypting it, and sending it to a remote server. This is indicative of a potential data exfiltration attempt. The deletion of the script file after execution could be an attempt to cover its tracks and avoid detection.

Figure 13.14: Explanation of script through LLM on the copilot portal

Featured prompts

Web portal gives you the features prompts through which you can ask area specific questions.

The following is the example of automatic highlight of the required prompt for a given context on which you are working:

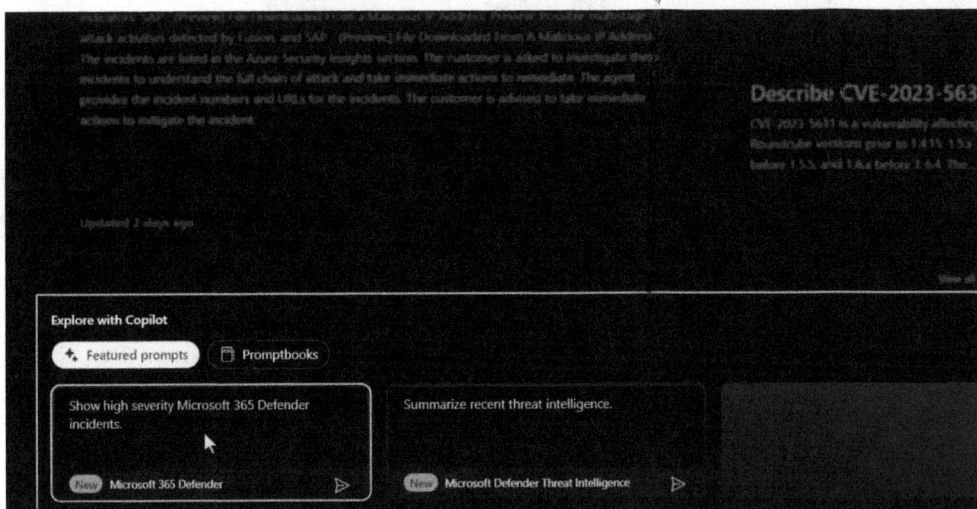

Figure 13.15: Featured prompt example

Security Copilot vs LLM models based comparison

Before Microsoft Security Copilot launch, there were customers who were trying to build similar functionality with their own custom solutions or solutions like Azure Copilot Models and Azure services. However, that lacked the domain specific capability that Copilot brings like strong accuracy using multiple models available internally and externally to provide better results.

The following figure showcases the well integration of LLM model on Security Copilot itself that also showcase that Security copilot uses more fine-tuned model instead of just merely relying on OpenAI GPT 4 model.

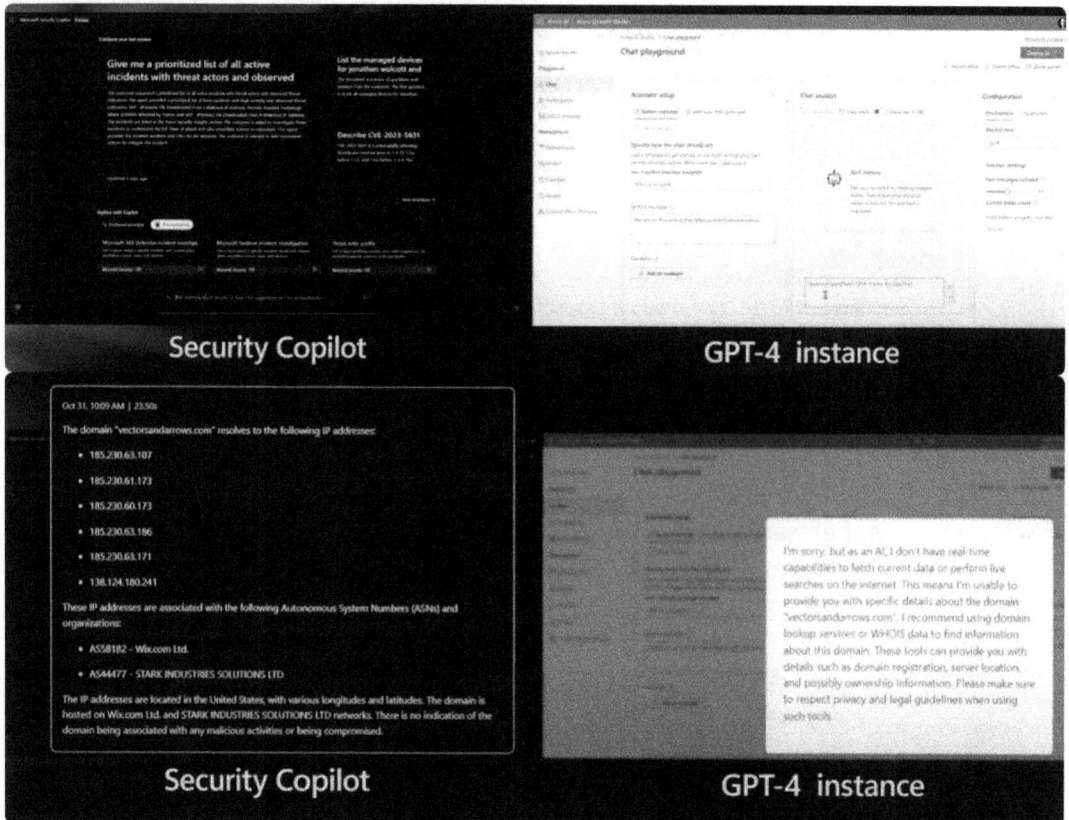

Figure 13.16: Example of LLM usage in Security Copilot vs. Azure GPT-4 based LLM usage

Promptbooks

It is a collection of prompts that can be executed from within Security Copilot. Promptbooks are designed to accomplish specific security-related tasks such as incident investigation, threat actor profile, suspicious script analysis, and vulnerability impact assessment. Each promptbook requires a specific input (for example, a code snippet or a threat actor name), such as:

- For instance, the *incident investigation promptbook* generates an executive report for a nontechnical audience that summarizes the investigation.
- *The threat actor profile promptbook* is a quick way to get an executive summary about a specific threat actor.
- The *vulnerability impact assessment promptbook* provides information about the impact of a specific vulnerability.

To use promptbook, type an asterisk (the "*" symbol) at the prompt bar to find the different promptbooks. Select a promptbook to open it and supply the required input. Security Copilot generates responses for each of the prompts, building on each response until it gets to the last prompt. The last prompt generates an executive report summarizing the investigation based on the responses.

The following figure showcases the promptbook screenshots from Security Copilot web portal:

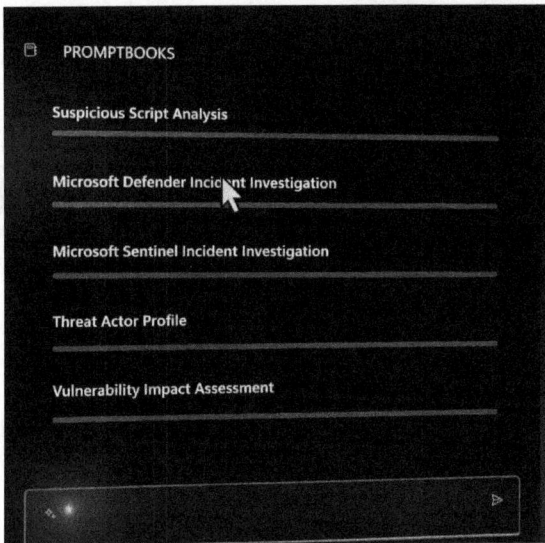

Figure 13.17: Prompt books

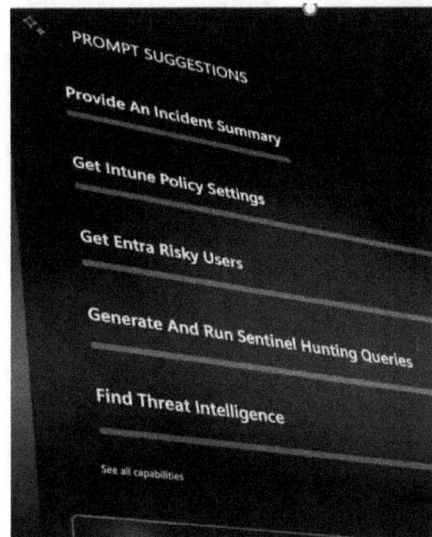

Figure 13.18: Prompt suggestions

Script analysis

It can perform suspicious script automatic analysis and can tell you if there is any malicious hidden intent coded in the script.

The following figure is a screenshot that gives reference of explanation of the suspicious script on the security copilot web portal itself:

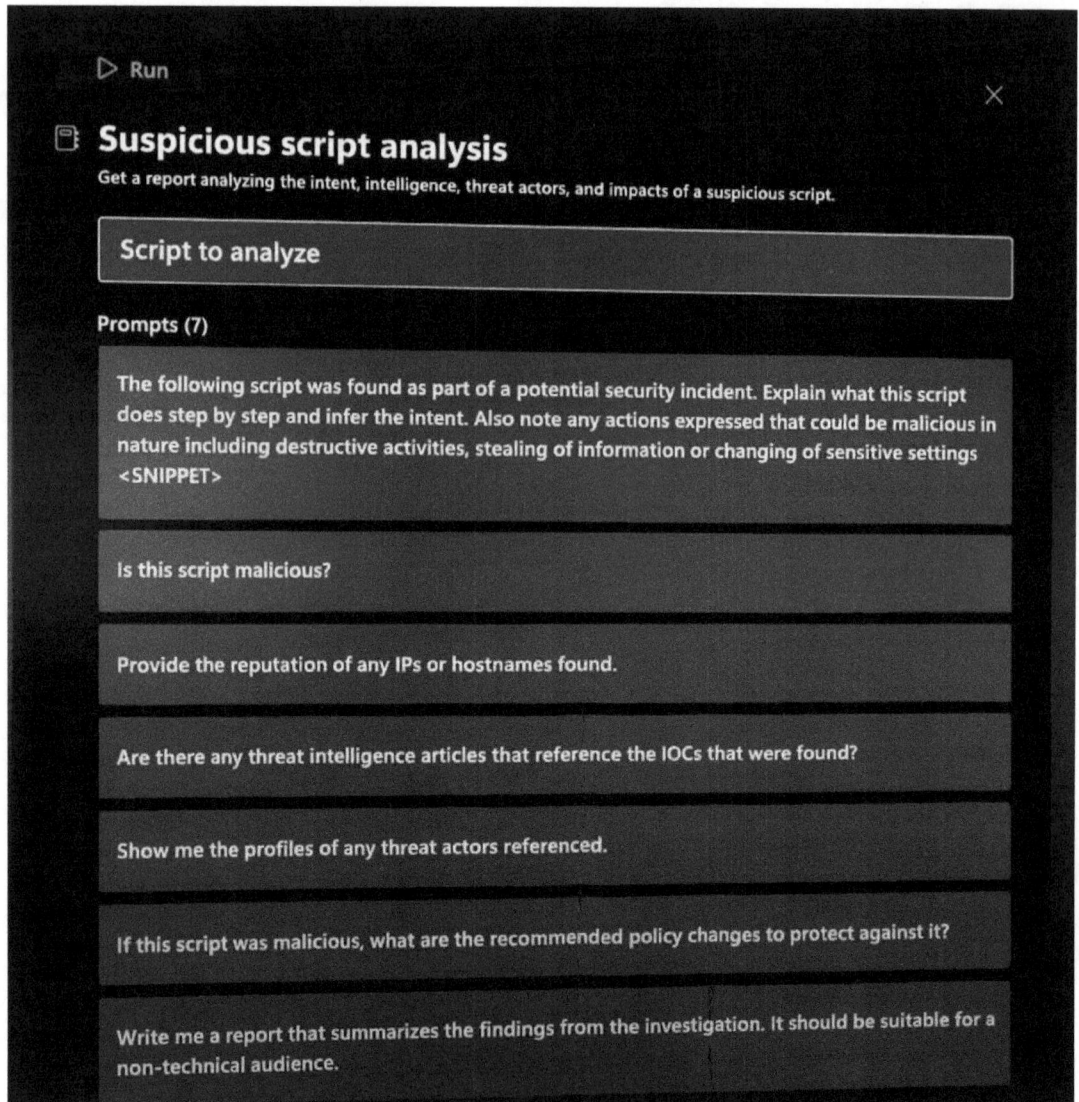

Figure 13.19: Security Copilot script analysis by LLM

Policy and other configuration generation

This feature is going to help a lot to all the security administrator as it has power to generate multiple security policies of multiple Microsoft security product, run hunting queries, generate examples etc., as shown in the following figure:

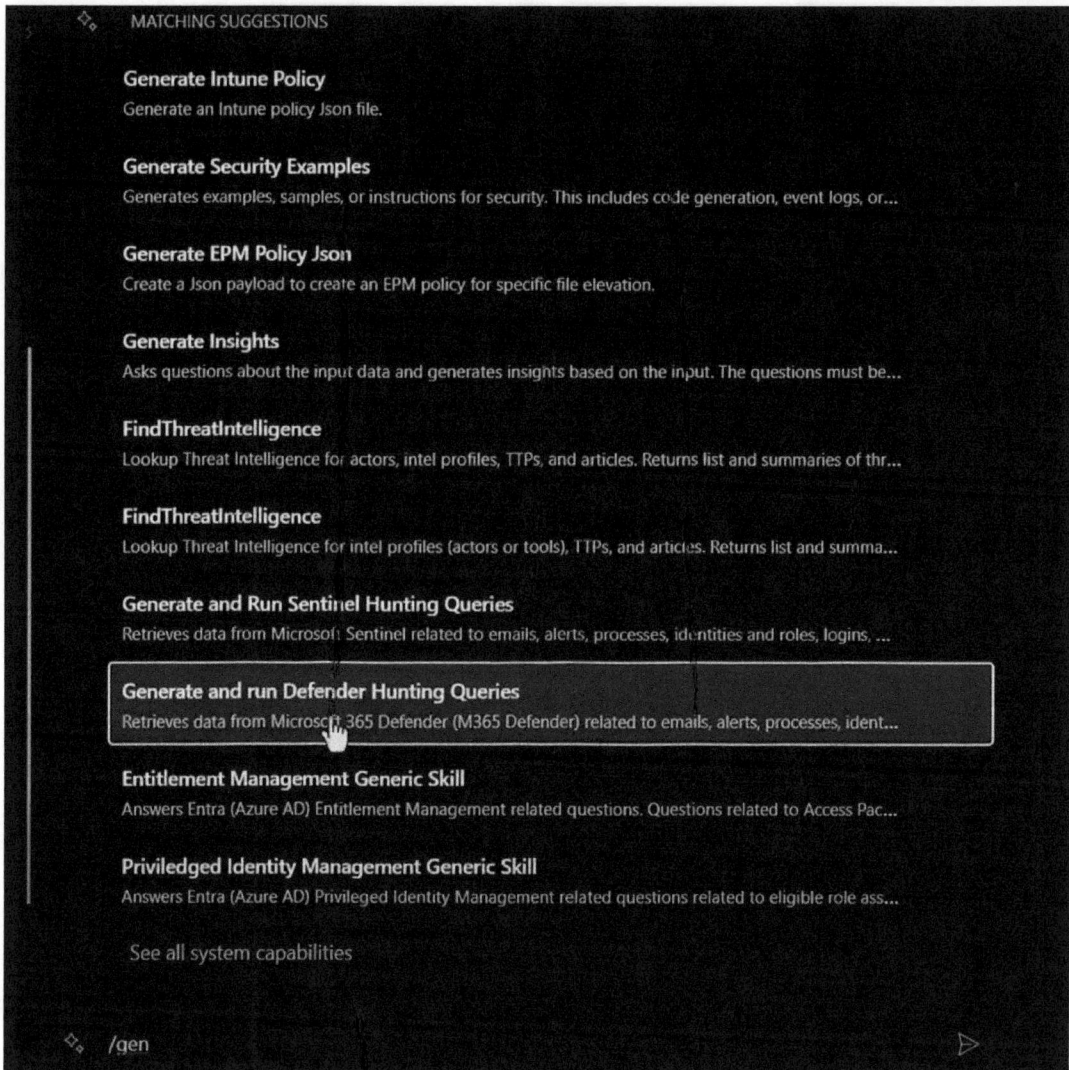

Figure 13.20: Security Policy recommendation by Security Copilot

Advanced hunting query generation and execution

It can automatically build advanced hunting quires and can execute to give you the result.

The following figure showcases given sample prompts that can generate advanced hunting KSQL quires:

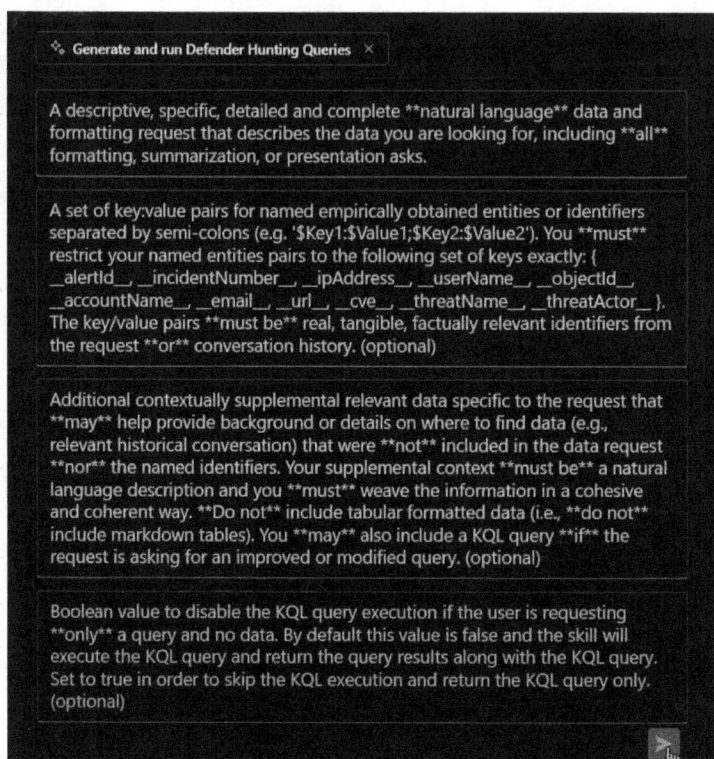

Figure 13.21: KSQL Prompts recommendation on Security Copilot

Incident corelation and summary generation

Multistage incidents can be corelated and summary can be easily provided.

The following figure showcases the timeline of multistage attack in more readable form and one of the features for executives to quickly get insight:

Timestamp	Title	Severity	Incident ID
2023-10-23T02:20:41.5168743Z	Multi-stage incident involving Initial access & Command and control including Ransomware on multiple endpoints reported by multiple sources	High	19388
2023-10-23T05:19:22.2635422Z	Multi-stage incident involving Initial access & Credential access on multiple endpoints reported by multiple sources	High	19447
2023-10-23T05:10:02.3002106Z	Password Spray involving one user	High	19445
2023-10-23T11:31:35.7568784Z	Multiple failed user logon attempts to a service involving one user	High	19467
2023-10-23T05:06:08.9102130Z	Multi-stage incident involving Privilege escalation including Ransomware on multiple endpoints reported by multiple sources	High	19444
2023-10-23T03:10:47.5002142Z	Multi-stage incident involving Credential access & Lateral movement on one endpoint reported by multiple sources	High	19423
2023-10-23T05:11:59.0702155Z	Multiple failed user logon attempts to a service involving one user	High	19446
2023-10-23T02:49:16.3435500Z	Potential human-operated malicious activity on one endpoint	High	19393

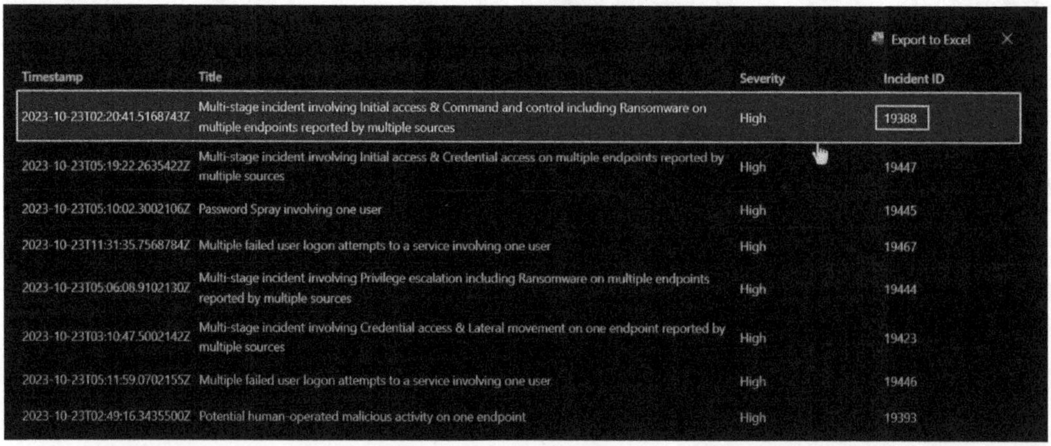

Figure 13.22: Incident corelation by Security Copilot

It can also show detailed synthesized incident summary, as shown in the following figure:

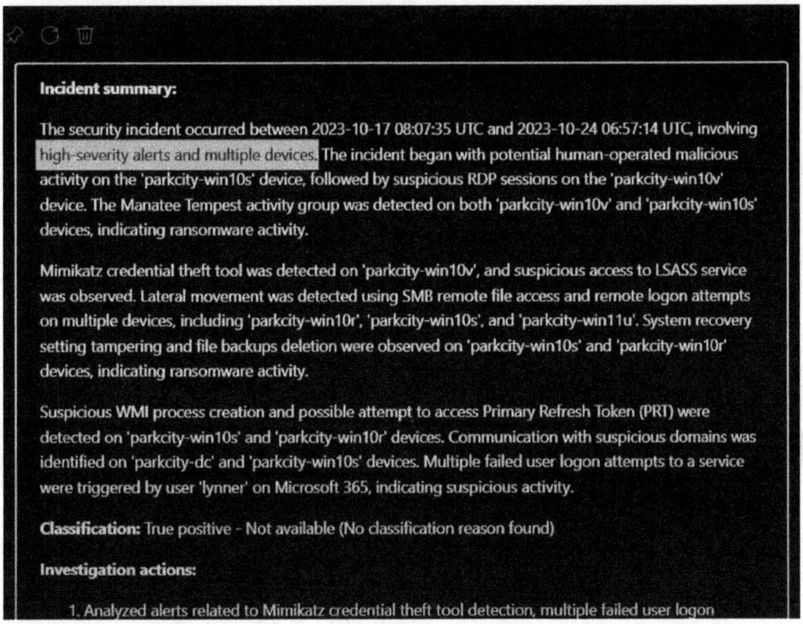

Figure 13.23: Detailed incident summary by Security Copilot

Multistage attack analysis

The following figure is the example of multistage corelation on the MDE web portal and now you can get more granular report on the copilot portal:

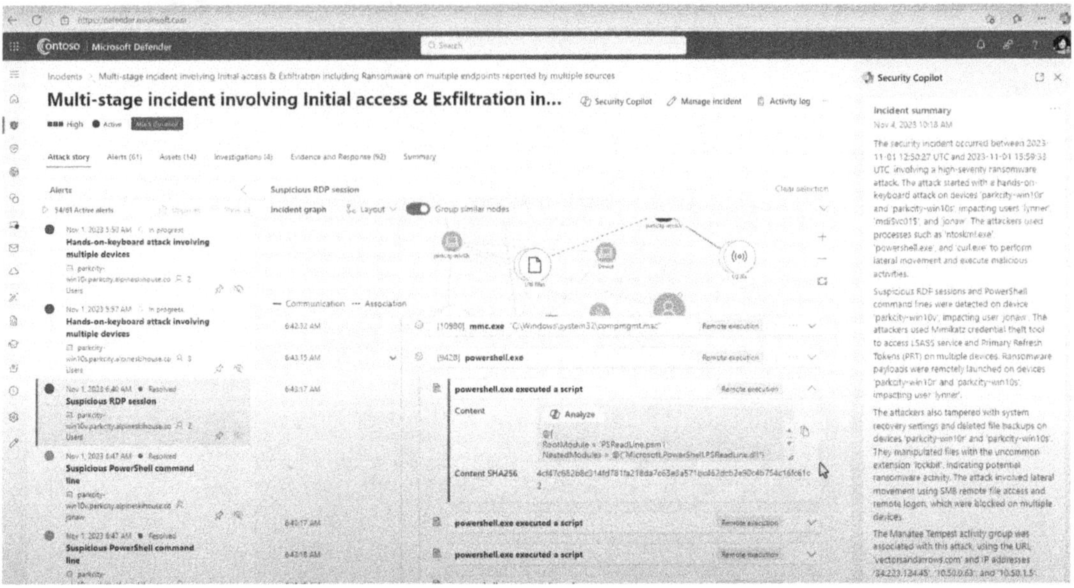

Figure 13.24: Multistage attack showcase on MDE portal

Remediation actions

It can automatically take remediation actions as shown in the following figure:

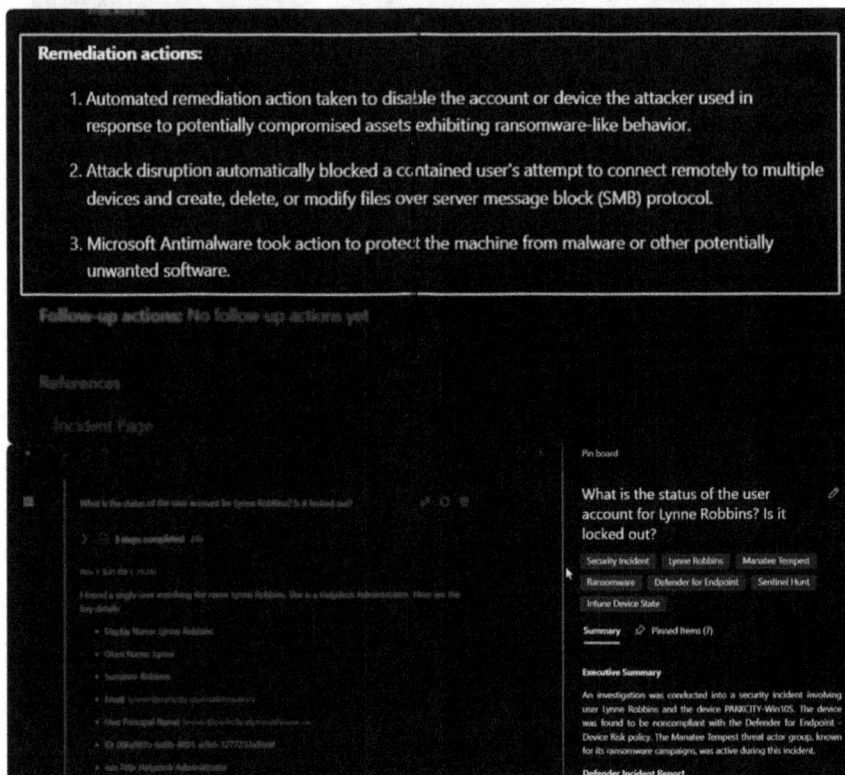

Figure 13.25: Recommendation given by Security Copilot

Aka.ms/Security Copilot

You can visit the following site to get the latest information about the general availability of the solution.

Figure 13.26: Highlight of Security Copilot URL

MS Entra interaction

Microsoft Entra is rebranded AAD solution that can help you to manage users, and you can directly ask and take actions from the Copilot web portal.

The following figure shows the screenshot reference where copilot is interacting with Microsoft Entra (a.k.a AAD) to query account status as it can help in taking automated unlocking or other required user action:

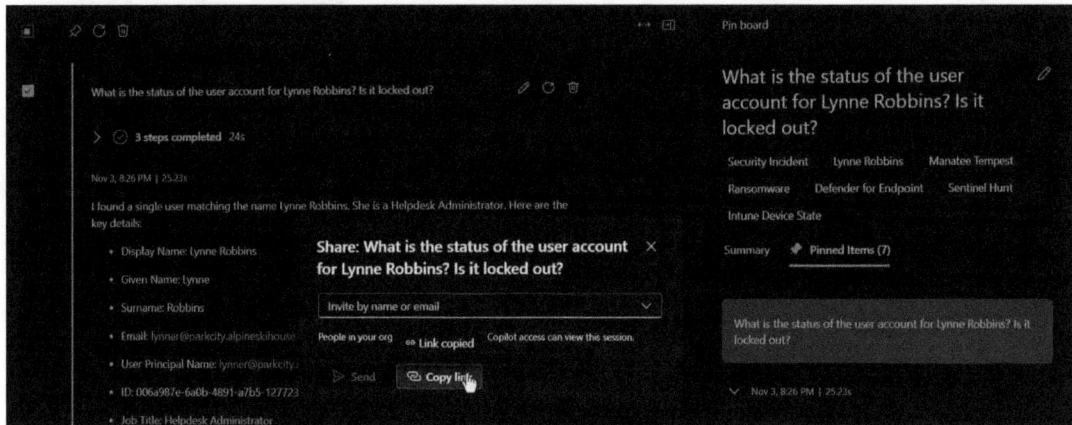

Figure 13.27: Security Copilot interaction of MS Entra for AD insight

Conclusion

In conclusion, this chapter has provided a thorough exploration of Microsoft's expansive security ecosystem, ranging from the breadth and depth of its product offerings to the strategic integration of AI/ML, with a particular focus on LLM and the revolutionary Microsoft Security Copilot. As we explored the future trends and innovations, the chapter underscored **Microsoft Defender for Endpoint's** (**MDE**) adaptability. Detailed insights into MTE and a comprehensive breakdown of Security Copilot's features, internal architecture, and functionality showcased its potential to transform SOC workflows. From script analysis to incident correlation and multi-stage attack analysis, the chapter has illuminated the power of Security Copilot in augmenting security operations. This exploration not only equips SOC analysts with a robust tool but also positions CISOs to gain quick and detailed insights into organizational security, marking a significant step forward in the evolving landscape of cybersecurity.

In the next chapter, you can find many practical configuration examples that got implemented in multiple production critical infrastructure like international airport management etc.

Join our book's Discord space

Join the book's Discord Workspace for Latest updates, Offers, Tech happenings around the world, New Release and Sessions with the Authors:

https://discord.bpbonline.com

CHAPTER 14

Practical Configuration Examples and Case Studies

Introduction

In the face of escalating cybersecurity threats, especially the increasing sophistication of ransomware attacks, the proper configuration of device security settings emerges as a critical line of defense. Recent statistics in end of *2023 highlight that misconfigurations contribute* to a substantial *21% of error-related breaches*, emphasizing the urgent need for solutions that streamline posture management.

Microsoft Defender for Endpoint, a proactive security tool designed to fortify organizational defenses by providing tailored recommendations for mitigating risks on at-risk devices. 7th November 2023 marks an exciting milestone as MDE team announced the general availability of simplified settings management within Defender for Endpoint, a significant step towards making prevention more accessible for their customers. This development aligns seamlessly with their *overarching mission*—to deliver not only comprehensive endpoint security but an experience that delights users.

> **Note: There are so many configurations and settings scattered across different MDE tools that we have covered in this book, and we cannot showcase all such settings, but this chapter will cover some of them and will set base for you to explore more.**

Structure

In this chapter, we will cover the following topics:

- MDE Security center features state
- MS Intune portal for Windows 10 configuration
- ASR coverage
- MS Intune ASR configuration
- High level ASR rules deployment steps
- ASR rules list by category
- ASR rule modes
- MDE agent configuration examples
- Configurations for Windows server
- Query language used internally and externally
- Deployment timelines

Objectives

The primary objective of this chapter is to empower readers with the practical knowledge needed to configure Microsoft Defender for Endpoint with precision and efficacy. Through exploration of real-world case studies, hands-on deployment scenarios, and a detailed examination of industry-specific implementations, the chapter seeks to provide a comprehensive understanding of endpoint security configurations. By the end, readers should feel confident in navigating the Microsoft Defender for Endpoint Security Centre and implementing configurations tailored to the specific needs and challenges of their respective environments.

MDE security center features state

The following table shows the top-level feature settings available to configure and gives you default configuration value so that you can tune it according to your organization's requirements:

Feature	Sub-feature	Feature state
Threat and vulnerability management	Dashboard	Default (Enabled)
	Organization exposure score	Default (Enabled)
	Secure score for devices	Default (Enabled)
	Security recommendations	Default (Enabled)
	Remediation, exception and blocked applications (trial)	Default (Enabled)
	Inventories (software) browser extensions, certificates, hardware and firmware (trial)	Default (Enabled)
	Weaknesses	Default (Enabled)
	Event timeline	Default (Enabled)
Endpoint detection and response	Dashboard	Default (Enabled)
	Incident and alerts queue	Default (Enabled)
	Device list	Default (Enabled)
	Take response actions	Default (Enabled)
Automated investigation and remediation		Default (Enabled)
Advanced hunting		Default (Enabled)
Next generation antivirus		Enabled
Attack surface reduction (16 ASR rules, Windows security experience, web protection, application control)		Audit mode (Enabled)
Account protection		Enabled

Table 14.1: MDE settings options on web portal

MDE alerts and advanced settings

The following table gives you recommended settings for various alerting and advanced settings available on the portal. These settings are recommended some of the SOC outsourcing companies to their customers.

Settings	Sub setting	Next sub setting	Action value
General	Data retention		Max. allowed – 180 days
	Advanced features	Live response	On
		Live response for servers	Off
		Live response unsigned script execution	Off
		Restrict correlation to within scoped device groups	Off
		Enable EDR in block mode	On
		Automatically resolve alerts	On
		Allow or block file	On
		Custom network indicators	On
		Tamper protection	On
		Show user details	On
		Skype for business integration	On
		Office 365 Threat Intelligence connection	On
		Microsoft Defender for Cloud Apps	On
		Web content filtering	On
		Download quarantined files	On
		Share endpoint alerts with Microsoft Compliance Center	On
		Authenticated telemetry	On
		Microsoft Intune connection	On
		Device discovery	On
		Preview features	On
		Microsoft Security Score	On
		Preview features	On
		Microsoft Threat Experts	Off
License			Default (Enabled)

Settings	Sub setting	Next sub setting	Action value
Email notification	Alerts	Add notification rule	Enabled
	Vulnerabilities	Add notification rule	Enabled
Auto remediation	Grouped Device	Remediation level	Full (Remediate Threat Automatically)
	Ungrouped device	Remediation level	Full (Remediate Threat Automatically)
Permissions	Roles	Default role Custom role	Project Team: MDE Administrator (Global Admin or Security Admin)
	Device groups	Grouped Ungrouped	Grouping structure are captured under 6.1 Clients – Grouping Structure
APIs	SIEM		Disabled
Rules	Alert suppression		Enabled
	Indicators	File hashes, IP address, URL'Domains, certificate	Default (Enabled)
	Process memory Indicators		Default (Enabled)
	Web Content Filtering		On (Need to define Policy)
	Automation upload	Content analysis (File extension names)	On
	Automation upload	Memory content analysis	On
		Memory content analysis	
	Automation folder exclusions		None
	Configuration management	Enforcement scope	Use MDE to enforce security configuration settings from Intune

Settings	Sub setting	Next sub setting	Action value
			Enable configuration management Windows client devices -ON Windows Server Devices - ON
			Security settings management for Microsoft Defender for Cloud onboarded devices - ON
			Manage Security settings using Configuration Manager - ON
Machine management	Onboarding		For Windows 10 & 2019 & above Servers
			Using onboarding Script. Deployment method: Intune/SCCM For Windows Servers 2012 & 2016
			Using Installation Package & onboarding Script. Deployment method: SCCM
			For Windows 7 & Windows Servers 2008 R2
			Using MMA Agent Package with MDE Workspace ID & Key
			Deployment Method: Intune /SCCM
			For Linux Using Onboarding Script method: Local/configuration tool

Settings	Sub setting	Next sub setting	Action value
	Offboarding		For Windows 10 & 2019 & above Servers
			Using onboarding Script. Deployment method: Intune/SCCM For Windows Servers 2012 & 2016
			Using Installation Package & onboarding Script. Deployment method: SCCM
			For Windows 7 & Windows Servers 2008 R2
			Using MMA Agent Package with MDE Workspace ID & Key
			Deployment Method: Intune /SCCM
			For Linux Using Onboarding Script method: Local/configuration tool
Network assessment	Assessment jobs		Default (Enabled)

Table 14.2: MDE Alert and Advanced settings on web portal page

MS Intune portal for Windows 10 configuration

Since MS Intune integrates with the MDE web portal, this section covers some device control configurations from the Intune portal.

Note: Implementation will be done by MS Endpoint manager (Intune) URL:

- **https://endpoint.microsoft.com**

MDE antivirus policy

Antivirus Policy plays a core role in endpoint security as this is the area that whole story of security product starts to protect you from various malwares.

The following table gives MDE Antivirus policy settings from Intune portal:

Settings	Action
Allow archive scanning	Allowed. Scans the archive files
Allow behavior monitoring	Allowed. Turns on real-time behavior monitoring
Allow cloud protection	Allowed. Turns on cloud protection
Allow email scanning	Allowed. Turns on email scanning
Allow Full Scan on Mapped Network Drives	Not Configured
Allow full scan removable drive scanning	Allowed. Scans removable drives
Allow intrusion prevention system	Allowed
Allow scanning of all downloaded files and attachments	Allowed
Allow realtime monitoring	Allowed. Turns on and runs the real-time monitoring service.
Allow scanning network files	Allowed. Scans network files
Allow script scanning	Allowed.
Allow user ui access	Not allowed. Prevents users from accessing UI
Avg CPU load factor	Configured – 45
Check for signatures before running scan	Enabled
Cloud block level	Not Configured
Cloud extended timeout	Configured – 50
Days to retain cleaned malware	Configured – 30
Disable catchup full scan	Enabled
Disable catchup quick scan	Enabled
Enable low CPU priority	Enabled
Enable network protection	Enabled (audit mode)
Excluded extensions	Not Configured
Excluded paths	Consolidated & attached below in this document
Excluded processes	Consolidated & attached below in this document
PUA protection	Audit mode
Real time scan direction	Monitor all files (bi-directional)
Scan parameter	Full scan

Settings	Action
Schedule quick scan time	Configured – 720
Schedule scan day	Friday
Schedule scan time	Configured – 720
Signature update fallback order	Not Configured
Signature update file share sourced	Not Configured
Signature update interval	Configured – 6
Submit samples consent	Send safe samples automatically
Disable local admin merge	Disable Local Admin Merge
Allow on access protection	Allowed
Remediation action for Severe threats	Block. Blocks file execution
Remediation action for Moderate severity threats	Quarantine. Moves files to quarantine
Remediation action for Low Severity threats	Clean. Service tries to recover files and try to disinfect
Remediation action for High severity threats	Block. Blocks file execution

Table 14.3: Intune Antivirus configuration settings

MDE disk encryption

Encrypting data at rest is crucial to protect against data theft risks and locking your disk with right encryption with various settings gives you the flexibility to manage such in your whole organization and majorly plays an important role in user desktop devices.

The following table gives Intune MDE disk encryption configuration setting:

Settings	Action
BitLocker base settings	
Enable full disk encryption for OS and fixed data drives	Yes
Require storage cards to be encrypted	Not Configured
Hide prompt about third-party encryption -	Yes
	Allow standard users to enable encryption during Autopilot - Yes

Settings	Action
Configure client-driven recovery password rotation	Disabled
BitLocker fixed drive settings	
BitLocker fixed drive policy	Configure
Fixed drive recovery	Configure
	Recovery key file creation - Blocked
	Set up BitLocker recovery package - Password and key.
	Require the device to backup recovery information to Azure Active Directory - enabled
	Recovery password creation - required
	Hide recovery options during BitLocker setup - Yes
	Activate BitLocker after storing recovery information - enabled.
	Prevent write access to fixed data drives without BitLocker protection - Unconfigured.
	Set encryption method for fixed data drives to AWS 128-bit XTS.
BitLocker OS drive settings	
BitLocker system drive policy	Configure
Startup authentication required	Yes
Compatible TPM startup	Required
Compatible TPM startup PIN	Blocked
Compatible TPM startup key	Blocked
Compatible TPM startup key and PIN	Blocked
Disable BitLocker on devices where TPM is incompatible	Yes
Enable preboot recovery message and URL	Not Configured
System Drive recovery	Configure
Recovery key file creation	Blocked
Configure BitLocker recovery package	Password and key

Settings	Action
Require device to back up recovery info to AZ AD	Yes
Recovery password creation	Required
Hide recovery options during BitLocker setup	Yes
Enable BitLocker after recovery information to store	Yes
Block the use of certificate-based data recovery agent (DRA)	Yes
Min Pin length	6
Configure Encryption method for Operating System Drives	AES 128Bit XTS
BitLocker removal drive settings	
BitLocker Removable drive policy	Configure
Configure encryption method for removal data	AES 128bit XTS
Block write access to removable data-drives not protected by BitLocker	Not configured
Block write access to devices configured in another org	Not configured

Table 14.4: MDE Disk Encryption configuration on Intune portal

MDE Windows security experience policy

The following table covers MDE windows security experience policy configuration on Intune portal:

Settings	Action
Tamper Protection (Device)	ON
Disable Account Protection UI	Not Configured
Disable App Browser UI	Not Configured
Disable Clear TPM Button	Enabled *The security processor troubleshooting page won't display a button to initiate the process of clearing the security processor (TPM).*

Settings	Action
Disable Security UI	Not Configured
Disable Family UI	Enable *Users are unable to view the display of the family options area in WD Security Center.*
Disable Health Ui	Not Configured
Disable Network UI	Not Configured
Disable Enhanced Notifications	Enable *WD Security Center only shows notifications that are deemed critical on clients.*
Disable TPM Firmware Update Warning	Disabled or Not Configured. *A warning will appear if the firmware of the security processor (TPM) needs updating for TPMs that have a vulnerability.*
Disable Virus Ui	Not Configured
Hide Ransomware Data Recovery	(Enable) The Ransomware data recovery area is concealed.
Hide Windows Security Notification Area Control	Not Configured
Enable Customized Toast	Not Configured
Enable in App Customization	Not Configured
Company name	Contoso
Email	support@contoso.com
Phone	TBD
URL	www.contoso.com

Table 14.5: Windows security experience policy configuration

Understanding ASR

In the ever-evolving landscape of cybersecurity, organizations face the constant challenge of fortifying their defenses against an array of sophisticated threats. **Microsoft Defender for Endpoint** (**MDE**) stands as a robust solution, offering a suite of advanced security features. Among these, **Attack Surface Reduction** (**ASR**) emerges as a pivotal component, reinforcing MDE's capabilities to proactively safeguard against attacks.

ASR is a proactive security feature designed to minimize the attack surface, limiting opportunities for adversaries to exploit vulnerabilities and compromise systems. Within the context of MDE, ASR focuses on reducing exposure to potential threats by controlling various aspects of the attack surface.

The following are the key features and capabilities:

- **Application control**: ASR empowers administrators to define and enforce policies on which applications are allowed to run. This ensures that only trusted and approved applications operate on endpoints, mitigating the risk of malicious software execution.

- **Code execution prevention**: ASR employs sophisticated techniques to prevent code execution in specific high-risk areas, such as Microsoft Office and script interpreters. This prevents the exploitation of these areas by malware seeking to execute arbitrary code.

- **Credential theft prevention**: ASR takes measures to prevent common techniques used by attackers to steal credentials. This includes blocking credential dumping tools and techniques, enhancing the security posture against lateral movement within the network.

- **Network protection**: ASR extends its influence to network traffic, enhancing protection against social engineering and malware. It works seamlessly with Microsoft Defender SmartScreen to thwart dangerous websites and connections.

The following are the benefits of ASR in MDE:

- **Proactive defense**: ASR adopts a proactive stance, anticipating potential attack vectors and fortifying the environment against emerging threats.

- **Reduced attack surface**: By controlling application execution and limiting code execution in critical areas, ASR significantly reduces the attack surface, minimizing opportunities for exploitation.

- **Credential protection**: Preventing credential theft is a crucial aspect of ASR, enhancing the overall resilience of the system against unauthorized access.

- **Network resilience**: ASR's network protection capabilities contribute to a more resilient defense against malicious websites and social engineering attempts.

MDE ASR policy and rules

Proactive actions are always better than reactive ones, and ASR provides such a proactive approach and MDE product has focused so much in this area and covers most of the corner cases that can set right posture of your organization Secure Score.

ASR coverage

ASR and ASR rules represent distinct concepts. ASR encompasses all the built-in and cloud-based security functionalities provided by Windows 10. These features collectively aim to reduce the potential entry points for attackers, thereby minimizing the attack surface. Essentially, ASR functions as a **Host Intrusion Prevention System** (**HIPS**), a term commonly used in the industry. Within Microsoft Defender ATP, ASR comprises the following components:

- Attack surface reduction rules
- Hardware based isolation
- Application control
- Exploit protection
- Network protection
- Web protection
- Controlled folder access
- Network firewall

The following figure represents the ASR coverage:

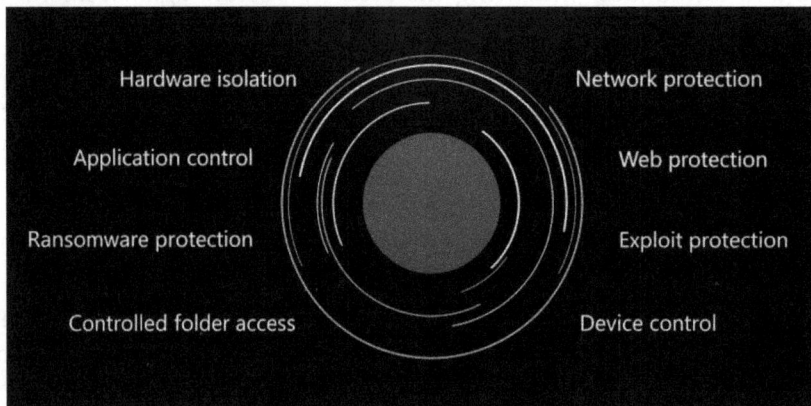

Figure 14.1: Items covered in ASR

Reference for ASR rule configuration: **https://techcommunity.microsoft.com/t5/microsoft-defender-for-endpoint/demystifying-attack-surface-reduction-rules-part-1/ba-p/1306420**

ASR rules

The following table lists various ASR rules that can be configured for different resources:

Attack surface reduction settings	Action
Email threats: Block executable content from email client and webmail	Enable (Audit mode)
Office threats: Block all Office application from creating child processes	Enable

Attack surface reduction settings	Action
Office threats: Block Office applications from creating executable content	Enable
Office threats: Block Office applications from injecting code into other processes	Enable
Office threats: Block Win32 API calls from Office macros	Enable
Scripting threats: Block JavaScript or VBScript from launching downloaded executable content	Enable
Scripting threats: Block execution of potentially obfuscated scripts	Enable
Ransomware threats: Use advanced protection against ransomware	Enable
Operating system threats: Block credential stealing from the Windows local security authority subsystem	Enable
Operating threats: Block executable files from running unless they meet a prevalence, age, or trusted list criteria's	Enable
External device threats: Block untrusted and unsigned processes that run from USB	Enable
Block persistence through WMI event subscription	Enable
Block process creations originating from PS Exec and WMI commands	Enable
Block Office communication application from creating child processes	Enable
Block Adobe Reader from creating child processes	Enable
Block abuse of exploited vulnerable signed drivers	Enable
Files and Folders to exclude from Attack Surface Reduction rules	<As per requirements>

Table 14.6: ASR configuration that can be configured from Intune portal

MS Intune ASR configuration

There are three major features available on Microsoft Defender ASR that are very helpful for prevention of attack:

- WD Application Control/Guard
- WD Exploit Guard
- WD System Guard

One of the key components of ASR is WD Application Control/Guard, which introduces a shift from traditional application trust models.

WD Application Guard

WD Application Control/Guard (WDAC) introduces a paradigm shift from the conventional application trust model, wherein all applications are inherently deemed trustworthy, to a more stringent model. In this new approach, applications must earn trust before being permitted to run, reducing the risk of sensitive information being compromised by malicious software.

Traditionally, processes initiated by a user inherit the same level of access to data as the user. This inherent trust can lead to the accidental or intentional execution of malicious software, resulting in potential data breaches. Application control addresses this vulnerability by requiring all executables on the system to undergo vetting before execution.

Vetting is primarily achieved through code signatures from software publishers. However, recognizing that not all Windows executables are properly signed, administrators can create a manifest encompassing all files on the system. This manifest is then authenticated by the organization and deployed to Windows Enterprise PCs. Consequently, executables not outlined in this policy file will be restricted from running once WDAC is activated. Additionally, WDAC policies extend their scope to block unsigned scripts, MSIs, and Windows PowerShell.

Application Control finds an optimal fit in environment with **Point of Service (PoS)** devices like sales terminals and ATMs, as well as server-based desktops (virtual desktop infrastructure). This is particularly advantageous in scenarios where the operating system remains relatively consistent across devices and undergoes infrequent updates. Notably, Microsoft assures that, given the signed nature of code available from Windows Update, Windows installs will continue to operate securely even as the OS and Microsoft applications receive updates.

However, organizations must deliberate on the integration of third-party applications that update regularly but lack proper signatures. This consideration is crucial for maintaining the integrity and security of the overall system.

The following figure showcases the new profile creation on Intune portal for ASR rules that can be later used to apply on devices:

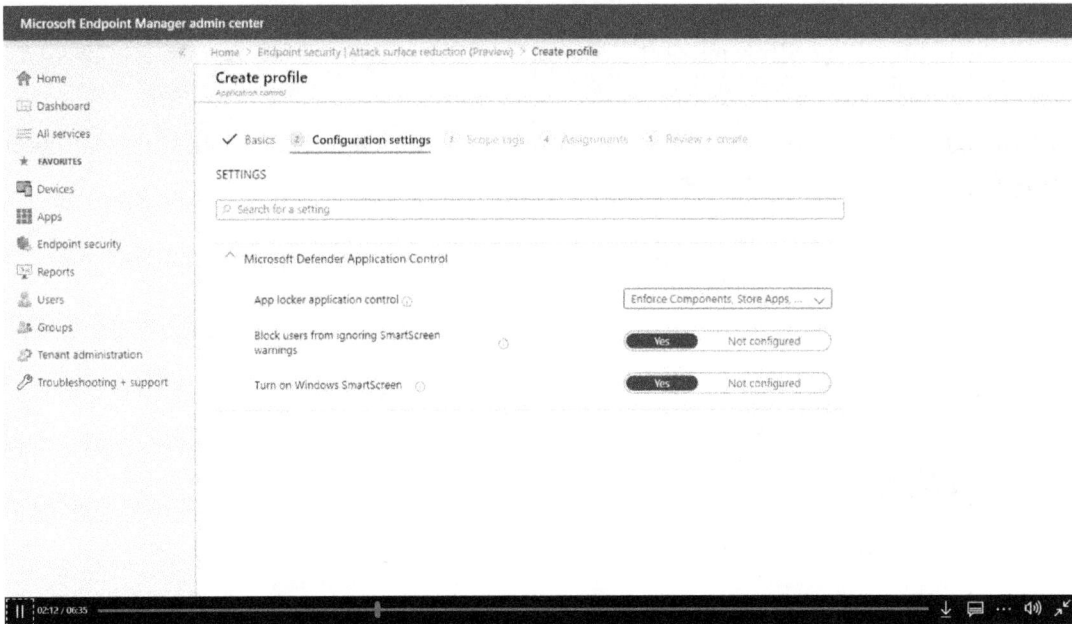

Figure 14.2: ASR configuration for WD Application

Windows Defender Application Guard, simply know as **Application Guard** is meticulously engineered to fortify against both historic and emerging cyber threats, ensuring sustained employee productivity. Leveraging Microsoft's innovative hardware isolation strategy, Application Guard aims to dismantle attackers' playbooks, rendering current assault methods ineffective.

Tailored for compatibility with Windows and Microsoft Edge, Application Guard functions as a shield, particularly when employees traverse the internet. It achieves this by isolating sites that fall outside enterprise-defined trust, thus fortifying your organization's cyber defenses. As the enterprise administrator, you wield the authority to enumerate trusted websites, cloud resources, and internal networks. Anything not explicitly endorsed on this list is automatically flagged as untrusted.

When an employee accesses an untrusted site using either Microsoft Edge or Internet Explorer, Application Guard swiftly responds by opening the site within a dedicated Hyper-V-enabled container. This container operates independently of the host operating system, ensuring a robust security layer. In the event that the accessed site harbors malicious elements, the host PC remains impervious, shielding enterprise data from potential compromise. The isolated container operates incognito, safeguarding employee enterprise credentials and thwarting any attempts by attackers to gain unauthorized access.

In essence, Windows Defender Application Guard stands as a formidable defense mechanism, aligning with Microsoft's commitment to perpetual innovation and security in the ever-evolving digital landscape.

The following figure showcases high level overview of hardware isolation of Microsoft Edge with the Windows Defender Application Guard.

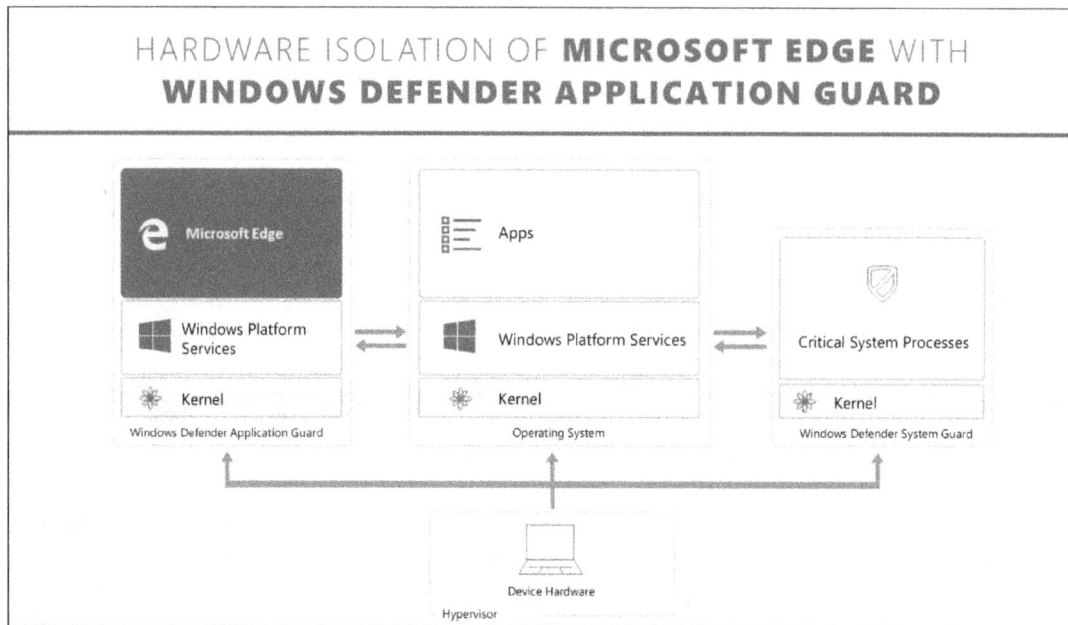

Figure 14.3: High level overview of Windows Defender Application Guard

The application guard is designed to cater to various device scenarios, including:

- Enterprise desktops
- Enterprise mobile laptops
- **Bring Your Own Device (BYOD)** mobile laptops
- Personal devices

Configuring Application Guard

To enable Application Guard in Microsoft Edge, use the following steps:

1. Launch control panel
2. Click on programs.
3. Choose the turn Windows features on or off link.
4. Check the **Windows Defender Application Guard** option. If that option is not available to select, it is probably because your hardware does not support this feature.

5. Select **OK**.

6. Select **Restart now**.

After the computer restarts, you can start a Microsoft Edge session using MD Application Guard by selecting the menu button on the top-right and then selecting the **New Application Guard window** option and using this all the session on the new window will be covered by it.

If you want to configure Application Guard features by using Microsoft Intune platform, you can do it by creating device configuration profile. This applies only to Windows 10 and later operating systems. When you select to create a new configuration profile, you should choose Endpoint protection as the profile type, and then select to configure MD Application Guard settings. This admin interface allows you to create more options than in Group Policy, and to configure Application Guard not just for Microsoft Edge but also for Office apps, as shown in the following figure:

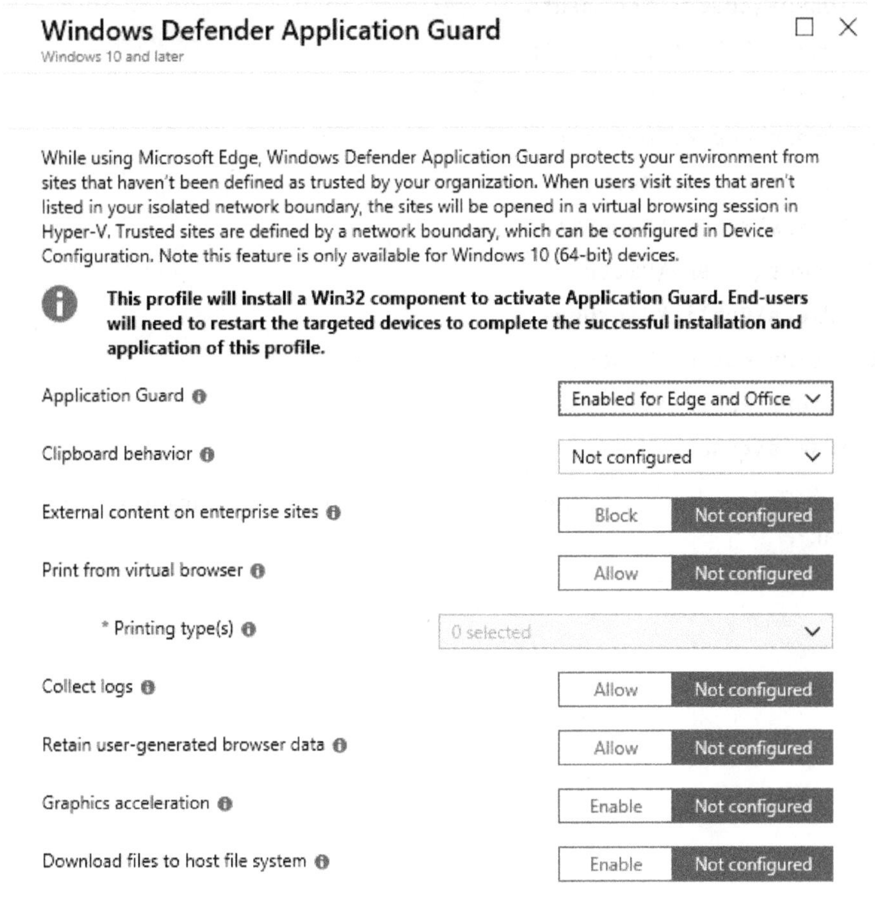

Figure 14.4: Windows Defender Application Guard configuratin page on Intune portal

Windows Exploit Guard

Windows Defender Exploit Guard, formerly known as WD Exploit Guard, introduces a suite of host intrusion prevention capabilities for Windows, empowering organizations to efficiently manage and diminish the attack surface of applications utilized by their workforce.

The key features of Microsoft Defender Exploit Guard are as follows:

- Exploit protection
- Attack surface reduction rules
- Network protection
- Controlled folder access

By default, the following folders are enabled for protection:

- `C:\Users\<user>\Documents`
- `C:\Users\Public\Documents`
- `C:\Users\Public\Music`
- `C:\Users\<user>\Desktop`
- `C:\Users\Public\Desktop`
- `C:\Users\<user>\Favorites`
- `C:\Users\<user>\Pictures`
- `C:\Users\Public\Pictures`
- `C:\Users\<user>\Videos`
- `C:\Users\Public\Videos`
- `C:\Users\<user>\Music`

The following figure showcases the endpoint protection configuration profile setting on Intune portal:

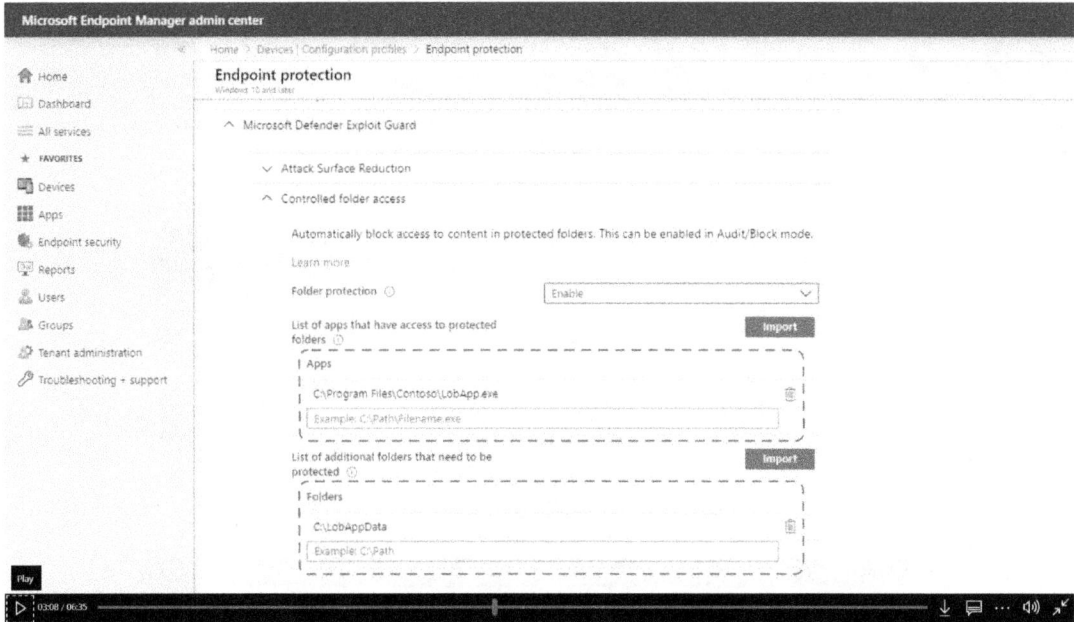

Figure 14.5: Exploit Guard protection configuration on intune portal for controlled folder access

Windows System Guard

Windows employs containers to create a secure isolation environment for critical system services and data, safeguarding them against compromise even in the event of an operating system breach. A specific container type, known as **Windows System Guard**, is utilized to fortify essential resources like the Windows authentication stack, single sign-on tokens, Windows Hello biometric stack, and the Virtual Trusted Platform Module.

WD System Guard consolidates existing Windows system integrity features into a singular system and lays the foundation for future investments in Windows security.

The following figure gives a high level overview of Windows Defender System Guard boot time integrity protection:

WINDOWS DEFENDER SYSTEM GUARD
BOOT TIME INTEGRITY PROTECTION

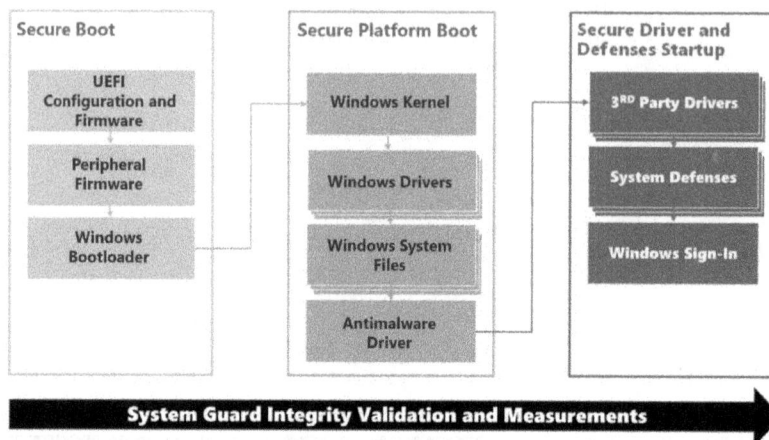

Figure 14.6: Windows Defender System Guard boot time integrity protection overview

Reference: https://learn.microsoft.com/en-us/training/modules/manage-microsoft-defender-endpoint/7-explore-windows-defender-system-guard

The primary objectives of MD system guard are:

- **Protecting and maintaining system integrity during startup**: Ensures the system's integrity from the moment it initiates the startup process.

- **Safeguarding system integrity post-startup**: Continues to uphold system integrity once the operating system is operational.

- **Verification of system integrity through attestation**: Provides mechanisms for both local and remote attestation to confirm the sustained integrity of the system.

- **Initiating system integrity during startup**: Ensures the integrity of the system during the startup phase, preventing potential compromises.

In the earlier days, particularly with Windows 7, attackers could persist and avoid detection by installing a boot kit or rootkit before the operating system initiated. This malicious software would gain a privileged position by starting before or during the boot process. However, with modern hardware meeting Windows 8 certification or higher, a hardware-based root of trust, part of the **Unified Extensible Firmware Interface (UEFI)** known as **Secure Boot**, prevents unauthorized firmware or software from initiating before the Windows bootloader.

After the successful verification and initialization of the device's firmware and Windows bootloader, the potential for attackers to compromise the system's integrity arises during the initiation of the remaining Windows operating system and defences. WD System Guard counteracts this risk by ensuring that exclusively consist of properly signed and secure Windows files and drivers, including third-party one's components, are allowed to start on the device. As the final step in the Windows boot process, System Guard launches the system's antimalware solution to scan all third-party drivers, concluding the boot process securely. In essence, WD System Guard guarantees a secure and uncompromised system startup before the activation of additional system defences.

Maintain integrity of the system after run time

Sustaining the integrity of the system during runtime has been a critical challenge, particularly in scenarios where an attacker, prior to Windows 10, exploited the system, obtained SYSTEM-level privileges, or compromised the kernel itself. In such instances, the potential for severe damage to the targeted system was significant. The level of control granted to an attacker in this context allowed them to manipulate and circumvent numerous, if not all, system defences. Despite the implementation of various development practices and technologies like WD Exploit Guard that have made attaining this level of privilege more challenging, there remains a necessity to uphold the integrity of the most sensitive Windows services and data, even in the face of an adversary securing the highest level of privilege.

The advent of Windows 10 brought forth the concept of **Virtualization-Based Security** (**VBS**), introducing a transformative approach to address this challenge. VBS enables the encapsulation of the most critical Windows services and data within hardware-based isolation, specifically within the WD System Guard container. This secure environment establishes a robust hardware-based security boundary, essential for safeguarding and preserving the integrity of pivotal system services during runtime. Notable examples of such critical services include Credential Guard, Device Guard, Virtual **Trusted Platform Module** (**TPM**), and integral components of WD Exploit Guard. Through the WD System Guard container, Microsoft has effectively fortified the runtime integrity of these services, mitigating the risk posed by adversaries wielding elevated privileges.

Validate platform integrity after Windows run time

Despite the robust protection offered by WD System Guard during boot and runtime, adopting an *assume breach* mindset becomes imperative even with cutting-edge security technologies. While organizations place trust in these technologies to perform their tasks effectively, there is a concurrent need to verify the successful accomplishment of their objectives. Relying solely on the platform to autonomously attest to its security state, without the potential for compromise, is not a prudent approach. Therefore, WD System Guard incorporates a set of technologies enabling the remote examination of the device's integrity.

During the Windows boot process, WD System Guard leverages the device's TPM 2.0 to capture a sequence of integrity measurements. This process and associated data are encapsulated in hardware isolation, detached from Windows, preventing tampering that might occur if the platform were compromised. These measurements, utilizing the TPM, evaluate the integrity of the device's firmware, hardware configuration state, and Windows boot-related components, among other aspects. Once the system is operational, WD System Guard secures and authenticates these measurements using the TPM.

Upon request, a management system such as Intune or Configuration Manager can retrieve these measurements for remote analysis. If the WD System Guard signals a lack of device integrity, the management system can initiate a series of actions, including denying the device access to critical resources. This proactive approach ensures that even in the face of potential compromise, organizations can maintain a vigilant stance toward the integrity of their Windows platform.

High level ASR rules deployment steps

As with any new, wide-scale implementation which could potentially impact your line-of-business operations, it is important to be methodical in your planning and implementation. Because of the powerful capabilities of ASR rules in preventing malware, careful planning and deployment of these rules is necessary to ensure they work best for your unique customer workflows.

The following figure shows the steps that gives overview to work in your environment, you need to plan, test, implement, and operationalize ASR rules carefully:

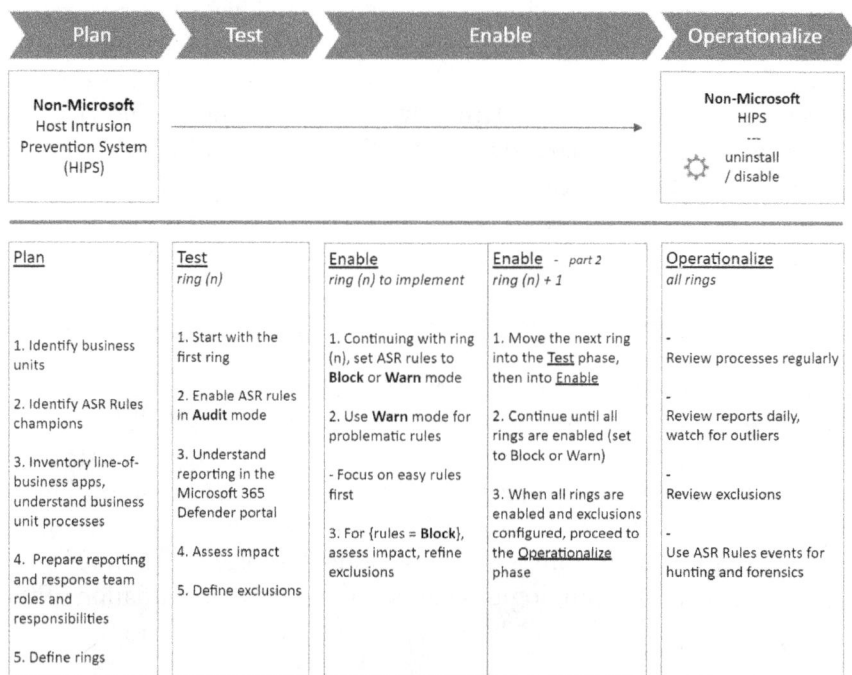

Plan	Test *ring (n)*	Enable *ring (n) to implement*	Enable - *part 2* *ring (n) + 1*	Operationalize *all rings*
1. Identify business units	1. Start with the first ring	1. Continuing with ring (n), set ASR rules to **Block** or **Warn** mode	1. Move the next ring into the Test phase, then into Enable	- Review processes regularly
2. Identify ASR Rules champions	2. Enable ASR rules in **Audit** mode	2. Use **Warn** mode for problematic rules	2. Continue until all rings are enabled (set to Block or Warn)	Review reports daily, watch for outliers
3. Inventory line-of-business apps, understand business unit processes	3. Understand reporting in the Microsoft 365 Defender portal	- Focus on easy rules first	3. When all rings are enabled and exclusions configured, proceed to the Operationalize phase	Review exclusions
4. Prepare reporting and response team roles and responsibilities	4. Assess impact	3. For {rules = **Block**}, assess impact, refine exclusions		Use ASR Rules events for hunting and forensics
5. Define rings	5. Define exclusions			

Figure 14.7: High level ASR rule deployment implementation step from planning to operationalize stage

ASR rules list by category

As outlined in user attack surface reduction rules to prevent malware infection, there are multiple attack surface reduction rules within MDE that you can enable to protect your organization. The following figure shows the rules broken out by category:

Polymorphic threats	Lateral movement & credential theft	Productivity apps rules	Email rules	Script rules	Misc rules
Block executable files from running unless they meet a prevalence (1000 machines), age, or trusted list criteria	Block process creations originating from PSExec and WMI commands	Block Office apps from creating executable content	Block executable content from email client and webmail	Block obfuscated JS/VBS/PS/macro code	Block abuse of exploited vulnerable signed drivers [1]
Block untrusted and unsigned processes that run from USB	Block credential stealing from the Windows local security authority subsystem (lsass.exe)[2]	Block Office apps from creating child processes	Block only Office communication applications from creating child processes	Block JS/VBS from launching downloaded executable content	
Use advanced protection against ransomware	Block persistence through WMI event subscription	Block Office apps from injecting code into other processes	Block Office communication apps from creating child processes		
		Block Adobe Reader from creating child processes			

Figure 14.8: Listing of ASR rule categories

ASR rule modes

The following are the four different configuration modes for ASR rule:

- **Not configured or disabled**: Indicates that the ASR rule has not been activated or has been turned off. The code for this state is 0.
- **Block**: Denotes the state in which the ASR rule is active. The code for this state is 1.
- **Audit**: Represents the state where the ASR rule is assessed for its potential impact on the organization or environment if enabled (set to block or warn). The code for this state is 2.
- **Warn**: Depicts the state where the ASR rule is enabled and provides a notification to the end-user, allowing them to bypass the block. The code for this state is 6.

MDE ASR policy for web protection

The following are the ASR policy configuration settings available on Intune portal for web protection:

Settings	Action
Enable network protection	Audit mode
Require SmartScreen for Microsoft Edge Legacy	Not Configured
Block malicious site access	Not Configured
Block unverified file download	Not Configured

Table 14.7: ASR policy configuration settings for web protection on Intune portal

MDE ASR policy for application control

The following table shows the ASR policy configuration settings available on Intune portal for Application control:

Settings	Action
App locker application control	Audit Components, Store Apps, and smart locker
Block users from ignoring SmartScreen warnings	Not Configured
Turn on Windows SmartScreen	Not Configured

Table 14.8: ASR policy configuration settings for Application control on Intune portal

Endpoint ASR Policy for detection and response

The following table shows the ASR policy configuration settings available on Intune portal for EDR:

Settings	Action
Block sample sharing for all files	Not Configured
Expedite telemetry reporting frequency	Not Configured

Table 14.9: ASR policy configuration settings for EDR on Intune portal

MDE ASR policy for account protection

Local user group membership policies help to add, remove, or replace members of local groups on Windows devices, as shown in the following table:

Local group	Group and user action	User selection type	Selected users/groups
Administrators	Add/update	Users/groups	Select users/groups

Table 14.10: ASR Policy configuration settings for Account Protection on Intune portal

MDE agent configuration examples

Configurations of MDE agent are very important to understand before you set it to *active* mode. Each organization can have different versions of these files, but we will give you high level overview and later you can download our version of configuration from the version control system used by us.

We are giving examples of RHEL Linux and Windows Server, but there is more configuration of macOS, iOS, Windows desktop etc.

Configurations for Linux RHEL

The configuration profile is a **.json** file containing entries distinguished by keys, representing preference names, along with corresponding values. The nature of these values varies; they can be straightforward, such as numerical values, or intricate, such as nested lists of preferences. To accomplish this, we must employ a configuration management tool to deploy a file named **mdatp_managed.json** to the directory **/etc/opt/microsoft/mdatp/managed/**.

We have created the following file for example **mde_rhel_configuration.json**:

```
{
    "antivirusEngine":{
        "enforcementLevel":"real_time",
        "behavior Monitoring":"enabled",
        "scanAfterDefinitionUpdate":true,
        "scanArchives":true,
        "maximumOnDemandScanThreads":2,
        "exclusionsMergePolicy":"merge",
        "exclusions":[

            {
```

```
            "$type":"excludedPath",
            "isDirectory":true,
            "path":"/var/log/*/"
        },
        {
            "$type":"excludedPath",
            "isDirectory":true,
            "path":"/opt/YOUR-OTHER-APP/*/"
        },
        {
            "$type":"excludedPath",
            "isDirectory":true,
            "path":"/etc/opt/microsoft/mdatp/*/"
        },
    ],
    "allowedThreats":[
        "<EXAMPLE DO NOT USE>EICAR-Test-File (not a virus)"
    ],
    "disallowedThreatActions":[
        "allow",
        "restore"
    ],
    "nonExecMountPolicy":"unmute",
    "unmonitoredFilesystems": ["nfs"],
    "threatTypeSettingsMergePolicy":"merge",
    "threatTypeSettings":[
        {
            "key":"potentially_unwanted_application",
            "value":"audit"
        },
        {
            "key":"archive_bomb",
            "value":"audit"
        }
    ]
},
```

```
"features":{
    "networkProtection":"disabled"
},
"networkProtection":{
    "enforcementLevel":"audit"
},
"cloudService":{
    "enabled":true,
    "diagnosticLevel":"optional",
    "automaticSampleSubmissionConsent":"safe",
    "automaticDefinitionUpdateEnabled":true,
    "proxy": "<EXAMPLE DO NOT USE>"
    }
}
```

Now, we will validate JSON file by running the following command:

```
# python -m json.tool mdatp_managed.json
```

After deploying the JSON file, if configuration does not reflect then we can run the following commands to start or restart the MDE service:

```
#sudo service mdatp start
#sudo service mdatp restart
```

Reference: https://learn.microsoft.com/en-us/microsoft-365/security/defender-endpoint/linux-preferences?view=o365-worldwide

Configurations for Windows server

We are listing implementation options deployed through MS Active Directory Group Policy by using the following ADMX template.

Example of one of Exploit Guard (Antivirus) ADMX:

```
<?xml version="1.0" encoding="utf-8"?>
<!--  (c) 2008 Microsoft Corporation  -->
<policyDefinitions xmlns:xsd="http://www.w3.org/2001/XMLSchema" xmlns:x-
si="http://www.w3.org/2001/XMLSchema-instance" revision="1.0" schemaVer-
sion="1.0" xmlns="http://schemas.microsoft.com/GroupPolicy/2006/07/Poli-
cyDefinitions">
  <policyNamespaces>
```

```
    <target prefix="expguard" namespace="Microsoft.Policies.ExploitGuard"
/>
    <using prefix="windows" namespace="Microsoft.Policies.Windows" />
  </policyNamespaces>
  <resources minRequiredRevision="1.0" />
  <categories>
    <category name="WindowsDefenderExploitGuard" displayName="$(string.Win-
dowsDefenderExploitGuard)">
      <parentCategory ref="windows:WindowsComponents" />
    </category>
    <category name="ExploitProtection" displayName="$(string.ExploitProtec-
tion)">
      <parentCategory ref="WindowsDefenderExploitGuard" />
    </category>
  </categories>
  <policies>
    <policy name="ExploitProtection_Name" class="Machine" display-
Name="$(string.ExploitProtection_Name)" explainText="$(string.Exploit-
Protection_Help)" key="Software\Policies\Microsoft\Windows Defender
ExploitGuard\Exploit Protection" presentation="$(presentation.ExploitPro-
tection_Name)">
      <parentCategory ref="ExploitProtection" />
      <supportedOn ref="windows:SUPPORTED_Windows_10_0_RS3" />
        <elements>
          <text id="ExploitProtection_Name" valueName="ExploitProtection-
Settings" required="true" maxLength="65535" />
        </elements>
    </policy>
  </policies>
</policyDefinitions>
```

Note: We have uploaded all the configuration on MDE book repository due the fact that it cannot be captured here in the text so please download from thereBelow you will find some overview of GPO Path that Administrators leverage to deploy settings through AD are captured here:

MDE ASR antivirus policy

The following table gives ASR Antivirus policy settings on Intune web portal:

Setting name	GPO path	State
Scan Archive Files	*Windows Components\Microsoft Defender Antivirus\Scan*	Enabled
Turn on behavior Monitoring	*Windows Components\Microsoft Defender Antivirus\Real-time Protection*	Enabled
Join Microsoft MAPS	*Windows Components\Microsoft Defender Antivirus\MAPS*	Enabled (Advanced MAPS)
Turn on e-mail scanning	*Windows Components\Microsoft Defender Antivirus\Scan*	Enabled
Run full scan on mapped network drives	*Windows Components\Microsoft Defender Antivirus\Scan*	Not Configured
Scan removable drives	*Windows Components\Microsoft Defender Antivirus\Scan*	Enabled
Allow Intrusion Prevention System	*Setting not available in GPO*	Setting not available in GPO
Scan all downloaded files and attachments	*Windows Components\Microsoft Defender Antivirus\Real-time Protection*	Enabled
Monitor file and program activity on your computer	*Windows Components\Microsoft Defender Antivirus\Real-time Protection*	Enabled
Scan network files	*Windows Components\Microsoft Defender Antivirus\Scan*	Enabled.
Allow Script Scanning	*Setting not available in GPO*	Setting not available in GPO
Enable headless UI mode	*Windows Components\Microsoft Defender Antivirus\Client Interface*	Enabled
Specify the maximum percentage of CPU utilization during a scan	*Windows Components\Microsoft Defender Antivirus\Scan*	Enabled - 45
Check for the latest virus and spyware security intelligence before running a scheduled scan	*Windows Components\Microsoft Defender Antivirus\Scan*	Enabled
Select cloud protection level	*Windows Components\Microsoft Defender Antivirus\MpEngine*	Not Configured

Setting name	GPO path	State
Configure extended cloud check	*Windows Components \ Microsoft Defender Antivirus \ MpEngine*	Enabled - 50
Days To Retain Cleaned Malware	*Setting not available in GPO*	Setting not available in GPO
Turn on catch-up full scan	*Windows Components \ Microsoft Defender Antivirus \ Scan*	Disabled
Turn on catch-up quick scan	*Windows Components \ Microsoft Defender Antivirus \ Scan*	Disabled
Configure low CPU priority for scheduled scans	*Windows Components \ Microsoft Defender Antivirus \ Scan*	Enabled
Prevent users and apps from accessing dangerous websites	*Windows Components \ Microsoft Defender Antivirus \ Microsoft Defender Exploit Guard \ Network Protection*	Enabled (audit mode)
Extension Exclusions	*Windows Components \ Microsoft Defender Antivirus \ Exclusions*	Not Configured
Path Exclusions	*Windows Components \ Microsoft Defender Antivirus \ Exclusions*	Consolidated & attached below in this document
Process Exclusions	*Windows Components \ Microsoft Defender Antivirus \ Exclusions*	Consolidated & attached below in this document
Configure detection for potentially unwanted applications	*Windows Components \ Microsoft Defender Antivirus*	Enabled (Audit Mode)
Real Time Scan Direction	*Setting not available in GPO*	Setting not available in GPO
Specify the scan type to use for a scheduled scan	*Windows Components \ Microsoft Defender Antivirus \ Scan*	Full scan
Specify the time for a daily quick scan	*Windows Components \ Microsoft Defender Antivirus \ Scan*	Configured - 180
Specify the day of the week to run a scheduled scan	*Windows Components \ Microsoft Defender Antivirus \ Scan*	Friday
Specify the time of day to run a scheduled scan	*Windows Components \ Microsoft Defender Antivirus \ Scan*	Configured - 1380

Setting name	GPO path	State
Define the order of sources for downloading security intelligence updates	*Windows Components\Microsoft Defender Antivirus\Security Intelligence Updates*	Not Configured
Define file shares for downloading security intelligence updates	*Windows Components\Microsoft Defender Antivirus\Security Intelligence Updates*	Not Configured
Specify the interval to check for security intelligence updates	*Windows Components\Microsoft Defender Antivirus\Security Intelligence Updates*	Enabled - 6
Send file samples when further analysis is required	*Windows Components\Microsoft Defender Antivirus\MAPS*	Send safe samples
Configure local administrator merge behavior for lists	*Windows Components\Microsoft Defender Antivirus*	Enabled
Allow On Access Protection	*Setting not available in GPO*	Setting not available in GPO
Specify threat alert levels at which default action should not be taken when detected	*Windows Components\Microsoft Defender Antivirus\Threats*	Low -1 Quarantine - 2
Specify threat alert levels at which default action should not be taken when detected	*Windows Components\Microsoft Defender Antivirus\Threats*	Medium - 2 Quarantine - 2
Specify threat alert levels at which default action should not be taken when detected	*Windows Components\Microsoft Defender Antivirus\Threats*	High – 4 Remove - 3
Specify threat alert levels at which default action should not be taken when detected	*Windows Components\Microsoft Defender Antivirus\Threats*	Severe – 5 Remove - 3

Table 14.11: ASR Antivirus policy settings on Intune web portal

MDE ASR Windows security experience policy

The following table gives ASR settings for Windows security Experience policy:

Settings name	GPO path	State
Tamper Protection (Device)	*Setting not available in GPO*	Setting not available in GPO
Hide the Account protection area	*Windows Components\Windows Security\Account protection*	Not Configured
Hide the App and browser protection area	*Windows Components\Windows Security\App and browser protection*	Not Configured
Disable the Clear TPM button	*Windows Components\Windows Security\Device security*	(Enabled)
Hide Windows Security Systray	*Windows Components\Windows Security\Systray*	Not Configured
Hide the Family options area	*Windows Components\Windows Security\Family options*	(Enable) Users are unable to view the family options area display in WD Security Center
Hide the Device performance and health area	*Windows Components\Windows Security\Device performance and health*	Not Configured
Hide the Firewall and network protection area	*Windows Components\Windows Security\Firewall and network protection*	Not Configured
Hide all notifications	*Windows Components\Windows Security\Notifications*	Enabled
Hide the TPM Firmware Update recommendation.	*Windows Components\Windows Security\Device security*	(Disable or Not configured) If the firmware of the security processor (TPM) has a vulnerability, a warning will be shown regarding the need for an update
Hide the Virus and threat protection area	*Windows Components\Windows Security\Virus and threat protection*	Not Configured
Hide the Ransomware data recovery area	*Windows Components\Windows Security\Virus and threat protection*	(Enable) The Ransomware data recovery area is hidden

Settings name	GPO path	State
Hide Windows Security Notification Area Control	*Setting not available in GPO*	Not Configured
Configure customized notifications	*Windows Components\Windows Security\Enterprise Customization*	Not Configured
Enable in App Customization	*Setting not available in GPO*	Not Configured
Specify contact company name	*Windows Components\Windows Security\Enterprise Customization*	Example Private Limited
Specify contact email address or Email ID	*Windows Components\Windows Security\Enterprise Customization*	support@ yourwebsite.com
Specify contact phone number or Skype ID	*Windows Components\Windows Security\Enterprise Customization*	TBD
Specify contact website	*Windows Components\Windows Security\Enterprise Customization*	www.yourwebsite. com

Table 14.12: ASR settings for Windows security Experience policy

MDE ASR policy rules

The following table shows one of ASR rule and different value names that can be configured under it:

Setting name	GPO path	State	
Configure Attack Surface Reduction rules	Windows Components\ Microsoft Defender Antivirus\Microsoft Defender Exploit Guard\Attack Surface Reduction	Enabled	
		Value Name	**Value**
		56a863a9-875e-4185-98a7-b882c64b5ce5	2
		7674ba52-37eb-4a4f-a9a1-f0f9a1619a2c	2
		d4f940ab-401b-4efc-aadc-ad5f3c50688a	2
		9e6c4e1f-7d60-472f-ba1a-a39ef669e4b2	2
		be9ba2d9-53ea-4cdc-84e5-9b1eeee46550	2
		01443614-cd74-433a-b99e-2ecdc07bfc25	2
		5beb7efe-fd9a-4556-801d-275e5ffc04cc	2
		d3e037e1-3eb8-44c8-a917-57927947596d	2
		3b576869-a4ec-4529-8536-b80a7769e899	2
		75668c1f-73b5-4cf0-bb93-3ecf5cb7cc84	2
		26190899-1602-49e8-8b27-eb1d0a1ce869	2

Setting name	GPO path	State	
		Value Name	**Value**
		e6db77e5-3df2-4cf1-b95a-636979351e5b	2
			2
		d1e49aac-8f56-4280-b9ba-993a6d77406c	2
		b2b3f03d-6a65-4f7b-a9c7-1c7ef74a9ba4	2
		92e97fa1-2edf-4476-bdd6-9dd0b4dddc7b	2
		c1db55ab-c21a-4637-bb3f-a12568109d35	2

Table 14.13: ASR rule for GPO path

The **value names** and **values** you see in the table correspond to specific **Attack Surface Reduction** (**ASR**) rules within MDE. Each rule is designed to block or audit certain behaviors that are commonly exploited by malware1. Here is how they work:

1. **Setting name**: This indicates the specific ASR rule being configured. For example, Configure Attack Surface Reduction rules is the setting that enables or disables these rules.

2. **GPO path**: This is the path in the Group Policy Management Console (GPMC) where the setting is located. It helps administrators locate and configure the rule within the policy framework.

3. **State**: This shows whether the rule is enabled or disabled. In your table, all rules are set to **"Enabled"** (indicated by the value **"2"**).

4. **Value name**: This is the unique identifier (GUID) for each ASR rule. Each GUID corresponds to a specific rule that targets particular behaviors or actions that malware might use.

5. **Value**: This is the action assigned to the rule. The value **"2"** typically means **"Enabled"**, meaning the rule is actively blocking or auditing the specified behavior.

For example, the rule with the GUID 56a863a9-875e-4185-98a7-b882c64b5ce5 might be designed to block executable files from running unless they meet certain criteria, such as being signed by a trusted publisher or being on a whitelist.

Query languages used internally and externally

We have listed three commonly used query languages across the security industry to search for various alerts:

- **KQL**: Kusto Querly Language is the far most used language internally by Microsoft and same they have added on the security web portal for end users. We have already covered KQL in detail in *Chapter 7, Defender SOC Investigating Threats* and just keeping a small reference for quick refresh

- **Splunk**: It is also one of the SIEM products that captured the SOC market so most of the SOC engineers are using Splunk queries to identify such threats.

- **Datadog**: Datadog is also trying to enter in SIEM market as this monitoring tool is heavily used in the industry and they do have powerfull query language that can be leveraged by SOC engineers. Datadog is not much famous as comparison to Splunk but it has possibility to grow in near future along with above mentioned two languages.

Deployment timelines

When it comes to outsourcing companies managing end-to-end MDE product installation and configuration, the typical timeline is around three months. This period includes several critical stages to ensure the deployment is smooth and efficient. Here is a breakdown of the key phases:

1. **Initial assessment (Week 1-2)**:
   - Understanding business requirements.
   - Performing a network and infrastructure assessment.
   - Planning the deployment strategy tailored to the specific needs.

2. **Preparation and setup (Week 3-6)**:
   - Procuring necessary software licenses and hardware.
   - Setting up the infrastructure, including servers, storage, and network configurations.
   - Preparing the deployment environment.

3. **Installation and configuration (Week 7-10)**:
   - Installing the MDE product on the designated systems.
   - Configuring the product to align with the security policies and business goals.
   - Integrating with existing systems and tools.

4. **Testing and validation (Week 11-12)**:
   - Conducting comprehensive testing to ensure all systems are functioning as expected.
   - Identifying and resolving any issues.
   - Validating the deployment with stakeholder approval.

5. **Training and hand-off (Week 13):**

    o   Providing training sessions for the internal team to manage and operate the MDE product effectively.

    o   Handing over documentation and any necessary support tools.

6. **Go-live and support (Week 14 onwards):**

    o   Officially going live with the deployed MDE product.

    o   Monitoring the system for initial issues.

    o   Offering ongoing support and maintenance as needed.

By breaking down the timeline into these stages, it becomes clear that each phase is crucial for the overall success of the deployment. This structured approach ensures that all necessary components are addressed methodically, resulting in a stable and efficient MDE product deployment within the usual three-month timeframe.

Conclusion

In this chapter, we have explored fundamental configurations and settings within the Microsoft Defender for Endpoint Security Center. From examining the intricate state of features to navigating advanced settings and policies covering antivirus, disk encryption, and attack surface reduction, we have presented a comprehensive roadmap for enhancing endpoint security. The incorporation of practical examples, agent configurations, and customized policies for various platforms, including Linux and Windows Server, highlights the flexibility and adaptability of Microsoft Defender for Endpoint. Through these insights, our aim has been to empower readers with the knowledge and tools to strengthen their organization's security posture, mitigating risks, and ensuring robust protection across diverse environments. As the threat landscape evolves, this chapter acts as a beacon, underscoring the significance of a proactive and multifaceted approach to endpoint security within the domain of Microsoft Defender for Endpoint.

This chapter can also be used by companies those who takes outsource work for MDE deployment in their organization at large scale as during writing of this book we talked to our many colleagues those who are working to successfully lead such deployment projects and such timeline and configuration information was shared by them and we give big thanks to our colleagues and friends who shared such valuable practical configuration for this book.

Index

www.ingramcontent.com/pod-product-compliance
Lightning Source LLC
Chambersburg PA
CBHW061740210326
41599CB00034B/6739

* 9 7 8 9 3 6 5 8 9 4 0 2 8 *